P9-DSZ-002

THE GREAT ROAD

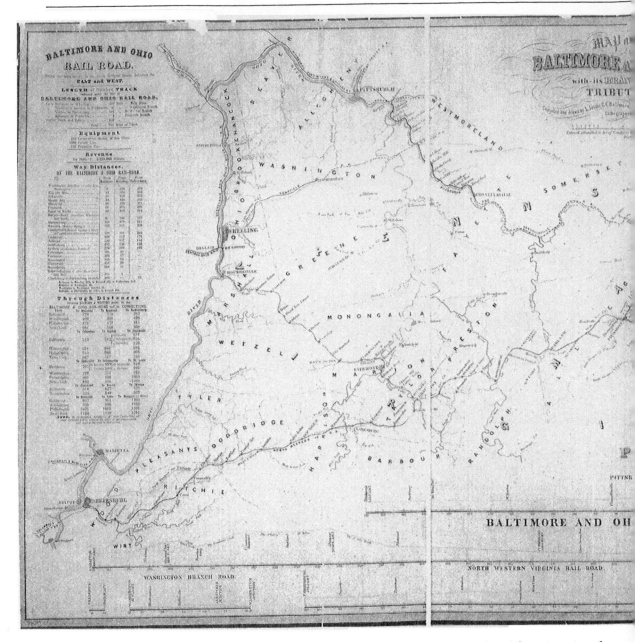

This 1858 map shows the entire extent of the Baltimore and Ohio Railroad from its point of origin to Wheeling, its initial destination on the Ohio River, with the Washington and Parkersburg branches, and the proposed route to Pittsburgh. *Special Collections, University of Maryland, College Park Libraries.*

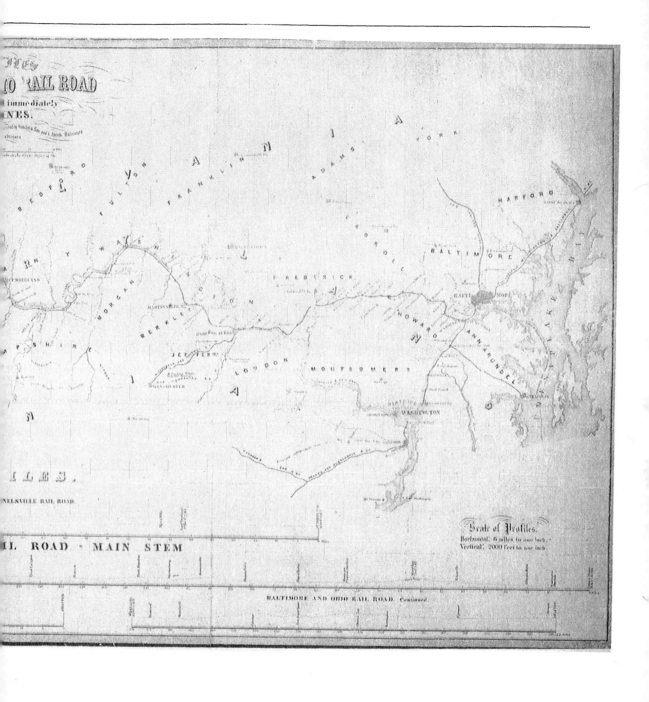

The Great Road

The Building of the Baltimore and Ohio,
the Nation's First Railroad,
1828-1853

JAMES D. DILTS

STANFORD UNIVERSITY PRESS
STANFORD, CALIFORNIA

Stanford University Press
Stanford, California

© 1993 by the Board of Trustees of the
Leland Stanford Junior University

Printed in the United States of America

CIP data are at the end of the book

Original printing 1993
Last figure below indicates year of this printing:
03

FOR JORDAN AND SUZANNAH

ACKNOWLEDGMENTS

SEVERAL YEARS AGO, I WALKED INTO THE OFFICE
of Robert M. Vogel, then curator of mechanical and civil engineering at the Smithsonian Institution, and told him that I was going to write a new history of the Baltimore and Ohio Railroad. He took me next door to meet John H. White, Jr., then the Smithsonian's curator of transportation. "He's going to write a book about the Baltimore and Ohio," said Vogel. White's response: "Now we're going to have to go through all that business about the Tom Thumb again." Over the longer than usual gestation period that followed, Vogel and White became supporters of the project, read sections of the manuscript, and offered many ideas for improvement. Both have since retired from the Smithsonian Institution to pursue their own varied interests, but without their informed assistance, the book would not have appeared in its present form.

Herbert H. Harwood, Jr., author of several fine works on the Baltimore and Ohio and other railroad subjects, gave me early encouragement and critical advice. John P. Hankey, curator at the B&O Railroad Museum, has proved a steadfast friend of this endeavor since its inception, from locating original documents to printing out the final manuscript. In between, I benefited from his encyclopedic knowledge of the B&O, his exposition of the museum's excellent collection of railroad equipment, and his expert guidance through the complex corporate hierarchy.

Spence Sullivan, corporate secretary for the Baltimore and Ohio, first unlocked for me the door to the "pipe space" under the roof of the B&O's Central Building in downtown Baltimore where the written history of the company dating back 150 years was stored on shelves that rose to the ceiling and in wooden filing cases stacked almost as high in the center of the room. Hays T. Watkins, chairman emeritus, CSX Corporation, and his assistants Howard Skidmore and Franklyn J. Carr, gave me complete access to these materials and an office in the Central Building in which to work. More recently, CSX Corporation, through the agency of Thomas E. Hoppin, vice president, corporate communications, granted subvention funds that helped me to complete the book and to purchase illustrations.

The late Howard Simpson, former president of the Baltimore and Ohio, shared his intimate knowledge of the twentieth-century railroad in several fascinating conversations. The late Vera Leclercq of the B&O's public relations staff and Anne Calhoun, archivist, Hays T. Watkins Research Library at the B&O Railroad Museum, provided additional information. These few individuals will have to represent the many administrators, supervisors, and trainmen who showed me the B&O's coal and other facilities in Baltimore, took me down into a deep mine near Fairmont, West Virginia, and pointed out landmarks from the locomotive and the caboose of a coal train on the way back to Baltimore, and who, almost without exception, cheerfully answered innumerable questions about their jobs on the railroad.

Others made the long stretches of track less lonely. Mark Reutter was an unfailingly energetic, intrepid, and knowledgeable companion on our trips through the Maryland and West Virginia countryside and devised workable solutions to several vexing problems. Justin Simpson walked the line with me near Baltimore and analyzed "versed sines" and other mathematical arcana. Martha J. Vill, my researcher, explored the various repositories of B&O Railroad documents and sifted through the most promising ones when I was starting out. Michael J. Trostel related little-known facts about James Carroll and Mount Clare. John Ferguson, Robert Alholm, and my other colleagues at the Maryland Institute, College of Art, and Ray Wise, Gary Turner, and Lucretia B. Fisher contributed sustenance of various kinds along the way. I was enlightened by the insights afforded by special consultants Kevin Donnelly and Mike Tammany. Phoebe B. Stanton, architectural historian and resident scholar at the George Peabody Library of the Johns Hopkins University, has been a mainstay from initial conception to completion. And my late father, M. S. Dilts, old artificer, stood me in good stead.

Librarians are both the inspirers and guardian angels of books. Jane Katz guided my search through the large collection of maps, manuscripts, and pamphlets relating to the B&O Railroad at the Evergreen House of the Johns Hopkins University. Cynthia Requardt, head of special collections, at the university's Milton S. Eisenhower Library, and Elizabeth Schaaf, archivist at its George Peabody Library, were also very helpful. Marcia Eisenstein and Ralph Clayton at the Enoch Pratt Free Library, and Karen Stuart, former librarian, Francis O'Neill, and Jeff Goldman, photographer, at the Maryland Historical Society, were indispensable aides during my many visits to those institutions over the years. I am particularly indebted to the Maryland Historical Society, from whose rich and extensive collections came much of the background material on individuals in the book, and whose administrators, J. Jefferson Miller, II, former director, Barbara W. Sarudy, former acting director, and George H. Callcott, former chairman of the publications committee, assisted me in obtaining grants that enabled me to finish the writing. The Engineering Society of Baltimore, Inc., opened their library and its excellent collection of Victorian engineering books and periodicals to me, and Joyce Koeneman, librarian at the Association of American Railroads in Washington, D.C., did the same. I would like to thank the staffs of the Peale Museum in Baltimore, the McKeldin Library of the University of Maryland, the National Archives, the Library of Congress, the National Portrait Gallery, the American Philosophical Society in Philadelphia, the New York Public Library, the New York Historical Society, the National Archives of Canada in Ottawa, and the Guildhall Library in the City of London. I am also grateful to John Orbell, archivist, Baring Brothers & Co., Limited, for taking me on a tour of the company headquarters and doing additional research in the Baring files.

Financial support for the production of this book came from the Allegheny Foundation, Pittsburgh, Pennsylvania; the CSX Corporation, Richmond, Virginia; and the B&O Railroad Historical Society, Baltimore, Maryland.

I am very grateful to the Stanford University Press: Norris Pope, acting director, who went far beyond the normal duties of an editor-in-chief to ensure that this manuscript made its way effectively into print; Shirley Taylor, whose careful, sympathetic editing slimmed down and speeded up the text; and associate editors Lynn Stewart and Nancy Lerer. Finally, I would like to thank my wife, Penelope Williamson, the alpha and omega of this project, who never lost faith.

JAMES D. DILTS

Baltimore, Maryland
April 1993

Contents

Photo sections follow pp. 80, 158, 264, and 388.

Chronology

Summer 1826	Serious railroad talks begin in Baltimore.
February 12, 1827	First meeting of Baltimore merchants to discuss railroad.
February 19, 1827	Second meeting results in decision to build railroad.
February 28, 1827	Maryland legislature incorporates Baltimore and Ohio Railroad Company.
March 8, 1827	Virginia legislature approves B&O Rr. charter.
March 20, 1827	City of Baltimore subscribes for 5,000 shares of B&O Rr. stock.
April 23, 1827	B&O Rr. Co. officially organized.
July 1827	Surveys begin.
February 27, 1828	Pennsylvania legislature approves B&O Rr. charter.
March 3, 1828	State of Maryland authorizes subscription for 5,000 shares of B&O Rr. stock.
April 1828	Engineers report on surveys.
May 23, 1828	Company adopts route, Baltimore to Potomac River.
June 10, 1828	Chesapeake and Ohio Canal Company files suit to stop B&O Rr. from acquiring more land along Potomac River.
June 23, 1828	B&O Rr. files similar suit against C&O Canal.
July 4, 1828	First stone laid for B&O Rr.
October 22, 1828	B&O engineers Jonathan Knight, William G. McNeill, and George W. Whistler leave to study railroads in England.
May 22, 1829	B&O engineers return from England.
July 11–August 6, 1829	First court hearing, B&O Rr. vs. C&O Canal.

October 6–14, 1829	B&O Rr.'s George Brown and Ross Winans attend locomotive trials held on Liverpool & Manchester Rr. at Rainhill, England.
October 1829	First track laid from Pratt Street to Carrollton Viaduct.
December 4, 1829	Patterson Viaduct officially opened.
December 21, 1829	Carrollton Viaduct officially opened.
May 22, 1830	B&O Rr. officially opened to Ellicotts Mills.
July 20, 1830	Benjamin H. Latrobe, Jr., starts job on B&O Rr.
August 24, 1830	Peter Cooper's locomotive makes first public appearance on B&O Rr.
August 28, 1830	Oliver Viaduct officially opened. Peter Cooper's locomotive runs to Ellicotts Mills and back.
September 20, 1830	Peter Cooper's locomotive races horse, and loses.
June 28, 1831	B&O Rr. conducts own version of Rainhill locomotive trials.
June 29, 1831	Irish laborers riot at Sykesville, Md.
October 10–25, 1831	Second court hearing, B&O Rr. vs. C&O Canal.
December 1, 1831	Frederick Branch officially opened.
December 30, 1831	C&O Canal wins third and final court hearing, allowing it to proceed alone along Potomac River from Point of Rocks to Harpers Ferry.
April 1, 1832	B&O Rr. completed to Point of Rocks, Md.
July 1832	Surveys begin for Washington Branch.
September 1832	Atlantic, first Grasshopper engine, put in service on B&O Rr.
October 1832	City extension completed from Mt. Clare to tidewater at City Block.
March 9, 1833	Maryland legislature passes law allowing B&O Rr. to build Washington Branch.
March 22, 1833	Maryland legislature authorizes B&O Rr. to build rail line along Potomac River from Point of Rocks to Harpers Ferry, effecting compromise with C&O Canal.
June 1833	President Andrew Jackson rides on B&O Rr. from Relay to Baltimore.
July 1833	Construction of Thomas Viaduct and Washington Branch begins.
June 1834	Irish laborers riot on Washington Branch.
November 12, 1834	John Reeder's locomotive American explodes.
November 18–26, 1834	More Washington Branch riots by Irish laborers.
December 1, 1834	B&O Rr. main line from Baltimore to Harpers Ferry officially opened.

December 2, 1834	Grasshopper locomotive Arabian pulls scheduled train over inclined planes at Parrs Spring Ridge.
May–June 1835	Surveys conducted, Cumberland to Wheeling and Pittsburgh.
July 4, 1835	Thomas Viaduct completed.
August 7–9, 1835	Bank riots in Baltimore.
August 25, 1835	Washington Branch officially opened.
September 27, 1835	Engineer Phineas Davis killed in locomotive accident on Washington Branch.
April–August 1836	Surveys conducted, Harpers Ferry to Brownsville, Pa.
April 26, 1836	City of Baltimore authorizes subscription for $3 million in B&O Rr. stock.
June 4, 1836	State of Maryland authorizes subscription for $3 million in B&O Rr. stock.
June 30, 1836	Philip E. Thomas resigns as B&O Rr. president.
December 1836	Bridge over Potomac River to Harpers Ferry completed.
December 27, 1836	B&O Rr. elects Louis McLane president.
April–October 1837	Surveys conducted, Harpers Ferry to Pittsburgh and Wheeling.
November 1837	Jonathan Knight and Benjamin H. Latrobe, Jr., make inspection tour of other railroads.
December 1837	B&O Rr. signs first contract with federal government to carry U.S. mail.
February 14, 1838	B&O Rr. decides to build main line from Harpers Ferry to Cumberland through Virginia.
March 1838	Surveys begin from Baltimore to Harpers Ferry to reconstruct Old Main Line and build new route over Parrs Spring Ridge avoiding inclined planes.
June 1838	Surveys begin from Wheeling eastward.
June–August 1838	Cumberland bituminous coal successfully tested in B&O locomotives.
November 1838–April 1839	Location surveys conducted from Harpers Ferry to Cumberland.
February–October 1839	Surveys conducted, Wills Creek–Casselman River area of Pennsylvania above Cumberland.
June 1, 1839	Locomotive Isaac McKim pulls first train on new route over Parrs Spring Ridge.
August 1839	Construction begins, Harpers Ferry to Cumberland.
August 24, 1839	Louis McLane leaves for England to market $3.2 million worth of State of Maryland bonds allocated to B&O Rr.
November 3, 1839	McLane, having deposited bonds with London's Baring Brothers & Co., returns from England.

February 1840	B&O Rr. issues scrip to finance construction, Harpers Ferry to Cumberland.
July 23–25, 1840	Baltimore shop workmen conduct first strike on B&O Rr.
May 30, 1842	B&O Rr. officially opened to Hancock, Md.
November 3, 1842	B&O Rr. officially opened to Cumberland, Md.
August–October 1843	Benjamin H. Latrobe, Jr., conducts surveys for a Virginia route, Cumberland to Parkersburg and Wheeling.
February 1844	B&O Rr. signs first contract for large-scale coal shipments with New York Coal and Iron Co., Mt. Savage, Md.
May 24, 1844	Samuel F. B. Morse sends first telegraph message from Washington to Baltimore along B&O's Washington Branch right-of-way.
July 16, 1845	Louis McLane, appointed minister to England by President Polk to deal with Oregon question, sails for England. Samuel Jones, Jr., appointed B&O Rr. president pro-tem.
October 1, 1846	McLane returns and is reelected B&O president.
March 6, 1847	Virginia legislature passes law providing right-of-way for B&O Rr. to Wheeling.
August 25, 1847	B&O stockholders approve Virginia act and route to Wheeling.
April 1848–January 1849	Location surveys conducted from Cumberland to Wheeling.
June 1848	First Winans Camel engine introduced on B&O Rr.
September 13, 1848	Louis McLane resigns as president of B&O Rr.
October 11, 1848	Thomas Swann elected president, B&O Rr.
May 23, 1849	Ground broken near Swanton, Md., for construction of B&O Rr. from Cumberland to Wheeling.
July 1849	Locust Point Branch and coal piers in Baltimore completed.
November 1849	Irish workmen riot at Kingwood Tunnel, Va.
November 14, 1849	B&O directors vote to put entire line from Cumberland to Wheeling under contract.
March 1850	Laborers strike and riot at Kingwood Tunnel.
September 1850	Arbitrators rule that B&O Rr. must follow Grave Creek route to Wheeling.
October 10, 1850	Chesapeake and Ohio Canal officially opened to Cumberland.
December 1850	Irish workmen riot near Cumberland.
January 1851	B&O Rr. sells remaining State of Maryland bonds

	held by Baring Brothers & Co., to New York's Brown Brothers & Co.
February 14, 1851	Virginia legislature charters Northwestern Virginia Railroad Company, which later becomes B&O Rr.'s Parkersburg Branch.
July 22, 1851	B&O Rr. excursion to Piedmont, Virginia.
November 1851	Work force reaches peak: 4,870 men, 995 horses.
May 8, 1852	Kingwood Tunnel completed.
June 22, 1852	B&O Rr. excursion to Fairmont, Virginia.
Fall 1852	Washington, D.C., station completed.
December 24, 1852	Track closed at Roseby's Rock, 25 miles below Wheeling.
January 13, 1853	B&O Rr. officially opened to Wheeling.
March 27, 1853	Eight people killed, several injured on Cheat River grade in worst accident in B&O Rr.'s 25-year history.
March 28, 1853	Board Tree Tunnel completed.
April 1, 1853	Railroad officially open for business, Baltimore to Wheeling.
June 7, 1853	Iron bridge completed over Monongahela River at Fairmont.
December 1853	Wheeling station completed.
November 1854	B&O Rr. opens through rail connections to Columbus and points west, via Central Ohio Rr.
May 1, 1857	Northwestern Virginia Railroad (Parkersburg Branch) completed. B&O Rr. gains access to Cincinnati and Saint Louis via Marietta & Cincinnati and Ohio & Mississippi Rr's.
June–July 1857	B&O Rr. excursion, Baltimore–Saint Louis, and return.

THE GREAT ROAD

"The United States themselves are essentially the greatest poem."

—Walt Whitman
Preface to *Leaves of Grass* (1855)

Prologue

IN THE HIERARCHY OF AMERICAN RIVERS, the Patapsco is a trifling stream. Its western branch rises about 40 miles west of Baltimore at a place called Parrs Spring, which is on a ridge of the same name that happens to be the highest point, and about midway, on a line leading west from the city to the Potomac River. The Patapsco flows generally eastward, emptying into a larger body of water—also called the Patapsco River—that is actually a drowned river valley, an arm of the bay that forms the city's harbor. At one time the Patapsco proper had its own deepwater port five miles or so upstream at Elkridge Landing, a flour-milling and tobacco-shipping center before it was eclipsed by Baltimore.

On its journey to tidewater, the Patapsco is sometimes straight and placid, but in other places it swings in wide loops past rocky hills and the husks of mill towns. It has picturesque beauty, but no panoramic rapids, no Great Falls or Palisades. In fact, other than an impressive capacity to flood—when, as if to assert its authority as a river, it sweeps away trees, bridges, or part of a town—the Patapsco has no distinction at all, except one: it was the route of the first real railroad built in America.

Waterways were the trade routes of the early 1800's. Lacking a decent river, Baltimore could not compete with New York, whose Hudson River delivered the trade of the Erie Canal to the city, or with Philadelphia, where the nearby Susquehanna, though it ended in Maryland, chiefly served Pennsylvania, or with Washington, which received products from the Western settlements by barge along the Potomac. And so, in a brilliant intellectual step, 25 businessmen of Baltimore decided to build a railroad, a river of iron that would go west from the Chesapeake Bay over the Allegheny Mountains—perhaps, some said, all the way to the west coast.

Even if their vision did not extend quite that far, it took courage in 1827 to reject the prevailing canal technology and choose a rudimentary form of mine transportation to fashion a long-distance internal improvement. The conception and founding of the Baltimore and Ohio was the single most important business decision made in

Maryland during the first half of the nineteenth century. Building the railroad became Baltimore's greatest civic project. It was considered a national endeavor at the time, and its history is to a large extent the history of all early American railroads.

The Baltimore and Ohio was "the Railroad University of the United States," said the *American Railroad Journal* in 1835. The company's annual reports were "a text book and their road and workshops have been as a lecture room to thousands." A decade later, the journal added that, although the company had paid the price for being a pioneer, "The spirit of the age is onward. Railroads tend to enlarge and liberalize the views of mankind." In 1853, after the B&O had reached the Ohio River, the journal still considered its annual report "a model of its kind, and well worthy the imitation of other companies."

Railroads, and certainly the Baltimore and Ohio, epitomized progress, not only in the development and extension of the Western frontier but in the revelation that personal travel and the delivery of freight could be dramatically faster, better, and cheaper. Even today, in the age of the superhighway and the jet airplane, railroads are still impressive in physical size and meaning in our lives. A train of loaded coal cars, at 20,000 tons or so, is the heaviest thing that moves on land. A modern passenger train is a mobile town with hundreds of inhabitants and all the accommodations necessary to travel 3,000 miles across the country.

The Baltimore and Ohio was the first leg of a national rail system. Its early engineers formed the core of the railroad engineering profession in America; their theories of survey and location laid the groundwork for future textbooks. Building the B&O Railroad through 200 miles of mountain wilderness between Cumberland and Wheeling was a major feat of civil engineering. The B&O imported and improved British rail technology and exported the technology (to Russia), one of the first American railroads to do so. It contributed to the domestic industrial revolution by developing the Georges Creek bituminous coal fields, which led to an exponential growth in Maryland's iron and coal industry and added greatly to the economy of the western part of the state.

These events prompted a simultaneous expansion of the port of Baltimore. The railroad left its mark not only on the city's urban geography but also on its eminent educational and cultural institutions. Baltimore's most important philanthropists—George Peabody, Enoch Pratt, William Walters, and Johns Hopkins—were involved with the B&O as investors, directors, or prime clients; the city's renowned university was founded on Baltimore and Ohio Railroad stock.

The B&O set other precedents. Probably the first instance of a bill being "railroaded" through a legislature was the passage of its charter in 1827 with the famous tax exemption. Low-ball estimates, construction cost overruns, bank scandals, proxy fights, bribery and corruption of public officials, the revolving door between government service and private consulting, political battles over the importation of foreign steel, and port rate differentials—the subjects of today's headlines—were also news then. The labyrinthine nature of Maryland politics has deep roots.

The enterprise has had several historians, initially William Prescott Smith, who wrote *A History and Description of the Baltimore and Ohio Railroad* (1853), the country's first railroad history. There have since been two full-length treatments: Edward Hungerford's centennial history, *The Story of the Baltimore and Ohio Railroad* (1928), and John Stover's *History of the Baltimore and Ohio Railroad* (1987), which brought the story up to the present. There have also been several specialized studies, most importantly, Milton Reizenstein, *The Economic History of the Baltimore and Ohio Railroad, 1827–1853* (1898); J. Snowden Bell, *The Early Motive Power of the Baltimore and Ohio Railroad* (1912); Festus P. Summers, *The Baltimore and Ohio in the Civil War* (1939); William Bruce Catton, "John W. Garrett of the Baltimore & Ohio: a Study in Seaport and Railroad Competition, 1820–1874" (unpublished Ph.D. dissertation, 1959); and Herbert H. Harwood, Jr., *Impossible Challenge, the Baltimore and Ohio Railroad in Maryland* (1979).

This book concentrates on the B&O as the prototypical American railroad during the critical period of its formation and construction. By allowing those who built the railroad to speak for themselves through their own and contemporary accounts, it emphasizes the many types of men who were involved: promoters, financiers, politicians, lawyers, newspaper editors, fixers and bagmen, civil engineers, inventors and mechanics, foremen, contractors, and feuding Irish laborers, who together built the first long-distance, general-purpose railroad in the United States. Their experiences have been gathered from thousands of pages of B&O records and from personal journals and diaries, private correspondence, and pamphlets and newspapers of the time, many of which have not been taken into account by earlier historians of this railroad. It is a story of youth and expansion rather than of maturity and decline, a record of great accomplishment, and severe personal sacrifice.

Some of these builders were giants of the Jacksonian era and of American history: Charles Carroll of Carrollton, who said that the only document he ever signed of greater consequence than the document to incorporate the Baltimore and Ohio Railroad was the Declaration of Independence; Roger Brooke Taney and Daniel Webster, who tried the railroad's, and the state's, "greatest case" against the Chesapeake and Ohio Canal; and Andrew Jackson himself, who stepped into a B&O coach in 1833 for the ride to Baltimore and became the first U.S. president to board a train. Two sons of America's famed early architect Benjamin Henry Latrobe spent their entire professional lives with the railroad: John H. B. Latrobe, the company's general counsel, and Benjamin H. Latrobe, Jr., its chief engineer. Both left voluminous accounts in their diaries and journals, the lawyer's more notable for its lacunae, the engineer's revealing the terrible personal cost of his initial triumph, the Thomas Viaduct, near Baltimore. Peter Cooper and Samuel F. B. Morse found the Baltimore and Ohio a convenient testing ground for their inventions. Alexander Brown and Sons, America's premier merchant bankers, rescued the railroad financially on more than one occasion. Even writers such as John Pendleton Kennedy had important roles to play.

Of those who actually laid the tracks and operated the trains, less is known, but some have stepped out of the shadows: John McCartney, the hard-swearing contractor who was the company's top performer until he drank himself out of a job; Caspar W. Wever, the construction superintendent and corporate intriguer whose early victories led him into a classic conflict-of-interest situation in which he sacrificed everything; the unassuming mechanic Phineas Davis, the B&O's first builder of locomotives, who lost his life on the line while testing one of his products; Owen Murphy and Samuel Raily, murderer and labor terrorist, respectively, prime instigators of the worst riots on the railroad; J. B. Ford, the company's long-suffering agent at Cumberland and Wheeling, who performed a crucial service shortly after the new line opened, when it suffered its first serious accident.

In 1828, when the railroad first pushed its way toward the west, Chicago was still a raw settlement; 25 years later, when it reached Wheeling, the citizens of Seattle had yet to fight their major battle with the Indians. The Baltimore entrepreneurs sensed that they were not just building a railroad. They were following George Washington's plan of binding together a young nation, commercially and politically, and they were tracing a route Washington himself had picked out. They expanded the country's horizons and opened up unfamiliar landscapes and new ways of looking at them.

The focus of this book is on the B&O as "the pioneer railroad of the country." It ends before the railroad extended its lines to Chicago and New York, reached "13 states and eight great cities," and took its place as one of the four major eastern trunk lines. The B&O's corporate existence terminated in 1987, some 160 years after it started. The Baltimore and Ohio is now part of CSX Corporation, one of the three largest railroad companies in the East (with Conrail and Norfolk-Southern). Yet in achieving its initial objective on the Ohio River, the railroad that began in Baltimore uniquely aided in the creation of what was the dominant form of transportation in America in the nineteenth century and is still a major force today.

Finally, this book is an exercise in local and regional history. The author has walked virtually the entire 380-mile length of the B&O Railroad's original main line between Baltimore and Wheeling, in an attempt to link with a common thread personality, place, name, landscape, and literature.

Part I

BALTIMORE TO HARPERS FERRY, 1827-1836

1

Procession

JULY 1828 BEGAN WITH TEMPERATURES IN THE
nineties, but there was a change in the weather, and the morning of Friday the Fourth
dawned cool and bright. By eight o'clock, the parade route was swarming with
people. Baltimore Street, the pride of the city, stretched away in a line of low, ram-
bling businesses and stores, occasionally interrupted by the three- or four-story brick
house of a merchant or the broader expanse of an inn or warehouse. The buildings
ended at the woods on the west side of town, where Franklin and Union squares
are now. On this day, people lined the route for about two miles, from Bond Street
on the east almost as far as the big meadow on the edge of the western city limits.
There, as the culmination of the festive occasion, they would witness the laying of
the cornerstone for the nation's first genuine railroad, the Baltimore and Ohio.

Many in the crowd had also been in the center of Baltimore the night before
to watch the scaffolding being put up on the sidewalks and window sashes removed
from buildings in preparation for viewing the parade while participating tradesmen
arranged their banners and floats. Two new marches written for the event were in
the sheet music racks at the publishers, tavern owners anticipated a horde of dry
throats, and enterprising merchants were selling everything from whiskey in special
flasks to window space from which to view the "novelty, elegance and diversity of
the procession."[1]

Visitors had been arriving in the city since the beginning of the week by steamboat from Easton and Annapolis and by stage from Washington, D.C. and neighboring states. For the past month, schools, fire companies, and delegations from the
various trades had been meeting regularly to mark out the details of the parade. The
order of march was to be the same as that of the industrial parade to promote domestic manufactures held in 1809.[2] Marchers would wear special badges designating
their trade or association. One badge showed the figure of History recording in the
American annals the beginning of a railroad.

Sunrise signaled the official beginning of the day's events. Cannons boomed, church bells pealed, and ships in the harbor ran up flags. Timothy Gardner, a Fells Point sea captain and commanding officer for the day of the *Union*, a miniature frigate 27 feet long with a six-foot beam mounted on a moving platform, had mustered his crew of ship captains dressed as seamen at 4:30 A.M. and was already moving as the reports of the great guns reverberated around the waterfront. The bakers, "those who are not ashamed of their profession," said the notice in the newspaper, gathered at the Shot Tower at five-thirty. The blacksmiths met at the courthouse on Calvert Street at the same time. Shortly thereafter, the Grand Lodge assembled at the nearby Masonic Hall. At six, there were three more cannon reports and these groups, along with about 40 others, each consisting of up to 100 members, began moving toward the place where the parade was to start.

That was at Benjamin H. Latrobe's domed Merchants Exchange, Gay and Water streets, around which were grouped the houses of the town's commercial aristocracy. While the fifes and drums waited at the Centre Market and marshals in blue coats guided the tradesmen's groups and the military and political associations to their places, Mayor Jacob Small, Jr., the members of the City Council, and the company directors and other officials descended the steps of the Exchange.

The parade followed a semicircular route, east on Water Street, north a few blocks on Bond, then west on Baltimore Street. The lead groups set off at seven o'clock, and 45 minutes later, having made the circuit, were passing Timothy Gardner and his shipmates aboard the *Union*, which had taken up a position a block north of the Exchange. They continued through the city with all the pomp and order of a medieval procession of the guilds—first a troop of horsemen, then laborers walking with their tools on their shoulders. Wendel Bollman, who started out as a carpenter and many years later became the B&O's Master of Road, marched in the parade, probably in this group; he was then a boy of fourteen. The workmen were followed by the Freemasons, wearing special aprons and insignias. At their head, drawn sword in his hand, was John H. B. Latrobe, 25, a son of the architect of the Exchange and of the city's magnificent new Catholic Cathedral. Latrobe and his friends, members of a youthful lodge of Masons, had not planned to participate in the long, dusty march out to the west side of town, but even they were swept up by the noise and excitement in front of the Masonic Hall and decided to join in. Another eyewitness to the event, William H. Brown, future author of a book on locomotives that would figure prominently in the Baltimore and Ohio legend, wrote of his experience, "Never in his life (and he has been present on many demonstrations on other occasions) has he witnessed a more magnificent display than was made on that day." [3]

The Freemasons were followed by the dignitaries—first an open landaulet pulled by four horses in which rode the "venerable" guest of honor, Charles Carroll of Carrollton, the last surviving signer of the Declaration of Independence, now nearly 90 years old, wraithlike, his silky white hair flowing back from his high forehead almost to his shoulders, and tied with a ribbon. Sitting beside him was the Revolutionary War hero General Samuel Smith, 75, who had defended the city against the British fourteen years earlier. He was a United States senator. Next came a barouche in which sat Andrew Stevenson, speaker of the U.S. House of Representatives; Maryland legislator Upton S. Heath, the orator of the day; and William Patterson, one of Baltimore's merchant princes.

Following on foot in two rows were the directors of the Baltimore and Ohio Railroad and their engineers. Among the former were Alexander Brown and Robert Oliver. A contemporary considered these three—Patterson, Brown, and Oliver—"the royal merchants of America," and compared them to the Medici.[4] Then came the carts and floats representing the trades and associations. Most of these were elaborate presentations, cleverly worked out to show the craft or trade and to entertain as well. In a group of farmers, James W. McCulloh, lawyer, politician, and financial manipulator, was the "winnower" in a scene depicting agriculture, part of a five-stage horse-drawn tableau. Another man milked a live cow under a real tree, while a third churned butter and several more engaged in a mock harvest. Gardeners dressed in white bore bouquets of flowers. There were millers and flour inspectors, bakers and victuallers. A master tailor and six journeymen on a stage pulled by four bay horses were busily finishing a coat made of cloth woven on the loom on the weavers' stage; it was to be presented to Charles Carroll of Carrollton at the end of the parade.

Another stage carried a deputation of blacksmiths and whitesmiths with the pick, hammer, shovel, and trowel that had been forged especially for the laying of the B&O cornerstone; the stage bore a complete forge, with an operating furnace and bellows. The carpenters' team towed a miniature Greek temple designed by William F. Small, the son of the mayor and the city's first professionally trained architect. In the center of the stonecutters' car, resting on a platform draped with green baize, was the cornerstone itself—a block of white marble about three feet long and two feet wide and a little over a foot high, with a removable top. In the small cavity inside there was a hermetically sealed glass cylinder that contained the B&O charter, copies of the day's newspapers, and a scroll listing the important names and dates.

Other cars illustrated more of the city's thriving trades. On a bedstead with wheels, a cabinetmaker and a carver assembled a cradle. There were tanners and curriers, hatters making hats to be presented to Carroll and Smith, machine makers with a lathe, coopers, saddlers with richly caparisoned horses led by grooms in Arabian costumes, and an elegant barouche for the coach makers with postilions in blue livery. The coppersmiths and allied metalworkers flung engraved tin tumblers to the crowd as they passed. The printers had a car sixteen feet long and nine feet wide equipped with a printing press, type cases, and barrels of water and wine for the thirsty. Hezekiah Niles, whose clear, vigorous prose had made his *Niles Weekly Register* one of the nation's most influential journals, was in charge of the printers, as he had been in the 1809 parade, and one of the passengers was Thomas Murphy, editor of the Baltimore *American*, an important daily newspaper. Two young men dressed as Mercury in flesh-colored tights and winged helmets handed out copies of the Declaration of Independence and an ode by Rufus Dawes, a lawyer and quondam poet, both printed during the parade.

Eight apprentices preceding the marching bookbinders carried the morocco-bound report of the railroad's engineers that was to be presented to Carroll. The eminent silversmith, Samuel Kirk, marched with the watchmakers, jewelers, silversmiths, and engravers with a display of their work; a group of fourteen men carried their specialty, Baltimore cut glass; and the maritime trades were represented by a huge contingent of ship carpenters and joiners, boat builders, block, pump, and rope makers, riggers, sailmakers, pilots, ship captains, mates, and seamen, with more platoons, carriages, and displays, and finally the miniature ship, the *Union*.

The whole parade took more than four hours to reach the open field south of the Frederick turnpike, near a shallow, rocky stream called the Gwynns Falls. In a pavilion that had been set up on a bisecting ridge, Carroll and the other guests sat waiting. Cavalry lined either side of the ridge, the stages of the professions were drawn up on the left, and the Masons formed a hollow square in front, surrounding an excavation.[5]

After some introductory formalities, the band played the new "Carrollton March," and John B. Morris, at 53 the youngest of the railroad's directors, stepped forward to address the waiting thousands. Philip E. Thomas, the railroad's president, was supposed to have made the speech, which John H. B. Latrobe had written, but he did not attend, perhaps owing to illness. "We have met to celebrate the laying of the first stone of the Baltimore and Ohio Railroad," Morris said. "We are about opening the channel through which the commerce of the mighty country beyond the Alleghany must seek the ocean. We are about affording facilities of intercourse between the east and the west, which will bind the one more closely to the other, beyond the power of an increased population or sectional differences to disunite. We are in fact commencing a new era in our history . . . and with abundant resources at their command, the Board of Directors find themselves within little more than a year after the incorporation of the company, fully prepared to commence the construction of the Great Road."[6]

When Morris finished, the two Mercurys came forward to take a copy of his remarks to the printers to reproduce for distribution to the crowd. Then several blacksmiths came with the tools, and the stonecutters brought up the cornerstone. While they were maneuvering it off the wagon and into position, Carroll, accompanied by Morris and the grand marshal, Samuel Sterett, left the pavilion and walked up to the excavation.

Carroll must have seemed a curious figure from a remote age as he stood in the bright sunlight, dressed in his standard costume of old-fashioned knee breeches, roquelaure, and buckled shoes. A patrician Irish Catholic, a powerful opponent of the abuses of the British crown in Maryland, a signer of the Declaration of Independence, a delegate to the first Continental Congress, a Maryland and United States senator, he was also a millionaire and one of the wealthiest men in the country. Carroll owned more than 25,000 acres of some of the richest farmland between Baltimore and the Potomac and held shares in turnpike and canal companies and the B&O Railroad. As he grasped the silver shovel presented by the blacksmiths, his countenance, said one reporter, was of "the brightest vivacity and pleasure." John H. B. Latrobe remembered him that day as "a spare, attenuated old man . . . small in size but active in his movements, with eyes still bright and sparkling, with a voice thin now and feeble, but clear and distinct as . . . [he] prophesied the success of the great work."[7]

Carroll, born just seven years after Baltimore's founding in 1730, made a few remarks recalling the appearance of the city when it was as new as the railroad. Then he sank his spade into the earth and stepped back. The Masons went about their rituals of measuring the cornerstone, pronouncing it "well formed, true and trusty," and anointing it with oil and wine, and scattering it with corn. They recited a benediction. Carroll remarked to one of his friends, "I consider this among the most important acts of my life, second only to my signing the Declaration of Independence, if even it be second to that."[8]

Carroll received the engineers' report and the beaver hat and chambray coat manufactured during the procession. Then he and Smith and several of the railroad directors went aboard the *Union* for refreshments before visiting some of the cars of the professions. Although Carroll drank only water, whiskey flowed freely as the celebrants made their way back to the city. At the head of the procession were two huge decorated carriages with more than 100 women passengers from the Union Factory, one of the state's oldest and largest cotton mills, located across the Patapsco River from Ellicotts Mills.

Timothy Gardner and Hezekiah Niles, who had started drinking toasts to each other at the field, guided their troops to town in some disarray. The printers wanted to accompany their friends the seamen to Fells Point, but they quit in confusion about halfway while the sailors on the *Union*, thoroughly drunk, pushed on. In town, there was further toasting among the tradesmen at Goddard's and the Vaux Hall Gardens, but "the day concluded with more decorum and quiet, than we remember to have seen on a like occasion," said the *American*, which estimated that between 5,000 and 6,000 artisans and others had marched and 50,000 to 70,000 people had watched. Virtually everyone in Baltimore had turned out, either as participant or spectator.

The next day's edition of *Niles Register* (July 5, 1828) summed up the mood of civic pride:

> The most splendid civic procession, perhaps, ever exhibited in America, took place in this city, yesterday, the 4th of July, on the occasion of laying the first or corner stone of the Baltimore and Ohio Rail Road, by Charles Carroll of Carrollton. . . . A glorious tribute was paid to one arm of the triumphant American System—internal improvement, in displaying the progress of the other, domestic manufactures, all the principal trades being represented, and in full operation, on their several stages, drawn by horses. Independence, Independence, Independence was shewn in every movement.

To many observers, particularly outside Baltimore, the proposal to build a railroad several hundred miles longer than any ever conceived, over a range of mountains higher than any so far encountered, by technical means as yet undefined, seemed foolhardy, or worse. "We're all crazy here in Baltimore," acknowledged the chorus of the "Song for the Day," printed in the *American*. The people of Philadelphia offered to send a supply of straitjackets to Baltimoreans affected by "the Rail-Road Mania." But people in the city were genuinely optimistic and excited. B&O President Philip E. Thomas wrote to an associate the day before the ceremony, "We are beginning full of confidence and fine spirits."[9] And in the detailed official version of the day's events that appeared, spread over one full page and most of the next in the *American* on Monday, July 7, 1828, the following incident was reported. Just after Carroll and Smith, in their carriage, had passed the *Union*, an aide to the parade marshal hailed the crew:

"Aide. 'Ship Ahoy!'

"Capt. G. 'Hallo!'

"Aide. 'What is the name of that ship, and by whom commanded?'

"Capt. G. 'The *Union*, Capt. Gardner!'

"Aide. 'From whence came you, and where bound?'

"Capt. G. 'From Baltimore, bound to the Ohio!'"

2

Reaching
Enchanted Ground

"NO ONE CAN PASS THROUGH OUR WESTERN REGIONS, and witness the marks of industry and enterprise, which everywhere meet the eye, without feeling almost as if he walked on enchanted ground, and that the wilderness had bowed to a more than mortal arm." Jared Sparks, the new editor of the *North American Review*, writing in 1825, found on the banks of the Ohio, the Wabash, the Mississippi, and the Missouri "towns, villages, innumerable cultivated farms, a teeming population, well organised governments, and all the details of commercial and social intercourse, established on a firm basis, and going into an harmonious operation, over an immense space of country, where thirty years ago scarcely a vestige of civilisation could be traced." Although growth in the East was less rapid, it was still impressive. Over the past 30 years, Philadelphia had tripled its population, New York had grown four times as large, and Baltimore, five times. "But among all the cities, whether of America or of the world, in modern or ancient times, there is no record of any one, which has sprung up so quickly to as high a degree of importance as Baltimore."[1]

Sparks (1789–1866), a native New Englander, had recently returned to Boston as owner and editor of the *North American Review*, but in his article "Baltimore," in the January 1825 issue of the *Review*, he wrote enthusiastically about the younger city where he had spent five years as pastor of the First Unitarian Church. He attributed Baltimore's rise to prominence to five conditions: its position as the major port on the Chesapeake Bay and the nearest market to the western country, its fast sailing ships, its trade with the West Indies, its staples of flour and tobacco, and finally, "the enterprising spirit of the people." He noted more than 60 grain mills and several cotton factories within 20 miles of the city, located on the fall line of the numerous streams, which occurred so conveniently close to tidewater that they were named "falls." Baltimore, he pointed out, was the beneficiary of good roads, being connected to Reisterstown, York, Belle Air, Havre de Grace, and Washington by "broad and well constructed avenues." A recently completed series of western turnpikes also joined the city to Cumberland and to the National Road that ran between there and Wheeling. Annual droves of livestock, especially hogs, were coming to Baltimore from the Ohio country, and the city's merchants were considering a line of freight wagons that would ply continuously, day and night, to Wheeling.

But more important to Baltimore's future as a trading and manufacturing center, Sparks indicated, were the "water communications" that were being discussed, particularly the "brilliant, and as some think rather dubious scheme" of joining the eastern and western waters by the Chesapeake and Ohio Canal, paralleling the Potomac. This scheme would benefit Georgetown, Washington, and Alexandria, but not enough for these competing grain ports to overtake Baltimore, especially if Baltimore built its own canal west to meet the C&O. To the north, the Chesapeake and Delaware Canal was almost finished through the isthmus that separated the bays, and Sparks expected it to help both Baltimore and its traditional trade rival, Philadelphia. Baltimore was also proposing another canal to the Susquehanna River near Harrisburg, to draw off the river trade before it could reach the Chesapeake, but Sparks doubted that it could be built soon because of its cost.

Sparks did not mention railroads in his article. In 1825 Baltimore, along with its competitors, was still in the acute stages of "Erie fever." New York was preparing to open its grand canal that fall, and the other East Coast ports, which feuded like Greek city-states for the western trade, were frantically trying to emulate it, despite New York's obvious geographic and financial advantages. Between these cities and the common goal lay the Appalachians—"the endless mountains," the Indians called them—a 1,600-mile-long chain stretching from the Saint Lawrence Valley to Alabama, with peaks more than a mile high near the northern and southern ends. They had long been regarded with admiration. "Those mighty High and great Mountaines trenching NE and SW," Marylander Augustine Herrman wrote in 1670, "is supposed to be the very middle Ridg of Northern America and the only Naturall Cause of the fierceness and extreme stormy Cold Winds that comes NW from thence all over this Continent and makes frost."[2] Jefferson in 1787 wrote that the Appalachians were indeed "the spine of the country."

The central portion of the chain, in southwestern New York, western Pennsylvania, and Maryland, Ohio, and Virginia, had lower summits. Albert Gallatin, Jefferson's Secretary of the Treasury, described them as consisting of "a succession of parallel ridges, following nearly the direction of the sea coast. . . . The ridge, which divides the Atlantic rivers from the western waters, generally known by the name of Allegheny, preserves throughout a nearly equal distance of 250 miles from the Atlantic ocean, and a nearly uniform elevation of 3,000 feet above the level of the sea."[3] The Alleghenies, "the place of the foot" in Indian terminology, were over 100 miles wide, and among their twisting crests and ravines, rampant vegetation, and winding, dark-colored streams even experienced surveyors became disoriented. It was the modest aim of the engineers and entrepreneurs of the early nineteenth century to connect these eastward- and westward-flowing waters, separated in Paleozoic times, when the first Allegheny rocks were thrust up 500 million years ago.

The first "commercial American" to grasp the potential of these rivers and translate his concepts into a policy of national expansion and unity through trade was George Washington. In 1783, the year peace with Great Britain was declared, after a tour of New York that included the Mohawk Valley, General Washington wrote the Marquis de Chastellux:

> I could not help taking a more contemplative and extensive view of the vast inland navigation of these United States, and could not but be struck with the immense diffusion and importance of it; and with the goodness of that Providence which has dealt his favors to us with so profuse a hand. Would to God we have wisdom enough to improve them! I shall not rest contented until I have explored the Western country, and traversed those lines (or great part of them) which have given bounds to a new empire.[4]

The following year, Washington, who owned or claimed almost 50,000 acres in several states, set out on horseback from Mount Vernon to view his own western lands and "to obtain information of the nearest and best communication between the eastern and western waters; and to facilitate as much as in me lay the inland navigation of the Potomack." Following the river to Cumberland, he continued into Pennsylvania on Braddock's Road, which he and the Virginians had helped the British general carve out of the wilderness in 1755, during the French and Indian War. That was when Washington first realized the necessity of making the Potomac navigable for military purposes. In 1784, he met "numbers of persons and pack horses going in with ginseng; and for salt and other articles in the markets below."[5]

On the far side of the mountains, Washington viewed the Virginia portion of the Cheat River that flowed into the Monongahela and on to Pittsburgh. The river was choked with huge boulders and constricted by forbidding hills full of briers. No one Washington talked to had accurate knowledge of the country between the navigable part of that river and the Potomac: "All seem to agree however that it is rough and a good way not to be found."[6] Washington went back by a more southerly route, crossed the Youghiogheny River, and in the Maryland Glades, having sent on his camp equipment, spent an uncomfortable night in the rain, "with no other shelter or cover than my cloak."[7]

At Mount Vernon, he summed up his findings in his diary and amplified them in a series of letters to Jefferson and Madison and the governors of Maryland and Virginia, among others. More than 40 years later, Pennsylvania Congressman Andrew Stewart, member of a House committee making a report on the Chesapeake and Ohio Canal, was astonished to find that in these documents Washington not only had anticipated the major internal improvements already completed or under construction but had identified their locations. "When he returned he made out a detailed and accurate report of the distances, the advantages and disadvantages of the several routes examined by him, and on comparing them he expressed, unequivocally, his opinion that the Potomac and Ohio offered the nearest and most practicable route" over the mountains, Stewart wrote, "and what is a most remarkable fact, he at that early day predicted the accomplishment of the New York Canal, and . . . also one through the Susquehannah, to Lake Erie":

> But a circumstance still more remarkable is, that among his manuscript papers, endorsed in his own hand writing, the committee have found a map exhibiting the whole route of the Chesapeake and Ohio Canal, indicating the practicable point of connexion, which appears to be the same recommended by the United States Board of Engineers in their report made to Congress at the last session!! This map also exhibits the route of a road or portage to connect the Eastern and Western Waters, commencing at Cumberland and terminating at the Youghiogheny, precisely at the point where the present Cumberland road strikes that river, and without any material deviation in the intermediate space.[8]

In other words, Washington had foreseen the routes that were to become New York's Erie Canal, Pennsylvania's Main Line of Internal Improvements, Maryland's National Road, and Washington, D.C.'s Chesapeake and Ohio Canal. The Baltimore and Ohio Railroad—a project that he could not have envisioned because the technology was unknown—proved to be the ultimate beneficiary of his mountain survey.

In the late 1780's, the immediate objective of better transportation was trade, for the furs of the Great Lakes country and for western agricultural produce, but Washington also saw the need for transportation as a way of giving purpose and direction to a weak and politically disorganized country. By expanding and unifying the American territories, the new nation would strengthen and protect itself against British and Spanish incursions and interference with its domestic trade alliances. Washington believed it was necessary "to apply the cement of interest to bind all parts of it together, by one indissoluble bond—particularly the middle states with the Country immediately back of them."[9]

To this end, Washington asked for surveys of the James and Potomac rivers to their sources in order to determine the best way over the mountains, and he encouraged private companies to make the rivers navigable. At the end of 1784, at a meeting of Maryland and Virginia delegates in Annapolis (Charles Carroll of Carrollton represented the Maryland Senate), the two states agreed to improve the Potomac for commerce. Meanwhile, Washington told Madison, Baltimore interests were backing a company to remove obstructions from the Maryland portion of the Susquehanna: "And this, I perceive, is all that can be obtained in behalf of Potomac from that quarter."[10]

More meetings between the two states culminated in a gathering at Mount Vernon in the spring of 1785 where an interstate agreement on commercial matters, the Mount Vernon Compact, was ratified. This led to further assemblies, including one in Annapolis the following year among the thirteen states, and ultimately to the Constitutional Convention at Philadelphia in 1787. The Maryland and Virginia legislatures passed laws providing for the establishment of a company to undertake the improvements, and after it was organized, Washington, who was named president of the Potomac Company, wrote to Lafayette, "We have opened the plains of Ohio to the poor, the needy and the oppressed of the Earth. . . . the ways are preparing, and the roads will be made easy." [11]

But making the roads was not easy. The Potomac Company's advertisements for contractors went unanswered, and they could not find an experienced canal engineer, so they gave inventor James Rumsey the work of deepening the channel in the river and constructing short canals with locks around the falls. He and his men began digging and attacked the rocks in the river with gunpowder, but the work force, mostly drunken ex-convicts exiled from England and sold in America as laborers, were so troublesome in the countryside that the company brought in indentured Irish servants and Negro slaves. Many of the servants ran off, and if caught, ran off again, and they fought with the Negroes. High water on the Potomac drove the workmen back. Many fell ill from fever. A year after work began, a frustrated Rumsey wrote to the company treasurer:

> Great Falls potowmack July 3d 1786. Sir We have been much Imposed upon the last Two weeks in the powder way (we had our Blowers, One Run off the other Blown up) we therefore was Obliged to have two new hands put to Blowing and there was much attention gave to them least Axedents should happen yet they used the powder Rather too Extravagent, But that was not all they have certainly stolen a Considerable Quantity. . . . Our hole troop is such Villains. [12]

Soon after writing this letter, Rumsey resigned. Washington, following his election to the Presidency in 1789, also withdrew from the Potomac Company, which entered a slow decline. Nevertheless, by 1792, the officers reported the completion of a canal around the Seneca Falls and a straight channel in the river from there to the Great Falls, created by removing the rocks and deepening the water with dams. Ten years later, they opened the locks at Great Falls, superintendent Leonard Harbaugh having finished the job that Rumsey started, and the company buoyantly declared its first, and last, dividend.

Over the next two decades expenses consistently outstripped tolls, and having spent from half to three quarters of a million dollars and almost 40 years in building short, unconnected canals and engaging in "fruitless efforts" to clear a channel in the shallow, rocky Potomac, the only result, according to an official report, was that goods and produce could be brought down the river in barges only six weeks out of the year, in the spring, when "the floods and freshets . . . gave the only navigation that was enjoyed." Still, the company had gained the important right-of-way up the Potomac River. [13] Other states imitated their example, with similar results. New York's Western Inland Lock Navigation Company, formed in 1792, made a survey to determine the best route for a canal to connect the Hudson River with the Great Lakes. In 1795, a short canal, less than a mile long, was opened around the Little Falls on the Mohawk, east of Utica, New York, and work was begun on another. But for a long time after that, all the tolls went to repairs and reconstruction.

Pennsylvania's "Society for promoting the improvement of roads and inland navigation" told the state legislature in 1791 that by making its western rivers navigable, they hoped "to combine the interests of all parts of the state and to cement them in a perpetual commercial and political union." Their engineers toured Rumsey's locks on the Potomac, regarded as engineering marvels of the time, and started building their own around Conewago Falls at Middletown, below Harrisburg, on the Susquehanna. By 1797, a company had circumvented the falls. However, in later years, boatmen ignored their crude canal, as well as another lower down built by Baltimore interests, and ran the river in arks.[14]

In conjunction with this lower canal, which stretched for nine miles in Maryland on the northeast side of the Susquehanna from the Pennsylvania line to the Bay, a 40-foot channel had been cleared in the river under the direction of Benjamin H. Latrobe. "Rocks of immense magnitude were therefore blown away," he said, making the 41-mile stretch from Columbia, Pennsylvania, to tidewater in Maryland somewhat less dangerous, so that lumber, iron, and farm products from the upper Susquehanna could be sent by boat down to Havre de Grace and from there to Baltimore. Even so, Latrobe said, "the whole ravine . . . contains only one furious torrent . . . and very skilful pilots, and many and stout hands, are required to carry a boat or an ark safely down." He concluded that "much remains still to be done, before this unfriendly river can be made fit for the common purposes of a convenient intercourse between the country, so immense in extent and population, which it waters, and the commercial cities." [15]

As Benjamin Franklin had observed, "Rivers are ungovernable things, especially in Hilly Countries. Canals are quiet and very manageable." [16] In the absence of accommodating rivers, Baltimore and Philadelphia had begun to reach out with turnpikes to the Susquehanna country and the west. Philadelphia built a stone-and-gravel turnpike, the nation's first, more than 60 miles to Lancaster in 1794 and nine years later extended it to the Susquehanna River at Columbia. By the early 1800's, Baltimore was building turnpikes to Gettysburg, Hanover, and York, towns traditionally oriented to Baltimore, and was starting to move west to Frederick. But Baltimore was ultimately forced to share the trade of the Susquehanna with Philadelphia.

Albert Gallatin noted the expansion of these new turnpikes in his widely discussed 1808 report on public roads and canals. Although his comprehensive plan of a federally sponsored system of internal improvements for the eastern United States was not destined to become government policy, it was an exemplary document. Besides an eloquent summary of Washington's theories, which established the terms for future discussion, it contained Benjamin H. Latrobe's report on railroads, the first ever submitted to Congress, and it described many projects that were later constructed and are still in use, including the inland waterway, and Route 1, the East Coast highway extending from Maine to Georgia. Gallatin recommended complete and extended public works: "Good roads and canals, will shorten distances, facilitate commercial and personal intercourse, and unite by a still more intimate community of interests, the most remote quarters of the United States. No other single operation, within the power of government, can more effectually tend to strengthen and perpetuate that union, which secures external independence, domestic peace, and internal liberty." [17] Moreover, only the federal government could supply the money necessary to lengthen the waterways and make them useful.

Nevertheless, Gallatin believed that trying to cross the mountains with canals was impracticable because of the principle of lock navigation, "which in order to effect the ascent, requires a greater supply of water in proportion to the height to be ascended, whilst the supply of water becomes less in the same proportion." The highest lock canal then known, on the Languedoc, in France, was 600 feet above sea level. The Alleghenies were 3,000 feet high. Therefore, although canals might be built alongside the rivers to a certain point, roads would have to carry the trade the rest of the way over the mountains. Alternatively, turnpikes could be built all the way from tidewater to the western waters. One exception, Gallatin noted, was the Hudson, in New York, where "a narrow and long bay . . . breaks through, or turns all the mountains, affording a tide navigation for vessels of 80 tons to Albany and Troy, 160 miles above New York. This peculiarity distinguishes the [Hudson] River from all the other bays and rivers of the United States. The tide in no other . . . comes within thirty miles of the Blue Ridge, or eastern chain of mountains." Above Troy, the Mohawk Valley extended west almost to Lake Ontario, and because the difference in elevation was less than 400 feet, "a canal navigation is practicable the whole distance." [18]

New York at that time led the other states in highway construction, Pennsylvania was extending its Lancaster Turnpike to Harrisburg, and in Maryland the Frederick Turnpike was being lengthened to Boonsboro, "beyond the Blue Ridge." From there, the road had been surveyed to Cumberland, where it would meet "the road laid out by the United States from Cumberland to Brownsville, on the Monongahela." This was the National Road, which Gallatin himself had proposed in 1802. The federal law that was passed that year making Ohio a state provided that a portion of the receipts from the sale of public lands be used to build east-west highways. In 1806, Congress, over the objections of Pennsylvania and Virginia, decided that the road would go from Cumberland to either Steubenville or Wheeling. The latter won out and surveys were made, but construction did not begin until five years later. The National Road was the first federally sponsored internal improvement and the first of four highways outlined by Gallatin to provide the mountain link between the eastern and western waters.

Gallatin included in his report two "communications," the first from his personal friend and fellow Jeffersonian Republican, Benjamin H. Latrobe; the second, from Robert Fulton. Latrobe described a railroad remarkably similar to the one that was begun in Baltimore 20 years later, but he did not, at the time, foresee much use for it. "The astonishing loads drawn upon rail roads by single horses in England, have induced many of our citizens to hope for their early application [in] our country," but aside from hauling coal or stone from the mine or quarry to the river—which was, in fact, the purpose of America's earliest railroads—he saw little chance for success for a rail line of the English sort. Rail lines might be useful in the mountains and other areas where canal construction and operation was difficult, but only as "the last resort." Although Latrobe was well aware of steam power, he was skeptical of its potential for moving carriages or boats and in this document he does not mention it at all.[19]

Fulton's comments had to do with roads and canals. Canals had cheaper rates and were better suited than roads to the long-distance movement of goods and produce, but roads were better for shorter, speedier travel. In Fulton's opinion, there was "no difficulty in carrying canals over our highest mountains": water could be brought up with steam engines from the valleys below, stored in reservoirs, and serve a dual purpose of irrigation. He described a way to haul canal boats over the mountains using stationary steam engines and inclined planes, a system that Pennsylvania later adopted.[20]

Although admitting some lack of time to study the question of canals, Fulton did, of course, know a good deal about steamboats. His side-mounted paddle-wheel vessel *Clermont*, built together with Robert R. Livingston, Jefferson's Minister to France, had just begun commercial service on the Hudson, and the two men already had their eyes on the western waters, especially the Mississippi.

Steamboats were a corollary of river improvements. In December 1787, eighteen months after resigning from the Potomac Company, James Rumsey had successfully demonstrated a steamboat off Shepherdstown, Virginia, that operated on the rocket principle, by which a steam-activated pump sucked in water through valves in the hull and forcefully ejected it from a pipe in the stern; and John Fitch, Rumsey's arch-rival, had made a similarly successful experiment on the Delaware River in August 1787, using side-mounted, steam-powered paddles. Fulton's chief rival, John Stevens, Livingston's brother-in-law, built the paddle-wheel boat *Phoenix* in 1808 and operated it for a time in defiance of the Livingston-Fulton Hudson River monopoly before establishing a regular service on the Delaware between Philadelphia and Trenton.

Three years after the Gallatin report, Fulton and Livingston entered a partnership with Benjamin H. Latrobe and Nicholas J. Roosevelt to build steamboats in Pittsburgh. Their initial effort, the *New Orleans*, built by Roosevelt and similar in design to Fulton's Hudson River craft, made the first steamboat trip down the Mississippi to New Orleans in the fall of 1811 with Roosevelt and his pregnant wife, Lydia, Latrobe's daughter, on board. Despite some perils—notably the earthquakes centering on New Madrid in what is now Missouri—the four-month trip was a success. After the boat completed its trip to New Orleans, it operated commercially between there and Natchez, earning tremendous profits.[21]

Partly because of the attention given the exploits of Roosevelt, Fulton refused to have anything more to do with him, and Latrobe gradually assumed a greater role in the Fulton-Livingston enterprise. Latrobe built at least two of several boats launched at Pittsburgh by the Fulton interests. But steamboat development on the Ohio and Mississippi was carried out by others more familiar with the characteristics and dangers of those rivers. Daniel French's *Enterprise*, a Pittsburgh-built stern-wheeler, made the first successful northward voyage from New Orleans to Louisville in 1815, and the following year, Henry M. Shreve built the *Washington* at Wheeling. This craft, which had a flat bottom and an upper deck replacing the hold, set a new pattern for shallow-draft vessels. By 1816, seventeen steamboats were running on the western rivers, including several that incorporated Shreve's radical design.

On the eastern side of the mountains, where the rivers were steep and rocky, Baltimoreans, determined to ascend the Susquehanna by some means, sent the first steamboat upriver to York Haven, Pennsylvania, in the summer of 1825. This vessel, called the *Susquehanna*, had a draft of just seven inches. The following year, two other vessels entered the contest: the *Pioneer* and America's first iron steamboat, *Codorus*, built at York by two engineers, John Elgar and Phineas Davis, who later were connected with the Baltimore and Ohio Railroad. The *Codorus* was 60 feet long and had a nine-foot beam; it weighed two to three tons and had a draft of less than one foot. With Elgar as captain, the *Codorus* steamed all the way up to Binghamton, New York, attended by delirious receptions along the way. Only months later, however, in May 1826, at Berwick Falls below Wilkes-Barre, the *Susquehanna*, driven back by the current, struck a wing dam. The boiler exploded and several people were killed. The disaster effectively ended such experiments on the Susquehanna, and if steamboats ever moved extensively on the upper Potomac, they have escaped the notice of that river's historians.

Baltimore still had its highways, but the year that the first section of the National Road was completed over the mountains, 1817, was also the year that steamboats proved commercially feasible on the western rivers and the year that the Erie Canal was begun. The Erie Canal project originated in the early 1800's when Gouverneur Morris, a United States senator from New York, proposed the idea of a continuous canal from the Hudson River to Lake Erie. DeWitt Clinton in an 1816 memorial to the New York legislature had argued the merits of the project. Canals could carry materials 30 times more cheaply than roads and therefore would open up more remote parts of the country to cultivation. New York would become "the greatest commercial city in the world." European canals, Clinton said, had been planned or built by monarchies, but "It remains for a free state to create a new era in history, and to erect a work, more stupendous, more magnificent, and more beneficial, than has hitherto been achieved by the human race. Character is as important to nations as to individuals, and the glory of a republic, founded on the promotion of the general good, is the common property of all its citizens." [22]

Construction started July 4, 1817, a date that set a precedent for future groundbreakings for internal improvements. When the first section, extending from Rome to Utica, opened in the fall of 1819, the excitement was tremendous. One eyewitness wrote: "The interest manifested by the whole country, as this new internal river rolled its first waves through the state, cannot be described. You might see people running across the fields, climbing on trees and fences, and crowding the bank of the canal to gaze upon the welcome sight." [23]

In a report made in 1818 to the Maryland legislature, state senator John Eager Howard, Jr., summed up Baltimore's situation. The National Road was now finished from Cumberland to Uniontown, Pennsylvania (and would be completed to Wheeling that year). The system of connecting turnpikes between Baltimore and

Cumberland was still not complete, nor had any provision been made for a ten-mile section between Boonsboro and Hagerstown. The Pennsylvania turnpikes between Philadelphia and Pittsburgh were also unfinished, but their wagon and immigrant traffic was already impressive. Maryland must connect the turnpikes "now lying in parts," Howard said, and he reproved the Baltimore merchants for looking across the ocean for trade instead of facing the other direction, toward "the nations growing up rapidly in the west." The Susquehanna and Potomac advocates were beginning to talk about canals. Perhaps Baltimore could build one. But Howard was skeptical of the usefulness of the Erie Canal, splendid though it was; he doubted it would ever be finished, and even if it was, it would freeze in the winter and would do little to overcome the great distance between New York City and the West.[24]

The merchants of other cities, perhaps not so skeptical, were at any rate hoping to compete with canals of their own. In Washington, the failure of the Potomac Company to do much to make that river navigable had prompted discussion of a full-length canal into the mountains. In 1820, Thomas Moore, engineer of the Virginia Board of Public Works, declared such a project practical, based on his survey. Other explorations and unsuccessful attempts to organize a new company followed until November 1823, when Charles Fenton Mercer, who was to the Chesapeake and Ohio Canal what Philip E. Thomas was to the Baltimore and Ohio Railroad, that is, its originator and first president, organized a three-day convention in Washington. The result was a proposal to build a continuous canal to Cumberland and beyond.

Philadelphia, meanwhile, had its own grand project of a canal that would link the city with Pittsburgh and Lake Erie. The scheme was based on an outline roughly sketched by Washington in his 1784 diary and and later amplified by Robert Morris in a publication (1791) of the Pennsylvania "Society for promoting the improvement of roads and inland navigation." Surveys had, in fact, been undertaken as early as 1762, and construction had been started around 1792 on some sections near Philadelphia. The present canal, however, was much more ambitious. Because Philadelphia lay at some distance from the Susquehanna, which ran perpendicular to the desired direction, the Pennylvania Canal would make use of a series of smaller streams and a variety of technical means to achieve its objective. The eastern link of this system, which became known as the Pennsylvania Main Line of Internal Improvements, was to consist of the Schuylkill Navigation from Philadelphia to Reading and the Union Canal from Reading, through Lebanon, to Middletown on the Susquehanna. The Union Canal was incorporated in 1811 and work began in earnest ten years after that.

Baltimore, located almost exactly halfway between the Susquehanna River, at the point where it enters the Chesapeake Bay, and the Potomac River, at Washington, looked naturally to these two rivers for its salvation. In 1823 there were two canal surveys to study the possibility of connecting Baltimore either with the Susquehanna at York Haven, Pennsylvania, or with the Potomac at some convenient point.

Setting out in the early summer, the Susquehanna survey commissioners, Theodorick Bland, George Winchester, and John Patterson, first interviewed Governor DeWitt Clinton in New York, then took a 140-mile ride on the Erie Canal before drifting back down the Susquehanna in an open, flat-bottomed boat from Oswego,

New York, to Harrisburg. They found the river south of Harrisburg as angry as Latrobe had left it. Boatmen guiding the arks and flatboats downriver always left Columbia in the morning with a pilot "and in five or six hours after having been committed to this mad torrent they are either dashed to pieces against the rocks, or safely moored," they said, "sixty miles below on the placid tide."[25]

A direct canal between Baltimore and the Susquehanna also presented some difficulties, chiefly because of a series of high, wide, dry ridges that lay across the route (which roughly followed the turnpike to York). The only path a canal could follow was the southwest edge of the river to Havre de Grace, thence along the bay shore to Baltimore, a difficult, circuitous, and somewhat redundant connection.[26]

The other route, leading west from Baltimore to the Potomac, was similarly obstructed by a high ridge west of the city. The surveyors of that route, among them William Howard, brother of John Eager Howard, Jr., and Isaac Briggs, who had worked on the Erie Canal, found only two gaps in the ridge—one a few miles north of Parrs Spring, source of the Patapsco River, and another at Westminster, Maryland. The surveyors preferred a route straight to the Potomac above Georgetown, reasoning that the boats on the C&O Canal would come on to Baltimore, which enjoyed quicker water access to the Bay than Washington.[27]

At a meeting at the Baltimore Exchange in December 1823, Robert Goodloe Harper, son-in-law of Charles Carroll of Carrollton and a man of influence in the community, made a "great speech" backing the Chesapeake and Ohio Canal and the recommended "connector" from Baltimore to the Potomac at Georgetown. George Winchester, the Susquehanna survey commissioner, championed with equal fervor a direct canal all the way to the Susquehanna. The animosity engendered by these two rival canal projects was later extended to the railroads that replaced them.

For the next few years, Baltimore watched and waited. The newspapers started talking about railroads. "Clinton" wondered whether, instead of a canal, a railroad could be built from Baltimore to York Haven, Pennsylvania.[28] The *American* editors suggested another possibility for a rail line along the turnpike route between Baltimore and Wheeling.[29]

Then in late October 1825, a grand artillery salute that reverberated for three hours and more than a thousand miles along the Mohawk and down the Hudson from Buffalo to Sandy Hook and back again inaugurated ten days of celebrations to commemorate the opening of the completed Erie Canal. The culmination was the arrival of a flotilla of canal barges off Manhattan. There were marches, balls, and fireworks. "The Deed is Done," said the *American*.[30]

At a statewide convention on internal improvements held at the Baltimore Exchange that December, with Charles Carroll of Carrollton in the chair, the delegates listened as the canal proponents ran through their case. The Erie Canal would deprive the city of the trade advantages it had gained from the National Road, they said. Also, although the turnpike from Baltimore to Wheeling had finally been completed two years before, about the same time the one between Philadelphia and Pittsburgh was finished, the highways were already too slow and expensive. The convention, hedging its bets, favored a canal from Baltimore to the Potomac to join the Chesapeake and Ohio Canal, and yet another scheme for a canal from Port Deposit, Maryland, on the northeast side of the Susquehanna—the site of Baltimore's earlier effort and Latrobe's work in the riverbed—to Harrisburg, where it would meet Pennsylvania's Main Line of Internal Improvements, going west.[31]

On December 14, 1825, the day of the convention, the *American* published an unsigned letter that summarized the city's dilemma: "Baltimore happens to be situated on a short river, very advantageous . . . as to the ocean; but not penetrating into the interior of the country;—for the aid of canals she can look to but two rivers . . . the Susquehanna and the Potomac, she must chuse between them, there is no alternative unless indeed her hopes are in the railroad system."

3

The Last Resort

HISTORIANS HAVE MADE MUCH OF THE IMPORTANCE
of the Erie Canal. Its opening has been called "the most decisive event in the history of American transportation." Another historian described the canal as "an act of faith, the demonstration of a spirit of enterprise that has few parallels in world history."[1] There was, of course, ample precedent for it in Europe, as many Americans knew. The Languedoc Canal in France, mentioned by Gallatin, had been completed more than a century earlier, in 1681; it was 148 miles long, a little over 600 feet above sea level, and had 119 locks. In England, the canal age that began in the mid-1700's had reached its height at the time the Erie Canal was built. Nevertheless, the Erie Canal was impressive. As constructed between the Hudson River and Lake Erie, the canal was 360 miles long and required only 82 locks to overcome the difference in elevation between Albany and Buffalo of about 550 feet. In fact, almost half of it, roughly between Utica and Rochester, was built on a level. But as America's longest and most expensive canal, it was quite rightly looked upon as an audacious project for the time.

Moreover, it was profitable. Even before the $7 million project opened in 1825, it had collected close to $1 million in tolls. In one early eight-month period, the Erie carried over 13,000 boats loaded with some 220,000 tons of merchandise and 40,000 passengers. Freight rates between Buffalo and New York fell from $100 to $5 a ton, and travel time was drastically reduced.

Not the least of the effects of the Erie Canal was the impetus it gave to Baltimore and other major seaboard cities to build their own public works. Philadelphia began constructing its "mongrel" system of canals and railroads in 1826. Also in 1826, Washington, by far the smallest of the seaboard cities but with a special significance and a unique location on a river that led to the west, placed its hopes in the Chesapeake and Ohio Canal. With marvelous confidence and grand delusion, Philadelphia and Washington actually believed that if they built their own canals to

25

Lake Erie, the shorter distance would allow them to capture some, if not all, of New York's trade.

In 1827, Baltimore, then the nation's fourth largest city after New York, Philadelphia, and Boston, adopted the railroad. When it began operations three years later, it became, as it turned out, the first planned, long-distance, general-purpose railroad in the world. The Baltimore and Ohio Railroad was in its own way quite as audacious as the Erie Canal. Although crude tramways had been used in England in connection with mines since the sixteenth century and the earliest locomotives had appeared there just after the beginning of the nineteenth, the first railroad in England, or anywhere, that used locomotives to haul passengers and freight, the 25-mile Stockton and Darlington, had opened just eighteen months before the merchants in Baltimore decided to build one of their own.

The principal American model for the Baltimore project was the railroad that ran three miles from the quarries at Quincy, Massachusetts, to the Neponset River and hauled granite for the Bunker Hill monument. Another short railroad was under construction at Mauch Chunk, Pennsylvania, that was to transport coal by gravity nine miles from the mine to the Lehigh River. The projectors of the Baltimore and Ohio were planning to build a railroad far longer than those—ten times longer than any in existence—over mountains 3,000 feet high. Their decision represented the rejection of the dominant canal technology, which they considered outmoded, and the application of a primitive form of mine transportation to a long-distance internal improvement to the west. It was an amazing intellectual step, no less daring because it was desperate.

The Baltimoreans made their choice amidst an exhausting and divisive controversy over canals and whether the Susquehanna or the Potomac was the proper means of reaching the west. They also closely monitored railroad developments in England, where the initial run of the first steam passenger train, pulled by George and Robert Stephenson's Locomotion on the Stockton and Darlington Railway on September 27, 1825, heralded the beginning of a new age of transportation. All that year, the newspapers were full of railroad talk, but Maryland was still preoccupied with canals and the plans of Philadelphia and Washington.

In February 1825, the three commissioners appointed by the legislature to examine the route of the Pennsylvania Canal submitted their report, recommending a continuous waterway 320 miles long from Middletown, the terminus of the Union Canal, to Pittsburgh. It would have 417 locks and a four-mile tunnel under the Allegheny summit. The route followed the Susquehanna and its western branch, the Juniata, and linked up with the Conemaugh and the Allegheny rivers on the other side of the mountains. The estimated cost was $3 million. The surveys continued that year and were extended to Lake Erie.[2]

Dissension began immediately after the report was issued. One of the commissioners disagreed with the others, arguing that the summit was no place for a canal or a tunnel. A month later, the Pennsylvania Society for the Promotion of Internal Improvements, an organization founded by Mathew Carey, publisher, bookseller, political economist, and pamphleteer, sent William Strickland to Europe to investigate the entire subject of canals and railroads. Carey was a friend and Philadelphia counterpart of Hezekiah Niles, but whereas Niles in his *Weekly Register* advocated railroads, Carey was a vigorous promoter of canals, and the members of the Internal Improvement Society, mostly businessmen, were also canal backers.

Strickland, an architect and engineer, trained by Benjamin H. Latrobe, had gained a national reputation for his Second Bank of the United States in Philadelphia, finished in 1824. Like the Society's members, he belonged to the Franklin Institute, and he was respected for his clear thinking. Strickland confined his investigation to England and Scotland. He procured plans and models of everything from locomotives to bridges and sought answers to such questions as whether steamboats were suitable for canals and how railroads were built. When the results of his inquiries began appearing in newspapers, it quickly became evident that his preferences were not those of the Society. His first published report, written from Edinburgh, June 5, 1825, appeared in the Baltimore *American* the following August 15: "As to the relative advantages of railways and canals in mountainous or level countries," he wrote, "there appears to be but one opinion among the ablest engineers in England; both modes of transportation have been practically tested, and although much wealth and commercial greatness have been produced by numerous canals, still railroads offer greater facilities for the conveyance of goods, with more *safety, speed,* and *economy.*"

Although this statement was edited out of the published version of Strickland's report that appeared in 1826, the report nonetheless unequivocally favored railroads. It was the first complete explanation of their construction to be published in the United States, and its 72 very clear and detailed illustrations included renderings of tunnels, locomotives, and cars. The advent of the locomotive, Strickland concluded in his report, "has greatly changed the relative value of railways and canals; and where a communication is to be made between places of commercial or manufacturing character, which maintain a constant intercourse, and where rapidity of transit becomes important . . . railways will receive a preference, in consequence of this very powerful auxiliary." He also noted that steamboats were not suited to canals because their wake washed out the banks.[3]

The House of Representatives took 25 copies of Strickland's report, the State of Maryland, ten, and among other subscribers were at least one future Baltimore and Ohio Railroad board member, Isaac McKim, and three future B&O engineers, William Howard, Jonathan Knight, and Stephen H. Long, in whose later writings on railroads, Strickland's theories are discernible.

All during Strickland's ten-month survey in England, the canal-railroad controversy raged in Pennsylvania. Despite Carey's appeal for moderation, the debate quickly became inflammatory. Carey wrote Strickland, "It is feared by many that [the railroad issue] will divide the friends of [internal improvements] and thus postpone, if not prevent, the commencement of the great work."[4] Carey himself, however, was carrying on a venomous newspaper argument with a pro-railroad antagonist, who called himself the "Examiner." His identity was unknown, but Carey suspected him of also being the author of a popular pamphlet entitled *Facts and Arguments in Favour of Adopting Railways in Preference to Canals in the State of Pennsylva-*

nia. Carey dropped any pretense of impartiality and mounted a furious attack in a counter-pamphlet in which he declared, "The canal spirit is increasing throughout the Union. . . . The proprietors of turnpike roads are alarmed, and yet when they were established, they were resisted on similar grounds; they destroyed transportation by pack horse. Steamboats encountered violent opposition from the owners of sloops and packets." [5]

Carey's side prevailed. Early in 1826 a new board of canal commissioners recommended to the Pennsylvania legislature a shorter canal route and a railroad instead of a tunnel at the summit. The legislature passed a bill authorizing the canal, and construction began at Columbia, Pennsylvania, on July 4, 1826. The old and narrow Union Canal that was originally to have formed the eastern end of the system was by then nearing completion between Philadelphia and Middletown, north of Columbia, but this was subsequently abandoned as being inadequate for the trade expected. The Philadelphia and Columbia Railroad eventually replaced the Union Canal as a practical link in the line, and in 1831 an ingenious system of inclined planes and stationary engines was selected to cross the 2,300-foot summit.

When it was finished, the 395-mile Pennsylvania Main Line of Internal Improvements consisted of 277 miles of canals with 174 locks and 118 miles of railroads. The cost was $12.1 million. The route from Philadelphia began with the railroad to Columbia, then followed canals along the Susquehanna and Juniata rivers to Hollidaysburg, where the boats and their cargoes were loaded on railroad cars for the 37-mile trip over the mountains on the Allegheny Portage Railroad. At Johnstown on the other side, canals again led along the Conemaugh and Allegheny rivers to Pittsburgh. In October 1834, the *Hit or Miss*, the first keelboat to cross the Alleghenies, landed at Pittsburgh and sailed for Saint Louis. But the system proved to be an operational nightmare. Even Mathew Carey, in 1828, became a convert to railroads after a ride on the railroad at Mauch Chunk, Pennsylvania, and in 1831, the Internal Improvement Committee of the Pennsylvania legislature admitted that their canal system had been a mistake, built in imitation of New York's. [6]

Maryland's struggle to make up its mind about the canal-railroad question was resolved sooner than Pennsylvania's, but it was in many ways quite as difficult and acrimonious, and the canal proponents were not won over quickly. Philadelphia had long been Baltimore's chief competitor for trade, and the Susquehanna, far more than the Potomac, was the trade link. In 1817, almost $2 million worth of grain, flour, whiskey, iron, coal, New York State salt, lumber, and other products floated down the Susquehanna River past York Haven in nearly 350 arks and 1,000 rafts. Since the Chesapeake and Delaware Canal was not then open, most of this trade came on to Baltimore. [7]

When John Eager Howard, Jr., wrote his pamphlet in 1818, he noted that for the past seventeen years, the entire trade of the Potomac had amounted to just slightly over $7 million, or little more than $400,000 per year. And it flowed not to Baltimore, but to Georgetown. "The wealth of Georgetown gives nothing to Maryland," he said, "the prosperity of Georgetown is that of the stranger." Therefore the city should concentrate its canal efforts to the north: "A good boat navigation to Columbia would in fact make Baltimore instead of Philadelphia, the capital of Pennsylvania," and the Susquehanna was the logical route. "The struggle for this noble river must be made by Baltimore."[8]

For the farmers and merchants of Gettysburg, Hanover, and York, Baltimore already was the trade capital of Pennsylvania. Strong business bonds had built up over the years to the point where a Pennsylvania assemblyman could declare "that he did not care if a wall 50 feet high were built round Philadelphia, for Baltimore was his market."[9] Gradually, the Susquehanna trade had assumed a triangular pattern. Every spring, as many as 1,500 arks came down the river, and its western branch, the Juniata, to Port Deposit, Maryland, where their cargoes were transferred to sloops bound for Baltimore. During other seasons, when there was not enough water to run the rapids, the cargoes went ashore at Columbia and were wagoned to Philadelphia. For the return trip, regardless of the time of year, Philadelphia supplied most of the merchandise, sending it back over the turnpikes to Columbia or Middletown, where it was put on boats and distributed to the upriver towns. For years, Pennsylvania frustrated Maryland's efforts to extend canals past the falls of the Susquehanna and farther up into its territory.

Outside Baltimore, however, the Potomac River trade was quite important to its potential beneficiaries. The Hagerstown farmer shipping a barrel of flour to Baltimore paid from $1 to $1.25 on the turnpikes, but it would cost him only five cents if he could send it to Georgetown by water. "A canal through the western counties of the state would relieve the people from the most distressing and onerous burdens," according to the report of the Maryland convention on internal improvements that was held in Baltimore in December 1825.[10]

The lack of transportation also hindered Washington and the other district cities of Georgetown and Alexandria, which were to some extent isolated by poor roads and the tortuous outlet to the Bay down the winding, shallow Potomac. Indeed, Washington lagged far behind the rest of the seaboard cities. Its growth and improvement, wrote Abner Lacock, a former U.S. senator and a Potomac enthusiast, "have not been equal to the expectations of the Nation, and its tardy progress to importance is a subject of considerable mortification to its friends. What forbids this place becoming a commercial and manufacturing city? Washington is more than 100 miles nearer the navigation of the Ohio River than Philadelphia, and has greatly the advantage of Baltimore."[11]

The answer was to be the continuous canal along the Potomac River. This became the lifework of Charles Fenton Mercer, self-appointed executor of George Washington's Potomac legacy. More than just an advocate, like Pennsylvania's Mathew Carey, he was the waterway's creator, developer, protector. Charles Fenton Mercer *was* the Chesapeake and Ohio Canal.

Mercer, a Virginian, born in Fredericksburg in 1778, was a lawyer, as his father and grandfather had been before him, and after he was elected to the Virginia legislature in 1810, he took a special interest in internal improvements. He was primarily responsible for the 1816 bill creating the Virginia Board of Public Works and a state fund for internal improvements. The board recommended a full-length canal along the Potomac. Mercer was elected to Congress in 1817, and in his maiden speech in the House of Representatives in 1818 he spoke on the constitutional question of using surplus federal funds for internal improvements. For the next five years he assiduously promoted his canal project.

In December 1822, after more surveys by Thomas Moore, who had done an early survey in 1820, and Isaac Briggs, the commissioners appointed by Virginia and Maryland reported that the Potomac Company had failed to comply with its charter and would be unable to do so. The Virginia legislature then incorporated the Potomac Canal Company to take over from George Washington's old organization, but the Maryland General Assembly declined to confirm the charter because it required a heavy state contribution and was opposed by Baltimore merchants. The Baltimore businessmen's objections were, as always, that the canal would mostly benefit their competitors in Washington, Georgetown, and Alexandria, and also that the bill would deny them the right to build their own waterway from Baltimore to connect with the Potomac canal, and, not the least, that Baltimore would lose in taxes as well as in commerce.

Mercer continued his efforts, rallying support for the canal among the Maryland counties that stood to gain from it and considering concessions to the Baltimore interests. He organized a series of meetings in towns along the river during the summer and fall of 1823, and in November of that year, under his direction, some 100 delegates from Maryland, Virginia, Pennsylvania, Ohio, and the District of Columbia met in the Supreme Court chamber in Washington for a three-day canal convention. The only Baltimorean who attended was William Howard, the surveyor and canal enthusiast, who was seated as an honorary member.

Mercer projected the canal to Cumberland, to Pittsburgh, to Lake Erie. The assembled delegates changed the name from the Potomac and Ohio Canal to the Union Canal, but discovering that there already was one of those in Pennyslvania, settled on the politically innocuous Chesapeake and Ohio Canal. Further to mollify Baltimore, the convention made a point of authorizing Maryland and the other states to build connecting canals. On the last day they established a Central Committee, with Mercer as chairman, to continue the effort, and thanked him for his "zeal, ability, and industry."

The cost had been rising steadily, from an estimated $1.1 million in 1820 for a canal from Washington to Cumberland, to $1.6 million in 1822, and to $2.75 million in 1823. The last estimate, by the 1823 C&O Canal Convention, for a waterway to the coal banks beyond Cumberland, was no more reliable than earlier ones, however.

Mercer was a personal friend of President Monroe, and Monroe in his year-end State of the Union address urged Congress to support engineering surveys and more exact cost estimates. The Virginia legislature, in January 1824, obliged by incorporating the Chesapeake and Ohio Canal. Maryland again refused to ratify the charter, essentially for the same reasons as before. After Congress allotted $30,000 for the surveys, teams of United States engineers began a three-year program of tracing the banks of the Potomac to Cumberland. Following the streams into the mountains to the north and west, they reached the rivers that flowed to Pittsburgh, just as Washington had done before them.

A year before the official survey began, James Shriver, member of an energetic and talented family of civil engineers and businessmen based in Cumberland, had on his own explored the favored summit line of the canal along Deep Creek to the Youghiogheny River. This was the most difficult portion of the route over the mountains traced by the bi-state commissioners in 1822. It led from Cumberland west along the Potomac to where the Savage River flowed into it, at what is now Bloomington, Maryland. From there it climbed 1,500 feet in fourteen miles following the Savage River up over the mountain of the same name to Crabtree Creek, then continued on to Deep Creek, the Youghiogheny, the Monongahela, and Pittsburgh.

Shriver concentrated on the area at the top, west of Savage or Backbone Mountain, the dividing ridge. These were the Maryland Glades, where Washington, sheltered by his cloak, had spent the night in the rain. Shriver thought the several thousand acres of mountain meadows were the beds of former lakes; they still flooded annually during the spring thaw. When he was there during the summer of 1823, the glades for miles along Deep Creek were covered with twelve to eighteen inches of water. Nearby, Shriver found coal, iron, and limestone and white pines 200 feet high and eight to twelve feet in circumference. At the Deep Creek falls, where the stream met the Youghiogheny, the mountain laurel was so thick and impenetrable that Shriver had to discontinue his levels. Shriver followed the Youghiogheny north to where it met the Casselman River and other streams at a place graphically named Turkeyfoot, now Confluence, Pennsylvania.[12] The Virginia and Maryland commissioners had recommended damming Deep Creek to create a reservoir three or four miles long and half a mile wide that would furnish water for a two-mile tunnel under the dividing ridge, and also for the canal locks. Shriver thought the man-made lake could itself be used as a canal.[13]

Official surveys began in earnest when three brigades of engineers took the field in the summer of 1824. The first brigade, led by Major John J. Abert of the Army's Corps of Topographical Engineers, examined the lower Potomac in July and August, but all the officers became sick and quit until the following spring. Up in the healthier air of the mountains, two groups labored to determine the best way of connecting the rivers. One group, under William Gibbs McNeill, also of the Topographical Corps, was made up of six West Point graduates, most of whom, in another few years, would show up on Baltimore and Ohio Railroad surveys. The other group, led by James Shriver, now in an official capacity, included Jonathan Knight and probably William Howard. While these men were trailing through the Maryland Glades that summer, Pennsylvania's commissioners were less than 50 miles away along the same Allegheny front, exploring another set of rivers with a similar purpose in mind.

These preliminary surveys showed that the Maryland bank of the Potomac was best suited for a canal and alluded to two other possible routes to carry it over the mountains. One led north of Cumberland along Wills Creek and followed the Casselman River to the Youghiogheny and Monongahela. The other, a southern alternative to the Deep Creek route, sought a connection with the Cheat River. When McNeill, Knight, and the others subsequently took up railroad surveying, their steps turned naturally to these familiar mountain streams.

The engineers set out again in the spring of 1825. Again, sickness suspended operations on the lower Potomac, but work continued at the summit throughout the year and was extended beyond Pittsburgh to Lake Erie. Shriver and his men that summer were pursuing Bear Creek, yet another tributary of the Youghiogheny north of Deep Creek. They found only a few settlers in the Glades, most of them hunters living in cabins in an "extremely wild and desolate place." The surrounding country-side exhibited "a complication of mountain and valley, hill and hollow," that was "almost incomprehensible," they said, but they assured their auditors, "Everything so far appears quite favorable to the grand project." [14]

While the canal surveyors were extending their fieldwork, Mercer had unre-mittingly pursued his political chores. The Maryland legislature finally confirmed the Chesapeake and Ohio charter in January 1825, Congress ratified it two months later, and in June, Philip E. Thomas of Baltimore was named a state C&O Canal commissioner.

But the question of the connection from Baltimore was still unresolved, the Maryland charter being deliberately obscure on the point, according to an anony-mous critic, possibly Benjamin C. Howard, another of the Howard brothers, who was a member of the Maryland House of Delegates. He offered a revealing glimpse of Mercer's aggressive tactics. Having rushed the C&O bill through Congress, Mercer wrote resolutions in Washington in the fall of 1825, carried them to Frederick, Mary-land, and presented them at a canal meeting that he had organized. This in turn led to the state convention on internal improvements held in Baltimore in December 1825, that was supposed to smooth matters over. [15]

The convention settled nothing. In March 1826, the Maryland legislature passed an internal improvement bill appropriating $500,000 each to three canals: the Chesa-peake and Ohio, a canal from Baltimore to the Potomac to connect with it, and a third to the Susquehanna River. There would be "a mighty contest," for the west-ern trade, the *American* predicted, "between the great state of Pennsylvania on the one side, and the Potomac interest, aided by . . . the national government, on the other." [16] Later that month, the *American* released the preliminary cost estimates for the Chesapeake and Ohio Canal from Washington to Pittsburgh and in its excite-ment exaggerated them to $30 million—a figure alarmingly greater than the canal advocates expected.

During the summer of 1826, the engineers concluded their surveys in the moun-tains and refined their plans and estimates. Much of the work was done by McNeill, who surveyed both the Deep Creek and Casselman River routes, Shriver having fallen "a victim to the sickness" that season. On October 23, 1826, the federal Board of Engineers for Internal Improvement made its report, based largely on McNeill's find-ings. McNeill had concluded that Deep Creek could not supply enough water for a canal across the summit, and that, although dams could be built, the Casselman River route would be cheaper. McNeill had also surveyed a four-mile tunnel through the ridge separating the eastward-flowing Wills Creek and the westward-flowing Casselman.

The final report, which had been released in stages throughout the year, was made public officially in December 1826. It divided the canal into three sections. The first, 185 miles from Georgetown to Cumberland, was to cost $8.2 million; the second, from Cumberland to the confluence of the Casselman and Youghiogheny rivers (Confluence, Pennsylvania), $10 million; and the third, from that point to Pittsburgh, $4.2 million.[17] That was a total estimated cost of $22.5 million for a 341-mile canal with almost 400 locks, more than on any other waterway, and a four-mile tunnel to overcome the Allegheny summit of over 2,500 feet. (The *American* editors, working with a partial report, had probably added the first section to the total to come up with their $30 million figure.)

Fearing public reaction to so expensive a project, Mercer and the other canal backers had been working in various ways to discredit the findings of the official report before it was released. Early in September, Mercer assured canal enthusiasts, "Most exaggerated and erroneous rumours of the probable cost of the proposed canal are giving way to corrected estimates and reports." It seemed to be just a matter of time before the embarrassing business was cleared up and work could start.[18] President John Quincy Adams officially transmitted the United States engineers' report to Congress on December 7, 1826. By the time the second Chesapeake and Ohio Canal convention ended in Washington three days later, Mercer had succeeded in casting doubt on the cost estimates.

This convention had almost twice as many delegates as the one in 1823, and among them were some important canal advocates. Henry Clay represented Washington, Francis Scott Key, Georgetown; Baltimore this time sent six delegates—Philip E. Thomas, Solomon Etting, Benjamin C. Howard, William Lorman, Isaac McKim, and Joseph W. Patterson. Most of these men had been pushing the bill for the Susquehanna Canal earlier in the year. All six would become directors of the Baltimore and Ohio Railroad.

The convention looked into the lingering legal controversy surrounding the canal connection from Baltimore and the possibility of substituting a railway with inclined planes and stationary engines, similar to the Pennsylvania system, from Cumberland over the mountains. But its main task was to lower the cost, and it succeeded, though not so thoroughly as to change the minds of the Baltimore contingent.

Since the C&O Canal costs were a major factor in the railroad decision, the way they were derived is significant. Essentially, they were based on the Erie Canal. At the time the first estimates for the C&O were prepared in the early 1820's, the construction cost for the then uncompleted Erie was about $12,500 per mile. Using this figure, Abner Lacock had actually offered to build a 188-mile canal from Washington to Cumberland for $2.5 million, allowing $500,000 for contingencies. More sophisticated engineers, such as William Howard, knew such a project would be a good deal more expensive.

Even so, this same canal was now to cost more than three times as much as the early estimates, according to the U.S. engineers' report. One reason was that it had become, under federal auspices, a grandiose project. "The Chesapeake and Ohio Canal is, in every point of view, more important than that of New York," Congressman Andrew Stewart declared, rationalizing the high preliminary cost figures in a report to Congress in May 1826. It was a national work "of the most magnificent and durable character," he said, "intended to last for ages to come." It would be wider and deeper than the Erie Canal, and because of the difference in topography, there would have to be more locks per mile, which added to the expense.[19]

Stewart was the logical choice to head the special committee appointed on the first day of the 1826 C&O Canal convention to review the U.S. engineers' report. The extremely detailed document of more than 100 pages that he turned in three days later shows that he was well prepared for his task. It included testimonials from "practical engineers" such as Abner Lacock, then working on the Pennsylvania canal system, who again offered to build the C&O Canal to Cumberland at his old figure. Stewart's committee criticized the canal's enlarged dimensions, attacked the engineers' estimates for labor and materials, quarreled with them over construction methods, and concluded "that the work can be done for less than one third of its [$8.2 million] estimated cost."[20]

And so the canal proponents gradually worked back to their original figure of about $2.5 million. The following year, they succeeded in hiring engineers who, on the basis of a new survey, said the waterway to Cumberland could be built for $4 or $4.5 million. That of course renewed the incentive, and in taking the low figure as sound, the canal spokesmen established a precedent for underestimating C&O Canal construction figures that was to cost the State of Maryland dearly.

Mercer was also setting a pattern for using his public office to further his private ambitions. When the Chesapeake and Ohio Canal Company was officially formed in June 1828, Mercer was elected its first president. He held the post until 1833. From 1823 to 1838, he was also a either a member or chairman of the House Committee on Roads and Canals, and in that capacity he did all he could to advance the cause of the quasi-private company he headed, a classic conflict of interest on a scale that would be unimaginable today but was evidently unremarkable at the time, although it was certainly noticed.

As time went on, one of Mercer's most constant critics was the Baltimore and Ohio Railroad. In the early days, the company complained sharply and often of the canal's unfair political advantage. When they were not crying foul, the Baltimore capitalists condescendingly dismissed Mercer as a social and intellectual inferior. But Mercer was an intelligent and skillful tactician who became their most effective, consistent adversary and a bitter personal enemy of Philip E. Thomas. The Baltimore and Ohio never accused Mercer of using his position to enrich himself. Indeed, Mercer claimed to have left the federal government a poor man and there was never a hint that his concern with internal improvements was anything but genuine. Certainly it was long standing and hard won. By 1828, it had taken him six full years to pass sixteen separate legislative acts in three states and the Congress to create the C&O Canal.

The Baltimoreans, although they had certainly benefited from all the work that Pennsylvania and the Potomac interests had done, respectively, in exploring alternative methods and routes for reaching the west, still had to decide what was best for Baltimore. When the local merchants met in January 1827 for their third biennial discussion of what was to be done, the mood was somber. This time, as they went over the old, familiar ground of whether to build a canal to the Susquehanna or to the Potomac, and by which route, the man in charge was Philip E. Thomas, who had been appointed by the mayor as chairman of the committee.

Thomas's report emphasized that the Susquehanna was the more pressing problem, because Pennsylvania's Main Line of Internal Improvements was already under construction. Should Baltimore try to draw off Philadelphia's trade by extending a canal along the southwest side of the Susquehanna to York Haven, or should it build one on the northeast side to Middletown, the termination of the Pennsylvania canal? Thomas commented, "These differences of opinion had degenerated into a mere controversy about the relative facilities for . . . a canal on this or that side of the river." [21]

The prospects for a waterway to the Potomac were no better. The legislature had chartered the Maryland Canal Company in March 1826, and William Howard, now working for the federal government, was in the midst of his second canal survey to connect Baltimore with the Potomac River. This survey had started in the summer of 1826, and Howard in his report a year later said that a 37-mile, $3 million canal between Baltimore and Georgetown was practical, but one to the Potomac River north of there was not. Of the various alternatives, the committee recommended the canal along the Susquehanna's northeast side to Middletown. But Thomas, reflecting the lack of enthusiasm, remarked wearily, "Forty years have elapsed since the first acts were passed for the improvement of the Potomac and the Susquehanna, and we are as yet in the wilderness." [22]

Thomas had already resigned as commissioner for the Chesapeake and Ohio Canal and turned to the counsel of George Brown. A month later, in February 1827, they organized the Baltimore and Ohio Railroad. Thomas later summed up the situation thus: "When the report of the United States engineers, transmitted to Congress, December 7th, 1826, and published, presented a detailed and intelligible view of [the canal's] character and difficulties, in place of the vague ideas, that had before been entertained with regard to it, all hopes of accomplishing the desired object by its means, were at once abandoned. The people of Baltimore, then, had but one course left; and they adopted the railroad system." [23]

4

Sons of Commerce

BY THE LATE SUMMER OF 1826, SERIOUS RAILROAD discussions were under way in Baltimore. Evan Thomas, the younger brother of Philip E. Thomas, was in England that summer to see the Stockton and Darlington Railway in operation, and after he returned he gave an enthusiastic report to a group of men who assembled for dinner at Belvidere, the Baltimore mansion of Colonel John Eager Howard.[1] Colonel Howard, then aged 74 and in failing health, was the father of William Howard, the canal surveyor who was also an architect-engineer, and of Benjamin C. Howard, member of the Maryland legislature, future congressman and railroad incorporator. His eldest son, John Eager, Jr., who as state senator in 1818 had reported on canals and turnpikes to the legislature, had died in 1822 of the fever, aged 34.

Philip and Evan Thomas were sons of a Quaker minister from Montgomery County, Maryland. In 1799, they served as ambassadors of the Friends to the Indians in Ohio. After a partnership in a hardware business with his brother-in-law and Evan, known as Thomas and George, and later as P. and E. Thomas and Sons, hardware merchants and importers, Philip branched out into banking and became involved in the affairs of his city. He advanced the state $25,000 to begin construction of Baltimore's Washington Monument; he served as the first president of the Mechanical Fire Company and as trustee of the almshouse; he was a founder of the Baltimore Library Company and an active participant in the State Temperance Society—a "philanthropic public character," as one foreign visitor described him. Where Evan was voluble and impulsive, Philip, five years his senior, was quiet and painstaking, but the popular conception of him as a good, gray banker was less than complete. When circumstances dictated, Philip E. Thomas could also be calculating and devious. At the time of the dinner at Belvidere, Thomas, then 50, was the cashier of the Mechanics Bank, which Alexander Brown and Sons had helped to establish and where George

Brown was a director. Together, over the months following the dinner, George Brown and Philip E. Thomas conceived the Baltimore and Ohio Railroad.

The Browns were in a unique position to appreciate Baltimore's dilemma with regard to internal improvements. Alexander Brown, the 62-year-old founder and patriarch, had emigrated in 1800 with his wife and eldest son, William, from northern Ireland because of the political unrest there, and in Baltimore, where he had relatives, he established himself in the linen business with stock he brought from Ireland. Two years later, the other three sons, George, John, and James, arrived in Baltimore. Eventually, all the sons were taken into the firm.

Their office was on the northwest corner of Baltimore and Calvert streets (the site, until the fire of 1904, of the Baltimore and Ohio Railroad's Central Building), opposite the present location of Alex. Brown and Sons, Inc. The company under that name dates from 1810 and is the oldest investment banking firm in the nation. About that time the eldest son, having returned to Great Britain, opened a branch office in Liverpool, William Brown and Company. John opened a branch of the business in Philadelphia in 1818, when Baltimore and Philadelphia were dueling over the western trade, and in 1825, a few months after the Erie Canal began operations, the New York office, run by James and known as Brown Brothers and Company, was ready for business. George stayed in the Baltimore headquarters with his father.

By 1826, Alex. Brown and Sons had virtually monopolized the linen business in the city as well as the foreign trade with Liverpool. They were also significant dealers in sterling exchange, cotton shippers, importers, shipowners, and merchant bankers. In the last function, they arranged the international shipments and sales of other traders, using bills of exchange that passed as currency. With their knowledge of domestic and foreign markets, widespread organization, and communications network (via sailing ship, steamer, and stagecoach), Alex. Brown and Sons became "America's foremost international banking enterprise in the nineteenth century," rivaling the Second Bank of the United States in the American foreign exchange markets and competing with Baring Brothers and Company, the London merchant bankers.

Of the four sons, George most closely resembled Alexander. He bore the same square, almost seraphic expression, and he was in the best position to absorb directly his father's bold but conservative approach to business. He took over the firm when its founder died in 1834. In the intervening years, the father and son immersed themselves completely in the new railroad. They were supplied with first-hand information from William, in Liverpool, to whom Alexander Brown once wrote, "In the management of one's business it is not only necessary to be correct, but not to be suspected of incorrectness."[2]

The two meetings of the city's commercial aristocracy in February 1827 that resulted in the formation of the Baltimore and Ohio Railroad took place at George Brown's house. This house, where the City Hall now stands, was at that time in the heart of Baltimore's social, cultural, and business center. The Merchants Exchange, where the Browns conducted their trading under the dome, was a few blocks south;

the Holliday Street Theater, from whose boxes and long, hard, wooden benches, they applauded the elder Booth and other entertainers, was just opposite, and Peale's Museum and the Library, with the assembly room above it, home of the Cotillon, were nearby.

The first gathering took place on February 12, and was brief and businesslike. Some two dozen mercantile leaders were called together to discuss "the best means of restoring to the City of Baltimore, that portion of the Western Trade, which has lately been diverted from it by the introduction of Steam navigation, and by other causes." William Patterson was named chairman, and George Brown and Philip E. Thomas presented "various documents and statements, illustrating the efficiency of Rail Roads," along with their advantages over turnpikes and canals. A committee was appointed to decide a course of action. George Brown, Philip E. Thomas, and Evan Thomas were on it, as were Benjamin C. Howard, Talbot Jones, Joseph W. Patterson, and John V. L. McMahon. The merchants agreed to meet again in a week.

The following Monday night, February 19, 1827, the group reassembled at George Brown's house and reviewed the document the committee had drafted. The "Proceedings of Sundry Citizens of Baltimore, convened for the purpose of devising the most efficient means of Improving the Intercourse between that City and the Western States" contained the decision to build the railroad, and the reasons for doing so. Philip E. Thomas signed the report, as chairman of the committee that produced it.[3]

The account begins by noting the efforts of Philadelphia and New York to gain the western trade and argues that the completion of a canal from the Chesapeake Bay to the Pennsylvania State Canal represents "all that we are now called upon to execute in reference to the River Susquehanna. But important as this trade is to Baltimore, it is certainly of minor consideration, when compared to the immense commerce which lies within our grasp to the West, provided we have the entreprize to profit by the advantages which our local situation gives us." Those advantages were geographic: "Baltimore lies 200 miles nearer to the navigable waters of the West than New York, and about 100 miles nearer to them than Philadelphia, to which may be added the important fact, that the easiest, and by far the most practicable route through the ridges of Mountains, which divide the Atlantic from the Western waters, is along the depression formed by the Potomac."

Pointedly ignoring Washington, D.C., the businessmen asserted that Baltimore's southern competitor for the trade of the west was New Orleans, and that they would have to share it with that city. There would be enough for both, they thought.

As to the best means of crossing the mountains, the planners looked to England, where the canals that had replaced the turnpikes were now themselves being superseded by railroads, 2,000 miles of which were finished or under construction. But they noted that even in England, the idea of building long-distance railroads was novel, and England's climate was more conducive to canals than America's. Here they would freeze in winter and stagnate in summer. If Great Britain was building railroads, "will it be wise in us to exhaust our resources upon a system which is now about to be abandoned in a country where the experiment of the two plans has been fairly and fully made?"

The three-mile Quincy Railroad near Boston, completed the previous fall, had cost $11,000 per mile, the committee reported, but they thought a similar one could be built for about a third less. Though their information on the subject was slight, it was "enough to leave no doubt upon their minds, that these roads are far better adapted to our situation and circumstances, than a Canal across the Mountains would be: they therefore recommend that measures be taken to construct a double Rail Road between the City of Baltimore and some suitable point on the Ohio River, by the most eligible route, and that a charter to incorporate a Company to execute this work be obtained as early as possible."

To support their opinion, the committee included a number of extracts from other reports; half of the "Proceedings" consists of such material. They quoted William Strickland on the power of locomotives from his report to the Pennsylvania Society for Internal Improvements, and William Jessop, an early builder of English tramways, whom Strickland had used as an authority. Another expert cited was Nicholas Wood, foreman of the Killingworth colliery in England, where George Stephenson's locomotives had been in daily use for many years, and whose *Practical Treatise on Rail-Roads* had appeared in London in 1825. The committee also quoted at length from a treatise by the English railroad enthusiast Thomas Gray entitled *Observations on a General Iron Rail Way or land steam-conveyance*. This work had already been through five editions, of which the committee had the latest, published in 1825.

Gray, the most outspoken advocate of railroads in England at the time, had started talking about them in 1816, gradually becoming convinced that his system "would revolutionize the whole face of the material world and of society." He published his treatise in 1820 and campaigned for a railroad between Liverpool and Manchester.[4] Gray was certain that railroads were vastly superior "in every respect, over all the present pitiful methods of conveyance by turnpike roads, canals, and coasting-traders." Railroads could be built at a fifth the cost of canals. They could convey goods, even fish and oysters (which intrigued the Baltimore railroad promoters), cheaper, quicker, more efficiently. Again, it was the locomotive that made the difference.

The title page of Gray's book features illustrations of cog-wheel engines pulling coaches and freight cars and a message:

> No Speed with this, can fleetest Horse compare,
> No weight like this, canal or Vessel bear,
> As this, will Commerce every way promote,
> To this, let Sons of Commerce grant their vote.

A map in the fifth edition of Gray's *Observations* shows proposed rail lines fanning out from London to Falmouth, Bristol, and Edinburgh on undeviating alignments straight as a ruler, for Gray believed that railroads could be built on a "direct line."

The Baltimore committee agreed with the statements of Gray and others about the cheaper cost of railroads, and they also brought in the report of the federal Board of Engineers for Internal Improvement to strengthen their economic case. They argued, for example, that if the U.S. engineers estimated that the C&O Canal would increase the value of land in the District of Columbia and the western states by a certain amount, the railroad, with Baltimore substituted for the District, would increase it more. If the canal would create, by virtue of its existence, a rise in trade, tonnage, and revenues, these figures could be applied equally to the railroad. The committee went on to state succinctly their own economic argument, in terms of the railroad's adding value to goods, stimulating production, and creating benefits at either end of the line:

> There are a great variety of articles, the product of the country west of the Alleghany Mountains, which are now of little value in those countries, on account of the heavy expense unavoidably incurred in the transportation of them, to a port whence they could be shipped to a foreign market. With the facilities afforded by this road many of those articles could not only bear a transportation to Baltimore, but while they would furnish a constant and increasing supply of freight upon the proposed road, they would become a source of great wealth to the people of the West.
>
> To illustrate the truth of this statement, it will only be necessary to refer to the single article of bread stuffs. A Barrel of flour for instance, which would now command five dollars in Baltimore, would not, as an article of export *to that market*, be worth at Wheeling, on the Ohio River, more than one dollar; the cost of its transportation from that place by the present means of conveyance being four dollars; Whereas upon the proposed Rail Road, the whole expense of transportation from the Ohio river to Baltimore, being estimated to be only at the rate of ten dollars per ton, the cost of carriage upon a barrel of flour would then be only one dollar; thus at once would its value, as an article of export, be enhanced in Ohio from one dollar to four dollars per barrel.

Cotton, "and coal from the Alleghany mountains near to Cumberland," would also be shipped to Baltimore. The committee thought "that there is no scale by which we would venture to calculate the ultimate extent of the trade, which would flow into the State of Maryland, upon the proposed Rail Road."

Their expectations were based on a growing population and an expanding nation, the prospects for which in 1827 seemed to them limitless. After a slow beginning, the westerly migration was now moving at a rate of about 30 miles a year. It had reached the junction of the Osage River with the Missouri, roughly halfway between Saint Louis and Kansas City, and "if not checked by some unforeseen circumstances, it will, within the next thirty years, reach the Rocky Mountains, or even to the Pacific Ocean. We have therefore, no reason to look for any falling off in this Trade, but on the contrary, for an increase of it."

The committee concluded its report with a call to connect Baltimore and the western states "by intersecting the contemplated Chesapeake and Ohio Canal within the District of Columbia, and by A DIRECT RAIL ROAD FROM BALTIMORE TO SOME ELIGIBLE POINT ON THE OHIO RIVER."

The tables in the appendix to the "Proceedings" summarized their case. The railroad was to be shorter, quicker, and cheaper to construct and transport goods on than the Chesapeake and Ohio Canal. Again, the source of the canal figures was the report of the U.S. engineers. If the connecting canal were built to Washington, the total distance from Baltimore to Pittsburgh via the C&O Canal would be 390 miles, but from Baltimore "to Wheeling or some other suitable point on the Ohio River," by railroad was only 250 miles. Since the turnpike distance between Baltimore and Wheeling was 252 miles, the Baltimore capitalists apparently planned to build their "direct railroad" parallel to the National Road.

The U.S. engineers had estimated the expense of the canal from Washington to Pittsburgh at $22.4 million. Giving the canal proponents the benefit of the doubt with regard to their revised cost projections, the Baltimore merchants allowed that it could be made for less than half that much, or $11 million. Adding $1 million for the Baltimore-Washington waterway, they arrived at a total canal cost of $12 million. But a 250-mile railroad from Baltimore to the Ohio River, at $20,000 a mile, "a very high estimate," they said, would be only $5 million.[5]

It would take a canal boat almost nine days to get from Pittsburgh, through Washington, to Baltimore, but the trains from the Ohio River would reach the city in about two and a half days. This conservative estimate was based on English reports of locomotives pulling coal cars at only four miles an hour. The cost of moving a ton of freight the 390 miles from Pittsburgh to Baltimore by canal, at one and a half cents per ton per mile, was $5.85. The railroad toll would be just $2.50, for 250 miles at one cent per ton per mile, but they planned to charge an additional three cents for transportation, making the true rate four cents per ton per mile, or $10 for moving a ton of freight the 250 miles between the Ohio River and Baltimore.

The group gathered at George Brown's house unanimously approved this report and appointed a 25-man committee to apply immediately to the Maryland legislature for an act to incorporate a joint stock company with the power to build the railroad. They were also to seek legislative approval in Pennsylvania and Virginia for the rail line to pass through those states. Charles Carroll of Carrollton headed the list. Other important members were Robert Oliver, Alexander Brown, and William Patterson, men of nearly equal wealth and prestige in the community; Philip E. Thomas and Benjamin C. Howard; ironmaster Charles Ridgely of Hampton; Isaac McKim, ex-congressman, owner of mills and sailing ships; Thomas Ellicott of Ellicotts Mills, president of the Union Bank; and William Lorman, another banker, who had interests in turnpike and steamboat companies.[6]

On the morning of February 19, 1827, the day the city's business leaders decided to build the Baltimore and Ohio Railroad, the *American* printed a letter, unsigned but so similar in its sentiments and language to those expressed in the "Proceedings" that its anonymous author must have been intimately involved with the railroad plans. It was in effect a ringing call to arms, rallying support for the railroad and scoffing at canal backers. A few days earlier, the Pennsylvania commissioners had turned in a voluminous report to the state legislature on the Susquehanna canal, and Mercer had been active in Congress since the beginning of the month pushing bills for the Chesapeake and Ohio Canal, but the latter, the correspondent maintained, even if completed the next day, would be no use to Baltimore: "*Depend upon it you will never see a canal between this city and the Ohio River.*" Rather, "You must look for some more permanent mode of intercourse; that mode must be a *rail road*, with locomotive and stationary engines, inclined planes, etc."

Until then, the newspapers had been totally absorbed in the canal plans. Only the week before, the *American* had indicated in its lead editorial that the most important thing for Baltimore was to intersect the Pennsylvania Canal and divert the Susquehanna trade to the city. But the newspapers quickly swung round. Within days, they were carrying ads noting that 1,500 copies of the "Proceedings" were on sale at twelve and a half cents a copy. The evening paper, the *Gazette*, described the pamphlet as containing "a collection of facts showing the superiority of rail-ways over Canals and turnpikes, and . . . that [a railroad] would make this city the great emporium for the immensely extensive trade of the West." Moreover, "The character, energy and enterprize of the highly respected gentlemen who have undertaken the business, are the surest guarantees to the public that, with proper legislative aid and the co-operation of the Citizens, the plan must succeed."[7]

The first and most important order of business for the new railroad was to draft a charter. The man chosen to do it was the brilliant but enigmatic young lawyer John Van Lear McMahon. He represented Baltimore in the Maryland House of Delegates, where he was on the internal improvement committee. McMahon was from Cumberland, the only son of an Irish Presbyterian farmer who had served several terms in the state legislature. Precocious and studious, he graduated from Princeton with top honors when he was just seventeen and was recommended for the ministry. McMahon became a lawyer instead, but when he began to practice in Baltimore, his overbearing attitude alienated the city's attorneys and judges. He retreated to Cumberland, honed his skills as a public speaker, and was elected to the legislature from Allegany County in 1823. His reputation as the "mountain orator" preceded him to Annapolis, where he arrived, still vain and affected, a strange figure "absurdly dressed in the guise of a mountain huntsman in a linsey-woolsey shirt and with a primitiveness and uncouth manner which indeed were no part of his nature."[8] McMahon quickly shed his pose and turned into an effective legislator. He worked on the railroad charter bill, advocated state aid for the Chesapeake and Ohio Canal, and argued for the removal of political restrictions on Maryland's Jews. By the end of the session, he was acknowledged as a major spokesman in the House. Completing his second term in 1825, he returned to Baltimore to practice law, and in 1827, at the age of 26, he was again elected to the legislature, from the city.[9]

Despite McMahon's eccentricity and probably in view of his stature in Annapolis, the business leadership of Baltimore decided he was just the man to draft the charter for the railroad. McMahon's charter, as passed by the legislature, contained 23 sections. The Baltimore and Ohio Railroad Company, as it was designated, was to have $3 million of capital stock in $100 shares with $1 million worth reserved for the State of Maryland and $500,000 worth for the City of Baltimore if the two political jurisdictions acted within a year. The remaining 15,000 shares could be subscribed for by corporations or individuals. The company would be organized when 10,000 shares had been sold. The amount of stock could be increased when necessary. The charter provided for twelve directors, with the state and city entitled to one additional director for each 2,500 shares of stock owned.

The charter specifically empowered the corporation to construct a railroad with a 66-foot right-of-way from Baltimore to the Ohio River. The officers were to have the right of eminent domain concerning both the land and the materials they needed to build it. There was ample provision for condemnation proceedings, court settlements, compensation for damages, and so on. The officers also had the power to place "all machines, wagons, vehicles, or carriages of any description whatsoever" on the road and to charge four cents per ton per mile for freight transported eastward and six cents westward. Passenger fares were set at three cents a mile. The company had entire jurisdiction over its road and equipment.[10]

The next provision was ultimately one of the most valuable, controversial, and imitated of all the provisions: the corporation's capital stock was to be considered "personal estate" and exempt from taxes by the states assenting to the law. The Maryland Court of Appeals later extended this tax exemption to all the railroad's property in the state. It was a benefit that despite numerous legal challenges remained virtually intact until 1987, when the B&O ceased to exist as a corporate entity.[11]

As McMahon was reading this section to the committee appointed to secure the charter, the blunt, florid-faced Robert Oliver stood up and said, "Stop man, you're asking for more than the Lord's prayer." McMahon replied with a smile that "it was all necessary, and the more they asked for, the more they would get."

"Right man, go on," said Oliver.[12]

The speed with which the incorporators pursued the railroad project—it took them just nine days from the time they formally decided to build it until they secured the charter—testifies to their renewed sense of purpose after years of frustrating canal discussions, and to their political influence. A very practical reason for their haste was that the legislatures in the other states where they hoped to pass the charter would, like Maryland's, shortly end their sessions.

Presumably no one except the railroad committee, neither the newspaper editors in Baltimore nor the legislators in Annapolis, had seen McMahon's draft when, on February 27, the august delegation representing much of the economic power of the nation's fourth-largest city presented itself at the state Capitol and was seated "within the bar," that is, on the floor of the House of Delegates itself. At least some of the politicians, however, must have known that the charter was coming because a careful plan had been worked out to pass it the same day, preferably with no discussion. If this was not the origin of the term "to railroad" a bill, it certainly was an early and prime example of the maneuver. But the planners evidently did not include Charles County's John G. Chapman, chairman of the Ways and Means Committee, who took the tax exemption as a personal challenge.

The Baltimore *Gazette*, published by lawyer William Gwynn, carried a full account of the debate that followed, perhaps written by Gwynn himself.[13] Gwynn was a good friend of Philip E. Thomas and he later drafted some of the railroad's legislation and acted as an intermediary in Annapolis. According to Gwynn's account, James W. McCulloh, the House speaker, a former bank speculator and future B&O

Railroad lobbyist and agent, after predicting that the proceedings they were about to embark on "would form a bright chapter in the history of Maryland," read the names of the signers of the memorial seeking passage of the charter, beginning with Charles Carroll of Carrollton. Carroll, it was reported, remarked when he added his name "that he only signed *one other document* in his life which he considered more important and essential to the interest of the state."

To expedite passage of the bill, the House of Delegates, on the motion of John S. Tyson, from Baltimore, voted to sit as a committee of the whole. The measure was read. Chapman said he would like to amend the bill by striking out the tax exemption and was ruled out of order. Tyson then asked "that the committee now rise and report the bill." Chapman professed astonishment at this: "In all his life he never heard of such a proceeding." He thought the House had voted itself a committee of the whole to consider the provisions of the bill, but that when he had offered to consider one of them, he was prevented from doing so, and now, "at this stage of the business, when . . . it had not yet been in order to propose an amendment to the bill, the gentleman makes his motion that a committee rise—Rise for what, Sir? to report a bill? The committee cannot report that bill—they have not considered it."

Furthermore, Chapman continued, he had known nothing of the contents of the bill until a moment ago when it was read for the first time. In other words, the delegates were being asked to approve, without debate, a measure they had not seen. McCulloh backed down. The House, to avoid a second reading of the entire bill, agreed to consider the offending section containing the tax exemption. There followed a full and free discussion of that one provision. Chapman stated his principle, that private property ought to be taxed for the support of government, and he clung to it like a lifeline as first McCulloh, then Thomas B. Hall, of Washington County, and finally Tyson tried to shake him loose.

McCulloh cited a precedent for the tax exemption provision in the charters of the Chesapeake and Ohio Canal and its ancestor, the Potomac Company, and he further pointed out that the capitalists were, after all, investing their own money, and that if Maryland taxed the railroad, the other states through which it passed could also do so, perhaps at ruinous rates because of sectional jealousy. Would the lawmakers prefer to reap the benefits of the railroad "by granting this little boon," or would they defeat the whole project through "coveting the pittance which might be derived from a tax on this stock?"

Chapman still maintained that it was unfair to tax "every humble planter or farmer, with his impoverished land on which he sustains a family," and exempt the stockholder, "who owns half a million of money in a rail road." The canal was different, because its promoters anticipated heavy government investment, which ought to be tax exempt. The railroad was being backed mainly by individuals who, though motivated by patriotism and public spirit, "undertake it because it is expected to be vastly profitable."

McCulloh defended them as "pioneers in a vast and expensive enterprise, as yet certainly *a speculation*." Chapman replied that his sole object was to leave to future generations the choice of taxing the railroad if it became profitable, or not doing so if it did not: "But pass the bill as it is reported, and you will exclude the state forever from any such discretion, however riches may pour into the lap of the stockholder, however severe the exigencies of the state—however oppressive the taxes on other . . . property, this is to be exempt and free."

Hall, taking up the defense, asked the legislators whether they would "for a petty, sordid consideration strangle the infant in its cradle," and Tyson rejoined the discussion, claiming their actions represented "life or death for the undertaking." He announced that the gentlemen from the railroad who were closely monitoring the debate had authorized him to state that the law would be unacceptable without the tax exemption. Chapman's motion was voted down.

There were further attempts to table the bill or lay it over for at least one night so that the members could have a chance to read it on their own, since they had just received it that morning, but these, too, were defeated. One delegate said he had "no idea of this precipitation in legislation."

Two minor qualifications were added. The first said that if the railroad was not begun in two years from the passage of the act and finished within Maryland in ten years, the charter would be null and void; the second, that other companies had the right to construct branch lines within the state. It was about 2:30 P.M. when the House of Delegates passed the bill, 59–10, Chapman voting for.

The measure was sent immediately to the Senate, where an attempt to have it printed failed. But the Senate passed the bill the next day, and the charter of the Baltimore and Ohio Railroad Company effectively became law on February 28, 1827. The *American* editors, after alluding to the "novel method adopted in the management of this business," said simply, "God Speed the Rail Road." [14]

Perhaps out of pride of authorship, McMahon himself took little part in the argument. McMahon's biographer claimed the B&O charter was "formed without a precedent, out of the fertility of his own brain"; John H. B. Latrobe said the document "was modelled mainly on the old turnpike charters." [15] There are also some similarities to contemporary British railroad charters. The projectors of the Baltimore and Ohio had a copy of the Liverpool and Manchester Railway charter.

The Virginia legislature, aided in its deliberations by a trio of B&O lobbyists, ratified the act including the tax exemption on March 8, 1827. They added one significant restriction that said the railroad must not strike the Ohio River at a point lower "than the mouth of the Little Kenhawa," at Parkersburg, Virginia.

Maryland's governor signed the bill on March 13, and the same day the Baltimore newspapers carried ads announcing that the sale of stock would begin in a week and would continue until the end of the month at the Mechanics Bank, where Philip E. Thomas and George Brown were officers, and also at banks in Frederick and Hagerstown. There were rumors that the entire 15,000 shares reserved for individuals would be sold the first day, and they almost were: 13,586 went in four hours.

It was a scene "which almost beggars description," John H. B. Latrobe recalled. "By this time public excitement had gone far beyond fever heat and reached the boiling point. Everybody wanted stock," he said. "Parents subscribed in the names of their children, and paid the dollar on each share that the rules prescribed. Before a survey had been made—before common sense had been consulted, even, the possession of stock in any quantity was regarded as provision for old age; and great was the scramble to obtain it. The excitement in Baltimore roused public attention elsewhere, and a railroad mania began to pervade the land." [16]

Almost as many shares, 13,387, were sold the last day as the first. Altogether, nearly 42,000 shares of stock were subscribed for during the twelve days, representing a capital investment of more than $4 million; the names of 23,000 stockholders were listed. Among them were Jacob Small, Jr., the mayor of Baltimore, and the City Council, which signed up for the city's full allotment of 5,000 shares on March 20, 1827, along with several incorporators of the railroad. Robert Oliver, Alexander Brown, and William Patterson took 500 shares apiece, as did Philip and Evan Thomas. Charles Carroll of Carrollton, Thomas Ellicott, Isaac McKim, Talbot Jones, and Charles Ridgely of Hampton, took lesser amounts. Just about everybody bought stock, from Robert Gilmor, the wealthy art collector (200 shares), to James W. and Abby McCulloh (5 shares each), to C. Meineke, the professor of music who was probably already at work on "The Railroad March" that he composed in honor of the B&O's start of construction.[17]

Because the stock was oversubscribed, purchasers were limited to fractions of a share. The excess money was refunded. A year later, the railroad issued an additional 15,000 shares and the original buyers received their full amount of stock. The supplementary stock issue was bought up almost as quickly as the first.

A few days before the subscription books were opened, Jonathan Knight, one of the engineers who conducted the early surveys for the C&O Canal in western Maryland, who was a member of the Pennsylvania legislature, reported a B&O charter ratification bill out of the Senate committee of internal improvement, which he chaired. But the state's lawmakers wanted to avoid a conflict with their own Main Line of Internal Improvements and declined to pass it that session.

Yet nothing could detract from the euphoria of the moment. Hezekiah Niles, intoxicated with the railroad's potential, predicted, "The time will soon come, when a person may pass from the city of Baltimore to some point on the Ohio river, with the same sort of certainty, ease and convenience, that he may make a voyage from Baltimore to Norfolk in a steam boat—that little travelling palaces will be prepared, in which persons may eat, drink, sit, stand or walk, and sleep, *just as they do in steam boats*. Why not?" [18]

The railroad is "bringing an empire to our doors," said the Baltimore *American*. During the spring of 1827, the newspaper reprinted comments coming from the West in support of the railroad. The Cincinnati *Register*, for example, wrote: "We are heartily tired of a Louisiana monopoly. . . . The West is as much concerned in [the railroad's] success as Baltimore herself." If, owing to Pennsylvania's rejection of the B&O charter, the railroad did not go to Pittsburgh, so much the better for Ohio, and for Baltimore. Nor did it have to go to Wheeling. The river was deeper farther south, just above the Little Kenhawa, at Marietta, where citizens were organizing to make it a railroad terminus. Chillicothe, on the Ohio Canal, which imagined itself a major metropolis of the future, backed the Marietta effort. These Ohio towns hoped to send their produce to Baltimore on the new railroad rather than to New York via the existing canals. The Wheeling *Gazette* derided Marietta's hopes but said diplomatically that wherever the railroad ended, "The value of our produce will be enhanced, and consequently the value of our lands." Marietta in turn hinted that Wheeling was offering the B&O $100,000 to end its line there. And so on. In these early reactions can be found the origins of disputes over routes and destinations that would perplex the company and wear down its officers and engineers for the next 20 years. In all, the West's enthusiasm for the railroad has "greatly surpassed our expectations," the *American* concluded.[19]

But it wasn't just the West. Attention north and south was focused on Baltimore. The Berkshire, Massachusetts, *Star* raved, "Pyramids . . . palaces and all the mere pride and pomp of man sink to insignificance before such a work as this . . . a single city has set on foot an enterprise . . . worthy of an empire." The Tuscumbia, Alabama, *Patriot* promised that Baltimore would become "the greatest commercial city in the United States," and Tuscumbia a major rail depot when Southern planters sent their cotton to Baltimore instead of to New Orleans.[20]

The requisite amount of stock having been sold, the Baltimore and Ohio Railroad was organized officially on April 23, 1827. On that day, the stockholders met at the Mechanics Bank at Calvert and Fayette streets at 9:00 A.M., and elected twelve directors: Charles Carroll of Carrollton, Robert Oliver, Alexander Brown, William Patterson, Philip E. Thomas, Isaac McKim, Thomas Ellicott, William Lorman, George Hoffman, John B. Morris, Talbot Jones, and William Steuart. The city appointed two directors to represent its stock, Solomon Etting and Patrick Macaulcy. The following day, the directors held their first board meeting and elected Thomas president. George Brown was later appointed company treasurer.

In December of that year, the B&O decided to ask the Maryland legislature to subscribe for the stock to which the state was entitled under the law. The railroad committee that had gone to Annapolis in the spring told the lawmakers that they were not seeking state funds but would be satisfied if the legislature granted the charter with all its benefits and powers; now, however, Thomas believed that Maryland should become a stockholder.

John V. L. McMahon was again instrumental in seeing that it did. In mid-February 1828, he produced a favorable report on behalf of the House internal improvement committee, and on February 28, the last day under the charter for the state to acquire B&O stock, he helped guide the bill that he had written through the House of Delegates. Some attempts were made to link it with a state subscription to the Chesapeake and Ohio Canal, but James W. McCulloh and John G. Chapman, who was now House Speaker, supported the bill. McMahon had arranged with a friendly steamboat captain to cancel a scheduled run on the pretext that the engines were out of order, and the Eastern Shore members were kept in their seats long enough to deliver a favorable vote. On March 3, after some senators who backed the measure had returned to Annapolis, it was called up in the Senate, passed, and became a law.[21]

The act directed the state to subscribe for 5,000 shares of B&O stock when the company certified that private investment had reached $3 million. It also provided that an additional 5,000 shares could be acquired later on. There were the usual restrictions: the railroad was to strike the Potomac somewhere between the Monocacy River and Cumberland and it was to go into Frederick, Washington, and Allegany counties.

At the same time that McMahon and the others were shepherding the stock subscription bill through the Maryland House of Delegates, Jonathan Knight was performing a similar function in the Pennsylvania legislature on the charter bill, having submitted it to Thomas beforehand for his comments. This time it passed, on February 27, 1828. The law, with yet another restriction, required the B&O, if it entered the state, to go directly or via a branch road to Pittsburgh.

Thus in a year—indeed, in little more than two months—the business leaders of Baltimore had inaugurated the first long-distance, general purpose railroad in the world, one that, for the time, was the equivalent of a transcontinental line; and they had established its legal and financial basis. Now, they thought, all that remained was to determine where to build it and what sort of motive power to employ.

5

The Train and the River

THE NEW COMPANY'S FIRST REAL ACT,

in June 1827, was to appoint a committee to determine how to build a railroad. The committee recommended that an engineer and other "suitable persons" ought to travel to Europe to examine the railroads there, particularly the plan of construction, machinery, and motive power, that is, whether they used horses, locomotives, or stationary steam engines. Similar information should be obtained from "authentic sources" in this country. And some directors ought to call on President John Quincy Adams and request some of the federal government's topographical engineers to make surveys between the Patapsco and Ohio rivers.

President Adams favored internal improvements, and he was sufficiently impressed by the views of Philip E. Thomas and two other directors on connecting the eastern and western sections of the United States with "free, speedy and cheap communication" to refer them to the Secretary of War, James Barbour, who had jurisdiction over the Topographical Engineers. Secretary Barbour said that because the railroad was a project "of national importance," the expense of the government engineers would be charged to the public appropriation for internal improvements.[1]

This was of particular moment to the railroad because although, at least in its formative stages, it did not lack capital, it and other early railroads did lack technical talent. The only real source of trained civil engineers, of which there were probably less than 50 in the country at the time, was the engineering school at West Point. The two-paragraph Survey Act of 1824, passed by the Monroe administration, authorized the President to order surveys of "such Roads and Canals as he may deem of national importance," designate government engineers to conduct them, and draw on a $30,000 fund set up to pay the cost.[2] The Chesapeake and Ohio Canal and the Baltimore and Ohio Railroad were two early beneficiaries of this act. The same U.S. Corps of Topographical Engineers actually conducted the surveys for both public works. The B&O shared the cost of the crews and equipment and later on paid the salaries of the most important federal engineers.

While they waited for the surveys to get under way, Philip E. Thomas, Alexander Brown, and Thomas Ellicott investigated the railroads in this country, such as they were. Even the two best-known ones, at Mauch Chunk, Pennsylvania, and Quincy, Massachusetts, were merely short coal- and stone-hauling lines operated by gravity and horsepower. Mauch Chunk, Pennsylvania, was quite a lively place in the 1820's, attracting visitors from this country and abroad who wanted to inspect the latest methods of mining and transporting coal. It was located on the Lehigh River, near Blue Mountain, about 25 miles northwest of Bethlehem. The coal descended from the mine to the water's edge by wagon and was barged down the Lehigh and Delaware rivers to Philadelphia.

The operation dated back to 1793, when several men bought about 10,000 acres in the Mauch Chunk area and started producing the first anthracite regularly mined in America. The venture was not a commercial success. The mine road was wretched, and the Lehigh, which as late as 1825 was described as "a mountain torrent" below Mauch Chunk, proved to be practically unnavigable. The company did manage to get a few barges to Philadelphia, but most of the coal ended up at the bottom of the river and the contractor who hauled it from the mine lost money.

Around 1817, Josiah White and Erskine Hazard, wire manufacturers near Philadelphia who had bought some of the coal and liked it, took over the operation. By various means, they improved the road and made the river navigable, and by 1823 their Lehigh Coal and Navigation Company had shipped over 2,000 tons of anthracite. The improvements were regarded as unique in their time. The road, which dropped about 100 feet per mile on its descent from the coal fields to the Lehigh, was constructed on a uniform grade, probably the first in the country. The decline was scarcely "perceptible to the eye," one visitor said. Another noticed that the horses pulled wagons up the gravel road "with a spirit as if they were on descending ground."[3]

The mechanism White used to tame the river was equally ingenious. With it, he created a series of induced floods similar to the natural ones the boatmen took advantage of in springtime on the Susquehanna and Potomac rivers to get their produce to market. The system was made up of eight dams at the worst shoals, equipped with White's special locks and gates. When raised, they backed the water up behind them and they could be instantly lowered. The coal was loaded into arks that were roped together and positioned behind one of the sluices. When an attendant on shore opened a valve, the gates dropped and the arks shot through on a sheet of water three or four feet deep, carrying them down to the next dam and so on to Easton where the Lehigh joined the Delaware.

The open-pit mine at the top of the hill covered four acres—"a solid mass of coal," said one distinguished European visitor (Bernhard, Duke of Saxe-Weimar). Miners pried the coal loose with hammers and wedges, sometimes in pieces weighing a ton. In an area of Pennsylvania that was still mostly wilderness, the town of Mauch Chunk had in less than ten years acquired roughly 2,000 inhabitants and had a school, a flour mill, a store, an inn, a tavern, and two sawmills constantly cutting lumber to build the coal barges. The barges could be knocked together in an hour and after they reached Philadelphia they could be dismantled and the lumber sold.[4]

When the B&O directors arrived at Mauch Chunk in late May 1827, the company was in the midst of building the 37-mile-long Lehigh Canal to Easton, which would replace the sluice gates. It was just completing the nine-mile railway that would be faster and cheaper to operate and would be a major improvement over the road to the mine. The railway had been built in five months; the workmen were still finishing parts of it.

The three-car train that carried the Baltimoreans and eleven other passengers to the top of the mountain was pulled by a single horse. The coal cars were open boxes with a capacity of one and a half tons of coal each; usually they ran in trains of fourteen or so, pulled by teams of horses and mules. The cars had wooden brake shoes activated by a vertical lever rising from the left front wheel. The levers were tied together and controlled by the driver, who stood on the last car. The coal trains were generally followed by the trains made up of the "pleasure carriages" with the visiting dignitaries, who paid 50 cents each for the trip up and back. Attached to the end of these would be a few cars containing the horses and mules, munching away at their feed troughs as they rode back down the mountain. They refused to walk down. When Thomas, Brown, and Ellicott descended, the trip took about 45 minutes, propelled by gravity and sometimes reaching a speed of 20 miles an hour.

At the bottom of the line, the coal cars were lowered on an inclined plane, a trestle covered with a shed at the lower end. The descending cars simultaneously pulled up several empty ones. The coal flowed into a chute from which it was dumped into the waiting boats below.

The railway was built for the most part on the continuous grade of the existing mine road. The pine rails, 20-foot lengths of four-by-six timber, were laid on edge three and a half feet apart on oak sleepers or ties. The ties were placed at four-foot intervals, and notched to receive the rails, which were held tight in the notches with wooden keys, or wedges. Iron rails, fourteen feet long, about one and a half inches wide, and a quarter inch thick were nailed to the inside top edges of the wooden ones. The iron carriage wheels, two and a half feet in diameter, had inside flanges and turned with the axles. The space between the rails was filled up with dirt to make a horse path and the curves on the railroad were banked.[5]

The B&O directors were enthusiastic. One of them wrote, "I had no idea before I saw it that a rail way was a thing of such easy construction." No more mechanical skill was required to make one "than is necessary to construct a common post and rail fence. I mean after the line is regulated and the route graded—and the cost will be far less than we had expected. I find that the grading of the road and the adaptation of the moving power to it, are in reality the only subjects of difficulty." The Mauch Chunk railway cost only about $2,750 a mile because the right-of-way was already in place.[6]

The Quincy Railroad outside Boston had been completed some seven months before the B&O officials saw it in June 1827. The construction of the line, three miles from the granite quarries in Quincy to the Neponset River, was similar to that at Mauch Chunk except that instead of a continuous grade it had several sections with different inclinations to accommodate the hilly terrain. The steepest was about 66 feet per mile, or 1.25 percent. The wooden rails were six-by-twelve-inch pine timbers laid on edge five feet apart. They rested on granite sleepers, which in turn sat on stone foundations that were sunk three feet into the ground, to prevent the rails from being displaced by frost. Wooden viaducts carried the line over ravines. The cars resembled farm wagons, with huge wheels, six and a half feet in diameter. Two horses could pull about 40 tons of stone. The rest of the journey to Boston was by barge.

So far, the B&O directors anticipated "no difficulty in constructing the proposed rail way from the City of Baltimore to the Ohio river," but they realized that the choice of the proper route should be made very carefully and that "much experience and science" would be needed to determine the motive power. The power had to be adapted to the railroad as laid out, or else the railroad had to be graded to suit the type of power used.

Since there were no locomotives in America at that time, all such study had to be carried on in Europe. As a preliminary, the company decided to make a reconnaissance of the potential routes. This was the task given to the three men whom Secretary Barbour assigned: Colonel Stephen H. Long, Captain William Gibbs McNeill, and William Howard. Together, these engineers possessed an intimate knowledge of the country between Baltimore and the Potomac and Ohio rivers and beyond. Howard, assisted by Frederick Harrison, Jr., had spent the past year surveying for the second time a connecting waterway through Maryland to the Chesapeake and Ohio Canal. Howard submitted his report only a few weeks before joining the railroad.

Both Howard and McNeill were familiar with the area beyond the Potomac extending to the western rivers. Howard had been a consultant to the engineers surveying the C&O Canal, and McNeill had spent much of the previous three years running those surveys and analyzing the results. In the summer of 1824, with a team of lieutenants just out of West Point, McNeill had tramped from Deep Creek, a tributary of the Youghiogheny, across the western Maryland Glades to the point where the Savage River ran down off the Allegheny Backbone to join the Potomac. The following year, they had ranged farther west, through some of the more rugged, less hospitable Appalachian terrain to the tributaries of the Cheat River and north along the Wills Creek–Casselman River route out of Cumberland.

McNeill and Dillahunty, one of the lieutenants, also, in 1826–27, had explored the prospects for a National Road from Cumberland to Washington through either Martinsburg or Winchester, Virginia, and McNeill had surveyed a set of rivers to the south, the Greenbrier, New, Gauley, and Kanawha, for Virginia's proposed James River and Kanawha Canal.[7] At about the same time, he and the other engineers began surveying for the Baltimore and Ohio Railroad. They were, in fact, often looking at the same rivers at different times of the year for rival projects.

Of the trio of engineers assigned to the B&O, Long had the most far-ranging view of the nation and its rivers. Eight years before, he had made a dramatic entrance upon the stage of American affairs when he arrived at Saint Louis aboard the *Western Engineer*, a bizarre steamboat of his own design, to lead the third major government expedition to the West after Lewis and Clark and Zebulon Pike. In the summer of 1819, this strange craft, armed and built to resemble a sea serpent to impress the Indians, proceeded farther up the Missouri River than any steamboat had ever gone before. The following year, Long led an expedition of 20 scientists and soldiers that crossed the Missouri at what is now Council Bluffs, Iowa, went west along the Platte River, and south skirting the Rockies, and returned following the rivers to Fort Smith on the Arkansas border—a journey of some 2,000 miles in three months. Along the way, they discovered Long's Peak, the highest point in what is now the Rocky Mountain National Park in Colorado. Besides valuable collections of insects, plants, and other specimens, they brought back a wealth of information about the two thirds of the continent west of the Mississippi that was but a faint concept at the time. The official narrative of the expedition contained the first illustrations of Indians and western landscapes that Americans had ever seen, and served as the literary inspiration for James Fenimore Cooper's *The Prairie*.[8] By the time Cooper's book appeared in 1827, Long was on his way to Baltimore. From his travels, he had gained a knowledge of the extent of the country, its terrain, and its major arteries of transportation that few of his contemporaries could match, and he understood the implications of this new empire.

Long had also taken a closer look at the Potomac country shortly before arriving in Baltimore when he and Trimble, one of the West Point lieutenants, in the summer and fall of 1826, considered the route for yet another scheme for a National Road between Washington and Buffalo. During that investigation, Long refamiliarized himself with the Blue Ridge that crossed the Potomac at Harpers Ferry, and, on the other side of it, the Cumberland Valley with its lovely farms and woodlands— "the garden of the middle and Southern States," he called it: "This beautiful district presents a waving aspect, ridges and valleys succeeding each other in grateful alternation."[9] Boonsboro, Williamsport, on the Potomac, and Hagerstown were the major settlements in the Maryland portion of the valley, which in Pennsylvania was called Cumberland and farther south, Shenandoah, or the Valley of Virginia.

The highway, like the one McNeill surveyed between Washington and Cumberland, was never built and probably for the same reason, that the countryside was too difficult. But Long's report on it is significant because it contains the basis of a theory of "equated distance." As it was fully developed, the theory involved calculating the mileage added to each route by having to go up and down hills and the additional power needed to pull loads over them compared with the distance and power required on a level road. Expressed in total miles or "equated distance," the comparison simplified the choice of the optimum or shortest route.

For his highway report, Long aggregated the ascents and descents on each route and compared them. "It may seem incredible," he said, but a road built on a direct line from Washington to Buffalo, that is, crossing the intervening hills with no greater than the four-degree grades specified by the federal government (which were quite steep, 368 feet per mile or 7 percent), would be 100 miles longer than the true distance between the two places based on latitude and longitude. "Every hill is to be regarded as an impediment, to be avoided if possible," he concluded.[10]

Rivers were the other major obstacle to roads. Long figured the expense of bridges and other construction costs in his survey results, which he arranged in a series of tables to make comparison easier. Caspar W. Wever, then superintendent of the National Road west of Wheeling, supplied the documents on which Long based his construction estimates. At this point, he only alluded to the cost of transportation. "We trust it will not be deemed irrelevant to intimate the facility of constructing a *Rail Road* from tide water, of Chesapeake Bay, across the entire range of the Alleghany mountains," Long added.[11]

Long submitted his highway report, including a section on wooden bridges, in February 1827, the same month the projectors of the Baltimore and Ohio Railroad announced their intention to build just such a "direct," 250-mile line to the west, presumably paralleling the National Road, and in April, in a letter to Thomas, he applied his theories of location to railroads. Comparing the cost of power, either horses or locomotives, on level and inclined railways, he concluded that "the cost of transportation on a rail-road will be greatly enhanced by the passage of hills."[12] Avoid them, Long reiterated, even at the expense of adding horizontal distance.

Therefore when Long, McNeill, and Howard began their B&O reconnaissance two months later, they did not strike out cross-country to lay out a straight-line railroad. They turned, with the approval of the board of directors, to the winding river valleys they knew so well. The board's instructions, likely written by the engineers themselves, called for the work to be done in two phases. First, they were to examine all reasonable routes from Baltimore striking the Potomac River Valley anywhere between Harpers Ferry and Cumberland. Then, while the most promising of these were being surveyed, they were to begin a reconnaissance of the area between the Potomac and Ohio rivers. On each route, the engineers were to note the ascents and descents in feet per mile; the location of the "valleys, hills, and precipices" in the neighborhood, and their elevations or depressions; the position and flow of all watercourses; "the character of the rocks, soils and aspect of the adjacent country"; the horizontal deviations from a straight line, and the places where inclined planes might be necessary, along with the availability of water for generating steam. Abrupt changes in elevation and sharp curves were to be avoided. Afterward, the most promising routes would be examined more closely, compared, and the best one chosen.[13]

This two-step approach became formalized in engineering textbooks as the reconnaissance and survey. The reconnaissance was a relatively quick study, done with simple instruments or none at all, of the topography of the entire area being considered for a road, particularly the ridges, valleys, and watercourses. To a practiced eye, the configuration of all these land features would indicate the best routes. "The direction and size of the watercourses will show at once the position of summits," one late-nineteenth-century engineering text pointed out.[14] The next step was to find the best way over the top to join the streams flowing in opposite directions on either side. The second part was the survey, conducted by teams made up of engineers, axmen, rodmen, and so on, using the compass, level, and chain, who compared in detail the various potential routes to determine the best. Finally, the location would be actually staked out on the ground.

The railroad officials seemed confident that the three engineers assigned to them by the federal government were well qualified to conduct the reconnaissance, but the surveys would require much careful work. As Thomas said, they felt they still lacked sufficient information concerning "the best ground for locating the road and secondly the most economical manner of employing moving power upon it." [15]

In early July 1827, with the permission of the War Department, Thomas sounded out Jonathan Knight on becoming chief engineer and examining the European railroads, particularly the motive power, as a preliminary to locating the route of the Baltimore and Ohio Railroad. Knight was then surveying the route for the extension of the National Road from Wheeling to Missouri, across land, Knight said, so flat that it made little difference what direction the road took. Knight's theory was that a straight route could be varied if the cost of construction were less, for example, to cross a river at a better angle, but never for political or commercial purposes. Knight declined Thomas's offer "for the moment," but within a year, after helping the railroad secure the passage of its charter bill in the Pennsylvania legislature, he came to work for the Baltimore and Ohio and made the trip to Europe.[16]

Several of the young Army lieutenants were called in to help with the work— Joshua Barney as Long's assistant, Dillahunty to aid McNeill and Howard. George Washington Whistler was requested, but he could not be spared from his present duties, the Army said. Isaac Ridgeway Trimble came in mid-July and was assigned to explore the country west of Cumberland. By the end of the first season (1827) most of the members of McNeill's brigade, who were simultaneously conducting canal surveys, were working on the railroad.

From nearby towns like Westminster, Maryland, and from others like Athens, Ohio, that were hundreds of miles away, letters poured in promoting the advantages of their locality for a railroad route. The citizens of Winchester, Virginia, conducted their own reconnaissance and included a map and topographical sketch. Dreams of instant wealth fired the minds of frontier speculators. One, writing from Sistersville, Virginia, on the Ohio midway between Parkersburg and Wheeling, begged Alexander Brown to tell him where the railroad would strike the river. "I will buy the land about that quarter and take it in the Rail Road stock and the advantages derived from the Land after the village would be laid out and the Lots sold should be divided equally among the company," he said excitedly. "My composition is rather ungrammatical but my meaning is good," he added.[17]

The municipalities requesting special consideration from the engineers were generally aligned straight west from Baltimore through Clarksburg and Parkersburg, Virginia, and on to Chillicothe and Cincinnati, Ohio; or on a route curving northward through Morgantown, Virginia, to Wheeling; or on two other trajectories to the north and south of these.

To the north, substantial interest in the Baltimore and Ohio arose in Pittsburgh, but Pennsylvania was temporarily not under consideration by the survey parties because the state legislature had not yet passed the charter bill. Although it did so in early 1828, by then the B&O officials were concerned with other matters and Pittsburgh had to wait. To the south, Charleston, Virginia, and other communities on the Great Kanawha River were equally intrigued with having the railroad come their way on a line that turned south at Harpers Ferry, passed through Winchester, and continued down the great Valley of Virginia until it crossed the mountains and followed various rivers before it met the Kanawha. The problem was that the Virginia charter prevented the railroad from striking the Ohio River lower down than the Little Kanawha at Parkersburg. The first three alignments, with minor variations, became important B&O routes; the last was adopted primarily by other railroads. From the West came an intriguing hint that the Baltimore railroad promoters were planning a true transcontinental route. The Scioto, Ohio, *Gazette* noted the B&O directors' "intention to extend this great commercial avenue to the ocean, westward, so soon as it shall have been completed to the Ohio river, and its utility . . . fairly and practically tested." [18]

Philip E. Thomas was cordial, politic, and noncommittal in his replies to all these groups. He invariably commended their zeal, said the company would benefit by consulting with them, spoke confidently of the railroad's completion, and sent along some literature, a copy of the charter and a report or two.

The negotiations with the Kanawha County (Charleston, Virginia), delegation revealed something of the strategy on both sides. In August 1827, James E. McFarland, a Virginia legislator, representing his clients at a meeting of the railroad's board of directors, presented a memorial asking for a survey down the Shenandoah Valley to the Great Kanawha, in exchange for a political effort to have the Virginia legislature remove the route restriction. The directors agreed, and Thomas assured McFarland of the company's intention to "examine every pass through the mountains which may be suggested" before choosing a route that would present "the fewest obstacles and involve the least expense." [19]

The B&O engineers did reconnoiter a route that led down the Shenandoah Valley and over the mountains to the Greenbrier, New, and Kanawha rivers, but despite the efforts of McFarland and others representing the Kanawha interests in the Virginia legislature, the restriction remained in the law. While these negotiations in Richmond were still going on in early 1828, Thomas wrote McFarland to explain his philosophy of trade and hopes for the railroad in challenging New York's commercial hegemony. The annual $40 million import trade of the United States, Thomas said, was concentrated in New York, where the goods were auctioned off, generating $12 million worth of duties. The importing merchants collected these duties and held them for as long as six months before they became due:

> A large portion of these goods being bought up and consumed in the South, we are thrown in debt to the East, not only for the amount of the original cost but also for the duties and other charges, which duties . . . are left without interest in the hands of the importers, several months before they are called upon to pay them and which, with the importers' profits of ten per cent, enables the East continually to keep

the South in its debt and to oppress its monied institutions. The almost exclusive enjoyment of this import trade naturally brings with it the return commerce.

We shall accordingly find . . . that the single city of New York has monopolized the exports of nearly one fourth of the entire cotton crop of the whole country, and by means of her great Western canal and other similar works . . . she is also making prodigious efforts to secure to herself the export of the productions of the Western States. . . . No nation or district, in fact, ever enjoyed the advantage of being carriers without becoming rich, and all experience shows that the dealers in, and carriers of either merchandize or agricultural productions, gain more nett profits than the growers or manufacturers.[20]

Thomas was confident that the railroad was the best means by which Virginia and Maryland, in a united effort, could "turn the tide of the immense western trade along the Road, to be divided between the ports of the two states and afford ample means of enriching both."[21] The major eastern cities wanted to retain their political influence as much as revive their commerce, and there is no doubt that sectional jealousy was a great influence on the B&O's determination to succeed. Pennsylvania had rejected the railroad's charter because of conflict with its own canal plans and the route restriction stayed in the Virginia law for the same reason.

Meanwhile, the engineers, reasonably above the political issues, were conducting the reconnaissance. McNeill and Howard had charge of the area between Baltimore and the Potomac, and Trimble, acting alone, handled the district from Cumberland to the Ohio along the Cheat and Little Kanawha rivers. Long was supposed to have covered this territory, but just before coming to Baltimore, while engaged with Trimble on yet another government road survey from Ohio to Alabama, he had fallen ill, apparently of the fever that made engineers and laborers dread the "sickly season" on the rivers. Long spent the rest of the summer and early fall convalescing.

McNeill and Howard turned in their first report in August 1827. They had traced the valley of the Patapsco River from the Baltimore harbor to Parrs Spring, the headwaters of its western branch where, as Howard already knew, there was a "favorable point" for crossing the ridge. From there, they had followed a roughly oval-shaped route in a clockwise direction that took them to Frederick, Harpers Ferry, Williamsport, Hagerstown, Thurmont (then called Mechanick's Town), Westminster, and back to Baltimore.

The main barriers, after Parrs Spring Ridge, were Catoctin Mountain, South Mountain, and the Blue Ridge, in that order. During the first 30 days, McNeill and Howard and their assistants, splitting up, examined most of the practical routes over or around them. They traveled on horseback, making topographic sketches in their notebooks, eating and sleeping for the most part in inns, taverns, or boardinghouses. They looked at three ways to overcome Catoctin Mountain: at the Point of Rocks, where the Potomac cut through it; near Frederick; and in the north at a place called Harman's Gap, between Thurmont and Hagerstown. The major rivers and streams they traced were the Patapsco, Bush and Bennett creeks, two westward-flowing tributaries of the Monocacy, the Potomac, Antietam Creek, and, in the Westminster area,

Pipe Creek and Sam's Creek. Sometimes they left the watercourses to consider direct routes, for example, crossing the Middletown Valley between Catoctin and South mountains and exploring Pleasant Valley between there and the Blue Ridge.

They believed they had sufficient information from the reconnaissance to conduct the full-scale surveys between Baltimore and the Potomac, but they did not think they could finish, during the same season, a reconnaissance of the territory beyond Cumberland to the Ohio River that would be detailed enough to satisfy all the localities and their special interests. They therefore recommended a quick examination of just four western routes. These were along the Potomac's north branch; down its south branch and over to the Little Kanawha; across the Shenandoah Valley to Winchester, then west through Clarksburg, Virginia; and following the Shenandoah Valley to its conclusion, then crossing the mountains to the Greenbrier and the Kanawha rivers.

With Long out of action, even by simplifying the project, McNeill and Howard could not both supervise the survey work in the east, where their guidance was needed because the surveys would be of a type "entirely novel to our assistants," and reconnoiter the Ohio country.[22] So they left to join Trimble in the west. The engineers were back in Baltimore again in November and despite their former misgivings were now convinced, based on eleven weeks in the field and their general knowledge of the tributaries of the Potomac and Ohio rivers, that they had examined every major route that could possibly be recommended. Then they told the capitalists what they wanted to hear. Although their reconnaissance was conducted by eye and might not be sustained by instrumental surveys, "We feel warranted in pronouncing that the Railroad from Baltimore to the Ohio is practicable, and that it can be accomplished at a reasonable expenditure of time and money."[23]

McNeill and the others felt that, even though it was late in the season, the eastern surveys should start immediately in Baltimore and be taken "as far as may be necessary to determine the general direction of the road from this city to the Potomac."[24] They had already called in Trimble, Barney, Dillahunty and Harrison, who had been working with them in the west, to begin surveying. Other young Army engineers, as well as Long, recovered from his illness, joined them, and within two months, that is, in January 1828, the initial surveys for the first major American railroad were completed. The surveyors, who suffered much "from being frosted," had looked at four routes from Baltimore. Two, in light of later developments, were significant. The first went north through the valleys of Jones Falls, Gwynns Falls, and the north branch of the Patapsco River and continued by Harman's Gap to Hagerstown and Williamsport. This route was adopted many years later by the Western Maryland Railroad.

The other left the city heading southwest, crossed the Gwynns Falls, and entering the Patapsco Valley at Elkridge, wound along it past Ellicotts Mills and up over the ridge at Parrs Spring. On the other side, the line followed Bush Creek to the Monocacy River south of Frederick, went across, and continued on a more or less direct alignment to the Point of Rocks. On May 23, 1828, when the board of directors formally adopted it, this became the route for the Baltimore and Ohio Railroad to the Potomac River.

Although detailed surveys of this route and its extension up the Potomac Valley were to continue for most of that year, sometimes at a frantic pace, the basic location for the railroad from Baltimore had been established. Its rationale and a description of what awaited them in the west were fully set forth in a report from the engineers, Long, McNeill, and Howard. It was their report, bound in morocco, that was carried in the parade and presented to Charles Carroll of Carrollton at the cornerstone-laying ceremonies on July 4, 1828.

The *Report of the Engineers on the Reconnoissance and Surveys* is divided into four major sections, dealing with a geographic view of the country, a description of the routes examined, a statement of principles governing the location and construction of railroads, and the conclusions drawn. Although the report had certain antecedents as a literary form, it was the earliest real railroad study produced in this country, and the quality and scope of its analysis served as models for the many others that followed.[25]

The engineers took as their arena of interest "a triangle whose base is formed by the Ohio River from the latitude of the southern Pennsylvania line [below Wheeling] to the mouth of the Great Kenhawa [at Point Pleasant, Virginia], and whose apex is at Baltimore." This was a huge slice of countryside, comprising over 7,000 square miles. "The most prominent geographical feature of this district is the great range of the Alleghany mountains, rising to the height of from 2,500 to 3,000 feet above tide, and extending in nearly a uniform direction to the northeast and southwest separating the waters of the Ohio from those of the Chesapeake." At their center was the "great master ridge, the control of which appears to have been so strong as to have governed the direction of every collection of rocks of even a few yards in extent."

Descending eastward, there were the Blue Ridge, South, and Catoctin mountains, the ridge at Parrs Spring, 800 feet in elevation, and finally, near Baltimore, the fall line. In the west, after the relatively uniform natural meadows of the Glades, another series of ridges descended to the Ohio. These mountains, "passing in a transverse direction to the general course of our work, offer the principal difficulty." But the hills themselves provided the means to overcome them, by way of the rivers that had broken through the ridges, producing "many facilities . . . for any work, for which it is desirable to maintain a nearly level line."

The landscape features, or works of nature, were ready-made for improvement by railroads, or "works of art." The mountains also contained large deposits of bituminous coal, "destined to be of the greatest importance to the Rail Road," both as fuel and as an article of transportation. It was fortunate that the coal beds were situated where the greatest amount of mechanical power would be needed, they said. An abundance of iron ore, building stone such as granite and marble, timber, and petroleum also existed along the proposed routes.

The major question about the route proceeding west from Baltimore had been where to cross Catoctin and South mountains. The northern route, through Westminster and Harman's Gap, was shorter, but the southern, via Parrs Spring and the Point of Rocks, was lower, and the "equated distance" made it the preferred choice. The railroad from the Point of Rocks north to Williamsport and west to Cumberland would therefore more or less follow the Potomac River Valley.

Leaving Cumberland, there were again a couple of good choices. One was to continue west along the Potomac to the Savage River and up over the Allegheny Backbone, climbing 1,680 feet in a little over sixteen miles. (At 105 feet per mile, this was a grade of 1.9 percent.) The other route led north, along Wills Creek and the Casselman River. Being prohibited at the time of the reconnaissance from entering Pennsylvania, the B&O engineers could not examine this route, but the Chesapeake and Ohio Canal surveys had indicated its potential as a line to Pittsburgh, and the B&O engineers thought it ought to be carefully surveyed at some point for the railroad.

Concerning the first, they said, "The valleys of Savage River and Crab-tree Creek [a stream flowing west on the other side of Backbone Mountain] are extremely rough and wild, and any work passing through them must of course be difficult; but as they had been minutely surveyed, and a canal through them pronounced . . . quite practicable, we may conclude a fortiori that a Rail Road may be made over the same ground." At the western edge of the Glades the line would have to dip down into the Cheat River Valley and climb back out. Here there were real problems in the form of steep descents to a distinctly unfriendly river, at least the portion of it the engineers were interested in. The tributaries of the Cheat, flowing down from the Alleghenies, were no better. Even hunters avoided these valleys, "the skill of the woodsman scarcely sufficing to extricate him, when once entangled in their mazes."

The river itself was full of boulders, many as big as a house and sometimes so close together "that we were often able to pass over by leaping from rock to rock. The mountains which form its banks, rise almost immediately from the water's edge . . . at an angle of 40 to 50 degrees, and ascending to the height of 700 to 800 feet. Such being the rough character of this valley . . . it is of course uninhabited: indeed . . . there is scarcely level ground enough [for] the foundation of a small cabin. Its wildness may be imagined, from the fact that we were for three days industriously occupied in making this distance of 16 miles. This was only accomplished—of course on foot, as no horse ever penetrated here—by clambering with excessive fatigue, over the rocks at the constant risk of falling from them, and by frequently fording the river."

William Howard and Frederick Harrison, Jr., probably made this arduous journey, and McNeill, Trimble, and Barney may have been in the party also. The neighborhood had not changed much since Washington passed through and declared that it was "rough and a good way not to be found." Such was their determination that the engineers claimed that a railroad could be built even here, although they admitted that protecting it from "avalanches of rock and timber . . . would be extremely difficult." The section of the river they were discussing extends roughly from Kingwood, West Virginia, almost to where the Cheat joins the Monongahela, a few miles north of the Pennsylvania state line. No railroad, or highway of any sort, was ever built through this part of the valley.

In the difficult country beyond the Cheat, Trimble, Barney, Harrison, and Dillahunty, blocked at times by mountain laurel so thick they could hardly get through it, explored other routes to the Tygart Valley River and the Monongahela, which flow north, and to the westward-flowing tributaries of the Ohio, such as the Little Kanawha. In just eight weeks, Trimble and Barney studied 38 different routes totaling 225 miles, estimating ascents and descents, the lengths of necessary bridges, and the availability of rock and timber for building. This mountainous region was so broken and the rivers so wild that there was talk of abandoning it altogether in favor of the southern route that another young Army lieutenant named Hazzard traced through the Shenandoah Valley to the Greenbrier and the Kanawha rivers.

However, at some point in the summer or fall of 1827, Harrison found himself in a more hospitable section of the Cheat River Valley not many miles south of where he and the others had spent three days clambering over the rocks. He looked at a creek called Salt Lick Run that descended on a relatively gentle slope to the river, figured it was the best of the available alternatives, and decided to explore a route connection to another stream called Snowy Creek, where McNeill two summers earlier had ended his canal surveys and left a benchmark. Harrison could not have known it at the time, but he had found the way for the railroad.

The section of the *Report* that dealt with construction, which was to follow the pattern of the Mauch Chunk and Quincy railroads, contained a rudimentary exercise in laying out curves by Walter B. Guion that after further refinement by Long became standard railroad practice. Wooden bridges were declared to be best; for motive power, locomotives were preferable to horses at speeds of over four miles an hour.

Long and Jonathan Knight, who had joined the B&O the same month the engineers' report was issued, April 1828, added a nice illustration of the "equated distance" formula in choosing the line from Baltimore to the Potomac. Trimble contributed a lyrical description of the mountains, the Glades, the river valleys, and their products. He summed up better than anyone where they had been and what they had done and why: "This region of country is marked by the boldness, the grandeur and ruggedness of its scenery, produced by steep and lofty mountain ridges and spurs, devious narrow and deep valleys and ravines, almost perpetually shaded by thin bounding mountains, inaccessible precipices, dense forests, impenetrable Laurel beds, and headlong impetuous water courses. These features are universal with the exception of that tract of beautiful country familiarly termed the Glades."

Trimble said it was impractical to try to run a railroad directly over the mountains or on the ridge tops: "The reasons for this must be apparent to anyone. After the general description of the country which has been given, when it is considered that not only the practicability but the beneficial operation of Rail Roads depends upon their general levelness or slight inclination and avoiding a frequent repitition of summits and abrupt ascents and descents; with this principle in view, the water courses, mostly uniform in their descent upon the line of least inclination from ridge to valley, present in any other than a level country the most eligible sites for the location of a Rail Road."

6

Inventing a Railroad

ONLY A MONTH BEFORE THE OFFICIAL START
of construction, Philip E. Thomas and the other directors of the Baltimore and Ohio
Railroad still did not know where the line was to begin, and they had yet to advertise
for contractors. Building materials had been called for, but then an unseemly dispute
had erupted within the local business community and in Congress between the company officers and the domestic suppliers of iron over the plan to import rails from
England. Furthermore, Thomas said, there was no longer any question that "we shall
have a conflict with the Chesapeake and Ohio Canal."[1] Thomas had already sent
the B&O's lawyers and surveyors racing to capture the narrow passes between the
Point of Rocks and Harpers Ferry, where the two great public works were destined
to meet. Even at the Baltimore end of the line, there was opposition to the place the
railroad had picked, "for obvious good reasons," to enter the city.

If there was unity anywhere, it was among the engineers. Two new members
who had joined the ranks in the spring of 1828, Jonathan Knight and Caspar Willis
Wever, were used to working together and they shared similar backgrounds. Knight
was a self-taught surveyor and mathematician who loved detailed computations, a
practicing politician, and a devout, teetotaling Quaker from Brownsville, Pennsylvania, near the National Road. He had done his first survey work on the road between
Cumberland and Wheeling in 1818 and had gone on to similar tasks for the Chesapeake and Ohio Canal. He had served six years in the state legislature (1822–28), and
in 1825 had been named commissioner to extend the National Road from Wheeling
to Illinois. He may have been forced by economic necessity to pursue two careers—
in 1828, he was 40 years old and had ten children—but after helping the B&O secure
its Pennsylvania charter two months before joining the railroad, Knight dropped
politics and did not take it up again until the 1850's when he served a single term in
Congress.

Wever, too, lacked professional training, but he had worked for Knight as superintendent on the National Road in Ohio, where he had been in charge of contractors. He had responsibility for relatively large sums of money ($5,000 to $10,000 at a time), and in some instances located sections of the road. There are indications that he had trouble rendering his accounts on time. Wever was a landowner on the Potomac River below Harpers Ferry.

In April 1828, the railroad hired Knight for $3,000 a year, and Wever at an annual salary of $2,000, as engineer and superintendent of construction, respectively. The company simultaneously added Stephen H. Long to the payroll at a rank and salary equal to Knight's. Knight and Long, with Thomas as ex-officio member, were the board of engineers. The next month, William Gibbs McNeill was hired at $1,500 a year.[2] Except for one important addition, the engineering team that was to lay out and build the first section of the Baltimore and Ohio Railroad was complete.

Long knew Knight not at all and Wever only slightly when they first got together. Wever was flattered to be offered a job on the B&O. "The fact that my friends Col. Long and Jonathan Knight are to be the active engineers is one of the strongest inducements to enter the service," he told Thomas. Wever added that he looked forward to working with them "in perfect harmony and satisfaction."[3] Alexander Brown wrote his son William in the Liverpool office that the new engineers were among "the ablest our country affords."[4] The ten topographical assistants, several of whom had already worked on surveys and had been handpicked by the company with the approval of the principal engineers, were also highly qualified. They were Frederick Harrison, Jr., Joshua Barney, Isaac Ridgeway Trimble, Walter Gwynn, William Cook, John N. Dillahunty, R. Edward Hazzard, John M. Fessenden, William B. Thompson, and Walter B. Guion. With the exception of Harrison, all had graduated from West Point. They were therefore among the best-trained engineers in the nation.

West Point and engineering were synonymous during the first half of the nineteenth century. The United States Military Academy and the U.S. Army Corps of Engineers, as they are presently known, were founded simultaneously in 1802, when there were virtually no trained engineers in America. In fact, in the beginning, the Corps of Engineers was the Military Academy, with the Chief Engineer serving as Superintendent. In 1816, a Corps of Topographical Engineers was established. Two years later, it was made part of the Army's Engineer Department. The Corps of Engineers traditionally dealt with fortifications and coastal defense and the topographers with exploring, mapping, and collecting data. However, their duties often overlapped, for the Army was as interested in good river and highway transportation as it was in forts. Members of the two groups were assigned interchangeably to both internal improvements and defense.

The engineers and the topographers coexisted uneasily, the former patronizing the latter, who were naturally resentful. Long, who taught mathematics at West Point in 1815–16, and McNeill, who was graduated in 1817, were topographical engineers. Knight and William Howard were civil, nonmilitary, engineers, although often employed by the federal government. Wever was a practical engineer and builder.[5]

The Survey Act of 1824, in assigning these Army engineers to plan bridges, roads, canals, and later, railroads, formally recognized a concept that was already a reality. It was one that Jefferson, Madison, Monroe, Calhoun, Clay, and John Quincy Adams had all subscribed to, namely, that the Military Academy should also train civil engineers to build public works in peacetime. The federal government was well aware of the commercial, political, and military aspects of internal improvements, and an engineer's training was not considered complete until he had gained experience on some of the larger ones. Those who worked for the Baltimore and Ohio were among the first to take the field. After gaining their initial experience in Baltimore, they formed the core of the new railroad engineering profession in America.[6]

The federal government assigned the B&O three brigades of engineers, roughly a dozen men. Their common task intensified before the ground-breaking ceremony. In May 1828, Long and Knight were at Williamsport on the Potomac. Barney, Gwynn, and Trimble were there also, getting ready to run experimental lines down the east bank of the river to Harpers Ferry, the Point of Rocks, and then east to Parrs Spring Ridge. McNeill, at the same time, was setting out in the opposite direction from Baltimore, with another brigade consisting of Cook, Hazzard, and Dillahunty, to survey the final location of the line to Ellicotts Mills and on up the Patapsco to the ridge. The surveys joined there, at the highest point between Baltimore and the Potomac. Although parts of the route, such as the one over the ridge itself, were not established until later (by Knight), McNeill essentially located the Baltimore and Ohio Railroad from the city to Parrs Spring Ridge. Long located the line from there to the Point of Rocks and Harpers Ferry.

Alexander Brown wrote, "It is a work of immense magnitude, and if not begun on the proper route, and conducted on the best plan, it would be very unfortunate." The idea was to decide on the location of the beginning of the railroad, and while the line was being built, to keep the survey teams out in front of the contractors. As Brown put it, "The intention of the company is to have from 10 to 20 miles of the road staked out, and to commence building bridges, grading, cutting down and filling up, as much as can be accomplished this season."[7] When the engineers were not in the field, they were in the office working on their maps and figures. The *American* editors stopped in one day and said they were aware of the importance of selecting the best route, but "We had no idea of the laborious detail necessary."[8]

Using the surveyor's compass, the level, and the 50-foot chain, the survey teams worked systematically, noting the horizontal angles, the elevations, and the distances they obtained in field books. Later, they translated the figures into points and lines on drawing paper to produce a three-dimensional representation of the railroad consisting of plats, or plans, showing the alignment as a series of precisely measured actual locations, and profiles, or sections, showing the elevations as a sequence of connected points above mean tide. This line oscillated rapidly because of the rise and fall of the countryside while through it rode the railroad on a relatively even level, reflecting cuts or fills. The topographers also mapped natural features such as hills, valleys, and watercourses.

As Long explained in his *Rail Road Manual* (1829), the best route was a perfectly straight, level, or "right" line, but since this was seldom feasible, horizontal deviations to avoid hills were to be effected by curves and vertical ones to allow changes in level by uniform inclinations.[9] A railroad route was thus a series of alternating curves and straight lines or, mathematically speaking, of arcs and tangents to them. The concept, apparently originated by Long at least in America, has been repeated in books on railroad surveying and engineering down to the present.

Long specified the maximum allowable curvature as 14.5 degrees, or about 400 feet radius. (The manual included tables so that an engineer laying out a line in the field could quickly determine whether a particular curve exceeded the limit.) This is a sharp curve and was so even by contemporary standards.[10]

Long formulated his theories as the surveys progressed. A team consisted of three engineers or assistants: one to reconnoiter the country in advance of the work, another to supervise the compass and chain measurements, and the third to take charge of the levels. There were men to carry, set up, and operate the instruments. Two were needed for the chain, plus a couple of vanemen (rodmen) to work with the leveler, and a few axmen to set stakes and benchmarks and cut brush out of the way so that clear sights could be obtained. With a baggageman, cook, wagoner, and attendant, the usual party came to fifteen men.

They traveled by horseback, with their instruments, drawing supplies, field cases, tools, saddles, iron kettles, tin coffeepots and candlesticks, barrels of provisions, wall tents, and pine tables and benches accompanying them in a large covered wagon pulled by four horses with an extra horse for the engineer on reconnaissance. They spent their days in the woods shouting numbers, directions, and "Tally" at each other, and nights playing the harmonica or the flute while the officers sketched in their tents. Nearby residents sometimes invited into their homes these French-speaking officers from West Point who were engaged in the first railroad survey in America.

When they had finished their fieldwork, the engineers returned to headquarters to study their maps and profiles to select the optimum combination of curve, tangent, and grade. They estimated the amounts of excavation, embankment, and bridging needed for the various alignments (the cost of construction), factored in as best they could the expense of motive power (the cost of transportation), and picked the route representing the least overall expenditure (which they inevitably referred to as the most "expedient"). Then they reversed the process, going back over the ground with their instruments, ranging out the line.

By the end of the summer of 1828, a 66-foot-wide path of hundreds of marked stakes flowed from the city toward the Patapsco River and up the valley to Ellicotts Mills. Some were numbered in sequence, indicating stations where instrument readings were taken. Others bore red-chalk bench marks. Still more, showing their elevation or depression from the level of the road, read "cut" or "fill."

But more than science was involved in choosing the starting point. In March 1828, Roger Brooke Taney, the railroad's counsel, after judging the charter inadequate regarding the extension of the line into the city, drafted a law, which the state passed, that permitted the railroad to begin anywhere in Baltimore as long as the mayor and the City Council gave their consent. That same month, James Carroll offered the directors free land for a depot, provided that the railroad began "on Tide

Water at Carroll's Point." [11] Carroll, a distant relative of Charles Carroll of Carrollton, had a 1,000-acre estate called Mount Clare, on the west side of Baltimore, that he was interested in developing industrially. It contained valuable timber, clay for bricks, and iron ore, and also, besides the Georgian mansion begun in 1756, one of the largest flour mills in the region and a shipyard where the Gwynns Falls met the Patapsco, at a peninsula called Carroll's Point. [12] The company told Carroll it would not accept land with any restrictions, whereupon he removed them and instead offered the railroad a right-of-way through his property and ten acres for a depot anywhere on it *except* at Carroll's Point.

In April 1828, the City Council passed a resolution making a counteroffer of two free blocks of municipally owned land if the company would lay tracks to it. These two blocks also were on the waterfront, but on the east side of Baltimore at the City Block, between the commercial center of town and Fells Point, the deep-water port. The two blocks were bounded by Fleet, Exeter, and Lancaster streets, and by Harford Dock, now Central Avenue. Four years passed before the B&O accepted this offer, but the city was on record as to where it wanted the railroad built.

Powerful interests coalesced around both of the proposed sites, and touched off a controversy that lingered for years. The issue was whether the railroad should benefit the west side or east side of the city, Mount Clare or Peter Cooper's real estate interests that were forming in southeast Baltimore. Those who favored Carroll's Point claimed that the head of the Middle Branch was the logical termination of the railroad's Patapsco Valley route. Most of the city's business was conducted on the west side, which was as close to the commercial center as the City Block. But the City Block was on land that had only been leveled and filled in 1826 and had not yet settled. Carroll said it was "the worst of all the possible spots for a depot," and the shallow depth of water would require constant dredging. [13]

The City Block proponents replied that the situation was no different on the Middle Branch, and furthermore that the neighborhood, surrounded by swamps, was pestilential. The "best interests of the present city of Baltimore, as it is now built," demanded the rejection of Carroll's Point, said Solomon Etting. [14] Etting, a city councilman, who was an original incorporator of the railroad and a city director, was one of several B&O directors who owned property along the route to the City Block. Etting argued that the railroad should enter the city "on some high point of ground" rather than "the nearest point to tidewater," because the latter choice might result in "building up a new city, to the destruction of the property of the present owners." [15] He may have been referring to the municipality, which owned stock in the railroad and wanted to promote its own port facilities at the City Block, or to the B&O directors like himself, who owned land along the route the railroad eventually took into town. Perhaps to both. But it was not the last time the Baltimore and Ohio's private concerns would be wrapped in the public interest.

Carroll charged that "influential characters" and the city itself had threatened to withhold their installments on the stock unless the choice was the right one. At any rate, at the end of May, the directors met in their offices above the Mechanics Bank to decide the question of whether or not to adopt formally the southern route by the Point of Rocks and to instruct the engineers to terminate it at the city limits, "at a point best calculated to distribute the trade throughout the town as now improved."[16]

Etting and director William Steuart proposed amendment after amendment, restricting the point of entry to a 75-foot elevation, or to a specific location, and prohibiting branch lines below it. They lost the vote when the board adopted the original resolution, but since the decision did not specify exactly where the railroad was to enter the city or end within it, the matter was still open. The directors all agreed that it should come in as high as possible with no lower branch lines. James Carroll never forgave them.

On June 2, 1828, the Board of Directors decided to begin building July 4—precisely where was still to be settled. The engineers' assignment was to choose a place that was far enough away from the built-up part of town for the line not to interfere with traffic on congested streets such as Pratt and Baltimore and high enough to allow the trade coming in from the west to flow like water down the branch line from the depot to the City Block.

The engineers ran their levels up as far as the Washington Monument, but after considering various possibilities, decided that an elevation between 60 and 70 feet was best. On June 23 they found the spot, elevation 65 feet, "between Gwynns run and Gwynns Falls in a field belonging to James Carroll." The site was on what was then the City Line. The arrangement was the railroad's first major land deal—a secret one—and it was a political coup for Thomas. He had maneuvered adroitly among the contending forces to wind up with Carroll's land and the city's preferred route.[17]

But if Thomas was inclined to gloat, circumstances would have prevented it, for no sooner had he secured one end of the line than the company was called on to answer a legal emergency at the other. The Chesapeake and Ohio Canal had obtained a court injunction against the railroad on June 11, and by June 23 the B&O had a similar injunction against the canal. Both court actions were designed to prevent the other company from acquiring any more land along the east bank of the Potomac River between the Point of Rocks and Cumberland. The Chesapeake and Ohio charged that the B&O was trying to "oust" the canal, but since the railroad already had the land, from the Point of Rocks to Harpers Ferry and beyond, as the *Gazette* pointed out, there would not even be a "temporary interruption."[18] The board of directors likewise felt that the dispute with the canal would not "in the least retard our operations." Thomas sent Long to start clearing obstructions on the riverbank so they could grade the line. The canal retaliated by trying to run Walter Gwynn off from his survey work in the area. Gradually the situation settled into a stalemate at the Point of Rocks.

It cannot be proved that the railroad tried to head off the canal at the narrow passes of the Potomac. The river route was best for the B&O, too. But if it was their purpose, they had ample prior knowledge. Thomas had been a canal commissioner and McNeill and several of the other engineers now working for the Baltimore and Ohio had conducted the canal survey. The Chesapeake and Ohio, unlike the railroad, was not yet fully organized and was therefore vulnerable.

At the same time, the canal could not have been unaware of the railroad's plans. The Point of Rocks route had been in the papers in January 1828 as one of the four the B&O was considering and again on May 8, when the engineers, in turning in their report on the reconnaissance and surveys, said it was the best choice. In fact, when the board of directors formally adopted it on May 23, the *Gazette* did not even consider it news.

It is more likely that the canal resented being outsmarted by the railroad, which had dispatched its lawyers and engineers to the river on May 12 "to obtain possession of the several passes from the mouth of Monocacy to Cumberland."[19] There were four strategically important places below Harpers Ferry where the hills were so close to the river that there was almost no shore. They were the Upper and Lower Point of Rocks, where the Potomac cut through the Catoctin Mountain, Miller's Narrows, and Elk Hill, where it parted the South Mountain and the Blue Ridge. The B&O's efforts to acquire these sites were not without comic overtones.

First, directors John B. Morris and Patrick Macauley examined the land records to see what rights the C&O Canal or the Potomac Company had along the river. John V. L. McMahon and John H. B. Latrobe handled most of the legal work, for $1,000 each. Roger Brooke Taney and William Gwynn provided strategy. The engineers were chiefly Long and McNeill, with Isaac R. Trimble, Walter Gwynn, and R. E. Hazzard.

This was Latrobe's introduction to railroad work. William Gwynn had recommended him to Thomas, who needed someone to do the job. In mid-May, Latrobe and Long set out on horseback from Frederick for the purpose of securing releases for right-of-way from residents along the proposed route. When they reached the Point of Rocks, Long headed upriver and Latrobe proceeded to call on the residents of the area around the Point of Rocks. By the time Latrobe had worked his way up to the people living at the Upper Point of Rocks, he was delivering his speech with confidence and getting all the releases he asked for. He went on north of Harpers Ferry and then returned to Baltimore. There, he found that the senior lawyers, anticipating a legal challenge from the canal, had decided that deeds were necessary.

So back Latrobe went, this time with his old West Point classmate Trimble, whose job it was to survey the land for legal descriptions. A third colleague rounded up two justices of the peace, who had to witness each transaction. The instructions were to condemn the land if they could not obtain signed deeds. It was "wearisome work," Latrobe said. He had to explain to the residents he had called on earlier why the releases were insufficient, and Trimble had to go over each property—as at James Hook's place at the Upper Point of Rocks: "beginning on a tract of bottom land at the lower extremity of a field . . . being the first clearing in the valley . . . above the upper point of Rocks: on the eastern shore of the Potomac River, and at a small hickory tree . . . marked with a blaze."[20]

From the Point of Rocks to Williamsport, the team surveyed and "described what railroads were often times to men whose knowledge of highways was confined to mountain paths, made diagrams of cars and tracks unlike anything that existed before, or which came afterwards, and were believed by an ignorance that was only greater than their own," Latrobe recalled.[21] All this strategy worked. Most of the right-of-way not only along the river but all the way from Baltimore to the Potomac was given outright to the railroad. "The Point of Rocks are safe," Thomas exulted at the end of May.[22]

The West Point engineers were now surveying with a vengeance, completing several properties a day. In a little over a week, they surveyed 43 separate parcels of land totaling more than 169 acres. On these lightning surveys, an unlikely team worked the territory between Williamsport and Cumberland: McMahon, the pompous mountain orator who did not care much for slogging along the riverbanks near Hancock, and McNeill, the fiery soldier who had been Andrew Jackson's aide during the Seminole campaign in Florida.

Surveys and property acquisition between Baltimore and the Point of Rocks continued until December 1829, when the entire line was located between those points and the surveys were suspended. In the meantime, the practical engineers had taken over. Wever started work with the railroad in July 1828, and after the formalities of the parade and celebration for the laying of the cornerstone, he and the board of engineers made plans for actual construction. In June, in notices printed in newspapers from Boston to Richmond, they had called for sealed bids from contractors for excavation and preliminary construction work. In mid-July they advertised again for grading and masonry on the first twelve miles of railroad, but the surveys were still incomplete and the early proposals were unsatisfactory. The first contracts were signed at the end of the month and construction began on July 28.

The first sections were difficult, for there were several obstacles between the cornerstone in James Carroll's field and the first objective, the Patapsco River. Right at the start was the Gwynns Falls, where a substantial bridge would be needed. Two miles beyond it, a ridge divided the Gwynns Falls from the Patapsco. It became known for the railroad's passage through it as the Deep Cut. Farther on was a lowland called Gadsby's Run; it would require some sort of structure to carry the line. The railroad would have to cross the Washington Turnpike twice, and another bridge would be needed in the Patapsco Valley.[23] When the engineers bored holes in the ridge they found that it was composed of alternate layers of clay and sand of indeterminate "hardness and tenacity." [24] The way through it would be in an open cut, three quarters of a mile long and 70 feet deep, which would require over 300,000 cubic yards of excavation. It was a fairly large order for the time. They mounted the attack with picks, shovels, and wheelbarrows.

The railroad got off to a slow start that first season. The contractors were new and hesitant, the workmen were inexperienced, and the machinery necessary for such large-scale excavation had yet to make its appearance on the Baltimore and Ohio. Besides, some of the supervisors were elsewhere. The War Department removed William Howard and his brigade from the B&O in July and assigned them to survey the railroad in South Carolina. Knight and Wever were away on personal business from August until mid-October, and then Knight was dispatched along with McNeill and George W. Whistler, whom the company had finally obtained from the federal government, to England to study railroads. (McNeill had been made a member of the board of engineers and had had his salary doubled to $3,000 a year.) That left Long and Wever to supervise construction. Within a month the army engineer and the practical highway superintendent came to a serious clash of opinions over the matter of bridges.

Ever since his early road surveys, Long had favored wooden bridges, mainly because of cost, and he continued to recommend them in his railroad reports. His current thinking was that they would be built on the Burr plan, that is, as a combination of arch and truss. On November 3, 1828, the board of directors ratified its earlier decision to construct wooden bridges across the Gwynns Falls and the Patapsco River. But just eleven days later, they changed their minds and decided on a stone viaduct at the Patapsco River, Wever having convinced them that because ample stone for building was available at the site, the cost would be lower. At the same meeting, owing to the influence of Alexander and George Brown (Long claimed), the directors decided they would cross the valley of Gadsby's Run with an earth embankment rather than with the wooden viaduct Long had proposed. At subsequent meetings, stone bridges were substituted for wooden ones elsewhere on the line.

Wever and the board members believed that stone bridges were more permanent than wooden structures, which could be damaged or destroyed by fire, rot, and the like; Long argued that wooden bridges could be replaced several times over before they equaled the initial cost of stone. He stuck to that opinion long after, although he had to abide by the company's decision, and he seldom missed an opportunity to remind the B&O officials of the expense, as costs began to rise.

Despite dismal weather, work continued through the winter on the excavations and embankments. The directors advertised for contractors to start grading at the Point of Rocks, but the C&O Canal obtained a second injunction prohibiting construction in Frederick, Washington, and Allegany counties, and that effectively put a stop to it.

The arrival of Ross Winans, a 32-year-old farmer of Dutch extraction from Sussex County, New Jersey, shortly before Christmas 1828 provided a welcome diversion. He brought with him his patented invention, a small working model of a railroad car with "friction wheel" movement. Winans demonstrated the 125-pound car on temporary tracks and captivated the directors and everyone else who saw it.

Thomas could scarcely contain himself. He wrote Knight and McNeill in England: "It will greatly excite your curiosity and astonishment to be informed that a plain country farmer has invented a rail road waggon [that] by means of a friction wheel is so easily moved upon a level rail way that one pound weight over a pulley draws [more than half a ton], and a single cord of sewing silk tied to the waggon was strong enough to draw [several weights totaling more than 700 lbs.] and your friend George Brown on top of them."[25] Alexander Brown climbed aboard the car and shoving himself along with his walking stick, got up to 10 or 12 miles an hour. Later on, the car was taken to a room on an upper floor of the Exchange where the weight and pulley experiments were repeated, with Charles Carroll of Carrollton, then 91 years old, and Hezekiah Niles among the participants.

A much larger car, weighing 1,600 pounds, was soon built and tested. "It answered our most sanguine expectations," Alexander Brown reported. "A man can easily push along 5 or 6 tons on a level road, and we really believe that a horse will draw 30 or 40 with ease."[26] The hope was that the Winans car would allow horses to pull double the tonnage at twice the speed of the best English cars. Brown considered the friction wheel "as great a discovery in land transportation, as steam was in river navigation," so revolutionary that steam power would not be needed on railroads. "There will be no use for Locomotive Engines where one horse can draw so much," Brown said.[27]

Very quickly, the B&O acquired, for $1,000 plus $1 a year for each wagon in use, the exclusive rights to Winans's friction wheel car. Just after New Year's, the car went to Washington, with Wever and some of the directors, to be demonstrated for members of Congress. Meanwhile, Winans was on his way to England with enthusiastic letters of support from Thomas and Brown, to secure British patent rights for his invention.

The friction wheel operated on a principle that somewhat resembled that of a primitive roller bearing. In its earliest version, the device consisted of secondary wheels, mounted on axles and a frame, that rode suspended from the axle ends of the main wheels. The inside rims of the secondary wheels (about half as large as the main wheels) rolled on the main axle ends and turned with them. Seen in motion from the side, the contrivance looked like one wagon riding atop another. In later versions, the secondary wheels were more compact, like journal bearings.[28]

The Browns became so enamored of the Winans car that they developed a fascination with wheels in general. At their urging, the directors decided to "make a practical demonstration of the effect of power acting upon a railway," and they had temporary tracks laid. The Winans cars were put to work moving earth at the Deep Cut.[29] Long, though he recognized the merits of Winans's invention, was scornful of the near-hysterical reaction it provoked in Baltimore. He mocked the directors' trip to Washington—the B&O was seeking a $1 million federal subscription to its stock at the time, which it did not get—and argued that a plain presentation of facts would have been better than "the display of a mere pygmy car, maneuvered by silken threads."[30]

The new cars performed well at the Deep Cut but developed problems that Alexander Brown thought could be rectified by improved fabrication and a better track. Long noticed that after the Winans cars had run 500 miles, the main axle ends and the inside rims of the secondary wheels were badly worn. Brown responded that Long was "very deficient in mechanical knowledge, except what he has learned from books."[31] Long was against the Winans cars from the beginning, Brown said, and "he will be mortified if they succeed, as it will place his opinion where it ought to be, in the background." Long felt that his skepticism of the friction wheel contributed more than anything else "to impair [the directors'] confidence in his abilities and their respect for his judgment."[32]

Long was right and the Browns were wrong about the Winans cars. Their success was spectacular but brief. When the B&O Railroad opened the following year, the "Pioneer" coach that led the first train to Ellicotts Mills rode on friction wheels, but the company was already experimenting with another device, developed by John Elgar, in which journal bearings ran in cast-iron boxes. Both Elgar and Winans became B&O assistant engineers, but it was Elgar's mechanism, conceptually superior and more durable because of less wear on the parts, that pointed the way to future railroad technology. By 1835, the B&O was changing over from friction wheels to plain journal bearings.

Winans had by then decided that the valuable part of his invention lay not in the friction wheel but in the outside bearing. The concept of friction wheels was not unique. Others had thought of it including William Howard, who came up with the idea while riding alone through the forests of western Maryland on reconnaissance for the B&O. Howard took out a patent just eleven days after Winans. Also, most importantly, the friction wheel was basically flawed and dangerous in that the main axles "floated" in the friction wheels and could cause derailments. Elgar's journal bearings locked the main axles in cast-iron boxes that were rigidly attached to the loaded cars, so that the axles were kept perpendicular to the track.[33]

After a few years of experiments, the company was as disillusioned with the friction wheel cars as at first they had been intoxicated. When Winans's agent sought a change in the agreement with the railroad, Thomas wrote back that the B&O did not owe "one cent to the patentee. On the contrary he is more indebted to us for the aid he has received towards perfecting his invention than we are to him for any benefit it has been to us."[34] Winans claimed that his friction wheels differed from the others by being outside the main wheels, and he also complained that George Stephenson had seen his car in England and built one like it, thereby denying him British patent rights to the outside bearing. In this he was apparently wrong. There is evidence that Stephenson had cars with outside bearings in axle boxes running on the Stockton and Darlington Railway in November 1828, a month after Winans patented his invention in America but before he arrived in England, or even got to Baltimore with it.[35] Certainly it is possible that the two men arrived at the same concept simultaneously.

In any case, following an investigation by counsel John H. B. Latrobe, the B&O in 1834 paid Winans an additional $5,000 for the use of his outside bearing and other improvements. The headstrong, litigious mechanic, or as Knight called him, the "ingenious inventor," could not have chosen a better sponsor of his railroad career. Winans became the B&O's chief supplier of locomotives, and although his engines worked better than his cars, they were every bit as peculiar.

While Winans and the other engineers investigated the latest in English railway technology, the construction work in Baltimore gathered momentum and the ill feeling between Long and Wever grew more intense. They could not even agree on the best way to dig.

The fall labor force of 700 to 800 was increased during the winter of 1828 to about 1,000 men. They were concentrated at the Deep Cut, filling the Winans cars and other railroad wagons with tons of dripping gravel, sand, and a tenacious substance that became known in countless contractors' claims as "indurated clay." As Hezekiah Niles said, solid rock would have been easier to remove: "The strongest man could not drive a sharp pick two inches into it."[36] The horses dragged the cars to spoil banks at either end of the cut where the material was dumped to form embankments to level the line. The winter was especially severe, and it was cold, wet, miserable work. Four men died in February 1829, the first casualties on the railroad. Patrick Hackett, Edward McGreary, Thomas Hewes, and Daniel Ragen, "all natives of Ireland," noted the newspapers, were crushed and suffocated at Vinegar Hill, just past Gadsby's Run, when a bank under which they were excavating collapsed. A month later, Alexander Turner, a contractor, was blown up and lost his right arm.

In May 1829, they were still only halfway through with the Deep Cut. The work force was doubled to 2,000 men, 300 horses, 200 carts—these in addition to the laborers, wagons, horses, and drivers hauling stone for the bridges. During the summer of 1829 they worked in shifts around the clock under torchlights. Long tried teams of oxen and plows to loosen the earth. Wever favored gunpowder and they ended up drilling and blasting their way through. As they dug down, they struck iron ore, carbonized trees, and then, at 70 feet, springs and quicksand.

To avoid the quicksand and drain the springs, they decided to allow a slight incline rather than the perfect level originally intended. However, to do it, some of the material already removed had to be replaced. The directors, especially Alexander Brown, took credit for the decision and blamed the engineers for the extra cost. Long and McNeill later maintained that the decision was theirs and that they could not have foreseen the conditions that led to it. The contractor defaulted and the company took over the project. It was a process that would be repeated many times.

By December 1829, after eighteen months of work, the Deep Cut was finished. It was more than 180 feet wide at the top, sloping down to the right-of-way 70 feet below. The cost was $122,000. "A vast amount of money has been expended more than ought to have been, by the ignorance of our engineers," was Alexander Brown's conclusion.[37]

Long and McNeill made the same charge against the company with regard to the stone bridges built over the Gwynns Falls and the Patapsco River. What drove the price up depends on which version of events, the engineers,' the directors,' or Wever's, is the most believable, yet there was little disagreement about the outcome. The bridge over the Gwynns Falls, originally conceived as a single arch of rough stone costing about $15,000, ended up as a two-arched structure of finished stone costing at least four times as much. The bridge in the Patapsco Valley was to have two arches and a similar price. When it was finished, it had four arches and had cost more than twice as much.[38]

The bridges were Wever's province. For assistants, he hired two men who had built bridges for him on the National Road, James Lloyd and John McCartney, the latter an aggressive, hard-drinking contractor. Over the next decade, McCartney would take on some of the railroad's toughest and most important construction projects. During the winter, Wever discussed his plans with McCartney, who hauled in some lumber for the arch supports (centering). But real work did not begin on either of the bridges until May 1829, shortly before Knight, McNeill, and Whistler returned to Baltimore from their seven-month fact-finding mission to England. They had seen nothing in England that caused them to doubt the efficiency of railroads or the location and method of construction adopted in Baltimore. "Upon the whole, we have every confidence we shall succeed with the Baltimore and Ohio rail-road," they said.[39]

Long's feud with Wever had flourished unabated during the absence of the other engineers, but now Long hoped for better cooperation. He took Knight and McNeill on a tour of the line. They agreed that the masonry of Wever's Gwynns Falls bridge was too expensive.

The excess cost was not all Wever's fault, although he was apparently too willing to indulge the requests of James Carroll, the owner of Mount Clare. Carroll wanted changes, and as his demands increased, Wever's designs for the bridge grew larger and more grandiose. Carroll first complained that the 50-foot arch planned by the railroad was too small to accommodate the stream during floods. The directors made it 80 feet and added a 12-foot arch on the far side for an existing road. Carroll did not like the roadway arch either, so the company enlarged it to 20 feet and altered its position. In the midst of these negotiations, which took place between April and July 1829, James Lloyd, the contractor, agreed to pay damages for draining Carroll's millpond and shutting down his mill in order to build the bridge. Wever, hoping to please Carroll, changed the specifications from local stone roughly laid up to dressed granite wagoned in from Ellicotts Mills and Port Deposit. But Carroll was never satisfied. He was, in fact, so upset about the structure's "having most contrary to my wishes and solicitations" been built so that it disrupted his business operations that he remembered it in his will, which he drew up about that time.[40]

At the Patapsco River, construction problems added to the cost of the bridge. Because neighborhood residents wanted roadways on either side, the original two arches were expanded to four. There was, as Wever had said, plenty of building stone nearby, and temporary railways brought it to the site. Eleven times John McCartney and his men built coffer dams to lay the pier foundations, and eleven times the river washed them away. The flooding Patapsco also undermined the banks at either end of the bridge, and massive guard walls had to be built. When the arches were at last closed, everybody got roaring drunk in the steep, rockbound valley, and McCartney baptized his kneeling laborers by pouring a pint of whiskey on their heads. (Six months later, Wever banned the use of "ardent spirits" on the line, but it had little noticeable effect, particularly on McCartney.)

Both bridges were finished and officially opened in December 1829. The first rails, sent over from England, had been laid several months earlier under Whistler's supervision. They ran from Pratt Street, which was as far as the railroad had been extended into the city, out to the Gwynns Falls bridge, officially named the Carrollton Viaduct on December 21, when Charles Carroll of Carrollton rode out from the city in the cars, ceremoniously laid the last stone, and crossed over with a group of company and other officials.

The Carrollton Viaduct was roughly 300 feet long, 26.5 feet wide, and 58 feet high, from the foundation to the top of the parapet. A powerful segmental arch, it was certainly the largest bridge to be seen in Baltimore at the time. Hezekiah Niles said it was "splendid," and the rest of the local press thought the structure both massive and graceful. Even Long acknowledged that it was "a magnificent Bridge, perhaps unequalled in this country."[41]

A few weeks earlier, on December 4, the Patapsco River bridge was officially opened by William Patterson in a similar ceremony. It was thereafter known as the Patterson Viaduct. The main arches each had a span of 55 feet and the roadway arches, 20 feet each. The bridge was about 375 feet long, 28 feet wide, and 46 feet high. Some of the massive granite blocks in the walls weighed seven tons each. Engineers and visitors agreed that its style of rustic masonry suited the picturesque scenery of the valley. "It would appear as if the Spirit of the Stream had presided at the plan and execution of the work," the *Gazette* reported.[42]

These handsome bridges had cost dearly, and their designer was under investigation by the railroad. At least within the company, the venomous dispute between construction superintendent Wever and Long and the board of engineers that had seethed below the surface was finally out in the open. Long and McNeill set forth their version of the events in May 1830 in a 400-page "Narrative of the Proceedings of the Board of Engineers," addressed to the stockholders. Although the pamphlet did not seem to attract much attention, perhaps because of its length but also, no doubt, because the opening of the railroad the same month rendered the discussion nugatory, it is in many ways a more revealing outline of what was involved in building the railroad during the early years than the voluminous company documents. Certainly it was a good lesson in how not to go about it.

The company never officially explained why the board of engineers had been created in the first place. It may well have been the idea of the engineers themselves: they were all associated in one way or another with the federal government, which had three-man boards of engineers to plan fortifications and internal improvements. The regulations that McNeill drew up for the B&O's version were based on the United States Corps of Engineers, and the company investigation that led to its dissolution had the aspect of a military tribunal.

Long traced the animosity between the board and the superintendent to their initial encounter. Incompetent and conniving were among the things he and McNeill called Wever as their difficult association developed, but there was more to it than that. They strongly implied that the contractors and agents under Wever's control had been involved in profiteering, collusion, and extortion and that the superintendent was not an innocent.

Wever made no written defense to these charges as such, but he did object indirectly to Long's "rigid formality" in requiring strict accounting for every expenditure. He admitted that construction costs on the first division (Baltimore to Ellicotts Mills) had been excessive and that "errors may have been committed," but he attributed them to changes in design and to the need to get a new and unfamiliar project built quickly. From the outset, the directors approved of Wever's actions, and he consulted the board of engineers only when it was necessary, which was seldom.[43]

McNeill's company-approved regulations, which made the superintendent subordinate to the board of engineers, had been an issue from the first meeting in June

1828. Wever insisted on having full control over the construction of the railroad, the contracts, the disbursement of funds, and changes in location, and over Long's strenuous opposition, Thomas and Knight sided with Wever. The pattern was thus set for the next eighteen months. When Long issued a set of instructions requiring Wever to submit contract forms, the superintendent gave himself sole authority to make agreements and pay contractors. Again Long objected and again he was voted down. He predicted a short life for their "associate existence."

Throughout the ensuing controversy, Long acted as if these guidelines were in effect, but Wever used them selectively. For example, the instructions gave Wever control over bridges under 20 feet in length, and soon ads for contractors to build stone bridges began appearing in newspapers as far away as Ohio. In October 1828, after Wever returned from his two-month leave of absence to conclude his affairs on the National Road, Long told him to lay the foundations for a wooden bridge over the Gwynns Falls. Instead, Wever began what Long called a "counterproject." When Knight, McNeill, and Whistler sailed for England, they left behind an uneasy and confused situation.

Thomas proposed a compromise. Long would work on the surveys for extending the railroad into the city, Thomas would supervise Wever's construction work, and when the engineers came back from England, they would reorganize. Reluctantly, Long agreed. He doubted Wever's qualifications as an engineer. "This arrogant pretender," he called him. That was in December 1828.

But Wever was no pretender. That month he rode up the Patapsco Valley with John McCartney to look at the bridge site. McCartney and Robert Wilson, who had built bridges on the National Road with James Lloyd, had been in Baltimore earlier in the year at Wever's request to make bridge proposals. Unsuccessful, they had returned to Ohio. After the directors substituted stone for wooden bridges they came back, again at Wever's suggestion. McCartney told Wever he would build the Patapsco River bridge for about $20,000. Wilson became Wever's superintendent of masonry. James Lloyd arrived later.

After the harsh winter and the wet spring, construction work accelerated all along the line. In May 1829, after the trio returned from England and the board of engineers was back in business, Thomas withdrew. Long moved at once to control Wever, but when he found Wever's accounts incomplete and declined to approve his monthly estimate of expenses, the directors approved them anyway. Wever was spending $20,000 to $30,000 a month, on what exactly the engineers were not sure.

Then, early in June 1829, Wever asked the board of engineers for assistance. The contractors were suffering, he said, their costs having risen much higher than the original contract prices. If they abandoned the work, the shock would idle laborers and discourage other contractors. Wever preferred to pay the present ones an extra amount and keep them on the job. He wanted the engineers' aid in determining how much.

McNeill and Whistler reviewed the state of the contracts from the city to the Forks of the Patapsco River, the end of the second division. They found that the price of labor had risen about 50 percent (from $8 to $10 a man per month to $12 to $14), that the contractors had encountered difficult clay and rock, and that changes in location and the substitution of stone for wooden bridges had escalated the cost. They agreed that a general failure of contractors would indeed be disastrous and estimated that an additional $45,000 would see them through.

The railroad directors also agreed, but they did not have the money. A $5 installment was called on the stock, due in November, advance payments acceptable. No one yet realized the extent of the problem. Thomas asked the engineers for more information. They succeeded in getting Wever to submit his first masonry documents on July 20, 1829, and made the figures the basis for their own report to the directors. This showed that although the railroad could be built the 66 miles from Baltimore to the Potomac River for just a little over the original estimate of $20,000 per mile, the cost of the first 13 miles to Ellicotts Mills would be more than $37,500 per mile. The engineers, the directors, and the newspapers tried to put the embarrassing figures in the best possible light. "The first step is the most difficult," Hezekiah Niles observed tactfully. He nonetheless considered the high initial cost an "extraordinary expenditure."[44]

Wever's documents provided the ammunition for McNeill's charges against him for making false reports. McNeill claimed that Wever, after all the design changes had been made in the bridges, had deliberately underestimated their true cost by $50,000. Wever's later reports tacitly acknowledged a discrepancy of about half that amount, but he maintained that the changes caused the increase. He may have lied. It is also likely that he did not know what the final figures would be.

Hardly anyone knew what was going on with the bridges. When the reconstituted board of engineers began delving into Wever's activities, they found that not only were there no written contracts, for Wever had verbal agreements with Lloyd and McCartney, but also there were no plans. The bridges were being designed as they went up. Long had offered to make drawings for the Patapsco River bridge and been rebuffed. Early in their investigation, the engineers found McCartney just starting work at the site and he had shown them "a very rough and unsightly draft of the western abutment," saying it was all he had. Evidently stung by this, Wever acquired a drawing board big enough to hold plans for all the bridges, but then announced that it was a waste of time "making pretty pictures," since a good practical engineer did not need written instructions. More was still to come. In September 1829, Wever told the directors he would need $180,000 over the next three months to finish the first two divisions of the railroad. The company had only $20,000 in cash, so a call went out to the "royal merchants," William Patterson, Robert Oliver, and Alexander Brown, to work with Thomas to raise the necessary money.

Long drafted yet another set of bylaws, taking the disbursement power away from Wever and giving it to the board of engineers. Thomas rejected them. The company's old friend William Gwynn, the *Gazette* editor, found it an opportune moment to ride out along the line. The work was progressing nicely, he reported, the "season of doubt" was over.[45] In fact, it was just beginning. The price of the stock was sliding and it would shortly become unsalable. Alexander Brown wrote to the English Brown branch, "We feel a little uneasy about the success of the road."[46]

At that point McNeill demanded Wever's suspension. It was just what the company needed. Thomas, who knew the true cost of the bridges, according to Whistler, wanted to keep it from the public until the stock installments came in and he could find some way to get rid of the board of engineers. Meanwhile, he dissembled, claiming Wever had deceived him and feigning amazement at what the engineers had found out. "He was distressed that the facts had been discovered, not that they existed," said Whistler. "Indeed he was so much distressed as to be quite sick." [47]

For their part, the directors were frantically trying to finish the work before there were further revelations about the expense. They focused on raising money. Some of the stockholders advanced notes in anticipation of their installments coming due. Eight of the directors, including Patterson, Oliver, Alexander Brown, and Thomas, put up individual notes of $12,500 each. George Brown, the company treasurer, borrowed close to $75,000 from the Mechanics Bank on these notes and was authorized to borrow up to the full $100,000 or get the money from the directors themselves, "in order that the completion of the road may be secured as fast as circumstances will admit." [48]

In the railroad's third annual report issued early in October 1829, Thomas repeated the reasons given by the engineers for the high initial cost and assured the stockholders that the rest of the line to the Ohio River would be built for the previously estimated cost of $20,000 a mile. The annual report of the board of engineers— their second and last—was more complete and more critical, especially of the bridge costs, than the company report, but restrained under the circumstances. Unlike the company's, it did not appear in the newspapers, and McNeill and Whistler claimed that it was suppressed.

Immediately after the reports were out, the five-man committee of directors appointed to investigate McNeill's charges began hearing testimony in the company's offices. Thomas sat in occasionally, but McNeill's chief questioner was a chill and austere Alexander Brown. "It's a very strange business, this, that the Board of Engineers should be giving us all this trouble, and putting themselves in opposition to the President and Directors of the Company," Brown said. "Don't you know, Sir, that the Board of Directors have a right to do as they please, they are supreme in this Company, Sir, they can even dismiss you or the whole Board of Engineers." McNeill replied that he had already offered to resign. [49]

Thomas, the mediator, stepped in. That was true, he said, but he wouldn't hear of it. "Capt. McNeill is a young man, and impetuous in his feelings, sometimes says things hastily, which he afterwards regrets, but is always willing to *apologize*," Thomas added. McNeill allowed that he had said nothing requiring explanation, let alone apology, and after a general clearing of throats, the proceedings continued.

McNeill, an outspoken and strong-willed man, gave the directors a full account of what had been uncovered. Although the committee voted against keeping a written record, McNeill kept his own. According to his account, the system under which the contractors arranged their prices informally with Wever as the work progressed encouraged corruption: Wever would ask, "John [McCartney], how much money do you want this week?" Long suspected McCartney of making a $10,000 profit (close to $100,000 in today's money) on the Patterson Viaduct, almost a third of the cost of the bridge.

McNeill also had doubts about Robert Wilson, Wever's masonry agent, who had estimated the progress of the work on which the payments were based. McNeill said there were strong indications that Wilson was financially involved with James Lloyd in the lucrative contract for the Carrollton Viaduct and that, after failing to buy out the contractor who was doing the work before Lloyd took it over, he used his position to force him out. Wever's false reports of the bridge costs had misled both the board of engineers and the board of directors, McNeill said.

The hearings wound down in December 1829. Alexander Brown predicted that all the members of the board of engineers except Knight—Wever's ally, who had taken little part in the controversy and was out of town during the hearings—would soon leave the railroad. The investigating committee's report to the rest of the board the following month called Wever a "faithful, devoted, and efficient servant" who had "honestly and satisfactorily accounted for every sum . . . placed in his hands."[50] After his contretemps with the board of engineers over his reports, Wever had by-passed the board and gone directly to the company with his vouchers for funds. The committee decided that the evidence against Robert Wilson was inconclusive. They acknowledged that McNeill had been motivated by his sense of duty.

On the whole, the committee sustained McNeill's charges: Wever had failed to comply with the rules and regulations, his reports were mere "shreds and patches," and his method of handling contracts "loose." But his duties were complicated and he needed some discretionary power, they said. Early on, the directors discovered "that a race for popularity was to be run with our more favored rival," and therefore they were worried less about economy than about finishing the railroad. Wever had driven on the contractors and had seen that the bridges were up in six months, and that was what they wanted.[51]

Within a few months, the board of engineers was defunct. Knight was appointed chief engineer in February 1830. Long resigned in March, terminating his career with the Baltimore and Ohio in a petty dispute with Thomas over his final pay and his refusal to return the engineers' journal of proceedings, which he was doubtless using to prepare his and McNeill's publication. (After protracted negotiations, Long returned the book five years later and received his back wages.) McNeill left in April. The railroad wanted him to stay, partly because of the knowledge he had acquired on his trip to England, but he said he could not work under Knight. Wever remained, and the company may have had occasion to recall these events when he and Charles Wilson, Robert's brother, collaborated some years later on a bridge farther on.

There was one last structure on the line that was nowhere mentioned in the official company records during this period. It was a small, wooden bridge that carried the Washington Turnpike over the railroad just beyond the Carrollton Viaduct. Long called it the Jackson Bridge, in honor of the President and perhaps in defiance of his employer's practice of naming big bridges for important directors. It was a wooden truss of Long's own design, 110 feet long, 24 feet wide, and 16 feet high. It was put together by half a dozen carpenters in five weeks at a cost of $1,670. The press described it as slender and bold, "like the flight of a bird over a valley."[52] Long calculated its capacity at 110 tons, but to dispel rumors of its lack of strength, had 80 head of cattle driven over it "at close gang," and received the testimonials of architects William F. Small, Robert Cary Long, and Robert Mills, the designer of the Washington Monument in Baltimore (and later of the Washington Monument in Washington, D.C.).[53]

The principles of the Jackson Bridge, which Long patented in 1830, were so far in advance of their time that not even Long himself fully appreciated their virtues. An important feature was the basis of the modern K-truss, widely used in bridges and high-rise buildings. The next major bridge (over the Monocacy River) that the railroad put under contract was also a wooden one, but it was designed by Lewis Wernwag.

Before the public was really aware of the controversy surrounding its construction, the railroad was running. The company began excursions from the Pratt Street depot to the Carrollton Viaduct in late December 1829, after experimenting with a variety of cars. Some of the earliest consisted of bodies similar to stagecoaches, with seats on the roof, built by coachmaker Richard Imlay and mounted on Winans's friction wheels. Another, described as a "market cart," looked like a Conestoga wagon minus the hoops and canvas cover. There were cars propelled by dogs, by man-powered cranks, by horses on treadmills, and by the wind. John Elgar built a light sail-car named the Hobus for Evan Thomas. Thomas went out with one of Alexander Brown's ship captains as a pilot and they got up to 20 miles an hour and might have gone faster had they dared. At the Pratt Street depot, congressmen, state legislators, and other important people vied for trips in the Imlay and Winans cars with "a vast crowd of boys, [who] with some danger to themselves, caused great annoyance to the respectable persons who had been invited to witness the exhibition." The reporter who covered the event thought there should have been railroad police to keep order and prevent accidents.[54]

At last, on May 22, 1830, with Charles Carroll of Carrollton and the other directors leading the way in Imlay's coach the Pioneer, pulled by a single horse, the Baltimore and Ohio Railroad officially opened for travel the thirteen miles to Ellicotts Mills.

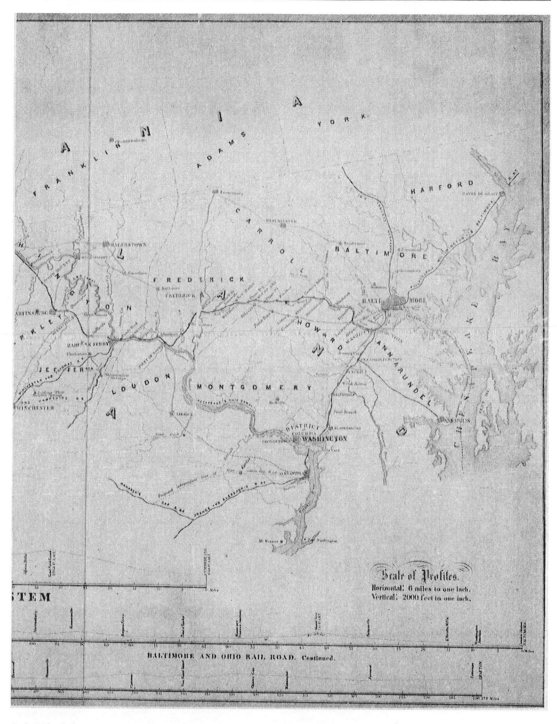

A detail of the 1858 map shows the B&O's route from Baltimore to Harpers Ferry and Martinsburg, and the Philadelphia, Wilmington, and Baltimore, and the Northern Central railroads, the National Road (Baltimore to Frederick and Hagerstown), and the Chesapeake and Ohio Canal. *Special Collections, University of Maryland, College Park Libraries.*

The skyline of Baltimore, 1872, from Federal Hill, showing Benjamin Henry Latrobe's cathedral with the dome and two towers, and the Washington Monument on the right. © *The B&O Railroad Museum, Inc., Collection.*

Philip E. Thomas *(top)*, hardware merchant and banker, and George Brown *(left)*, the banker son of Alexander Brown, originated the Baltimore and Ohio Railroad in 1827. Thomas, the B&O's first president, is seen in a rare daguerreotype, taken probably in the early 1850's, and Brown, the company's first treasurer, in a lithograph made for publication in 1853. *Thomas: Private collection; Brown: © The B&O Railroad Museum, Inc., Collection.*

When he laid the first stone for the B&O Railroad on July 4, 1828, Charles Carroll of Carrollton said it was "among the most important acts of my life, second only to my signing the Declaration of Independence, if even it be second to that." A wealthy landowner, Carroll was an original B&O director. *Oil painting, circa 1815–20, by Rembrandt Peale, Baltimore Museum of Art, Bequest of Ellen Howard Bayard.*

Almost everyone in Baltimore marched in or watched the four-hour parade and accompanying pageantry that preceded the B&O's ground breaking. The "Rail Road March" by C. Meineke was one of two songs composed for the occasion. *T. Edward Hambleton Collection, Peale Museum, Baltimore City Life Museums.*

Alexander Brown *(right)*, founder of
Alex. Brown & Sons, and Robert Oliver
(bottom left), owner of western
Maryland coal lands, marched in the pa-
rade as railroad directors, while another
B&O director and merchant prince,
William Patterson *(bottom right)*, rode in
a carriage. Philip Hone considered these
three the city's "royal merchants," and
compared them to the Medici. *Brown:
Engraving; Oliver: Oil painting, circa
1827, by John Wesley Jarvis; Patterson:
Oil painting, 1821, by Thomas Sully;
Maryland Historical Society, Baltimore.*

The Lehigh Coal and Navigation Company's nine-mile railway at Mauch Chunk, Pennsylvania, was one of the few that existed in America when the B&O began; three company directors rode the line, operated by gravity and horse-power, in May 1827. Karl Bodmer, at the start of his tour of the American West with Prince Maximilian in 1832, did a water-color of the inclined plane, the arks, and the community at Mauch Chunk. *Joslyn Art Museum, Omaha, Nebraska, Gift of the Enron Art Foundation.*

Baltimore civil engineer William Howard, in 1823, surveyed two routes for a canal from Baltimore to connect with the Chesapeake and Ohio Canal, planned to parallel the Potomac River from Washington, D.C., to the west. Howard later conducted railroad surveys along both alignments; the B&O's main line and its Washington Branch generally followed the two canal routes. © *The B&O Railroad Museum, Inc., Collection.*

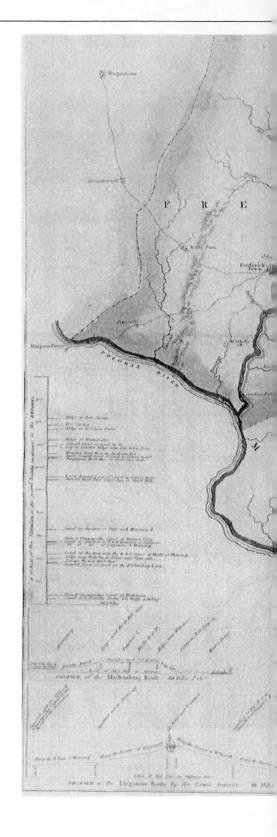

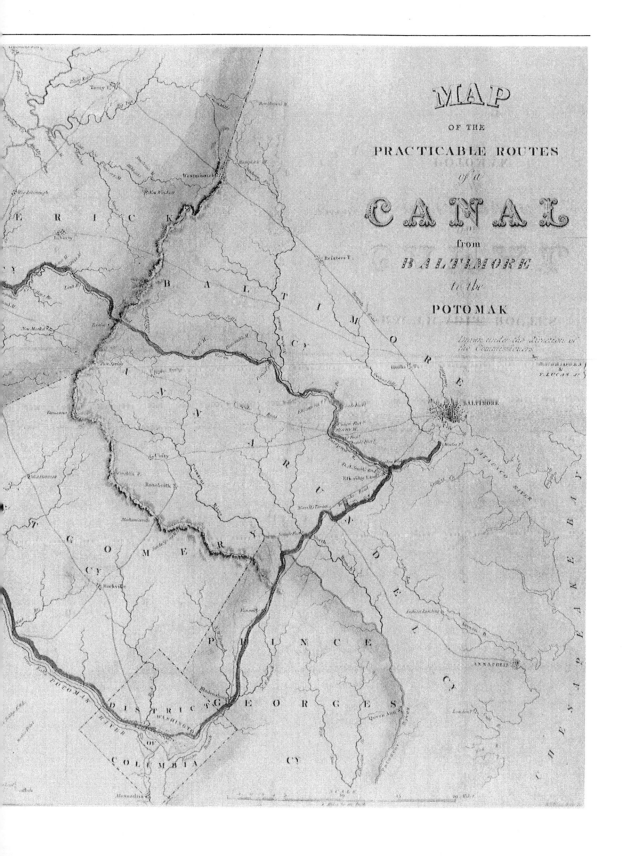

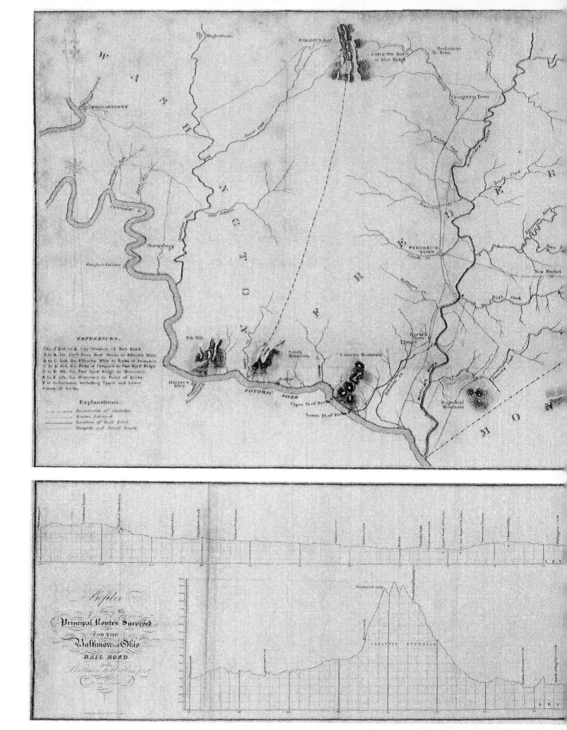

Joshua Barney, a West Point-trained engineer, aided in surveying routes for the B&O between Baltimore and the Potomac and drew this map *(top)* for the 1828 annual report. The accompanying profiles *(bottom)* show the two highest points, Parrs Spring Ridge and Harman's Gap in Catoctin Mountain; the railroad chose the lower one. © *The B&O Railroad Museum, Inc., Collection.*

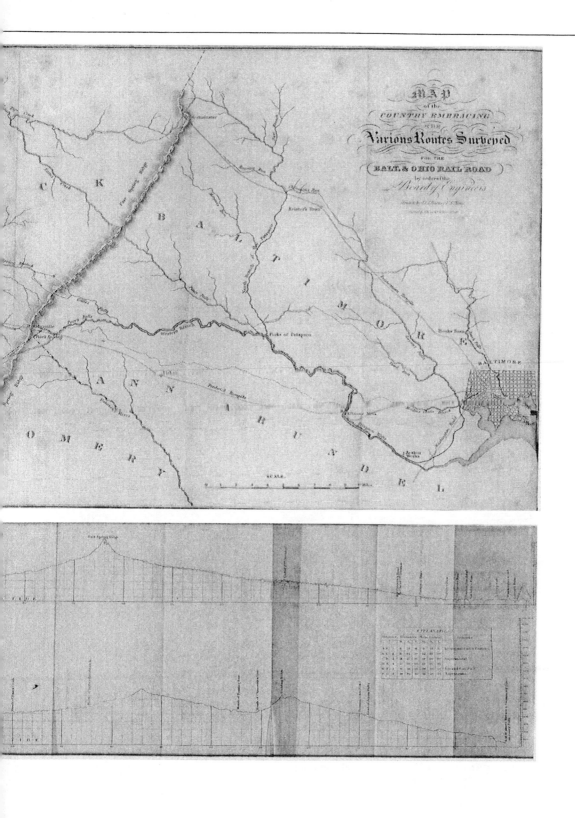

Isaac Ridgeway Trimble, another West Point graduate, participated in the initial B&O Railroad surveys and wrote luminous descriptions of the mountain landscape. He later became a railroad engineer for other lines, but was aboard the B&O train that officially opened the line to Wheeling in January 1853. *1852 oil painting by Samuel Waugh of New York, Maryland Historical Society, Baltimore.*

Benjamin Henry Latrobe, *(left)* architect and engineer, submitted the first report on railroads to the United States Congress in 1808, and his sons Benjamin H. Latrobe, Jr. *(bottom left)*, and John H. B. Latrobe *(bottom right)* spent virtually their entire professional careers with the B&O Railroad. Benjamin, an engineer, laid out the route from Harpers Ferry to Wheeling; John, a lawyer, made many of the political deals that enabled the line to be built. *B. H. Latrobe: portrait, circa 1816, by Rembrandt Peale; B. H. Latrobe, Jr.: 1861 photograph; J. H. B. Latrobe: 1879 photograph; Maryland Historical Society, Baltimore.*

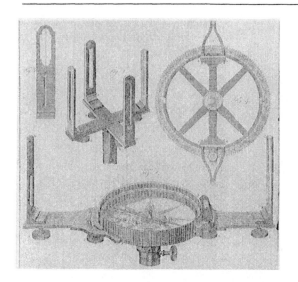

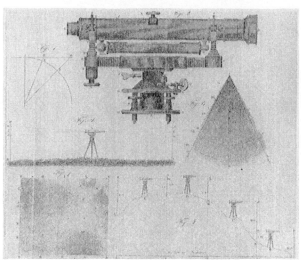

The surveyor's compass *(top left)* and the level *(top right)* (with the fifty-foot chain) were the instruments used for the first B&O surveys. The railroad soon added the transit *(bottom)*, invented in 1831, which could perform the functions of all three. The drawings are from *Elements of Surveying and Navigation* (1870), by Charles Davies, first published in 1830 as a textbook for West Point, where Davies trained many of the future B&O surveyors. *The Engineering Society of Baltimore.*

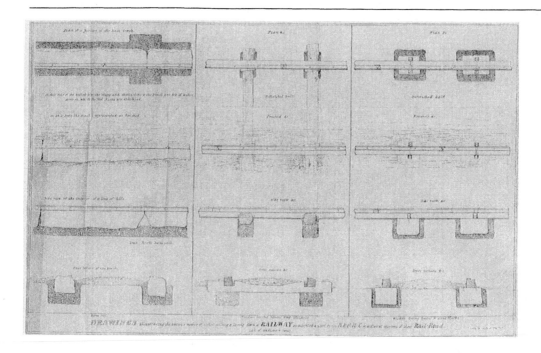

The B&O experimented with all three methods of track laying *(top)* before adopting the one in the center. They were drawn by Benjamin H. Latrobe, Jr., and printed in the 1831 annual report. In 1972, Hurricane Agnes uncovered the stone blocks and sills *(bottom)* along the Patapsco near the site of the Patterson Viaduct. *Drawing: © The B&O Railroad Museum, Inc., Collection; photograph: John P. Hankey.*

The early horse-drawn railroad using Richard Imlay's stagecoach-style cars was very pastoral for the first thirteen miles from Baltimore to Ellicotts Mills, which opened officially May 22, 1830. The Carrollton Viaduct *(top left)* crossed the Gwynns Falls, the Patterson Viaduct *(bottom)* bridged the Patapsco beyond Buzzard's Rock *(top right)*, and the Tarpean Rock *(top, opposite)* was just past Ellicotts Mills. The map *(bottom, opposite)* is from the 1828 B&O annual report. *Carrollton Viaduct, Buzzard's Rock, and Tarpean Rock: T. Edward Hambleton Collection, Peale Museum, Baltimore City Life Museums; Patterson Viaduct: © The B&O Railroad Museum, Inc., Collection; map: Maryland Historical Society, Baltimore.*

TARPEAN ROCK.
BALTO & OHIO R.R.

1831.

Lith. & Published, by Endicott & Swett, Graphic Hall Balto

for the Methodist Protestant.

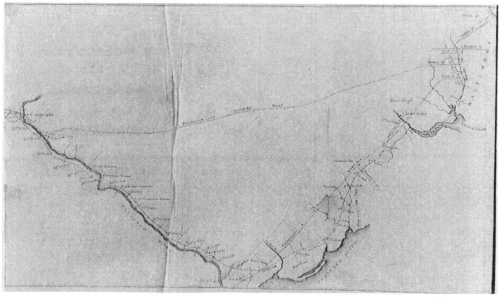

The early freight cars looked as if they belonged on a highway rather than on a railroad. Benjamin H. Latrobe, Jr., drew the illustration of the car *(right)* used to transport flour and of Ross Winans's friction wheel *(bottom)* for the 1831 annual report. *Flour car: Peale Museum, Baltimore City Life Museums; friction wheel: © The B&O Railroad Museum, Inc., Collection.*

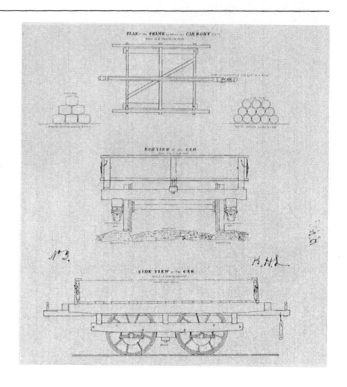

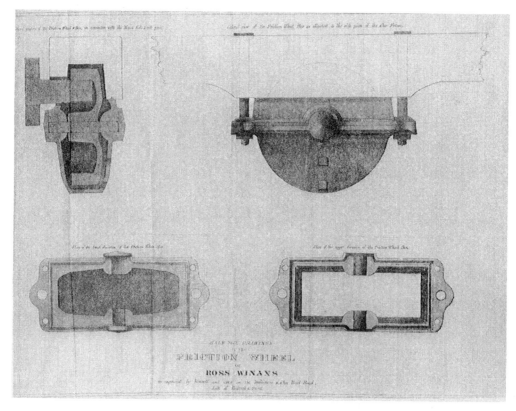

7

The Triumph of Steam

THE BALTIMORE AND OHIO BEGAN CONSTRUCTION
before the steam engine became an integral part of the railroad. The latter event
took place in the fall of 1829 at the British Rainhill trials where George and Robert
Stephenson's Rocket demonstrated conclusively that the locomotive could provide
fast, safe, and efficient transportation.

The steam engine was invented in England, so it was natural for the Baltimoreans to turn there for inspiration, as they had for the railroad itself. The B&O and
other American companies sent observers to Rainhill. Some U.S. firms ordered British
engines, but after a preliminary flirtation with them the B&O decided to procure
domestic models and held their own locomotive trials a year and a half later. Few
could see in those early machines at Rainhill the device that was to become the most
visible symbol of the Industrial Revolution, one that would link cities and countries
and revolutionize almost every aspect of society. The steam locomotive fascinated and
influenced generations of writers, artists, and musicians, not to mention mechanical
engineers.

The steam engine and the railroad may not have been synonymous before Rainhill, but they shared the common ancestry of coal and iron. One of the traditional
uses of steam engines in England was to pump the water from deep mines. Crude
tramways hauled the coal from the mine to the pier and coincident developments in
the iron industry had important effects on both steam engines and tramways. By the
1820's, the Boulton & Watt Cornish engines used to drain the mines had become
gargantuan. Pistons made eight-foot strokes, fifteen or so a minute, in cylinders that
were over five feet in diameter. A three-story building was required to house the
boiler and engine and to hold up the cast-iron beam, which weighed several tons.
They were huge, sluggish machines using low-pressure steam, at two to three pounds
per square inch.[1]

To make the steam engine move on land required a mechanism that was relatively small and fast, and high-pressure steam. One of the inventors of such a machine was an American, Oliver Evans (1755–1819). The other was his British contemporary, Richard Trevithick (1771–1833).

Evans was a wagon maker's apprentice from Newport, Delaware. He conceived his Columbian engine at age eighteen and proposed using it to power boats and vehicles, but his ideas were ridiculed. He also devised water-powered improvements to milling machinery that completely mechanized the functions of a flour mill. (The system is now regarded as the world's first automated production line.) In 1786, Evans petitioned the Pennsylvania legislature for the exclusive rights to the use of his mill inventions and steam carriages in that state. A legislative committee listened patiently while he described the mill improvements, he said, "but my representations concerning steam waggons made them think me insane." [2] The Maryland General Assembly was more receptive the following year and approved Evans's petition for both millworks and steam carriages. The members believed, as a Baltimore legislator put it, "that the grant could injure no one, for he did not think that any man in the world had thought of such a thing before." Afterward, the grateful inventor felt "bound in honor to the State of Maryland to produce a steam waggon." [3]

Within two years, Evans had his Columbian engine running in a Philadelphia shop. Its horizontal boiler was about fifteen feet long and three feet in diameter and had a central flue. There was a six-inch-diameter vertical cylinder with an eighteen-inch stroke. In 1803, Evans decided he could more profitably employ his engine in mills, but he did not give up the idea of using it to run steam carriages. Nor did his critics abandon their doubts. One of his severest detractors was Benjamin H. Latrobe, America's reigning steam engine expert. Latrobe had just designed the country's first steam-powered waterworks for Philadelphia. Like James Watt, however, Latrobe was peculiarly myopic concerning the possibilities of high-pressure steam.

Evans discussed his plans with Latrobe "who publicly pronounced them chimerical, and attempted to demonstrate the absurdity of my principles," in an address to the American Philosophical Society in May 1803. "I was one of the persons alluded to as being seized with the *steam mania* conceiving that waggons and boats could be propelled by steam engines," Evans said. [4]

Evans's moment of victory was at hand, however. Philadelphia hired him about this time to build a dredge to deepen the water around the city docks. By the summer of 1805, Evans had completed the *Oruktor Amphibolos*, or Amphibious Digger. This flat-bottomed scow, as ponderous as its name, was 30 feet long and 12 feet wide and weighed 20 tons. The engine, with an iron boiler set on bricks, was of the Grasshopper type. A vertical piston, five inches in diameter with a nineteen-inch stroke, moved a horizontal beam that pivoted at one end and powered a long connecting rod attached to geared wheels at the other.

The inventor drove this leviathan up to Centre Square (now Penn Square, the site of City Hall), and puffed and clanked triumphantly around Latrobe's waterworks engine house for days. Then he trundled down to the waterfront where the dredge floated off its road wheels and churned downriver into a unique status as America's first steam-powered vehicle. Evans never built another, but he did turn out some 50 stationary engines that weighed one fourth as much as others, operated at pressures of 100 to 150 psi, and used steam expansively, that is, by shutting off the supply when the stroke was partly complete and letting the expansion of the steam push the piston the rest of the way.

Evans was a consistent advocate of railroads and something of a prophet. In 1813 he promised:

> The time will come when people will travel in stages moved by steam engines from one city to another almost as fast as birds can fly, fifteen or twenty miles in an hour . . . a carriage will set out from Washington in the morning, the passengers will breakfast in Baltimore, dine at Philadelphia, and sup at New York the same day. To accomplish this, two sets of railways will be laid (so nearly level as not in any place to deviate more than two degrees from a horizontal line), made of wood or iron . . . so that [the carriages] may pass each other in different directions, and travel by night as well as by day; and the passengers will sleep in these stages as comfortably as they now do in [steamboats].[5]

Richard Trevithick was likewise unable to capitalize on his invention, but for quite different reasons.[6] He was the son of a mine manager in Cornwall, and at the age of eighteen, like Evans, began to design steam engines. Within three years he had built a high-pressure engine that eventually became a serious rival of the Boulton and Watt type for all sorts of industrial uses. It had a horizontal boiler with an internal U-shaped flue, faintly similar to the one developed by Evans. Trevithick's boiler permitted the use of much higher steam pressures than Watt's, up to 60 psi, and allowed his Cornish engine to work expansively.

Realizing that he could also use it to drive a carriage on the highway, Trevithick first did so successfully in 1801. In February 1804, he ran the world's first locomotive on the Penydarren railway, at Merthyr Tydfil, Wales, on a bet. He won the bet, but the engine broke several of the cast-iron plate rails and finally ran off the track. It had a cylinder recessed in the boiler to keep it hot, a safety valve, and a forced draft operated by exhaust steam sent up the chimney.

Four years later, Trevithick ran a demonstration locomotive called Catch-me-who-can around a circular track in London at twelve miles an hour, advertising it as "Mechanical Power Subduing Animal Speed." It attracted little public attention, however, and having proved that steam traction was practical on railways, the volatile inventor dropped the project and immersed himself in several farsighted but unprofitable schemes such as building a steam thresher and developing plans for iron ships. Trevithick died penniless in 1833. His life, said biographer Samuel Smiles, was "but a series of beginnings."[7]

After the mixed success of the first locomotive, there were several attempts to improve upon it that resulted in some strange and wonderful machines. George Stephenson saw many of them in operation. Like the other early British locomotive builders who were products either of the coalfields or of the iron foundries, Stephenson, born in 1781, a colliery fireman's son, grew up surrounded by steam engines. The house where he was born near Newcastle was only yards from the Wylam tramway, where as a child he watched horses pulling coal wagons past the door. Stephenson took a job tending a coal-pit pumping engine. He did not learn to read and write until he was eighteen.

Stephenson built his first locomotive in 1814 for the owners of the Killingworth Colliery, where he had become the engine-wright. It was named the Blucher after another Newcastle coal pit. Stephenson then joined forces with a Newcastle iron foundry and during the next several years built sixteen increasingly sophisticated locomotives. George Stephenson made sure that Robert, his son, born in 1803, acquired the education that he had missed, and Robert, in turn, tutored his father in science and engineering, handled his correspondence, and eventually joined his expanding enterprises. It was this father-and-son team that from the coal tramway, the steam engine, and the iron foundry, created the modern railroad.

By the 1820's, few engineers in the British coalfields could match George Stephenson's experience and ability. He had built close to 40 stationary engines to pump water and raise coal from mines and to operate inclined planes of his own design. He had surveyed and equipped with locomotives half a dozen colliery lines, including those at Killingworth and Hetton. In 1821, he was the logical choice as the engineer for the Stockton and Darlington Railway.

The promoters had proposed this 25-mile tramway between the towns in the north of England mainly to haul coal by horsepower, but after Stephenson convinced them to try locomotives, they expanded their plans to include passengers. Stephenson brought his son, Robert, in to help with the surveys. The Locomotion that pulled the first train on September 27, 1825, was fabricated by Robert Stephenson and Company, the newly organized Newcastle firm of engine builders.

The Stockton and Darlington was the first freight- and passenger-carrying railroad to employ locomotives. Their performance was disappointing at first, so the engines were used to haul coal and the passengers traveled in horse-drawn coaches. Thus, the real significance of the line was as a halfway step from the colliery tramways to the first general-purpose railroad to use locomotives exclusively.

That was the Liverpool and Manchester. William Jessop, the engineer who developed the edge rail and the flanged wheel, made a tramway survey between the two cities in 1797. Thomas Gray aggressively advocated the connection in his book on railroads. The Liverpool and Manchester Railroad was conceived in 1821. Robert Stephenson again participated in the early surveys and his father was hired as engineer in 1824. The story of the hostile encounters between George Stephenson and the landowners and canal proprietors who bitterly opposed the project, his humiliation before a committee of Parliament, and his ultimate engineering triumph has been told often and well.[8]

But the Stephensons had to wage another battle before their final victory at Rainhill. Among the reasons for the defeat of the Liverpool and Manchester Railway Act in Parliament in 1825 was the backers' insistence on the use of locomotives, to which there was substantial public opposition. The enemies of the locomotive believed that it was too fast, frightened horses, and might explode.

The act was approved in May 1826, but because an antilocomotive faction had developed within the railroad's board of directors, the question of motive power remained undecided, although it was considered formally at least five times in as many years and was argued in three separate reports. The planners of the Baltimore and Ohio Railroad closely followed this debate. Some of the Liverpool and Manchester's representatives, among them Henry Booth, who became the railroad's treasurer and first historian, had visited the Stockton and Darlington, then under construction, in May 1824, and also had looked at the Killingworth and Hetton lines near Newcastle. The latter were hybrid systems, worked by a combination of horsepower, stationary engines at inclined planes, and locomotives on the level sections. The committee concluded that locomotives would be best for the Liverpool and Manchester.

In October of the same year they issued their prospectus and in it noted the recent arrival in Liverpool of "a gentleman from the United States . . . with whom it is a principal object to collect the necessary information [to establish] a Railway, to connect the great rivers Potomac and Ohio."[9] (The visitor may have been either Evan Thomas or William Howard.) Charles Sylvester, a British engineer, inspected the Newcastle lines for the Liverpool and Manchester and confirmed the preference for locomotives in his report, a copy of which is in the B&O files.[10]

In January 1825, locomotive speed and power trials were conducted at Killingworth and Hetton by several of England's leading engineers including Sylvester, George Stephenson, John U. Rastrick, James Walker, and Nicholas Wood, the superintendent of the Killingworth colliery whose treatise on railroads had been studied by the projectors of the Baltimore and Ohio. After the political battles with the canal proprietors were fought and won and construction began on the Liverpool and Manchester Railway, the motive power question again became paramount.

Booth and two other directors returned to the Stockton and Darlington in the fall of 1828 to see it in operation. They agreed that horsepower was not appropriate for the Liverpool and Manchester, but the rest of their report was inconclusive. George and Robert Stephenson with Joseph Locke, one of the resident engineers, made a similar fact-finding expedition to Newcastle. They knew what they wanted. Locomotives were best, they said.

As a way out of this dilemma, the board assigned two outside engineers, James Walker and John U. Rastrick, to investigate the issue. One of their major sources was Benjamin Thompson, the chief proponent of stationary engines. That was in December 1828, and the Liverpool and Manchester directors noted in their minutes that month the presence of three American engineers who would witness some of the Newcastle experiments: Jonathan Knight, William Gibbs McNeill, and George Washington Whistler, of the Baltimore and Ohio Railroad.

Alexander Brown had introduced them by letter to William and James Brown and Company as "engineers engaged in constructing our great Railway. They visit England with a view of obtaining all the practical information on that subject, with the improvements recently introduced in construction as well as the moving power thereon." The Liverpool office was to open an account of 2,000 pounds sterling for their use, roughly $9,500 at the then current rate of exchange, and to help them meet the "practical men" of England.[11]

For the next five months—a critical period in the development of railroads—Knight, McNeill, and Whistler consulted with the Stephensons, Wood, Thompson, Hackworth, and the other prominent engineers and toured several rail lines with them. McNeill and Whistler had been friends since West Point and had much in common. Whistler, the son of an Army captain, had graduated in 1819, two years after McNeill. In 1831, he married McNeill's sister Anna; the painter James McNeill Whistler was their firstborn son. On the English trip, Whistler was disdainful of many of his uneducated British colleagues, though he was pleasantly surprised by the elder Stephenson, "a common digger in the Newcastle coal pits [who] took to engineering instinctively. Certainly the coal pits have lost a man." He thought Thompson (the uncle of William B. Thompson, one of the B&O's West Point–trained topographical engineers) "conceited beyond measure." Wood was a gentleman, Whistler said, whose book on railroads "speaks for him as an engineer"; Hackworth, who had often been discussed in the B&O offices, was "another engineer by instinct . . . a blacksmith [whose] engineering consists in tinkering and refining locomotive engines on the Stockton and Darlington Railway."[12]

The three B&O engineers began their tour in the Newcastle area in early December 1828, accompanying the Stephensons to the various railroads to compare engine types. "We shall have the opportunity to hear fully the arguments on either side," they reported to Thomas.[13] During the next several weeks they saw stationary engines in use for several miles on one railway and locomotives hauling loaded coal trains up the inclined planes on the Killingworth and the Stockton and Darlington lines. Hackworth was their guide on the latter railroad, where they were pulled over hills and around curves "nearly as quick as ours on the Patapsco."[14] They measured the curves and by counting the revolutions of the locomotive wheels and marking the time, they estimated their speed at ten to fifteen miles an hour.

Whistler rode on Stephenson's engine, the Locomotion. Timing the piston strokes with his watch, he checked the speed and power loss through curves and inclines, which was not excessive. All in all, everything they saw and heard from the English engineers, with whom they discussed the details of engine design, encouraged their belief that locomotives "may be advantageously introduced on our road."[15] They walked the length of the Liverpool and Manchester Railroad and saw construction crews working day and night by torchlight at deep excavations, while temporary railways hauled away the spoil. Great stone bridges, such as the Sankey Viaduct, were rising. So was the expense. The Liverpool and Manchester cost, conservatively, over $60,000 a mile. George Stephenson had designed the line for locomotives, so "cuts and embankments have been unavoidable. Indeed they extend thro'out the whole line," the engineers wrote to Thomas.[16] Since the Baltimore company now subscribed to this heavy and permanent construction philosophy, what they saw in England inspired Knight, McNeill, and Whistler "to look forward with confidence to the successful accomplishment of the B&O R Road."[17]

In March 1829, shortly before the American engineers returned to the United States, Walker and Rastrick turned in their consultants' report on motive power to the Liverpool and Manchester Railroad. It slightly favored stationary engines as the more economical, though with such faint enthusiasm that it hardly amounted to an endorsement. The report also contained the seeds of its own undoing. This is how Benjamin Thompson's system, an abbreviated version of which was in operation on a colliery line, would work:

> The plan consists in placing Steam Engines at intervals of one or one and a half mile along the whole line of Railway, and having ropes running on rollers, placed between the rails, to extend from one Engine to the other, by which the waggons are drawn forward. When a train of waggons leaves a station, it takes along with it another rope, technically called the "*tail-rope*," which serves to bring back the next train which is moving in the contrary direction; the rope which drew the first train then becomes the "*tail-rope*," and is drawn back by the former, which then becomes the "*head-rope*." This is called the reciprocating system.[18]

Walker included an equally confusing drawing of the trains changing tracks at the engine stations, "which, if not altogether impracticable, is certainly very complex," observed Robert Stephenson.[19] Finally, the report pointed out that an accident, or the failure of any of the stationary engines or ropes, would stop the entire line, whereas a locomotive problem would affect only a single train. Walker captured this in a striking simile: "The one system is like a number of short unconnected chains, the other resembles a chain extending from Liverpool to Manchester, the failure of one link of which would derange the whole."[20]

Robert Stephenson turned this argument to his advantage in a counterreport, issued within six weeks and also in the B&O files. "Rely upon it," he told a correspondent, "locomotives shall not be cowardly given up. I will fight for them until the last. They are worthy of a conflict."[21] This report, by Robert Stephenson and Joseph Locke, of course championed the locomotive and found the other system, "this long chain of connected power . . . requisite to preserve the communication between two of the most important towns in the kingdom . . . totally unfitted for a public Railway."[22]

In the end, the Liverpool and Manchester directors set aside the engineers' recondite comparisons. Noting another admission in the Walker-Rastrick report—that locomotives were capable of greater improvement than stationary engines and that a premium might be encouraging—they decided in April 1829 to offer a prize of 500 pounds, roughly $2,400 at the time, "for the most improved Locomotive engine." Knight, McNeill, and Whistler missed the Rainhill trials held October 6–14, 1829, but Ross Winans, who had followed them to England and introduced himself early in the year, was still there. A self-propelled version of his friction-wheel car, operated by two passengers turning winches, was tested at thirteen miles an hour on the Liverpool and Manchester that summer and was one of many strange contraptions that took part in the Rainhill festivities.

The rules for the competition called for engines weighing no more than six tons to pull three times their own weight on a level railway consistently at ten miles an hour with a steam pressure not exceeding 50 pounds per square inch. The engines were to have springs and six wheels, or four wheels if they weighed four and a half tons or less. They were to consume their own smoke and have two safety valves, one of them out of reach of the engineman. The winner would be the engine that pulled the load at the greatest speed with the least expense.[23]

The site of the trials was a two-mile straightaway between two inclined planes located nine miles east of Liverpool. Toward one end of the testing ground was the Rainhill bridge that carried the Liverpool-Manchester turnpike over the railroad. The judges were Nicholas Wood, author and engineer; John U. Rastrick, of Stourbridge, engineer and locomotive designer; and John Kennedy, a mill owner and railroad promoter. A crowd of at least ten thousand turned out at Rainhill on the first day of the trials. Besides Ross Winans, the B&O's George Brown was there; also E. L. Miller of the South Carolina Railroad, and Horatio Allen, who had been named its chief engineer.

Five "running coaches" were listed for the trials. The main ones were the Novelty, in copper and blue, by Braithwaite and Ericsson, of London; Timothy Hackworth of Darlington's Sans Pareil, green, yellow, and black; and the Rocket by Robert Stephenson, Newcastle, yellow and black with a white chimney. The other two entries were the Perseverance by Mr. Burstall of Edinburgh, and the Cycloped, a horse treadmill entered by Thomas G. Brandreth, a diehard locomotive opponent on the Liverpool and Manchester board.

Burstall's engine was the only one that was not on exhibit as the trials began. It fell off the wagon bringing it to the site and was damaged. Although its designer got it running the last day of the competition, he realized that it was not in the same league with the others and withdrew it. Brandreth's entry, the Cycloped, clearly did not fulfill the contest rules, but Brandreth was nevertheless allowed to demonstrate the machine the first day and he got it going five miles an hour with 50 people clinging to the wagons. Ross Winans and six passengers also operated his friction-wheel car, not very fast compared with the locomotives, said the Liverpool *Mercury*, but fast enough "considering that it was put in motion by human power."[24]

The real competitors therefore were the Novelty, the Sans Pareil, and the Rocket and their "ordeal," as the judges termed it, lasted eight days. Except that all three engines ran on four wheels, their principles of design could not have been more dissimilar. The favorite was the Novelty, a light, compact, three-ton vehicle that carried its own fuel and water. It was really a London-style highway steam carriage adapted to the railroad.

The engine featured a vertical boiler with a horizontal extension enclosing an S-shaped flue that ran underneath the entire carriage and ended in a narrow smoke pipe. A mechanical bellows supplied a forced draft to the furnace. The drive operated through connecting rods to a crank-axle from two vertical cylinders. The first day, "its beautiful workmanship excited universal admiration. . . . Almost at once it darted off at the amazing velocity of twenty-eight miles an hour," according to the London *Mechanics Magazine*.[25] The Liverpool *Mercury* said "It seemed to fly as it were on the wings of the wind."[26]

But its appearance proved deceptive. The Novelty had no guts, George Stephenson said. On the second day of its test, the engine had made only one trial trip when a muffled explosion and a shower of sparks and flame erupted from the machinery mounted underneath the carriage. The mechanical bellows had blown out. The day after that, the four-ton Rocket, with George Stephenson and his son, Robert, at the controls, pulled the assigned load over the course the proper number of times at the required speed.

The Rocket, which Robert Stephenson had built and tested at his Newcastle works, had a multitubular boiler that was six feet long and three feet in diameter containing 25 three-inch copper fire tubes. The tube plates at either end were connected by long stay-bolts for added strength. The multitubular boiler, the basic form used in all steam locomotives, was the concept of Henry Booth, but George Stephenson contributed ideas for its fabrication. The two cylinders, eight inches in diameter with a fifteen-inch stroke, angled up toward the rear of the engine and were directly connected by crank-pins to the large forward driving wheels. The exhaust steam was sent into a tall chimney, creating a strong draft. The fact that the boiler produced ample steam and did not leak was a large part of the Rocket's success. The Novelty tried a second time two days later and again lasted only a single trip. The boiler feed pump failed, throwing water all around, and the engine was effectively out of the running. Afterward, to show the London skeptics what a real locomotive could do, George Stephenson unhooked his tender and sent the Rocket charging past the grandstand at 30 miles an hour.

Timothy Hackworth's locomotive, the Sans Pareil, a machine with a short, fat boiler with a U-shaped flue, vertical cylinders, and direct connections to the axle cranks, exceeded the weight limit and had no springs, but the judges permitted it to run. The forced draft using waste steam was so powerful that it threw burning coke straight out of the chimney; its fuel consumption was three times that of the Rocket. The trial lasted only two hours because the pump that supplied water to the boiler quit, and the locomotive expired in a huge cloud of steam in front of the grandstand. Hackworth requested a second chance, but because the Sans Pareil did not meet the company's specifications and wasted fuel, the judges said no. The quickly rebuilt Novelty did run a short while on the final day of the trials, until the boiler gave up once again. Only the Rocket survived the "ordeal." Since it had also pulled passenger coaches at speed several times up the inclined planes at Rainhill, in effect canceling the Liverpool and Manchester's planned use of stationary engines there, the Stephenson victory should have been complete.

But the Liverpool *Mercury* awarded "the grand prize of public opinion" to Braithwaite and Ericsson, because "however imperfect the present works of the machine may be, it is beyond a doubt, and we believe we speak the opinion of nine-tenths of the engineers and scientific men now in Liverpool, that it is the principal and arrangement of this London engine which will be followed in the construction of all future locomotives."[27]

This preference influenced decisions by both the Liverpool and Manchester and the Baltimore and Ohio. On the British railroad, the stationary engine faction, having been defeated by the Stephensons, took up the cause for their competitor. The company bought the Rocket and ordered four more Stephenson locomotives, but at the insistence of the minority faction, they also bought two Braithwaite and Ericsson engines similar to the Novelty, which proved also to be failures.

Before Knight, McNeill, and Whistler left Baltimore on their mission to England, the Baltimore and Ohio had decided to obtain "one of the best and most approved" English locomotives, and shortly before they returned home, the engineers reported that they were considering a Stephenson engine. Some time that year, the Stephensons did build and dispatch a locomotive for the B&O, but it was involved in some sort of shipboard accident, recovered, and disposed of in England.[28] About the time this happened, in December 1829, Alexander Brown instructed the Liverpool office to consult Braithwaite and Ericsson and explore the purchase of "a Light Engine . . . of the most improved make."[29] This was perhaps on the advice of George Brown, who had seen the Novelty at Rainhill. Ross Winans was still in England, and that same month, the Novelty pulled his wagons, along with the Stephensons', in friction tests. (Both Brown and Winans had also ridden the Rocket.)

The last railroad investigator to visit England on the B&O's behalf was Evan Thomas. He arrived in mid-April 1830, just as Ross Winans was leaving. Thomas reported that the Liverpool and Manchester's board was divided over types of locomotives and that public opinion still favored Braithwaite and Ericsson's engine. Whether the B&O actually ordered one is not known. If they did, it never reached America.

It was not understood until much later that with the Rocket at Rainhill, the Stephensons had designed the prototype of the steam locomotive, and that in triumphing over other forms of motive power, they had created the modern railroad. In many ways, the Liverpool and Manchester served as the model for the Baltimore and Ohio, which appropriated a good deal of British rail technology, except for the engines. Instead, native mechanical engineers, Peter Cooper, Phineas Davis, and Ross Winans, produced machines that were quite unlike anything developed elsewhere. They had one saving grace—they worked.

The two railroads opened officially in 1830. The B&O was the first to begin operations, with horse-drawn carriages, on May 22. The Liverpool and Manchester's inaugural, using the Stephenson engines, was on September 15. The Baltimore and Ohio ran its first locomotive that same summer. It became as well known as the Rocket owing to an event the account of which, through frequent publication, has become part of the nation's history. Who has not heard of the celebrated and symbolic race between Peter Cooper's engine and the "gallant gray" of Stockton and Stokes?

In the summer of 1830, Cooper, then 39, was a prosperous but relatively inconspicuous New York businessman and a talented, though uneducated, mechanic, a combination craftsman, inventor, and manufacturer. Glue, produced in his New York factory, had started him on the road to financial success. Foundries and philanthropy came later. His varied experience did not include railroads before he came to Maryland, and Cooper seems to have avoided them after this brief but significant phase in his career. The reasons why a glue manufacturer from Manhattan should be in Baltimore building a locomotive are fairly straightforward; the doubts arise over what happened next. Yet nothing he did subsequently, with the exception of founding Cooper Union, made him more famous or admired than the engine he built and ran for the Baltimore and Ohio Railroad.

By the time he first arrived in Baltimore in 1828, Cooper had shown himself to be a daring, if somewhat accident-prone, inventor. In the course of work or youthful adventure, he had toppled from beams and ladders, survived three near-drownings in as many bodies of water around New York and had the scars, missing teeth, and cracked ribs to prove it. An explosion while he was working on a flying machine had nearly cost him an eye, and he was not in Baltimore very long when igniting gases blew him through the open door of a charcoal kiln.

The inventions varied from a crude washing machine to a musical, mechanical cradle, patented in 1815. There was a lawnmower, a remote-controlled, wire-guided torpedo boat with a six-to-eight-mile range, a machine to harness the tides, an endless chain to pull vessels through canals, and more patents in 1820 and 1828 for converting a steam engine's reciprocating motion to rotative without using a crank. Cooper regarded the crank as mechanically inefficient; the 1828 patent declared that the engine, which also employed a chain, was suitable for "land carriages." He built not just models but operating versions of these devices, and he believed in all of them although none except the lawnmower, which was patented by someone else, ever came into practical use. His crankless, chain-driven engine proved unworkable after a brief trial in Baltimore, yet Cooper was still convinced 45 years later that the principle was worthwhile and upbraided a reporter who criticized his canal plan, claiming he had never "made a failure."

Cooper went to Baltimore because of the railroad. In the summer of 1828, excited by its prospects, he and two acquaintances, Francis Price and Ely Moore, decided to buy property in Baltimore. They expected to profit from the increase in land values that would result from the B&O's successful completion. Cooper visited the city and arranged to buy 3,000 acres of land in Canton, in southeast Baltimore, including three miles of shoreline from Fells Point to Lazaretto Point, opposite Fort McHenry, for $105,000. Having put down $20,000, some of it borrowed, as his share of the initial payment, Cooper went back to New York. He returned six months later to discover that Price and Moore had not paid their shares and had used the money he advanced for taxes to live on. It cost him another $18,000 to buy out the two frauds. Cooper found other investors in Boston, New York, and Baltimore, and in December 1828 they made plans to develop the land.

The Canton Company was incorporated March 11, 1829. Besides Cooper, the original investors included William Patterson and Robert Oliver, two of the "royal merchants" who were B&O directors, and Columbus O'Donnell, a railroad stockholder whose estate, named Canton, constituted the bulk of the property. John H. B. Latrobe and William Gwynn, lawyers for the railroad, became Canton Company directors in 1831 and Gwynn served as the organization's first president. The Canton Company was a real estate firm whose aim was to develop a planned industrial community consisting of homes, businesses, warehouses, and piers. The B&O's Caspar Wever provided the survey and plat.

By 1830, Cooper had built several large charcoal kilns and anticipated making charcoal iron with ore dug at Lazaretto Point. The following year, he had Baltimore machinist George W. Johnson install a forge. His goal was evidently to sell rails to the B&O, but the iron Cooper produced could not compete with the cheaper and better rails the company was already importing from England. With piers built and streets laid out, the Canton Company sold its first house lots in 1833.

The impact of this formidable new presence in the city was dramatic. Charles Ridgely of Hampton opposed its charter, claiming the industrial development would ruin the view of the river from his Baltimore townhouse. But because Ridgely, an ironmaster, also wanted to sell rails to the B&O, competition was more likely the issue. James Carroll, the proprietor of Mount Clare, who was trying to channel the B&O route to benefit his West Baltimore waterfront property, similarly objected to the formation of the Canton Company, charging that they would "create a monopoly of power, resident as it were, in one man, and do as they please with the Railroad." [30] By 1832, the B&O had built its line to the City Block, well away from Carroll's piers, but not reaching the Canton Company's either. [31]

What Cooper wanted to do with the railroad initially, he said, was prove that locomotives could run on it. It was an open question in the summer of 1830 whether the B&O's grades of eighteen feet per mile and sharp curves of 250–300 feet radius would permit steam power to be used. There was so much doubt among the major investors that some were on the brink of pulling out, Cooper recalled 45 years later in a speech to the Master Mechanics Association in New York:

> They had learned from their own experience, as well as from the opinions of competent engineers from England that no road could be successfully run with locomotives on which there were curves of less than three hundred feet radius. The company were plunged into despair, and the principal stockholders determined that they would no longer pay up the assessment on their stock. In the abandonment of that road I saw the defeat of my enterprise. It would have been a terrible defeat to me, for I saw that the growth of the city of Baltimore depended upon the success of that road, and I had purchased that tract with a view of taking advantage of the rapid growth of the city. . . . I said to the President and a few of the directors who were principally interested that if they would hold on, and not sacrifice their stock for a little while, I would put a small locomotive on which, I thought, could pull a train around those short curves. . . . I happened to have an engine in my factory, which I took on to Baltimore, and with some old wheels that I got at the railroad shops, I rigged up a temporary locomotive. [32]

Cooper's first model made use of his invention to convert reciprocating to rotative motion. There is no clear explanation, including the inventor's, of how this machine operated, but it employed a system of ratchets and pawls. The piston powered a chain mechanism that alternately bypassed and engaged cogged wheels and raked them forward, producing continuous motion. Although the cast-iron parts wore rapidly and kept breaking, Cooper did manage to make one midsummer trip, starting from Mt. Clare: "On a Saturday evening just before dark, I got up steam, when Mr. George Brown, and the President of the Road stept on the engine and rode out a mile or more which was the only opportunity I had to run the engine in that shape." [33]

He soon adopted a more conventional arrangement of connecting rod, crank, and spur and pinion gears to increase the speed. The wheels were just 30 inches in diameter. At that point, vandals broke into the shop and stole the copper off the engine to sell for scrap. Cooper replaced it, using iron gun barrels for boiler tubes. A fan blower powered by a belt passing around a drum on one of the axles provided a draft in the firebox. The rebuilt engine made its first public appearance on the B&O on August 24, 1830, and transported about a dozen people out to Relay, seven miles from the city. Architect Robert Cary Long was aboard. They went twelve to fourteen miles an hour and burned bituminous coal, coke, and wood, "each used according to circumstances and fancy," they said in their published report.[34]

The dedication of the Oliver Viaduct, the second great stone bridge in the Patapsco Valley, at Ellicotts Mills, the following Saturday, August 28, provided Cooper with the opportunity to show what his engine could do. At ten o'clock that morning, he left Mt. Clare with about six people riding on the locomotive and eighteen more in a passenger coach in front of it. Philip E. Thomas, Robert Oliver, for whom the viaduct was to be named, John H. B. Latrobe, and the reporter for the Baltimore *Gazette*, who unfortunately left the train at Relay, were among the passengers that day. As they pulled out, the steam was blowing off through the safety valves so fast "that I thought all of the water would go out of the boiler," said Cooper. "I knew that the boiler was strong, so I put my hand on them and held them down." [35] (Cooper was lucky.) The morning was fine and the small, one-ton engine, not much larger than a railroad handcar, performed well. It got up to eighteen miles an hour whereupon several of the men pulled out notebooks and wrote their names and a few connected sentences to prove that normal human activities could be carried on at such dizzying speeds.

"Insignificant as that little engine was," Cooper continued, "we made the trip of thirteen miles in an hour and twelve minutes . . . and demonstrated that a locomotive could be made which could go around those short curves, the thing that I set out to do." Lunch was probably at the trackside hotel where the stagecoaches stopped in the center of Ellicotts Mills, a picturesque village that resembled an Italian hill town. It was the initial terminus of the Baltimore and Ohio Railroad. Ellicotts Mills had been founded in 1772 by brothers Joseph, Andrew, and John Ellicott, who had purchased mill sites in a wild and inaccessible part of the Patapsco Valley. They brought their equipment mainly by ship from Bucks County, Pennsylvania, to Elkridge Landing, went from there over a rough country road and hand-carried everything the last mile through the forest. Backed by Charles Carroll of Carrollton, the Ellicotts built the largest flour mill in the colonies; they also had wharves in Baltimore, and they built good roads between there and Frederick.

At 2:00 P.M., everyone gathered outside the hotel to watch Oliver ceremoniously place the bridge keystone and to listen to Thomas's remarks. The granite bridge, designed by Caspar W. Wever and built by Simon Frieze in about 100 days at an estimated cost of $21,830, carried the B&O line over the Frederick Turnpike and a small stream, Ellicotts Branch, on three 20-foot arches. It was 123 feet long, 26 feet wide, and fifteen feet above the roadway. Thomas did not mention the laborers who had been killed and injured three days before when a car full of stone that had been excavated from the Tarpean Rock, a massive formation just beyond the bridge, rolled off the end of a temporary railway onto men working below. Instead, he congratulated the contractor for his speed, the workmen for their abstinence, and the neighborhood residents on their forbearance.

The train did not start back until six o'clock. Benjamin H. Latrobe, Jr., who began his career with the Baltimore and Ohio that summer and was stationed at Ellicotts Mills, followed the engine a little way down the tracks, "after it had started with much puffing and leaking of steam from some of its joints." [36] His brother, John H. B. Latrobe, rode the train back to Baltimore and recorded the following event:

> But the triumph of this Tom Thumb engine was not altogether without a drawback. The great stage proprietors of the day were Stockton and Stokes; and on this occasion a gallant gray of great beauty and power was driven by them from town, attached to another car on the second track . . . and met the engine at the Relay House on its way back. From this point it was determined to have a race home; and, the start being even, away went horse and engine, the snort of the one and the puff of the other keeping time and tune. At first the gray had the best of it, for *his* steam would be applied to the greatest advantage on the instant, while the engine had to wait until the rotation of the wheels set the blower to work. The horse was perhaps a quarter of a mile ahead when the safety valve of the engine lifted and the thin blue vapor issuing from it showed an excess of steam. The blower whistled, the steam blew off in vapory clouds, the pace increased, the passengers shouted, the engine gained on the horse, soon it lapped him—the silk was plied—the race was neck and neck, nose and nose—then the engine passed the horse, and a great hurrah hailed the victory. But it was not repeated; for just at this time, when the gray's master was about giving up, the band which drove the pulley, which drove the blower, slipped from the drum, the safety valve ceased to scream, and the engine for want of breath began to wheeze and pant. In vain Mr. Cooper, who was his own engineman and fireman, lacerated his hands in attempting to replace the band upon the wheel; in vain he tried to urge the fire with light wood; the horse gained on the machine, and passed it; and although the band was presently replaced, and steam again did its best, the horse was too far ahead to be overtaken, and came in the winner of the race. But the real victory was with Mr. Cooper, notwithstanding.[37]

A wonderful story, but did it really happen? Latrobe was the first to relate the incident in his 1868 speech to the Maryland Institute. Cooper confirmed it in 1882, but in a curiously offhand way. Contemporary accounts of his engine do not specifically mention a race with a horse, nor was it recalled in print by anyone who was there. Still, there was ample precedent for such an encounter.

The press may have considered the event unremarkable. Stagecoaches and steamboats raced routinely, in Baltimore and elsewhere, but made the papers only if an accident resulted. The following summer, when a horse treadmill built by James

Stimpson was being tested on the B&O and ran into a cow, spilling Hezekiah Niles, William Gwynn, and the other editors into a ditch, the incident received wide coverage. A few years earlier, Stephenson's Locomotion, on the Stockton and Darlington Railway, had raced a stagecoach on the adjacent turnpike and come in the winner by about 100 yards.

The race on the B&O probably did not take place on August 28, as Latrobe indicated. The more likely date is September 20, 1830, when Charles Carroll of Carrollton celebrated his ninety-third birthday by taking a ride on the railroad with other dignitaries. "On the return of the guests to Baltimore, they were met by Mr. Cooper's Locomotive Engine," the *Gazette* reported. Speed trials were conducted, during which the engine's "connecting band" (the belt powering the fan blower) broke.[38]

When questioned in 1882 by a reporter who hinted that the Tom Thumb had been beaten, Cooper responded: "Yes—no—not exactly; they tried a little race one day. . . . It was some time after our first experiments; we had been out several times, when the men, whose horses had been out there, came on the track to try paces with us, but it didn't amount to anything. It was rather funny, and the locomotive got out of gear."[39]

Cooper was less reticent about the building of the engine and its importance to the railroad. He repeated the story many times, refining it as he went, until at the end, he had put the locomotive, which he called the Tom Thumb, together himself in a coachmaker's shop, breaking the stocks off muskets to obtain the gun barrels for the boiler tubes. And by running the machine around the railroad's tight curves, he had single-handedly rescued the Baltimore and Ohio from bankruptcy. Actually, Cooper had received a good deal of assistance in building his engine, which did not have a name until Latrobe gave it one in his 1868 speech, and although there was some concern about whether or not steam power could be used on the B&O's sharply curving alignment, the situation was not nearly so drastic as Cooper made it out to be.

The carriage of Cooper's engine was made by Richard Imlay, who was then building passenger coaches for the railroad. George Gillingham and Ross Winans, respectively, contributed journal boxes for the forward axle and friction wheels for the rear one. The two later joined forces to manufacture B&O locomotives. The boiler was produced by Charles Reeder, the city's first builder of steam engines. He had opened his plant in the Federal Hill area fifteen years before and provided the power for some of the early Chesapeake Bay steamboats. He also built locomotives later on for the B&O. His first one exploded, killing the engineman (who had fastened down the safety valve) and ending Reeder's career with the railroad. At least two machine shops, Mayger and Washington's and George W. Johnson's, performed additional services. Johnson, who provided the forge for Cooper's ironworks, and Baltimore-born James Millholland, his eighteen-year-old apprentice, eliminated Cooper's chain drive and made the locomotive operable. Millholland subsequently designed engines for the Reading Railroad.[40]

Although small, the engine was powerful. Ross Winans, who was aboard for the trip out to Ellicotts Mills for the dedication of the viaduct, compared it favorably with Stephenson's Rocket. Reeder's vertical boiler, containing 53 tubes, was about 20 inches in diameter, five or six feet high. The single cylinder was also upright, only 3.25 inches in diameter with a 14.25-inch stroke. Separated from the boiler, it was held in place by a light, pyramidal frame. There was no tender, for the locomotive carried its own water and anthracite coal, which was determined to be the proper fuel. The steam pressure was roughly 50 pounds per square inch and the engine developed about one to one-and-a-half horsepower.

Judging from the relieved comments that followed its successful trials, there had definitely been some question about the effect of the B&O's sharp curves on motive power. Jonathan Knight said in the 1830 Annual Report, "Whatever doubts may have been entertained of the applicability of locomotive engines on a Rail Way, the curvatures of which have a radius of 400 feet, none can remain after the recent, triumphant demonstration with an experimental engine constructed by Peter Cooper of New York." And Thomas agreed: "All doubt is removed of our being able to employ locomotive Engines, upon the Baltimore and Ohio Railroad."[41]

Yet there is no evidence, as claimed by Cooper, of the principal officers abandoning their investment and the B&O going bankrupt. There was general concern in late 1829 and early 1830 over the escalating cost of construction, but the installments were being paid on the stock. Far from forsaking the railroad, Philip E. Thomas, Alexander Brown, and other influential directors were putting up their own money to keep the enterprise afloat until the line could open. When it did, on May 22, 1830, it was an immediate success, with horsepower.

The B&O's grades of eighteen feet to the mile, or 0.3 percent, and curves of 400-foot radius, 14 degrees, or worse, alluded to by Cooper, doubtless appeared formidable in 1830. Knight, McNeill, and Whistler had seen the Locomotion on the Stockton and Darlington Railway pull loaded trains up inclines four times as steep and around curves just as sharp, with only a slight loss of speed. But since George Stephenson had laid out the Liverpool and Manchester so level (its two inclines of 55 feet per mile, or one percent, were originally planned to be worked by stationary engines) and so straight (the curves were seldom sharper than 12,600-foot radius, or less than half a degree), and because that line was the current exemplar, the issue could well have provoked anxiety in Baltimore.[42]

Cooper later may have exaggerated the importance of conquering the B&O's grades and curves with his experimental engine to compensate for his failed enterprise to sell operating locomotives to the railroad. He never mentioned it in his voluminous recollections, but about a year after his triumph, Cooper contracted with the company to build six engines at $4,000 each. He reneged on the contract, claiming that "unexpected circumstances . . . prevented [him] from producing an Engine equal to his expectations or the wants of the company."[43] It was one of his few defeats as an entrepreneur. The first working locomotive he built was also his last.

Cooper's engine nevertheless had profound significance for the Baltimore and Ohio at the time. Besides convincing the company of the efficacy of steam power on their railroad, it inspired them to seek American-made locomotives rather than British models. Cooper's precedent of the vertical boiler, particularly suitable for short-wheelbase locomotives, which do better in curves, remained a prominent feature of B&O engines for most of the next decade. In 1833, Cooper sold the company the rights to his vertical boiler for $1,000.[44]

There had been two previous instances of locomotives operating in America. The first was a novelty; the second, a trial that ended in failure. Neither machine ever went into actual service. John Stevens ran an engine weighing less than a ton around a circular track in Hoboken, New Jersey, in 1826 as a demonstration, much like Richard Trevithick's Catch-me-who-can in London. The first real locomotive to operate in America was the British Stourbridge Lion built by the firm of John U. Rastrick, one of the Liverpool and Manchester's motive power consultants and a Rainhill judge.

The Lion was built for the Delaware and Hudson Canal Company, which shipped coal from Pennsylvania to New York along a system of artificial waterways that connected the two rivers. A railway had been constructed through a sixteen-mile mountainous section between Carbondale and Honesdale, Pennsylvania, that was unsuited for a canal. Horatio Allen, the company's engineer, had made his own inspection tour of British railways in early 1828 and ordered the Lion. It arrived in New York in May 1829 and was sent down by canal to Honesdale; Allen himself ran it on the railroad in August and September 1829.

The locomotive weighed seven tons. When Allen took it over the line, the weight on the lightly built wooden viaducts of the Delaware and Hudson popped out the fastenings holding the rails. Company officials, fearing that their structures would collapse under regular locomotive service, had the Stourbridge Lion removed from the tracks and stored. That experience seemed to justify the Baltimore and Ohio's decision to build stone bridges and permanent embankments instead of wooden structures. The *Gazette*, commenting on the Delaware and Hudson fiasco, congratulated the Baltimoreans on their good fortune, and observed, "The question of expense alone caused a difficulty."[45]

Although put together as a trial model, Cooper's engine was still pulling passenger trains six months after its first run. It therefore represented a transition in American locomotive development between Stevens's experiment and the first American engine built for actual railroad service, the Best Friend. This locomotive was also ordered on the recommendation of Horatio Allen. Shortly before attending the Rainhill trials, Allen had been named the engineer of the South Carolina Railroad. The Best Friend was produced by New York's West Point Foundry in 1830 and ran for the first time on the South Carolina Railroad in November of that year.[46]

In January 1831, the Baltimore and Ohio, wishing to obtain "a supply of Locomotive Steam Engines of *American manufacture*, adapted to their road," decided to hold its own Rainhill competition and advertised a prize of $4,000 for the best entry. The engines had to burn coal or coke, consume their own smoke, weigh no more than three and a half tons and be able to pull fifteen tons on a level road "day by day." They were to have four wheels, springs, and a four-foot wheelbase "in order to suit curves of short radius." The wheels themselves could be two and a half to four feet in diameter. The steam pressure was to be 100 pounds per square inch or less, preferably less, and the boiler was to have two safety valves, one of them out of reach of the engineman. In deciding the victor, the advertisement said, "the company will take into consideration their respective weights, and all other things being equal, will adjudge a preference to the Engine weighing the least." The advertisements appeared in New York, Philadelphia, and Pittsburgh papers. One of the purposes was to stimulate American mechanics, and in this they succeeded, for there were several entries and a clear winner, just as there had been in England.[47]

The contest was set for June 1, 1831, but experimental trials were permitted on the line before then. Within six weeks of the announcement, the first engine arrived in Baltimore by wagon. It was Phineas Davis and Israel Gartner's York, built in the Pennsylvania town of the same name. It had a vertical boiler that, instead of tubes, had suspended in the middle a thick, round disk called a "cheese," which was filled with water. Two vertical cylinders were mounted on the sides of the boiler. The power was transmitted through connecting rods to a diamond-shaped iron truss that coupled the wheels and drove them by crank pins.

Neither the "cheese" boiler nor the iron truss worked very well. Because of the insufficient heating surface, the boiler did not produce enough steam, and the length of the piston stroke was uneven because the engine bounced up and down on its springs while the truss remained fixed to the wheels. Even so, in February 1831, the York was tested at 15 miles an hour. Ross Winans helped to rebuild the locomotive. By June it had a multitubular boiler and spur-and-pinion gearing along the lines of Cooper's engine. With these improvements, the York managed to get up to 30 miles an hour.

Meanwhile, as other contestants arrived, the line between Baltimore and Ellicotts Mills became a proving ground for railroad motive power with horsecars and horse treadmills, sail-cars, and Peter Cooper's engine. In March, Philadelphian Ezekiel Childs, a watchmaker like Phineas Davis, tested a "rotary" engine. This was a turbine-driven locomotive with a vertical boiler and an ingenious valve arrangement. The B&O judges did not think it suitable for the road and offered to buy it for yard service, but Childs refused and went back to Philadelphia in a huff.

The railroad postponed the trials to the end of June, evidently to allow for late arrivals. One was a locomotive assembled by William T. James of New York. He had been building highway steam carriages when he heard about the B&O trials and went to work. His engine had the peculiar upright conical boiler that he favored and two vertical cylinders that powered an elaborate overhead rod-and-crank system that ultimately drove the wheels. On June 28, after further delays and breakdowns, a contest of sorts took place between Phineas Davis and William T. James.

There was a large crowd at Mt. Clare to see the engines run. Davis's engine "started from the Depot with a car attached, containing nearly forty passengers, and swept past with astonishing velocity," according to the *Gazette*, "and returned with the same speed, averaging . . . twenty miles an hour."[48] James's engine then made its run to the Carrollton Viaduct and returned, but at a slower speed, perhaps, as the *Gazette* noted, because of the difference in fuel—pine wood rather than the anthracite coal burned by the York. And that was about it. The company records state laconically that of the engines that ran, "only one . . . has been made to answer any good purpose." That was the York. The next month it was in regular service, hauling passenger trains to Ellicotts Mills.[49]

Another engine that was in Baltimore for the trials was one built by George Welsh of Gettysburg "upon an entirely new principle," though what exactly it was and whether it ever ran are not known. William T. James, whose son was killed when his engine ran over him as he was adjusting a switch, rebuilt the machine the following year, using angled cylinders, a simpler transmission, and a highly advanced valve motion that allowed for the expansive working of steam. The valve gear, similar to link motion, was years ahead of its time, but James's conical boiler was weak. Soon after arriving in Baltimore in 1833, it exploded.

Two other engines were produced in the wake of the trials, both with horizontal boilers. One was built in 1832 by George W. Johnson and James Millholland, who had revised Cooper's design. It had vertical cylinders and walking beams. And Stacy Costill (or Costell), another watchmaker from Philadelphia, built an engine the same year with oscillating cylinders under the boiler and other oddities. But Phineas Davis had long since claimed the prize.

In August 1831, he told the directors that his engine was in regular service "without the occurrence of more casualties or interruptions" than any other machinery. He set forth its qualifications in terms of speed, power, fuel consumption, and costs, and requested compensation. They decided to pay him $3,500 for his engine and offer him $2,000 a year as superintendent of machinery. Davis declined the job offer, preferring to work as an independent contractor, whereupon the railroad gave the job to George Gillingham.

The York proved to be too light to climb the grades, however, and could only work a few days at a time. When the B&O signed a contract with Davis and Gartner in the fall of 1831 to build two new engines, at $4,000 each, one geared for fast passenger trains and the other for slow freight service, they were specified to weigh four and a half tons. "Take care that [they] are strong enough and have plenty of steam power," Thomas told Davis.[50]

The first of these engines, put on the road in September 1832, was the Atlantic. Winans, who had helped to modify the York, aided in its design. The engine had an upright, tubular boiler, a fan to produce a draft powered by the exhaust steam, and two vertical cylinders each ten inches in diameter with a 20-inch stroke. They activated lever beams, attached at one end to the top of the boiler and at the other to long connecting rods that operated the wheel cranks through spur-and-pinion gearing. The Atlantic was the prototype of many Grasshopper engines to follow.

The Baltimore and Ohio had evolved a unique locomotive, based on the design of Oliver Evans 30 years earlier, and was fulfilling the predictions of Evans and his champion, Hezekiah Niles, who vowed in his first article on the B&O in 1827: "Thus will scientific power conquer space, and even the Alleganies sink . . . beneath the pressure of unconquered steam."[51]

8

A Race for Popularity

IT WAS AN IMPERIAL ENTERPRISE, A GREAT ARTERY
leading from the capital of the United States over the mountains to the Ohio River
and beyond, to the Great Lakes. Grander than the Erie Canal, it was a truly national
endeavor, joining the country together economically just as the first patriot had envisioned. And when it was finished, the city named for him would take its place among
the other eastern seaports as a major center of commerce. These were the hopes for
the Chesapeake and Ohio Canal when it broke ground on July 4, 1828, the same day
that the Baltimore and Ohio Railroad was laying its cornerstone in James Carroll's
field near the Gwynns Falls.

The weather was equally fine in Washington as a flotilla of steamboats made its
way up the Potomac. The passengers were President John Quincy Adams, members
of his cabinet, senators and congressmen, and virtually every available foreign diplomat in the city. Crowds followed them on the riverbanks. "The sun shone now and
then from the clear blue heavens through the fleecy clouds," the Washington *National
Intelligencer* wrote, in the first of many rapturous episodes it would compose on
behalf of the canal. Nature herself "seemed to smile upon the scene." [1]

The ceremonies took place at a powder magazine at the head of the Little Falls.
Some spectators climbed trees for a better view and thousands more watched from the
nearby hills as the mayor of Georgetown presented the ceremonial spade to Charles
Fenton Mercer, president of the canal company. Mercer began his speech: "There
are moments in the progress of time, which are the counters of whole ages. There are
events, the monuments of which, surviving every other memorial of human existence,
eternise the nation to whose history they belong, after all other vestiges of its glory
have disappeared from the globe. At such a moment have we now arrived. Such a
monument we are now to found." [2]

Mercer passed the spade to President Adams, who stuck it in the ground and hit a root. Adams tried again, with the same result. Then he threw down the shovel and took off his coat. Nothing in his lackluster speech that day equaled the dramatic impact of this action on the crowd, most of whom were too far away to hear anyway. They "raised a loud and unanimous cheering, which continued for some time after Mr. Adams had mastered the difficulty."[3]

At the time of their respective ceremonies, both the canal and the railroad were already competing for funds and public recognition, and for the Potomac route. They continued to compete for five years, on the river and in the mountains, in the Congress, the state legislature, and the courtroom. The fight, indeed, went on for much of the nineteenth century. The controversy was "a barrier as difficult to overcome as the ridges of the Alleganies," said the B&O's first historian, William Prescott Smith, and its effect on both public works and the State of Maryland was profound.[4]

Yet even as adversaries, the canal and railroad had many similarities. Certainly they both encountered the same kinds of obstructions in their early days. Even before the first construction contracts for the Chesapeake and Ohio were let, in September 1828, the company officers and stockholders disagreed over where the canal should end, at the Little Falls over the District line in Maryland where the ground-breaking was held, or lower down, closer to Washington's commercial center. The district cities of Washington, Georgetown, and Alexandria each wanted the benefit of the terminus, while Georgetown property owners led by Francis Scott Key vehemently opposed the canal through their neighborhood. Mercer and his staff overrode the resistance in Georgetown and arranged a compromise to end the canal at Rock Creek.

There were also arguments among the company's engineers and directors reminiscent of the ones in Baltimore. The canal had a three-man board of engineers whose subordinates often went over their heads to deal directly with company officials, who in turn sometimes overruled the qualified engineers they had hired. The C&O encountered the same underground conditions, rock and "indurated clay," that drove up expenses on the railroad, and with labor costs rising, contractors were forced to abandon the work unless they received more money.

The higher costs also reflected the fact that it was a different canal from the one originally planned. Engineers had initially proposed a waterway 32 feet wide at the surface and four feet deep. The 1823 C&O Canal Convention adopted a 40-foot width, the size of the Erie Canal. The United States engineers in their report three years later raised this to 48 feet with a five-foot depth, and the company directors eventually decided on a canal that was 60 feet wide at the surface, 42 feet wide at the bottom, and six feet deep. The cross-section, or "prism," of the canal was therefore more than twice the size first contemplated, and twice as large, also, as the New York, Pennsylvania, and Ohio canals. The rationale was that a larger canal offered lower water resistance and more efficient use of power. Parts of the waterway as built were grander still. The five-mile section from Georgetown to the Little Falls was actually 70 feet wide and seven feet deep.

The company's charter required that 100 miles be finished in five years. By June 1829, when the C&O issued its first annual report, 48 miles were under contract between Georgetown and the Point of Rocks, where construction was halted by the various court suits. Two thousand men with 400 horses and 80 oxen to pull the plows and scrapers were excavating the canal.

The charter (in Pennsylvania) also stipulated that half of the $1 million United States stock subscription, the money that enabled the canal to undertake such large-scale construction, be spent on its western section. Mercer was anxious to get started in the mountains, not only to maintain the national character of the work but also to challenge the railroad in that sector, so he dispatched Nathan S. Roberts, who was to have an important role in the controversy, to conduct surveys between Cumberland and Pittsburgh.

Isaac Ridgeway Trimble had been there on a similar assignment for the Baltimore and Ohio Railroad in early 1829, several months ahead of Roberts. The railroad had already completed its western reconnaissance by then, but the first reconnaissance in Pennsylvania had to await approval of the charter. Trimble was one of the most outstanding of the B&O's young West Point engineers. He entered the academy at the age of fourteen, and soon after graduating in 1822 he was surveying canals, roads, and railroads for the Corps of Topographical Engineers. He subsequently, after his B&O experience, left the army to become chief engineer and superintendent of several rail lines, including the Baltimore and Susquehanna and the Philadelphia, Wilmington, and Baltimore.[5]

Trimble also wrote poetry, poorly it is said, but in his hands, the prosaic topographical memoir listing boundaries, prominent features, rivers, trees, rocks and soils, natural products, towns and native inhabitants became a literary art form. His description of the prospect from the Allegheny summit, twelve miles northwest of Cumberland, early in 1829 gives a good idea of the kind of terrain the transportation pioneers were facing:

> A view from Savage Mountain westward, presents in bold and regular outline, about eight miles distant, the Allegany ridge or mountain (so called in that part of the country), which has about the same elevation and bearing as Savage Mountain. The country between these two mountain ridges, being depressed but a few hundred feet below them, may be termed the High Table Land of the Alleganies in this quarter . . . a broken and hilly country. It is covered with a dense growth of Pine, Spruce, Hemlock, Oak, etc. with scarcely a cultivated spot to indicate the abode of civilization. Westward of the Allegany ridge the country sinks near one thousand feet below its summit, possessing much greater uniformity of surface and richness of soil, than are usually met with in mountainous districts. It is in a high state of cultivation, and thickly inhabited by industrious Germans.[6]

Noting that "the Potomac has already done what man could never have effected, in breaking through the numerous mountain ridges between tide water and the summit," Trimble, from his Olympian vantage point, decided that "it is here that the relative value of Rail Roads and Canals . . . must be tested."[7]

In May 1829, Nathan S. Roberts and Alfred Cruger, an assistant, restudied the C&O route along Wills Creek and the Casselman River first explored by McNeill.

Roberts, who had located part of the Erie Canal, began work for the Chesapeake and Ohio in 1827 when, with James Geddes, he revised the original high estimate and breathed new life into the project. Based on their resurvey of the canal, Roberts and Geddes had said that the section from Georgetown to Cumberland could be built for $4.5 million, rather than the $8.2 million estimated by McNeill and the other U.S. engineers.

Benjamin Wright, formerly chief engineer of the Erie Canal, had turned down the job of revising the figures because he did not want to offend those who made the original estimates. However, in June 1828, he accepted the job of chief engineer for the Chesapeake and Ohio. Wright, Roberts, and a third man formed the canal's board of engineers.

Roberts, as chief engineer for the Pennsylvania Canal, had recently examined the line for the Allegheny Portage Railroad connecting its eastern and western sections. Mercer wanted him to perform a similar assignment for the C&O, whose charter authorized it to substitute a railroad over the mountains. But Roberts decided to postpone the railroad survey and concentrate on the canal route and the proposed four-mile tunnel under the Pennsylvania summit of the Alleghenies. Faced with "a continued forest of various kinds of valuable timber, intermixed with a thick growth of laurel, which is the most tedious of all shrubbery to run a line through," he and Cruger could make only a mile a day on their survey above Cumberland.[8]

Roberts's report on the canal tunnel in the fall of 1829 outlined a formidable task: he estimated that it would take 120 men working around the clock for thirteen and a half years, at a cost of $1.6 million, to drive a hole fourteen feet high, 22 feet wide, and four miles long through the slate and sandstone ridge that divided Wills Creek from the Casselman River. Mercer had already signed up 77 fellow House members seeking Presidential authorization to use the army to build it. They argued that such subterranean labor was good training because it would "impart additional strength to the arm of the soldier, and render him more formidable to his enemy." President Jackson, through his Secretary of War, refused the authorization, saying, "It is doubtful whether the obligations of a soldier impose upon him, as a duty, the performance of such work."[9]

Jackson, unlike his predecessor, was not an advocate of internal improvements, and Mercer was on less friendly terms with him than he had been with Adams. When Mercer continued to press for federal assistance to begin the western section, he got a stinging rebuke from Jackson's treasury secretary, Samuel D. Ingham: in seeking "to entangle the affairs of this company with those of the government," Ingham said, Mercer was imperious and condescending. "He had long since taken possession, in imagination, of the Treasury . . . and now he has another project, to get hold of the army, to tunnel through the Alleghany mountains . . . the Government is, in fact, deemed a secondary concern, and of but little account, except to aid the gentleman's schemes in making roads and canals."[10]

The testing ground for canals and railroads proved to be at the Point of Rocks, "a place soon to become more talked about than any other spot in the Blue Mountains," wrote John H. B. Latrobe.[11] By 1829, the preliminary skirmishing between the competing public works was well under way and they had instituted the policy of reciprocal delay and harassment, with intermittent periods of reconciliation, that was to characterize their relationship for the next several decades. It began on June 10, 1828, when the canal filed suit in the Washington County court and obtained an injunction preventing the railroad from acquiring any more right-of-way on the Maryland shore of the Potomac in Frederick, Washington, and Allegany counties. The canal's lawyers, William Price and Walter Jones, claimed that their charter entitled them to the exclusive use of the land on both sides of the river and gave them the preemptive right to their specified route from Georgetown to Cumberland. They said the railroad had located its line deliberately to thwart them.

The B&O retaliated June 23, by successfully suing in Maryland's High Court of Chancery to stop the Chesapeake and Ohio from doing the same thing. Roger Brooke Taney, William Gwynn, John H. B. Latrobe, and John V. L. McMahon filed two ancillary proceedings during the next two days. All three suits, later combined into one, sought to protect the right-of-way that the railroad had bought, condemned, or located its route on. The Baltimore and Ohio asserted that it was proceeding under its charter rights to build a railroad and not "merely" to stop the canal; that the C&O was the true obstructionist because its agents were trying to buy up the same land the B&O had already arranged to buy from George Snouffer, James Hook, Peter Miller, and the rest; and that neither the Potomac Company nor the Chesapeake and Ohio Canal Company had a prior right to the route.

Mercer went to Baltimore in November 1828 with Walter Jones to see whether the railroad would agree to bring the case to trial. Mercer discovered that it would not, but would instead prefer to wait until both projects were built and operating to the Point of Rocks. Then the public could decide which one provided the best transportation. If the railroad was chosen—and the B&O spokesmen had little doubt that it would be—the canal should stop there and allow them to proceed. Mercer's main objection, he said, was that the C&O could not just stop at the Point of Rocks; if it did, the 26 miles below there to Seneca Creek would be without water since the next canal feeder was at Harpers Ferry.

Philip E. Thomas's account of the meeting is rather different. He said Mercer and Jones met with John H. B. Latrobe in an attempt to agree on a statement of facts without surrendering the rights of their respective companies, but that the first fact the C&O Canal president wanted the B&O to agree to was "the moral, if not physical, impossibility of the canal and rail road proceeding, side by side, along the Maryland shore of the Potomac."[12] That was unacceptable to the railroad, and the meeting ended. Mercer came away feeling the B&O "would interpose every legal obstacle in their power . . . to retard the progress of the Canal."[13]

And indeed the railroad, apparently unworried, advertised for contracts and began work that same month. This brought a second C&O injunction, issued in December 1828 by the Washington County court, prohibiting the railroad from building anywhere within Frederick, Washington, and Allegany counties, "particularly past and by the Point of Rocks."

Into the negotiations at this juncture stepped one of the most accomplished and unscrupulous political operatives of that or any age. James William McCulloh had already entered the pages of history as the protagonist in *McCulloch v. Maryland*, the Supreme Court case made famous by Chief Justice Marshall's classic assertion of the implied powers of the Constitution and of national sovereignty over states' rights, incorporating the memorable phrase, "The power to tax involves the power to destroy." Marshall borrowed it from Daniel Webster, one of several outstanding lawyers who argued the case. Some of the others were Attorney General William Wirt and Walter Jones. All three were to meet in the canal-railroad court proceedings, which has been called "Maryland's greatest case." [14]

McCulloch v. Maryland revolved around the state's effort to impose a heavy tax on the Baltimore branch of the Bank of the United States, an unpopular institution in the south and west. McCulloh (the spelling varied) was the cashier of the Baltimore branch, which refused to pay the tax and urged a court test. Marshall in his celebrated opinion issued on March 6, 1819, declared the state tax unconstitutional. But the basic principles he enunciated so brilliantly were more than a little ironic in view of the activities that had been taking place in the bank in Baltimore.

Mismanagement and irregularities were prevalent throughout the national banking system, but there was outright fraud and embezzlement in the Baltimore branch of the U.S. Bank. The problems came to light with the completion of a congressional investigation two months before the Supreme Court's decision. One of the investigators was a future B&O president, Congressman Louis McLane, who spent four days in Baltimore questioning McCulloh and James A. Buchanan, president of the Baltimore branch. Buchanan and his cousin Samuel Smith, then a congressman, were partners in Smith and Buchanan, one of the country's largest shipping firms, and Buchanan was reputed to control a "club" of speculators that was systematically looting the Baltimore branch.

Even for the age, the extent of the speculators' malversation was extraordinary. Essentially, they were making unsecured loans to themselves from the bank's deposits to finance their own business and speculative investments and to acquire bank stock. McCulloh, Buchanan, and George Williams, a director in whose firm McCulloh received his training, together grabbed off bank stock worth $4.5 million. McCulloh discovered a way to lend himself $85,000 without Buchanan's knowledge. At the end, their total unsecured indebtedness was $1.4 million. McCulloh's share was $429,000.

In May 1819, the City Bank, another Baltimore bank, failed as a result of its speculation in U.S. Bank stock. In the general panic that followed, about 100 Baltimore businesses failed, including the most prominent of all, Smith and Buchanan. Buchanan left town. McCulloh blithely claimed he was just an employee. One observer noted that "these destroyers of Widows, and Orphans, affect to consider themselves as persecuted men. McCulloh for example struts about in all the pride and gaiety belonging to an honest heart." [15] Existing laws were vague concerning their offenses. Buchanan and McCulloh were tried for conspiracy to defraud the Bank of the United States and acquitted, but the city's reputation suffered for years.

Nonetheless, when McCulloh ran for the General Assembly in 1825, he won, and the year after that he was made Speaker of the House of Delegates, just in time to oversee the passage of the B&O charter with its tax exemption intact. He also promoted the C&O Canal's legislation. He stepped down as Speaker in 1827 but remained in the legislature and took up the practice of law. In ten years' time, during which there were unique services rendered to both railroad and canal, he had created the prototype of the Maryland political fixer and bagman.

The compromise between the feuding corporations that McCulloh first proposed in February 1829 was clear and reasonable. Both companies would have their engineers, working together, locate the canal and railroad at the four difficult passes between the Point of Rocks and Harpers Ferry and estimate the cost of constructing them jointly and independently. They would calculate the extra cost of building the works concurrently and the firms would agree that this additional expense constituted the sole difference between them. McCulloh, offering to function as a go-between, told Mercer he would ask the railroad to submit such a proposal for an "amicable agreement."

The canal board thought it was a good idea and in a spirit of compromise withdrew their second injunction insofar as it affected the construction of the B&O line in Frederick County east of the disputed ground. "This measure of conciliation is duly appreciated," Thomas replied.[16]

McCulloh evidently did present his scheme to the railroad officials, but they did not act on it. A court would have to order the joint surveys. Both Thomas and McCulloh subsequently claimed to have misplaced the documents spelling out the compromise. In fact, Thomas denied knowledge of any overture for an amicable settlement, other than the one Mercer and Jones discussed with Latrobe in November 1828. "Nothing therefore remained," he said piously, "but 'to await the slow course of the law.'"[17] The only thing the railroad offered was a place of disengagement. Thomas proposed a separation of several hundred yards where the two lines collided on the property of George Snouffer and Mercer agreed. The companies waited there at the Point of Rocks, but they were not idle. To the east and south, construction and the war of words continued.

In May 1828, the Chesapeake and Ohio had received the $1 million federal stock subscription that made Mercer's idea a reality. Twice over the next two years, the railroad, too, tried to obtain federal funds, but their friends in Congress were unable to outmaneuver Mercer, who as a member (or chairman) of the House committee that reviewed their requests had great influence in the Senate. The B&O made its first request for funds in December 1828. Charles Carroll of Carrollton headed the list of signers of the short document, followed by Thomas, the trio of "royal merchants," William Patterson, Robert Oliver, and Alexander Brown, and the other directors. The company said it had a capital stock of $4 million—made up of $3 million from individuals or corporations and $1 million from the State of Maryland and the City of Baltimore—and estimated that its line would cost $6–7 million. The document did not mention the canal, whose ratio of stock ownership was almost exactly the reverse: of the C&O's $3.6 million capital, $3 million came from public sources and $600,000 from private subscribers. The United States and the City of Washington had $1 million in stock each; Maryland, $500,000; Alexandria and Georgetown, $250,000 each.

The Senate Committee on Roads and Canals in early 1829 reported a bill providing $1 million for the railroad's western section. Mercer's House committee did not act, claiming it was too late in the session. However, its members did make what Thomas called "a highly flattering report." They were impressed with the railroad's backers, "gentlemen of wealth, high character, and great enterprise," but they were also concerned about the legal controversy. Someone—it could only have been Mercer—had told them the C&O's right to construct a railroad in the mountains might prevent the B&O from building one there. Mercer was busily writing his own memorials to Congress, accusing the railroad of interfering with the canal route yet all the while maintaining he was not hostile to the B&O or trying to hinder its attempts to obtain federal funds. No bill passed.

In December 1829, the railroad made another, more urgent, request. They pointed out that three miles of track had been laid and the grading and bridges finished on about 26 miles, and that locomotives were on the horizon. Thomas went to Washington early in 1830 to plead the company's cause. He invited Mercer to join him before the House committee, but the canal president snubbed him, claiming he had confused the dates. Thomas accused him of deception. Thomas said that, although Mercer had told him to press his bill in the Senate and had promised that when it came to the House he would support it, he had instead gone to the Senate before him and worked hard to undermine his bill. A series of formal notes between the two, a kind of verbal adagio, confirmed the end of their professional friendship.[18]

Thomas's effort was successful in getting a bill passed in the House providing $350,000 to help build the railroad to the Point of Rocks, but again it was too late and the measure died in the other branch. Thomas blamed Mercer. "In both of the applications," he said, "this company was met by the most decided and inveterate opposition, on the part of the Chesapeake and Ohio Canal company, chiefly through its president." The City of Baltimore made up the funds necessary to reach the Potomac by paying its stock installments in advance and took a mortgage on the railroad.[19]

In early 1829, the Chesapeake and Ohio petitioned the Maryland General Assembly, the railroad's home territory, for three amendments to its charter: to acquire and dispose of excess land, to sell water power, and to eliminate bridges, substituting ferries. Mercer's stated reason was that without bridges, two- and three-story boats could lift the passenger high above the insects and noxious vapors lurking at the canal's surface into the fresh air and sunshine where he would have "an unobstructed view of the country around him."[20] The B&O quite understandably regarded Mercer's memorial as an attack and alerted its forces in Annapolis to study the measure carefully and stop it from being forced through. "Should the bill contain a provision to prevent the erection of bridges across the canal, it may totally defeat the railroad," Thomas warned McMahon.[21]

The C&O proposals stirred up controversy not only among the mill owners along the Potomac but also among the canal's own stockholders. The Baltimore press was predictably hostile. Mercer, asserting that his ideas had been "entirely misconceived," withdrew the memorial. Nevertheless, he was back the following year asking for the same things, plus permission to start construction of the canal west of Cumberland before the eastern section was finished, which was prohibited by the Maryland charter. Again he was turned down.

Meanwhile, in July 1829, Mercer informed the B&O that his company would ask the Chancellor of Maryland to dismiss the railroad's year-old injunctions. Lawyers from both sides sparred for almost two weeks, in the heat of an Annapolis summer, from July 21 to August 6, in the first of three court hearings. The legal talent was impressive. William Wirt, the former attorney general, Walter Jones, and Mercer himself represented the Chesapeake and Ohio. The B&O sent five lawyers, headed by Roger Brooke Taney. The others were William Gwynn, Reverdy Johnson, John V. L. McMahon, and John H. B. Latrobe. Although only three of them actually argued the case, Mercer felt outnumbered, the more so because some of the canal's attorneys who were expected in Annapolis, including Francis Scott Key, did not show up and those who did were in some disarray.

For two days, Latrobe, the junior counsel, outlined the Baltimore and Ohio's position, which was essentially that its injunctions should be kept in force pending a final decision on which company had the prior right to the route. Wirt, who was ill as the case got under way, started to do the same thing for the canal but was unable to continue and turned the reading of the company's voluminous documents over to Mercer. Mercer spent a morning poring over the various laws and surveys before he, too, was forced to give up and ask for time to straighten them out. The court adjourned for an afternoon. Mercer then took another day and a half to summarize the history of the canal. The C&O lawyers looked to Jones for relief, but Jones turned out to be less than expected. Wirt wrote to his wife:

> This morning to my great relief Mr. Jones came. Mr. Mercer has been reading the documents yesterday and today, and tomorrow Jones says he will go on, so as to give him till Monday. How he can go on is to me incomprehensible. In his way from Washington in a hack yesterday he got [plastered?] at a mill about seven miles from this, stayed there all night among the mail bags, pigs, chickens, and dirty children, got no sleep, he says, came here before breakfast, quite haggard, has not seen a paper in this cause for months, and now instead of preparing for his argument, he is playing cards in the cloak room, and yet he has to go on in the morning in this cause on which millions depend. Mercer is in great disgust with him.[22]

Jones recovered over the weekend and when Mercer at last sat down, he stood up. Jones's rhetorical skills were directed toward making a case against the railroad as a conspirator that had, first of all, "studiously masked and concealed" its intention to obstruct the C&O by announcing a shorter and more direct route to the west than the C&O's: "The direct route, proposed for the Rail Road, as contrasted with the circuitous route chosen for the canal, was vauntingly printed in capitals" [in the "Proceedings of Sundry Citizens"] and its various advantages reiterated in every form calculated to illustrate the superiority of the rail road over the canal.[23]

The canal's lawyers said the Baltimore and Ohio told the Maryland legislature that their line lay through Westminster and Williamsport. Moreover, when it became obvious in May 1828 that the Chesapeake and Ohio was about to become an active corporation, the railroad decided, without prior surveys, "to pounce upon the route and site chosen for the canal." The B&O's engineers and attorneys at the river, "proceeding with the utmost haste and secrecy," told some landowners they were just making experiments and that the only reason they wanted the property was so the surveyors could pass through. Latrobe and McMahon no doubt listened with amusement as their opponents described "agents riding about and ranging the country with ceaseless activity day and night, hunting up the proprietors of the ground on the route, and soliciting from them cessions for the railroad [so that] the party more resembled a partizan corps . . . guarding against surprize, on the flank of an enemy, than persons engaged in the ordinary business either of contract or of civil engineering."

It was true, of course, that every one of the six Baltimore delegates to the 1826 C&O Canal Convention, including Thomas, had left to form the railroad, and also that six of the canal's surveyors, including McNeill, took part in the B&O reconnaissance. The rival corporation had adopted the C&O's idea of building a great artery to the West, lured away some of their potential investors, and had raided their engineers, and now, worst of all, coveted their route.

Both Mercer and Jones firmly believed that if the canal was intercepted by the railroad at the Point of Rocks, it would "be entirely stopped and defeated," or forced across the Potomac on an expensive aqueduct: "There is no necessary or proper connexion or dependence between the rail road and the river whereas the river is . . . the lifeblood of the canal."

Wirt, who concluded the case for the Chesapeake and Ohio, had recently resigned after twelve years as U.S. attorney general. Wirt was also well known as an author of "polite literature." The anonymous *Letters of a British Spy* (1803), purporting to be the leisurely observations of Virginia society by an English visitor, had been very popular, and Wirt had written other books, culminating in 1817 with *Sketches of the Life and Character of Patrick Henry*, a patriotic biography chiefly memorable for words the author assigned his subject: "Give me liberty or give me death." As a lawyer, he was known for his oratory. He had prosecuted Aaron Burr. Latrobe remembered Wirt as industrious rather than brilliant. From the window of his Annapolis hotel room he could watch Wirt in his room across the courtyard on the hot summer evenings during the hearings "in his shirt sleeves, busily engaged in writing" his arguments for the next day's court session.[24] But things across the courtyard were less tranquil than they seemed from a distance. Wirt, troubled by a poor stomach, was a sick man. He wrote to his wife:

> I took my old breakfast of boiled milk and crackers with pepper, salt and lager. I ate dinner two plates of mutton broth . . . I believe I shall eat no supper. I have been on court from 12 to 3. Jones has been speaking and will go on again tomorrow. How long he will go on I don't know. I must be prepared to follow him. And I have

been so much indisposed that I have not yet finished my notes which I must do forthwith. I shall begin again with the blue pills tonight and the quinine tomorrow morning.[25]

Wirt in his argument in court the next afternoon maintained that the Chesapeake and Ohio Canal Company filed the first suit to protect their prior right of choice of a route, guaranteed by their charter and the Potomac Company's. "The whole controversy turns on the existence or non-existence of this prior right of choice," he said, and this could be determined only by a comparison of the railroad and canal charters. The B&O thought this question should be postponed to a final hearing, hoping that court-ordered surveys would show that the two public works could both squeeze by the narrow places along the river, but Wirt was against this: "Do not keep our works hung up, by this injunction, and cause us to lose months and years for the proposed surveys which . . . must, at last bring you back to the very question which is now presented. By our charter we are to choose our own route. Where does the Court of Chancery of Maryland get the right to choose it for us?"[26]

The canal company wanted an immediate final decision, but Johnson and Taney, who finished the Baltimore and Ohio's court presentation, successfully argued against it. Johnson, 33, was on his way to a national reputation as a politician and constitutional lawyer, and Taney, 52, Maryland's attorney general, would be named U.S. attorney general before the case was over. Latrobe described Taney as having "a face without one good feature, a mouth unusually large, in which were discolored and irregular teeth, the gums of which were visible when he smiled, dressed always in black, his clothes sitting ill upon him." He was "a gaunt, ungainly man," with the hollow voice of a consumptive. "And yet, when he began to speak, you never thought of his personal appearance, so clear, so simple, so admirably arranged, were his low voiced words."[27] The future chief justice of the Supreme Court wore himself out with a four-hour speech on a sweltering morning and the court had to adjourn for another day before he could continue.

Theodorick Bland, the chancellor, issued his decision September 24, 1829, in favor of the railroad. He said that the Baltimore and Ohio had got there first and was entitled to the right-of-way. The canal company, rather than answering the railroad's complaint, had instead amassed "a multitude of acts, proceedings, and papers" to prove their claim that the B&O had illegally cut them off at the pass.[28]

Bland further said that the canal company's injunction obtained in the Washington County court had no connection with this case, and that the railroad's injunction therefore continued in force. Wirt's question of prior right was, he indicated, "new matter." (Wirt had submitted it as a supplemental argument.) If surveys showed the railroad would exclude the canal at the Point of Rocks, then the court could decide later whether the C&O had "a priority of right, to the choice and selection of the route." The B&O attorneys informed Thomas that the decision was "all that we could have desired." Each of them received a fee of $500, and Taney, $200 extra for drafting the railroad's argument.

In December, the canal's lawyers asked Bland to order the surveys, but only of enough of the route "to show the impossibility of the two works passing along the Maryland side of the Potomac" above the Point of Rocks.[29] Bland issued the survey order in January 1830 and commissioned the B&O's Jonathan Knight and Nathan S. Roberts from the Chesapeake and Ohio to conduct it. Because at that time the canal and railroad both intended to follow the river to Cumberland, Bland wanted maps and profiles for the entire route.

Then the canal made another overture to the railroad. If the engineers did find enough room between the Point of Rocks and Harpers Ferry, and if "the two works can go on socially along the river," perhaps they could be located and built together.[30] Thomas objected to that, using his former argument that there was no need for both public works to be constructed beyond the Point of Rocks—only the best one, which, clearly, was the railroad: "I have never for a moment doubted of the superiority of rail roads over canals for . . . transportation in our country," he told a correspondent.[31]

Thomas, buoyed by news of the successful Rainhill trials, invited Mercer and the canal directors to Baltimore to become converts, and even suggested that the two companies merge and build the railroad. Mercer was not persuaded, but the two executives did manage to collaborate on a set of instructions for their engineers. They were to concentrate on the narrow passes, and when they got to Harpers Ferry were to report on whether it was practical to build the two works from the Point of Rocks, the width of ground that each would require, and the additional expense for joint construction. They were then to continue their surveys along the river.

Knight met Roberts and his party of surveyors at James Hook's place in March 1830, and they spent a day looking over the Point of Rocks. Knight then went on to Harpers Ferry to search for his assistants, and not finding them, went to Frederick, then back to the river, and then to Baltimore, leaving Roberts alone to lay out the line of the canal. Roberts told Mercer, "I began to feel my situation very unpleasant."[32]

What Knight did not know was that the man who was assigned to help him— William G. McNeill—was quitting the railroad. McNeill, embittered by the breakup of the B&O's board of engineers and the ascendancy of Wever, told Thomas he refused to take any job that was "dependent upon a consultation with, or the opinions of, Mr. Knight." Thomas said that was unacceptable, and McNeill resigned.[33]

When Knight returned to the surveys, he was principally aided by one of Roberts's assistants (Wever, although assigned, having proved unavailable). By April, Roberts had worked his way up to Peter Miller's place, near Wever's mill (Weverton, Maryland), about three miles below Harpers Ferry. He wrote Mercer, "The whole collision at the Point of Rocks does not exceed ⅞ of a mile, and from there to within two miles of Harpers Ferry, the lines will not, I believe, come in contact so as to cost any extra expense to either company." The section he was talking about was the eight miles in the middle. No part of the route, Roberts said, "will make a more beautiful canal."[34] A month later, he was less optimistic. Further examination had revealed problems at the lower Point of Rocks, where, Roberts said, "It will be a hard case for both those works to pass side by side, and it can be done only at a great expense [to] the Canal," which might be forced into the river. Even so, he hoped they could adjust their differences.[35]

Altogether, Roberts and Knight spent three and a half months, from March 17 to July 4, 1830, and $2,600 surveying and mapping the twelve-mile route from the Point of Rocks to Harpers Ferry. In this distance, the canal and railroad collided at four major locations, totaling a little over two miles. These were at the upper and lower Point of Rocks at Catoctin Mountain, Miller's Narrows just past South Mountain between what is now Weverton and Sandy Hook, and Harpers Ferry Narrows, across from the town at the Blue Ridge. Roberts estimated that surveys of the remaining 127 miles to Cumberland, where there were twice as many problem areas proportionally, would take six years and cost nearly $60,000. For that and other reasons, these surveys were never made.

"We united in opinion, that it was practicable to construct both the contemplated works through the narrow passes," Roberts and Knight said in their report, written from Harpers Ferry. They had surveyed independent lines for the canal and railroad, determined where they clashed, and realigned the routes at those points "by laying the Rail road further into the Rocks, and the canal further into the river." They believed that the materials excavated for the first could be used to build the second, and they recommended that both should be constructed simultaneously by the same contractor. The total extra cost of this would be about $12,600.[36]

On the basis of this report, Thomas seemed to go along with the canal's suggestion that the two companies should collaborate on building their works as far as Harpers Ferry. In August 1830, three C&O Canal negotiators arrived in Baltimore for a meeting with the railroad officials. The following day, Thomas expanded his ideas in a formal, eight-point proposal. The most controversial provision was that the two companies, after reaching Harpers Ferry, should continue the same joint survey and construction procedure to Cumberland. The C&O negotiators thought this was unreasonable, and furthermore the time-consuming and expensive surveys might show that it could not be done.

Mercer's opinion was clear: "Regarding the compromise to Harpers Ferry, as precluded by . . . your late *ultimatum* we are not only willing but anxious to submit our controversy, without further delay to the . . . legal tribunals." Thomas declared the negotiations at an end on November 16, 1830.[37] Both sides remained convinced of the merits of their own project, Mercer citing "the superiority of the Chesapeake and Ohio Canal, to any other mode of transportation applicable to the valley of the Potomac."[38] The first section of the canal, from the Little Falls to Seneca, opened the same month, and at once the adversaries fell to quarreling again over the stopping place at the Point of Rocks.

Mercer, meanwhile, had been active on another front. He printed up Wirt's court argument on the canal's prior rights, added some other material, and laid the results, some 180 pages, on the desks of Congress in mid-May 1830, just when the railroad was trying to keep alive its second request for federal funds. Thomas, caught by surprise, managed a hastily produced eight-page rejoinder in which the Baltimore and Ohio's lawyers admitted they had insufficient time to answer the canal's ex parte argument in print before the current session ended.

What followed was a paper campaign for the hearts and minds of Congress, the stockholders, and anybody else who cared to wade through the documents. During this bitter and protracted battle of the pamphlets, each company claimed for itself the most Christian forbearance and at the same time castigated the other for the virulence of its attacks upon the rival firm. At the end of the year, after the negotiations collapsed, the railroad issued an 80-page pamphlet containing the letters back and forth and the B&O's interpretation of events. The canal responded in 1831 with a pamphlet almost twice as long, incorporating more correspondence, and corrections of the B&O's version. Official reports and memorials to Congress, newspaper essays, and verbal assaults were all used to sway public opinion.

The comparative advantages of canals and railroads were exhaustively examined. Knight, using the figures he and Roberts had worked up during their joint survey, stated that canals could cost at least twice as much to build as railroads. Because different physical laws applied, railroad speeds four times faster than those possible on canals had already been reached. The cost of transportation, using locomotives, might be half that for canals. Railroads could go places canals could not, such as up in the mountains, where there was little water. They could operate year-round, whereas canals would be closed half the year because of floods, droughts, and cold weather. Thomas submitted these arguments in a report to the Maryland Legislature in January 1831 in which he reviewed the whole controversy. In a counterreport for the canal company, Mercer dismissed Knight—"his facts are inconsistent . . . his assertions are without proof; and his principles have been refuted"—and talked of experiments in Scotland where horses had pulled canal boats at fifteen miles an hour without injuring the banks, and he said steamboats were being tried. Each company claimed that its construction costs were lower than the other's, but in fact they were running about the same, $30,000 a mile.

The newspapers aired all the issues and became so full of canal-railroad polemics that they began apologizing to their readers, but they went on printing them anyway. In a typical exchange on the relative value of the two systems, the Baltimore *American* and the Washington *National Intelligencer* discussed, under the general topics of the facility, certainty, economy, and velocity of transportation: the effects of weather, load weight, speed, horsepower, locomotives, and monopoly, whether railroads were suitable for hauling the heavy products of farms and mines, whether canals were adaptable to the speeds required for passengers, and which was the better for military purposes.

Not an accident or labor dispute took place on the Baltimore and Ohio that was not dissected in detail by the Washington papers, and the Baltimore press did the same for whatever happened on the canal. On the whole, the editors behaved with more decorum and good humor than the executives, and despite occasional lapses into overwrought prose, maintained their journalistic objectivity. For example, in the summer of 1831, William Gwynn, editor of the Baltimore *Gazette*, by invitation joined Joseph Gales, Jr., and William W. Seaton, editors of the Washington *National Intelligencer*, at Georgetown and rode with them on the canal packet *Charles Fenton Mercer* up to Seneca Creek and back. The construction, particularly the locks, was excellent, he reported, and the route along the Potomac and through the natural ravine around the Great Falls "excited great and continual interest [rendering] our first visit to this magnificent work (for it truly is so) highly delightful."[39]

In the fall, Gales returned the favor by taking a ride on the railroad, with Gwynn and the B&O's George Brown. The Washingtonians had underestimated its capacity to haul heavy materials, said the *National Intelligencer*. The scale of the work was less spectacular than the canal's, but still respectable. The newspaper expressed its "admiration of this stupendous undertaking of our neighbors [in] the Monumental City, which deserves so richly to be rewarded for it . . . we will imitate the courtesy of our Baltimore friend when he visited our Canal, and would not allow himself to say anything disparaging of it."[40]

No such mutual consideration animated the companies that season as their attorneys returned to Bland's High Court of Chancery.[41] The basic questions facing them were the same ones that Wirt had posed the last time around: which company was organized first, and which one had the prior right to the route? They were not simple questions to answer.

For the Baltimore and Ohio, the situation was fairly straightforward. Maryland had approved its charter on February 28, 1827, according to which the company was to become incorporated when one third of its $3 million in stock was subscribed for. That goal had been achieved by March 31 of the same year and the company was duly organized on April 23, 1827. The B&O formally adopted the Point of Rocks route May 23, 1828.

The Chesapeake and Ohio's corporate history was slightly more complicated. Maryland had approved its charter January 31, 1825, as had also Congress and the Potomac Company, on March 3 and March 16, respectively, of the same year. The C&O was to become incorporated when one fourth of its $6 million in capital stock was subscribed for. Washington, Georgetown, and Alexandria signed up for the required amount, $1.5 million worth, on November 14, 1827, even though none of them was empowered to make such subscriptions, or, indeed, had the money to do so. However, the canal had sold $562,700 worth of stock to private subscribers by the time Congress, on May 24, 1828, approved a subscription of $1 million and also passed a law giving the District cities the powers they lacked. The company was organized on June 20 and formally adopted its route on June 26, 1828. Later that year, the Potomac Company transferred its rights to the new organization.

The dates would indicate that the railroad company was the first to fulfill the incorporation requirements and choose its route, but did that guarantee it the prior right? The answer depended on whether the Potomac Company's charter included the power to make a continuous canal and whether the charter had lapsed before being turned over to the Chesapeake and Ohio.

The lawyers argued for two full weeks, from October 10 to 25, 1831, one day longer than the hearing in July-August 1829. The cast had changed slightly. Mercer was replaced by Alexander C. Magruder, president of St. John's College, Annapolis. Magruder, Wirt, and Jones upheld the canal's side. Taney, who had been named U.S. attorney general, Gwynn, Johnson, and Latrobe were back for the railroad. Only McMahon was missing. The B&O formally ended its relationship with the Pride of western Maryland about that time, paying him $500 for the year's work, and put Daniel Webster on retainer for the same amount.

It was generally understood that regardless of Chancellor Bland's decision, the case would be taken to the Court of Appeals, and when Bland again favored the railroad, on November 9, 1831, the companies made preparations for the final round.[42] The six judges of the appeals court were thought to be evenly divided on the issue. Therefore, a tie vote would confirm Bland's decision and make the railroad the winner. Near the end of November 1831, William Bond Martin, one of the judges favorable to the B&O, became ill. Walter Jones then asked the Court of Appeals to hear the case out of turn, because the C&O had less than two years left to finish 100 miles of canal or forfeit their charter and therefore the future existence of the company was at stake. Reverdy Johnson vigorously opposed the request, but the court moved up the hearing to December 26.

Just two lawyers were to be permitted to speak for each side. For the canal, they were Jones and Magruder; for the railroad, Webster and Johnson. Wirt was sick again, and because Taney was unable to attend on such short notice, the B&O asked Webster to take his place. John H. B. Latrobe, who accompanied Webster to Annapolis and shared rooms with him there, wrote an interesting account of the experience:

> One would have thought that, as my mission was to cram Mr. Webster and his duty was to be crammed, the case to be argued would be our sole subject of conversation. On the contrary we but rarely spoke of it, after I had stated in a general way what had taken place before the Chancellor, and rehearsed as well as I could, from my notes, the argument of . . . Wirt and Jones. Sometimes I would begin on the case as we sat before our big fire, and Mr. Webster would apparently be listening, so far at least as to keep his great dark eyes fixed on mine; when instead of replying to me he would start some topic that had filled his thoughts while I was speaking, and go off in an entirely different direction from the controversy that had brought him to Annapolis.[43]

Latrobe was clearly in awe of Webster, though perhaps no more so than the rest of the country. At the time of the trial, Webster, about to turn 50, was at the height of his powers, just a year past his Union-glorifying triumph over Robert Y. Hayne, Calhoun's spokesman, in the United States Senate. He was a magnetic speaker with an imposing presence. Webster's reputation declined as he became known as the spokesman for the rich and powerful and his once-magnificent oratory degenerated into what Emerson called "noble explosions of sound." But for many, including Latrobe, who considered him the greatest man he had ever met, Webster was the nation's leading lawyer, its foremost political orator, and the best-known American of his time.[44]

The Court of Appeals met on the second floor of the statehouse in Annapolis, and on particularly cold days all the judges came down from the bench to gather around the fireplace. On the morning of Friday, December 30, 1831, the courtroom filled early with members of the legislature and others eager to witness the living legend's first appearance in the Maryland courts. He did not disappoint them. Latrobe commented on "the Doric purity of his language." William Gwynn's *Gazette* described how, during a four-hour speech, Webster, a supporter of internal improvements, "was once or twice decidedly eloquent. But certainly his great merit was the masterly manner [in which] he presented the history of these two rival companies, the course of legislation pursued in relation to both of them, and the clear and manly style in which he exhibited to the court their respective legal rights."[45]

Five days later the Court of Appeals decided three to two in favor of the canal, reversing Chancellor Bland and dismissing the railroad's injunction. No appeal was possible.

Webster had thought they would win. The company said later it was pleased with his performance. Taney believed the court had determined beforehand to decide the case against the railroad and had taken advantage of the absence of Martin, who objected to the advance of the hearing date, to do so. The *Gazette* mentioned "a concurrence of unusual circumstances" and recommended that the B&O apply for redress to the legislature, many of whose members had been in court and had heard the arguments.[46]

Chief Judge John Buchanan found that the operative date of the C&O's incorporation was the earlier of the choices, November 14, 1827 (although the Baltimore and Ohio had been incorporated and organized before that). "The question then presented for the consideration of this court is, whether the Chesapeake and Ohio Canal Company, has a priority of right, in the choice of selection of ground for the route and site of the canal in the valley of the Potomac," Buchanan said. The answer was yes, because the C&O's rights were in abeyance until it became organized, based on the Potomac Company's charter, which did include the power to construct a continuous canal and had not lapsed.[47]

Benjamin C. Howard wrote Latrobe that the Potomac interest had "proved too strong even in the Temple of Justice, into which prejudice has crept, hiding itself beneath the sacred ermine," and it was too bad the B&O had not adopted his policy "of prolonging the suit and keeping the canal below the Point of Rocks. It would have perished by starvation. . . . I have constantly said that you must look upon the Mercerian spirit of the Canal Co. as utterly intolerant, as wishing for your destruction."[48]

The railroad had, of course, been rather of the same mind toward the canal. Now, in this crisis, the B&O was, by turns, resolute, appeasing, and, as always, resourceful. Although Thomas confessed to Howard that he did not know which way to turn, or whether they would ever get past the Point of Rocks, he was determined to find a way out. The B&O offered to bear the whole additional cost of joint construction from the Point of Rocks to Harpers Ferry if it could bridge the canal before crossing the river, preferably at Harpers Ferry. The C&O rejected joint construction as more trouble than it was worth, but it did agree to a crossing, provided it was below the Point of Rocks.

The B&O asked the Maryland legislature to release them from the requirement to construct the road into Washington and Allegany counties. The lawmakers, at least, were agreeable.[49] Meanwhile, the company explored alternative routes. Thomas thought either the opposite bank of the Potomac or the Shenandoah were the best choices. He made overtures to the Virginia legislature to remove the restriction requiring the B&O to strike the Ohio no lower down than Parkersburg. Since a new route would probably be more expensive, the railroad sought $500,000 each from the City of Baltimore and the federal government. "The chance of getting a subscription is certainly worse than before the decision of the court," Congressman Howard wrote a Baltimore friend: "The route is not now designated. They are bound out westerly somewhere, no one knows where. This is favourable for an exploring voyage, but not for an Investment."[50]

The Chesapeake and Ohio wanted nothing, for the moment, except the satisfaction of having the railroad admit defeat. According to Mercer, the C&O received the court's decision with "unfeigned satisfaction," and he immediately advertised for contractors to construct the canal from the Point of Rocks to Williamsport. They let the first contracts, to Harpers Ferry, on March 14, 1832, the same day they rejected the railroad's proposal.

Thomas was worried that the canal would place its line in such a way that rails could not be laid beside it, a suspicion partly confirmed by one of the C&O engineers, who said they "located the Canal as if the Rail road Company had never been in existence," but then asserted that the changes were insignificant.[51] Concerned that the C&O was acquiring land at the Point of Rocks to cut them off from the Potomac trade, Thomas told Wever to take countermeasures. They "are buying up the shores of the river to get command of them," Thomas said dolefully. "I expect all kinds of open and secret hostility from the Canal Company."[52] Wever accordingly made himself as obnoxious as possible to the C&O throughout 1832, stirring up the local residents to require a ferry, docks, and a road for the transfer of freight at the Point of Rocks and frustrating the canal in its attempt to acquire the right-of-way through his mill below Miller's Narrows.

The Point of Rocks was of little consequence to the B&O except as a means to reach Harpers Ferry, the gateway to the routes to the west and the strategic key to the trade of the Shenandoah Valley. For the railroad to cross the Potomac at the Point of Rocks, where it was wider than at Harpers Ferry, would require a more expensive viaduct, and it would also mean having to cross the Shenandoah to reach their objective. The B&O admitted, several times in fact, that they had made a tactical error in not accepting the canal's earlier offer to compromise.

In mid-March 1832, the Maryland legislature stepped in, requesting a meeting of the canal stockholders to reconsider the railroad's proposal. The state, having invested $500,000 in each project, wanted to see both of them built, preferably in Maryland rather than in Virginia. Maryland's agent, representing its C&O stock, was Benjamin S. Forrest. His most outspoken opponent was Richard S. Coxe, chairman of the canal stockholders' committee. The politicking and vote trading were intense and the editors and pamphleteers cranked up the presses once again.

Thomas provided Forrest with plenty of railroad reports and philosophy. As the C&O Canal committee and stockholder meetings continued in Washington through the spring and summer of 1832, the state agent made certain concessions and refinements in the B&O's offer, but with little effect. Mercer, merely implacable at first, had become vindictive. He was finally in a position to avenge the slights he had suffered for years from Baltimore's condescending merchant princes and their incessant claims for the railroad's technological superiority.

The canal company said it did not care if Thomas made a mistake in refusing their earlier offer of cooperation. The reading, at one of the canal meetings, of Thomas's pre-trial admission that if the railroad won the court case, it would proceed up the Potomac to Harpers Ferry on the land it already owned without regard to the canal, and if it lost, would cross over into Virginia at the Point of Rocks, created a sensation.

Although Maryland's governor and its U.S. senators and congressmen urged the Chesapeake and Ohio to be accommodating, the canal company, admitting that it feared the competition of the railroad in the Potomac Valley, seemed determined to prevent it from going there. Their decision, ratified by the stockholders on August 4, 1832, contained most of Thomas's original ideas and gave them a nice ironic twist: the railroad should terminate at the Point of Rocks, at least until 1840, and its funds should be used to finish the canal to Cumberland. In their minds, the winner of the contest to determine the superior transportation system was the company that had triumphed in court.

The railroad at once declined this insulting proposition, and Thomas told Forrest that their only recourse was the legislature. Yet he believed the Chesapeake and Ohio might disregard even the General Assembly if there was a prospect of obtaining funds elsewhere. "They seem almost reckless of consequences," he wrote Benjamin C. Howard.[53]

As the year turned, the two companies were still bickering in their official reports about relative costs and efficiency and who was delaying whom. The C&O applied to Congress again, unsuccessfully, for $1.4 million to build the canal to Cumberland. There would be no further federal aid. They made their customary appeals to the state government for grants and favors, but Maryland's patience was wearing thin. Hezekiah Niles hoped the canal "will get a lesson on courtesy and accommodation from the legislature of the state."[54]

Governor George Howard (another of the Howard brothers), in his annual address to the General Assembly in January 1833, recommended denying further help to the canal until it allowed the railroad to pass. The lawmakers agreed. The Committees on Internal Improvement for the Senate and House of Delegates issued stern reports the following month. The Senate suggested that the companies give up trying to strangle each other. The canal would yield or face legislative sanctions.

The House internal improvement committee visited the battleground and took testimony from Jonathan Knight and Alfred Cruger to determine whether the canal line had indeed been shifted to block the railroad. The testimony was at odds: Knight maintained that although the canal line now under construction had been moved, the railroad could still be built beside it; Cruger magnified the problems of joint construction.

Delegate William D. Merrick, the committee chairman, felt there was still room for both works, and he suggested that if the canal remained adamant, legislative approval of funds, a charter extension, and the requested rights to sell water power and acquire excess land would become highly problematic. He also threatened a state investigation, a possible court suit to abrogate the present charter, and nonpayment of Maryland's stock subscription. The carrot came after the stick. If the canal cooperated, the state would extend the charter for two years, call off the investigation, and make its subscription payments. The committee drafted a proposed agreement and set a deadline.

Mercer was not about to give up, but the strain was beginning to tell. At the end of February 1833, in an exhausted state, he addressed a joint session of the General Assembly for three and a half hours. The experience left him wringing wet and very embittered. "As to the threats of Maryland or rather of the miserable committee of her legislature we regard them now with contempt," he defiantly told a Virginia friend. In Annapolis, he said Knight was cunning and Thomas and Wever "full of malignity," and all of them "so elated by the ruining [of] our whole project that they made no proposals whatever of compromise" but instead told everyone "that they had done so and that I had flatly rejected them."[55]

Thomas applied pressure also in Washington and Richmond where the C&O was also seeking funds. The City of Washington, unable to pay its stock subscription of $250,000 to the canal, had requested a federal loan. Thomas's plea to Congress not to grant the loan while the canal remained recalcitrant drew an outraged response from Mercer and two of the B&O's most intransigent opponents, Richard S. Coxe and Walter Jones, who complained of interference in the city's affairs. Thomas then tried to influence the Virginia legislature, which was considering a $250,000 grant to the canal, to make the grant contingent upon the C&O's assent to the railroad's free passage. Henry Clay and other influential members of Congress urged Mercer to make a settlement.

Mercer and John H. B. Latrobe met in Annapolis in February or March 1833—accidentally, according to Latrobe. Mercer sought a compromise and they worked one out in a day or so with a joint committee of the Senate and House of Delegates, headed, respectively, by Charles F. Mayer and Bene S. Pigman. Mercer was clear about two things: he did not want the railroad in the Potomac Valley above Harpers Ferry, and he wanted money, but the state declined to make a further subscription.

The bill went through several versions. The act the legislature passed in late March 1833 authorized the railroad to build its line from the Point of Rocks to Harpers Ferry, where it was to cross into Virginia and "not occupy the Maryland shore of the river Potomac" above that point.[56] Both public works had to be reduced in width to squeeze by the narrow passes, where a board fence was to separate the locomotives from the horses tracking the boats. The canal company finally received authority to start the western section and to sell water power. The railroad was permitted to subscribe for 2,500 shares of C&O stock. The two companies had to agree formally to the terms by May 10, 1833.

The stockholders and the general public were opposed to the railroad's buying stock in the canal, Thomas said, as officers from the two companies met in April to work out further details of the compromise, and he hoped the C&O would not insist on it. They did not. The private agreement the negotiators concluded, which replaced the first section of the law, stipulated a payment for damages instead of a subscription, which Mercer considered roughly equivalent. The B&O agreed to pay the canal $266,000 for grading a little over four miles of railroad line at the narrow passes. Mercer also extracted their promise "not to continue the rail road further up the valley of the Potomac than Harpers Ferry" until the canal was finished to Cumberland, or until 1840.[57] The C&O charter required the canal to reach Cumberland by then.

The B&O board of directors adopted this agreement May 6, 1833, and the stockholders approved it, along with the law, two days later, when they met at the Exchange. James W. McCulloh, who seemed to materialize whenever there was a deal to be struck, played a central role in the meeting. Afterward, he carried the signed documents to Washington where the canal's stockholders gathered at the City Hall to vote their approval on May 9, and then he delivered them to the Governor's office in Annapolis in time to meet the deadline. "A compromise is therefore at last effected in this long-standing controversy," the *American* reported.[58] It was five years, almost to the day, since the railroad had first sent its agents to the river.

Thomas had not addressed Mercer since he rejected the canal president's humiliating proposal nine months earlier. Its premise, that the railroad surrender and help build the canal to Cumberland, was part of the current agreement. Now he wrote him a warm letter, hoping they could forget their past hostility and join in a common effort. Thomas even liked Mercer's idea of replacing the board fence with a hedge of evergreen.

In his annual report in that summer of 1833, the C&O president treated the resolution of the conflict as a victory for the canal. And so it was. They had won the psychological war and humbled the mighty. Some day, Mercer said, the twelve miles where the two public works were in conflict "will dwindle into a point, not of collision between embittered rivals, but of union between generous friends." It was his last report. Barely a month later, Mercer was replaced by John H. Eaton, a Jackson intimate, in yet another unsuccessful attempt to obtain federal funds.[59]

Thomas was so infused with the new spirit of cooperation that he became a canal advocate and also began to resist the idea of extending the railroad. He talked of helping the canal get to Cumberland, so that it could bring coal to the railroad and carry rail freight to the west. Mentally exhausted, he offered his resignation that fall, but the board would not accept it.

Twelve months later, in the Annual Report, after a year in which Alexander Brown and John H. B. Latrobe had found themselves in the unlikely situation of appealing for canal funds in Baltimore while Thomas was doing the same thing in Annapolis, the B&O president said the true interest of the railroad, the city, and the state "now lies in the completion of the Chesapeake and Ohio Canal to Cumberland." From there, the railroad could cross the mountains to the Ohio River and together they would form a unique transportation system. "If at any future day," Thomas continued, "the state of the trade should justify it, freed from the condition that now fixes Harpers Ferry as the western limit on the Potomac, the road might be brought down the River, and the continuous Rail Road communication, as first designed, be finally accomplished."[60] Charles Fenton Mercer could not have said it better.

9

Men of Iron

A CANAL IS A SERIES OF ARTIFICIAL LAKES
separated by elevators, and when the Chesapeake and Ohio began, the principles of hydraulic engineering were well understood. The C&O Canal, basically an earthen ditch, had stone locks with wooden gates that allowed the boats to change levels. Its masonry aqueducts, quite as impressive as the railroad's bridges, carried the waterway over the tributaries of the Potomac. But the building methods were not in dispute and the materials were generally at hand.

A railroad is technologically much more sophisticated than a canal in terms of structure and equipment. Yet at the time the Baltimore and Ohio started, there were in America no established procedures for building or running a railroad. As the directors said later, everything was "new, crude, and doubtful." [1] Construction materials, especially iron, which was most essential, were often not available in sufficient quantity on a local basis. The B&O advertised in November 1827 for domestic iron and other materials needed to lay the track, but ended up importing British rails owing to the shortage of local supply, the company said. The quarrel that arose over the B&O's importation of foreign rails divided friends of the project in Baltimore as it followed a typically convoluted path through the company offices and the Congress.

The railroad's original call for materials included "rolled iron bars . . . 15 feet long," and they intended to obtain them from American producers, Philip E. Thomas asserted. [2] But before the first supplier could reply in writing, the B&O had begun to explore the possibility of importing rails free of duty. Congress in early 1828, in response to mounting pressure to protect domestic manufactures from cheaper British goods, was debating an increase of the duty on iron and other products. Rolled bar iron was to be subject to an advance from the existing duty of $30 a ton, but rails that were trimmed and punched in a certain way were to be classified as "manufactured iron" and would pay an ad valorem rate of only 25 percent. This favorable ruling for trimmed rails had been granted by the Treasury Department in December

1827, mainly in response to the petition of John Bolton, president of the Delaware and Hudson Canal Company, which incorporated a short railroad line. The B&O, the D&H, the South Carolina Railroad, and other early lines appealed to Congress to drop the duty altogether, and their memorials to this effect became part of the general debate that preceded the passage of the so-called Tariff of Abominations in May 1828.

Both the Delaware and Hudson and the B&O also had in mind buying British locomotives, and the D&H had already sent their engineer, Horatio Allen, on a three-month trip to England in January 1828, nine months before the three B&O engineers left on their mission. Allen's job was to investigate the British railways, supervise the production of iron for the fifteen-mile railroad portion of the Delaware and Hudson, and arrange for purchase of four locomotives, one of which turned out to be the Stourbridge Lion.

Thomas and Bolton, whose companies had remarkably similar experiences in their attempts to obtain domestic iron, collaborated on overcoming the political opposition to importing British rails. The ones the B&O eventually ordered were almost the same as those Allen specified for the D&H. The South Carolina Railroad also ordered the same type.

The three railroads made their applications to Congress in the spring of 1828. The B&O argued that in view of the number of lines projected in the United States and the amount of domestic iron produced, trying to buy enough rails locally would drive the price up and force the purchasers to go abroad. The Delaware and Hudson, which needed just 360 tons of rails, said they had received only two American offers to supply them and that the lower of the two bids was for more than $120 a ton—twice as much as the cost of importing British rails. Furthermore, one of the oldest U.S. iron manufacturers, which had no connection with the D&H, had advised them to buy in England because American mills did not have the capability of producing good rails.

William Patterson, the "royal merchant" and railroad director, had two sons in the iron business, Joseph W. and Edward. Patterson recommended that the B&O ask Congress for help. Maryland's Sam Smith, who presented their memorial in the Senate, and Baltimore representative John Barney, a son of naval hero Joshua Barney, were the point men for the ensuing campaign. Barney thought they might win if they could show "that the country cannot furnish the iron as fast as it may be required," and management set out to prove that this was the case.[3]

The B&O needed 15,000 tons of rails, or 1,500 tons a year, since under their charter they had ten years to build the railroad. It was impossible for the company to get them in America, Thomas told Senator Smith. Although there had been numerous offers to supply large amounts of wood and stone cheaply, "we received from the whole United States but two proposals for iron, and these were for a small quantity and at a price 100 per cent higher than the Liverpool and Manchester Railroad Company pay."[4] Thomas enclosed a letter from Joseph W. Patterson, who said there were several Maryland mills capable of rolling bar iron, including his own, located at Joppa on the Gunpowder River. He would "make the rails faster than the Baltimore and Ohio Company could . . . lay them down," Patterson maintained, if only he could get enough iron from the furnaces. Patterson added that there was an annual national shortage of 25–30,000 tons of iron.[5]

The B&O concentrated its early efforts on Smith's duty-free iron bill in the Senate. It passed in April 1828, but Thomas anticipated strenuous opposition in the House from domestic iron manufacturers and railroad opponents. He outlined the situation in letters to the local congressmen and incorporated many of his comments in a public statement he wrote for the Baltimore *Gazette*, in which he noted that of the bids the B&O had received, the lowest was for $100 a ton, whereas they could get English rails at $57, or $70 including the 25 percent ad valorem charge for importing them. He also cited Patterson's figures on a national shortage of iron and added what appeared to be a gratuitous challenge: "It is therefore obvious that the company must obtain their supplies from abroad, and the iron masters in this country, under existing circumstances, can have no interest whatever in the matter."[6]

The campaign soon gained momentum on both sides. The B&O had received two bids. The first, from Baltimore, was to supply 30 tons of rails a month for $106 a ton. The second, from out of town, was too vague to consider seriously. Thomas told Sam Smith that if they could not get what they wanted—cheap foreign iron—they would abandon the project altogether. It was the same tactic employed in Annapolis when the tax exemption was under attack. Thomas then called a special meeting of the directors to report a move in the Senate, backed by American manufacturers, to levy a straight duty of $37 a ton on imported rails—which would make them almost as expensive as domestic ones. At Smith's suggestion, he requested statements from local producers of the amount of iron they could supply and at what cost.

Within a day or two, a carefully selected list of Baltimore mills reported their inability to make the rails, except at prohibitive prices. The Pattersons repeated their earlier comments about the lack of sufficient raw material. Ex-congressman Isaac McKim, a B&O director who operated a rolling mill in Baltimore, declined to make a bid for the same reason. And Thomas Ellicott, a former board member and president of the Avalon Company, another rolling mill located in the Patapsco Valley just past Relay, told the railroad officers, "[I] cannot furnish the iron upon as cheap terms as it can be imported, even if the present duty be exacted upon it."[7]

Thomas took Joseph W. Patterson and Solomon Etting with him to Washington to present their case in Congress. The Baltimore *American* printed articles favoring the duty-free importation of iron that bore signs of Thomas's fertile powers of reasoning and clearly implied that if the railroad companies were forced to buy their rails at home, the lines would not be built. It was British iron or no American railroads. The Senate defeated the measure, 23–22.

While the action moved to the House, powerful local adversaries emerged. One was a Baltimore ironmaster whose political strategy was as devious as anything ever conceived by Thomas, "our serpentine president," as Benjamin H. Latrobe, Jr., once called him.[8] The other opponent was Hezekiah Niles.

The iron controversy put Niles in a predicament. He had been a consistent backer of the Baltimore and Ohio, but he was at the same time a dedicated protectionist. Although the B&O's intention to import rails would benefit internal improvements, one principle of Henry Clay's tripartite American system, it would violate the other two, a high tariff and the promotion of American manufactures. Niles was an unswerving advocate of the American system and in this instance he came out against the railroad. Niles's *Weekly Register*, which he had been publishing since 1811, had a wide readership, not just locally but nationally, including Presidents and other persons of influence. The Quaker editor was almost unique among American journalists of his day. His paper was nonpartisan, scrupulously fair and accurate, and editorially independent. It carried no advertising, nor were the news columns for sale. Therefore, what Niles had to say about his favorite topic, the tariff, carried a good deal of weight.[9]

Niles had the previous year published an address to the people of the United States on the American system in which he censured British colonialist economic policies and their American adherents and, by extension, all enemies of the tariff. Only 20 years had passed, he said, since "the last of the race died in Maryland, a foolish old man, who yet continued to ship his tobacco to a factor in England, as before the revolution, and to receive from thence supplies of the most trifling articles for his family use—such as tea, sugar, coffee, pepper, mustard, and all farming utensils and articles of clothing, packed up and forwarded as they had been at the period of the first settlement of the state."[10] It must therefore have been with particular anguish that Niles felt called on to reply to a veiled personal attack in William Gwynn's newspaper. The article concerned the B&O's application to Congress to import duty-free British rails. "No real friend to Baltimore" would oppose it, the *Gazette* said, referring to Niles.[11] Niles's reply was to reprint the whole of the article, noting that some people were less provincial than others in their thinking about important national measures, did not balance the propriety of an action against its effect on someone else's pocket, and believed that it might benefit the public interest in this case to spend $100 at home rather than $50 abroad.[12]

These were exactly the sentiments of Charles Ridgely of Hampton, the one Baltimore ironmaster with close connections to the company (an original incorporator) whose statement of his ability to supply rails the B&O had not solicited. Ridgely presented it anyway, but not to the railroad. He organized his campaign just as Thomas was discussing with John Barney the possibility of having someone from out of state introduce the duty-free iron bill in the House to help give it a national character, after which "You would then come in, in aid of the measure, with less charge of local or sectional interest."[13] Barney settled on George McDuffie of South Carolina, an arm-waving ranter whose harangues embodied the South's hostility to the tariff. McDuffie called the duty on iron a heavy, permanent, and universal tax that would benefit only the few hundred ironmasters in the United States.

Many of the ironmasters were concentrated in Philadelphia, the nation's center of iron production. In mid-May 1828, Pennsylvania Congressman James Buchanan, the future President, introduced their memorial opposing the B&O's bill to import British rails without paying duty. Although Charles Ridgely of Hampton was not named specifically, the well-to-do Baltimore landowner-ironmaster, a former governor of Maryland, was suspected of fomenting the opposition in Philadelphia through his business connections there.[14] The Pennsylvanians maintained that their state legislature would not have passed the B&O's charter if the company's advocates had not promised that the railroad would create a large market for their iron. Allowing the B&O to bring in cheap foreign rails not only would upset the balance of trade and depress domestic prices, it would spread "disaster" and "utter ruin" over the American iron establishment, they said.

Ridgely then announced through his agents that the original offer from Baltimore to supply the B&O with 360 tons of rails a year had been his and that the company itself had dictated the low figure, saying that it was all the iron they could use. The agents, Henry B. Chew and James Tucker (the latter was general manager of the Ridgely forges), told Congressman Buchanan in writing how they had visited the B&O offices over the Mechanics Bank in January 1828, at Ridgely's request. There, Thomas and Stephen H. Long had shown them a model of the rail, and told them "that only 30 tons of iron, per month, would be wanted for the first year." [15] The agents said that Ridgely had therefore limited his bid to that amount, although he would have liked to supply a much larger quantity. Indeed, they said, the mill could produce 3,380 tons of rolled bar iron a year, which was almost three times more than what the railroad had publicly stated it had to have.

Barney was worried. "I am grieved to find that the most serious and effectual opposition to our bill comes from the City of Baltimore," he wrote to Thomas. "This letter will militate seriously against us." [16] Ridgely was a member of the landed gentry and an ironmaster on the grand scale. His 12,000-acre Hampton plantation north of the city, larger and more splendid than any in the Baltimore area with the possible exception of Doughoregan Manor, the ancestral home of Charles Carroll of Carrollton, had vast farmlands in addition to the furnace and forge at Northampton. The Hampton mansion, where he lived in grand style, had fourteen bedrooms and there were extensive gardens. The estate had more than 300 slaves. Ridgely raised thoroughbred horses and entertained lavishly.[17] No doubt the profits from furnishing rails to the Baltimore and Ohio Railroad would have sustained this grand life indefinitely, but Ridgely's failed bid was his final gesture as a captain of industry.

While William Gwynn's *Gazette* went after the Philadelphia ironmasters— "gratuitous hostility . . . prompted by a spirit of sectional jealousy and rivalship," the newspaper said—Thomas rounded up affidavits from George Brown, Stephen H. Long, and others, denying that the conversations described by Ridgely's representatives ever took place. (Brown, as president of the Mechanics Bank, shared an office with the president of the Baltimore and Ohio.) Thomas even talked about going to court.

He sent Barney a statement from Henry Thompson, Ridgely's sales agent, asserting that the forges had produced only a little over 400 tons of iron annually for the past three years and had turned away orders for more. "I trust this will satisfy every one that the iron makers in this country, with 100 per cent usual profits, cannot, nor ought to expect to supply our road," Thomas said.[18] But when Barney tried to maneuver the duty-free iron bill to a floor vote in the House, he was ruled out of order and the bill failed.

Besides the furnace and foundry at Northampton, which were mostly shut down in 1827, Ridgely had another ironworks on Curtis Creek, south of Baltimore, and several forges. In 1827, his various facilities processed about 1,400 tons of pig iron. If that amount of raw material could have been converted entirely into rails, Ridgely very well might have been capable of supplying the necessary quantity to the Baltimore and Ohio. Whether or not he was telling the truth about the forced bid is uncertain. Certainly the railroad was disingenuous. Some of the B&O's most powerful backers expected to import British iron before bids for the domestic product were even called for. In February 1827, Alexander Brown sent a letter to the Liverpool office in which he mentioned railroads for the first time and said, "An application will no doubt be made to Congress to permit Iron (for this purpose exclusively) to be imported free of duty, whether it's granted or not there can be no doubt that large quantities will be imported."[19] William and James Brown and Co. shipped, and the Alex. Brown and Sons organization garnered lucrative commissions on, nearly all the rails ordered by the B&O, the Delaware and Hudson, the South Carolina Railroad, and other pioneering American lines.

After the excitement died down, the rail situation returned to the status quo. Under the Tariff of Abominations that John Quincy Adams signed in May 1828, the duty on imported bar iron was raised to $37 a ton, but imported rails were specifically exempted, though they were still subject to the 25 percent ad valorem charge.[20] According to one estimate, the difference was worth over $400,000 to the railroad.

In the fall of 1828, Thomas wrote William and James Brown and Co., Liverpool, with the B&O's initial order for "wrought iron plate rails" and the necessary fittings, to be designated by Knight and McNeill, who, with Whistler, were just arriving in England. Fifty tons were to be shipped immediately and another 450 tons in lots over the next year "as fast as [they] can be procured."[21] At the end of 1828, the directors briefly entertained the idea of again asking Congress for permission to import the rails without paying duty, but after talking with members of both houses, thought better of it and requested a stock subscription instead.

The first British rails arrived in Baltimore in June 1829. They were half an inch thick, two and a quarter inches wide, and fifteen feet long. The iron was slightly rounded on top, holes had been punched every eighteen inches, and the ends were cut to fit together in a special joint. Thomas, anticipating an attempt to impose the bar iron duty, again sought the help of John Bolton of the Delaware and Hudson, who had already brought in foreign rails. Bolton forwarded his correspondence with the Treasury Department showing that they were properly classified as manufactured iron. "The documents have at once removed all difficulties and our iron is admitted to entry at an ad valorum [*sic*] duty of 25 p cent," Thomas reported back.[22]

By September 1829, the B&O had imported all 500 tons of rails at $58 a ton. Alex. Brown and Sons provided the financing, but since the cost of construction had depleted the railroad's cash reserves, Thomas asked Alexander Brown if he could defer payment "until the funds of the company shall be more flush."[23] Later that year, the railroad paid back the money.

A few months later, Thomas requested the Brown office in Liverpool to ship ten tons of "patent rails precisely such as are used in laying the Liverpool and Manchester Rail Road."[24] He also ordered the necessary fixtures for these—cast-iron spikes, chairs to hold the ends of the rails, and wedges to keep the rail ends tight—and twelve sets of crossings and switches for turnouts. The price came to almost $3,000. These patent rails were edge rails rather than flat rails, similar in section to those used today. The B&O did not adopt them, however, because, as Jonathan Knight made clear in his engineering report that year, they required too much iron, about 31 tons per mile. The railroad could lay a mile of track with just 22 tons of the wrought-iron plate rails it was importing, but the ten tons of patent rails would have laid only about a third of a mile of track. The B&O evidently used the patent rails for sidings.

In April 1830, Thomas ordered 500 more tons of the flat rails through the Brown organization. He complained that raised ridges around the holes in the last shipment, probably caused by the punching operation, produced "constant jolting in the carriages," and asked that the defect be remedied. Thomas enclosed an illustration showing how the ends of the new rails were to be cut diagonally to fit together. He ordered one-eighth-inch-thick wrought-iron plates that would be placed under the joints, like chairs, to hold the ends of the rails and keep them from digging into the supports. That fall, Jonathan Knight told him that the company did not have enough iron to lay the double track to Ellicotts Mills and the single track from there to Parrs Spring Ridge and would need 1,600 additional tons the following year. In the fall of 1831, Thomas ordered 700 more tons of rails and 25,000 wrought-iron plates.

The Baltimore and Ohio tried several methods of track laying based mainly on English practice, but in the end, as with locomotives, they set their own course. Iron being expensive and other materials relatively cheap in the United States, the B&O and other early lines decided on wooden or stone rails (stringers), topped with thin metal strips. The B&O engineers at first preferred stone rails plated with iron, believing these would be more stable and permanent. Iron-plated wooden rails, laid on sleepers (ties), were to be used only temporarily—for example, on embankments until the dirt settled—after which they could be replaced with stone. Stephen H. Long recommended stone rails after seeing them on the Quincy Railroad in Massachusetts, where they had been substituted for the wooden ones first laid down.[25]

The first rails the B&O laid in October 1829 were wood and iron, set at a gauge of four feet, six inches. The rails went from Pratt Street about a mile and a half to the Carrollton Viaduct. George W. Whistler supervised the construction, "from day light till dark—having the constant benefit of the opinions and suggestions of all the gentlemen of leisure in the town."[26] Wendel Bollman, the B&O's future master of road, was a fifteen-year-old carpenter when he helped Whistler lay this track. Another section of wood and iron rails ran for roughly the same distance beyond the Patterson Viaduct over the Patapsco River. It was used to haul construction materials for the bridge. A third stretch was put in at Ellicotts Mills to aid in the building of the Oliver Viaduct.

In the spring of 1830, the company decided to extend the first track from the Carrollton Viaduct to Ellicotts Mills. For seven and a half miles, roughly to Relay, it would rest on wooden sleepers and from there, for the remaining five and a half miles, on stone blocks. The directors offered $100 to the contractor who could build the best section of railway within the specified time. The First Division, which ran approximately from the viaduct to the mills, was split up into 26 half-mile sections.

At the same time, they rebuilt the original one and a half miles of track for wheels with inside flanges. When these rails were first laid in the fall of 1829, the iron was put on the outside edges of the wooden stringers because the flanges were then on the outside of the wheels, an arrangement that suited the Winans cars. But putting the flanges inside, as the British did, made it easier to cone the wheels, that is, to bevel the area where the tire meets the flange so that the wheels turned better through curves. In January 1830, after correspondence with William Brown in England, Knight decided it was best after all "not to depart from the English practice in this respect."[27]

At the end of that month, Alexander Brown informed his son, "It has been determined by Mr. Knight, who is now our chief engineer, that our road will be calculated for inside flanges and the same breadth of the L'pool and Manchester."[28] To give the flanges extra play, Knight at first established the new gauge of the Baltimore and Ohio at four feet, nine and a half inches, but at least by the time the Washington Branch was under construction four years later, the B&O had adopted George Stephenson's gauge of four feet, eight and a half inches, which he had specified for the Liverpool and Manchester Railway. This eventually became the universal standard.

A few days before the B&O opened to the general public, on May 24, 1830, with service to Ellicotts Mills, the directors authorized a second track, also with wooden rails and sleepers. It would extend to where the line crossed the Washington Turnpike before Relay, at a place called Vinegar Hill, about six and a half miles from the Carrollton Viaduct. The rest of that track was to be laid on stone sills. In July, they gave John McCartney the contract and hired two more contractors, William Hinks and Smith & Temperly, to lay a stone track on the twelve-mile Second Division, which ran from Ellicotts Mills to the forks of the Patapsco River. These men were reluctant to sign, "alleging that more work is required than they expected."[29] The company made the contract terms less stringent, but it was not an auspicious beginning. They let contracts for the graduation and masonry on the Third Division, extending seventeen miles from the Forks of Patapsco to Parrs Spring Ridge, thus keeping one group of contractors out in front of those laying the rails, just as the engineers had preceded the first construction crews.

On July 20, 1830, Knight sent up the line to Ellicotts Mills a young man, 24, with a note in plain language, to John D. Steel (or Steele), an assistant engineer: "I have appointed the bearer, Benj. H. Latrobe, an assistant and have instructed him, for the present, to cooperate with thee on the 2nd Division. Thee will find him a pleasant, agreeable and useful companion. Thee will most freely explain to him everything within thy knowledge in relation to the important business in which thou art engaged."[30] So began the Baltimore and Ohio Railroad career of the man who superintended the track laying beyond Ellicotts Mills that fall and eventually replaced Knight as chief engineer.

The nature of the railroad changed as it was built. Between Baltimore and Relay, roughly, the structure of the two tracks was wooden. In the Patapsco Valley, stone was available for construction and no large embankments were planned. Therefore, from about Relay to Ellicotts Mills one track consisted of wooden rails laid on stone blocks and the other of stone rails. Once past the mills, it was intended to construct both tracks entirely of stone. In all cases, iron rails formed the running surface.

One of the start-up contractors was John Ready, a carpenter who had headed the team laying the first rails for Whistler. He then made a proposal of his own, which Jonathan Knight liked. "His price is $3.50 per perch in length of the road for laying down a single track, exclusive of horse path," Knight told Thomas. "He will do the necessary digging and place the stone under the bearings of the sleepers, prepare and lay the sleepers, make the keys, lay the string pieces, and put on the iron rails, the materials being found him on the ground."[31] In other words, Ready would lay a wooden track, the railroad supplying him with wood, broken stone, and iron rails and fixtures. A perch, in linear measure, is sixteen and a half feet, the same as a pole or rod, and so the contractor's price was $1,120 per mile.

Ready later won one of the track-laying awards. This is the work that the contractor and his men were required to perform for their money. First, along the graded right-of-way, they dug two rows of holes, about one cubic foot in size and roughly five feet between the rows. They connected the holes across the line of road with shallow trenches and filled the excavation with small pieces of stone—no larger than could pass through a two-inch ring—which they either compacted with a roller or rammed down with a huge wooden block with four handles, requiring as many men to lift it. After that, they laid down cedar or oak sleepers, roughly the size of modern railroad ties, at four-foot intervals on the transverse trenches, carefully adjusting them with a spirit level. The sleepers were deeply notched at the ends to hold the rails, the notches sitting directly over the pits filled with broken stone. They were also cut down in the center for the horsepath.

The stringers were of yellow pine, six inches square and anywhere from 12 to 40 feet long—substantial timbers. These were placed in the notches and secured with foot-long wooden wedges driven in on the inside with mauls. The earth was removed from beneath the stringers to prevent rot and the joints rested on sleepers.

The iron rails, which were attached next, were set in a little from the inside edges of the wooden stringers and their ends spiked down through the wrought-iron plates. Finally, the projecting wood was chamfered off with an adze so that it would not come in contact with the wheel flanges. The space between the rails was filled in with dirt and compacted by the horses' hooves before being covered with gravel to form the horsepath. On the large embankments, such as Gadsby's Run, longitudinal timbers rather than broken stone were placed under the sleepers. This helped to preserve the level of the rails and made it easier to raise the tracks again after the embankment had settled. One track dropped a total of four feet over a six-month period.

On the section built with stone blocks, two pieces of granite took the place of one sleeper. The blocks were about twelve by eighteen inches and a foot thick, and they weighed an average 200 pounds each. To help support them and keep them from sinking too far, the pits of broken stone were made larger than those for the wooden sleepers and special care was taken in leveling.

On the Liverpool and Manchester Railway, where the system of large stone blocks was used, George Stephenson had devised a method to settle them using a five-foot-high wooden tripod and a 20-foot pole. With the lever and a chain, one man could jerk the stone a foot or so in the air and drop it while his partner threw sand or fine gravel underneath it until it was firmly seated. Between Relay and Ellicotts Mills, the stones may have been placed in this manner, or else simply pried up with shovels while the material was shoved underneath and then pounded back down with mauls or the wooden ram.

A couple of holes, several inches deep and a half-inch or so in diameter, had to be drilled in each block so that wooden plugs could be inserted in them to hold the spikes. This would be done by two or three men, one holding and turning a long chisel-point or star drill called a jumper and the others swinging three-to-five-pound iron hammers known as stone hammers. A blacksmith followed the track crews with a portable forge to sharpen the drills.

The wooden stringer was attached to each stone block with two cast-iron "knees," as Knight called them, one on each side. These were pieces of angle iron with holes, like a shelf bracket, spiked into the stringer and the wooden plugs in the stone blocks. Finally, the iron rails were put on and the track finished off as before.

It was slow, painstaking work, but the stone rails were worse. "The heavier the stone sills are, the better," Knight said, but handling them was a very difficult job for the workmen. The stones ranged from twelve to eighteen inches on a side and from three to 20 feet in length. The smallest weighed less than 500 pounds; the largest were well over two tons. These granite monoliths had to be split out at the quarries near Ellicotts Mills, hauled to the construction site by wagon, maneuvered with the primitive cranes onto stone boats (crude sledges made of boards nailed to heavy timbers), dragged by oxen or horses to the end of the rail line, and manhandled into place. They were laid flat, rather than on edge, in longitudinal trenches half-filled with broken stone and gravel, since, as Knight had proved by mathematical formula, if they were laid on edge in curves they would tend to overturn under the centrifugal force of the trains. The sills were then leveled with the heavy wooden rammer, several inches of the top surface were dressed smooth to receive the rails, and the ends squared to make tight joints. Holes were drilled and plugged every eighteen inches so that the rails could be spiked down. The inside edges of the stone sills were chamfered, as the wooden stringers had been.

All this had to be done "in a correct, substantial, and workmanlike manner."

The contractors, who had to submit personal recommendations in writing with their proposals, received partial payments as the work progressed, but the company withheld the final 25 percent until the contract was satisfactorily completed.[32]

John McCartney's contract to lay stone rails differed from John Ready's in that McCartney was to supply all the material except the iron and was also to keep the line in good order for one year after it was finished. His price was accordingly about three times as high, $10.75 per perch. Shortly after McCartney started work in July 1830, Hezekiah Niles visited the site, near Vinegar Hill, and saw that the granite sills were "deposited along the greater part of the track, and the parties of workmen are engaged at different points in the various operations of dressing, laying and drilling, and affixing the iron."[33]

Another visitor that year, Englishman James Boardman, studied the living conditions of the laborers:

> I was happy to observe, on looking into their temporary wooden cabins, which are erected at different stations on the road, that, although there appeared a good deal of wild disorder in the domestic arrangements, and the total absence of what the English cottager would term comfort, there was no lack of the means to live; which was the more important as philoprogenitiveness seemed the order of the day.
>
> Every hovel had its swarm of children, its barrel of superfine flour, flitch of bacon, and stone bottle of the "creature," and the interstices were filled up with pigs and poultry.[34]

Boardman noted that one of these collections of windowless huts, with their flour-barrel chimneys, was grandly called Dublin.

These were the Irish. They were witty and violent, garrulous drinkers, vicious fighters, who built turnpikes, canals, and railroads across half a continent. Their reward was 50 cents a day, with a few glasses of whiskey and a shanty to lie down in. They battled regularly over everything—politics, religion, and jobs, or for the hell of it. The magnificent stone structures that are their monuments are barely visible nowadays among the shopping malls and superhighways, yet the fury of their passage will outlast even these. They were genuine wild men.

Irish immigration to America peaked after the potato famine of the late 1840's, but there had been other famines and upheavals in Ireland, each followed by an exodus. The newspaper stories of the late 1820's repeated a familiar threnody of excess population, "bad government," expatriate landlords, displaced tenants, political and religious violence, ignorance, poverty, disease. The Irish took their troubles and not much else aboard the "coffin ships" that brought them to Boston, New York, Philadelphia, and Baltimore. Two-thirds of a million Irishmen came to America in the 1830's and two-thirds of them were laborers. Many were recruited by the companies that built the National Road and the Erie Canal, and many more by the railroads. There was an Irish Emigrant Association in Baltimore before 1818, and there were other Vinegar Hills in Ohio and Illinois, the last one named for a famous site in County Wexford, Ireland. (Vinegar was also used to disinfect the ships.)

The Irish were highly respected as workmen, literally "the cutting edge of the frontier," as one historian put it,[35] but they brought with them their feuds and secret societies and a tradition of terrorizing their rivals for jobs. The progress of most of the great public works is marked by a series of battles between the Fardowns from Ulster and the Corkonians from the south, or between the Connaught men and the Longfords, rivals from the Irish midlands. When the Irish were not fighting among themselves, they took on the Negroes, their major competitors in the labor market, who fully reciprocated their hatred and contempt, or the Germans, also traditional opponents. Some of their riots were really unorganized strikes over nonpayment of wages and bad working conditions.

The Irish continued the outbreaks of labor violence that began in the 1700's when some 50,000 ex-convicts were shipped from England to America to be sold as servants, the bulk of them arriving in Virginia and Maryland, sometimes at the rate of 700 a year.[36] They constituted James Rumsey's work force that terrified the natives around the Great Falls of the Potomac where they were digging a canal. Even when the labor force was not made up of ex-convicts, it was often unruly, particularly in remote areas. As the internal improvements program accelerated and laborers were in demand, they became all the more restive. Canvass White, the engineer at Mauch Chunk, Pennsylvania, reported that his workmen were not responsive to authority, were ready to march on the slightest provocation, and were of a "migratory disposition."[37]

The Chesapeake and Ohio Canal in 1829, less well capitalized than the B&O Railroad and greatly in need of cheap labor, placed advertisements in British, German, and Dutch newspapers offering "Meat three times a day, a plenty of bread and vegetable, with a reasonable allowance of liquor and eight, ten, or twelve dollars a month for wages."[38] Their agent in Great Britain, who offered free passage in exchange for three- or four-month indentures, signed up several hundred English and Irish workers, including miners, masons, blacksmiths, and carpenters.

The voyage was horrible, the working conditions when they arrived almost as bad. The overseer of one ship referred to his passengers as "clowns," "brutes," and "frauds," and it was a rare contractor who lived up to the promises made in the ads. There was fever on the river and disorders among the workers. Many grew sick, others absconded. Their contracts proved unenforceable, even though the fugitive slave and servant laws were invoked.

The ships docked at Alexandria or Georgetown to prevent the men being lured to the railroad, but some of them ended up there anyway. In October 1829, a group of indentured workmen was arrested in Baltimore. A mob gathered and helped them escape. That month another ship arrived in the Potomac with almost 200 more "of the plagues." After that, the experiment was stopped. Charles Fenton Mercer of the C&O Canal attributed its failure in part to "the vicinity of other public works, offering higher wages." In 1829, and again in 1830, the C&O considered buying slaves to work on the canal, but rejected the idea.[39]

The Baltimore and Ohio adopted its usual supercilious tone. Thomas assured Walter Smith, a C&O official, that they would return any indentured canal employees discovered working on the railroad: "This company has not at any period found the smallest difficulty in obtaining as many labourers as was desired and that at the present there are many more offering than we can employ."[40] The reason was simple enough: better pay. Wages for canal laborers in 1829 averaged $10 a month, whereas the B&O paid $12 to $14. And although Thomas was opposed to the Chesapeake and Ohio bringing in slaves from Virginia to work on the canal, he found nothing wrong about putting Maryland slaves to work on the B&O alongside the Irish and the Germans.[41]

In the summer of 1829, a couple of B&O contractors went along the canal line passing out handbills offering higher wages in Baltimore. Their counterparts on the C&O beat one and threw the other into the Potomac, not once but several times. But when a canal contractor retaliated by coming to Baltimore and offering railroad workers $2 a month more than they were earning, he was "neither ducked nor drubbed," sniffed the *Gazette*.[42] Nor did any workers leave the railroad line.

Still, the B&O had plenty of problems with its own workforce during these years. They began when John Salmon, a contractor on the City Division, from Pratt Street to the Carrollton Viaduct, failed to pay his workmen, causing "much discontent and confusion." The company made good half of their claims against Salmon, put the laborers on the payroll for a few days, and prevented a riot. In August 1829, Niles reported a man killed and several wounded "in a broil." A contractor, not Salmon, was severely beaten and his dwelling demolished. The *American* a few days later dismissed the reports as exaggerated. No one was murdered and the problem was due to "quarrels, wholly among the workmen, generally when after the labours of the day, they have met at taverns—or grog shops." Niles retracted the story, saying he had based it on another paper's hasty and inaccurate account.[43] There were those as well as a steady stream of anti-Irish stories from such sheets as the Maryland *Gazette*, a weekly published in Annapolis: "Paddy's Ride on the Railway," or "Shillelah Fight in Ireland."

The Irish were exploited at every turn. A self-appointed agent named Nathaniel G. Drake set himself up in Boston at the end of 1829 to provide laborers to the B&O. He charged 30 or 40 Irish immigrants $1 or $2 each, plus their passage, handed out certificates of employment and sent them on to Baltimore, where some may have found jobs on the railroad. The next 100 or 200 were not so lucky. Drake actually induced them to sell their pickaxes and other tools to pay their travel expenses and then absconded with the money. It was as cruel a fraud as any they had ever heard of, said the Baltimore *Gazette*: "The effects of this deceit upon these poor laborers will be almost ruinous, and for the perpetrator of it, if detected, scarcely any punishment would be too severe."[44]

But they gave as good as they got. Early in 1830, taking advantage of the legislature's repeal of a law making it illegal to cut down and carry off wood, the cart men abandoned the railroad and attacked the forests. "I am told they have not left one tree standing," on a particular 80-acre tract, Thomas told Upton S. Heath in Annapolis, to whom he appealed for legislative intervention. Another landowner informed Thomas "that he had 8 or 10 men stationed through his woods to protect the timber and that one of them . . . was nearly murdered by some of these Banditti."

Moreover, Thomas said: "About 150 of these people broke off from work upon the 10th section of the rail road near to Elkridge Landing and have fallen upon the lands of Charles Warfield from which they will soon clear all the wood. When ordered off they bid defiance and when sued they go to jail and clear out leaving the prosecutor to pay the cost."[45]

Warfield had, it seems, suffered a long series of abuses at the hands of the Baltimore and Ohio Railroad. His land was located in the low-lying valley of Gadsby's Run, a small tributary of the Patapsco between the Deep Cut and the railroad's second crossing of the Washington Turnpike, and Warfield could not understand why the line was crossing the Washington Turnpike at all when it was supposed to go west. Especially he did not like what it did to his property. The railroad went straight through it, cutting the lane from his house to the turnpike almost in half and blocking his view of his farm with an embankment 60 feet high.

In a pamphlet that he apparently wrote in desperation, Warfield listed his grievances: the B&O's agents, illegally and without proper notice, had trespassed on his cornfields, put up shanties for their laborers, and then could not even tell him how much of his land they wanted for the line. Wever answered that he had no control over the route, which was laid out by the board of engineers, and moved on. On such occasions, the superintendent of construction found the board of engineers useful. The contractors listened and made promises but did nothing. Warfield said some proprietors might welcome the B&O, but he did not. He wanted fair compensation for his losses and mentioned a figure of $5,000. The company at that point was especially anxious to avoid paying damages because the right-of-way had initially been given to them.

Under the circumstances, Warfield showed remarkable restraint. He was not trying to interfere with anyone's livelihood, he maintained, "especially a poor man, be him an Irishman or otherwise," but his own rights were being violated. The railroad might cut down his fruit trees and his timber, occupy his buildings, improperly use his stone (Warfield's lane and millrace, as well as Gadsby's Run, all had to be bridged under the embankment), consume his hay and grain, and so ruin his plantation that he might be disposed to sell it for half its value and he would still protest: "For the present, I purpose to have as little intercourse as possible with these people."[46]

Thomas failed to mollify him and finally contractor John Gray decided to give it a try. Gray was "a sharp little Irishman" who had named the nearby cluster of workmen's shanties Vinegar Hill. Hearing that Warfield had written another pamphlet containing some odd religious theories, Gray got hold of a copy, read it through, and called on the author for an exegesis. One of the things he wanted to know was "whether a part of the writer's body was, in fact, as stated in the work, of the color of a grain of new wheat." A bottle or two may have appeared about that time and Gray so ingratiated himself with the owner that he gave the contractor permission to do what he wanted with the land. However, this did not stop Warfield from later claiming $5,500 in damages against the railroad for their excavations, injury to his crops, and destruction of his fruit trees.[47]

But not even the Irish could charm the stones into place. The granite sills proved almost impossible to put down.[48] In the fall of 1830, the contractors began complaining that they could not lay the rails for the prices agreed on. It was a repetition of the previous year when the stone viaducts, the "indurated clay" at the Deep Cut, and the heavy embankment at Gadsby's Run proved more than they bargained for and led to numerous failures.

Knight had been gone all that spring, surveying the joint route for the railroad and canal on the Potomac River. The track laying was mainly supervised by James P. Stabler, his principal assistant, a Quaker relative of Thomas's. Knight returned in July. In September 1830, he, Stabler, and Thomas talked it over and agreed to give the contractors more money. There was trouble all along the line. McCartney was having difficulty laying the stone rails on the First Division, William Hinks had similar problems on the Second, and even the men excavating in soft ground for the graduation and masonry on the Third were not moving ahead.

McCartney was upset because the contractors laying the rails on the Second Division had negotiated a better arrangement than he had. Only one-fifth of their total price was withheld until completion whereas he was under the one-fourth provision. Knight put him on the same footing as the others. Still, Knight told Thomas: "the price is full low." McCartney also thought that William Pollock, another of Knight's assistants, was underestimating the stone sills McCartney had quarried, a major component of his contract payments. Later in the fall, the directors found that retaining 20 percent of the contract price was still too much of a burden and gave McCartney and Hinks each an extra $1,000.

At the end of January 1831, McCartney, one of the company's most consistent contractors, was just completing his six and a half miles of stone rails to Ellicotts Mills. Hinks was going nowhere from there, so the directors canceled his contract and gave it to Enoch Sweat and Co. The price was now $11.75 per rod.

The stone rails were proving a real problem: difficult to quarry, time consuming and expensive to haul to the site, and devilish to deal with. With one stroke, a workman could undo the labor of several days by driving a spike too hard into one of the locust plugs in the stone and splitting it. The company still thought it was using the right material: "It is believed that no Rail way extant will compare in point of permanency with the *Granite and Iron way*, now being laid," Knight told the stockholders.[49] "The continuous stone rail is believed to be the best known, and superior to the iron rail, in use in Europe," Thomas assured Maryland legislators in early 1831.[50] Stabler, however, said he was disappointed at the slow progress: between Baltimore and Ellicotts Mills, it had taken one month to lay ten miles of wooden rails and six months to lay six miles of stone track.[51] Wever decided it was time to impose a ban on whiskey. He had forbidden the use of "ardent spirits" in the contracts let in July 1830. That fall, the ban became official along the entire line. Wever made it a moral crusade and both he and Knight fired men for drinking on the job. Generally, however, prohibition worked about as well as it did on the canal. There were worse riots than ever because there were always taverns nearby.

These circumstances combined to produce the affair at Sykes's Mill (Sykesville, Maryland) in June 1831. It involved Irish laborers, plenty of whiskey, and no pay for hard work, a volatile mixture every bit as explosive as the black powder used to bring down the cliffs and one that the railroad directors, after the initial experience, came to regard with awe and respect.

The situation was, as usual, complicated. In late September 1830, the B&O had given Truxton Lyon, a Pennsylvanian, the contract to lay the first track of stone rails on the entire Third Division, which extended seventeen miles from the Forks of Patapsco to Parrs Spring Ridge. He was to be finished by July 1, 1831. In hindsight, the engineers felt they should have given the work to several contractors, but they thought at the time that one man might be able to work the quarries more efficiently. Lyon had come highly recommended and had started work that winter with enthusiasm.

In the spring, some workmen complained about him to Jacob Small, Jr. Small was an architect who had just finished a term as mayor of Baltimore and been hired as the B&O's superintendent of construction. (After that Wever became superintendent of graduation and masonry.) Small continued to receive bad reports about Lyon. At the same time, William Pollock, the resident engineer, was submitting returns showing that the contractor was working harder than ever and had almost quarried enough stone sills to complete the whole track. Small said the only reason Lyon was not dismissed was because of Pollock's estimates. It didn't seem fair to take the contract away from him when he had finished the toughest part of the job.

On June 20, 1831, a Monday, Lyon's workmen walked off the job, claiming he owed them money. They threatened to destroy the railroad if they were not paid. Stabler was there and said he would look into it. He returned to Baltimore, checked Lyon's account, and again, based on Pollock's figures, estimated that the company still owed him about $2,000. John H. B. Latrobe went out to the Third Division the same day and promised the workmen there that $2,000 would be distributed among them.

The following day, Stabler, back on the line, discovered that Lyon, who had decamped, instead of owing the laborers and boardinghouse keepers $3,000, as he claimed, owed them three times as much. Furthermore, he found that the number of stone sills Lyon had quarried was only a little over half the amount Pollock had given him credit for. In other words, far from owing Lyon $2,000, the company had actually overpaid him. Management found no collusion between the contractor and the resident engineer, although "he certainly suffered himself to be deceived or imposed upon," Small noted. It is hard to see why the railroad officials retained such faith in Pollock. McCartney had already told them he could not count.

A week went by, during which there were further audits in Baltimore and an uneasy truce out on the line. Small made a lengthy presentation to Thomas showing that "all the contractors who have laid stone rails . . . have lost by their contracts." John McCartney was out $3,000; William Hinks, the same amount; David Smith and Co. (of Smith & Temperly), $4,000. Small said stone rails could not be laid at the contract prices; $14 a rod was about right. If they recomputed Lyon's work using the revised figure, they would again owe him $2,000 and could pay the men that much.[52]

But Truxton Lyon, always a step ahead, had returned to Sykes's Mill in the meantime and had told his workmen that the railroad really owed him $9,000—the exact amount of his debts. And so when Stabler and Mr. Shriver, the new resident engineer, started back on June 28, after the directors had approved the $2,000 payment, they were already several days late and several thousand dollars short. The next day, they could induce only two of the 100 men to accept their reduced $20 "dividends." The few others who might have gone along were threatened with violence. The rest marched past them and began tearing up the sills and culverts. Then, having undone a good day's work, the Irish returned to their shebeens and shanties to await developments. The hapless Stabler arrived back in Baltimore early in the afternoon and swore out a warrant. The sheriff, accompanied by George Patterson, the only man he could find for a posse, began the 25-mile trip to the Forks of Patapsco. The next morning, June 30, they arrived to find real trouble:

> They had not proceeded very far down the road when they were met by the workmen to the number of 135 marching with their stone hammers and other tools, with a handkerchief on a pole for a flag, under the command of one of their number, named Hugh Reily, to whom they appeared to pay implicit obedience. One of them seized the reins of the Sheriff's horse and refused to let him proceed, and all were totally regardless of his authority, and injunctions.[53]

The sheriff sent an express message from Sykes's Mill to Baltimore calling out the militia. At nine o'clock that evening, 100 members of the Light Brigade slogged in a driving rain through streets ankle-deep with water to muster at Mt. Clare. They left an hour later and rode through the night in the railroad cars nearly to the Forks of Patapsco where the usable track ended at the construction site. There they got out and marched seven miles up the Third Division until they reached Sykes's Mill, around daylight. They surprised the rioters asleep in the shanties, arrested 50 including Reily, and brought them back to Baltimore. The next day they arrested eighteen more and the riot was broken.

The damage was substantial. From the Forks of Patapsco to Sykes's Mill, on eighteen sections, extending for roughly nine miles, the stone sills had been broken, both on the line and in the quarries, the iron torn off, the culverts defaced, and the wooden rails that were to be laid on the embankments, burned. The rioters had been planning to blow up the new stone bridge over the west branch of the Patapsco River below Sykesville, near what is now the Henryton Tunnel, on the day they were arrested. The damages totaled $6,000. Most of the laborers except the ringleaders were shortly released from jail and returned to work, the company having in the interim sent out provisions for their wives and children. Three weeks after the riot, in a letter printed in the *American*, Lyon claimed it had all been a mistake—the company's.[54]

Hardly a month later, in mid-August 1831, the Irish and the Negroes squared off for a two-day battle near New Market where they were at work on the railroad's Fourth Division. Twenty ringleaders were arrested and 400 Irishmen massed to release them, threatening the town. They were dissuaded by Wever and John McElroy, a Catholic priest, and by the timely arrival of a contingent of militia from Frederick.

These men, too, went back to work the next day, after the priest made bail for the prisoners. The railroad gave Father McElroy $100 for the charity of his choice and Knight issued elaborate instructions to Small as to how the contractors were to lay the stone sills and how the resident engineers were to count them.

Lyon's old contract, including the ruined track, was turned over to John Littlejohn. By September 1831, he had laid three miles of stone rails and had lost nearly $3,000. It was the same up and down the line. Enoch Sweat was digging trenches through solid rock on the Second Division and losing more money. John Gray was in trouble on the Fourth. The price for laying the granite sills was now up to $15 a rod. "All confidence seems to be destroyed," Stabler reported.[55]

So, at last, the company decided to lay the rest of the track with wooden rails. The reason given was the lack of suitable stone. Altogether, only 34 or so miles of stone rails were laid: six and a half miles of a single track from near Relay to Ellicotts Mills by John McCartney, close to 22 miles of double track between there and the Forks of Patapsco by Smith & Temperly and Enoch Sweat & Co., and five and a half more miles between the Forks and Sykes's Mill by John Littlejohn.

These 34 miles were costly in many ways. John Gray, the clever little Irish contractor who had pacified Charles Warfield, ruined his health. William Smith, of Smith & Temperly, lost his life on the work, and David Smith, his partner, went to prison for not paying his debts. The trains passed on as did those whose names went unrecorded. In time, even the iron rails disappeared and only the stones remained.[56]

10

City Extension, Frederick Branch

THE BALTIMORE AND OHIO'S CONFLICT
with the Chesapeake and Ohio Canal from 1828 to 1833 effectively barred the railroad from the Potomac River, and during those years the company concentrated on extending the tracks closer to home, east through the city streets to tidewater, west to Frederick and the Point of Rocks, and south to Washington.

All these projects were controversial, none more so than the first. Few things stimulated the competitive jealousies of Baltimore's merchants, stirred up political hostilities among its ward chieftains, or upset the hackers and draymen quite as much as the proposal to bring the railroad into the city. The argument was a continuation of the old one over where the B&O was to begin and whether the extension into town should serve the east side or the west side. James Carroll eagerly returned to the struggle. After he died, his son, heir, and namesake, a city councilman, carried on in the same combative spirit.

The relationship between James Carroll and the Baltimore and Ohio Railroad can be considered as a prototypical Baltimore land deal, but one that went sour. It was one of the first and most significant in terms of the city's development. Much of Baltimore's present urban geography can be traced to this early railroad decision. For Carroll the romance ended quickly once the company in the spring of 1828 accepted his offer of land for a depot on his 1,000-acre manor, but declined his request to start the railroad at tidewater on Carroll's Point, another part of his property.

Carroll had inherited Mount Clare from his uncle, Charles Carroll, Barrister.[1] He was 67 when the railroad began, a widower who lived alone in the Georgian-Palladian villa that sat atop a small hill overlooking wheat fields and orchards and served as a landmark to ships sailing up the Patapsco River. The estate also had racing stables, flour mills, and the remains of the family shipyard at Carroll's Point at tidewater a mile away across sloping pastures. Carroll had plans for the industrial development of Mount Clare and hoped the railroad would benefit his potential port facilities on the Patapsco's Middle Branch. When it did not, Carroll became an enemy of the B&O. He quarreled belligerently and often with the B&O engineers and sporadically harassed the company with pseudonymous pamphlets and newspaper articles concerning its chosen route.

In the fall of 1830, two and a half years after his first offer to convey a right-of-way and land for a depot, Carroll began to have second thoughts. The railroad by that time had been brought into the city only as far as Pratt Street, at the corner of his estate. It is fairly clear, reading between the lines, that Carroll still hoped to have the line go to Carroll's Point on the Middle Branch; when the B&O still refused, he tried to renege on the agreement, but the company had it in writing and held him to it, maintaining that his early letters were legally binding. Carroll reluctantly surrendered the property in December 1830. Thereafter, he opposed any route for the railroad except his own.

The company's actions in the affair were hardly magnanimous. Thomas kept the Baltimore and Ohio Railroad's first major land deal a secret even from the directors, officially anyway, until eighteen months after the fact. He censored the Board of Engineers' report on which the decision to extend the railroad into the city was based by removing the section that mentioned Carroll's donation of property. Stephen H. Long, who favored the Carroll's Point route, responded that for what they spent to make Mount Clare usable, they could have bought their own land.[2]

Thomas was, it is true, under heavy pressure not only from the City of Baltimore but also from influential stockholders and property owners. City officials envisioned a productive and expanding depot at the municipally owned City Block on the east side of town, and the property owners along the route stood to profit. Also, there was a general feeling among the downtown Baltimore faction that the businesses and shipping facilities concentrated at the inner harbor, or "the basin" as it was then known, should not be threatened by the creation of a potential new city at Carroll's Point.

For these reasons, Thomas instructed the engineers to locate the railroad in a way "best calculated to distribute the trade throughout the town as now improved." These same engineers, who had selected the railroad's starting place at the city line in James Carroll's field, had also explored routes from there into the city, having at the outset, in June 1828, ruled out such principal business streets as Pratt and Baltimore—"utterly inadmissable" for a railroad, they said—in favor of a line that would go in a northeasterly direction almost up to the Washington Monument and then circle around the built-up part of town before coming back down to the City Block. Their findings were a matter of public record.[3]

In January 1829, James Carroll stated his case in his first pamphlet, "The Claim of the Western Navigation of the City of Baltimore to a Rail Road Deposit," signing it, hopefully or facetiously, "A Friend to the Railroad." The next month, the engineers further defined their chosen route, "passing the high grounds situated between Pascault's Row and Centre street, by means of a tunnel about half a mile long," crossing Jones Falls and ending at Belair Road. The tracks would consist of "a series of curbstones . . . plated with iron." This was also publicized while Carroll, under the pen name "Civis," and his friends kept up a running criticism of it and its most likely beneficiary, the Canton Company. In March 1829, the City Council authorized the railroad to construct the line as far as Baltimore Street, but they built it only to Pratt Street.[4] In the fall, they added a few structures for a depot there—a temporary shed over the tracks that was knocked together by contractor John Ready out of old boards salvaged from the workmen's shanties—and built an eight-foot-high fence around the entire yard.

The B&O decided that summer that public convenience demanded the continuation of the railroad into Baltimore. Jonathan Knight was ordered to examine "all the avenues and streets" and once again to pick the best route to "accommodate the trade of the city as now improved."[5] When it was heard that Knight had been seen in Pratt Street with Thomas Poppleton, an English surveyor who had produced a well-known map of the city a few years back, it was immediately assumed that the railroad was coming down Pratt Street to the water. The rumor quickly escalated into a major political issue and public controversy and James Carroll decided it was an opportune time to speak out. "The scheme is fraught with immense mischief to a great portion of the city, particularly to persons owning property on Pratt street," he said at a meeting he organized at the Union Engine House. The tracks were to be laid on curbstones raised above the pavement, blocking vehicular traffic and interfering with the markets: "No lady will ever come into Pratt street in her carriage and shop across a railway." Baltimore would become a place of transit rather than a center of business, he continued, with the draymen and carters, "the bone and sinew of the community," forced out of work as the freight rolled by to "the sickly vicinity of the city block."[6]

The battle of the wards erupted shortly after Knight made his report in early February 1831, recommending, as expected, a railroad down either Pratt Street or Camden Street to the basin and on to the City Block. Poppleton drew a map to accompany the report, which featured one of the earliest views of the Mt. Clare depot, with a list of nearby property owners. While the company sought municipal authorization, Thomas assured the City Council that the locomotives would go no farther than Mt. Clare. From there, horses would pull the trains through the streets and the rails would cause "not the smallest interruption to the general travel." The tracks were described as continuous stone sills with iron rails, raised two inches above street level. The benefits of the railroad would be distributed by branch lines to all parts of the town "as now improved," he said.[7]

Carroll in a deluge of letters to the editor using various noms de plume stirred up the public by predicting flooded streets caused by drainage problems from the raised tracks, and, indeed, general ruination. He scoffed at the turntables the company was considering using to get around the tight curves—"gentlemen riding in railroad cars" through Baltimore, being turned at the street corners "on a whirligig"—and warned of trouble ahead: "Doubt and alarm are created in the minds of many of our citizens, sectional jealousies are excited, the city is divided, and one part of it arrayed against the other."[8]

Ward meetings were going on all over town. Notices in the newspaper cried,

"Citizens of Old Town Awake! Will you sleep while you see such exertions are making to carry the Rail-road down Pratt street to tide water to the exclusion of Old Town."[9] Hezekiah Niles ran a meeting in the Seventh Ward that endorsed the Pratt Street route, and Talbot Jones, a member of the B&O's first board of directors, signed up against it in the Tenth. Even brothers were divided over the issue. Charles Howard was in favor while William Howard was opposed and both owned Pratt Street property.

The northern section of the city felt not only left out but betrayed. The Tenth Ward was particularly opposed to the Pratt Street route and fought it vigorously. It reprinted the 1829 Baltimore ordinance and the exchanges between company and city officials at the time, and claimed that the railroad had committed itself to a northern route ending at Belair Road and should be held to it. In fact, these documents show that, although the company sent the engineers' report of February 1829 to the City Council as the basis for the proposed legislation, the directors did not themselves formally adopt the northern route and, indeed, probably had no intention of building the line. Furthermore, although they sought and received authorization to construct the railroad to Baltimore Street on that alignment, they may never have meant to do that either, since they stopped several blocks short. One of the alternatives the engineers looked at then was "a Branch by Pratt street to the basin."[10]

Far from suggesting that Thomas and his associates may have been dissembling, an anonymous stockholder defending the company accused a few selfish residents in the Tenth Ward of demagoguery in trying to capture the line for themselves when they had no financial stake in it. His point was well taken, for another group in the Tenth Ward backed the Pratt Street route. The same phenomenon occurred in other wards and the debate degenerated into an intramural squabble in each one over which faction, pro or con, truly represented the people's interests. Satires of the meetings began appearing in the papers.

The City Council debated the bill in March 1831. The Baltimore and Ohio had powerful friends in the council, including John B. Morris, a railroad director who was president of the first branch, and Joshua I. Cohen, Jr., a councilman who later joined the B&O board. The chief opposition on the council was James Carroll, Jr., but he lost his motion for an indefinite postponement of the measure. After several more days of debate, it passed the first branch, 18–6, the three northern wards (the city had twelve at that time) all voting no. A few days later the second branch approved it.

The day before the bill passed, April 1, 1831, Jacob Small, Jr., resigned as mayor of Baltimore to become superintendent of depots for the Baltimore and Ohio Railroad. One of his first jobs was supervising the laying of the track down Pratt Street. His replacement as mayor, William Steuart, resigned as a B&O director to take the job. The door had opened to those moving back and forth between public service and private enterprise.

The law authorized the company to extend the main line to the City Block and to lay tracks in a number of downtown streets, including Charles, Camden, Howard, and Paca, but it limited the railroad to the use of horsepower and further stipulated that if at any time the tracks became an obstruction to the ordinary use of the streets, the city could require the company to correct the problem or remove the tracks.

John McCartney got the job of laying the stone rails. William Patterson bought several properties at Pratt and Charles streets, including some tobacco warehouses, and offered them at cost to the B&O for a downtown depot. By October 1831, the tracks had been laid to Light Street at the basin (the inner harbor), and passengers could buy tickets and board the cars at the Three Tuns Tavern, Pratt and Paca streets. According to the newspapers, the freight system was supposed to function in the following manner. A horse would pull the railroad car to its destination on a spur line where a turntable in the street would "enable the consignee, in three minutes, to place the loaded car in his warehouse." If no spur line existed, a crane at Mt. Clare would lift the car body off the railroad wheels onto a dray and the merchandise would be delivered.[11]

The idea was good, but what happened was that the railroad cars sat around in the streets, and by the spring of 1832, the City Council and the company were back in negotiations. The B&O sought protection from "idle and mischievous persons wantonly running their cars over the railways in the streets, to the imminent peril of their own lives as well as damage to the company," and the council passed a law requiring the cars to be chained up when not in use.[12] With regard to the spur lines themselves, the railroad said it did not want to be involved in anything more than connecting them to the main stem. The directors recommended that the municipality hire John McCartney to build the first one up Howard Street.

McCartney was one of the first to take advantage of the City Extension. Because the streets near the City Block area were not paved or even graded, McCartney had to lay a wooden track down President Street to the wharf. He offered to do this at his own expense, so "that he might be enabled to convey a large quantity of granite, directly on shipboard, which he had contracted to deliver for exportation."[13] The board approved and McCartney built the track not to the City Block proper, which was still unusable raw land, but to a nearby square, rented temporarily from the city, bounded by President, Aliceanna, and Lancaster streets, and Falls Avenue. In October 1832, when the two-mile track from Mt. Clare to this deepwater site was finished, McCartney's granite was waiting and the B&O inaugurated the first major sea-rail interchange in the United States. The same month, the railroad moved its passenger depot downtown to Charles and Camden streets.

The City Block proper—the two squares bounded by Fleet, Exeter, and Lancaster streets, and Harford Dock, now Central Avenue—was not ready for the railroad until early 1835, when the B&O moved its facilities there. That was about the time the campaign to remove the tracks in Pratt Street shifted into high gear.

It was odd that the final attempt to force the railroad out of downtown Baltimore was instigated by the same man, Solomon Etting, who, as a city councilman and B&O director in 1828 had led the effort to adopt the route through the city that was finally chosen at the expense of Carroll's Point. Moreover, his ally in 1835 was James Carroll, Jr., who had inherited the bulk of the Mt. Clare estate, including the mansion, from his father. Etting was no longer a councilman or a railroad director in the spring of 1835, but he still owned property on Pratt Street and by that time he thought the tracks were a nuisance. Carroll was still a city councilman and also owned property on Pratt Street. Etting, Carroll, and some 70 other property owners petitioned the council for the removal of the Pratt Street line and all the branches, as provided for by law. Although their main argument was that the tracks caused traffic problems and interfered with a sewer drain at Howard Street, producing a great stench in the summertime, they were probably really objecting to the railroad itself, since indications are that McCartney had actually laid the stone sills with their iron rails flush with the existing pavement.[14] Several hundred Irish hackmen, draymen, and carters also sought redress, charging that while the city levied a fee for their licenses, "a large business for which we have been paying a heavy tax, has been transferred to a *monopoly*, who now enjoy exclusive privileges over certain parts of the streets, without contributing one dollar for taxation to the city."[15] But other factions of the community rallied to the railroad's support, saying that it had increased commerce, reduced freight charges, and stimulated real estate values in Baltimore. Carroll was outvoted in the council, and the tracks stayed in Pratt Street.[16]

In many ways, the problems of the City Extension were repeated in the Frederick project, the B&O's first real branch line, when similar controversies arose over the railroad's route and its potential economic impact. Frederick was the conservative capital of the rich piedmont farming country of the surrounding Monocacy and Middletown valleys, lying within the hazy shadows of the Blue Ridge. The town, settled in the mid-eighteenth century by Pennsylvania Germans, had a population of about 5,000 in the early 1830's and was a trading center for agricultural products. It had developed an early and profitable association with Baltimore through the National Road, and its businessmen, naturally expecting to be on the railroad's main line, had subscribed eagerly for stock and showed the B&O engineers favorable routes. They simultaneously explored a connection with the C&O Canal.

Thomas began to express doubts in the summer of 1829 that the railroad would pass directly through Frederick. He promised a citizens' committee that if it did not, the company would build a branch line to town and construct a depot at the same time that they were building the main stem. Following the strict railroad survey logic of the time, the engineers did bypass the state's largest inland city in order to take advantage of a better route a few miles to the south along Bush Creek. In November 1830, the Frederick municipal authorities agreed to give the railroad, at no charge, a depot site and three miles of right-of-way to it from the main line. Deciding that the depot should be located on six acres of Lewis Birely's lot at the city line on the southeast side, they then began to worry about what might happen when it was. Did the B&O intend to compete with the Frederick commission merchants? No, Thomas assured them.

That fall, Wever's ads for contractors brought 200 road makers and bridge builders to town, as construction on the main line crept closer to the Monocacy River. Six months went by before work actually began on the Frederick Branch, during which company officials worked out the details with the municipal authorities. The plan was much like Baltimore's. The engines were to stop at the outer depot, located at a sufficient elevation so that lateral railways could be built "into all parts of the City of Frederick as now improved."[17] From Birely's lot, with its yards and workshops, horses would pull the trains along All Saints Street to an inner station in the center of town. The city also donated a lot for this inner depot, the right-of-way to it, and the construction and maintenance of the line. However, there were counter-offers of land from others, just as there were in Baltimore, and further municipal misgivings about conveying title to the property once everybody had agreed.[18]

In the spring of 1831, population, rents, and business establishments increased in Frederick in anticipation of the start of construction. Before it began in July, Thomas wrote often to his foreman, Caspar W. Wever, warning him that the procrastination of the Frederick authorities and the greed of the county landholders might be the worst they had yet encountered. He recommended the usual combination of friendly persuasion and subtle hints, to move the depot out of town, for example. "Negotiations may be better than war," he said at one point. It was his credo.[19]

The Frederick Branch was not long—a little less than three and a half miles—and was a single track that began on the western shore of the Monocacy River, traced its edge for about a mile, then headed northwest, crossing Carroll Creek, and ended at Birely's lot, 60 railroad miles from Pratt Street in Baltimore. It was finished in five months. There was some heavy work, including "one long and deep excavation through solid limestone rock," done by contractors J. & D. Cahoon.[20] The official opening was on December 1, 1831. Two weeks before, about 100 B&O and Baltimore city officials and their guests made a railroad excursion to the inclined planes at Parrs Spring Ridge, the ridge that, rising abruptly to an elevation of over 800 feet some 40 railroad miles from Baltimore, sweeps in a great arc across the state.[21] The Patapsco River, which the engineers had been following west on a relatively gentle grade, ends there. On the other side, Bush Creek leads again through level country to the Monocacy River, which flows to the Potomac. Knight, Long, and the others knew in 1828 that to get over Parrs Spring Ridge they would need inclined planes and stationary power. The only other place they anticipated using such a system was at Great Backbone Mountain, the Allegheny Summit.

Within a horizontal distance of three and a half miles, Parrs Spring Ridge rises and falls, at a somewhat steeper rate on the west side, a total of 420 feet. This is an average of 120 feet per mile, representing a 2.25 percent grade. The engineers believed at the time that a locomotive could not climb a steeper grade than 30 feet per mile, or 0.6 percent. There were a number of theories as to how to overcome such obstacles. An early one was to run a continuous chain or rope around pulleys at the top and bottom of the incline so that one train coming down the hill could pull another one up. There was one of these so-called "self-acting planes" on Pennsylvania's Mauch Chunk Railroad, part of the Lehigh Coal and Navigation Company. Moncure Robinson patented a similar system using water as a counterweight; this system was used, along with stationary engines, on the 37-mile Allegheny Portage Railroad from Hollidaysburg to Johnstown, Pennsylvania, and entire canal boats were lifted over the mountains.[22]

Long had helped Robinson lay out the Allegheny route, and he and McNeill had discussed inclined planes when they were just starting out with the Baltimore and Ohio. In early 1827, Long calculated the time it would take locomotives, horses, or stationary engines to pull different loads up varying inclines. McNeill, in his typically brusque manner, later described the stationary equipment:

> The machinery of an Inclined Plane is exceedingly simple [consisting] merely of *sheeves* or rollers placed at convenient intervals in the middle of the road-track to sustain the rope or chain to which the wagons are attached . . . the operation of the Engine throughout the length of the Plane must be so obvious, that it is scarcely necessary to say that by means of a rope (or chain) one end of which being attached to a train of wagons and the other end to the "Drum" around which the rope is wound by the action of the engine, the train is caused to ascend.[23]

Knight, McNeill, and Whistler had also discussed these schemes in England in 1829 when they met Benjamin Thompson, the chief advocate of stationary engines for railroads, and George Stephenson, who had designed several inclined planes and was using locomotives to pull trains over the easier ones. Ahead of his time as usual, Stephenson was also recommending pusher or helper engines for the heavier grades, the technique still in use. But by the fall of 1831, when Knight located and supervised the construction of the inclined planes at Parrs Spring Ridge, Long and McNeill were gone. Knight agonized over various plans and admitted late in the game that he still could not determine exactly where to position the stationary engines with respect to the tracks until he knew how the power was to be transmitted to the trains.

Knight laid out four inclined planes, two on each side of the ridge, numbered from east to west. They were perfectly straight to give free play to the ropes or chains and were separated by level sections on which the stationary steam engines would be located. The company wanted four of these, three of 45 horsepower each for Planes 1, 2, and 4, and a 60-hp engine for the steeper Plane No. 3. Ross Winans was in charge of the machinery, which was to be supplied by the Mattawan Company of New York. The first set of equipment was due to arrive in November 1831 and a temporary building was erected to house it.

The 100 or so gentlemen who marched over Parrs Spring Ridge in mid-November saw rails laid on most of the line.[24] They hiked up Plane No. 1, which was 2,150 feet long and had a rise of 80 feet (3.7 percent), and came to the first level. Following the railroad as it curved to the left, they crossed the Frederick Turnpike and a small stream on a twin-arched stone viaduct, then turned to the right again to Plane No. 2—3,000 feet long, climbing 100 feet (3.3 percent). At the summit, there was a level space 600 feet across, where the railroad passed under a county road that ran along the top of the ridge. Plane No. 3 then fell 160 feet over a length of 3,200 feet (5 percent) to another level and curve in the line leading to Plane No. 4, some 1,900 feet long, dropping 81 feet (4.3 per cent).[25]

A couple of accidents happened as the construction crews rushed to finish the line in time for the opening. The wooden brake failed on one car loaded with clay and carried a lone workman, frightened "almost out of his senses," down with it for almost a mile before stopping. Another clay car got loose on Plane No. 2 with two men aboard, only one of whom remained when it got to the bottom. The other was thrown off "like a tangent" when the car hit the curve between the planes.[26] Hezekiah Niles reported a fatal accident on the Quincy Railroad in which a broken chain on one of its steep inclines, up to 27 percent, sent a car hurtling down, off the tracks, and over a 30-foot drop, and he confessed that, for some time, he never crossed the Baltimore and Ohio's inclined planes "without some degree of apprehension."[27]

On the day of the official opening of the Frederick Branch, the ground was covered by a light snow that had fallen during the night. The dignitaries—including the governor, George Howard, and the mayor of Baltimore, William Steuart, but not President Andrew Jackson, who had declined Thomas's invitation—rode in four carriages, each drawn by a single horse, with the Frederick leading the way. A reporter for the Frederick *Examiner* pronounced it "the most beautiful car that has yet been built in this country. It is papered and curtained within and has windows on each side. In shape and general appearance it looks more like a house on wheels than a traveling vehicle."[28] The Frederick may have been one of the new eight-wheel passenger coaches that the B&O began experimenting with in the summer of 1831, very different from the Imlay stagecoach-style cars in use up to that time.[29] The first of these, the Columbus, designed either by Ross Winans or by Conduce Gatch, the railroad's master carpenter (both claimed credit for it), was about 24 feet long; it had doors at each end, square windows, and longitudinal benches that seated about 40 persons.

The train from Baltimore wound its way, deep in the shadow of the valley, along the ice-edged Patapsco River, whose snow islands contrasted sharply with the dark and sinuous stream. It passed the new station at Ellicotts Mills, designed by Jacob Small, Jr., and built by John McCartney out of the local dull-gray granite.[30] It went by the Union Factory to Marriottsville, then continued on a long, straight stretch after Sykesville, where Wever had rerouted the river into a new channel and used the excavated earth to form the railroad embankment. At Parrs Spring Ridge, on the level before Plane No. 2, a pair of horses was added to each car. At the summit, they passed under an arch decorated with inscriptions. Eighteen miles distant lay the foothills of the Alleghenies, Catoctin and South mountains and the Blue Ridge. The extra horses were taken off, "breakers" were added under the cars, and "a trusty man [was] placed behind the car, to assist in the regulation of the wheels by bearing on them, in proportion to the grades." At the Monocacy River, they stopped to admire the new bridge, 350 feet long, 24 feet wide, and 38 feet above the level of the stream, that had been built by Lewis Wernwag and his two sons. Its three wooden arched deck trusses rested on stone abutments and piers.

Meanwhile, a procession of Frederick burghers headed from the downtown Talbott's Hotel toward the depot, where they formed a welcoming avenue several hundred yards long on either side of the tracks. At two o'clock the sentinel at Cahoon's Cut signaled the approach of the train, and a volley of artillery echoed along the Monocacy. All the crowd could see at first was the American flag fluttering along the top edge of the excavation, but in a few minutes the Frederick, bearing the flag, came into view. The band struck up "Hail, Columbia," and there were three cheers for the "incongruous spectacle." Richard Potts, the chairman of the Frederick committee of arrangements, climbed onto a car in the "rough plank house" that served as a temporary structure over the tracks. He gave a speech, and then Thomas responded at some length that they were glad to be there, and then everybody marched back to the hotel for dinner.

Flour, Frederick's chief product, began to flow almost immediately. Four thousand barrels were shipped by the B&O in an eleven-day period in January 1832. This represented a saving of $2,000 to the Frederick farmers, but they thought it was not enough and they appealed to the legislature for lower rates. Thomas exploded. Was this the B&O's reward for spending $70,000 on the Frederick Branch and charging lower rates than any other U.S. railroad?: "The attack upon us from Frederick is amongst the most unkind returns for a benefit conferred that I have ever in my life witnessed." [31]

The rate fight with the farmers blew over quickly after Thomas reassured the Frederick commission merchants, again, that he was not in competition with them. Operations also settled into a routine at the planes, even though the machinery that was due in November 1831, before the opening of the Frederick Branch, did not arrive until the following August, a year after it was ordered. Thomas reviewed the consequences in an angry letter to the Mattawan Company. Owing to their failure to deliver the equipment on time, he said, the B&O was "thrown into very serious embarrassment" and forced either to substitute horse power or to suspend operations. [32] The railroad paid the supplier for $4,100 worth of cast iron wheels and sheaves that eventually arrived, but then did not get around to installing them until about 1835. The horsepower that Thomas described as a "temporary expedient" continued to be used for many years after December 1834, when for the first time a locomotive pulled a scheduled train over the inclined planes at Parrs Spring Ridge.

The B&O records are vague concerning their operation, but in 1837, horses, locomotives, and stationary steam engines all seem to have been employed. That year, an assistant engineer, John R. Niernsee, later a well-known Baltimore architect, traversed the planes and reported, "The cars were raised to [the summit] by means of a stationary steam engine and an endless steel rope; they were lowered the same way on the other side." [33] In 1838–39, the engineers relocated the line at the ridge to accommodate locomotives and reported difficulty in selling the "Old Castings from the inclined planes." [34]

From the beginning, the system was expensive to operate by any means. During the first few months of 1832, while manual brakes were being added to the cars, the company's income dropped under the burden of having to pay for extra horses to haul the trains up and extra men to brake them on the way down. The B&O did not use mechanical brakes until 1835, when they were installed on the Washington Branch cars, the earliest known use of such brakes.

Past the planes and the Frederick Branch, the railroad followed a straight route for about ten miles from the Monocacy down to the Point of Rocks. The line was opened to that place on April 1, 1832. On April 20, the first trainload of Potomac flour, some 300–400 barrels, arrived in Baltimore. Three days later, the Columbus, with 50 passengers, made the first trip west to the Point of Rocks.[35]

11

Road to Washington

THE WASHINGTON BRANCH, AS IT CAME TO BE KNOWN, was even more problematic than the City Extension or the Frederick Branch, and because national and state pressures were involved, the stakes assumed greater urgency. The idea for a rail line from Baltimore to Washington was not new with the Baltimore and Ohio Railroad. Early in 1828, even before the company had broken ground for the main line, the Washington and Baltimore Turnpike Road Company had had a law passed in Annapolis allowing them to build a railroad between the two cities, and Congress had approved similar legislation.[1]

The turnpike was notoriously uncomfortable at any time of the year—hot and dusty in the summer, a frozen, bone-jarring bed of stones in winter, and a quagmire whenever it rained. Benjamin H. Latrobe, who as a road commissioner in 1810 had planned and surveyed one of the first sections between Capitol Hill and Bladensburg, himself, along with his family, was thoroughly drenched on one occasion when their carriage from Baltimore to Washington was almost swamped fording a rain-swollen stream between Elkridge and Waterloo.[2]

The turnpike was finished in 1825, and it eventually formed part of Route 1, the great post road linking the major Eastern cities. But in the best of times, the ride to Washington still took five or six hours and in the worst, two or three times as long. A railroad would cut the journey to two hours. Hezekiah Niles looked forward to eating breakfast in Baltimore, riding to the capital to hear the debates in Congress, and being back home for dinner with his family the same night. What a contrast, he said, to the time "when the mail stage would leave Baltimore before daylight (in the winter season), and by dint of great exertion reach [Washington], at 9 or 10 o'clock that night. In fact, it was often the case, after wet thawing weather, that the stage did not arrive [there] until the day following, and sometimes even late on that day."[3] E. T. Coke, a British Army lieutenant, described a trip he made on the turnpike from Baltimore to Washington in the early 1830's, during which the stagecoach driver tore full tilt down the hills, drove furiously across the numerous ravines and streams that cut the road, and dashed "over rough stones and tottering bridges that would have cracked every spring in an English carriage." They ran into thunderstorms and got to Washington that night soaked and exhausted.[4]

But there was no practical alternative. In 1830, some 40,000 stagecoach passengers, an average of 100 a day, spent $2.75 each to travel the turnpike between Baltimore and Washington.[5] In the same year, 2,600 people made the journey between the cities by Chesapeake Bay steamboat, roughly 200 water miles, paying about $9.85 for a trip that took 24 to 48 hours. Some actually enjoyed it; as one enthusiast said, the trip was like flying along "in a fine floating tavern" at fifteen miles an hour, "and if your business consists in reading or writing, there is absolutely a *gain of time.*"[6]

The second attempt to find a faster method came in 1829, when the Maryland legislature passed a law incorporating the Washington and Baltimore Rail Road Company. This company may have been a proxy for the Baltimore and Ohio, since of the eleven commissioners on its board, four had close ties with the B&O—William Patterson, William Lorman, John B. Morris, and George Brown. At least one other, however, John S. Hollins, was allied with the Baltimore and Susquehanna Railroad, a competing and sometimes hostile line that began construction a year after the Baltimore and Ohio. Its destination was York, Pennsylvania, and ultimately the Susquehanna River.

Neither of these preliminary acts concerning a railroad between Baltimore and Washington was implemented, but the groundwork had been laid. A flurry of newspaper debate preceded the decision of the B&O to build the Washington Branch. Some critics felt that the company lacked the charter powers and the funds to do so and should not deviate from building the railroad to the west. However, the charter gave the B&O the right to construct "lateral rail roads," although it also provided that other companies could connect their own railroads within the state to the Baltimore and Ohio. Others said loan funds were available and warned that if the B&O did not make the Washington Branch, "some other persons will."[7]

At the B&O board meeting on December 6, 1830, William Patterson, at the behest of Thomas, advanced the proposal to build the line.[8] The motion passed unanimously, and after ordering Jonathan Knight to make a reconnaissance of the route, the company sent a memorial to Congress seeking authority to construct a branch line that would terminate at some convenient point within the District of Columbia. The directors were confident that they could get the funds to build it without interfering with the progress of the main line. By January 5, 1831, when the board met again, Thomas had arranged to borrow up to $1 million in construction money from Nicholas Biddle, president of the Bank of the United States.

At the January meeting, however, the directors discussed the terms of Biddle's loan but took no action on it. For various reasons, the Bank of the United States was under some suspicion, and it may be that Thomas had been warned, probably by Congressman Benjamin C. Howard and Roger B. Taney, who was months away from assuming a cabinet post, that there were political problems. President Jackson had already suggested the establishment of a new bank with strictly limited powers, and the early skirmishing in what was to become the "bank war" was under way. At any rate, the day after the board meeting, Thomas advised Biddle that the company would postpone action on the loan until Congress had passed the B&O's legislation. He did defend the funding concept in a reply to Congressman Howard, saying he understood that the U.S. Bank had lent money to similar enterprises in other states. "No complaint was ever heard against the bank on account of these loans and it does seem most curious that any exception should now be taken against a loan to the Rail Road Company," Thomas said. "I can see no political sin," he added, "even if the object be to promote a public improvement in which the whole nation has a most vital interest." [9]

Opposition was mounting in the Maryland legislature, however, and the B&O decided to try to make Maryland a partner in the venture. It might not succeed, but if it did, it would provide an alternative source of construction funds and effectively block their competitors. In informing the legislature of their intent, Thomas said: "The Rail Road Company, as a corporation, feel no particular anxiety to be the makers of the road, should the State be desirous of constructing it. . . . Or, if the state prefer it, the company will make the whole road themselves." [10] Or they might share the cost. Thomas proposed various ways in which this could be done by means of complex exchanges of B&O and State of Maryland stock. One alternative would be for the state to provide up to $1 million in financing, with the choice later on, after the Washington Branch was finished and operating, of either becoming part owner or getting its money back.

Patrick Macauley, a city councilman, B&O director, and Washington Branch advocate, was particularly incensed about the resolution introduced in Annapolis to have the state build the line. "We have made one fifth of the way at a most enormous expense," he told Benjamin C. Howard. "To go and make a road alongside of this as the resolution proposes, would be the repetition of one of those acts of folly which have so often brought the schemes of internal improvement into disrepute." [11] He intimated that the B&O's political enemies in Annapolis and Washington were already working to defeat the railroad's legislative program. One of those he named did in fact lobby Howard to change the federal bill so that the state, as well as the company, could extend a railroad into the capital.

Finally the congressman heard from his brother, William, the civil engineer, on the subject. William Howard and William Gibbs McNeill had been asked by the Maryland House of Delegates to analyze the feasibility of a state railroad from Baltimore to Washington. One of their proposals was indeed to make an entirely new line. William Howard said the information might help his brother "in the delicate situation between conflicting interests in which you are placed." [12] Despite the pressure, Congressman Howard expertly steered the Baltimore and Ohio Railroad's bill around the pitfalls in the House of Representatives by using an artful blend of resistance and compromise. In mid-January 1831, the measure emerged relatively unscathed from the House District Committee, before which Thomas had made a successful appearance. The next scene of political activity was the Maryland House of Delegates.

Thomas made his views more explicit in an inspirational message to the legislators that he sent to Annapolis with William Steuart, the mayor of Baltimore. The railroad president wished the State of Maryland to be partners with the B&O in building the Washington Branch or else lend it $1 million worth of 4.5 percent state stock so the company could build it. "It is generally understood that the state has no desire to make the road herself," he said.[13]

At the same time, the Washington turnpike company and the old Washington and Baltimore Rail Road Company resumed their efforts to build their own rail lines to the capital. Besides the B&O's bill to build the Washington Branch in partnership with the state, there was a fourth bill calling for the state to build the line by itself, in spite of Thomas's understanding of the matter. The legislators were bewildered. A newspaper correspondent put the situation in perspective: "One party wishes to connect the scheme with the present turnpike company; another to sell a charter to the highest bidder; and another to make the road by the state." But they all had one object: "To have no rail-road at all, or to prevent a union between the state and the Baltimore and Ohio Railroad Company."[14]

Two teams of engineers were in the field studying the project on behalf of the state and the B&O, respectively, and each had its backers. "The Balt. & Ohio Railroad Co. are certainly the most impudent corporation in existence," Charles Howard informed Benjamin C. Howard:

> You know that the Dr. [their brother William Howard] and McNeill were requested by the Committee on Internal Improvement to procure information for them. Well, the Railroad Co. have volunteered by their agents at Annapolis "to furnish the Legislature with all the information they want, *as soon as Jonathan Knight returns to town*." . . . Is it not almost inconceivable that they [the B&O Railroad] should ask the state to trust them for data on which to decide whether they [the State of Maryland] will enter into the scheme in opposition to the Co?[15]

Both engineering reports were finished on January 22, 1831. Jonathan Knight and Benjamin H. Latrobe, Jr., used William Howard's 1827 survey for a canal between Baltimore and Washington as the basis for their examinations. "It will appear that the country along the immediate vicinity of the canal line, as run by Dr. Howard, will afford a good route for the rail road," Knight told the B&O directors.[16] The same canal survey also provided the foundation for the competing report by William Howard and William Gibbs McNeill to the Maryland legislature. In many ways it was a more thorough job than the B&O's. Howard and McNeill said they would branch off from the main stem about six miles from the city, but that a completely new line could also be run all the way into Baltimore with a terminal closer to the center of town than the B&O's Pratt Street depot.[17]

William Howard was of two minds about canals and railroads. At the 1823 convention in Washington for the Chesapeake and Ohio Canal, he had been the sole

Baltimore representative, and ever since then he had been a consistent advocate of a canal from Baltimore to connect with the C&O Canal. He had also surveyed two potential routes on behalf of Maryland canal interests. One of these routes, going west from the city over Parrs Spring Ridge and down to the mouth of the Monocacy River, had become the route of the B&O's main line; Howard had, in fact, surveyed it for the B&O with McNeill. The second, more preferable, canal route went from Baltimore to Georgetown. Howard had now resurveyed that line, again with McNeill, again for a railroad, but not for the B&O. William Howard wrote his brother, in Congress:

> I enclose you a copy of the report of Capt. McNeill and myself, relative to the proposed railway from here to Washington. We have offered to make the road, 34 miles from Gadsbys Run to the General Post Office in Washington in 3 years for $650,000; the road not to be deemed complete until we shall have placed on it a locomotive engine, to carry a reasonable number of passengers from one city to the other within two hours. I do not know what the legislature will do. The feeling in favour of the state undertaking it is gaining ground: but I believe the greater part of the members feel the responsibility too great to make such a decision.[18]

In a handwritten note to future historians that he left among the company records, Thomas characterized the whole thing as a subversive attack. "The report of Dr. W. Howard and W. G. McNeill was a measure brought about by the enemies of the Baltimore and Ohio Rail Road under the combined influence of the Susquehanna Rail road & Chesapeake & Ohio Canal Companies and was intended as a *contre coup* to defeat the Washington Rail Road, to which measure these Engineers kindly lent their cordial aid."[19] The next engineering assignment for McNeill, who had left the B&O on less than friendly terms, was to locate the Baltimore and Susquehanna Railroad.

In mid-February, the House of Representatives again took up the Washington Branch bill. Congressman Howard defended the measure against attempts to table it until the Annapolis legislators figured out what they wanted to do, and he defused the situation by adding a provision that would allow the State of Maryland to build the railroad into the capital. The House shortly passed the bill.

The strife continued in Annapolis until, like a shaft of sunlight, a bill calling for the B&O to build the Washington Branch came over to the House of Delegates from the Maryland Senate where it had been introduced by Upton S. Heath, a steady friend of the railroad. After more days of bitter wrangling, it was approved. Congress shortly passed its first Baltimore and Ohio Railroad act. The company now had its laws, but still no money.

Thomas wrote Biddle at the U.S. Bank formally declining the $1 million loan but borrowing a more modest $200,000 for main line construction funds. Thomas told Biddle that the Washington Branch had been postponed. The obstacle was the new state law, which gave Maryland, with no commitment of public funds, the right to acquire over 60 percent of the Washington Branch stock after the B&O had paid to build the line and to receive a portion of the net profits. The act also authorized the turnpike owners to subscribe to $100,000 worth of the stock. It did, however, give the B&O Railroad "the undisputed pre-emptive right" to construct the Washington Branch. But the company clearly wanted better legislation, and it did little on the Washington Branch for the next few years except conduct surveys.

The first real engineering assignment for Benjamin H. Latrobe, Jr., was to lead one of the Washington Branch survey parties from July to September 1831. The work was suspended when several of the men became seriously ill from "bilious fever," near the Patuxent River. Early in 1832, Knight submitted a report on the preliminary surveys for the Washington Branch. He intended to make the line as straight as possible for locomotives, but there were three ridges that had to be got over: Merrill's Ridge, which divided the Patapsco and the Patuxent rivers at Waterloo; Patuxent Ridge, between Savage and Laurel, which separated the two branches of the Patuxent; and Snowden's Ridge past Contee, where the Patuxent and the Potomac went their separate ways. A fourth ridge was located within the District of Columbia, called Duel Ridge after the bloody encounters that had taken place there. The railroad line passed through the dueling grounds themselves, a gloomy ravine surrounded by tall cedar and maple trees.

Thomas submitted Knight's report to the Maryland legislature and asked for a state subscription. Instead, he got an act permitting the railroad to sell stock in the Washington Branch and to borrow money to build it by mortgaging the property with stockholder approval. The City of Baltimore was authorized to subscribe for 5,000 shares. The State of Maryland reserved its rights to acquire stock and share in the profits later on, but its own contribution was not specified. Thomas declared that this new law was hardly more acceptable than the previous one had been, and with Washington in mind, he hinted that the B&O would carry the mail free if the federal government would subscribe to the stock. The idea stayed alive for a year and then died, as had all the other B&O requests for U.S. funds. Meanwhile, the company went on with the engineering work. In the spring of 1832, Knight instructed Latrobe to locate the Washington Branch, and for the next year, Latrobe and the survey teams worked hard and carefully.

Finally, on March 9, 1833, the Maryland legislature passed a law that provided the public funds the company had been waiting for. State Senator Charles F. Mayer from Baltimore was credited with steering it through the upper house. The preamble clearly stated that the problem with the previous legislation had been uncertainty over the state's contribution, which had scared off other investors, and without money the railroad could not be built. The particulars were equally clear: the Washington Branch stock was to be "separate and distinct" from other B&O stock; when private subscriptions totaled $1 million, the state would subscribe for $500,000 worth; the company itself was permitted to buy any stock that was unsold at the end of 30 days, and the City of Baltimore and the turnpike company could exercise their options to buy within six months. (Neither did.) The one-way passenger rate was set at $2.50, up from $1.50 in the 1831 act, and the state was to receive 20 percent of the gross passenger receipts.[20]

Thomas said that the new law provided for "the commencement of the work without further delay,"[21] yet when the subscription books were opened on Saturday, April 6, 1833 at the Mechanics Bank in Baltimore and the Bank of the Metropolis in Washington, there were few takers. Of the 10,000 shares offered at $100 each, only 612 were sold over the next month; most of those went to Stockton and Stokes, the stage proprietors. The B&O was now realizing full well that the commercial fever that had gripped investors when it first offered stock in 1827 had been cooled by hard times. Therefore, instead of waiting for the City of Baltimore and the turnpike company to exercise their six-month options to acquire stock, the railroad company, on May 8, held a meeting at the Exchange, at which the stockholders, by an overwhelming vote, authorized the directors to borrow the money necessary to buy the stock themselves by mortgaging the company's property. The stockholders also approved the legislative act effecting a compromise with the Chesapeake and Ohio Canal.

The most crucial month for the Washington Branch was July 1833, when the financial arrangements were completed, construction began, and Jonathan Knight submitted his final engineering report. This document, eloquent in its estimate of the effects of the Washington Branch and exhaustive in its detail, took up 126 printed pages in the annual report that year. Knight was totally confident of the economic success of the new facility. It would revolutionize the shipping of freight between Baltimore and Washington. Whereas merchants had formerly been sending their goods over the turnpike at a cost of $9 to $10 a ton and a span of two to three days, or by water, taking a few days in a steamboat or a week in a sloop at up to $5 a ton, in railroad cars on the Washington Branch, both time and money would be less: five hours, and roughly $1.50 a ton. Moreover, Knight said, "A merchant or consignee will know, within fifteen minutes, when his goods will arrive, and the risk will be nothing." Passenger service would yield even greater revenues. Knight anticipated 400 passengers a day—a substantial increase over the 125 daily stagecoach passengers then on the turnpike. The fare would be reduced from $3 to $2.50 and travel time would be cut to two hours. "All travellers upon business or pleasure visiting the Capital of the Union from the states West, North, and East as well as all those from the Southern states, travelling through the Seat of Government, will pass and repass upon this railway," he predicted.

The Washington Branch was a project of national significance that embodied the spirit of the age, and it would be an important link in a continuous rail line that would one day extend from New York to the capital: "It is impossible to form in advance any adequate conception of the degree of improvement in the arts and the facilities of trade and intercourse, and of the effects of these upon wealth, in a nation advancing with unprecedented vigor and enterprise, and which at the same time is comparatively of such recent origin as the United States."

Knight outlined his plan to lay a cheap first track on oak logs and sleepers obtained in the immediate neighborhood and use it to haul the materials for a second, more expensive track of yellow pine sills, sleepers, and stringers. The running surface was to be 35-pound edge rail with a flat base. What they actually built was a single track of the better, yellow pine version, with some log sidings in the cuts through the ridges, topped with 40-pound T-rail, essentially in the modern configuration. The line was not double-tracked until the 1860's.

The most salient feature of the report was a set of calculations that Knight, who loved numbers, produced in an effort to help the directors choose a route. There were twelve alternatives, but only two main ones. The upper route mostly followed the turnpike (the present Route 1), passing near the mills at Savage and Laurel. The lower route, nearer the Chesapeake Bay, traversed a more rural countryside. In fact, there was no substantial difference between the two main choices, and the others were only variations of those two, five for each one. Benjamin H. Latrobe, Jr., did the surveys, levels, and drawings. Thomas, taking note of the massive detail, commented that the nature of the ground between the two cities required precise surveys and exact comparisons. (The route traces the fall line dividing the coastal plain from the pied-mont plateau.) He may indeed have requested ample documentation, knowing that the choice would be controversial in that the upper alignment favored manufacturers and the lower one, agricultural interests.

At any rate, Knight, with meticulous precision, compared the costs of ten dif-ferent track-laying methods, the expenses of operating locomotives and cars, and the costs of running them over each of the twelve different routes, turning what ought to have been a fairly straightforward engineering assignment into such a complicated and bewildering analysis that it took a committee of directors seven weeks to un-ravel the results. The committee expressed its bafflement diplomatically: "To render justice to the report, and at the same time disengage it of the minute calculations introduced to sustain the Engineer's conclusions, and to reduce the question to such a space as to render it susceptible of being generally appreciated, the committee have had [a] table prepared." This table showed that the upper route was slightly shorter, the lower a little cheaper to build; the upper, faster to travel; the lower, less costly to repair, and so on. "The committee forbear to pursue the comparison further," the members reported. They recommended the upper route, and that was adopted.[22]

The financial package seemed almost simple by comparison. Thomas had made preliminary arrangements with Thomas Ellicott, former B&O director who was now the president of the Union Bank of Maryland, to borrow up to $1 million to invest in the Washington Branch. He had also arranged with state officials to receive Mary-land's $500,000 stock subscription. The $1.5 million total made up the estimated construction cost. In July 1833, after the Union Bank agreed to furnish the first half of the loan beginning that fall, the railroad advertised for contractors.

PANORAMIC VIEW OF THE SCENERY ON THE PATAPSCO

ELLICOTTS MILLS, MD.

Washington Irving was so upset by the encroaching mills and railroad in the Patapsco River Valley in the 1850's, when this view was made, that he wrote his friend John Pendleton Kennedy, a former B&O director, to recommend that chateaus be built instead: "All the cotton lords should live in baronial castles on the cliff; and the cotton spinners should be virtuous peasantry of both sexes, in silk shirts and smallclothes and straw hats with long ribbons and should do nothing but sing songs and choruses and dance on the margin of the river." The Patterson Viaduct is shown, bottom, Ellicotts Mills and the Tarpean Rock in the middle distance, and Elysville (now Daniels) in the upper left. *Maryland Historical Society, Baltimore.*

The Carrollton Viaduct, completed December 1829, is the oldest railroad bridge in the United States. When this photograph was taken for an 1872 promotional album showing the B&O's line "from the Lakes to the Sea," the arched opening for the wagon road on the left side had halfway silted up; it has since completely disappeared. © *The B&O Railroad Museum, Inc., Collection.*

This rare photograph *(left)* of the 1829 Patterson Viaduct was taken before 1866, when the two central arches were destroyed in a flood; an 1872 photograph *(bottom)* shows the Bollman truss bridge that replaced them. A track re-alignment in 1903 left the bridge abandoned, and today all that remains of the original viaduct in this still-bucolic area is a single roadway arch. *1866 photo: Wilgus Collection; 1872 photo:* © *The B&O Railroad Museum, Inc., Collection.*

Peter Cooper *(left)*, as a successful businessman and philanthropist late in life, often reminisced about the locomotive he built and ran for the B&O Railroad in 1830 and its famous race with the horse, which the horse won. He thus added to the controversy that has arisen over the engine and the event. © *The B&O Railroad Museum, Inc., Collection.*

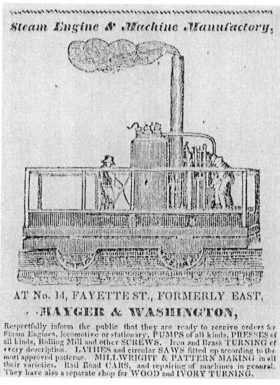

Steam Engine & Machine Manufactory,

AT No. 14, FAYETTE ST., FORMERLY EAST,

MAYGER & WASHINGTON,

Respectfully inform the public that they are ready to receive orders for Steam Engines, locomotive or stationary, PUMPS of all kinds, PRESSES of all kinds, Rolling Mill and other SCREWS, Iron and Brass TURNING of every description. LATHES and circular SAWS fitted up according to the most approved patterns. MILLWRIGHT & PATTERN MAKING in all their varieties. Rail Road CARS, and repairing of machines in general. They have also a separate shop for WOOD and IVORY TURNING.

The only known contemporary drawing of Cooper's engine appears in this 1831 advertisement *(left)* for a machine shop that worked on the locomotive, which Cooper later said he built himself, although he could not remember much about it. John H. B. and Benjamin H. Latrobe, Jr., and Ross Winans later collaborated on some accurate drawings *(opposite)* of the engine that appeared in William H. Brown's 1871 *History of the First Locomotives in America. Cooper ad: © The B&O Railroad Museum, Inc., Collection; engine drawings: The Enoch Pratt Free Library, Baltimore.*

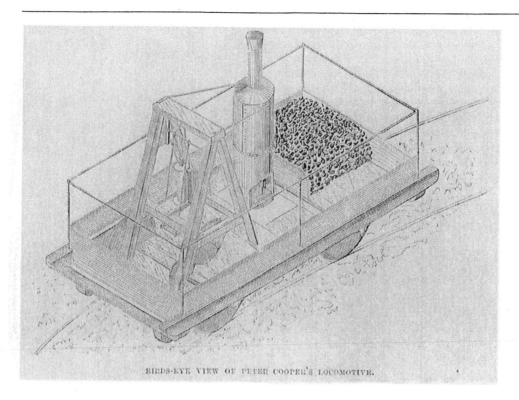

BIRDS-EYE VIEW OF PETER COOPER'S LOCOMOTIVE.

Fig. 9.

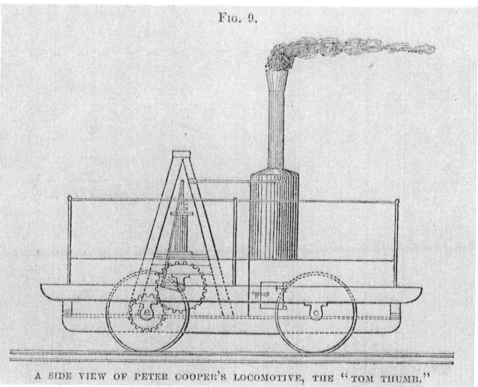

A SIDE VIEW OF PETER COOPER'S LOCOMOTIVE, THE "TOM THUMB."

James Carroll, proprietor of Mount Clare, had a falling out with the B&O over Carroll's secret donation of a right-of-way through his estate and a depot site at Pratt Street in exchange for a branch line to his proposed port facility at Carroll's Point, seen on the map *(right)* from his 1829 pamphlet. The B&O instead extended its line down Pratt Street to the Basin (Inner Harbor), past the property of several company directors, shown on the map *(overleaf)* from the 1831 annual report. © *The B&O Railroad Museum, Inc., Collection.*

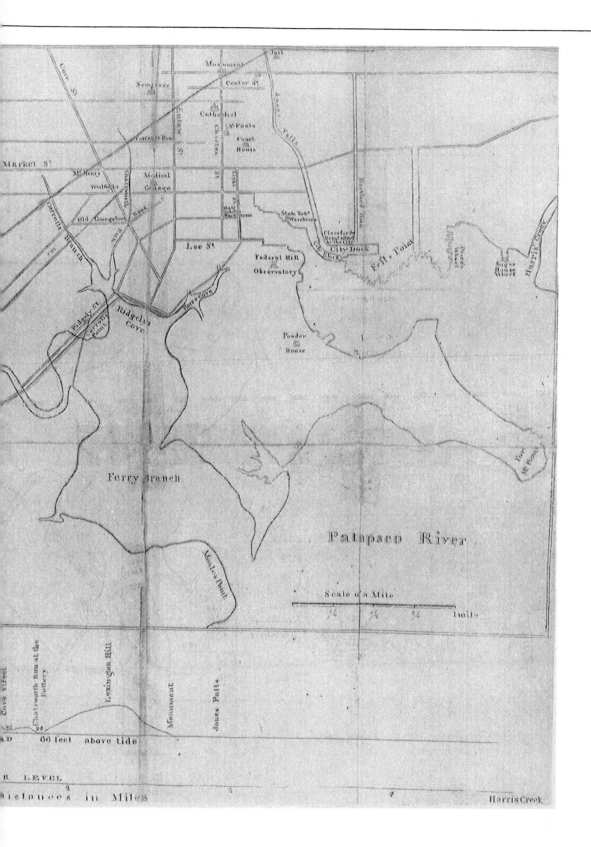

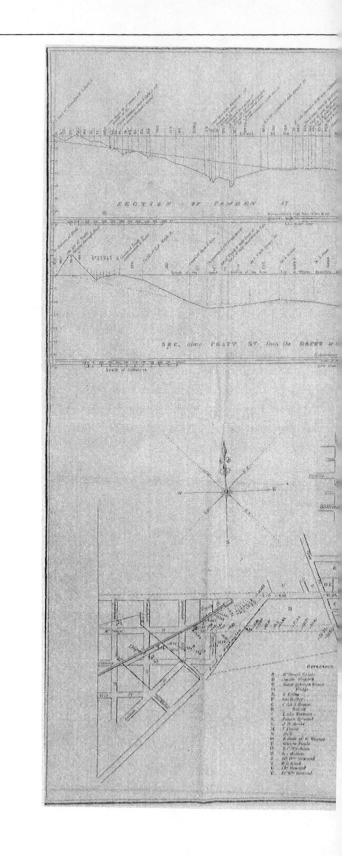

Plan and Profiles
Illustrating the Report of
J. KNIGHT Ch Engr BALTE OHIO R. ROCO
upon the Subject of the extension of that Rail Road
into the CITY of BALTE as now Improved

BASIN

NOTE

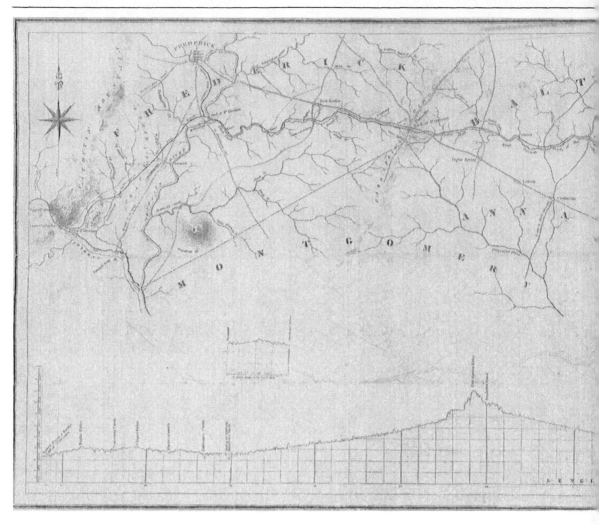

The map of the railroad route between Baltimore and the Potomac River is from the B&O's 1831 annual report. © *The B&O Railroad Museum, Inc., Collection.*

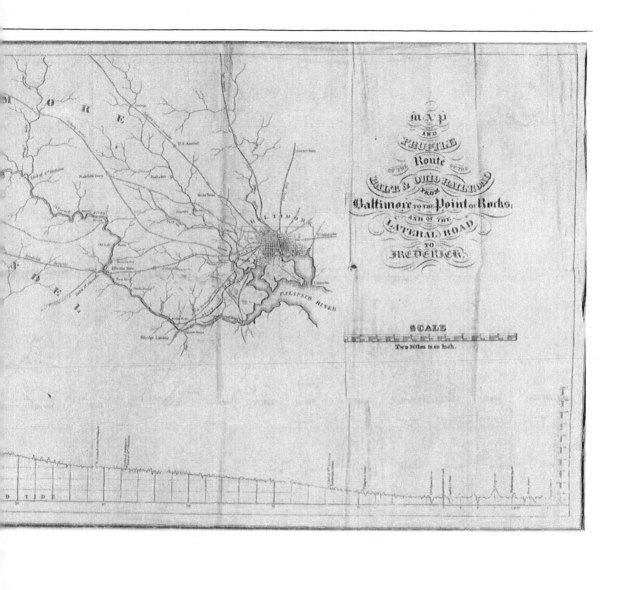

MAP AND PROFILE Route OF THE OF THE BALT. & OHIO RAILROAD FROM Baltimore TO THE Point OF Rocks; AND OF THE LATERAL ROAD TO FREDERICK.

SCALE

Two Miles to an Inch.

No man, it was said, was as great as Daniel Webster looked: "That amorphous crag-like face; the dull black eyes under the precipice of brows, like dull anthracite furnaces, needing only to be blown; the mastiff mouth accurately closed; I have not traced so much of silent Berserkir rage that I remember in any man," wrote Thomas Carlyle. Webster argued the B&O's case against the C&O Canal before the Maryland Court of Appeals in *1833*—and lost. *1874 steel engraving after a daguerreotype, The Granger Collection, New York.*

Roger Brooke Taney, future Chief Justice of the Supreme Court, was another of the railroad's lawyers during its five-year legal battle with the canal over the right-of-way along the Potomac River between the Point of Rocks and Harpers Ferry. *Oil painting, 1860, Maryland Historical Society, Baltimore.*

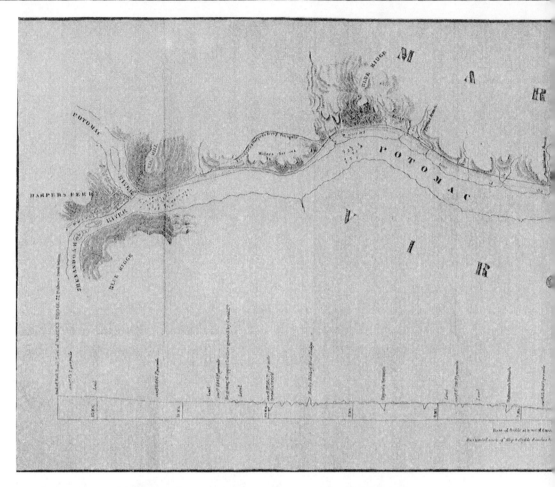

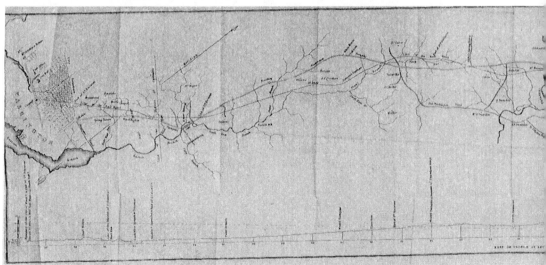

The Maryland legislature effected a compromise between the railroad and the canal in 1833 that allowed both to be built through the disputed twelve miles between the Point of Rocks and Harpers Ferry. The map *(top)* is from the B&O's 1834 annual report. © *The B&O Railroad Museum, Inc., Collection.*

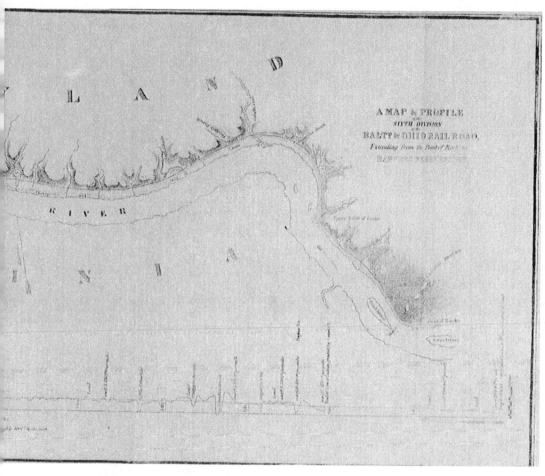

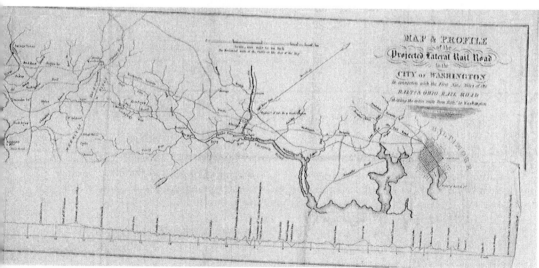

Benjamin H. Latrobe, Jr., supervised the surveys for the B&O's Washington Branch and drew this map *(bottom)* for the 1833 annual report. He laid out the last section between Bladensburg and Washington by aligning it with the dome on the U.S. Capitol, rebuilt by his father after the British burned it in 1814. © *The B&O Railroad Museum, Inc., Collection.*

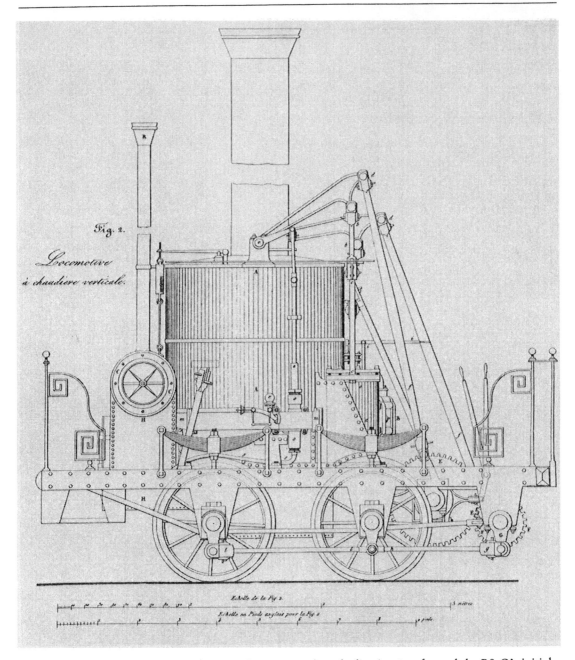

Fig. 2.

*Locomotive
à chaudière verticale.*

The Grasshopper locomotives that first appeared on the line in 1832 formed the B&O's initial complement of power. This model, illustrated in Michel Chevalier, *History and Description of the Channels of Communication of the United States*, 1841, was built about 1836 by Gillingham and Winans. *Herbert H. Harwood, Jr., Collection.*

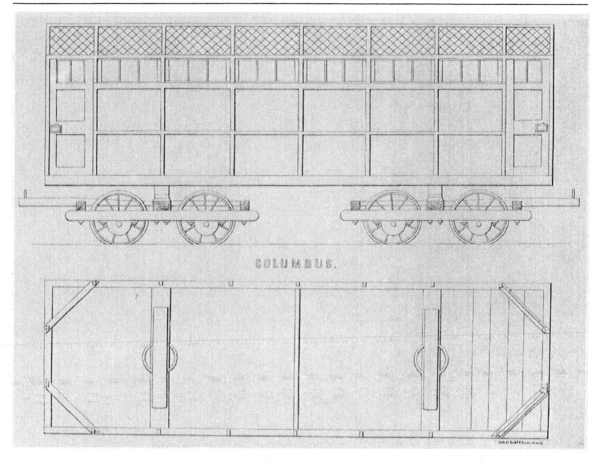

COLUMBUS.

The Columbus, roughly 24 feet long and seating 40 passengers, was the first eight-wheeled passenger car built by the B&O in 1831. Ross Winans had this and other drawings made for an 1850's patent suit in which he claimed to be the inventor of the eight-wheeled car. (He lost.) Conduce Gatch, the B&O's master carpenter, also claimed credit for the design of the Columbus. *Peale Museum, Baltimore City Life Museums.*

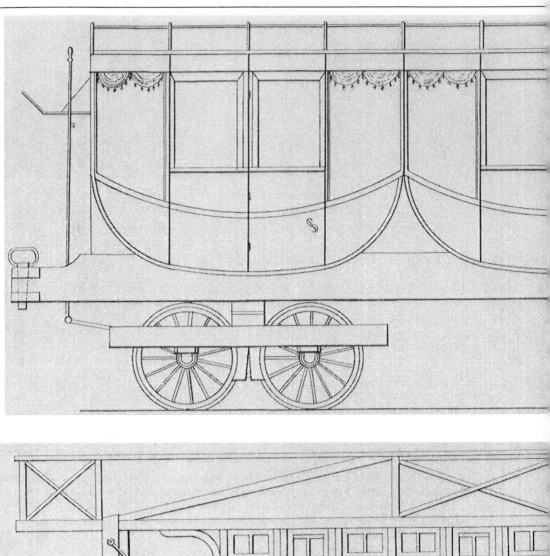

The B&O built the Winchester *(top)* in 1832, with three stagecoach-style bodies, and the Dromedary *(bottom)* in 1834, with a drop frame, overhead truss, and space for cordwood on the right, as experimental eight-wheeled cars. Both were in the train pulled by Davis and Gartner's Grasshopper engines when the B&O opened its line to Harpers Ferry in December 1834. *Peale Museum, Baltimore City Life Museums.*

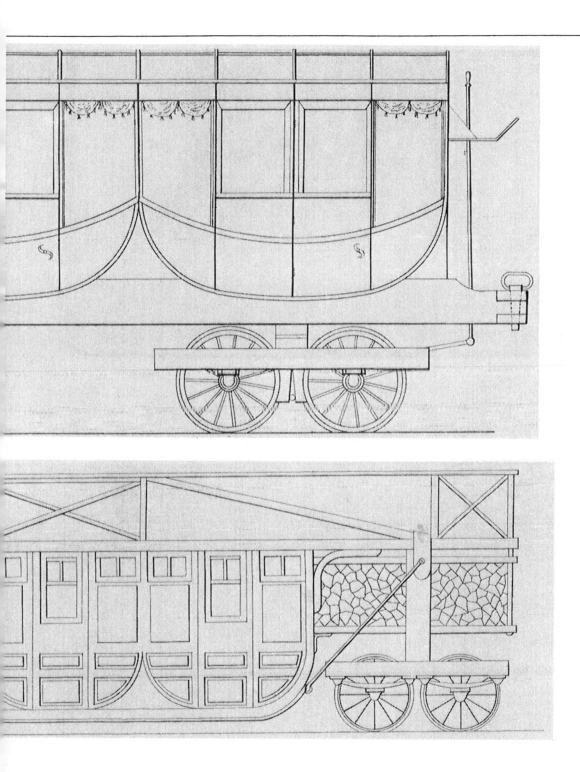

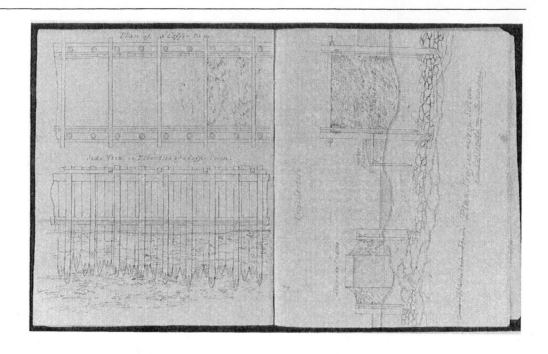

Three pages from Benjamin H. Latrobe, Jr.'s notebook, "Bridges," 1833 *(opposite)*, show the proper method for building cofferdams and one bay of Latrobe's Thomas Viaduct *(above)* for the B&O. *Drawings: Maryland Historical Society, Baltimore; photograph: © The B&O Railroad Museum, Inc., Collection.*

THE THOM

across the · Patapsco · River on the Washington branch of the · Baltimore

Whole length of Bridge and Wing Walls 700 feet. Arches 58 feet 4 inches span. Chord line 612 feet. Height 59 feet
radius of which the arches are chords. Piers at the

A grasshopper engine and train move across the Thomas Viaduct toward the obelisk on
the far side that commemorates the builders. Thomas Campbell's 1835 lithograph was
based on a sketch by John H. B. Latrobe; it lists the official dimensions of the bridge.
© *The B&O Railroad Museum, Inc., Collection.*

VIADUCT,

Ohio Rail Road Designed by Benj. H. Latrobe, Civil Engr.

and Roadway raised from the surface of the water. The plan of the Bridge is a curve of 1273 feet
feet thick, and at the water line 63 feet

The Thomas Viaduct, with Benjamin H. Latrobe, Jr.'s specially designed iron railing, as it appeared in 1872. © *The B&O Railroad Museum, Inc., Collection.*

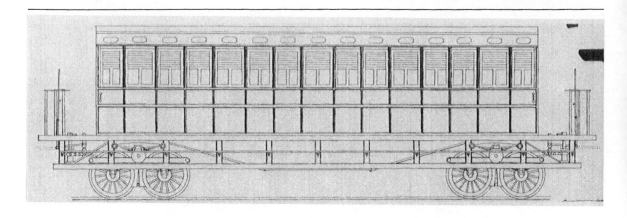

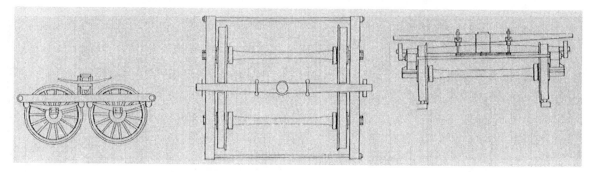

The eight-wheeled coaches that the B&O built for the Washington Branch in 1835 were the prototype of the American railroad passenger car. They were 37 feet long, weighed six tons, seated 44 people, and had mechanical brakes designed by Evan Thomas. *Peale Museum, Baltimore City Life Museums.*

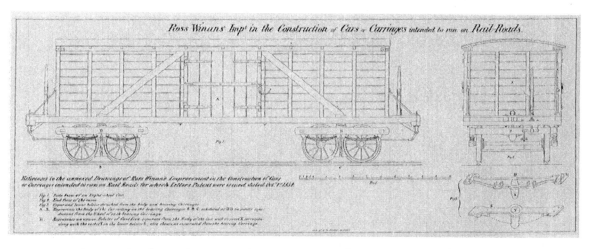

An early B&O freight car illustrating the improvements of Ross Winans. *Peale Museum, Baltimore City Life Museums.*

The Annapolis Junction *(top)* and Bladensburg *(left)* stations on the Washington Branch, and Frederick Junction *(bottom)* on the Old Main Line, 1872. © *The D&O Railroad Museum, Inc., Collection.*

Before tunnels at the Point of Rocks were built in 1868, the railroad skirted the cliff where the telegraph poles are in this 1872 photograph; it was literally on top of the canal. © *The B&O Railroad Museum, Inc., Collection.*

A canal boat and at least three trains under steam power are visible in this circa 1920 view of Harpers Ferry, where the Shenandoah (left) joins the Potomac River and the Winchester & Potomac Railroad (Valley Branch) meets the B&O's main line. The Bollman truss bridge in the foreground was built on the piers of the B&O's original 1836 crossing. The one next to it was erected in 1894 when the railroad tunneled Maryland Heights. The cleared space beyond was the site of the federal arsenal, burned during the Civil War and never rebuilt. *Maryland Historical Society, Baltimore.*

Between 1850 and 1870, the timber truss bridge built for the B&O in 1836 by Benjamin H. Latrobe, Jr., and Lewis Wernwag was replaced by the Bollman truss shown here where the Winchester & Potomac Railroad met the Baltimore and Ohio to cross the Potomac River and the C&O Canal. The 1872 view looks south with Maryland Heights at the left. © *The B&O Railroad Museum, Inc., Collection.*

Wendel Bollman, born in Baltimore, marched in the 1828 parade that inaugurated the B&O, became a carpenter for the company and later its master-of-road. The developer of the Bollman truss was the pioneer builder of iron railroad bridges in America.
© *The B&O Railroad Museum, Inc., Collection.*

✇ 12 ✇

The Thomas Viaduct

THE CONSTRUCTION OF THE WASHINGTON BRANCH began July 1, 1833, when the directors authorized John McCartney, the low bidder and an able, hard-working contractor, to start work at the bridge. The selection of Benjamin H. Latrobe, Jr., an inexperienced, 26-year-old surveyor, trained in the law, to design the bridge seems surprising, but inasmuch as Latrobe's journals, official records, and the press do not discuss the matter, the choice apparently did not surprise anyone at the time. There may, however, have been an implicit understanding between the railroad and its new engineer (who had never built a bridge or even taken a formal engineering course) to create a monumental structure, because that is what they did.

Thomas almost did not stay in office long enough to see the completion of the great bridge that was named for him. He submitted his resignation in the fall of 1833, declaring that he had wanted to retire for years and since the controversy with the canal company was over he thought it an opportune moment. He was urged to stay on, and he said he would, for a time.[1]

Benjamin Henry Latrobe, Jr., was the youngest son of the great architect who introduced the Greek Revival style into America with his design for the Bank of Pennsylvania (1798) in Philadelphia. He also designed, with Nicholas Roosevelt, the Philadelphia Waterworks (1801), the nation's first steam-powered municipal water supply system. Benjamin H. Latrobe (1764–1820) was the first of a succession of architect-engineers in the United States. He was Yorkshire-born, and he received his professional training from the best English teachers—first under John Smeaton, the first modern civil engineer, and then under William Jessop when Jessop was inventing the edge rail and the inside flange, and finally under Samuel Pepys Cockerell in London. In 1795, devastated by the deaths of his wife, infant, and mother, he left England and came to America. His two surviving children by his first wife, Lydia and Henry, came five years later, after he had married Mary Elizabeth Hazlehurst, the daughter of a prominent merchant in Philadelphia. John H. B. (1803–91) and Benjamin Henry, Jr. (1806–78), and a daughter, Julia, were the children of this second marriage.

In 1803, after Benjamin H. Latrobe completed a survey of the lower portion of the Susquehanna River and worked for a time as the engineer of the Chesapeake and Delaware Canal, President Thomas Jefferson named him surveyor of public buildings. In that position, Latrobe undertook to complete the United States Capitol, which had been rather badly handled by several designers, and he rebuilt it after the British burned it in 1814. Much of this work has since been covered over by that of his successors, but the old House and Senate chambers, as well as the original Supreme Court, with its annular vaults and Latrobe's distinctive corncob and tobacco leaf capitals, can still be seen and admired. While he was working on the Capitol, Latrobe was also designing the Roman Catholic Cathedral in Baltimore (1805–18), perhaps his finest work. There was an unsuccessful interlude in Pittsburgh, building steamboats for Robert Fulton, which resulted in personal bankruptcy, and finally, another steam-powered water supply project for New Orleans. Benjamin H. Latrobe died there, of yellow fever, September 3, 1820, three years after the death there of his eldest son, also of yellow fever.

Toward the end of his own career, John H. B. Latrobe summarized his father's attainments as "an artist as well as an architect, botanist, geologist, entomologist, mathematician, poet, musician, and composer, speaking nearly every modern language, and an admirable Greek and Latin scholar."[2] The architect Latrobe kept a journal, a habit he had acquired from his own father. He passed on the idea and the journals themselves to his children and they continued the tradition. Latrobe's journals contained his travel notes and diaries. With the accompanying watercolor sketchbooks, they compose a unique physical and cultural landscape of America during the Federal period.

Both John H. B. Latrobe and Benjamin H. Latrobe, Jr., inherited much of their father's diversity of talent and his good taste. They were educated at home and then at schools in Washington and Baltimore. John went on to West Point but left, prior to graduation, after his father's death to help support the family, not as an engineer but in the law, first in the Baltimore office of his father's close friend Robert Goodloe Harper, then on his own, all the while supplementing his income by free-lance writing and illustrating. Benjamin, after finishing his schooling, also began to study law, and after being admitted to the Baltimore bar he practiced for a time with John. But the practice was hardly big enough for two, and so Benjamin went to Salem County, New Jersey, where his mother owned some woodland property. After three years, during which he practiced law a bit and learned something about timber and surveying, he returned to Baltimore. John was now a lawyer for the B&O, and he got Benjamin his first job on the railroad, as an assistant on the line past Ellicotts Mills. That was in July 1830. "It was a swap between us," John explained later. "I had been educated as an engineer and became a lawyer, and he, educated as a lawyer, became an engineer."[3]

The Latrobe brothers spent virtually their entire professional careers, which spanned much of the nineteenth century, with the Baltimore and Ohio Railroad. Benjamin, in the process, became America's pioneer railroad engineer; John made many of the financial and political arrangements that enabled the line to be built. "The two sons were a remarkable pair," Talbot Hamlin, Latrobe's biographer, says, "and it is interesting to see how they carried on many of the talents of their father." [4]

The bridge that Benjamin H. Latrobe, Jr., designed to cross the Patapsco River Valley between Relay and Elkridge, at the beginning of the Washington Branch, was unprecedented in America. When it was completed on July 4, 1835, at a cost of about $200,000, it became the nation's largest bridge and the first built on a curving alignment. The viaduct of rustic masonry was 704 feet long, including the approaches, and 26 feet wide. The roadway was 66 feet above water level and each of the eight arches spanned a little over 58 feet. The piers, 15 feet thick at the waterline, tapering in to 10 feet at the spring of the arch, were faced with engaged columns and capitals. At both ends of the bridge there were huge stone abutments with battered walls and buttresses. [5]

The configuration was dictated by the curve of the line at that point, which had a radius of 1,273 feet, 4.5 degrees, and was the sharpest on the Washington Branch. The curve resulted from the railroad's choice of a route that crossed the Patapsco at a place called the Hockley Mill. This route made it possible to use a long stretch of the main line before branching off, although an alternative route that would have crossed the river slightly below the Washington Turnpike bridge over the Patapsco at Elkridge Landing would have been much shorter and straighter. The railroad may originally have contemplated the more direct alignment requiring a smaller bridge, but sometime between April 1832, when Latrobe began his surveys for the Washington Branch, and May 1833 when the directors adopted the location and let the contract for the bridge, they changed their minds. The change may have had something to do with wanting to cross the flood-prone river at a higher level. Acquiring the right-of-way in the plain below had been difficult and expensive. The company was at that time engaged in a dispute with a congregation at Elkridge Landing whose exorbitant demands for damages to their wooden meetinghouse had prompted the engineers to conduct a sham survey for a line to avoid the protesters and perhaps induce them to lower their price.

The directors may have received a better offer from their colleague John McKim, Jr., owner of the Hockley Mill, although they later paid him $2,500 in damages. Rebecca Smith owned the property on the Relay side of the river where the bridge was to be located. The railroad gave her $1,000 for the right-of-way, the use of her existing bridge at the spot, and a spring of water near the junction of the Baltimore and Ohio's main line and its Washington Branch.

Certainly the Hockley Mill site was the more spectacular, but it posed difficult engineering problems. For example, because of the curve, the dimensions of the arches would vary on opposite sides of the bridge. Latrobe's solution was to lay out the lateral faces of the seven piers on radial lines, making them wedge-shaped in plan, so that he did not have to construct the arches on a skew. He also used elliptical, two-centered arches instead of semicircular, or Roman, ones, a sophisticated form more in keeping with Renaissance bridge design than classical. The "basket-handle" shape of the arch is emphasized by the tapering piers. The result has been called "a superb work of architecture as well as of engineering."[6]

In style, the Thomas Viaduct rather closely resembled the Liverpool and Manchester Railway's $200,000 Sankey Viaduct, completed a few years earlier with similar dimensions. That bridge lifted the railroad over the Sankey Canal on high piers with pilasters. The major difference was that it was built of brick, with stone facings, topped by a stone parapet. Knight had observed the Sankey Viaduct under construction during his visit to England with the other B&O engineers. Latrobe had not visited it, but he may have seen illustrations of it.[7]

Although he did not actually plan his structure while it was being built, as Wever did the Carrollton and Patterson viaducts, Latrobe, whose father had been a great advocate of stone bridges, learned as he went along. "How frequently we are led to the acquisition of knowledge by being called on to impart it to others," he wrote in his notebook. In August 1833, even as the workmen were starting the foundations for the abutments and piers, Latrobe, feeling deficient in architectural drafting and terminology, visited Colonel James Kearney and the staff of the U. S. Topographical Corps in Washington, D.C. to discuss technical matters. Colonel Kearney lent him books on bridges by Jean-Rodolphe Perronet (1708–94), the first director of France's Ecole des Ponts et Chaussées and designer of the Pont de la Concorde in Paris. The initial entry in Latrobe's notebook titled "Bridges," dated August 1833, described Perronet's bridge at Neuilly-sur-Seine, which had five elliptical arches. Latrobe drew its first pier and coffer dam, with a service bridge, in plan, a masterful pen-and-ink delineation. There is also a perspective view of another Perronet bridge, in his father's "outline style," and a rough sketch of one bay of what appears to be the Thomas Viaduct, showing ashlar stone piers, pilasters, an elliptical arch, and an iron railing. Latrobe indicated elsewhere in his notebooks that he had fully assimilated Perronet's theory of the interdependence of arches.[8] He read other books as well, on engineering, steam engines, and especially on cast iron and steel, and he visited other bridge sites. On a trip to Philadelphia in September 1833, Latrobe walked across Lewis Wernwag's Permanent Bridge on the Schuylkill, making drawings and measurements, and he went out in a bateau to the coffer dam around one of the piers for the Columbia Rail Road bridge, then under construction.

The credit for supervising the construction of the great bridge over the Patapsco River has usually been given to Wever, but Latrobe deserves an equal share. He functioned as what would today be called the project engineer, appearing regularly at the site throughout the construction period, consulting with the contractor, and making plans or decisions on the spot. Others who played major roles included his brother John, Robert Wilson, the superintendent of masonry, and, of course, McCartney and his workmen. But mainly it was the engineer himself who oversaw the building of the viaduct, and whose health deteriorated markedly under the strain and anxiety.

At the very beginning, Latrobe had to fend off Wever and his interminable plots. For aesthetic reasons, Latrobe had designed a stone parapet to top the structure, but Thomas wanted to substitute a cheaper iron railing. Latrobe noted, "Wever has been at work as I suspected poisoning his mind about the Bridge, but it will soon be beyond his reach." He prepared an estimate showing that stone was in fact less costly, and Thomas seemed to agree but Wever continued to try to skirt around Latrobe, who wrote in his journal, "His lordship is very cold in his manner towards me and I am as distantly civil to him." After he discovered that Wever had been asking questions of his staff so that he could impress the directors with his knowledge of the bridge and appear as well informed as the engineer, he wrote, "I have instructed my men to refer him to me on all such occasions." [9]

Yet the two men were able to sustain a professional working relationship, and when the Thomas Viaduct was finished, Wever praised it highly in his section of the 1835 annual report, calling it "that stupendous structure," and pointing out that "The beautiful and imposing design of that viaduct, was furnished by B. H. Latrobe, Esq., Civil Engineer." [10] Latrobe himself felt that the real heroes of the bridge were the men who built it, only a few of whom escaped anonymity and those mainly by dying. There were at least two deaths and several serious injuries. "The public good in works of this kind is purchased sometimes by much individual suffering," he noted. [11]

The Thomas Viaduct contained 63,000 tons of granite, representing over three-fourths of all the stone used on the entire Washington Branch, which included a number of bridges. The stone came from the quarries at Ellicotts Mills. McCartney worked some of them. The granite moved on spur lines extending into the quarries, down the main line to Relay, and out on a timber trestle that McCartney built across the floor of the valley. From there it was lowered by crude cranes called shears to the men building the piers in the cofferdams below. The lime for the mortar came also by railroad from Frederick County. The sand was dredged from the river bottom.

The granite was heavy, dense, and indestructible. Each stone was about one and a half feet high, three feet wide, and two feet deep, and might weigh three-quarters of a ton. Latrobe wrote admiringly of McCartney: "The contractor has begun this great work with a spirit worthy of it. His train of cars running across his service bridge by their own gravity makes quite a show." [12] But McCartney's cofferdams did not look like the beautiful ones Latrobe had drawn in his notebook, that is, double rows of pilings lined with timber and with the space in between filled by stone and clay. Instead, the contractor drove in a single temporary row of plank, and as fast as he and his men could throw it out, the muddy river streamed back in. They set the bottom course of masonry for the north abutment in a foot of water. The foundations for the second and third piers actually had to be laid in the river. Latrobe thought McCartney had made a mistake in leaving them to the last.

Work began August 8, 1833, and even with the difficulties, by the end of September all the piers and both abutments were under construction. They were founded on rock, or as close to it as it was possible to get. The worst by far was the second pier. "In laying the lowest course of stones the workmen were up to their chins in water and the proper packing of the stones together was a matter of no little difficulty," Latrobe recorded in his journal. The following month, the river flooded and inundated the works.

The first casualty occurred in early September, when, just as they were leaving for the day, "a poor fellow at work on the 5th pier was badly hurt by the fall of a large stone from the wooden bridge above," Latrobe reported. "His right arm . . . was terribly lacerated. He is an Irishman *without* a family fortunately." In mid-October another workman lost his footing on the temporary bridge and fell, breaking an arm, a leg, and some ribs. John H. B. Latrobe was on his way to Relay in a train pulled by the Traveller engine when it happened. They picked up the injured man, turned around, and brought him into town at 20 miles an hour.[13]

Then, in late November, the south end of the wooden trestle collapsed at the Hockley Mill, dropping three stone cars and a man named Jacob Cauders into the millrace. Cauders died of a massive head injury three weeks later, leaving a wife and two children. Latrobe knew him: "He was an excellent fellow and I had him last spring as an axeman for a few days." Latrobe spent the day after the accident at the same spot, "working in mud and water in the 7th pier in the head race of the mills. I have never worked under more uncomfortable circumstances. To have to make the nicest measurements upon the roughest ground is a worrying & troublesome thing in the extreme." The day after that, Latrobe wrote, "The south abutment begins to look like the plan and it does my heart good to see the features of my design beginning to appear. May I live to see this structure raised. It will ensure something like immortality to my memory for it will stand as long as the valley and its hemming hills remain in their places."[14]

The year ended with heavy rains and more floods; a landslide carried away about 50 feet of track near McCartney's turnout at the temporary bridge. The contractor had already left for Ohio to bring back his family. "He had better let them stay where they are," Latrobe observed darkly.[15]

Latrobe genuinely admired McCartney's ferocious energy and ability as a builder, but he was often exasperated by his excessive drinking, on the job and off. Latrobe's journals are full of references to McCartney at the bridge, "a little tipsy, but pushing on his men at a great rate," or down inside the leaking cofferdams beside them, "working at it himself like a Trojan." Another heavy drinker was Patrick King, "a droll old chap, a stumpy little man with a queer countenance, and dialect yet very honest and obliging." King helped McCartney cut the line through the hill at Relay. "He has done much work for the company, but seems sick of his present job," Latrobe noted. "He is about giving up his work on account of inadequate price. The little fellow consoles himself for his losses by pretty regular potations."[16]

King's problem was the same material that drove up labor costs at the Deep Cut, a mixed sort of "indurated clay." Latrobe, who found it both fascinating and repellent, described it thus: "The red rather the toughest, the black very sticky and very pervious to water. The yellow quite soapy in its look and texture. . . . Also a blue sand mixed with clay of the same color." Digging it out was unbelievably tedious.

"The pick brings away a piece not larger than the doubled fist at each blow, and when the material becomes penetrated by water, the difficulty is increased for it becomes still more tenacious."[17]

The wheelbarrow men and the cart men, pick and shovel laborers who excavated the material and hauled it away to be dumped, were the lower end of the hierarchy of workmen at the bridge. They were tough, hardened by years of physical toil and abuse and not averse to a little exploitation of their own, or retaliation against those whom they saw as their oppressors, usually the nearest foreman. A few years back, the cart men on the railroad had decimated the nearby forests to sell the wood, and there was now a specific prohibition in the state law for the Washington Branch against cutting timber "without the consent of the owner." Not too long before that, convict laborers, wheelbarrow men building the Frederick Road near Baltimore, had bludgeoned two overseers to death.

Latrobe made several estimates about the labor costs: for example, "A good laborer can excavate and throw into a cart or barrow 15 cub. yds. per day of 10 hours." Knight worked out a complex series of formulas involving two horses and one cart, or one man and two carts, and so on. But there were too many variables to come up with a consistent figure. The workmen, Latrobe noticed, tried to load as little as possible into the carts. Although the figures are contradictory, it appears that at the start of the work on the bridge, the wage for these laborers was $24 a month for a ten-hour-day, six-day week of numbing labor. By November 1833, wages had dropped to between $8 and $13 a month and found—that is, free food and lodging, worth roughly $8 a month—and no pay for rainy or idle days. When work started again, in February 1834, McCartney told Latrobe that he was paying his laborers $15 a month, "the man finding himself." Therefore, in six months, wages had dropped from $1 a day to 63 cents for hundreds of Irish and German workmen.[18]

Stonecutters, the elite of the labor force, were paid at a much higher rate—$2.50 a day in September 1833. In one day, a good stonecutter could dress sixteen cubic feet of the rustic masonry used for the Thomas Viaduct. There was enough granite in the structure to keep 75 or 100 of them busy for two years. There was also a large crew of carpenters at the bridge to put up the cofferdams and the temporary wooden centers for the arches, which supported the masonry until the arches were finished and the mortar had set. Wage rates for the carpenters would have been somewhere between those for the laborers and those for the masons. All the workmen lived in the local taverns and boardinghouses, or in the hundreds of shanties strung out beside the tracks, or in four large "house cars" that moved from site to site along the railroad line.

The tempo of construction accelerated in the spring of 1834, while the mishaps and liquor consumption continued at a steady pace. Latrobe instructed McCartney to erect all the centers and arches at once instead of two or three at a time, but because it was impossible to do that until the piers were in place, a spiderweb of timber falsework spread out between the finished piers while work resumed on the two in the river. In May, while making measurements at the third pier, "A car fell from the [service] bridge loaded with stone, close by us, the crash and splash was terrific," Latrobe said. "It fell into the river by the cofferdam." McCartney was now drinking so heavily that Latrobe predicted he would be dead in ten years if he kept it up. "It is a pity for he is a very intelligent, enterprising, and good hearted fellow," he noted—when he was sober, that is. When he was not, which was usually the case, the construction foreman was blunt and coarse. "What a compound of elevation and grossness of character the man is," Latrobe wrote.[19]

By June, half of the centers for the arches were in place. The next month they addressed in earnest the foundation for the difficult second pier. Latrobe's journal entry for July 15, 1834, reads:

> Went out again to the bridge and remained there till 6½ o'clock in the evening. McCartney hard at work driving everything on. The scene was a very busy one. Within the space occupied by the cofferdam about 40 feet long by 25 feet broad, upwards of 100 men were at work pumping, bailing, scraping the bottom or laying the stone. Numerous small leaks at the upstream end of the dam let in a good deal of water, yet they reduced its quantity till it was within a foot of the bottom. About 5 o'clock however a serious opening took place in the upper end and the water burst up from under the embankment so rapidly that further effort to keep it out was useless. So McCartney broke off to repair his defenses.[20]

Two days later, Latrobe reported: "Went to the bridge as usual. . . . Everything went well till about 4 o'clock when a heavy gust came up and a tremendous rain fell accompanied by severe lightning and thunder. All work was stopped and the river at 6 o'clock was running over the whole of the cofferdam and sweeping everything before it. This was truly mortifying as McCartney had nearly secured the weak point of his dam."[21]

Nerves frayed under these setbacks and the heat as temperatures rose to the mid-90's. One of the foremen, a man named Kincaid, went to the hospital with a mental breakdown, and the tempers of the engineer and the contractor overflowed at last. Latrobe criticized McCartney's work, McCartney "got miffed and behaved like a hot headed fool," Latrobe said. "I was provoked myself at first and spoke sharply to him but afterwards unwilling to quarrel . . . I got him into a good temper again."[22]

By the end of the month, the second pier had cleared the surface of the water. They had been able to get the foundation within a foot of the rock but not on it. Latrobe expected the pier to settle a few inches. It did, as he discovered when he took his levels of the pier tops and abutments a few months later, muttering to himself, with unusual asperity, that using true scientific principles would have been preferable "to the blundering guess work of a mere practical mechanick like the builder of this bridge. If his cofferdams had been well built in the first place, he might have worked dry & comfortable."[23] But the piers were finished. In August, the stone arches were being raised between some and the last centers placed between the rest. McCartney now planned to bring his temporary railroad out over the bridge itself.

In September, Latrobe was dismayed to learn that the directors had revived the plan for the iron railing. He argued against it, and lost, but held his temper and ended up designing it. The cast- and wrought-iron railing was set into large granite blocks installed over the tops of the piers, saving the railroad $1,830 and affording Latrobe the opportunity to utter his father's common complaint, that ignorant interference by budget-minded clients (or others) resulted in inferior designs. Latrobe objected to the iron railing because it was too light for the masonry bridge, but he made the best of the situation. His neoclassical design, consisting of narrow panels containing circles atop X's, is simple and effective. From track level, it resembles a walking stick figure.[24]

The other news, that the contractors had misread the plans and had begun improvising, was another familiar theme, and it distressed Latrobe even more. The slope of the wing walls and buttresses was coming out wrong because Robert Wilson, the masonry superintendent, had started them too close to the base of the bridge. Latrobe blamed McCartney also. Again, he made the best of the problem by altering the design to make the elements thinner, but he was not happy: "It is intolerable that a work intended to last for ages should in the building be thus spoiled by the mistakes of ignorant mechanics. If I had been entrusted with its sole superintendency as I ought to have been, nothing of this kind would have occurred." Six months earlier Latrobe had praised Wilson as "a very industrious attentive man. I would rather have him as an assistant than any one I know of."[25]

The bridge having been officially named the Thomas Viaduct, the railroad president asked the designer to make a drawing of it, with the surrounding scenery, that could be lithographed and distributed bearing both their names. "How much better the *Latrobe* viaduct would sound," Benjamin Latrobe, Jr., mused. His brother John did the actual drawing, choosing the south end as his vantage point, and the lithograph was executed by Thomas Campbell. Campbell's lithograph, published in January 1835, remains the best contemporary view of the bridge and gives the official dimensions.

In mid-October, as Latrobe was planning a monument, a simple obelisk to be put up at the bridge, the viaduct claimed its final victim. What he wrote on the occasion is probably as plain and sincere a tribute as any construction worker who died in the line of duty ever received:

> There was a man killed yesterday by a fall from the centre of the 1st arch. He was knocked off by the slipping of the foot of one of a pair of sheers he was assisting to put up, and was precipitated to the ground a height of about [55] feet, where he struck his head upon a stone and rebounded several feet. His skull was fractured and he sustained other injuries which in about an hour terminated his existence. He was a laborer by the name of Barney Dougherty and has not left a family fortunately. He was buried today, all hands attending his body as far as Vinegar Hill on its way to the Catholic graveyard near Baltimore. What a sympathy there is between these rough men. It was affecting to see [his] fellow laborers dressed in their best going in a body to escort him a part of the way upon his long journey.[26]

Rain and the funeral slowed McCartney down, but he closed the arches in early November 1834. The train from Frederick stopped briefly at Relay to let the passengers get down and watch. When Latrobe made his measurements that month, he determined that the greatest variance between the height of any two of the eight arches was a considerable nine and one-half inches. The northern four arches, the last closed, had settled the most. However, it would not affect the appearance of the structure, he said.

The critics agreed. The Baltimore *Gazette* said, "This great work, which surpasses any thing of the kind yet executed in America . . . combines all the necessary strength with great lightness of appearance."[27] By February 1835, however, months before the bridge was declared completed, alarming cracks had developed. Benjamin Latrobe, Jr., wrote, "John came in great alarm this morning to tell me that Campbell the artist had reported to him that one of the piers of the Thomas Viaduct had cracked and the bridge showed signs of giving way." They raced out to Relay, but after examining the structure from one end to the other, Benjamin declared, "The cracks which had scared Campbell were principally in some stones of the south abutment. I had seen them two months ago."[28] He explained to his brother that the mason in charge had put small chips of stone, or iron wedges used to split the granite, under the courses to level them, and the pressure of the weight on these points of support had caused some of the huge blocks to fracture. In addition, a soft stone in one of the arches had cracked, but the foundation had not yielded and the bridge was as solid as it looked. Relieved, they returned to Baltimore, but Benjamin admitted that he was shaken by the experience.

The final additions to the Thomas Viaduct were the coping, the iron railing, and the obelisk that Benjamin Latrobe, Jr., designed and McCartney paid for. Putney and Woods, quarry operators at Ellicotts Mills, supplied the beautiful light-colored granite for the monument. They also built it. The cast-and-wrought-iron railing, fabricated at the Savage Factory nearby, and the monument were put up in June 1835. After watching him wrestle with the latter one morning, Latrobe noted with satisfaction that it was the same old McCartney. "He has no contrivance but does everything by main force and was working like Jehu himself and swearing correspondingly at his men." One thing was different though. McCartney was now constantly drunk. Once Latrobe thought he was going to fall off the bridge. He was glad the contractor would soon leave Baltimore for good, he said, because even though his cleverness and good nature still showed through, his condition was indeed "piteous."[29]

The monument listed the principals involved in the Thomas Viaduct, its dates of construction, and the names of the B&O directors. Three of the most important were dead by the time their names were engraved in the fall of 1835: Alexander Brown, Robert Oliver, and William Patterson, the trio of "royal merchants," whose wealth, prestige, and influence had meant so much to the railroad during its early days.

The Thomas Viaduct was declared completed July 4, 1835. There appears to have been no ceremony until the official opening of the Washington Branch the following August 25. For its designer, the completion of the bridge embodied professional triumph and personal tragedy. Latrobe and his wife, his cousin Ellen Hazlehurst, had had a second son in June, born with birth defects; in August 1835, the baby died, after an agonizing eight weeks of suffering.

Benjamin Latrobe's own health seemed tied directly to the fate of his bridge. It worsened when work on the Thomas Viaduct began and improved when it was finished, although he had a brief relapse a few months afterward. His diaries contain a complete account of his symptoms and the supposed cures, many of which actually exacerbated his condition. He complained most often about rheumatic shoulder and chest pains, particularly around the heart, palpitations, excited circulation, shortness of breath, indigestion, and fainting. He often woke up in the middle of the night with his heart pounding and the blood racing through his veins. He also had headaches and hearing loss. For these ailments he was bled, cupped, and physicked (purged). He scourged his chest and back with a variety of mustard, hemlock, and tartar plasters, ointments, and poultices, which inflamed his skin. He applied camphor, asafetida, hartshorn, and sulphur. He drank everything from sarsaparilla to turpentine, which made him good and sick, including snakeroot tea and a vile concoction of Iceland moss that caused a raging headache. He wore flannel drawers and put garlic cloves in his ears to improve his hearing. They produced sores instead. He was looking forward to trying "beehive blistering and galvanism." He took several kinds of pills, ranging from the commercially available Hygeian, Lees, and Morrison's pills to special combinations of quinine, lye, and morphine, finally settling on morphine, plus laudanum. This cured his headaches and gave him happy dreams, and gradually his other symptoms receded.[30]

Benjamin H. Latrobe, Jr., left the B&O on July 1, 1835, and did not return until a year later, when he was made engineer of location at $3,000 a year. In the interim he did some work for the company, but his main job was to finish the survey of the Baltimore and Port Deposit Railroad between the City Block, where it connected with the B&O, and the Susquehanna River.[31]

The "valley and its hemming hills" have remained in place, and the Thomas Viaduct is now an important part of this section of the Patapsco River Valley. Most of the original railing on the east side of the bridge is intact, but an anchoring stone block from the top of one of the piers lies at the foot of the north abutment. Some of the most dramatic changes have occurred in the stream bed where the bridge piers, built at an angle to the direction of the flow, have diverted the course of the river, creating a gravel bank and an island.[32] The Patapsco has seen major floods, including one in 1866 that destroyed most of the Patterson Viaduct upstream, but Latrobe's bridge has stood firm and still carries heavy railroad traffic.

∞ 13 ∞

The Bank War

WHILE HIS BROTHER WAS BUILDING THE GREAT BRIDGE, John H. B. Latrobe organized the means to pay for it and stepped into the middle of the "bank war." It revolved around Andrew Jackson and Nicholas Biddle, but the Baltimore and Ohio Railroad was a prime participant.

Jackson became the first President to ride on a railroad, in June 1833, when he took a short trip on the Baltimore and Ohio from Relay to Baltimore. But he had no great love for them, he explained to Benjamin H. Latrobe, Jr., during a brief meeting at "the Big House" in Washington that summer. Railroads might be useful between commercial cities or to connect the seaboard with the interior, but the President did not think they were any great help to the individual farmer, and he doubted that there would be any federal funds to extend the B&O beyond Harpers Ferry.

But Jackson, who once was badly burned in a speculative venture, loved banks even less, and least of all Nicholas Biddle's Bank of the United States. Despite Marshall's decision in *McCulloch* v. *Maryland*, Andrew Jackson and Roger B. Taney, his attorney general since June 1831, believed Biddle's bank was unconstitutional. By the summer of 1833, they had reached a crucial stage of their plan to destroy "the Monster."

The Second Bank of the United States, in whose Baltimore branch James W. McCulloh had toiled profitably fifteen years earlier, was not a federal institution, as many thought, but a private corporation. It did, however, hold a charter from the federal government, which owned 20 percent of the stock, and it had the sole right to receive federal deposits. The bank, with headquarters in Philadelphia and 29 branches around the country, provided credit to approved businesses, circulated banknotes that functioned as a national medium of exchange, and restrained inflation by checking the speculative inclinations of the state banks. It exercised the sort of centralized control over the nation's monetary policy that the Federal Reserve System does today. It also made loans to its political friends.

In January 1832, Biddle, convinced that further attempts to placate Jackson were futile, technically began the "bank war" by applying for a renewal of his charter four years before the old one was due to expire. Congress passed the recharter act and Jackson vetoed it that summer. Taney had a hand in writing the veto message. Although the economic reasoning was dubious, the document was brilliant in its political intent. Jackson took his resounding reelection in the fall as a mandate and decided to implement his ultimate plan to remove the government deposits. Biddle responded by calling in loans and raising interest rates to cover the loss, but he overcompensated in assuming that causing a financial panic would force the return of the federal funds. Nothing but public suffering would produce the needed effect on Congress, he said.

Biddle, a Philadelphia patrician, had powerful advocates in Washington, notably Clay and Webster, as well as strong backing in the financial community. But Jackson had workingmen, state bankers, and ultimately, the votes in Congress. "The bank is trying to kill me," he told Van Buren, "but I will kill it." [1] A primary influence on the 1833 debate within the administration that preceded the removal of the government deposits was Taney's good friend Thomas Ellicott, president of the Union Bank of Maryland. Ellicott offered the services of his own Baltimore institution, in which Taney was a stockholder. The decision was made. When neither Louis McLane nor his successor as treasury secretary would order the removal of the deposits, Jackson appointed Taney Secretary of the Treasury in September 1833. Taney ordered the deposits removed effective October 1. Six state banks were chosen initially as substitute depositories; Jackson's opponents called them his "pet banks." There was one in Baltimore, the Union Bank.

The federal government stopped depositing money in the Bank of the United States and continued its withdrawals. Beginning in August 1833, for the next seven months, Biddle lost $8 million dollars in total deposits. Through November 1834, when he relaxed credit again, he reduced his loans by $18 million. Interest rates went from 6 to 15 percent, and as the depression deepened, money became unavailable, companies failed, and men were thrown out of work. Businessmen and bankers called on Jackson seeking a restoration of the deposits and an end to the crisis. "Go to Nicholas Biddle," he told them. Eventually they did.

While the president of the Bank of the United States sat in his beautiful Greek Revival headquarters on Chestnut Street in Philadelphia, designed by Benjamin H. Latrobe's pupil William Strickland, "as calm as a summer's morning, with his directors around him, receiving his salary, with everything moving on harmoniously," as one of his Senate supporters put it, the laborers on the B&O's Washington Branch watched the competition for their jobs increase and their wages fall.[2] The railroad was desperately short of funds.

Meanwhile, relations had grown strained between Taney and Thomas Ellicott at the Union Bank, which soon turned into the most troublesome of the pet banks. During this period, it was an incubator of self-dealing and speculation among its officers and came perilously close to failing. The Baltimore and Ohio Railroad was intimately involved in its activities. During the sixteen or so months of the Biddle panic, the flow of cash, which was in short supply because of Biddle's constriction of credit, and the exchange of securities among the United States Bank, the Union Bank, Alex. Brown and Sons, the State of Maryland, the City of Baltimore, and the Baltimore and Ohio Railroad grew into an elaborate network. The railroad seems to have called on every conceivable source of funds, and enough of them came through to enable it to keep going.

In the summer of 1833, first of all, the Union Bank agreed to provide the needed cash to begin the Washington Branch in exchange for long-term railroad bonds. Alex. Brown and Sons did the same in early 1834 by buying the State of Maryland securities during the darkest period of the depression. About that time, things got so confused that a committee of railroad directors was sent to call on Thomas Ellicott, who had offered $125,000 for some securities, "and explain to him the difference between the stock that his offer alludes to and the stock that the company are to receive [from the state]."[3]

In this web of exchange, there were a few major events, beginning in April 1831, when the B&O, for the moment putting the Washington Branch aside, declined the offer of a $1 million construction loan from the Bank of the United States and instead took a one-year loan of $200,000 for the main line. After a year, the loan was extended, and in October of the same year, the Union Bank lent the railroad $200,000 so that it could pay off the Bank of the United States. The loan from the Union Bank was due in mid-1833, and it also was extended.

Under the $1 million agreement with the Union Bank arranged in July 1833, the railroad borrowed an initial $500,000, the money to be made available in quarterly installments of $100,000 each, beginning October 1, 1833; the bank was then to provide the remaining $500,000 any time the B&O required it. As the railroad withdrew the funds, it was to deposit an equivalent amount of 6 percent B&O bonds and the company was to give a lien on its property. The securities covering the first half of the loan were made redeemable in January 1854, and those for the second half in January 1845.

However, by the time the Union Bank was to provide the last $500,000, its political and economic fortunes had so fallen that it was obliged to try and back out. It solved the problem by selling these bonds to the Mechanics Bank. John M. Gordon, the Union Bank's new cashier, who was brought in after it was reorganized, claimed the mortgage was never executed. John H. B. Latrobe, who drafted an early prospectus for the sale of these bonds, said the certificates themselves pledged the property and revenues of the main stem and the Washington Branch as security. There is some evidence that the paperwork for the loan was not completed for another nine years.[4]

Latrobe, the counsel for the railroad, and Reverdy Johnson, attorney for the Union Bank, prepared the original loan agreement and stock certificates, although both men were at the same time working for the other company, in a classic conflict of interest. In October 1833, when the first $100,000 changed hands, Latrobe, who was already a Union Bank director and lawyer, was installed on their finance committee. The same month, Johnson was retained as a B&O attorney. Also that month, Taney, who had no knowledge of the Union Bank's investment in railroad securities, gave

Ellicott $300,000 in contingency drafts on the Bank of the United States; he gave the other pet banks similar drafts. His purpose, evidently, was to arm them against an attack by Biddle, who might present large quantities of their notes for redemption in specie, or otherwise cause trouble, and he made clear that the secret drafts were to be cashed only in such an emergency.

But the temptation proved too strong. Ellicott's bank was not the only pet bank to cash the drafts and use the money for other purposes, but it was the first. It is likely—though not certain—that the initial funds for the construction of the Washington Branch came from this source, in a very roundabout way. Ellicott was simultaneously buying Bank of Maryland stock, one of Reverdy Johnson's favorite causes, through which the Union Bank became the owner of a huge block of Tennessee bonds. Taney was also unaware of this, but Biddle let him know that the drafts had been cashed and Ellicott was called to Washington for an accounting. Amos Kendall, a member of Jackson's "kitchen cabinet" who witnessed the scene, reported that Ellicott stammered incoherently under Taney's cross-examination and at last confessed to using the drafts for speculation.

The commercial relationships between the officers of these various institutions were interesting, to put it mildly. Thomas Ellicott was an incorporator and one of the original directors of the B&O Railroad. Evan T. Ellicott, his nephew, and a current B&O director, was the president of the Bank of Maryland. This was basically a reputable institution until the summer of 1832 when Evan T. Ellicott, Evan Poultney, Reverdy Johnson, John Glenn, and some others took it over, using the bank's own funds to purchase the stock. Thomas Ellicott was also involved in the takeover. Besides the Tennessee bonds, they began acquiring Union Bank stock, expecting a rise in value when it became a "pet bank."

The shenanigans at the Bank of Maryland are too obscure and too tedious to recount, but they bore an uncanny resemblance to the Maryland savings and loan scandals of the 1980's, in that they involved using the institution's own assets to gain control of it, attracting depositors by paying premiums (in the case of the Bank of Maryland, the inducement was 5 percent interest on accounts, a banking innovation in Baltimore), insider loans made with little or no security, intentionally complicated transactions to confuse auditors and deflect responsibility, and, toward the end, repudiation of the agreement among the original cabal and ultimate collapse. The feverish expansion of the Bank of Maryland and other financial institutions had been fueled by the anticipated decline in the Bank of the United States, just as the latest savings and loan scandals in Maryland and other states were inspired by federal deregulation.

The Bank of Maryland failed on March 24, 1834. There was an immediate run on its counterpart, the Union Bank. Thomas Ellicott had been named trustee of the Bank of Maryland. The run lasted from morning until four o'clock in the afternoon. John H. B. Latrobe was there, helping to count out silver from the boxes. "A crowd assembled opposite in the street, on the pavement, on the steps, in the passages, and even in the Banking Room," he said. "Men and women, black and white, brought forward their notes and asked for silver and by the time the doors were closed more than $20,000 had been redeemed with specie." The lawyer dryly concluded his journal entry: "Fine day, for the weather." Said Benjamin: "I wish my brother was well clear of Tom Ellicott and his bank."[5]

Although John H. B. Latrobe was evidently not a major speculator, he was a central figure in many of these financial deals. Philip E. Thomas, Thomas Ellicott, and Evan Poultney were already linked by family ties and commerce, but as the agent for both corporations, the lawyer Latrobe probably also had a hand in bringing the Baltimore and Ohio Railroad and the Union Bank together. From September 1833, when the federal deposits arrived at the Union Bank, to March 1834, when the Bank of Maryland failed, Latrobe had regular meetings with the officers of the railroad and both banking institutions on related business matters. He spent long evenings in conference with Thomas Ellicott and Reverdy Johnson. On a combined railroad-bank lobbying trip to Washington in December 1833, he met with Taney and consented to write an article on the removal of the deposits for the Jackson paper in Baltimore, the *Republican*. "Agreeing as we do in Politics our conversation was full and confidential," he noted in his journal.[6]

In early 1834, John H. B. Latrobe made three lobbying trips to Annapolis on behalf of the Union Bank in an attempt to convince the state treasurer and the legislature to increase its capital stock. He drafted the legislation. He cajoled the politicians with oysters and terrapins, wine and song, staying up to two and three in the morning with them, as was (and still is) the Annapolis custom, to "royster and make merry." He conducted secret negotiations with the Senate finance committee, taking care to keep the discussions out of the journal and out of the newspapers. He offered the state treasurer roughly $20,000 on behalf of the bank in exchange for the passage of its program and was turned down by the committee and the state treasurer because the offer was too low.[7]

The day after the failure of the Bank of Maryland and the mob scene at the Union Bank, after his nerves had steadied, John H. B. Latrobe confessed, "I never saw a run on a bank before: and I can now say that it is by no means a pleasant sight even to an unconcerned spectator." Latrobe was not exactly unconcerned, however: he was a director of the Union Bank and he owned stock in it, which he later sold at a loss, and he was indebted to it as well as to the Bank of Maryland, where he maintained his checking account. When that institution failed, he had to borrow $50 from Jonathan Knight. Altogether, he lost only $71 of his own funds. His banking connections protected him from further damage. The total loss from the collapse of the Bank of Maryland, borne mainly by the middle and lower classes, was about $3 million. Latrobe was similarly reticent in his assessment of the demise, saying only that Evan Poultney had "more imagination than judgment."[8]

Two months later, when the Maryland Savings Institution went under, Benjamin H. Latrobe, Jr., a Whig, lost several hundred dollars and was a little more outspoken. Tarring and feathering or at least hanging in effigy would be appropriate "for the scheming, swindling scoundrels who have thus robbed the poor," he said.[9] Yet when still another bank collapsed, along with "two or three other rag shops," as Hezekiah Niles called them, the depositors bore their misfortune stoically, for a time.[10]

Taney assigned Reverdy Johnson and Charles Howard, in May 1834, to investigate the Union Bank's affairs and help him determine whether it warranted retention as a depository for the government's funds. Johnson immediately wrote Biddle, to whom he was personally indebted for $10,000, and laid out a duplicitous scheme. If Biddle made a loan to the Union Bank on the Tennessee bonds, Thomas Ellicott might relinquish the government deposits and declare the whole idea a failure. Perhaps such an assertion by Jackson's and Taney's favorite pet bank would sway Congress to restore the deposits to the Bank of the United States.

Biddle not only declined to make the loan, he also advised the Union Bank to dump the Tennessee bonds at whatever cost, get rid of its railroad securities, and escape the contract to provide further loans to the B&O. The investigation never amounted to much either. A year later, Charles Howard was still asking John H. B. Latrobe for his recollections of Thomas Ellicott's connection with the Union Bank and the railroad loan. Latrobe procrastinated. It is doubtful that he ever answered the questions.

During the dark days in early 1834, as the Union Bank's influence and utility spiraled downward, the B&O turned to Alex. Brown and Sons, which, as usual, had little use for speculators. "We had no confidence in any of these institutions and are not invested for one dollar," they said after the bank crashes.[11] The Union Bank did make the first two $100,000 payments under the $1 million loan agreement, but effectively handled the third, due April 1, 1834, by canceling half of its previous $200,000 loan to the railroad. It is unclear whether the Union Bank made any more payments before arranging with the Mechanics Bank to take over the second half of the $1 million loan. The other part of the financial package, the state's $500,000 subscription to the Washington Branch, was received in the form of 4.5 percent State of Maryland stock in the fall of 1833. In January 1834, Biddle refused to lend the railroad money on this stock, and since, according to Thomas, they could not sell it except at a loss of up to 15 percent, the B&O lobbied the Maryland legislature to change it to a 5 percent stock. But the state was running a deficit, and before the lawmakers could comply, the railroad hit rock bottom. "I fear the company will be much embarrassed for the means to meet their engagements with contractors for the construction of the Washington road," George Brown told Thomas. The Mechanics Bank could not advance them any more money, and "If the Union Bank should be able to give us $100,000 on the first of April, it will not be in time to meet the expenditures upon this road."[12]

On February 4, 1834, Thomas wrote John B. Morris in Annapolis, "If we do not get the aid we ask, we must at once stop work as we are without the funds to proceed further."[13] Two days later, the Maryland legislature passed a law that in essence made the state's $500,000 subscription to the Washington Branch a 5 percent stock and turned it over to the railroad. The same month, the company received almost $200,000 more in 5 percent bonds, $125,000 from the State of Maryland and

$70,000 from the City of Baltimore, representing the remainder of their unpaid stock subscriptions to the B&O Railroad. The negotiation with the city was particularly convoluted. The Baltimore and Ohio appears to have subscribed to a municipal loan, thus enabling the city to issue its bonds to the company.

Thomas Ellicott at the Union Bank bid on the $500,000 batch of State of Maryland stock, but Alex. Brown and Sons made the B&O a better offer. They said they would take it at par and begin $50,000 monthly payments immediately. That was in mid-February 1834. In the succeeding months, as the Bank of Maryland went under, the Union Bank showed little interest in the $200,000 in state and municipal bonds. On April 1, 1834, Alex. Brown and Sons took the bulk of these securities as well, at 98 percent, paying $25,000 a month, starting right away.

Three days later, Alexander Brown was dead at 69. The cause was pneumonia contracted while presiding over a merchants' meeting at the Exchange in the wake of the Bank of Maryland's failure. During his lifetime, he had been the Baltimore and Ohio Railroad's most resolute backer and the major source of stability in Baltimore's volatile banking community. For Thomas and others it was a personal loss. "The decease of our estimable friend Alexander Brown is felt here to be a severe public calamity," Thomas wrote a correspondent. "I have no recollection of so deep a gloom having ever heretofore been thrown over this city by the death of an individual. He was universally known and enjoyed the unlimited confidence of the whole community." [14]

The B&O directors at their next meeting paid tribute to "the head of an opulent house," who possessed "a mind outstripping the march of events and anticipating the slow process of ages." [15] Thomas confided to George Brown that he had depended on Alexander Brown's kindness and judgment and felt like a family member in his sorrow. The B&O treasurer resigned the following month to take over Alex. Brown and Sons in Baltimore. That summer, the Union Bank stockholders, including Taney, decided they had had enough of Thomas Ellicott and replaced him with Hugh W. Evans, a B&O director. John H. B. Latrobe was ousted as well. Ellicott wisely decided to retire to his wife's estate in Avondale, Pennsylvania.

The mercantile community pressured Nicholas Biddle to relent, and he did so in the fall, making credit available again on reasonable terms, and the panic was officially over. By the end of the year, the railroad was not alone in reporting better economic times. A renewed effort by Webster and Clay in Congress failed to win Biddle a new charter and the Jacksonians had won the "bank war."

Its effects were less tidily concluded. During 1834, amid general unemployment and social unrest, the Irish conducted their own war on the Washington Branch. Although much of their quarreling was, at least to begin with, among themselves, as it had always been, their declining fortunes mirrored the railroad's, and the railroad eventually became a kind of target. "The money market remains under great pressure," Thomas told a correspondent at the beginning of the year. Labor was abundant and prices low, he informed another a month later, and a few days after that, wrote, "the money market is becoming daily more pressed." [16] Another month went by and there was a minor disturbance among the workmen. Charles S. Ridgely, a general of the Maryland militia who lived at Elkridge, helped to restore order.

Thomas thought the "deluded men" did not understand their "true interests": the B&O had kept them on during the winter when there was little work and now that the company could get all the labor it wanted at cheap rates, which was all they could afford to pay, the workers ought not complain.[17] In April 1834, it was the "money concerns of the country" that were "disordered,"[18] and a week later Thomas warned Wever that the contractors' practice of paying the workmen in depreciated bank paper had to be stopped.

Throughout the year rival groups of Irish laborers on the various public works terrified their local communities. The earliest encounter of any size occurred in January 1834 on the C&O Canal at Williamsport when about 300 men of Cork met and were defeated by roughly twice as many Fardowns. There were numerous deaths. Federal troops were called out from Fort McHenry to restore order. Benjamin Latrobe, who was on the Potomac refining the joint railroad-canal line between the Point of Rocks and Harpers Ferry, witnessed some of the battle preparations from a tavern, where he and his survey crew were staying in Berlin (now Brunswick), below Williamsport. "The [survey] party came in about sunset," he reported, "and just as they arrived, a band of 75 or 80 of the Corkonians came trudging up the towpath. I counted them from the window. About 15 guns were in their possession and Lord knows how many pistols, dirks, and knives. They marched in quick time and were soon out of sight."[19] The inhabitants, fearing that the Corkonians would return and attack them, sent the children to nearby homes, and about fifteen men from the neighborhood gathered in the evening with their fowling pieces and hatchets to protect the tavern. They kept everyone up all night by constantly running upstairs to the garret to spot the attackers, but the only Irishman who appeared was an unfortunate traveler who blundered into the midst of the posse and was put under house arrest.

It was the B&O Railroad's turn that summer when several hundred members from each of the same two factions squared off on the Washington Branch. The riot began on a Sunday evening in mid-June and was mostly over by Wednesday. There were four deaths, including a woman. General Ridgely was again called out on Monday morning and spent the next three days with about 60 local militiamen under arms, marching back and forth between Waterloo and Vansville trying to separate the feuding parties. The local militia was later joined by a company from Baltimore. At Laurel, the Fardowns wrecked and burned their opponents' shanties. The Corkonians counterattacked at Waterloo and drove the others into the woods and fields. In the end, both sides welcomed Ridgely as a mediator. Several rioters were arrested and jailed at Annapolis and the militia remained on the Washington Branch for several more days to ensure tranquillity.

In the early fall, Thomas informed Trueman Belt, a B&O construction manager,[20] that the Irish workmen were massing to attack the Germans at Snowden's Ridge, the southernmost of the three low hills on the Washington Branch in Maryland. A few days later, he asked Amos A. Williams, a B&O state director and agent at the Savage Factory, to consider concentrating the German laborers at one location for their own protection. There was also construction at Merrill's Ridge, the north-ernmost hill, near Waterloo, under Jonathan Jessop (or Jessup), in a section known as Jessop's Cut.[21] But when the Irish exploded for the last time in 1834, it was at the center elevation, Patuxent Ridge, between Savage and Laurel.

John Watson was the company's "energetic and competent" manager of con-struction at that location. Like Wever, he had previously been a superintendent on the National Road. Early in September, irregularities and disorders were reported at Watson's station. On Monday, November 17, 1834, the B&O awarded him an exca-vation contract for another part of the line, through Duel Ridge, within the District of Columbia. His low bid of 25 cents a yard was a very cheap price.

The next evening eight or ten laborers attacked Watson and a contractor named John Gorman at Gorman's shanty. They clubbed Watson to the ground and with their dirks wounded Gorman, so seriously that for a time it was thought he would not recover. During the excitement, Watson managed to crawl away on his hands and knees and hide behind a tree. He then dragged himself to his own shanty two miles off, where he lay in bed all the next day. His friends encouraged him to leave the area, but he refused, so a dozen or more stayed with him that night, includ-ing William Mercer, his assistant, Smith, a company clerk, and two foremen named Callon and Welsh.

The excavation through the ridge where Watson's shanty was located began a short way past the Little Patuxent River. Heading south from this point, the line entered an elongated S-curve. The cut itself was almost a mile in length and 20 or so feet deep. It was just about finished. Workmen's shanties and construction equipment were still scattered about. Through this raw work site late Wednesday, about 30 armed men moved silently and purposefully. Between midnight and 1:00 A.M. Thursday morning, November 20, 1834, they surrounded Watson's shanty. Then they stormed in shouting, "Where is Watson?" "Where is Mercer?" They dragged men outside and beat them, and left Watson dazed under a horse trough to pursue other victims. Mercer and Smith found Watson and carried him back into the shanty. He crawled up to the second floor and managed to pull himself up onto the ceiling joists over-head. Then the attackers grabbed Mercer, marched him around the shanty, forced him to kneel and say his prayers, and then either shot him four times or clubbed him to death. (Accounts vary.) They almost gave up the search for Watson, tramping through the house, upstairs and down, until one man who had lingered on the second floor noticed blood dripping onto the floorboards from above, and brought the rest back with a shout. Watson had no chance. He was beaten and then flung headfirst down the stairs. At the bottom, they held a firebrand to his face to make sure he was dead. The gang then broke open some desks and trunks. They stole watches, cloth-ing, and $11 in cash, which was all that was left. During the pandemonium, Smith, the clerk, had managed to scoop up $4,300 in payroll funds and escape. Outside, the marauders fired a final volley before dispersing.

The others escaped also. When the attack began, Welsh jumped out the second story window and as he landed, someone cried, "Shoot the damned rascal." He was hit two times, once in the face, but got away. The *American* on Friday said Callon had been killed as well. He stopped by the office the day after the notice appeared to say it was premature and told his story. As he had burst barefoot from the cabin door with his dog, someone fired a horse pistol, missing him, killing the dog, and so terrifying Callon that he ran full speed for several miles, stopping only when he noticed that his feet and legs were lacerated and swollen.[22]

The Savage Factory's Amos Williams informed Thomas of the murders the same day. Although the railroad was later criticized for being indecisive, the president acted swiftly. He notified Wever at the Point of Rocks and asked him to come in and take charge of the company's property at Patuxent Ridge, but Wever, recovering from a "severe bilious fever," demurred. The day after the murders, Thomas convened an emergency meeting of the directors. They decided to spend $500 in an attempt to find the perpetrators. Later that day, Thomas sent word to Amos Williams—whom he had asked to safeguard the books and papers at Watson's shanty—that the company wanted to keep its activities secret to avoid retaliation. A "sagacious, experienced, and intrepid" Baltimore police officer named G. Riggs carried the president's note to the Savage Factory. The Baltimore and Ohio Railroad's first undercover agent was going to work.[23]

Riggs may have been all that Thomas said he was, but after two days he reported that he hadn't a clue regarding the identity of the killers. The workers, meanwhile, menaced the community. They took possession of Mrs. Harrison's tavern, the Half way, at Laurel Saturday night, drinking and fighting, and broke into Wheelock's store, a mile away, to carry off what was left, the owner having thoughtfully removed most of the stock.

On Monday, November 24, five days after the murders, Thomas decided to call out the militia. Benjamin Latrobe shouldered a musket and marched from Waterloo with a group of 30 men to search the shanties at Jessop's and Watson's sections. No arrests were made Monday, but on Tuesday reinforcements arrived from the city, and by Wednesday roughly 300 rioters had been captured and returned to Baltimore. The murderers were surely among them, according to military spokesmen.

But the citizens of Anne Arundel and Prince Georges counties had had enough. At a large and angry meeting at Merrill's tavern in Waterloo on Wednesday they condemned the workmen and their employers. The neighborhoods near the Washington Branch had been "the scene of successive riots, dangers, and bloodshed" since construction began, they said, leading up to the recent "murders of the most wanton, diabolical, and atrocious character." The laborers were "a gang of ruffians and murderers" who had formed "secret associations" to accomplish their "hellish plots." The railroad should fire them all. Since the company had not discovered the murderers and because the workers were now threatening the general public, the citizens intended to "muster a sufficient force and drive every Irishman off the road from the Patapsco to the Patuxent."[24]

Thomas took the vigilantes' anger seriously—they threatened to destroy the shanties at Jessop's and Watson's sections where the workmen were concentrated—and pleaded with Amos Williams, coordinator of the effort to secure the company's property and restore order, to give the laborers time to remove their belongings first. To do anything else might invite more damage to the railroad and the community. "These people are revengeful, vindictive, and unrelenting," Thomas said.[25]

The newspapers leaped to defend the company, saying the citizens were ignorant of its early efforts to determine who the murderers were and that the people at the meeting were more responsible for maintaining the peace than the railroad was. The Irish responded by setting fire to a stable at Waterloo the night after the meeting. The flames damaged Merrill's tavern and house. The next Saturday, some of the rioters, on their way home after being freed from jail in Baltimore, refused to pay the toll at Dennis A. Smith's turnpike bridge over the Patapsco. When they pushed through the gate, the tollkeeper shot one of them, but not fatally. More militia were sent to keep order at the bridge.

The following Tuesday, almost two weeks after the murders, as the residents held their second meeting at Waterloo to protest newspaper accounts saying that they had criticized the company unfairly, someone burned the nearby stable of Edward Jess, killing two horses, his only possessions of value. Jess was a laborer on the railroad and seemingly the target of others. By December 11, three weeks after the event, all but a dozen of the prisoners had been examined and let go, just a few of the several hundred shanties remained standing, and the workers had been scattered to Washington and Baltimore.

Only one voice spoke for the workers. The Baltimore *Republican*, the Jackson paper, blamed the company. If the railroad were wiser in picking contractors and if the contracts were more liberal, there would be no problems because "too much hard labor would not be exacted from the laborer, to make amends for the badness of their contract, which from the first had no hope of being profitable," the newspaper's correspondent said. "Then would we be spared the disagreeableness of seeing three hundred persons marched through our city, whose patched and tattered garments, whose long and squalid beards, and emaciated countenance, plainly indicated that they had suffered the greatest privations." Some might be ignorant, others sick from living and working in "chinky shantees or marshy grounds," yet they were not, as they had been characterized, a gang of ruffians: "If they remonstrate, they are told to quit the work, but perhaps disease has unfitted them for another emigration; and is this a time to tell them to begone?" The correspondent pointed out that some of the Irish had helped to tear down the shanties and had joined the local companies of volunteers in a search for the murderers.[26]

A critic in the *Republican* defended the company, saying that it had put its own superintendents at the most difficult construction sites on the Washington Branch, namely the three ridges, to avoid frauds and absconding contractors and to guarantee workmen their pay. They had been paid and if it was too little, it was too bad. The money was no worse than on other public works or there would not have been an oversupply of labor. Some 30 years earlier, Benjamin H. Latrobe had offered a more enlightened view of the workmen on the New Orleans water works: "Distress and want of employ has made many of them sots; few have saved their characters, most of them hate, envy, and calumniate each other, for they are all fighting for the scanty means of support which the city affords."[27]

The railroad riots, the community's anxiety, and winter weather combined to produce a suspension of work on the Washington Branch. At the end of January 1835, Owen Murphy, Patrick Gallagher, and Terence Coyle were indicted and tried in Annapolis for the murder of John Watson. Murphy was convicted of first degree murder and sentenced to death by hanging, at the spot where Watson was killed. Both Gallagher and Coyle were found guilty of second degree murder and both received sentences of eighteen years hard labor, including a year of solitary confinement. They were also later tried and found guilty of the same charge in the death of William Mercer. Samuel Raily, an accessory to the murder of Watson, escaped to New Orleans and three years later died of injuries sustained in a fight with a man who threatened to expose him as a labor terrorist.

The judge at the trial of Owen Murphy, after remarking that Murphy and the others, during "the stillest, darkest hour of the night . . . stole forth from your dens in the execution of a plot long before meditated," could find no motive, other than an allusion to the feuds of Ireland transplanted to the United States. Some attributed the riots to whiskey, handed out by contractors to inspire greater effort. Hezekiah Niles said they were due to ignorance, prejudice, and the Irish tradition of violence. But the motives were there.

John Gorman, the contractor who was wounded in the initial attack but recovered, had been robbed earlier of $1,200 and had accused some of his hands. Both Watson and Mercer were Irish, but as Orangemen were despised by the others. Watson had obtained his contract for the section of the Washington Branch through Duel Ridge in the District by offering a very cheap rate for excavation and had fired a number of his workers at Patuxent Ridge for being lazy and unruly. Some of them had found work at Jessop's Cut through Merrill's Ridge. When William Mercer was about to be struck down in front of the shanty, his assailants shouted, "You will recollect the cart men you discharged."

In the spring of the following year near Bladensburg, German laborers attacked a group of fellow German workmen with muskets, wounding half a dozen. The riot was the result of a demand for higher wages. Those assaulted were content with the existing rates. The Irish erupted again in July 1835, when they burned the tavern at Waterloo. So they were the normal human motives of profit and revenge, not so different from the motives of those who conducted the "bank war."

In August 1835, shortly before the Washington Branch officially opened, the "bank war" was brought home with particular fury to Baltimore. The public, "made weary and disgusted" by a battle of the pamphlets among the principals and trustees of the failed Bank of Maryland who were supposedly investigating its affairs, took matters into their own hands. For three days, Friday through Sunday, August 7–9, 1835, the downtown area was in tumult. "Society seems everywhere unhinged," said Hezekiah Niles, who had predicted mob rule.[28] When it was over, eight to ten people, some of whom were onlookers, had been shot dead in the streets by the militia. Reverdy Johnson's house in Monument Square was a shattered hulk. So were the houses of John Glenn, B&O directors Evan T. Ellicott and John B. Morris, the latter a Bank of Maryland trustee, and several others. Their elegant furnishings and libraries were scattered in the street and burned, and their stocks of expensive wines sold off or consumed by the rioters. Mayor Jesse Hunt, who had been implicated in the bank scandals, resigned after his house was sacked. Order was restored only when 83-year-old Samuel Smith rallied the citizens and put them under arms. Smith was later elected mayor.

A handbill posted on the third day of the rioting said: "Fellow Citizens—Let us pause. Last night we have nobly shown what robbers are to expect at the hands of Baltimoreans, but let us stop now, and give them a chance, once more, to make restitution, and if they can, to justify themselves. . . . If innocent, we have done them wrong, but if guilty, and they do not make restitution to the Widow and Orphan to the full extent of their means, let us visit them with the just indignation of an injured community." The bill was signed, "One of the People."[29]

Benjamin H. Latrobe, Jr., who had been away surveying during the worst of the rioting, returned on Sunday and went to a meeting called at the Exchange to rally the citizens who favored restoring peace to the city. Nobody came. That evening, the rioters discarded the masks they had worn the night before and went about their work with impunity. Latrobe noted that most of the spectators implicitly sympathized with them:

> I went down to see the demolition of Johnson's elegant house in Monument Square. The sight was as full of picturesque grandeur as it was of heart sickening horror. The magnificent furniture, consisting of large and costly bedsteads, bureaux, tables, chairs, looking glasses and all the other paraphernalia of an elegantly provided mansion was pitched from the windows, the sashes and frames of which were previously knocked out, and as it fell with quickly successive crashes upon the pavement below, was heaped upon the pile which blazed at the base of the Battle Monument with fierce and flickering lustre, illuminating with intense brilliance the beautiful little column and the classic statue it supported, and throwing a broad stream of light upon the lofty edifices ranged around the square.[30]

An immense crowd watched impassively as the marauders waved their spoils triumphantly from the shattered windows.

Latrobe said the violence was instigated by a group of butchers who had lost heavily in the failure of the Bank of Maryland and had sworn vengeance, to the point of hiring and training a cadre of 50 or so young rowdies to lead the attack while the butchers stood by in the crowd to help out if needed. Several persons were arrested, tried, convicted, and jailed for rioting. John M. Gordon, the new cashier of the Union Bank, attended the trials in December 1835. "Black Hawk was convicted today," he reported. "The great bear that struck terror into the hearts of 80,000 people was a mere youth, good natured, smart, and fond of fun, and I have no doubt entered into the mob merely as a frolick. . . . He had put a curtain ring in his coat in front and a piece of gilding in his hat and those spoils of a bed chamber were as appalling at the time as the tomahawks and green scalp. Red Jacket was still more contemptible, a stupid Dutch paver." [31]

Six months later, the governor pardoned the jailed rioters. Johnson, Morris, Glenn, and the others were afterward reimbursed for their losses by a special act of the legislature. Johnson received almost $41,000. Evan Poultney and his accomplices were acquitted on charges of looting the Bank of Maryland. The *National Gazette* said the affair was "very atrocious as a mere pulling down of houses, but as a punishment of these individuals for an alleged offence, it is neither unmerited nor unprovoked." [32]

After things had quieted down on the railroad, Jonathan Jessop finished what little remained of Watson's work at Patuxent Ridge and Trueman Belt took over the contract he never began, within the District. In the spring of 1835, Congress and the City of Washington passed laws providing for the extension of the railroad into the capital. The initial terminus was a former boardinghouse at Pennsylvania Avenue and Second Street, NW, but the city's legislation provided that locomotives could go no farther than New Jersey Avenue and C Street, a few blocks short.

Benjamin H. Latrobe, Jr., had laid out the route, lining it up from Bladensburg to strike his father's dome on the Capitol, although it hardly followed a straight line within the District. He was closely involved with the agonizing right-of-way negotiations there, as he had been for the entire Washington Branch. Particularly troublesome was a tailor named John Sinon, who extracted $10,000 from the company for his lot and house, which the B&O then tore down for its approach to the station.

The new T-rails from England, unloaded at the City Block, moved over the line through Baltimore, across the Thomas Viaduct, and down the graduated right-of-way to the end of the line, where the crews laid them down in a single track. There were not enough T-rails for the sidings, so strap rails were substituted. Meanwhile, Knight oversaw the completion, in Phineas Davis's shops at the Mt. Clare depot, of four new Grasshopper engines and several new eight-wheeled coaches developed by Ross Winans, among the first such cars introduced on an American railroad. On July 1, Thomas and some of the directors took a ride to the District line near Bladensburg. Service to that point began on July 20.

The Washington Branch cars were a little over 37 feet long, nine feet wide, and about seven feet high. They weighed roughly six tons and accommodated 44 people. The coaches rode on two four-wheeled trucks, with steel leaf springs. Their brakes, evidently the earliest examples of a mechanical braking system, were designed by Evan Thomas. The two trucks, attached to the car body with rose bolts, improved the equilibrium of the coach on curves, as well as the safety of the passengers, because if one wheel or axle broke, the car would stay on the tracks. Another major advantage over the old models, whose four wheels were set close together to diminish friction on curves, was that the eight-wheeled cars could be made any convenient length. [33] The new cars had a center aisle with seats on either side, windows that went up and down, and handsome details. Hezekiah Niles, an aging but undiminished enthusiast, praised these coaches, "with their broad seats, with their high stuffed, well inclined backs and wide leg-room," as "the most commodious we have ever travelled in, and we have lately been in a good many." [34]

Benjamin H. Latrobe, Jr., was one of the 800 people from Baltimore who traveled to the capital on August 25, 1835, to open the Washington Branch officially. The celebration started at the Charles Street depot in downtown Baltimore. From there, seventeen of the new eight-wheeled cars built for the Washington service, each pulled by four gray horses, proceeded to the Mt. Clare depot, where they were assembled into trains of four and five cars, and the new Washington Branch engines, named after Presidents George Washington, John Adams, Thomas Jefferson, and James Madison, were attached for the journey to the capital.

Hezekiah Niles, who of course was aboard for the trip, called the Thomas Viaduct "the most beautiful triumph of art that we ever saw." [35] Benjamin Latrobe, unusually laconic, only noted several delays. The citizens and the corporate authorities of Washington, Georgetown, and Alexandria had come out from the District by train to welcome the Baltimoreans at Bladensburg. W. A. Bradley, the mayor of Washington, said the new line was "among the first steps in that grand policy which seeks to unite this great country by bands of political and social interest, of mutual dependence, respect, and support, which alone can render our union firm and enduring." Philip E. Thomas remarked on the new spirit of cooperation between Washington and Baltimore: since they had become "competitors, without being opponents, friendship, not jealousy, is the feeling that should hereafter exist between them, as hand in hand, either by Canal or Rail Road, or by both in connexion, they effect that communication with the West which they simultaneously commenced." [36]

Andrew Jackson, in a white hat, watched the formalities from a nearby hill with a party of friends. Thousands of cheering spectators lined the route as the trains pulled into Washington. From the temporary end of the line near First and B streets, at the northwest corner of the Capitol, bands led the way to the nearby Gadsby's and Brown's hotels. There, what the papers described as a sumptuous repast awaited the guests. Benjamin Latrobe noted: "At Gadsby's we dined on a meagre supply of cold viands, and at Brown's found a greater abundance of everything." John H. B. Latrobe made a speech that was admired and the mayor of Washington remembered their father. "It was an exciting day to me," Benjamin H. Latrobe, Jr., said. [37] The Baltimore city officials called on the President, and at 4:30 P.M. everybody boarded the trains. Two hours and twenty minutes later, they were back home in Baltimore.

The 30-mile Washington Branch had cost four years, eight lives, and $1,493,797.

14

The Bridge at Harpers Ferry

THE FIRST BRIDGE OVER THE POTOMAC RIVER
to Harpers Ferry, carrying the turnpike from Frederick, opened in 1829. Five years
passed. Then the Baltimore and Ohio Railroad arrived on the opposite shore. The
railroad soon crossed the river, somewhat unsteadily, on a new structure, and there
it stopped. Another five years went by before the rails headed west again. In the
meantime the Chesapeake and Ohio Canal, which achieved Harpers Ferry about a
year ahead of the railroad and continued up the Maryland side of the Potomac, had
passed Hancock and was on its way to Cumberland, just 50 miles farther.

The reasons for the B&O's hesitation were more than physical, but the obstacles that nature had placed before them were formidable enough. Harpers Ferry
was located at the throat of a funnel. Below it in Maryland, extending to a small
opening at the Point of Rocks, lay a long, thin neck of land, gripped tightly at top
and bottom by the river and the hills, like a pair of hands. In the middle, around the
town of Berlin, the level land bulged out. Through this entire passage the railroad
and the canal were forced to proceed side by side. For two miles at either end, they
were literally on top of each other, and in one very constricted section across from
Harpers Ferry, the railroad, the canal, and the turnpike were all squeezed together
into a space 100 feet wide. It was, the B&O's weary president said, like running a
gauntlet.

Harpers Ferry was the gateway to the Ohio country and the key to the routes
leading to the West. Across the Potomac beckoned the abundant agricultural products of the great Valley of Virginia and the rich Cumberland coal deposits, and,
beyond, the Western waters. But for a time, even the near shore in Maryland seemed
unattainable.

The town occupied the foot of a low hill where the Potomac and the Shenandoah joined. These two turbulent rivers poured through a ragged tear in the mountain
and flowed down through the serene countryside that lay back of the Blue Ridge.

The Indians had named the great valley Shenandoah, "Daughter of the Stars."[1] The Shenandoah River, running north through the valley, ended in a rocky staircase that descended to join the Potomac at the traditional "trading place" of the tribes. Together, through several geologic periods, the waters had scoured the land. The land then rose slowly, leaving a deep notch in the Blue Ridge and towering masses of dark rock on either side. The traveler on the Frederick turnpike skirted the base of the 1,000-foot-high Maryland Heights on the eastern shore, "its terrible precipices hanging in fragments over you," Thomas Jefferson said. On the Virginia side, Chimney Rock stood like a sentinel at the edge of the gorge. Harpers Ferry is a wild, windswept place with a strange and violent history.

A century before the railroad got to town, Robert Harper, a Philadelphia merchant and millwright, passed by chance through the Hole, as the gap in the ridge was then known, and was enraptured by the rugged scenery. He bought rights from its only inhabitant, Peter Stephens, a German squatter who operated a crude ferry with an Indian associate named Gutterman Tom. Harper took over the ferry operation and opened a mill. By the time of the Revolution, nearby forges such as the Antietam Iron Works were producing raw material and arms. George Washington, intrigued by the water power potential, recommended Harpers Ferry as the site of a federal arsenal. The new armory began making muskets in 1796. One of their first customers was the Lewis and Clark Expedition, which was outfitted with rifles, tomahawks, and knives.

In 1811, John H. Hall developed the first successful breech-loading flintlock rifle. Six years later he was producing them at Harpers Ferry. About this time, Laura Wager, Harper's niece, supervised the carving of 44 steps out of the solid cliff leading to the upper levels of the community. By 1827, the armory consisted of thirteen government buildings, laid out mostly along the Potomac. Four of them, housing Hall's Rifles, were located on Virginius Island, on the Shenandoah.

When the B&O finally got there, Harpers Ferry was on the verge of becoming the Potomac Valley's leading factory town. Only Wheeling was destined to be more important in Virginia as an industrial and transportation center. Indeed, so successful were the local capitalists that when two British visitors climbed Laura Wager's stone steps to Jefferson's Rock in 1835, their eyes were assaulted by the denuded hills, their noses by the reek of coal smoke, and their ears by clanking hammers. "A most abominable village," they said.[2]

The Point of Rocks, at the bottom of the neck of the funnel, was worse. The town grew rapidly after the railroad came down the Monocacy Valley from Frederick in the spring of 1832, met the Potomac River, and turned right. Between the turn and the actual Point of Rocks where Catoctin Mountain, a spur of the Blue Ridge, struck the Potomac, the tracks ran through a mile-long flat. At the far end of it, near the hill itself, a raffish frontier village of taverns, freight depots, and boardinghouses sprang up. The Chesapeake and Ohio Canal had also arrived. Before the two works were completed to Harpers Ferry, the railroad and canal interchanged river freight at the Point of Rocks. As they always did, stagecoach lines greeted the B&O at its latest terminus to carry the passengers on from there. If they were only going to Harpers

Ferry, they could also choose between two competing lines of packets running on the canal.

Since the railroad clearly intended to "arrest" the produce coming down the Potomac and bring it to Baltimore before it could be transferred to the canal and sent on to Washington, there was some rough-and-ready competition at the Point of Rocks. In fact, Philip E. Thomas instructed Caspar W. Wever, his construction chief, to have the line open to the Point of Rocks before the river ice broke up in the spring of 1832 so that they could capture the trade. Besides flour and other agricultural products, building materials such as lime, timber, and stone were soon being shipped by rail to Baltimore. However, complaints about the business practices at the Point of Rocks multiplied during the first eighteen months of operation until one of the warehouse proprietors defalcated, leaving both the railroad and its customers holding the bag and the system was changed.[3]

Benjamin H. Latrobe, Jr., first visited the spot on reconnaissance in November 1830 before the coming of the railroad. He made several sketches of the ridge, not "in your style of excellence," he told his brother John, "but in a way that would give some idea of that scene of natural grandeur, whose equal I have never beheld."[4] Three years later, he was back as a surveyor. Canal contractors were blasting the narrow passes and the booming echoes from the hills were magnificent, Latrobe thought, as he rode on horseback down the muddy towpath and into town at dusk. But he was more than usually morose as he crept into his miserable rented pallet at 10:00 P.M. that Saturday night: "Such nasty beds I never saw, not half made up and the sheet actually brown with dirt. This Point of Rocks is a horrid hole, the habitation of a set of sharpers who assemble there to make money by a swindling sort of commerce. So beastly looking a village is to be found nowhere. The streets are made of mud and the almost impending mountain under which the little town stands, casts with its forest of pines a dismal shadow over the spot."[5]

The strategic twelve miles of riverfront between the Point of Rocks and Harpers Ferry had served as the canal-railroad dueling ground for five years, but the engineers of the two companies had always looked upon the rivalry as a professional problem that could be overcome. Unlike the feuding principals, they had started off on a friendly note in the summer of 1830 when the B&O's Jonathan Knight and Nathan S. Roberts of the C&O agreed for the first time at Harpers Ferry that both works could be built through the narrow passes along the Potomac. For the most part, their behavior had continued to be a model of professional decorum. The two rival firms had also become friends, or at least they had reached a compromise under the dictates of the Maryland legislature. After that happened in the summer of 1833, the long stalemate at the Point of Rocks ended, and with the canal's cooperation, the railroad began to make up for lost time.

Philip E. Thomas and John H. Eaton first arranged to examine the four difficult passes at the Upper and Lower Point of Rocks, and Millers and Harpers Ferry Narrows. Eaton, a former cabinet member, had just been appointed to succeed Charles Fenton Mercer as head of the Chesapeake and Ohio Canal, but whereas the always-belligerent Mercer regarded the canal as a personal crusade, Eaton seemed quite indifferent; indeed, he appeared distracted during the single year he was in office before being named governor of Florida. He was replaced by George C. Washington.

As part of the official agreement, the Chesapeake and Ohio was to build both the canal and the railroad through the four miles of narrow passes and the B&O was to pay them $266,000 for doing it. This work was soon under way. Wever was sent out to locate the railroad line through the eight miles in the middle, centering on Berlin, about halfway between the Point of Rocks and Harpers Ferry. Knight and the C&O's Alfred Cruger made some changes in the alignment and the B&O adopted it. Meanwhile, both firms were acquiring right-of-way.

The canal had used its one-year grace period between the favorable decision in the Court of Appeals and the legislative act enabling the railroad to proceed, to move ahead with construction and property acquisition. The first land they condemned near Harpers Ferry belonged to Gerard Bond Wager, spokesman for the descendants of Robert Harper. The Wagers also controlled the old ferry landings on both sides of the Potomac that were presently linked by Wager's Bridge, the first one to cross the river. Wager was an opponent of the canal and a friend of the railroad. In extracting maximum damage payments from the C&O, he evidently set a precedent for other landowners, because by the time the canal got up past Williamsport, "the excessive and enormous damages given in Maryland by juries" prompted them to begin surveys on the Virginia side of the river.[6]

But Wager also demanded maximum consideration from the railroad. It took the B&O three years to acquire the property rights they needed from him and his relatives, who, knowing that the railroad had nowhere else to go, wrested every possible concession before coming to terms. The upper Potomac Valley was closed to the B&O under the agreement with the canal company, and if they crossed the river below town, they would have to bridge the Shenandoah to reach it. In the summer of 1833, the railroad also opened negotiations with the Frederick and Harpers Ferry Turnpike Company, since it was going to be necessary to construct the rail line over part of the turnpike roadbed to get to Wager's Bridge. This was within the 100-foot wide "gauntlet" the railroad cars would have to run between the canal boats and the stagecoaches that were already there. A further complication was that the railroad and the turnpike then had to swing out over the canal and the river and meet another railroad on the opposite side.[7]

Thomas was used to intricate negotiations, but the political complexities of reconciling the interests of three different common carriers and a bridge proprietor were the worst yet. The Chesapeake and Ohio Canal was now the least of his concerns. In fact it proved to be the railroad's most valuable ally in negotiating the crucial distance between the Point of Rocks and Harpers Ferry. Thomas became so enamored of the new collaboration that he turned into a more energetic advocate of the C&O's programs than its own officials.

Like Wager, the turnpike company started out by being unreasonable, Thomas complained to John Bruce, his contact on the Potomac, and he confessed that they had "almost become dispirited under the accumulated expenditures and difficulties before us."[8] Thomas brushed aside suggestions that talks on the turnpike and on the bridge should be combined, and instead he let Wager and the bridge wait and turned the highway negotiations over to the canal company, which was handling the joint construction through this section under their agreement and also needed some of the turnpike's roadbed for its own line. Thomas paced constantly on the sidelines and occasionally stepped in, as he did in the fall of 1833 when the turnpike president's son threatened a lawsuit unless the railroad met his father's demands for compensation. Thomas "declined to pay them anything," and referred the turnpike company to the C&O. The year ended with the question still unsettled. The railroad president disliked the delay, he said, "as we dare not come under any contract with the bridge proprietors until we are out of the hands of the turnpike company."[9]

The new year somehow brought a change of heart, and in the spring of 1834, the Maryland legislature passed a law allowing the turnpike to shift its location in the area and the B&O to be constructed on the old alignment. The canal built the new roadway and paid the turnpike company $7,000, with the railroad sharing some of the cost of the indemnity. It had taken a year to reach the intricate finale of what Thomas called "this vexatious affair."[10]

The railroad was at last at the riverbank, its objective in sight. Thomas asked Wager to name his price, but Wager demurred, even as the canal and railroad corps geared up to complete the surveys and the acquisition of right-of-way. The work of the engineers—Benjamin H. Latrobe, Jr., for the railroad and Charles B. Fisk for the canal—had to be ratified by the officers of the two firms, but this was a relatively simple matter in the new atmosphere of consent.

Benjamin Latrobe was now living the life of an itinerant engineer. He was simultaneously surveying or building bridges on three rivers, the Potomac, the Susquehanna, and the Patapsco, for two railroads, the Baltimore and Ohio and the Baltimore and Port Deposit. It meant daily exposure to all sorts of weather and long, jarring rides on horseback or in rattling stages and railroad coaches. He slept in tents, ate in taverns, sat around in boardinghouses. But the money was good and he loved the life, judging from the evocative descriptions of it that he left in his journals. The mattress may have crawled with bedbugs the night before, but the dawn brought fresh adventures in unspoiled territory or evanescent views of familiar landscapes.

Throughout the 1830's when he was not on the road, Latrobe, his wife, Ellen, and their two young children rented rooms. They moved often, generally twice a year. One summer, they stayed at the Widow McLaughlin's in Ellicotts Mills, for $6 a week. It was quiet, airy, and secluded compared with the city. "The situation is delightful," said Latrobe, making a sketch. "The scenery around it is really lovely, such beautiful swelling green slopes, such pretty rivulets, such fine foliage, such picturesque groups of grey and mossy rock, and such comfortable and prettily disposed houses all about. I am delighted at the idea of getting Ellen here. We can take such charming walks."[11] The next winter they were back in Baltimore, at Mrs. Woodyear's, on Holliday street, a favorite stop. One day the temperature was 20 degrees—inside.

Latrobe bought some flannel underwear and a pair of "India rubbers" for his sojourn on the Potomac during the winter of 1834, working with Fisk. He spent the better part of a week being sick, went back to Baltimore, and returned when the Irish were rioting on the canal up at Williamsport. He and Fisk got their work done anyway. They went over the middle eight miles on either side of Berlin, where the canal wanted to make more changes in Wever's location of the railroad line, and discussed how to get the trains onto Wager's Bridge at Harpers Ferry. By April, progress was apparent, and springtime on the river was beautiful. Latrobe, at Berlin waiting for the canal packet, was captivated by "the bright rich verdure of the young grain, the lovely pink of the peach blossom, and the exquisite white of the cherry, the pearly grey of the rock, the deep green of the pines and cedars, the soft haze that covers the neighboring mountains." Except at a few locations, such as the major aqueducts, the canal was open to Harpers Ferry and in fact was finished but not yet filled with water to a point 26 miles above the town. The packet that came by Berlin was an old river keelboat captained by Wager himself, "a free and easy, vulgar sort of a fellow," according to Latrobe, who was competing with the other line of packets, although there was not yet enough business for one: "He goes up and down every day, planting himself most pompously in the prow, or playing the helmsman with equal importance." [12]

Latrobe and Fisk and the survey crew spent most of April 1834 making the final adjustments in the location of the railroad line between the Upper Point of Rocks and Millers Narrows. Sometimes they shifted the railroad farther from the canal as they did at the Catoctin Aqueduct, where the C&O wanted to build some warehouses. In the center of the town of Berlin, they moved it closer. At the end of the month, near Wever's Mill, they pronounced themselves satisfied. Latrobe toured Hall's Rifle Factory with the proprietor and took a trip upriver with Fisk to the vicinity of the C&O's Antietam Aqueduct, where the shoreline was so precipitous and rock-bound that there was barely room for the canal and none at all for a railroad. Always he remarked on the scenery, the sun highlighting one of the peaks as the wind scoured the mist from the amphitheatrical hills at Harpers Ferry, or the full moon rising over Loudoun Heights across the Shenandoah.

"We have finally adjusted with the canal company the location of the railway between the upper Point of Rocks and Millers Narrows," Thomas reported in mid-1834.[13] The railroad withdrew Wever's old alignment, substituting that of Fisk and Latrobe. The C&O ratified it. Thus ended the deadlock over the twelve miles to Harpers Ferry, which had occupied half a dozen years and as many civil engineers. Circumstances forced the Baltimore and Ohio Railroad across the river at Harpers Ferry. The company would have preferred to travel alongside the canal all the way to Cumberland on the Maryland side. They had no particular place to go once they got to Virginia, although there was nothing to stop them from going in any direction they chose, but they did have one immediate goal and that was to link up with the Winchester and Potomac Railroad.

This was a line running from Winchester, Virginia, 30 miles northwest to

Harpers Ferry. Chartered in 1831, the company began construction in 1833 and finished it three years later. The railroad turned out to be something of a misfit, but that was hardly the intention when it began. Winchester, established a century before, had developed an early packhorse trade with the back country as far away as Tennessee, and it was the traditional shipping point for Shenandoah Valley wheat, which went mostly to Alexandria by wagon. However, between the town and the turnpike were fifteen miles of a "foundering morass" of road. Within months after the Baltimore business leaders announced their intention to build a railroad, a committee from Winchester sent notice that they would like to be on the route.

When they realized that they would not be, they chartered their own railroad company and asked Thomas for a subscription. He declined, but nevertheless pledged Baltimore's support, and later the B&O helped the W&P Railroad to acquire loan funds and rails. The company was capitalized at $300,000, or $10,000 per mile. John Bruce, a local spokesman who hoped the railroad would increase land values and encourage settlement in the Valley, was made president. He became Thomas's confidant.

Winchester in 1834 was a town of 4,000 with one church, a courthouse, and a general air of neglect. The merchants of the town counted on their impending railroad connection to the Potomac and a major highway under construction, the Northwestern Turnpike to Parkersburg on the Ohio River (present Route 50), to move them to a brighter destiny. Thomas was equally hopeful. Besides gaining "a great share of the produce of the rich valley of Virginia," the Baltimore and Ohio wanted to meet the Winchester and Potomac at Harpers Ferry because railroad promoters were already talking about extending the latter line from Winchester to Staunton, 100 miles farther south in the valley. If they succeeded and if a few more links were added, the B&O might intersect the proposed James River and Kanawha improvements in Virginia and in that way reach the Ohio River.[14]

Thomas had always thought of Wager's bridge as the junction point between the two railroads. Moncure Robinson, head engineer for the Winchester and Potomac Railroad, disagreed. He told Thomas and Latrobe early in 1834 that they should build their own crossing because it would be difficult for locomotives to negotiate the curve at Wager's bridge, which left the Maryland shore at a 90-degree angle. Robinson's opinions were respected. Although he was largely self-taught as an engineer, he had completed a three-year tour of European public works and had built bridges and railroads, including a nineteen-span bridge on the Town lattice plan across the James River for the Richmond and Petersburg Railroad.[15] While supervising the Winchester and Potomac, Robinson was also planning his major work, the Philadelphia and Reading Railroad, for which he designed a 1,900-foot tunnel and a stone bridge with four 72-foot spans.

Robinson and Latrobe met briefly at Harpers Ferry. Robinson, 31, was tall and handsome. He had cold, gray eyes, an aquiline nose, and a scar on the left side of his face that ran from the corner of his mouth to his ear. Women found him fascinating; Latrobe disliked him instantly. He thought Robinson conceited and superficial, but he did admire "a plagued fine eye which I would give something to have."[16] Collectively, the Winchester and Potomac engineers did not regard the B&O engineering staff very highly, and they liked nothing at all about the railroad, starting with the tracks and engines. Thomas was relieved when the W&P Railroad agreed to make their line the same gauge. Gradually, however, the Baltimore and Ohio came around to Robinson's point of view concerning the bridge.

While he was making his peace with the turnpike and canal companies in early 1834, Thomas also tried to set up meetings with Wager; but Wager was a Jefferson County delegate to the Virginia legislature at Richmond and was unavailable until the spring. And when the directors of the two railroads did meet with him in the spring at Harpers Ferry to examine the site, they were unable to come to an agreement. That summer, after an inspection of Wager's bridge revealed that it was in poor condition, the two railroad presidents decided to construct their own bridge downstream.[17] The cost, including a better alignment, would be $85,000, not all that much more than the cost of paying Wager to use his bridge: $15,000 for the privilege of laying a track over it (on which he planned to levy tolls) and building a depot on his land, and $25–30,000 for reconditioning the structure, which had been built by Lewis Wernwag. Wager would, of course, demand payment for the approaches to the new railroad bridge, but Thomas hoped that if they gave him a highway lane on the structure on which he could charge people for crossing, he might turn over the approaches for free. The B&O president wrote to Bruce that the arrangement "will render their property worth three times as much as it would have before sold for, and I think they ought to be content." He added that it would not only indemnify the Wagers against loss, but "greatly overpay them."[18]

Wager did not think so. He now asked $7,000, but with guarantees regarding accommodations for the depot, his right to charge tolls, and maintenance of the bridge. He also offered to let the railroad use the old bridge for free until the new one was finished. The Baltimore and Ohio got it in writing and drafted a contract incorporating Wager's terms, but on the day set for the signing, December 15, 1834, Wager did not appear.

As the negotiations continued at the bridge, the railroad line slowly advanced from the Point of Rocks. This work had actually begun in June 1833, when the C&O Canal let the first contracts for the joint construction at the four miles of narrow passes. Under the legal agreement, they had until May 1834 to complete it. But they did not. The waterway was open, but the tracks were not laid when Hezekiah Niles made an excursion that month from Baltimore to Harpers Ferry via B&O coach and canal packet. He regarded the 80-mile trip, which took ten or eleven hours, as swift and refreshing, "uniting in this pleasant little journey all that is most sublime and beautiful in the works of nature, with the most sublime and beautiful of the works of art, condensing, as it were, every variety of mountain or valley, rocks piled on rocks, or fertile plains, mighty streams or silver rivulets—viaducts and aqueducts, and all that interests us in the construction of railroads or canals."[19]

The Chesapeake and Ohio, with the railroad's consent, gave their contractors more time. The Baltimore and Ohio later did the same for its men when they were unable to meet the contract deadlines. The executives could not fairly have acted otherwise, for what the construction crews faced was not of their making. The rock along this stretch of the Potomac is primarily dark limestone, white quartz, and granite. The limestone at the Point of Rocks was the so-called Potomac marble that Benjamin H. Latrobe used for the columns in the old House of Representatives in Washington. All this had to be drilled, blasted, and cleared away. Some was cut and used for huge retaining walls that formed one side of the canal with a narrow shelf on top for the railroad.[20]

The B&O built some of these walls, and quickly. Wever oversaw the work. He informed the directors early in 1834 that a wall was needed below Millers Narrows, 200 feet long and eight feet high, before they let the water into the canal in a few days. Thomas told him to put it under contract immediately. The board also authorized Wever to hire one of his children as a clerk and approved a contract with the construction superintendent and Peter Miller (of the Narrows) to supply oak and chestnut sleepers for the track.

Work was also slowed by an outbreak of cholera. Cholera had decimated the canal's construction forces on the Potomac in 1832, and it recurred in 1833 on the canal and again in 1834, when many railroad workers were stricken. This was not one of the vague "river fevers" that commonly broke out during the summer and fall "sickly season." Those were generally typhoid or dysentery or a variety of others and one usually survived them. This was Asiatic cholera and it was often fatal. The onset of the disease in Maryland was part of a worldwide epidemic that had gradually made its way from India across Europe and Asia. By the spring of 1832, the local newspapers were tracing its progress with morbid fascination. In April that year, it killed nineteen people in Glasgow, Scotland. The press noted that the Glasgow guild of cotton spinners was sending its idle members to the United States. Many had already shipped out of Liverpool. The cholera struck London and Dublin in May, in June it was at Rouen, and later that same month in Montreal where it was "sweeping off the emigrants and other people of the lower orders to a most alarming extent." Detroit and New York were hard hit by the disease in July. The following month, Norfolk and Baltimore, along with the upper Eastern Shore and Washington County, were affected. In September, there were 33 deaths in Baltimore (16 whites, 17 blacks), 10 in Washington, and 7 in Frederick.[21]

Many more canal workers probably would have died from cholera in 1832 had not so many of them fled in fear of it. "Its mortality in the valley of the Potomac bore, indeed, no proportion to the terror which its approach inspired," noted Charles Fenton Mercer, then the Chesapeake and Ohio's president.[22] The symptoms built up over a few days or struck suddenly, culminating in violent diarrhea and vomiting, followed by severe stomach pains and agonizing cramps of the legs and abdomen. The victim grew cold, literally turned blue, and usually died the same day.[23] "If the board but imagine the panic produced by a mans turning black and dying in twenty four hours in the very room where his comrades are to sleep or to dine they will readily conceive the utility of separating the sick, dying and dead from the living," said Mercer.[24] The canal company hired a doctor and set up a rude hospital; when this proved inadequate, they tried to rent an old mill building from Wever to house the hospital, but Wever's terms were so outrageous that they settled for some cabins and shanties near Harpers Ferry instead.

The cholera ranged up and down the river from Williamsport to the Point of Rocks. A mill owner at Shepherdstown reported 30 deaths within a few days. "The poor Exiles of Erin are flying in every direction," he said, "by the last of this week you will not have a working man on the whole line." The lawyer for the C&O in Frederick reported, "They are dying in all parts of Washington County at the distance of 5 to 15 miles from the river. I myself saw numbers of them in carts & on foot making their way towards Pennsylvania." "Humanity is outraged," said a canal official. "Men deserted by their friends or comrades, have been left to die in the fields, the highways, or in the neighboring barns & stables; in some instances . . . when the disease has attacked them, the invalid has been enticed from the shandee & left to die under the shade of some tree."[25] Once the disease had struck, there was little that anyone could do except try to ease the victim's misery, and the nurses often became ill themselves. The best protection was good sanitation, but the sanitation in the shanty towns was primitive and the drinking water came from the rivers and streams.[26]

In 1834, the Baltimore papers reported a "light visitation" by the cholera. It caused 71 deaths in the city that year, but the rumors were exaggerated, according to the press.[27] On the river, however, where the canal crews had mostly finished their work and the railroad laborers were now struggling to get to Harpers Ferry, it was the same story all over again.

John Littlejohn and his workmen were among those that suffered. Littlejohn, a diligent contractor who had laid the last of the stone rails on the main line and worked on the Washington Branch, signed a contract in November 1833 to build the railroad bridge over Catoctin Creek, where the C&O Canal had a large aqueduct, just up the line from the Point of Rocks. Mrs. Donovan kept the tavern there, dispensing free advice with the hard-boiled eggs and cheese and crackers, and in the spring of 1834 she predicted a sickly time on the river. Littlejohn began work there that summer, in a proverbially unhealthy spot, and the cholera returned. The railroad hired a doctor and assigned Wever to set up a hospital of sorts, as the canal had done. The doctor received $100 a month and was to provide his own medicine. Actually, the man they recruited for the job had been doing that for some time. He was James D. Quinn, a hulking, slovenly, one-eyed Irish drunk, and "a mad mick for sure."[28] Quinn had recently stayed late at the tavern, wrecked his gig, and otherwise misbehaved when Benjamin Latrobe met him earlier that year on the train to Baltimore from the Point of Rocks and was surprised to discover that although the doctor looked evil and smelled worse, he was able to converse intelligently about his profession with the usual Irish "ease and nonchalance."[29]

Sixty-five of Littlejohn's men "fell a sacrifice" to the cholera that summer. Littlejohn himself, his son, and Wever became gravely ill, but recovered. Littlejohn's partners deserted him and filed suit to stop the company from making further payments to the contractor. An arbitrator's audit revealed that Littlejohn was not due any money. In fact, he had lost $7,700 under the contract. When they found there were no funds to claim, but rather a deficiency to make up, the partners quickly disappeared, leaving Littlejohn to cover the loss.

Toward the end of the year, Littlejohn took over the work of another man who had abandoned his contract for laying rails from the Point of Rocks to Berlin. Littlejohn got the job done, but because of his many difficulties, he did not finish it on time and forfeited a portion of the contract price. After the B&O deducted his advances and the amount forfeited, they owed Littlejohn some $350, while he was indebted to his men for about $2,000. Because the situation was familiar, it was no less dangerous.

"The conduct of unpaid laborers on a former occasion and their recent turbulent and outrageous acts [on the Washington Branch], gives room for apprehensions about the safety of the Rail track and other property of the company, unless the laborers be speedily paid," Wever informed Thomas. "The expediency of paying the laborers is therefore respectfully suggested." The board, in no mood for further confrontation, promply remitted Littlejohn's forfeitures and advanced him the money to pay his crew.[30]

The directors later investigated Littlejohn's petition for redress and awarded him $3,000 in partial compensation for his losses, and they gave him a formal and sincere tribute. The investigation revealed that Littlejohn had been unable to start work at the Catoctin Creek bridge for seven months after he had contracted to build it because the railroad alignment was not finally settled until May 1834. That meant that he was building the piers during the worst possible time on the river. The delay also required him to pay higher wages, because by then the entire line from the Point of Rocks to Harpers Ferry was under contract and labor was in demand.

Although ill himself, he persisted while his workmen sickened and died and his partners abandoned him. Littlejohn could legally have given up his contract. Instead, he took on another. By completing the Catoctin bridge and laying the rails he had actually enabled the line to be finished. Management's appreciation and gratitude showed through the official language of their report, which recognized Littlejohn's "great efforts to meet the wishes of the Stockholders and Directors under circumstances so unfavourable to himself."[31]

Thomas wrote Wever at the end of November 1834, "As I suppose our board will want to open the line to Harpers Ferry with some little eclat, I wish thee to inform me as early as possible of the day it can be travelled—we must have time to invite the Governor of this state, the canal president & the Winchester board." Wever set the date for December 1, then had second thoughts, but Thomas told him he had already sent out the invitations. "We have consequently now no recourse *but to get it done*," he said.[32]

And so, on the designated day, the president and directors of the railroad, Baltimore's mayor and city council, the newspaper editors and assorted guests, about 100 in all, left Baltimore at eight in the morning for Harpers Ferry. They traveled in four coaches, including the Dromedary and the Winchester, pulled by Phineas Davis's

Mercury engine. The party crossed the inclined planes by horsepower. On the other side another locomotive, the Arabian, was waiting with steam up to take them on from there. William Gwynn Jones, the new editor of the *Gazette*, wrote glowingly of the canal:

> The substantial, and, at the same time, elegant construction of the locks of the magnificent Canal—its beautiful Viaduct over the Catoctin Creek—and more especially the boats laden with produce so frequently passing [and] from which, occasionally, portions of their cargoes are transferred to the Rail road for transportation to the Baltimore market—furnish inducements for visiting the Point of Rocks, which will only be exceeded in interest by the sublime scenery at the junction of the Potomac and Shenandoah.[33]

The ride to the ferry was more thrilling than Thomas's formal report to the B&O directors indicated. Benjamin H. Latrobe, Jr., took it three weeks later and after passing the Point of Rocks, climbed on top of the car for a better view. He was "much gratified by the extreme beauty of the long and gentle curvatures which I had last spring taken so much pains to locate," he said, but his hair stood on end as the train whirled along so close to the cliffs that the widest cars touched the rock.[34]

Thomas, in his official statement to the board on the railroad's latest achievement, briefly noted "that the Locomotive Arabian, on her return from Frederick yesterday drew over the planes at Parrs Spring Ridge besides her tender, two cars loaded with passengers."[35] Thus for the first time, on December 2, 1834, an engine pulled a scheduled train over the ridge. This event proved far more significant to the railroad than the opening of the line to Harpers Ferry. It marked the real beginning of the end of horsepower on the Baltimore and Ohio.

Phineas Davis's Arabian was the latest of a series of Grasshopper engines that began with the six-and-a-half-ton Atlantic, a locomotive that was put on the line in the fall of 1832 to haul passengers out to the inclined planes. The Atlantic was shortly followed by the Indian Chief, a slower, more powerful engine built for freight. Horses still provided the main motive power for the railroad; on the grades, travelers might see them contentedly riding down behind their trains on platform cars, as they did on the Mauch Chunk Railroad, to pick up their burdens at the bottom. The top speed that horses could pull a passenger train was 10 mph. The Atlantic could go 20 mph easily, although it was generally run slower. But the real argument against horsepower was its cost, which was twice as much as steam. The B&O determined that it could run the Atlantic for $16 a day, including $8 for a ton of anthracite coal, $2 for an engineer, and $1.50 for his assistant. The locomotive did the same work as 42 horses and 12 men, which, with the required stables, hostlers, feed, and so on, cost the company $33 a day.

Horses and mules had been thought to be more efficient for hauling freight trains at slower speeds, but traction experiments conducted between Baltimore and Relay in January 1833, by George Gillingham, the superintendent of machinery, and Ross Winans, assistant engineer, followed by Knight's customarily exhaustive analysis, demonstrated conclusively that locomotives were superior for this purpose also.

"It would appear from the foregoing calculations, that Locomotive Engines will afford the most economical power at all times, and more decidedly so when the trade is fluctuating," Knight reported to the directors. He recommended that they acquire sufficient engines to transport both passengers and freight.[36]

There were a couple of brief flirtations with outside technology that summer. One was with William Norris, who had just formed the American Steam Carriage Company in Philadelphia; Stephen H. Long was his engineer. The other had to do with manufacturers of iron boiler tubes in Birmingham, England. Yet in the end the B&O acquired its locomotives and components from local producers. Norris objected to the company's requirement that all four wheels be powered. This was fortunate, because Long's locomotive designs did not ultimately prove successful. The B&O disliked the quality of the foreign boiler tubes and canceled the order.

The Atlantic, by the fall of 1833, had gone 13,000 miles, but since there were only a few other engines on the line, "the entire horse establishment had still to be maintained," Knight explained in the annual report.[37] John H. B. Latrobe wrote the president's message that year and in it favorably compared the B&O's anthracite-burning, vertical-boiler engines with British locomotives, the boiler tubes of which, he said, often failed and required expensive replacement; the Atlantic had run for a year without bursting a single tube.[38] The Indian Chief, the slower companion of the Atlantic, was less successful. It had axle cranks instead of wheel cranks. After one of these broke, the engine was remodeled and improved somewhat along the lines of the Atlantic, and given a new name, the Traveller.[39]

Phineas Davis and Charles Reeder received contracts in the fall of 1833 to produce the new locomotives. Their design was to be similar to the Traveller. The specifications called for four wheels, a weight of eight tons, and an ability to pull a 50-ton load on a level track at 15 mph. The engines were to burn anthracite coal. The delivery date was August 1834 and the cost, $4,400 each. Davis's contract was for five engines, Reeder's for three.

Davis and Reeder were among the prime movers of steamboat travel in the United States, but their careers with the Baltimore and Ohio Railroad were relatively brief and tragic. Davis, like Ross Winans before him, had a rural background and an early interest in mechanics. After leaving his native New Hampshire, he worked six years for Jonathan Jessop, who was then a watchmaker and road contractor in York, Pennsylvania, and after that for Israel Gartner (or Gardner), who had a foundry and machine shop for making steam engines. They fabricated a few stationary ones, according to Davis's designs, then started work on the *Codorus*, the first iron steamboat built in the United States. John Elgar made the hull. Davis & Gartner provided the engine, a six-foot-tall high pressure (100 psi), vertical boiler that burned Pennsylvania anthracite coal. Jessop and Elgar induced Davis to enter the B&O's engine competition, and when Davis brought his trial locomotive, the York, to the city in 1831, Jessop was already a contractor on the main line and Elgar was an assistant engineer of machinery. Jessop became a B&O construction manager and contractor on the Washington Branch and was named assistant superintendent of machinery in 1835. Elgar invented the B&O's journal bearing, was involved in the development of the chilled cast-iron wheel, and designed switches and turntables for the railroad. He left the company in 1832 but later worked as a consultant for Benjamin H. Latrobe, Jr. Elgar claimed to have recommended to Knight in 1831 the idea of replacing the inclined planes at Parrs Spring Ridge with a uniform grade for locomotives.[40]

Davis, who had returned to York after his engine's successful debut and remained there to build the Atlantic and the Indian Chief, came back to Baltimore around the summer of 1833 when the B&O, having decided definitely on steam power, hired John Gillingham to erect a forge, machine shop, and other facilities at the Mt. Clare depot for the construction of engines and cars. Charles Reeder was just starting to work also. Reeder and Davis shared a maritime tradition and evidently had some sort of brief professional association because they made what seems to have been a joint proposal in February 1833 to build engines for the B&O. In the fall of that year the two men worked together in the same Baltimore shop, rebuilding the Indian Chief into the Traveller.

Reeder, a native of Bucks County, Pennsylvania, trained as a carpenter and millwright, had appeared in Baltimore in 1813 as an apprentice to engine builder Daniel Large of Philadelphia. His job was to install Large's engine in the locally built *Chesapeake*, the first steamboat to operate commercially on the Bay. Reeder stayed on in Baltimore. He fought at the Battle of North Point in 1814 and then, there being no marine engine works in the city, started one in the Federal Hill area, near his home. He built the engine for the city's second steamboat, the *Experiment*, in 1816 and many others that powered most of the early steamboat traffic on the Bay. His first work for the B&O was the boiler for Peter Cooper's engine.

The machines assembled for the Baltimore and Ohio by Phineas Davis and to a limited extent by Charles Reeder were the railroad's first complement of power. The first new engine on the tracks in July 1834 was Davis's Arabian, followed that fall by his Mercury, and by Reeder's American and Antelope. The company officers were pleased and in an unusually expansive mood as they made their annual report that year. Thomas admitted that they had been occasionally censured for not immediately adopting Stephenson-type locomotives, by critics who thought such engines would work as well on the Baltimore and Ohio's curving alignment as they did on the Liverpool and Manchester's straightaway track. Now, added Jonathan Knight, they had silenced their detractors. Following his customary close analysis of the new engines and their technical improvements, the chief engineer concluded: "From what has been related, it will appear that the Company have fully succeeded in procuring the construction, in this country, of locomotive steam engines fitted to use Anthracite coal as the fuel, and capable of plying successfully upon a railway having quickly turning curves, upon radii even so small as 400 feet; that these engines have all the power requisite upon railways, and that they appear to be substantial and durable."[41] Knight, who usually let numbers speak for him, then exultantly proclaimed in plain English their collective accomplishment: "We have power in abundance, and have speed at command; the machinery is beautiful and works admirably."

Phineas Davis's new Grasshopper engine, the Arabian, was a good illustration of a collaborative effort that featured several innovations. George Gillingham and Ross Winans helped Davis put it together, incorporating elements they all had worked on. Davis patented and deeded two of these to the company. The first was a method of powering the fan to create the draft needed to fire the slow-burning anthracite coal. It was operated directly by waste steam from the cylinders and could be controlled by the amount of steam applied. (Peter Cooper's fan had been driven by a pulley whose belt had slipped during the race with the horse.)

The second was a method for producing better wheels, including the cast-iron locomotive drivers, three feet in diameter. Originally these wheels were made of soft metal, but with heavier engines and cars they broke constantly. The breaks occurred usually in the area of the tire and the cone, which received the most wear. "Chilling" or case-hardening these areas in the casting process was known at the time, but Winans and Davis both devised effective variations of the process.[42] While the new engines were being put in service in the fall of 1834, the railroad asked Davis and Reeder, whose remaking of the Indian Chief into the Traveller had doubled the power of the engine, to do the same for the Atlantic. Davis took on the job alone, for $1,500.

The physical appearance of all of the new locomotives as well as the cars benefited from the design drawings and suggestions of John H. B. Latrobe. He was responsible for the "tasteful embellishments in the external form and finish."[43] They were strange and wonderful machines. The engines stood fourteen feet, six inches, from track level to the tops of the smokestacks and were about as long as they were tall. The wheelbase, on the other hand, was a scant four feet. Their prototype, the Arabian, weighed seven and a half tons. Its vertical, anthracite-burning boiler was 64 inches high and 52 inches in diameter and contained 400 tubes. The tops of the tubes projected several inches above the surface of the water, thus drying and superheating the steam whose normal pressure was 50 psi. The vertical cylinders were twelve inches in diameter and 22 inches long. It was as if a one-room, single-story, multi-ton log cabin with a chimney rested on a small four-wheeled wagon. A teakettle on wheels might be a better analogy. But there was a purpose, because the engines were built specifically for the railroad in question. They were of comparatively moderate weight to run lightly over the track, which was easily deranged, and short-coupled to be usable on curves, even the 60-foot-radius turns at the street corners in Baltimore.

The Grasshopper's motion, a side effect of its design, was something of a drawback. Despite the relatively small wheels, the center of gravity was still too high, and combined with the vertical action of the pistons and the thrashing of the long connecting rods, which was communicated to the springs, this imbalance resulted in a definite up-and-down as well as forward movement. It is indeed a wonder that, at the speeds at which they were driven, they managed to hold on at all as they jumped and flailed their way down the tracks.

With Winans, Gillingham, and some others, Benjamin H. Latrobe, Jr., went for an autumn ride in the Frederick train behind one of Reeder's machines, "which worked well and made the valley echo with its rapid blasts of steam escaping from its trumpet-mouthed pipe," he said.[44] It was not long before the new engines started leaving the rails in a series of sensational wrecks. In early September 1834, the Arabian, coming out of the city, hit a stone on a curve, broke a flange, and tumbled over a high bank, dragging the tender along. The water tank flew out of the tender frame and the engine made a complete somersault before burying itself nose first in the soft earth. Miraculously, there were no casualties. The engineer bailed out halfway down and the coaches, with roughly 100 passengers inside, remained on the tracks.[45]

More accidents followed. Then Charles Reeder's American, with engineer John Neff, a fireman, and a conductor aboard, pulled out of Mt. Clare one morning with fourteen cars loaded with freight for Ellicotts Mills. They had not gone far when Neff decided that an excess amount of water in the boiler was causing it to foam up and mix with the steam, so he closed off the water pump and increased the steam pressure by screwing down the safety valve. The train was moving slowly through the Deep Cut at four to five miles an hour when Neff, still dissatisfied with the state of things in the boiler, throttled down, shutting off the flow of steam to the cylinders and stopping the train. There was a 30-second hesitation, and then the ash pan and the fire grate were driven down to the ground so forcefully that they shattered. The engine, separating itself from the tender and the rest of the cars, rose like a rocket from the rails and flopped over on its side. Neff was killed instantly. The fireman was injured, but the conductor was unhurt.

Although Knight's investigation contained excessively tedious discussions of precisely how far Neff had screwed down the safety valve, and so on, it had some startling revelations. Knight calculated that there must have been at least 100 tons of steam pressure in the boiler when it exploded with a force that ripped apart the quarter-inch, wrought-iron boiler plate "like curtains of canvas thrown with a gust of wind." Knight also found that there were no stay or tie bolts in the section where the rupture occurred. Knight concluded that Neff, besides ignoring the laws of physics, had mismanaged the operation of the locomotive, but the boiler had also been defectively constructed, and either cause might have produced the explosion and possibly both did. He recommended two safety valves, one out of reach of the engineer, and said future boilers should "be properly stayed at the fire place with suitable bolts."[46]

The American exploded November 12, 1834, exactly one year after Reeder received the contract to build it. The explosion effectively ended his career as a manufacturer of locomotives for the B&O Railroad. Several months past the event, about the time the company gave Mary Ann Neff, the widow of the late engineer, $60 in back wages, they paid Reeder for the Antelope and a repaired American, but simultaneously canceled the contract for the third engine. The B&O soon depreciated the two locomotives heavily, saying they were "nearly new but of little use."[47] Thomas finally offered them for a small sum to John Bruce, president of the Winchester and Potomac Railroad.[48]

The new machines posed a danger as well to a group of travelers who were not welcome on the railroad. They used it as a common highway for riding on horseback or driving stock. Some even had custom wagons made up with short axles, so the wheels would stay within the rails. Many found it cheaper to use the railroad than pay tolls on the turnpike, particularly where the line ran parallel to the Frederick Road. These free riders were outraged when the company announced, with the advent of the steam locomotive, that it would enforce the charter provision against trespassers. George W. Warfield, near Sykesville, informed Thomas that he and his neighbors would take their frustrations out on the railroad itself. Thomas responded that railroads were by nature ill-suited to "promiscuous travel," which endangered everyone. If such travel persisted and accidents resulted, the responsibility would not lie with the company because the community had been warned.

At the B&O's request, the Maryland legislature passed a measure in the spring of 1834 establishing a fine of $5 for each offense of riding on horseback or in carriages other than the company's, leading horses, mules, or oxen, or driving cattle, hogs, or sheep anywhere on the railroad except in the streets of Baltimore and Frederick and in the narrow passes across from Harpers Ferry where there was a bull ring. The law was effective, but a year later, amid more threats of violence, there was an effort in Annapolis at repeal.

Thomas objected on the ground that there were so many curves on the main line that the engineer often could not see 50 yards ahead, and the embankments and cuts on the Washington Branch made it just as perilous. "Persons may say that they are willing to run the risk, but the danger unfortunately is not confined to themselves," he reminded a Baltimore delegate. "If the engine should . . . be thrown off the track by coming in contact with a horse and rider, and the persons in the cars behind be seriously injured, no satisfaction will be furnished to them by knowing that the cause of the accident is killed or as bad off as themselves."[49] The law, slightly refined, stayed on the books.

When, in the spring of 1836, the Baltimore and Ohio Railroad decided that it had enough locomotives to use them exclusively to pull trains on either side of Parrs Spring Ridge, the company closed its relay stations and sold the horses. They dispensed with 70 car horses and 14 teams of wagon stock which, with their hostlers and drivers, came to 154 animals and 27 men.

15

The Eight Million Bill

THE FINAL VICTORY OF STEAM POWER
on the Baltimore and Ohio Railroad coincided with the most humiliating period
of its collaboration with the Chesapeake and Ohio Canal. Throughout 1834, in a
perverse kind of corporate reciprocity, the B&O did a great deal to promote its traditional rival. It was now clear that if the canal helped the railroad to reach and cross
the river at Harpers Ferry, the railroad would support the canal in its efforts to get
to Cumberland.

Thomas's letters to John H. Eaton, the C&O president, in January 1834 demonstrated the extent to which the formerly self-sufficient railroad had been humbled
by necessity. Although the chronically underfunded canal was even harder hit by
the "Biddle Panic" than the B&O, Thomas, to cement relations, lobbied for additional state aid for the stricken waterway. He told Eaton it might help if he came to
Annapolis, because the legislators did not understand why no one from the C&O
Canal was there to represent its interests. Thomas even offered to accompany Eaton
from Baltimore in the steamboat. Eaton saw no need to come. In Baltimore, however, prominent citizens did their best to aid the C&O's apathetic effort to raise
public funds. Alexander Brown and John H. B. Latrobe announced their support for
building the canal to Cumberland, once the two works had reached Harpers Ferry.
Pittsburgh people wondered whether the railroad builders were giving up.[1]

There was no money that winter for the C&O, but the Baltimore and Ohio's
efforts paid off. Eaton's engineers, directors, and stockholders, who could have frustrated every step for the railroad, instead smoothed the way to Harpers Ferry. From
rivals they had become mutual promoters, Thomas told Eaton. Then in the spring of
1834, Eaton left the company to become governor of Florida. By the summer, the canal
was in fiscal straits and had suspended construction above Williamsport. Thomas,
still cooperating, told a C&O official that the canal would ultimately succeed "provided those to whom the enterprise is committed do not become disheartened or

discouraged." They should be "firm, steady, and determined," and most of all think of some way to draw public attention to their work of completing the waterway to the coal mines.[2]

In September 1834, Thomas went to Philadelphia with George C. Washington, the new C&O president, on a private fund-raising trip to assure lenders of the harmony between the two companies. Nicholas Biddle's Bank of the United States lent the Chesapeake and Ohio $200,000 that month, which enabled the company to finish its work to dam no. 5 above Williamsport. In the annual report that year, Thomas, at his most conciliatory, stated that the true interest of the B&O stockholders, the city, and the state lay in the completion of the C&O Canal to Cumberland; the railroad, he added, had no intention of continuing its line up the Potomac Valley but would extend it from Cumberland where the canal ended. But the ramifications of its new policy of appeasement were rapidly overtaking the B&O in the form of renewed interest in the canal project.

In October 1834, soon after Thomas's ill-advised statement in the annual report, a large meeting took place at the Cumberland courthouse to consider ways of bringing the Chesapeake and Ohio to their city so that the Allegany County mines could ship their bituminous coal east to the industries at Harpers Ferry and the consumers in Washington, D.C. Canal proponents argued that the B&O itself wanted the canal built to Cumberland and was not interested in shipping coal by rail. The western Maryland spokesmen called for a canal convention to be held in Baltimore in December and elected delegates to it. Other more distant voices were heard. In Wheeling, the *Times* began agitating for the promised extension of the railroad over the mountains from Cumberland to the Ohio River. The Mobile *Register* noted that a good B&O route from Harpers Ferry would be through the Valley of Virginia and Tennessee to New Orleans.[3]

Thomas specified the quid pro quo in a letter to the C&O president in Washington: "We have happily succeeded in eliciting a decided feeling here in favor of the completion of the canal to Cumberland, and if the canal directors will only accommodate the rail road in 'friendly and cordial spirit,' ... between the Point of Rocks & Harpers Ferry, & thence across the canal and river, they will have the firm support of this entire section of the state."[4]

Although the Baltimore and Ohio was stronger financially than the C&O Canal and had never actually stopped construction, it appeared to many to be a loser. Its stock price had sunk to a low of $35 a share, workers were rioting on the Washington Branch, and the halt at Harpers Ferry seemed to many to signify a loss of momentum. Taking advantage of this hiatus, the Baltimore and Susquehanna Railroad, the B&O's northern rival, again found it an opportune time to intervene. In their last encounter, the Baltimore and Susquehanna had tried to derail the Washington Branch. Now its adherents, before the Baltimore convention, circulated a paper that interpreted the B&O's accommodation as weakness. After quoting Thomas's statement from the annual report, they commented, "This proposition after all that has passed, and coming from the source it does, is calculated to excite surprize." They argued about whether it was a political ploy, decided it was not, and concluded that the

Baltimore and Ohio had "neither the moral nor physical power" to go any farther than Harpers Ferry.[5] The Baltimore and Susquehanna spokesmen wanted to see the canal finished to Cumberland, but they believed it would take too long to build it that far and then continue over the mountains with a railroad, especially since Pennsylvania had already reached the Ohio River with a similar canal-railroad system. Rather, there should be a link with the Pennsylvania Main Line of Internal Improvements— via the Baltimore and Susquehanna Railroad.[6]

Except for the destination, the Baltimore and Susquehanna line was an exact copy of the Baltimore and Ohio. In five years it had proceeded ten miles from Baltimore to around Cockeysville. It was 50 miles farther to York, where a canal led to the Susquehanna River. The Pennsylvania legislature in 1834 passed an act authorizing the continuation of the line within their state and the company's backers felt it could be built in eighteen months for $1 million if Maryland provided the funds. Finishing it would bring the Susquehanna trade to Baltimore and provide the quickest and cheapest means of reaching the west.

Almost 200 delegates attended the convention that began December 8, 1834, at the Masonic Temple in Baltimore. Half a dozen Maryland counties were represented, plus Baltimore City, and there were also delegations from Pennsylvania, Virginia, and Ohio. Thomas and several others represented the B&O, and George C. Washington and Charles Fenton Mercer were there for the C&O. Nothing of real consequence happened at the convention, but committees were named to estimate the cost and time necessary to complete the canal and to ask the City of Baltimore, the states of Maryland, Virginia, and Pennsylvania, and the Congress for the funds to do so.

After several months of work, the results of the committees' findings appeared in a long report, the most significant part of which, from the B&O's point of view, was that the president of the Baltimore and Ohio Railroad was put in the demeaning position of seeking money from the mayor and city council of Baltimore to complete the Chesapeake and Ohio Canal. "The question now is not whether it would be preferable to continue the rail-road beyond the mouth of the Shenandoah, or to exchange it, at that place, for the canal, but it is whether the only present, practicable mode of reaching the base of the Alleghanies, with works of internal improvement, shall be adopted," Thomas said.[7]

Mercer reported that it had cost $4.5 million to build the Chesapeake and Ohio the first 109 miles from Washington to above Williamsport, where they were halted for lack of funds, and it would cost $2 million more to finish the 78 remaining miles to Cumberland. Early in 1835, the canal company asked the Maryland legislature for the necessary $2 million; at the same time, Thomas, in an extraordinary gesture of capitulation, informed the governor: "The completion of the railroad to Harpers Ferry suspends for the present the further prosecution of the work on the main stem," and the state could therefore capitalize sooner on its investment in Maryland's two greatest works of internal improvement by finishing the canal.[8]

Thomas thought, correctly, that the C&O could get the $2 million from the State of Maryland: the bill, which also provided $1 million for finishing the Baltimore and Susquehanna Railroad to York, easily cleared the House. It was held up in the other branch by John B. Morris, a B&O director and state senator, but after some heavy lobbying by the mayor of Baltimore and others, it finally passed the Senate. The law authorized the sale of $2 million in State of Maryland stock with the proceeds to go to the C&O as a loan at 6 percent interest, in exchange for a mortgage on its property and revenues. The Maryland securities were sold at a premium of 17 percent, "and thus," as one critic said, "the entering wedge was made for the present large debt of the State."[9] Even Richard S. Coxe, formerly a bitter opponent of the Baltimore and Ohio Railroad, was won over by its new tactics. The railroad company, its stockholders, and the people of Baltimore had buried the "ancient controversies," he said, and the canal's improved fortunes were due to the help of their former rivals: "With such friends to cheer, and such auxiliaries to aid us, our progress must be onward."[10]

Charles B. Fisk and the other canal surveyors moved out toward Cumberland, the contractors following in their wake. Behind them the water was let into the portion of the canal that had been finished but not yet opened. At Williamsport, the local newspaper wrote: "It was a glorious sight to see the numerous boats as they lay in the basin by night, each illuminated by a glowing coal fire, which cast a long level of light across the water; and the silence of night was not unpleasantly interrupted by the cries of the hoarse boatmen, as they were disturbed from their moorings by new arrivals, and driven to closer contact with their neighbors."[11]

The Baltimore and Ohio's engineers were also out surveying early in 1835, but in different directions. Latrobe spent a cold, snowy week in February reconnoitering a route from Chambersburg, Pennsylvania, through Hagerstown, and down Pleasant Valley to Wever's Mill, on the Potomac.[12] To further Chambersburg's interest in rail service, the Pennsylvania legislature that year approved the construction of a canal from Maryland up along the Susquehanna River, on the condition that Maryland allow a railroad from Pennsylvania to meet the Baltimore and Ohio at Hagerstown.

In April 1835, Jonathan Knight was given the much more important assignment of reconnoitering the country between Cumberland and the Monongahela River and the routes to Wheeling and Pittsburgh. The B&O was thinking then of building their line from Cumberland to Brownsville, Pennsylvania, where the National Road crossed the Monongahela. Brownsville is roughly equidistant from Wheeling and Pittsburgh and branch lines could be extended to each city. Knight left the following month for a six-week mountain tour. As it drew to a close, Hezekiah Niles reported good news. Knight had found three passes with ascents of 94 feet per mile (1.8 percent), an elevation, Niles said, "that our *Baltimore* locomotives will overcome without any sort of difficulty."[13] Knight in his official report confirmed that locomotives could cross the mountains without the use of inclined planes and stationary power, and he described the routes to Wheeling and Pittsburgh as feasible.

At Harpers Ferry, the canal company obligingly allowed the railroad to construct a permanent bridge over its facility there, instead of the movable one required by the 1833 compromise act, and to build a large pier in the towpath. (In the Mercer era, the mere mention of such a crossing would have provoked a tirade, followed by a lawsuit.) Wager, however, now was asking for a two-cent rebate on every barrel of flour shipped on the railroad from his depot. The directors gave in, even making the rebate retroactive to the time they opened trade at Harpers Ferry, but there was further delay. "Pray look after Wager," Thomas pleaded with John Bruce in the spring in 1835. "I am quite worried with the long procrastination of this business with him." [14]

The delay was not all Wager's fault, for the railroad had been slow in getting a power-of-attorney agreement to him after John H. B. Latrobe lost the first one as the result of a fire in the Atheneum Building where his office was located, but Wager was slow to return it, and Thomas warned him, "Pray do not defer this matter any longer." [15] But at last, Wager did sign an agreement allowing the railroad to build a new bridge on his land and to use his old bridge in the meantime. The contract incorporated some further provisions favorable to the proprietor. As of June 1, 1835, all that remained was to get the co-owners—Wager's brother and sister, and the sister's husband, in Ohio—to sign. This was very nearly not done, but when N. H. Swayne, the brother-in-law in Ohio, refused to sign the agreement and demanded compensatory damages for the loss of tolls on the existing bridge after the new Potomac Viaduct was opened, Thomas once again demonstrated his powers of persuasion. He notified Swayne that although the directors would honor the agreement negotiated by Wager in his behalf, they refused to pay more or do anything else "that admits the right to compensation for consequential damages as claimed by thee. . . . I cannot close this letter without warmly reciprocating the kind feelings to myself individually expressed by thee and assuring thee of the regret with which I find my official relations bringing me in opposition to thee in the matter in question." [16] Thomas told Wager that the railroad intended to proceed with the construction of the new bridge under the existing agreement, and Swayne soon capitulated. Although the company did not finally execute the contract for another six months, when they paid $2,333 each to the three Harper heirs, their way was now clear to cross the Potomac River.

Latrobe had already begun the bridge design, although he left the B&O officially in July 1835, when the Thomas Viaduct was completed, to spend a year as chief engineer of the Baltimore and Port Deposit Railroad. He continued to work on the bridge design, and in July 1836 he returned to the Baltimore and Ohio as superintendent of the bridge at Harpers Ferry and their engineer of location.

On a trip to Harpers Ferry in the fall of 1835, Latrobe met "old Lewis Wernwag." Wernwag, 66, invited him to his shop to see a new kind of bridge. A fierce southeast wind, bearing rain, blew through the Potomac passes like a hurricane and chased the surveyors from the river the next day. Latrobe spent most of it with Wernwag, "examining his models & amusing & edifying myself with his conversation. . . . Wernwag is certainly a most uncommon man. His conceptions of complicated machinery are exceedingly clear and ingenious. He is a thorough-bred German in his dialect & manners and knew my father 35 years ago." [17]

Lewis Wernwag, German-born but American-trained, was one of three preeminent builders of long-span wooden truss bridges in the United States at the turn of the nineteenth century. (The others were Timothy Palmer and Theodore Burr.) His reputation was based on the bold and elegant single-span, arched truss, the Colossus, that leaped the Schuylkill River at Fairmount, in Philadelphia. This bridge, completed in 1812, was 340 feet long, the longest single-arch bridge in the United States and one of the longest in the world.

The Colossus was Wernwag's third bridge. In 1813 Wernwag bridged the Delaware River near New Hope, Pennsylvania, with six 175-foot spans, using a truss system that employed parallel top and bottom chords incorporating an arch (like the Burr truss), vertical timber posts, and diagonal iron ties. In the next ten years he built bridges across the Allegheny and the Monongahela at Pittsburgh and over the Susquehanna at Conowingo, Maryland,[18] and in 1824, no doubt attracted by the area's water power and lack of bridges, he set up shop on Virginius Island, near the Hall's Rifles factory, at Harpers Ferry. With his sons, William and Lewis, Jr., he was soon at work on Wager's bridge. It opened five years later. In 1831, the Wernwags built the Monocacy Bridge for the Baltimore and Ohio. That bridge used the arch and truss principle, but the model he submitted for the B&O's Potomac Viaduct in the fall of 1835 was quite different; it was based on the celebrated timber bridge over the River Rhine at Schaffhausen, Switzerland, built by the Grubenmann brothers some 80 years earlier.[19]

Latrobe and Wernwag worked together on the design for the B&O's span at Harpers Ferry. Its final form, which supplanted the arch in the truss with a series of straight, inclined timber struts, had a lasting effect on the younger man's thinking about timber and iron structures. As he recorded in his journal around that time, "It seems destined that I should deal in all sorts of bridges."[20] Contracts were let and work began on the bridge.

A short time after the two bridge designers held their productive meeting at Harpers Ferry, another prominent B&O engineer came to the end of the line. Phineas Davis, having recently finished a new locomotive, took it and some of his workmen on a Sunday ride to Washington. The date was September 27, 1835. They were on the way back when the accident occurred. The end of a rail, displaced by a broken chair, caught the flange of a wheel and threw the locomotive off the track. The tender jackknifed. Davis, who had been riding on it, was killed instantly, his head crushed by the tender wheel. No one else was hurt.[21]

The incident dramatized the dangers of early rail travel. The chairs and other iron track fixtures for the Washington Branch were designed by Jonathan Knight and produced by Phineas Davis himself and Amos A. Williams of the Savage Factory. The main problem seems to have been the new edge rails. Knight also designed these and the company obtained them from British sources through the Alex. Brown and Sons organization. No sooner had they started to arrive in the fall of 1834, than Thomas began complaining about their longitudinal flaws and rough ends. He told the Browns that the fifteen-foot rails conformed neither to the specifications nor to the pattern. The width of the base varied so much that the ends had to be taken down with a chisel before they could be laid in the chairs, through which they were spiked down to the yellow pine stringers underneath. The tops and bottoms were so warped that unless the rails were straightened, the end of one might stick up an inch higher than its neighbor. They were bad enough to cause the railroad to seek an indemnity from the manufacturer and to bill the Brown organization $5,500 for straightening the rails.

Speed was also a factor in the accident. The engine was running at full power. Davis was on the tender to observe its operation. In his annual report that year, written within days of Phineas Davis's death, Knight noted that the locomotives were normally run to Washington at 20 mph. He thought even that was too fast considering the raw state of the embankments and the liability of the track to derangement, "as with the utmost care, unequal settlings of the rails will occur, and may have an evil effect before a re-adjustment can take place." He recommended a top speed of 15 mph.[22]

Davis died at 35, leaving a wife and two young children. The railroad eulogized its first successful producer of locomotives in the 1835 annual report, then quickly moved on. George Gillingham resigned as superintendent of machinery. He and Ross Winans assumed the free use of the railroad's Mt. Clare shops. The locomotives for the Baltimore and Ohio were now to be built, at $5,500 each, by Gillingham & Winans. They would also furnish the cast-iron wheels. Jonathan Jessop replaced Gillingham, and the company paid Israel Gartner, Davis's partner, who had never lived in Baltimore or taken an active part in the building of engines, $5,700 for the shop machinery.

Buoyed by the knowledge from Knight's reconnaissance that the locomotives would be able to cross the mountains unassisted, and with earnings increasing on the lines that were finished to Frederick, Harpers Ferry, and most recently, Washington, the price of B&O stock rose to $75 a share. The company opened transfer offices in New York and Philadelphia, but then closed them several months later for lack of business.

The other signals the Baltimore and Ohio Railroad sent to outside observers in the fall of 1835 were just as mixed. Hezekiah Niles, heralding the return of peace to the city and the bustle of trade in the streets, proclaimed, "Our great railroad *must* go on," but there was no such clear commitment from the company itself.[23] Instead, in the 1835 annual report, Thomas still talked favorably about building the C&O Canal to Cumberland and the B&O Railroad through the Valley of Virginia to the James River and Kanawha Railroad, or to the New Orleans and Nashville Railroad, both of which were under construction. At the same time, he mentioned a continuous rail line from Baltimore to Wheeling and Pittsburgh, which would cost $4.6 million and would be paid for primarily by the City of Baltimore, the State of Maryland, and the two destination cities. Wheeling, too, had offered a stock subscription of $250,000 toward the B&O's completion, and Thomas intimated that if there was more interest from the West, the company would get on with the job.

The B&O declared a dividend that fall for the first time in two years, but it was only 1.5 percent and the disappointed investors vowed they would not put up more capital. The price of shares plummeted. The *American* observed gloomily, "The prospect of the speedy and energetic extension of the Road has become clouded."[24]

Thomas was feeling the strain of years of crisis and the debasing tactics necessary to placate the C&O Canal. He told a correspondent, "My health has latterly been much broken and quite infirm," and he confided to John H. B. Latrobe that he wanted to resign.[25] Latrobe tried to dissuade him: Thomas "complained much of the unpopularity of the company. The drudgery that was imposed on him. The complaints that were made out of doors, etc.," but Latrobe assured him that although the low dividend had annoyed the public, times would get better and if he quit now, the company's improved fortunes would be attributed to his having left.[26]

The initiative Thomas hoped for from the West soon appeared. The movement began in Brownsville, Pennsylvania, with a call for a railroad meeting to be held there November 25, 1835. It was just about a year after the canal convention in Baltimore, the impetus for which had come from Cumberland. The Brownsville gathering had the similar purpose of publicizing the need to complete the railroad at least from Cumberland to the Ohio River. The usual preliminary meetings were held in Baltimore to drum up interest and select delegates. The lawyer Latrobe was named to represent the railroad. He declined to go, pleading prior commitments.

Among the 150 or so people who attended the three-day Brownsville railroad convention, there were only ten from Baltimore, including John Pendleton Kennedy and the ubiquitous James W. McCulloh. Director William Steuart was the lone B&O representative. The chairman was Andrew Stewart, former Pennsylvania congressman and one of the originators of the C&O Canal. Most of the delegates were from Wheeling, Pittsburgh, and Brownsville, and from the Williamsport and Cumberland areas of Maryland. They all agreed that completing the rail line from Cumberland would greatly benefit local agriculture and industry.

The convention was lackluster for most of the Baltimoreans except John Pendleton Kennedy, who went to Brownsville as a lawyer, politician, and novelist, delivered an eloquent address, and came back as "A Man of the Times." The letters he wrote on his return for the Baltimore *American* had an immediate and electrifying effect on his fellow citizens.[27] Kennedy's message was clear: "The time for decisive and energetic action towards the completion of the Rail Road to the Ohio has arrived. The road *must* be completed—and speedily, for we have no time to lose. It must be completed, *no matter at what cost*. The city has credit . . . the present generation are able to pay interest; let the next generation pay the principal."

Kennedy brought up the old arguments—that the New York and Pennsylvania canals were stealing Baltimore's flour and tobacco trade, and that Washington, Richmond, and Charleston had plans to make off with the rest. He mercilessly shamed the city for not trying hard enough, and he promised that if they only made an effort, they would have support: "The people of the West are ready to help you. . . . They have invited you to come on: at Brownsville they have invited you." Addressing "A Baltimorean," a disgruntled B&O stockholder who favored a city connection to the Pennsylvania canals and whose arguments were mostly innuendo, he said:

> It is needless for you and me to discuss the value of the Pennsylvania canals to Baltimore, because the town has already decided that they will go to them; and the means are now provided. Now what do you want? Are you going to ask for more money? Do you want the citizens to do anything? Let us know, and perhaps we will

help you. Or do you want, my dear sir, *to stop the Baltimore and Ohio Railroad, and say it shall not go to the Ohio?*

"A Man of the Times" was clear about what he wanted:

> *First*—An entire railway to the Ohio is better than a route partly by land and partly by water. Therefore the Baltimore and Ohio Railroad ought to be carried through without interruption.
> *Second*—When carried through it will be better than the route of the Pennsylvania canals, because they have a portage over the mountains.
> *Third*—The route through Pennsylvania will be better by way of the Chesapeake and the canal from tide, than by the Susquehanna Rail Road.
> *Fourth*—It is very important to make a canal from the Potomac to Baltimore.

The way to accomplish all this was through public money, not private capital, he said.

On the day the above letter appeared, December 17, 1835, the Baltimore and Ohio Railroad recaptured its sense of mission. The board of directors established a special five-man committee, with Thomas as one of the members, "to employ such assistance as they may deem necessary towards obtaining the requisite funds for the immediate recommencement and vigorous prosecution of this undertaking according to its original plan and purposes."[28]

After the New Year, Benjamin H. Latrobe, Jr., noticed "much warm feeling" in favor of extending the railroad. Kennedy generated most of it. He addressed a large Saturday night gathering of the Brownsville delegation and other citizens at Baltimore's Masonic Hall. He helped to organize a series of ward meetings where more speeches were given and signatures were gathered. John H. B. Latrobe spoke at one. The organizers did their work well. When they were through, 6,000 B&O stockholders and Baltimore property owners had signed a memorial asking for $1 million. It was presented to the city council.

The rejuvenated railroad promoters simultaneously went to work in Annapolis, and their accomplishment during the chaotic December 1835 and May 1836 sessions of the Maryland General Assembly would be debated for years to come. It was the next to the last hurrah for the canal-railroad combination. But their triumphant joint effort was almost undone at the beginning by the Chesapeake and Ohio. It seemed that Mercer had grossly underestimated the amount of money that would be needed to complete the canal to Cumberland. Thus, when the representatives of the Baltimore and Ohio arrived in Annapolis in January 1836 also seeking funds, they found the political atmosphere poisoned by doubt about internal improvements.

Mercer had based his $2 million estimate for the last 78 miles to Cumberland on a year-old survey by C&O engineer Alfred Cruger, who in early 1834 had estimated the cost of building the next 27 miles, starting at dam no. 5 above Williamsport, at $636,000, or about $23,600 per mile. In the summer of 1835, soon after the legislature approved the $2 million loan to the canal, the company resurveyed the entire 78 miles and discovered that the funds needed to build the first 27 miles had risen to over $1 million, mainly because of higher labor costs and the relocation of the canal to a more elevated level, away from the river. The whole 78 miles would now cost $3.9 million, or $50,000 per mile, almost double what Mercer had said a year earlier. The new figures brought the total cost of the 187-mile canal from Washington to Cumberland to $8.8 million, roughly $600,000 more than the United States engineers had forecast ten years earlier in an estimate that was vigorously disputed by Mercer at the time.[29]

A joint House-Senate committee established to investigate the C&O's "false estimates" learned from George C. Washington, the C&O president, and other canal officials that of the first $1 million in state loan funds, the C&O had spent over $500,000 to pay its debts, about $170,000 for repairs, and roughly $120,000 on new construction. To queries about not knowing then that the cost estimates were incorrect, the C&O officials replied that they thought the money would be sufficient to build the canal to Cumberland, although no one believed that it would also cover their debt payments and repair costs.

The Baltimore and Ohio submitted its case to the General Assembly in late February 1836. Thomas informed the legislators that the B&O had spent $3,250,000 of their initial $4 million capital stock to build and equip 82 miles of main line railroad. A 400-mile railroad would cost a total of at least $8 million, he said, and the $750,000 in private installments yet to be called in was not enough to finish the job. He also talked about how the B&O had pioneered in a new venture under adverse circumstances and had made it work, and now the people of Maryland and the West were demanding that the remainder of the line be built. He emphasized that the company depended on the state for the funds, but he did not name a specific figure. Privately, Thomas told McCulloh that the B&O would not resume construction until they had the means to conclude it. He added that the State of Maryland could depend "upon a company which never has deceived it and which I may modestly say is not capable of doing it."[30]

Within days, the legislature passed an enabling act authorizing the City of Baltimore to subscribe, not just for the suggested $1 million, but for $3 million in Baltimore and Ohio stock, to borrow the funds to pay for it, and to levy a property tax to cover the principal and interest. The city council began debating the issue. The railroad soon asked the State of Maryland for a similar stock subscription, but the method by which they arrived at the figure was even more casual than the canal's. In early March 1836, at the City Hotel in Annapolis, John H. B. Latrobe fell into conversation with Charles B. Fisk, the C&O engineer who had conducted the waterway's most recent surveys. Fisk told him that $3 million would finish the Chesapeake and Ohio to Cumberland and Latrobe adopted the same figure, "when it followed almost as a matter of course that I should not ask for less for the railroad."

Latrobe next encountered the cunning and unscrupulous James W. McCulloh, who officially represented the canal and secretly the railroad. "Upon comparing notes, it was found that each of the companies would like to have three million dollars," Latrobe recalled. McCulloh believed the state's credit would easily sustain a large bond issue. "Accordingly, after much consultation," said Latrobe, "I undertook to write the internal improvement part of the report and Mr. McCulloh the financial part, which having been read to and approved by the chairman of the committee of ways and means, was presented to the House of Delegates and became the basis of the celebrated Eight Million bill."[31]

William D. Merrick, the ways and means committee chairman, delivered the report Latrobe referred to on March 9, 1836. The House of Delegates ordered a thousand copies printed. Two days later, the Baltimore *American* devoted almost a full page to reprinting what the editors called an able, luminous, and cheering document.[32] Its principles provided an outline for legislative debate and set the state's finances on a controversial course. In a grand manner reminiscent of Washington's Olympian view of an internal improvement system for the eastern United States, the report set forth a plan for Maryland that would make it the equal of New York, Pennsylvania, or any other competitor. Since one of the several branches of the system passed through all but four of the 20 counties in Maryland, there would be ample political support.[33]

Thus Maryland was asked to appropriate $8 million, in the form of stock subscriptions, for internal improvements: $3 million each for the Chesapeake and Ohio Canal and the Baltimore and Ohio Railroad, $1 million for the Eastern Shore Railroad (Elkton to Somerset and Worcester counties), and $500,000 each for the Maryland Canal (the Cross-Cut from the C&O to Baltimore) and the Annapolis Canal (from Washington to the state capital).

Although the legislators were alarmed that the Chesapeake and Ohio had underestimated the cost to Cumberland and needed more money, the committee seemed satisfied that the officials who submitted the estimate had been as much imposed upon by its "vague and uncertain character" as had been the lawmakers themselves and that the company had not spent the state loan funds improperly. And in any case, they said, the current estimate of nearly $3 million could be relied on and Maryland had little choice but to provide it. Unless it had further aid, the canal would expire unfinished and be unable to repay the loan or even the interest, and the state's previous investment of $500,000 in C&O stock would be a total loss.

On the other hand, the canal would succeed if it were built just to Cumberland to carry coal. However, the railroad, regarded mainly as a passenger line, had to be extended to the Ohio River, according to the report. The 318 miles of track remaining to be built beyond Harpers Ferry would cost almost $7 million (at $22,000 per mile). In recommending a $3 million state stock subscription to the B&O, the committee realized that if the city made its maximum allowable contribution and the unpaid installments were called in, it would just about make up the required amount. "So large a portion of the State's capital and credit have been embarked on the construction of Rail Roads and Canals, that these works now constitute the leading feature of the fiscal policy of the State," Merrick observed.[34]

Merrick's report graphically described the principal line of Maryland's internal improvement system as a huge checkmark made backward through the state's territory. It began at Elkton, followed the shoreline of the Chesapeake Bay down to Baltimore, its lowest point, then moved west, tracing a course along the arc of the

Potomac Valley to Cumberland and beyond: "This line may be termed the axis of the system, and its extension beyond the limits of the State to the west, would reach Wheeling and Pittsburgh [and] thence be carried on to Michigan city and Chicago, at the head of Lake Michigan. . . . The eastern prolongation of the same line, would pass through Philadelphia, New York, and Boston. . . . If [all] the lines here indicated are drawn upon a map of the State, it will be seen that there is not a county which is not in near proximity to some one or other of them." [35]

The same day the committee chairman delivered his report in Annapolis, the First Branch of the Baltimore city council passed a measure effectively doubling the number of railroad directors Baltimore was entitled to and giving the municipality a majority on the board, based on the city's new stock subscription. The newspapers countered immediately. The *American* was outraged: "This is a virtual rejection by that branch of the [state] law recently passed authorising the City to subscribe three millions to the Rail Road"; patronage issue, sneered the *Gazette*; "Party engine," added Hezekiah Niles.[36] The "Man of the Times" found it again necessary to take up his pen: "First, I tell you the town is perfectly satisfied that you should act under the law as it stands," he wrote. "Secondly, the delay is hurtful: we want action, action— immediate action." [37]

The councilmen got the message. The measure was immediately quashed in the Second Branch, and a few days later, the city council overwhelmingly approved a resolution directing the mayor to subscribe for $3 million of Baltimore and Ohio stock, with the proviso that the whole sum be used to build the railroad "in an unbroken line from Harpers Ferry." The council also issued a long report, clearly patterned on Merrick's, containing the basis for their action. The headline in the *Chronicle* read: "Three Millions To The Rail Road," and the editors opined that "the future prosperity of Baltimore depends entirely upon the completion of this road to the waters of the Ohio." [38]

The council did not pass the actual ordinance establishing the city's subscription until April 26, 1836. A week after their de facto decision to support the railroad, however, they were guests at a company-staged locomotive demonstration, "the experiment being performed for their satisfaction as the 3 millions was voted by them on the strength of the alleged power of these engines," said Benjamin H. Latrobe, Jr., who witnessed the trial.[39]

The start was inauspicious. It was a raw, windy morning on Tuesday, March 22, 1836, when the party of about 40, mostly made up of city councilmen, climbed into the cars and set out for the inclined planes behind the locomotive Andrew Jackson. At Marriottsville, the engine derailed after running over and killing a horse that jumped into the path of the train from the adjoining track where it had been hauling freight. Past Sykesville, they ran into an ox cart and the tender was thrown off the track. At Parrs Spring Ridge, the engineman was supposed to cut loose the single eight-wheeled car and proceed with the three four-wheeled ones. Instead, he climbed the first and most of the second planes with the entire train. Within 30 feet of the summit, he dropped off the smaller cars. Then, starting from a dead stop, he drew the passengers up the rest of the way. On the trip back down, two cars full of pig iron were added to the consist. The engineer, using the locomotive's power alone, without brakes, halted several times to demonstrate his control of the train.

The fan providing the draft broke down at Ellicotts Mills on the return to Baltimore and they had to stop several times to get the fire going again, delaying their arrival in the city until nine in the evening. Despite their misadventures and a full twelve hours on the road, the councilmen regarded the engine trials as a complete success. The locomotives had pulled 20 to 25 tons to the top of the hill and held back 33 tons on the way down. Their report was enthusiastic:

> It is now a matter of common parlance to assert that the Alleghanies can be passed by locomotive engines by the Potomac route, without the use of stationary power; and your committee entertain no doubt of the fact. It is this which gives to Baltimore the vantage ground in the competition with her sister cities, for the western trade; and yet this is owing, not more to the geographical depressions of the mountain range, than to the engines perfected by the company. . . . While nature, therefore, has done much to facilitate the intercourse of Baltimore with the west, the Baltimore and Ohio Rail Road Company has not done less.[40]

Meanwhile, in Annapolis, the debate on the Eight Million bill was about to begin. It was delayed by such grave affairs of state as the indemnity for Reverdy Johnson, whose house was sacked during the Baltimore Bank Riots the previous year.[41] The legislature was scheduled to adjourn, *sine die*, on Saturday, April 2, 1836, and the Eight Million bill, which had already been special-ordered several times, was not finally taken up until the Tuesday before. W. T. Wootton, chairman of the joint House-Senate committee investigating the canal loan, tried to move things along that first day by declaring that although they hadn't time to make a full report, "From the known character and probity of the parties, the committee are satisfied that the error was one of judgment, not of design—that the canal company had no intention to mislead or deceive the Legislature."[42] He urged an end to the controversy; more argument only meant further delay.

For the next two days, the fortunes of the bill seesawed as its opponents, led by Thomas G. Pratt, Prince Georges County, crippled it with amendments, and its backers, headed by ways and means chairman Merrick, from Charles County, succeeded in having some of them reconsidered and rejected. On Thursday, March 31, Pratt and Merrick went at it for several hours on the House floor and at 6:00 P.M. the members voted 35–34 to refer the Eight Million bill to the next General Assembly. For the delegates at least, that was a relatively painless method of dispatching it. The *American*, which had predicted victory, called the news "disastrous"; Daniel Cobb, Annapolis correspondent of the *Gazette*, who had been more cautious, wrote, "The hopes of the friends of Internal Improvement are blasted by the rejection of the Bill reported by the Commitee of Ways and Means. I am too much grieved to say more."[43] Hezekiah Niles observed matter-of-factly that the bill was considered too late in the session and amended to death through sectional jealousy.

The reaction from the Baltimore business community was instantaneous, and sufficiently alarmed to change the legislature's plans for adjournment. Merchants and property holders, meeting at the Exchange, formed a 25-man committee including John Pendleton Kennedy, George Brown, and Isaac McKim, Jr., which chartered a steamboat and sailed for Annapolis to hector the delegates into reconsidering their vote. The next day, Saturday, the House debated a reconsideration of the bill. Merrick introduced a substitute measure requested by the Baltimore committee. "The scene in the house which did not adjourn till 10 oclock at night was most exciting," said Benjamin H. Latrobe, Jr. "We shall hear tomorrow or next day. Great excitement prevails in regard to what is considered the last hope of Baltimore, the passage of the bill."[44] The best that could be arranged before the General Assembly adjourned on Monday, April 4, however, was a compromise to convene an extra session of the legislature beginning the fourth Monday in May.

There was a general feeling that the Eight Million bill would pass the next time. To make sure that it did, some positive steps were taken. On April 5, the railroad ordered surveys west of Harpers Ferry. The next day, another gathering was held at the Exchange. John Pendleton Kennedy once again addressed the group and got its approval for a huge internal improvement convention that would meet in Baltimore before the start of the special session. Mayor Samuel Smith backed the idea and issued an "Address of the City of Baltimore to the People of Maryland," in which he implored every Maryland town, city, and election district to send delegates.

Thus, on May 2, 1836, at the Universalist Church on St. Paul Street, almost 450 delegates gathered for a three-day convention. Thirteen Maryland counties were represented, and there were sizable groups from Wheeling and Pittsburgh. Baltimore's delegation of 50, the largest, included all the expected names—railroad officials, lawyers, prominent business and political leaders. There was only minor dissension, mainly from Frederick, which opposed everything except the canals near them. John H. B. Latrobe objected to a resolution backed by Hagerstown requiring the railroad to be built entirely within Maryland, but then went along in the interest of unity. The delegates emphatically endorsed state aid for internal improvements and adjourned.

The Maryland legislature convened May 23, 1836, for its first summer session since 1813, when the British fleet menaced shipping and towns on the Chesapeake Bay. The *Gazette* considered the current situation equally serious in terms of the welfare of the state.[45] The session began on a sour note in the form of a minority report from the joint committee that had investigated the loan to the canal company. It censured the C&O for misuse of funds. In the course of their research, the members had queried both Mercer and Washington. Mercer, true to form, had defended the cost estimates and evaded the question of how the money was spent and had gone out of his way to extol the virtues of canals and to deliver an ill-tempered diatribe against the railroad. Mercer had given "ten of the best years of my life," to the Chesapeake and Ohio Canal, he said. Now the price of its continued existence was more cooperation and perhaps even further joint construction with the hated Baltimore and Ohio Railroad: "I made the [1833] compromise which you witnessed to save the canal from the vengeance of your State councils then excited against it to an extent threatening not merely the loss of countenance and favor but actual and serious persecution. If I write frankly, your candour will excuse mine." Otherwise, Mercer continued, he never would have given up the C&O's rights and interests.[46]

Washington's response to the minority's charges was that the canal company had to clear its debts, including those to landowners, before it could get on with building the waterway to Cumberland under the $2 million state loan. "Would a wise Legislature have required or expected the company to have recommenced its work by throwing bankruptcy and ruin upon its contractors and laborers, and all with whom they were connected?" he asked.[47]

In the welter of documents produced by the canal company to justify its actions and in the confusing reports and counterreports of the legislative committees, whose findings were mainly politically motivated, a few things are evident. One is that the C&O officials made different statements at different times about what they intended to do with the $2 million. Another is that, although Mercer, a past master at understating construction costs, may not have submitted "false estimates," the cost figures he used were at least outdated. And finally, the Chesapeake and Ohio may not have deliberately set out to deceive the Maryland legislature, but that is what they accomplished. Mercer's own words, in the only document the C&O offered as the basis for the state loan, were that the funds would be used for construction of the canal to Cumberland. It is just as plain that the legislature intended the money to be so used, because the act established penalties if it were not. But they were not invoked and the discussion moved on.

William D. Merrick again championed the Eight Million bill. Thomas G. Pratt still opposed it. He and his allies used the canal's sloppy accounting to bludgeon the railroad. No B&O survey had been made from Harpers Ferry to the western waters, they said, on which to base a cost estimate "which would be entitled to the least confidence."[48] Nonetheless, at the end of a week the bill had survived a series of test votes and the newspapers were saying it would clear the House by a ten-vote majority. There was no Senate opposition.

The Baltimore and Ohio had a four-man lobbying team in the State House and there were other factors at work, but their opponents were not finished yet. Assuming a defensive posture, they took up delaying tactics. Early in June, Cobb, of the *Gazette*, informed his editor, Gwynn, that Merrick was working to change the House rules:

> Something of the kind is necessary or there is no knowing how long the session will last. The enemies of the bill make new propositions and amendments and substitutes at every step, then follow long speeches, from six or eight members, then points of order of trivial moment, which consume hours in their being discussed, until the house, wearied out of patience, and blinded by the various and conflicting subjects before it, all at the same time, adjourns to witness the same captious opposition on the next day. In this way, the House has stood for the last three days without moving one step in advance.[49]

The day after Cobb wrote that report, the House passed the bill by a vote of

48–29, the Senate confirmed it, and "An Act for the Promotion of Internal Improvement" became a law June 4, 1836. The railroad, taking no chances, paid a steamboat captain $50 to deliver a sick delegate, express, to Annapolis so that he could vote. Pratt, the measure's prime antagonist, evidently took a walk because his vote was not recorded.

A week later, meeting again at the Exchange, this time to plan a victory celebration, Baltimore's civic leaders first chose a dinner for the governor and the legislature, with a 100-gun salute, the ringing of bells, and a display of flags throughout the city; but it was thought that a more public commemoration was required, so a large parade was scheduled instead for the Fourth of July. In Wheeling, the excitement was more spontaneous. When the news reached there, the bells began to ring, and instantly, "as if by magic, numberless lights were seen gleaming from every quarter," said the Wheeling *Gazette*. "The hill in the rear of the city was lighted up by an immense bonfire, and a number of arches were thrown across the streets, on which were hung a variety of lamps, with almost every device which ingenuity could suggest. Many beautiful transparencies, which had been prepared on the day preceding, and on which the words, 'Maryland,' 'Rail-roads,' 'Merrick,' etc. were very prominent, attracted universal admiration." [50]

The fate of the Eight Million bill overshadowed the opening of the Winchester and Potomac Railroad in mid-March 1836 when about 50 guests left Harpers Ferry in two cars pulled by the Tennessee, a British import, followed by the Thomas Jefferson, an engine borrowed from the B&O. At Winchester bands played, artillery boomed, and there were the usual florid speeches from the two railroad presidents, followed by a big dinner at the Virginia House and a return trip the next day.

But there was still no connection between the lines at Harpers Ferry. Because of the lack of warehouses on the Maryland side, the goods were stored in closed cars. By May, almost 170 of them were waiting there to be unloaded, snarling transportation. About that time, Thomas was advised that the level of the Winchester and Potomac was coming in three feet below the grade of the Baltimore and Ohio where the tracks were supposed to meet. His solution was to split the difference by lowering the end of the Harpers Ferry bridge and raising the W&P embankment, but it was a sign of things to come.

Thomas's health was now failing rapidly. "I have today crawled back to the office, but am little able to attend to business," he wrote an associate.[51] On June 30, 1836, a few weeks after the final passage of the Eight Million bill, Philip E. Thomas made good his long-standing wish to resign as president of the Baltimore and Ohio Railroad. (He remained as a director until October 1838.) Joseph W. Patterson, the son of William Patterson, one of Baltimore's "royal merchants," replaced him, serving as president pro tem. The board accepted the resignation with profound regret: "On the commencement of this work, of which he has been, in fact, the father and projector, everything connected with its construction was new, crude, and doubtful, with little light to guide the way, and that derived from distant and uncertain sources." [52]

Caspar W. Wever, the B&O's construction foreman for eight years, resigned the same day. His reasons for leaving are unrecorded, but the board thanked him for "the faithful and able manner in which he has conducted the affairs of the company," and wished him well.[53] Wever may have left on account of a company reorganization that took place at the same time, in which H. W. Fitzhugh, a superintendent with broad fiscal powers, was brought in to serve under the new president, and Benjamin H. Latrobe, Jr., was named engineer of location in charge of the surveys. But Wever's resignation may have had something to do with the bridge at Harpers Ferry.

As designed by Latrobe and Lewis Wernwag, the bridge was a seven-span structure, 830 feet long, supported by six undressed masonry piers, with abutments at either end. The Baltimore and Ohio built the Maryland abutment, and the Winchester and Potomac, the Virginia one. The structure incorporated a roadway for the Wagers that they could charge toll on, and a tracking path to lead boats over from the Shenandoah River and into the C&O Canal. Charles Wilson received the masonry contract in the fall of 1835 and went to work on the piers. Wernwag got the job of building the wooden superstructure the next spring. In May 1836, Benjamin Latrobe took his wife, Ellen, on a business trip to Harpers Ferry. It was a miserable experience. They arrived in a downpour, could not see the scenery from Jefferson's Rock, and went back the next day. But Latrobe got a good enough look at the bridge to see that the masonry was not right: "The work is rough and the design not adhered to in the forms of the piers. It will be strong however. Wernwag is preparing for the superstructure, which he will frame at Wever's Mill, 3 miles below the scite."[54]

In August 1836, after Latrobe returned to the B&O and was made superintendent of the Potomac Viaduct, he went with some of the directors to inspect the bridge, on which the first of the wooden arches was now complete. The company accepted the structure. Latrobe commented, "It is a beautiful combination of timbers, but the lumber of which it is built is rough stuff."[55] The bridge was finished about December 1836. It had cost at least the estimated $85,000 and possibly a great deal more. Within a month, Latrobe knew something was wrong. In January 1837, he fought his way to Harpers Ferry through a snowstorm, going the final distance in a sleigh on the turnpike and then on foot because the drifts had shut down the railroad. A two-day trip turned into five; by the time it was over he had devised a plan to correct the problem at the bridge, which was lack of stability under load, but before he could do anything, the weight of the wooden superstructure had cracked the heads of the piers. The cause was poor masonry. It would cost several thousand dollars to repair the damage. Latrobe was glad he was not to blame, because "this part of the work was done under Wever by one of his pets who is I think not much honester than himself."[56]

That was in March 1837. After Latrobe made his report, in which he recommended banding the pier heads with iron, the board of directors named a committee to investigate the problems. The chairman was John Pendleton Kennedy, a new board member. Latrobe and his friend Charles B. Fisk, engineer of the C&O Canal, along with Knight, made a detailed examination of the Harpers Ferry bridge. By the time they presented their findings, two months later, the cracks in the pier heads had worsened to the point where iron bands would not do the job. Some of the foundations were actually washing away. Most of the five piers in the river would have to be completely rebuilt, which meant supporting the wooden superstructure on temporary trestles, an expensive and time-consuming operation.

The engineers attributed the failure to "defective workmanship and materials." The stone used in the foundations and skewbacks was too small and just thrown together, they noted, wondering "why so efficient a Contractor and one who had previously performed so well upon the Bridge work of the company as Charles Wilson, should have made on this occasion work so defective."[57]

Gradually, the investigating committee pieced together the story of what had happened at the bridge. Latrobe's design, as he already knew, had not been followed. The style of masonry, the size of the stone, and the dimensions of the foundations had all been changed and the man who had issued the change order was Caspar W. Wever. He did it at the start of construction, actually the day before the bids were approved. Wever had solicited three of these: from John Littlejohn, Lamb & Lukens, and Charles Wilson. Littlejohn, the conscientious builder who had finished the Catoctin Viaduct against all odds, was the low bidder. Charles Wilson submitted the highest one and was awarded the contract. (Wilson's brother Robert, now one of Knight's superintendents, had been Wever's masonry agent when the company investigated the excessive cost and other problems at the great stone bridges near Baltimore.) Charles Wilson's contract stipulated that the railroad would haul the stone he used for free. Littlejohn had made no such demand.

Lamb & Lukens got the job of constructing the Virginia abutment for the Winchester and Potomac Railroad. They built it according to Latrobe's original specifications, with stone obtained nearby at moderate expense, and produced "a permanent and most substantial" structure. Wilson might have done the same. Instead, he brought inferior stone for the piers almost three miles on the railroad, at the company's expense, from quarries owned by Wever, who charged him a much higher price than he would have paid for better material at Harpers Ferry. Needless to say, Wever's poor-quality stone was better suited to the type of masonry he had substituted for Latrobe's.

For some reason, the committee members found Wever's flagrant conflict of interest surprising. They should have realized that he had already, with their collaboration, graduated from self-dealing to nepotism. He had previously supplied materials to the railroad and hired his own children and the board had approved. But he had never caused a bridge to fail or cost them several thousand dollars in repair bills. The investigators believed Wever and Wilson had been in collusion. They asked John H. B. Latrobe to determine the legal liability of the superintendent and the contractor.

Latrobe's findings, presented in October 1837, showed that the company itself had authorized Wever's suggested change in the style of masonry because it was presumed to be cheaper. Therefore, he was not liable. Latrobe found no tangible evidence of collusion between Wever and Wilson before the contract was signed; ergo, there was no fraud on the company. Nor was Wever culpable for lack of supervision at the construction site, not when his superiors had sent him off on surveys west of Harpers Ferry while the piers were being built and praised the "faithful and able manner" in which he conducted the company's business. "My opinion therefore is, that the late superintendent of Graduation and Masonry is not legally responsible to the Company for damages growing out of the defects in the masonry of the Bridge at Harpers Ferry."

The next question was whether Charles Wilson, the contractor, could be brought to account for the shoddy construction. Latrobe learned that Wilson had been open about the kind of work he was doing at Harpers Ferry—had, indeed, told one of the Wagers that the style of masonry Wever insisted on would not stand; that he, Wilson, did not care about the work because nobody was supervising it; and that he was in a hurry to get his money, knowing that when the bridge gave way, he would not get any more jobs. In other words, the contractor had not fraudulently hidden the bridge's defects—quite the contrary. Latrobe summed up the fiasco this way:

> The defective character of the work itself furnishes, I think, no such proof as would be required to sustain an action. It was done in open day, on the line of a public thoroughfare, close to the town of Harper's Ferry with the Rail Road belonging to the company running up to it, with agents of the company all about it,—all circumstances apparently inconsistent with the idea of such concealment of defects, or knowingly of insufficient construction, as would amount to a fraud on the Company sufficient to make the contractor responsible in damages.[58]

Thus, after ten years of effort, the Baltimore and Ohio Railroad crossed the river at Harpers Ferry.

Part II

Harpers Ferry to Cumberland, 1836-1848

✺ 16 ✺

McLane,
the Politician

THE MAN THE BALTIMORE AND OHIO RAILROAD
chose to lead them farther west was very different from the benign Philip E. Thomas.
He was probably less competent. He was definitely less calm. John H. B. Latrobe was
one of the first to greet the new head of the railroad, and he came to know Louis
McLane well over the next decade or so. "He was not a pleasant person to get along
with. He was peremptory and at times uncertain, and would not abide opposition
or differences of opinion," Latrobe said. "I did not regard Mr. McLane as having
the soundest judgment. . . . I never was quite sure that he took much interest in his
office." Latrobe did admit, however, that he had never met anyone, including Daniel
Webster, "who possessed in the same degree the faculty of stating a case clearly."[1]

Latrobe considered McLane as not primarily an attorney, or a politician, though
he was both those things, but a statesman. McLane genuinely deserved the title. After
a dozen years in Congress, he had served successively as Andrew Jackson's ambassador to England, treasury secretary, and secretary of state. He was a Washington
insider, and in London, where he was much admired, he moved in the highest diplomatic and financial circles. McLane was, indeed, a natural aristocrat, and he made
an easy transition from the embassy to the corporate boardroom. McLane resigned
from public life in 1834 and then demonstrated his administrative ability in the private sector by remaking New Jersey's Morris Canal and Banking Company, which
was the plaything of speculators, into a respectable and profitable concern. Although
the records are not very clear on the matter, it was probably this accomplishment as
much as anything that prompted the Baltimore and Ohio Railroad to choose him as
its new president. McLane seemed to embody what the B&O felt was needed at the
time, a high-priced, outside executive who had good connections and could market
the large and crucial bond package they were counting on to extend the railroad from
Harpers Ferry to the Ohio River.

The directors appointed McLane president in the waning days of 1836 at a salary of $6,000 per year (twice what Philip E. Thomas had been making but equivalent to McLane's Morris Canal salary). Joseph W. Patterson, having served six months as president pro tem, resigned, but he remained on the board, along with Philip E. Thomas, until October 1838.

John H. B. Latrobe, Patterson, and another director took a stagecoach to New York a few days after Christmas to inform McLane of his appointment and explain the railroad's state of affairs. They had dinner with him and returned almost immediately. Neither Latrobe nor McLane had much to say about the meeting, but McLane apparently asked for time to review his present situation and study the B&O's charter, reports, and the 1836 Eight Million bill. Thomas, alluding to the choice of his successor, said, "We calculate largely on his efficiency and hope he will give great additional confidence to our undertaking." Hezekiah Niles was also hopeful: "The energy, talents, and weight of character which this gentleman will bring to his new duties, assure us that the great work will now be successfully prosecuted."[2]

McLane officially resigned from the Morris Canal at the end of January 1837 and accepted the job in Baltimore, but he asked for a few months to straighten out his affairs in New York. He attended his first B&O board meeting in early February, served as president for a day, and left again. In March, he was back saying that things had deteriorated in New York and he might not be able to come at all. The B&O directors did not like that, and the meeting ended inconclusively. The Morris Canal then reelected him president, McLane having promised not to leave until they found a replacement, which they had not done. Finally, in June, after Patterson had written him that, although the board understood that "uncontrollable and unforeseen circumstances" had kept McLane in New York, "at the same time they trust and believe that before long you will be able to remove permanently to our city,"[3] the new chief executive arrived in Baltimore. Patterson filled in for him in the interim, aided occasionally by Thomas, but for the first half of 1837, it was not exactly clear who was president of the Baltimore and Ohio Railroad.

Not everyone shared John H. B. Latrobe's edgy opinion of Louis McLane. New York's Philip Hone described him as "one of the most agreeable and able men I ever knew." Andrew Jackson said he was "a fair, honorable man."[4] Although he stood just five feet, five inches tall, imperial measure, McLane had commanding presence. His hair, curling loosely around his ears, framed a high forehead. There was a bulbous nose, a wide, straight mouth, and a strong jaw stiffly emphasized by his high starched collars. McLane's gaze was direct and uncompromising, autocratic one might say. He had been named Louis, for the king of France, by his father, Allan McLane. The father had had a distinguished career during the Revolutionary War, mainly as a scout for LaFayette and Washington. Louis, born May 28, 1784, was one of three children who survived out of a total of fourteen. Louis McLane and his wife, Catherine, eventually had thirteen children of their own; twelve lived, one of whom, Robert, later followed a similar career as a Congressman, diplomat, and railroad official.

Louis McLane was appointed a midshipman at age fifteen and cruised for a year on a frigate, but resigned in 1802, a victim of seasickness. He returned to Wilmington, attended Newark College, studied and practiced law, fought a duel with a fellow student, and was elected to the House of Representatives in 1817. There, he served on the ways and means committee under chairman Samuel Smith, of Baltimore, who became a lifelong friend. After five years, McLane took over as committee chairman. In 1827, the year the Baltimore and Ohio Railroad was incorporated, he was elected to the United States Senate. As a senator, he opposed the federal government's provision of engineers for the B&O surveys but backed the bill to import duty-free iron. McLane generally favored internal improvements, and specifically, the National Road, the Chesapeake and Ohio Canal (because he believed the nation's capital ought to have a project to match those of New York and Baltimore), as well as his favorite Chesapeake and Delaware Canal.

In the summer of 1828, just about the time the railroad was breaking ground, McLane bought a Georgian mansion surrounded by 1,000 acres of land below Elkton, in Cecil County, Maryland. His wife's family's ancestral estate, it was once part of a much larger tract originally surveyed in the seventeenth century by the legendary Augustine Herrman, of Prague. It was called Bohemia.[5] The following year, frustrated in his efforts to obtain a seat on the Supreme Court or a cabinet post, although Martin Van Buren lobbied vigorously for him, McLane settled ungraciously for an appointment as minister to England. "For a truly great man, he has more littleness about him than usual," was Van Buren's comment.[6] McLane's major worry was money. Although the $9,000 annual salary was very generous for the time, being ambassador to England was also a rich man's job in 1829, and besides having to support his wife and ten children in London, he had to pay the costs for entertainment and running the embassy. (He was allowed an additional $9,000 moving expenses.)

Washington Irving, legation secretary, recorded McLane's diplomatic triumph in London. His major objective in England was opening American trade with the West Indies on the same equal and reciprocal basis enjoyed by the British. He accomplished it in the fall of 1830. The day the arrangements were completed, McLane attended a court dinner. "The King [William IV] was particularly attentive to him, drank wine with him, and the second time, as a kind of toast to him, gave, 'Perpetual peace between my country and yours,'" Irving reported. "Our diplomatic situation therefore at this Court is as favorable and gratifying as we could desire, being treated with marked respect and friendliness by the Royal family, and by the various members of the Administration." "After dinner," Irving continued, "the King and Mr. McLane became so thick that some of the *corps diplomatique* showed symptoms of jealousy. The King took to him specially, when he found he had begun the world by being a Midshipman."[7]

While his secretary attracted artists, writers, and musicians to the embassy, McLane got to know such influential neighbors as Joshua Bates, a Bostonian who through adroit capital manipulation had become a full partner in Baring Brothers & Company, the premier merchant banking house in Europe. The firm was then headed by Alexander Baring, Lord Ashburton. Meanwhile, through the embassy apartments and drawing rooms paraded a full range of Southern exotics. Among these were Baltimore's Caton sisters, the so-called "Three Graces," granddaughters of Charles Carroll of Carrollton, in game pursuit of titled Englishmen. McLane's British idyll ended in mid-1831 when he was called home to become secretary of the treasury during a general cabinet shake-up following the Peggy Eaton scandal. Van Buren took his place in London and Roger B. Taney was named attorney general. McLane and Taney began sparring almost immediately for Jackson's favor as the "bank war" heated up. McLane was in principle friendly to Nicholas Biddle's Bank of the United States and opposed to removing the federal deposits, but at the same time, he believed some sanctions might be taken against Biddle in return for his political transgressions. Taney, meanwhile, was the most implacable enemy of the U.S. Bank in the Jackson administration.

McLane still hoped for a seat on the Supreme Court and therefore wanted to retain the President's favor. He negotiated the political minefield brilliantly for two years, but by mid-1833 he could no longer escape the pressure for removing the deposits. In another major cabinet reshuffle, which he worked out, McLane became Secretary of State and his handpicked successor, William J. Duane, took over as Treasury secretary. When Duane also refused to remove the federal deposits from the U.S. Bank, Jackson dismissed him and brought in Taney, who gave the order. Thereafter, McLane's national political career drew swiftly to a close. As Treasury secretary, in 1832, he issued an important report on American manufactures; as Secretary of State, he introduced orderly operational procedures for the first time and dealt with Mexico and Great Britain on boundary questions. But in mid-1834 McLane resigned in a cabinet dispute with Van Buren, who had come to recognize him as a challenger. Although McLane was still considered a candidate for Supreme Court Justice, Taney had supplanted him in Jackson's esteem, and it was Taney rather than McLane who was appointed to the court in January 1835.

Taney described McLane as being "an ambitious man [who] loved power, and aspired to the presidency which he confidently expected to reach." McLane was politically skillful: "He was an accomplished diplomatist, and exercised as much diplomacy in Washington to carry his measures as he would at a foreign court; and he had a remarkable talent at managing men with whom he came in contact, who were inferior to himself in strength of mind or firmness of purpose. He had great tact, and always knew whether he should address himself to the patriotism, the magnanimity, the pride, the vanity, the hopes or the fears of the person on whom he wished to operate."[8]

McLane was elected president of the Morris Canal and Banking Company in May 1835. The canal, which was completed in 1831 after a decade of construction, was used primarily to transport coal from the Pennsylvania anthracite fields at Mauch Chunk via the Lehigh canal system to New Jersey and New York. It meandered 90 miles across New Jersey, from Phillipsburg, on the Delaware River, via Lake Hopatcong, to Newark, and in 1836, to Jersey City. The waterway had 34 locks and 23 inclined planes to go up and over an elevation of 914 feet. When McLane assumed control the canal was in debt and needed repairs, and it had never paid a dividend.[9] The company charter also contained valuable banking privileges. The bank, in New York, had hardly begun operations in 1825 when it was taken over by speculators. A year later, four of the directors were indicted for conspiracy to defraud and there were other scandals that made the bank's name a curse on Wall Street. Just a few months before McLane arrived, a group of inside traders created a corner in Morris stock, the first ever in the market. They drove its price up spectacularly before they were disbanded.

Then in 1835, some New York merchants acquired control of the Morris and brought in McLane to clean house. He was attracted by the $6,000 annual salary. They were inspired by his name and reputation. One of the directors was Washington Irving. McLane first traveled the length of the canal all the way up the Lehigh to Mauch Chunk to see the problems for himself. He developed simultaneous programs for economy and expansion and lobbied for them in Trenton. By July 1836, the Morris Canal showed a profit of close to $275,000, the stock had almost doubled in price, and the company paid its first dividend. McLane also reduced the firm's debt and aggressively enlarged its role in interstate banking. But during the six months between the time the Baltimore and Ohio Railroad offered McLane the job and when he finally left the Morris Canal to begin it, the nationwide fever of speculation that had built up over the past several years broke. An economic panic ensued. McLane was reluctant to leave the Morris Canal in the midst of a crisis. He lingered to put together a financial rescue package for the firm through Biddle's U.S. Bank. Finally, in June 1837, the canal company let him go, with a $9,300 bonus for staying with them through trying times.

Louis McLane was 52 years old when he took over the Baltimore and Ohio Railroad. Speaking five years later, he referred to it as "the wreck." The company's expenses exceeded its income, the work was stalled at Harpers Ferry, and the railroad's chartered powers were about to expire. "The Main Stem to Harpers Ferry, was in a state of utter dilapidation," McLane said. The company was in debt, stock installments were being used to cover operating costs, and the engines and cars could not handle the existing trade, especially at Parrs Spring Ridge, which was still a barrier to efficient operation. "Public confidence, not only in the extension of the work westward, but in the working of the existing road, appeared to be entirely withdrawn," said its new administrator.[10] This was a very stark assessment, rendered five years after the fact, by a railroad executive highlighting his record of achievement, yet even at the time it was obvious that the euphoria surrounding the passage of the Eight Million bill in the summer of 1836 had dissipated. The B&O officials did everything the law required, but their program foundered on the one thing they could not control, the national economy, which was lurching toward the Panic of 1837.

Certainly the act passed by the Maryland General Assembly in 1836, which provided $3 million to the Baltimore and Ohio, removed some of the restraints that had slowed the railroad's progress, but it also imposed a number of new restrictions that complicated their plans. For example, it repealed the 1833 legal restriction preventing the B&O from building in the Potomac Valley above Harpers Ferry until the canal was completed to Cumberland or until 1840, when the C&O's charter required that it be finished to that point. At the same time, the act said that the company must construct the line through Boonsborough, Hagerstown, and Cumberland, or forfeit $1 million. The latter requirement was added to the law as a concession to the Washington County delegation whose votes were needed to pass it.[11] The new law also modified another stricture the B&O had accepted as part of its 1833 compromise with the canal, that is, to install a high board fence separating the two works along the narrow passes of the Potomac before using locomotives between the Point of Rocks and Harpers Ferry. The purpose of the fence was to keep the engines "from frightening the horses or mules tracking the canal boats."[12] A year after the B&O opened the line, it still had not built the fence, because, it said, it would "make the Railroad a great ditch for the snow and wash from the hills."[13] Consequently, steam power was not used for part of the distance along the Potomac. Later on, the C&O relented. The 1836 act allowed the substitution of a post and rail fence on the Potomac side of the canal where the banks were steep and the sudden appearance of a locomotive might startle the horses and drive them off into the river. In November 1836, Knight and Fisk, the commissioners, agreed on about three miles of fence. The railroad paid the canal $2,700 to put it up and began running engines to Harpers Ferry.

The main subject of the act, clearly, was money. Whereas the Baltimore City ordinance to provide $3 million to the Baltimore and Ohio only required the railroad to certify that there was nothing to stop it legally from building beyond Harpers Ferry, the state had more stringent qualifications. The law said that before Maryland made any payments, the B&O had to demonstrate that the city and state funds and the additional amounts expected from Pittsburgh and Wheeling were sufficient to complete the railroad to the Ohio River. To do this, the company needed engineers' estimates, which meant surveys. Both the Baltimore and Ohio and the Chesapeake and Ohio had to guarantee the state a 6 percent annual dividend on profits, and the railroad was permitted to raise its passenger rates one cent a mile. Nor would the state turn over any funds to either of its internal improvement projects until the Maryland Canal Company proved that it had sold enough stock to ensure completion "by the most northern practicable route."[14]

The project to build a canal between the Patapsco and the Potomac rivers had, of course, been around at least since 1818. The 1836 endeavor was the third of five attempts to make it a reality. John Eager Howard, Jr., was one of the first to note that a company had been chartered to build a canal from Baltimore to Georgetown. After the Chesapeake and Ohio Canal picked up momentum in the early 1820's, Baltimore merchants decided they wanted a canal connection farther north, up toward Harpers Ferry, so they could intercept the boat traffic before it got to Washington. When William Howard and Isaac Briggs surveyed west of Baltimore for the first time in 1823, they found unfavorable topography and insufficient water for a canal. It was possible, they said, that an 81-mile waterway could be built along the Patapsco-Monocacy route, with a tunnel under Parrs Spring Ridge, for $1.8 million, but they preferred another alignment from Baltimore to a point above Georgetown, reasoning that merchants there would forward their goods to Baltimore because of its closer proximity to Chesapeake Bay.

William Howard explored this route more thoroughly in 1826–27, when another Maryland Canal Company was chartered. His survey report said that a 44-mile waterway from Baltimore to Bladensburg and then over to Georgetown could be built for almost $3 million. It strongly indicated that a canal from Baltimore to the Potomac River anywhere north of Georgetown was impractical. Discouraged by the cost, the Maryland legislature the following year withdrew its support for the project.

The inhospitable geography west of Baltimore for canals contributed to the formation of the Baltimore and Ohio Railroad. The main line to the Potomac River, as well as the Washington Branch, generally followed the paths of Howard's original canal surveys, which he later retraced for the B&O and other railroad interests. Although these rail lines were both operating by 1836, Baltimore businessmen were still worried about losing trade to Washington especially in heavy, bulky items. They believed that once placed on the C&O canal, these items would continue on it to Georgetown and Alexandria as surely as water flows downhill. The answer was a lateral canal. "But will [our purpose] be secured by a connection with the Chesapeake and Ohio Canal with the District of Columbia? We think not." [15] Mistrusting Howard's theory that Baltimore's better access to the Bay would outweigh the added time and expense of shipping articles another 40 miles from Washington to Baltimore, the local merchants wanted to return to the old Patapsco-Monocacy route.

Although Baltimore interests were successful in making the lateral canal an integral part of the Eight Million Bill, the District forces remained skeptical, and the C&O stockholders voiced their objections before ratifying it. The state was compelling the Maryland Canal Company "to avoid selecting for its site the route through the District of Columbia, by holding out a pledge of a subscription of $500,000 on condition that another shall be adopted," said Richard S. Coxe, the B&O's old adversary. He thought the 1823 and 1826–27 surveys had established the superiority of the District route and the unsuitability of any other.[16] Yet within two weeks of Coxe's critical statements, both firms had approved the 1836 act and the Maryland Canal Company not only was organized but had sold all its stock. Once again, the former rivals decided to submerge their differences in favor of mutual gain by calling on their favorite double agent, the gray eminence of Maryland public improvements, James W. McCulloh.

McCulloh was one of the organizers of the Maryland Canal Company. It was a dummy corporation that existed only on paper. The president was William Krebs and the other directors were Daniel Cobb, Samuel Jones, Jr., Charles F. Mayer, and Richard Caton. Krebs was an acquaintance of the Latrobe brothers, as were lawyers Mayer and Caton. Cobb was the Baltimore *Gazette*'s excitable legislative correspondent, and Jones was soon to be named one of the commissioners for selling the Maryland bonds. According to one commentator, the subscribers "may have been spirits from heaven or ghosts from hell," but they never turned over any money.[17] Another said three very real Baltimoreans signed up for the entire $3 million in Maryland Canal Company stock, "although they had not the ability to pay as many cents." [18]

Four new surveys in as many years for both the city and the state only confirmed Howard's conclusion of 1823, that the summit levels of the routes north of Georgetown lacked sufficient water for a canal. Some engineers said it would be feasible to build one along Seneca Creek for either $6 or $12 million, depending on the alignment; the latter figure represented a cost of $500,000 a mile and effectively ended the discussion. The idea of a Cross Cut was resuscitated in the 1850's and again in the 1870's, but it foundered ultimately on politics. Baltimore did not want to build a canal to Washington, and Washington did not want it built anywhere else.

In September 1836, the B&O and C&O concluded a private agreement on engineering specifications, and after the railroad certified to the city that the legal obstacles barring its further extension had been removed, Baltimore and Maryland made their stock subscriptions to the railroad.[19] Finally, the Internal Improvement Act provided for the appointment of "three discreet, competent, and suitable persons," to go to Europe as commissioners and negotiate the sale of the $8 million worth of 6 percent State of Maryland bonds on the most favorable terms.[20] The securities were to be sold at no less than a 20 percent premium over par. The governor appointed the bond commissioners in December 1836. They were Judge John Buchanan, of Washington County (the Chief Judge of the Court of Appeals who had ruled against the railroad in the canal case), Thomas L. Emory, of Queen Anne's County, and Samuel Jones, Jr., of Baltimore. The last, having been named a state senator, resigned almost immediately, and George Peabody asked for the job and was accepted. "It is my intention to embark for Europe in a few weeks and many of my friends think my services in that country would be useful in negotiating the Eight Million loan," Peabody told a member of the legislature.[21] He sailed in February 1837.

The next month, John H. B. Latrobe and Reverdy Johnson drew up a contract with Buchanan and Emory. It said that if the commissioners were unsuccessful in marketing the loan, they would sell $3 million worth of the bonds to the railroad at par plus the 20 percent premium. The C&O Canal made a similar arrangement with the commissioners. Patterson signed the contract for the B&O, which subsequently proved to be a political embarrassment to McLane. Robert Gilmor, Jr., the art collector and patron, introduced the two commissioners to Baring Brothers & Company by mail. Buchanan left New York June 1, 1837, carrying 1,600 state stock certificates worth $5,000 each. He arrived in Liverpool 20 days later. Emory followed and the railroad heard no more of them until the end of the year.

Even if they knew where they wanted to build it, the B&O lacked the funds during this period to construct the line west of Harpers Ferry. Therefore, they spent what money they could raise on surveys and studies. The surveys traversed two spacious and confounding theaters of eastern American geography: the Potomac Valley, with its meandering bends, between Harpers Ferry and Cumberland, and the blue-shadowed mountain glades of the Allegheny plateau extending to the Ohio River.

Knight, for six weeks in the summer of 1835, became the first B&O surveyor to return to these high, winding, misty valleys since William Howard, William Gibbs McNeill, and the young army engineers had scrambled over the rocks and cut their way through the mountain laurel eight years before when the railroad was just starting out. Then Isaac Ridgeway Trimble had gone back for a second look in 1829. In his summer 1835 survey, Knight reexamined the several routes between Cumberland and Wheeling, which had requested the surveys to their city as well as to Pittsburgh. Although Knight had not taken part in the original mountain reconnaissance for the

B&O, he was thoroughly familiar with the territory, having experienced it in his initial surveys for the National Road and the Chesapeake and Ohio Canal. The canal routes in the mountains, like the ones near Baltimore, were eminently adaptable to railroads. Knight studied particularly the major ones out of Cumberland that had been defined a decade earlier by McNeill and James Shriver on behalf of the C&O. The first led north through the Narrows, and west along Wills Creek and the Cassel-man River to Turkey Foot (Confluence, Pennsylvania), and from there pursued the Youghiogheny River. The other headed south from Cumberland, along the Potomac, before turning west to climb the Great Backbone Mountain via the Savage River and Crabtree Creek. It then took a couple of paths through the Glades either to the Youghiogheny or the Cheat. North of the Pennsylvania line, the routes joined for a time along a stretch of the Monongahela River near Brownsville, then split again, one continuing north along the river to Pittsburgh and the other following Grave or Wheeling Creek west to Wheeling.

In his report Knight acknowledged his debt to McNeill's explorations. He quoted Trimble's luminous descriptions of the hill and basin landscape and added a few of his own. He reexamined James Shriver's Bear Creek route, starting at John McHenry's place (now McHenry, Maryland, at the head of Deep Creek Lake), to the Youghiogheny. Along Bear Creek's wild and rugged twelve-mile descent through Winding Ridge to that river, Knight found no greater evidence of civilization than Shriver had encountered in the area ten years before. Knight said the creek bank, "the formation of which is alternately of clay and loose sandstone rock, or both combined, is clothed with dense forests of oak, birch, spruce, etc., and with thickets of laurel, hard to penetrate, and hiding from the view the swiftly speeding waters whose perpetual roarings upon the ear announce the rapid and incessant fall along their rocky course."[22] To the southwest, he looked again at the gentle slope of Snowy Creek and Salt Lick Run down to the Cheat River that Frederick Harrison, Jr., had discerned in the early fall of 1827 as a good route for the B&O Railroad. Knight thought it still was.

Knight's map, drawn by Henry R. Hazlehurst, the cousin and brother-in-law of Benjamin H. Latrobe, Jr., was a good representation of the fractured, bewilderingly complicated mountain area. Knight's survey report, issued in the fall of 1835, nonetheless pronounced these jumbled ridges passable by locomotives. The report was an important factor in shocking the Baltimore and Ohio out of its lethargy. After a winter of being alternately flayed and inspired by the pen of John Pendleton Kennedy, the leadership recovered its sense of purpose and ordered surveys the following spring all the way from Harpers Ferry to the Allegheny summit and beyond.

They started almost immediately. Benjamin H. Latrobe, Jr., assumed their supervision in July 1836. That month Knight and his new engineer of location left Frederick on horseback to visit the survey teams. They took the National Road through Boonsboro to Hagerstown, where John D. Steele was camped, went on to Clear Spring and Hancock, reaching there in two days, and the next night were on top of Town Hill with a man named Carroll, a poor but proud owner of 16,000 acres he had acquired as vacant land with no other expense than a survey. The following day, they picked up Hazlehurst, who had finished his reconnaissance on Fifteen Mile Creek. The trio pushed on to Cumberland. From there, with another surveyor named Oliver C. Morris, they went to call on William P. Swann, up near Sand Patch on Wills Creek in Pennsylvania. They found him "looking like a bandit in the Appenines in his mountain fastness. His camp was on the banks of a roaring torrent, a great freshet in which a few days before had nearly swept him off," Latrobe said. Knight left then to visit his family in Pennsylvania and Latrobe remained at the summit for several days, circuiting among the surveyors' camps on his hired mare, which was going blind. He got soaked by showers and posted to Frostburg one afternoon over the top of the mountain, "by a gloomy wood road with scarce light enough to guide me, and fancying I heard rattle snakes jingling their bells among the bushes."[23]

He was back in Baltimore in twelve days while the work continued in the field. Steele, Hazlehurst, Morris, and Swann led the four survey brigades. Each fourteen-man brigade consisted of the leader, at $1,500 a year; a compass surveyor and a leveler, $2.50 a day apiece; two calculators and four vane bearers, $1.50 each; two chain men and two axmen, who were $1-a-day laborers; and a camp cook, at $16 a month. It cost over $500 a week to keep four survey teams in the field. The first two teams, active between Harpers Ferry and Cumberland, confined themselves largely to the Maryland side of the Potomac River. Steele and Wever, before the latter resigned in July 1836, considered a couple of inland routes via Pleasant Valley either from Weverton or from Antietam Creek above Harpers Ferry. Their purpose was to avoid the canal and fulfill the legal requirement to conduct the B&O line through Boonsboro and Hagerstown. Steele and Hazlehurst looked briefly at an alignment in Virginia that started at Harpers Ferry, crossed the Great Valley to Martinsburg, then headed back to the river and on into Cumberland. In August, Latrobe removed Steele's brigade from the Potomac because of the sickness and sent the surveyors to relocate the line at Parrs Spring Ridge. The engineers now believed the ridge could be passed by locomotives on a uniform grade.

From North Mountain to Sideling Hill the railroad would have to accompany the C&O Canal along the Potomac River in Maryland, running another gauntlet at Hancock where the National Road also squeezed through the narrowest portion of the state. Between Orleans and Oldtown, roughly, Hazlehurst examined a cross-country cutoff along Fifteen Mile Creek that would avoid the Potomac bends entirely. After that, the two rival works would again proceed side by side into Cumberland, unless the B&O took an entirely different route through Virginia.

Beyond Cumberland, Morris and Swann followed up on Knight's work of the previous year. It was so exact that Latrobe had "little more to do than to direct the instrumental survey of the routes indicated in his report," he said. In his first report as engineer of location, Latrobe complimented Knight on his professional ability to discriminate among various places in "a region of singularly perplexed topography."[24] In November 1836, Latrobe tried to see if they could run a railroad line directly from Frederick to Hagerstown by tunneling the Blue Ridge. That brought the season's survey work to an end.

The Baltimore and Ohio still clung to the Maryland shore of the Potomac River as its rightful path. As Knight told Thomas in early 1837, "It has not been ascertained whether the road will be made to cross the Potomac into [Virginia] between Harpers Ferry and Cumberland."[25] But the surveys that began again in the spring of 1837 broadened the company's vision. The surveyors ranged more widely on both sides of the river and expanded the mountain explorations beyond Cumberland, far into Pennsylvania.

Five survey parties took the field. One explored a line in Maryland that left the B&O tracks above the Point of Rocks, crossed the Middletown Valley, and proceeded by a tunnel under South Mountain to Boonsboro and Hagerstown. Across the Potomac in Virginia, Hazlehurst's brigade tried to find a way out of Harpers Ferry. They looked at three, including two to Martinsburg, via the Winchester and Potomac Railroad to Halltown, or along Elk Run and Tuscarora Creek. Up in the mountains, beyond the western Maryland border in Virginia, in the country that George Washington had described as "rough, and a good way not to be found," Steele's party was on Muddy and Big Sandy creeks, tributaries of the Cheat in the all but impassable section where the riverbed was full of house-sized boulders. Beyond there, in the far southwestern corner of Pennsylvania, they went down Ten Mile Creek from the Monongahela and over the ridge to Wheeling Creek. Morris was also in Pennsylvania on the Casselman and the Youghiogheny, at Turkeyfoot and Connellsville. John Blount surveyed a line to Pittsburgh along the Monongahela; and John Small, Jr., the Potomac and Savage river area around Westernport, Maryland. Latrobe visited the various brigades again in the fall of 1837 and this time stayed six weeks with them.

Altogether, in the two years spent completing the preliminary surveys to the Ohio River, the engineers had covered almost 1,500 miles of potential railroad routes. "One third at least of this distance, consists of lines lying upon high and steep mountain slopes, generally covered with loose rocks, and clothed with a thick forest, or in the beds of narrow ravines, overgrown with dense thickets of laurel," Latrobe said. "It is necessary to make this observation, that the difficulties and causes of delay attending these surveys may be duly appreciated."[26] The mountain lines were run at an agreed-on, uniform grade, according to the engineer's instructions, slowly and carefully enough to provide an accurate cost estimate. When this was finished, dollar figures would enable the board of directors to decide finally on the railroad's location. McLane next assigned Knight and Latrobe to study other railroads "with a view to the adoption of the best mode of reconstructing the Baltimore and Ohio Railroad."[27] They were to look particularly at locomotives, operations, methods of accountability, and staffs and salaries.

After McLane took over the railroad in July 1837, economy was definitely the order of the day. A year had passed since the City of Baltimore and the State of Maryland had promised $6 million in new financing, but so far none of that money had actually been provided. The new president alluded to their situation in October 1837, in his first annual report. Although the B&O had raised its rates in the spring, net revenues had not increased proportionately. This was caused by "the failure of the crops, and the serious interruption in the general business of the community; which have been equally operative in other parts of the country," McLane said.[28] His news was hardly surprising. Business generally was already feeling the effects of the economic crisis that would turn into the worst depression the United States had so far experienced. What became known as the Panic of 1837 actually began in Great Britain. Peabody as he sailed for England as a bond commissioner in February 1837 had been alerted by a financial associate who told him to "prepare for a gale . . . as sure as fate evil times are coming on us." [29]

The reasons for the Panic of 1837 were diverse, but they had their roots in the bank war and in the wild speculation in land and overinvestment in internal improvements that ensued. Inflation seemed beneficial for a while. Between 1835 and 1837, America was out of debt, for the first and only time. The surplus in the Treasury from the sale of public land was actually redistributed to the states. Inspired by the success of such ventures as the Erie Canal and attracted by high interest rates, British bankers invested heavily in American enterprises. They transferred almost $9 million in specie to the United States between 1833 and 1836. Eastern railroads and canals generated by British pounds and wildcat banks fueled by the sale of public land in the West sustained an almost magical prosperity.

But the unsound business practices that accompanied the removal of the federal funds from the United States Bank and their deposit in the pet banks expanded during this period. In Mississippi, the seventeen banks of the state floated $6 million in notes based on $300,000 in specie in the vaults. By the end of 1837, the currency of the state of Michigan was so chaotic that the legislature appointed three commissioners to straighten things out. But the cashiers outwitted them: "Specie which they counted at one bank was packed up and sent on ahead to be counted by them at the next," one historian said.[30] Both Mississippi and Michigan repudiated their foreign debts, but in the latter state, as in Illinois and other states in the West, the bank frauds and worthless currency went hand in hand with the wholesale giveaway of public land. From 1835 to 1837, somewhere around 40 million acres of land were sold off, 75 percent of it to speculators, many of whom were in league with dishonest government agents at the land offices and paid for the acreage with borrowed banknotes before dealing it off at handsome markups. Phantom towns and paper cities, linked by mythical rail lines, sprang up to lure Eastern investors and then vanished before the buyers could get there to claim their lots. President Andrew Jackson, attempting to correct the situation before he left office, described the process. "The banks let out the notes to speculators, they were paid to the receivers, and immediately returned to the banks to be sent out again, being merely instruments to transfer to the speculator the most valuable public lands," he said. "Indeed, each speculation furnished means for another." [31]

The same thing was happening with urban land in the East. A share of Canton Company stock, whose par value of $50 was based on filled land near the harbor in Baltimore, sold for $210 in Boston and $260 in New York. Maryland's banks were basically sound, but the state had invested more in internal improvements than any other state of its size and population, and Baltimore, too, was burdened with a huge municipal debt, primarily for internal improvements. Prior to the $2 million state loan to the C&O Canal in 1834, Maryland's entire funded debt was just $1.9 million.

Over 90 percent of the debt was due to internal improvements: $1 million for the B&O Railroad, $625,000 for the C&O Canal, and $100,000 for the Baltimore and Susquehanna Railroad. Through 1837, Maryland took on an additional $12 million in debt, most of it for canals and railroads. Six years later, according to the governor, the state "was staggering under a load of undertakings that would have taxed the financial resources of the whole kingdom of Great Britain."[32]

Theoretically, these projects would not tax the citizens of Maryland because revenues were supposed to cover the debt service, but substantial profits could not begin until years later when the internal improvements were finished. As one B&O executive commented, "There is hardly a railroad in the country, that has been completed, that is not now realizing a handsome return on the cost of its construction: and the chief reason why this is not done by the Baltimore and Ohio Rail Road, is, that it is *not completed*."[33]

Meanwhile, Congress had passed the Deposit Act, recommended by Henry Clay and the Whigs. It would redistribute some $40 million in surplus funds from the sale of public lands to the states, in installments. The Jackson administration had also issued the Specie Circular, stipulating that in the future only hard money or notes from specie-paying banks would be acceptable in payment for those lands. In August 1836, the Bank of England began to curtail credit to the British merchant bankers active in American trade, including Baring Brothers & Co. and William and James Brown & Co. It did not stem the drain of gold. By fall, there was a run on British banks and a few bank failures. In January 1837, the first installment of $9.4 million in surplus funds was withdrawn from the deposit banks and sent out to the states. The Specie Circular drew more real currency away from the Eastern banks, which raised interest rates and called loans to cover the losses. March 1837 marked the real beginning of the panic in England, when British banks demanded large remittances in gold from American merchants. During April and May, banks failed in Boston and New York and business was reported "prostrate" in the United States.

The spring and summer in Liverpool were nearly fatal to William and James Brown & Co., which received crucial aid from George Peabody, who traveled 500 miles in five days and used his personal prestige to obtain financial guarantees for the firm. When the rescue was complete, there was a public outpouring of joy and relief in Liverpool. William Brown wrote Peabody: "To you my dear Sir I feel much indebted for the lively interest you have taken & the Friendship you have shewn throughout a Crisis that has almost killed me with anxiety."[34]

But the situation in the United States had grown worse. Van Buren replaced Jackson as President and the second installment under the Deposit Act went out to the states. The price of cotton fell by half. The levee was deserted in New Orleans. Over 150 businesses in New York had closed their doors. On May 10, 1837, after a bank failure, the rest of New York's banks suspended specie payments (refused to redeem their notes in silver). The next day, banks in Philadelphia and Baltimore followed suit. The Panic of 1837 had officially begun.

While McLane remained in New York to assist the Morris Canal, the Baltimore and Ohio Railroad made plans to print scrip in small denominations, from five cents to a dollar. Whether the company actually did so at this time is not clear, but the City of Baltimore and the C&O Canal did issue these so-called "shinplasters." The B&O borrowed almost $50,000 from local banks to keep its surveys and other operations going. Adding to the economic malaise was an invasion of the Hessian fly that devastated the wheat crop in Maryland and neighboring states in the summer of 1837. Grain had to be imported from Europe. There were flour riots in New York. "The poor man and the laborer, as usual, bore the brunt of the catastrophe," and by the fall, the *Niles Register* reported most of the Eastern factories closed, their employees discharged. Irish laborers rioted several times on the Chesapeake and Ohio Canal and would have done so on the railroad except that they were not working.[35]

The assessment of blame for the economic downtown was well under way, along predictable lines. Whig merchants meeting in New York traced the disaster to the federal government's interference with business interests and the currency and the destruction of the Bank of the United States. Democratic workmen who gathered in Baltimore denounced the U.S. Bank and all banks as a "well-matured system of fraud and deception" that enriched the few and impoverished the many.[36] There was a slight recovery when the New York banks began making specie payments again in May 1838, a year after they had first suspended them, and others went along, but that was followed by a second round of speculation, another suspension of specie payments, and finally a deep depression that spread throughout the country. Banks and farms failed in the West and this time not even Nicholas Biddle survived.

In March 1836, one day before its federal charter expired, Pennsylvania had incorporated the Bank of the United States as a state bank. The action was controversial in that it involved a charge of legislative bribery, of which the bank was exonerated. Some three years later, Biddle, who saw the Panic of 1837 as a means to regain his position as the nation's chief banker and perhaps even to restore the ancien régime, suddenly resigned, mentioning the state of his health and noting that the institution was doing so well it no longer needed him. The bank suspended specie payments again in the summer of 1839, and other banks were forced to do the same. The failure was particularly devastating for Baltimore, which had provided $4 million of the U.S. Bank's original capital, all of which was lost. A stockholders' investigation uncovered misuse and misappropriation of funds by the officers, some of which was attributed to Biddle's policies. Swisher, Taney's biographer, says: "The bank permanently closed its doors, and was the object of lawsuits for many years thereafter. Biddle and others were indicted for conspiracy to defraud the stockholders. They were arrested, but were released on writs of habeas corpus from friendly judges. They were never punished."[37]

With nowhere to go, in the midst of an economic depression, Louis McLane and the Baltimore and Ohio Railroad made what adjustments and improvements they could. Two of the president's primary concerns were abolishing the inclined planes at Parrs Spring Ridge and obtaining better locomotives. The company had anticipated getting rid of the planes ever since Phineas Davis's locomotive the Arabian proved them obsolete in December 1834. But it was not until the day after the successful demonstration of engine power at Parrs Spring Ridge for the city council, in March

1836, that the decision was made to relocate the line there. Six months later, Steele's brigade, sickened by the Potomac fevers, began surveying for the new alignment. In January 1837, the Maryland legislature approved the relocation. Right-of-way acquisition and construction started in the spring of 1838.

The locomotives were constantly being improved. In the fall of 1835, Ross Winans showed John H. B. Latrobe his plans for a locomotive with horizontal cylinders. Knight believed the new arrangement would increase the engine's stability and longevity. The directors agreed, and the Grasshopper became the Crab. By the fall of 1836, four Crab engines, including the Phineas Davis, were put in service. They weighed eight tons each, a little heavier than the Grasshoppers. The external diameter of the cylinders and boilers was slightly increased, to 12.5 and 55 inches, respectively. The number of boiler tubes was raised to 450, and along with the wrought-iron ones, some copper tubes were tried in the Phineas Davis. The horizontal position of the cylinders lowered the center of gravity by a foot, thus making the locomotive more stable.[38]

As McLane was assuming the president's chair in July 1837, Winans patented his new engine design and listed its virtues. He explained that the Grasshopper's vertical cylinders and high center of gravity caused "the Baltimore engine to become at very high velocities alarmingly unsteady, so that indeed it would seem to bounce, rather than roll along the rails." This fault had been very apparent, and he had sought a remedy: "My invention consists of an arrangement by which I combine the prominent advantages and best qualities of both the engines here described, while I get rid of the objections . . . to produce a machine, which, to the steadiness of the English engine, proceeding from the lowness of its center of gravity and the horizontal action of its pistons, unites the great power of the Baltimore engine."[39] Winans incorporated other improvements in his patent, including elaborations of Phineas Davis's ideas for preheating the boiler feed water and regulating the furnace draft by controlling the waste steam powering the fan.

The Crab was well named. Instead of the Grasshopper's long legs, there were now side-mounted cylinders that operated the spur-and-pinion gears and ultimately the wheel cranks. Because of the intermediate gearing, two sets of connecting rods worked away on either side of the locomotive, rather than one set as in conventionally connected engines. This gave it a busy and contrary appearance and a peculiar scuttling action.

McLane was singularly unimpressed. Two months after Winans formally introduced his new locomotive, the board voted to end its contract with Gillingham & Winans for building and repairing the company's engines. Although the directors did not get around to canceling the contract formally until December 1838 and in the meantime Gillingham and Winans added four more Crabs to the company's fleet, the railroad now thought it would be cheaper to do all repairs in its own shops and that better locomotives might result from "opening the field of competition."[40]

The first outside manufacturer selected was William Norris of Philadelphia. The company had had dealings with Norris earlier, but Norris's new engine, the Lafayette, which the B&O tested in September 1837, was radically different from anything so far seen on the railroad. It had a horizontal boiler and six wheels, and it was also bigger and heavier than other B&O engines, weighing over ten tons, and it was directly connected, with no intermediate gearing. The boiler was of the Bury type, containing 78 two-inch-diameter tubes, with a domed "haystack" firebox that burned wood. The angled cylinders were each 10.5 inches in diameter with an eighteen-inch stroke, joined by single connecting rods to the wheel cranks. The drive wheels were four feet in diameter, a foot larger than the ones used on the Grasshopper and the Crab. There was a four-wheel swiveling truck under the smokebox. The ensemble was called a "one-armed Billy."

The B&O's renewed interest in William Norris was doubtless prompted by the remarkable and widely publicized feat of his prototype engine the George Washington, which in July 1836 pulled a sixteen-ton load up a steep, 7 percent grade on the Philadelphia and Columbia Railroad at 16 mph. By that time, Stephen H. Long had left the firm and been replaced as engineer by Joseph Harrison, Jr., who actually designed the locomotives.[41] In December 1837, after detailed tests of the Lafayette's power, speed, and economy, the B&O bought the Norris engine for $6,500 but required the wheels to be rebuilt out of iron and made smaller to take the curves, and set at the proper gauge to fit the B&O tracks. During the next two years the railroad bought seven more Norris engines, and despite a disagreement with Gillingham & Winans about purchasing the second Crab engine, the company eventually ended up buying eight of those also. The railroad began testing two other engines, the Baltimore and the Carroll, produced by Mathias W. Baldwin of Philadelphia, who was to become the most celebrated American locomotive builder of all.

McLane closed out the year of his arrival at the Baltimore and Ohio by successfully negotiating the railroad's first contract with the federal government to carry "the great Southern mail" from Baltimore to Washington, for $12,000 a year. The arrangement ended three years of intermittent offers and refusals by both parties. The B&O felt the postmaster general's proposals over the years were too cheap and onerous to make the service worthwhile; meanwhile, it had carried the mail anyway to Washington, Frederick, and Harpers Ferry, but as a subcontractor to Stockton and Stokes, the stagecoach operators.

McLane also learned in December 1837 that the bond commissioners had been unable to dispose of the state bonds in Europe. The railroad president asked for a report on the negotiations and the reasons for their failure. The governor also requested a report, and as the new year opened, the Maryland legislature began an investigation of the private contracts executed in March 1837 between the bond commissioners and the railroad and canal companies. These documents said that if the commissioners failed to negotiate the loan, they would dispose of the bonds to the two firms. The legislative investigation was to determine whether the state should honor the contracts. McLane was subpoenaed to appear before the House ways and means committee.

Buchanan and Emory said they knew when they left that there would be difficulty in negotiating the loan because of the depressed economy. They claimed certain discretionary powers under the 1836 act and felt that the best way to implement the state's policy of supporting internal improvements was to turn the bonds over to the companies, hence the contracts. After Buchanan and Emory met Peabody in London, the three commissioners had tried to dispose of the bonds there. Not having any luck, they went on to Paris, Antwerp, and Amsterdam in August 1837, but were no more successful. Buchanan and Emory left that fall, arriving in New York in early December. When the two commissioners got back to Baltimore, they deposited the bonds in the Union Bank.

McLane went down to Annapolis and testified in early February 1838, armed with the minutes of the directors' meetings and other documents. He said the railroad's contract with the commissioners was signed before he got to Baltimore. In response to other questions, he replied that the B&O had no control over the formation of the phony Maryland Canal Company and that the railroad had not yet selected a route west of Harpers Ferry.

In the end, the legislature decided to ratify the private contracts between the bond commissioners and the B&O and C&O because not to do so would mean more problems and delays. The companies were to pay for the bonds: $120 for each $100 worth. The Maryland General Assembly then passed a second and somewhat contradictory set of resolutions, saying the C&O Canal could have $2.5 million in bonds in exchange for a receipt. The remaining $500,000 worth were to be held as security for payment of the 20 percent premium. These bonds could "at any time be sold or hypothecated," said the State of Maryland.[42]

The canal, which had remained under construction throughout the panic and was therefore even more overextended than usual, literally could not wait to get its hands on these securities. The C&O quickly appointed George Peabody its agent, and under their instructions he began selling them off. The B&O had less interest in the bonds at the time, since it was not yet building the line to Cumberland, but preparations were under way. On February 14, 1838, Benjamin H. Latrobe, Jr., presented to the board his analysis of the routes west of Harpers Ferry. Based on it, the directors decided that day in effect to forsake Maryland, build their main line through Virginia, and ask that state to pay 40 percent of the cost. Latrobe's report, which summarized two years of surveys, came to over 150 printed pages, including a contribution from Knight.[43] Latrobe cited as a model Knight's exhaustive study of the Washington Branch five years before.

Latrobe's analysis began at the Little Catoctin Creek, where the line to Hagerstown, if it were built, might leave the Potomac River above the Point of Rocks. It ended about 100 feet beyond the mouth of Wheeling Creek in Wheeling, Virginia (where the B&O's first terminal in that city was actually constructed in 1853). Other parts of Latrobe's report were just as prescient concerning the Baltimore and Ohio's eventual alignment. For example, Latrobe foresaw a major division point at Cumberland, where "the routes over the Allegany summit, the one by Wills Creek, and the other by the North Branch of Potomac," would diverge. His principles for comparing the various routes were their actual lengths with the ascents and curves factored in "for the equation of the distance to a level and straight line," the cost of construction, repairs, and motive power, and the incidental advantages arising from the neighboring population, products, or the proximity of other transportation lines.[44]

The Hagerstown route, Latrobe said, would cost the railroad almost as much in increased construction expenses as the $1 million penalty they would have to pay if they did not build it. His preferred alignment started at the western end of the bridge at Harpers Ferry, followed the riverbank, skirting the federal arsenal buildings, to Elk Branch, turned inland, and crossed most of the great Valley of Virginia to Tuscarora Run, which it traced into Martinsburg. The railroad left there in almost a straight line to the narrows of North Mountain where it joined the Potomac River again and proceeded along the southern bank. Below Hancock, the route struck the bends of the Potomac. It cut off the first and biggest with a tunnel, swung around following the riverbank to Paw Paw, and continued until it crossed the Potomac back into Maryland about six miles below Cumberland. Latrobe estimated that building this 100-mile segment from Harpers Ferry would cost about $3 million.

Out of Cumberland, Latrobe once again ran over the familiar Wills Creek–Casselman–Youghiogheny River northern route through Pennsylvania via Sand Patch, Turkeyfoot (Confluence), and Connellsville to Wheeling and Pittsburgh; and the southern alignment, climbing the Alleghenies by way of the Savage River, and across the mountain meadows to the Cheat and the Monongahela. The report described this remote section of the route in detail:

> The part of Alleghany county through which the Southern route would pass is one of much beauty and interest—especially that which lies west of the Little Backbone, where are found those elevated natural meadows, so well known under the name of the Glades, and upon which vast herds of cattle are annually pastured upon a wild grass. . . . The mineral wealth of this region is also undoubtedly great, though as yet undeveloped. The few roads in this district and the sparseness of the population make it an especially favorable subject for the improving influences of a great thoroughfare.[45]

The northern route beyond Cumberland was the shortest, cheapest, and best. Latrobe estimated the total cost of the line from Harpers Ferry to Wheeling at about $8 million, and the branch from Connellsville to Pittsburgh at roughly $1.5 million. He described the trains that would one day appear in the mountains carrying passengers from Baltimore to the Ohio River in 24 hours and freight in 48. One of the latter, with a twelve-ton engine and a dozen cars, would weigh a total of 102 tons (about half the weight of a single modern coal car, fully loaded).

Knight in his section of the report mostly agreed with the younger engineer's opinions, although he preferred a somewhat different route through the glades of western Maryland. As for the portion between Harpers Ferry and Cumberland, from a comparison of the many alignments studied, "a very decided balance appears in favor of the route on the Virginia side of the Potomac, and such a result might have been expected in consequence of the preoccupancy of the Maryland shore by the Chesapeake and Ohio Canal," Knight said.[46]

In early March 1838, the board of directors ordered Latrobe's report printed confidentially. The company did not officially lift the embargo until November 1839. While a State Senate committee called for detailed survey information on the Maryland route to Hagerstown, Louis McLane, John Spear Nicholas, and John Pendleton Kennedy made plans to go to Richmond to lobby the Virginia legislature for money for their secret new route through Virginia.

17

Three Statesmen

THE THREE RAILROAD AMBASSADORS GOT OFF
the steamboat in the late afternoon, crossed the confused tangle of docks and mill-races that made up Shockoe Slip, and found their lodgings at the Eagle. There they were joined by Jonathan Knight. The following morning, Wednesday, March 14, 1838, they climbed the hill to Thomas Jefferson's Capitol Square and its temple of politics that dominated the city like the Acropolis. It was eleven years to the day since the Baltimore and Ohio's first official delegation to Richmond had returned with the Virginia legislature's ratification of their charter. Under that charter, the time limit for completing the railroad, which was ten years from the start of construction, was about to expire in Virginia. In 1836, Maryland had extended its deadline for another five years. Time, money, and getting to Wheeling were therefore uppermost in the minds of the three men from Baltimore.

All three—Louis McLane, John Spear Nicholas, and John Pendleton Kennedy—had a wide political acquaintance in Richmond. Nicholas's father, Judge Philip Norborne Nicholas, was a leader of the Richmond Junto, the narrow, inbred clique of eminent bankers, judges, and newspaper editors who controlled the Virginia Jackson party and ran it like a latter-day, big-city machine. Nicholas and Kennedy, both lawyers, had been appointed state directors of the B&O Railroad a year earlier. Kennedy, then 42, was still the most enthusiastic and most effective promoter of the Baltimore and Ohio Railroad. After his pamphleteering as the "Man of the Times" and speech making at important gatherings, along with Knight's western surveys, stirred the company out of its somnolence at Harpers Ferry and rallied public opinion to help pass the Eight Million bill, the B&O gave him their standard $500 lobbyist's payment.

Kennedy had been brought up on the border between North and South and was considered a skirmisher on the frontiers of his several professions. He was the son of a failed Baltimore merchant, who had emigrated from northern Ireland. His mother was of English extraction, descended from a distinguished family of Virginia planter-aristocrats. Later on, as Kennedy became the political spokesman for Baltimore commercial interests, he simultaneously labored to recapture in his writing the fading, genteel life of the Southern plantation that he knew as a youth.

He attended school in Baltimore with the sons of William Patterson and Alexander Brown, spent the summers with relatives near Martinsburg, Virginia, began to write, studied law, marched off to war in 1814 with Maryland's Fifth Regiment.[1] He left a hilarious account of the early campaign in his journals. It turned serious when the British light brigade drove the poorly led Fifth Regiment from the field at Bladensburg and he lost his musket in the melee while bearing off a comrade, James W. McCulloh, whose leg had been broken by a bullet.[2] Another acquaintance Kennedy made during the 1814 campaign was George Peabody.

Kennedy then practiced law, but according to John H. B. Latrobe, who became his lifelong friend, he was "too much addicted to politics and literature to make a distinguished lawyer."[3] In 1820, Kennedy was elected to the Maryland legislature. In the House of Delegates, he chaired the important committee on internal improvements and turned into such a vigorous champion of canals, particularly the Chesapeake and Ohio, that it cost him his seat. After claiming that the C&O was "an undertaking that could only be achieved with the wealth of an empire," Kennedy still cast his vote, in 1823, for state support.[4] The bill failed that year, mainly because of Baltimore's opposition, but his constituents were so infuriated with his vote that they effectively retired him. At subsequent meetings in the city, he still continued to argue for the C&O Canal to be built at state and federal expense.

Kennedy lost an election for Congress, succeeded as an attorney in spite of himself (the Union Bank was a prime client), and received some money from a rich Philadelphia uncle. In 1829 he married Elizabeth Gray, the daughter of Edward Gray, a wealthy Whig mill owner with a country seat on the Patapsco, a mile or so below Ellicotts Mills. Kennedy had been a zealous Jacksonian, but in the early 1830's he became disillusioned with Jackson and the party's hostility to internal improvements and began aggressively promoting Henry Clay's American System and the Whig principles of a central bank, a protective tariff, and distribution of the proceeds from the sale of public lands. Gray was so appreciative and generous regarding his new son-in-law's conversion that Kennedy effectively withdrew from his law practice and devoted the next decade to writing. Between 1832 and 1838, he published *Swallow Barn, Horse-Shoe Robinson,* and *Rob of the Bowl.*[5]

McLane, Nicholas, and Kennedy remained in Richmond for twelve days in the spring of 1838, conferring with members of the legislature and attending several large dinner parties with them. There were over 50 guests at one of their levees. They met Governor David Campbell and the city's important judges, bankers, and industrialists. Their major obstacle was John Bruce, president of the Winchester and Potomac Railroad, who, after promising to do everything he could to help the B&O lobbyists pass its legislative program, instead tried to frustrate them at every turn.[6]

The Winchester and Potomac's main problem in 1838 was that it did not go anywhere, except to Winchester. That year's legislative session in Richmond marked the beginning of its campaign to be acquired by the Baltimore and Ohio. When that failed, the Winchester & Potomac turned to obstructionism at Harpers Ferry. The railroad finally succeeded in being bought out by the B&O in 1848 and was eventually extended farther up the Valley of Virginia.

Shortly after Kennedy got home, the Virginia legislature passed a law that would provide the Baltimore and Ohio Railroad with a stock subscription of $1,058,000— an amount that represented roughly 40 percent of the estimated cost of building the B&O line through the state from Harpers Ferry to Cumberland. The act also extended the time for finishing the railroad in Virginia for five years, to July 4, 1843. But there were a great many conditions attached. For one thing, the state's subscription was contingent upon another from Wheeling for $1 million. Also, the line had to be completed to Wheeling before Virginia would hand over the money, and there were numerous restrictions against interfering with the Winchester & Potomac Railroad at Harpers Ferry. The previous year, the Richmond legislators had approved a $300,000 stock subscription to the B&O with similar conditions. Shortly after John H. B. Latrobe began negotiations with Wheeling's John McLure about that city's financial support, the Wheeling mayor and city council approved an ordinance providing the $1 million stock subscription, yet again with terms that were onerous. In May 1838 the B&O stockholders rejected the subscription and thereby also the Virginia law.

Meanwhile, enthusiasm for the Baltimore and Ohio was growing in Pittsburgh. The railroad responded, initiating a pattern that it followed for many years with its two municipal suitors. When the romance cooled in one, it was time to try the other and make the first jealous. When McLane, Fielding Lucas, Jr., Amos A. Williams, and another director went up to Pittsburgh that summer, they found that the enthusiasm was not very strong after all, and by the fall, the directors had made their peace with the Wheeling ordinance and the stockholders had accepted the Virginia law.

In the 1838 annual report, delayed until December of that year, McLane officially announced the new Virginia route. By referring cryptically to the bumbling opposition at Richmond, he made it seem as if the Virginia legislature had forced the alignment on the B&O, and he maintained that the company had to cross the Potomac River at Harpers Ferry and proceed through Virginia or else forfeit Wheeling as a destination. McLane was probably hoping to mask the railroad's desertion of Hagerstown and assuage the resentment of the people there at being abandoned, and he perhaps even hoped to escape the $1 million penalty for not constructing the line through Maryland. But there is no doubt that his main purpose in turning to Virginia was to avoid a connection with the Franklin Railroad, completed in 1838 between Hagerstown and Chambersburg, Pennsylvania. From there, the Cumberland Valley Railroad went on to Harrisburg. By means of these routes, eastbound passengers and trade headed for Baltimore on the National Road were already being diverted to Philadelphia. Another advantage of leaving the state of Maryland at Harpers Ferry would be to avoid further confrontation with the canal.[7]

This stratagem seems fairly transparent. After all, if the company had not wanted to build the railroad through Virginia, it would not have sought legislation to do so, nor would it have dispatched a right-of-way agent, C. C. Starbuck, to start buying land three months before the trio of railroad representatives made their trip to Richmond. But it did not fool Hagerstown or Washington County. The citizens, feeling betrayed by Baltimore, at least wanted their $1 million. In 1839, McLane hinted at a compromise, but the next year, Hagerstown announced a suit against the B&O. The year after that, the company had a Maryland law passed repealing the requirement that the railroad go through Boonsboro and Hagerstown and abrogating any suit.[8] Nevertheless, Washington County pursued the Baltimore and Ohio all the way to the Supreme Court, where the county lost.

McLane in his 1838 annual report showed that the stock subscriptions from Baltimore and Maryland, Wheeling and Virginia totaled roughly $8.4 million. This was about $1 million short of the estimated construction cost to the Ohio River, but the Baltimore funds were not yet available, the Maryland securities were still in the Union Bank, and Virginia's promises to pay when the railroad was finished were hardly certain. The only real money available to the B&O was the $450,000 that it could get by calling for the last $15 per share owed by the stockholders, and these funds were to be used to reconstruct the existing line.

Early in 1839, McLane joined C&O Canal president George C. Washington in seeking a modification of the Eight Million bill to make the Maryland bonds easier to sell. George Peabody had suggested that 5 percent sterling bonds with interest payable in London might be more marketable than the 6 percent dollar bonds. In April 1839 the legislature approved the conversion. The new bonds were turned over to the companies, which were to pay the interest for three years in exchange for Maryland's dropping the premium requirement. The state took mortgages on the canal and railroad properties as well as on their future profits. Virginia relaxed its legal restrictions a little and Baltimore authorized a public tax to help pay for its support of the railroad.

In the summer of 1839, as the financial panic took a turn for the worse, the Baltimore and Ohio completed its fiscal strategy. Baltimore's subscription to the B&O was in the form of a 6 percent city stock. On a pledge of this stock, the company would borrow from the local banks an initial $500,000 to begin construction from Harpers Ferry to Cumberland. Next it would market the Maryland sterling bonds and apply the proceeds to building the railroad from Cumberland to Wheeling. There was some opposition, led by John White, a dissident city director and former cashier of the Baltimore branch of the U.S. Bank, who objected to selling the bonds, "the money market being extremely depressed," but he was voted down.[9] (According to Kennedy, White entertained hopes of replacing McLane as president.)

The Baltimore and Ohio Railroad paid to engrave the new state bonds and to hire extra people to fill them out. When it came time to select an agent to market them, they did not have far to look. The B&O offered the mission to McLane, "a gentleman combining in himself qualifications for it rarely to be met with." The finance committee acknowledged McLane's acquaintance with politicians and bankers on both sides of the Atlantic, his "skill and intelligence in conducting the affairs of the Company . . . his intimate knowledge of its wants and resources," all of which tended to point him out as "the most competent and suitable agent for the business under consideration."[10]

McLane had, in fact, been anticipating the mission since the spring, when he decided that it was an appropriate time to renew his association with his friend from his days as ambassador to England, Joshua Bates of Baring Brothers & Co. "Although our correspondence has been a long time interrupted, I hope I may be [permitted?] from the acquaintance that I had the pleasure to make with you in London, in addressing you this communication," McLane prudently began his letter to Bates. He intimated that the mission to London could be personally quite profitable. And he discreetly inquired whether Baring Brothers & Co. might be interested in $3.2 million worth of Maryland sterling bonds.[11] The railroad gave McLane a free hand in disposing of the bonds "by sale or hypothecation." He would receive an $8,000 advance and another $8,000 if he was successful. This was in addition to his annual salary of $6,000. He would also be reimbursed for any fees paid to foreign bankers or agents.[12] But McLane accepted the mission to London, "from a desire to advance the work with which he was connected rather than any expectation of pecuniary advantage," he said.[13]

He left New York August 24, 1839 on the steamer *Liverpool*. "You will find him just as you left him in Portsmouth in June, 1831," a mutual acquaintance wrote to Joshua Bates the same day, "The same kind, generous, warmhearted, intelligent, polished man and will I am quite sure welcome [him] in England."[14] McLane landed in Liverpool on September 8 after a voyage during which, "shattered and reduced" by seasickness, he had lived on toast dipped in coffee.[15] George Peabody, who was in England representing the Chesapeake and Ohio Canal, still had some of the canal's original $3 million in state bonds, plus an additional $1,375,000 subscription that had been approved by the Maryland legislature earlier that year. McLane, with the railroad bonds, and Peabody, with the canal's, separately found their way to the same address, 8 Bishopsgate, City of London.

Peabody had prospered mightily in the 25 years since he soldiered with John Pendleton Kennedy in 1814. His career was about to take a quantum jump from dry goods merchant to international financier. The mechanism proved to be the Maryland bonds. They were the base on which Peabody built his fortune as a merchant banker. His firm, George Peabody and Company, evolved into the House of Morgan, America's most important private bank. The fortune enabled him, toward the end of his life, to establish the Peabody Institute in Baltimore (the plan for which was developed by John Pendleton Kennedy), and more modest Peabody Institutes in three other cities and also to endow three institutions of higher learning, found three science museums and seven libraries, and create extensive education programs for the American South, as well as housing for London's poor. The total amount of the bequests came to over $7 million. Peabody was, indeed, America's first great philanthropist, and he had a direct philanthropic influence on Enoch Pratt, who created Baltimore's public library, and on Johns Hopkins, the founder of the city's major university, medical school, and hospital.[16]

George Peabody was the original rags to riches, Horatio Alger hero. He came from a large family of British ancestry and slender means. There was some schooling, a job as a storekeeper's apprentice at age eleven, and a few years spent peddling goods on horseback in an enterprise with his uncle in Washington, D.C. During his twelve-day career as a soldier against the British in 1814, Peabody met Elisha Riggs, who had a dry goods business in Georgetown. Riggs brought Peabody in as a junior partner. A year later, they moved the business to Baltimore. Peabody took it over in 1829 when Riggs retired. Riggs's nephew replaced him, but the firm became Peabody, Riggs & Co.

When the Baltimore and Ohio Railroad began in 1827, George Peabody was one of the original subscribers, for 122 shares (over $12,000 worth). Peabody, Riggs & Co. also acquired stock in the C&O Canal. That same year, Peabody made his first trip to Europe as a company buyer. Alex. Brown & Sons introduced him to the Liverpool branch of the firm, which opened a $70,000 line of credit for him. Ten years later, when the Panic of 1837 struck the Liverpool branch, Peabody was able to return the favor. Peabody ranged throughout Great Britain and the continent buying Scottish woolens, Irish linens, and Italian silks for the U.S. market. On one European tour, he and a companion covered 10,000 miles in fifteen months by eating their meals in carriages and traveling day and night.[17] By 1832, Peabody had amassed $135,000, and by the late 1830's, when the fortunes of Peabody, Riggs & Co. went into decline with the panic, he had settled permanently in England and assumed the functions of a merchant banker, engaging in the commission business and dealing in bills of exchange. George Peabody & Co. opened its City office (at 31 Moorgate Street) in 1838, the year before McLane arrived on his mission.[18]

When they first appointed him their agent in April 1838, the Chesapeake and Ohio Canal had sent Peabody half of their Maryland bonds, $1.5 million worth, with instructions to sell them for a good price if he could and if not to hypothecate them for a loan. When he found that he could not dispose of them without a loss, Peabody pledged the bonds as security for short-term notes and sent over the first remittance: 40,000 pounds in gold (roughly $178,000). The canal company was also borrowing on the bonds from Baltimore and New York banks. "There followed one of the most disastrous episodes in the canal's history," said its historian: a "frenzy of hypothecation."[19]

Dealing in Maryland securities on behalf of the canal was becoming "heavy business," Peabody said that summer. The London financial markets were flooded with the bonds of other states, but the canal's construction expenses were running $100,000 a month and George C. Washington, the president, simultaneously complained that Peabody was not sending over enough money and was pledging the bonds at too low a price. Early in 1839, Peabody's loans were being called. He was personally advancing funds to the canal. The Chesapeake and Ohio, condemned for jeopardizing the state's credit by dumping the securities, voted in a new president and board of directors. They continued the same policy. The new C&O president, with an annual salary of $3,500, was Francis Thomas. Thomas was simultaneously running for a fifth term as a Maryland congressman on the Democratic ticket, which at that time implied an indifference to internal improvements. Thomas won the election, though his political enemies claimed that he had denounced the Eight Million bill.

On July 4, 1839, Thomas sent Peabody more than $400,000 worth of the freshly minted sterling bonds and promised more. So much money had been spent on the canal already, the company thought that "it would be better policy, to take even less than par for the securities we have to offer, than to postpone to a distant day the completion of the great work," Thomas told Peabody.[20] Without waiting for a reply, Thomas drew $80,000 to meet "most urgent demands upon the company." He also issued $240,000 worth of canal scrip that year.

Peabody's partner warned him about Thomas's "loose and irregular" business habits, and Peabody asked the canal company not to make any further draws on him and to return the $80,000. Instead, they withdrew an additional $185,000 without authorization. Francis Thomas told Peabody to sell off the bonds at their market value, which was rapidly falling. A list of Peabody's bond sales in 1839 shows the price slipping from 85 in August to 70 in November. To Peabody's remonstrances, Thomas replied, "the work must go on,"[21] and indeed the Chesapeake and Ohio Canal had again ranged far ahead of the railroad. In May 1839 the waterway was opened to Hancock and the company was trying desperately to complete the last 50 and most difficult miles, from dam no. 6 above Hancock to Cumberland. This section included a tunnel that was more than half a mile long and almost 400 feet down, through the solid blue slate of the Paw Paw Ridge. The company had already spent $8.6 million building the first 136 miles of canal and estimated that they needed $3 million more to reach Cumberland, which they expected to do by the spring of 1841, but the directors realized that the only way to pay the interest on the loans was to finish construction and start revenues flowing. They were also afraid that if they stopped work, the canal would expire in a welter of suits from suppliers and contractors.

In Europe, Peabody had his own problems in the evaporating market for the securities. The U.S. Bank and the Morris Canal, both heavy speculators in the bonds of Michigan, Mississippi, and other states, were going under while their agents made the rounds of the same lenders. "Everything connected with America is in bad odour," Peabody said.[22] Just about that time, Louis McLane stepped off the steamer in Liverpool with $3 million more in Maryland bonds to sell for the B&O Railroad.

"Here I am in smoky London, and, in the midst of all its population, solitary & lonely," McLane wrote his son at the end of September 1839. "I find London unusually thin; indeed so entirely deserted is it that . . . I really feel quite desolate."[23] Believing that his mission would fail, he made plans to come home. McLane was in England for almost six weeks and spent about half the time in London. A week before he left, he made an arrangement with the only man he really needed to see, his friend Joshua Bates, partner in Baring Brothers & Co. Philanthropy was just one of the ways in which Bates, who was instrumental in founding the Boston Public Library, resembled George Peabody. Bates was also a dry, methodical financier. "While I am in business, I like and wish to play the game well," he once said.[24] Bates supervised the day-to-day commercial operations and served as the American specialist at Baring Brothers & Co.

Their offices were in a four-story plain brick building with an ornate entrance at 8 Bishopsgate, corner of Threadneedle Street, City of London, the insular and tradition-bound enclave of merchant bankers, stock and commodity exchanges, guilds and livery companies, banks and insurance firms compressed into the square mile that was the old Roman and medieval walled city. As George Peabody said, it was "the greatest money market in the world,"[25] and the Barings were not only the leading "American House" but first among "the Princes of the City." No firm was older or more august. Founded in 1763 by a German immigrant, they had financed the Louisiana Purchase, among other transactions. "There are six great powers in Europe: England, France, Prussia, Austria, Russia, and the Baring Brothers," said Richelieu.[26] Indeed, the Barings wielded more political influence and had greater capital resources than many countries. "Nothing is more like itself, nothing less like anything else, than a Baring," one admirer said. "Strong, sensible, self-reliant men . . . not subtle or mentally agile but endowed with that curious combination of character which lends authority even to doubtful decisions."[27] Thomas Baring, Joshua Bates, and Humphrey St. John Mildmay were the ruling triumvirate at Baring Brothers & Co. when McLane offered them the Maryland bonds on behalf of the B&O Railroad, and on October 12, 1839, they took every one.

The Barings agreed to hold the $3.2 million worth of bonds and not sell them at less than 85. In the meantime, they would advance the amounts that were needed for construction of the railroad west of Harpers Ferry. When McLane boarded the *Great Western* a week later for the return voyage to the United States, he took with him the first $200,000 advance. But the promise of the financial backing of the House of Baring was worth much more. (The Baltimore and Ohio paid McLane $8,000 for his handling of the bond negotiation.)[28] Peabody disposed of the rest of his Maryland bonds to the Baring Brothers also, selling them $2.8 million worth at 70 on November 27, 1839. The Barings now controlled the majority of the Maryland bonds issued to the railroad and canal. With no more distressed sales, the price soon rose to 82.5 and earned Baring Brothers & Co. a tidy profit. As for Peabody, he told Francis Thomas, the C&O president, "I feel a relief by the negotiation I have effected that words cannot express."[29]

Over the following decade, several American states including Maryland suspended interest payments on their debts, and some, including Michigan and Mississippi, repudiated their debts entirely. Peabody meanwhile worked hard for resumption, especially in Maryland. He also became the largest speculator in Europe in depreciated American securities. When Maryland and most of the other states did resume paying interest and the value of the bonds rose, Peabody made a great deal of money. In 1847, the governor of Maryland publicly thanked him for upholding the state's credit. The fact that Peabody never claimed his commission on the Maryland bond sale only added to his esteem. All in all, it was an excellent example of enlightened self-interest.[30]

McLane arrived in New York on November 3, 1839. Ten days later he was explaining the results of his mission to London to the B&O directors. The bonds were safe with the Barings, but the railroad still lacked sufficient funds to extend the tracks to Cumberland, although it had let construction contracts and work had started. They should now look into issuing scrip, McLane said. The finance committee agreed. McLane's mission would have been even more successful "had the negotiation of the whole state loan been confided to one person instead of permitting it to be divided among and offered for sale by various parties underbidding each other in an oppressed and falling market," they said in an obvious reference to Peabody. But even though the times were depressed and the banks had again suspended specie payments, the railroad directors still thought that "light may be made to appear through the darkness." The committee recommended using the $3 million Baltimore stock subscription as the basis for issuing company certificates, commonly called "shinplasters."[31]

Over the objections of John White, the recusant city director, the board voted to issue $100,000 in scrip immediately in small denominations of $1 to $10. They planned to print no more than $500,000 worth altogether. The company would use these certificates to pay the contractors for their work and the landowners for their right-of-way, and while they were at it, provide the community with a reliable medium of exchange. When one person had accumulated $100 worth of the scrip, he or she could take it to the commissioners, who would redeem it in City of Baltimore 6 percent stock; that person would then presumably hold the city stock, in the same way that Baring Brothers & Co. were holding the state bonds, and could sell it at a profit when the economy returned to normal. The system would thus "form a great savings Bank," the railroad directors said; it would also require a common laborer to become a capitalist. "The expedient may not be successful; but the stake is too great, and the crisis too urgent," not to try it, said McLane in the 1839 annual report, which also appeared late, on New Year's Day, 1840.[32]

The next day, Maryland's first popularly elected governor, William Grason, made these events the basis for his maiden speech to the legislature. Grason was an Eastern Shore farmer, a graduate of Saint John's College, Annapolis, and a Jacksonian. The state was $15 million in debt, and all but $300,000 of it was the result of internal improvements, he said. Of the companies that had benefited from the Eight Million Loan, the Baltimore and Ohio was the only one that had paid the interest. The Chesapeake and Ohio Canal was $25,000 short on its 1839 interest payment. The Baltimore and Susquehanna Railroad, which owed the state $75,082.50 that year, had paid only the $82.50. These two companies had insufficient net revenues to cover their interest payments and the state had no income tax to make up the deficit.[33] Moreover, the C&O, by disposing of its share of the bonds to domestic and foreign banks, "to be held as pledges for temporary loans, or sold . . . for whatever discredited stock would bring in a depressed market," had squandered the means of finishing the work to Cumberland. As for the additional $3 million that was once again necessary, Grason doubted "whether so large an addition could be made to the public debt, without entirely prostrating the credit of the state."

The governor also had some harsh words for the B&O. He praised its conservative fiscal approach, then condemned it for being as fiscally irresponsible as the canal, in particular because the bond arrangement allowed the House of Baring to sell the Maryland securities with no restrictions as to time or price as a means of covering its advances to the B&O of 10,000 pounds sterling per month (about $444,000), starting in February 1840. (The company issued the scrip in the hope of avoiding the use of these advances.) "In making this arrangement with the Barings, the [B&O] has entered into the system of hypothecation, which has been so disastrous to the credit of the state," the governor said. Moreover, by undertaking construction without funds, the railroad "has abandoned the prudent and cautious policy which has generally characterized its proceedings." Grason said he intended to warn the legislators against increasing the public debt by further investment in internal improvements: "The opinion may be held by some few, that this debt is not binding on the state; and by others, that if binding, it will never be paid, because the people will not consent to be taxed." Maryland must honor her debts, the governor said. He characterized the plan to issue company scrip as a desperate measure that might work for a while, but would further derange the currency.[34]

The speech caused a furor. In response, the B&O called in John Pendleton Kennedy, whose pen could be counted on to explain their side to the lawmakers. Kennedy set up a committee of five directors—three Jacksonians and two Whigs—to produce a document that he, a known partisan, wrote himself. The 24-page pamphlet that the B&O issued authoritatively denied the governor's three major points—that the B&O had abandoned prudent fiscal policy, depressed the state's credit by introducing more bonds into the market, and engaged in hypothecation. Kennedy asserted that, on the contrary, city funds had advanced the construction so far, the placement of the state bonds with the Barings had actually elevated Maryland's credit, and there had been no hypothecation because no money had been raised on them (a statement that was not strictly true). He drew a fine distinction between canal-style hypothecation, or pledging securities without delivery, and the railroad's "stipulation for advances from an agent."[35]

Kennedy was proud of his performance, which "gives the Governor, in truth, but little quarter." The Baltimore *Sun*, which had sided with the governor, now decided that Grason "must have either lacked correct information or have misunderstood the nature of the arrangement effected abroad." The state's chief executive naturally issued a rejoinder, "and a precious piece of *after dinner* thunder it is!" Kennedy noted gleefully.[36]

Historians have had a tendency to dismiss Governor William Grason as a "political Jeremiah."[37] Pessimists are seldom popular, but they are sometimes right.

18

Engines in the Hills

BEFORE THEY CHALLENGED THE ALLEGHENIES,
the Baltimore and Ohio Railroad mastered their last obstacle in the piedmont—the
inclined planes at Parrs Spring Ridge; and while they were about it, they rebuilt the
Old Main Line to Harpers Ferry.

In November 1837, B&O president Louis McLane sent Jonathan Knight and
Benjamin H. Latrobe, Jr., on an inspection tour of other railroads to determine how
best to reconstruct and operate the line between Baltimore and Harpers Ferry. They
spent about a month traveling in the middle Atlantic states and New England. The
closest railroad was the Baltimore and Port Deposit, for which Latrobe had done
the surveys. This railroad had been connected to the B&O at President and Fleet
streets, near the City Block, and it extended from there through Canton and on up to
Havre de Grace. On the far side of the Susquehanna, other lines reached Philadelphia.
Beyond the Delaware, on New Jersey's Camden and Amboy Railroad, Knight and
Latrobe saw John Stevens's "H-rail," similar to the standard T-rail, which Stevens
had invented and had produced in England. Some of these rails were laid on the old-
fashioned stone blocks and some were on sleepers resting on planks supported by
ballast.

Knight and Latrobe recommended the latter method for the B&O in their report, the first part of which, concerning the track, was released in January 1838. (The
second section, dealing with engines, appeared five months later.) Both engineers
were firm in their opinion about the efficacy of laying sleepers on planks topped by
rails: "Success has nowhere attended the stone block method of laying rails in the
United States." The main trouble was that stone blocks were difficult to keep in gauge
and were hard on engines and cars.[1] They recommended that the new track between
Baltimore and Harpers Ferry should be laid on a solid foundation consisting of six
inches of broken stone, small enough to pass through a two-inch ring, followed by

three-by-six-inch sills, at least seven feet long and laid end to end, and on top of these, sleepers or crossties of the same length, six inches square, spaced every two or three feet, and fastened down. The H-rails, weighing 50 pounds per yard, with their ends joined in chairs, would be spiked to the ties, and the interstices in the wooden structure filled up with ballast. Curves would be banked. Knight and Latrobe estimated the cost at almost $10,000 a mile and recommended a resurvey of the Old Main Line from Mt. Clare to Harpers Ferry.

Survey teams started out in March 1838, some headed east from the Potomac, others west from Baltimore. They met near Parrs Spring Ridge, as they had on the original surveys. Latrobe gave John D. Steele, one of his favorite assistant engineers who had reconnoitered the route in the fall of 1836, the job of locating the new alignment over the ridge. It was to be a little over a mile north of the inclined planes and have a maximum grade of 80 feet per mile, or 1.5 percent.

Another purpose of the reconstruction program was to straighten out the line. A major problem area was at Elysville, just up the river from Ellicotts Mills, where, Latrobe noted, "a great bend in the present road is found, the most abruptly curved part of which has a radius of 318 feet."[2] Latrobe instructed Henry R. Hazlehurst, his brother-in-law, to survey a shorter alignment through the neck of land that the B&O's original route had curved around. This route would require two new bridges over the Patapsco River. Latrobe also sent all-purpose engineer James Murray on a road trip to assemble the timber for the track. Latrobe figured they needed over a million linear feet of the three-by-six-inch undersills alone. He preferred locust and mulberry or else cedar, sassafras, juniper, or cypress, all of which resisted rot and held spikes better than other kinds of wood.[3] Murray was to explore the Baltimore market first, then the locust country on the Susquehanna River up into Pennsylvania, the Potomac Valley ranging into Virginia, and the eastern and western shores of Maryland, then Delaware, and maybe southern New Jersey for red cedar, and finally lower Virginia, on both sides of the Chesapeake Bay, for red and white cedar, juniper, and cypress. After a four-month search, Murray wound up in Norfolk, having gone through all the potential sources and arranging for enough timber to lay 60 miles of track. Management decided to reconstruct only 20 miles that year, however. The B&O ordered 25 tons of plate rails and fixtures, probably for sidings, from A&G Ralston, Philadelphia; spikes from the Troy Iron Works, New York; and the heavy H-rails from England through the Alex. Brown & Sons organization.

Securing the right-of-way was always an adventure. Both sides had grown more sophisticated in the decade since the landowners gave up their land readily and the company dispatched such casual agents as John Gray, the Irish contractor from Vinegar Hill, to charm Charles Warfield into allowing the B&O to do pretty much what they wanted to on his property near Relay. Shortly before he died in 1832 at age 95, Charles Carroll of Carrollton, a man who seldom let principle interfere with profit, extracted $3,376.33 from the company whose cornerstone he laid, for the right-of-way through his manor in Frederick County. It was the largest such single payment up to that time,[4] but the record was soon surpassed. By the time the B&O got to

Washington in 1835, the bill for the 30-mile right-of-way to the city line was $90,000, and within the district, tailor John Sinon alone held them up for $10,000 for his strategically placed house and lot known as Sinon's Corner.

The B&O preferred doing almost anything to avoid paying money for land on which to lay their tracks. In exchange for land, they offered proprietors a variety of favors, including contracts for materials and construction, deals on switches and depots, occasionally a package arrangement. For example, after Thomas B. Dorsey, a farmer on the Patapsco River two miles beyond Elysville, allowed the B&O to cross his property, the railroad constructed seven sidings and let him use a "burthen car" on the line. It was perhaps sufficient recompense for having destroyed his mill seat and the value of about 50 acres of his farm that was separated from the rest. The company also aided him "by reason of the great quantity of wood consumed from his land by the contractors and their labourers . . . and of the burning of his fence rails and woodland and other injuries inflicted upon him, and also by reason of the demolition of his lime kiln (the centre of the railroad passing over it)." Dorsey apparently was mollified, for afterward, he offered to supply water to the engines and earned a depot.[5]

Similarly, by withholding benefits, the railroad punished those who declined to play by their rules. The Elys, owners of the cotton factory two miles downstream from Dorsey, argued with the company for a decade over a switch and a depot for their town. Following some minor disagreements, the B&O had granted both in the early 1830's and the relationship was smooth until the time of the realignment and the new bridges. "The notions of the Messrs. Ely are quite in the extreme," Latrobe complained in the spring of 1838,[6] but he did not understand why. The Elys—Thomas, Hugh, and Asher—had told Hazlehurst that they favored the new alignment because it bridged the river to their limestone quarries, but when McLane took over the negotiations from the local right-of-way agent, he accused the Elys of demanding exorbitant prices. The railroad condemned the land. The Elys reluctantly accepted the court award for the right-of-way but evidently delayed transferring the property, and then criticized the bridge locations. This prompted Latrobe to remind the Elys that they had initially expressed satisfaction with those as well, in statements corroborated by witnesses. Besides, it was too late to change them, he said. "The Bridges & grad'n. at Elysville have been commenced after much delay," Latrobe reported to Knight in July 1838. "The damages awarded to the Messrs. Ely were $1,916 which they required to be paid in *specie* and are giving us all the annoyance they can in the carrying on of the works."[7] When the job was done a year later, the Elys requested a switch to replace the one that was bypassed by the new line. The company said no. The Elys then offered to build it themselves. Not until they permanently conveyed the right-of-way through Elysville, the board replied.

At Parrs Spring Ridge, in the summer of 1838, Latrobe encountered Henry Buzzard. He was a landowner who understood the game. His property was at the summit of the ridge, and the B&O's new line avoiding the planes would cross it, with a deep excavation. Buzzard accepted this and a payment of $250 with no complaint. "You will in the receipt for the money on the deed, express it to be in full not only for the *land* as described but for all claims for fencing and damages arising from the construction and operations of the rail road," Latrobe warned his right-of-way agent.[8] The excavation cut across two existing roads, which needed to be shifted to the end of it. One of them formed the county boundary. After Buzzard gave his permission, state commissioners would decide his compensation. "Nevertheless if Buzzard insists upon something at once you may agree to the extent of $25," Latrobe told his assistant engineer at the ridge. "But he will hardly I should think be so grasping especially if you throw out a hint that his obliging the co. in this regard will probably forward his views in respect to the proposed depot at the Summit."[9]

The railroad gave its contingent approval for the depot and Buzzard spent the winter maturing his ideas. In the spring of 1839, he accompanied Latrobe to the top of Parrs Spring Ridge. At the summit, "an understanding took place between us," Latrobe told James Murray, "in regards to the manner in which we should locate the 4 acres of grounds which Mr. B. has made a donation to the Company."[10] Latrobe's letter included a map showing the key elements of Buzzard's scheme. They were a new house on a hill overlooking the intersection of the railroad and the relocated county roads at the end of the deep cut, a wagon yard and depot on either side of the highway, and a tavern beyond the tracks.

At Elysville, the bargaining process was adversarial and extended, but the work proceeded swiftly. At Parrs Spring Ridge, quite the opposite occurred: construction began at both places in the summer of 1838 and the excavated materials from one were used to build the other. Contractor Roseby Carr hauled puddling clay from the deep cut at the ridge to throw into the cofferdams being built in the Patapsco River at Elysville to raise the bridge piers. Latrobe did not drive the contractors too hard in July and August that year because of the "intense heat," and also because of a shortage of labor. In September, he began to lean on Putney, Riddle, and McMurphy, who were doing the graduation and masonry at Elysville. Put more men and carts on, Latrobe insisted. If the contractors were having trouble attracting laborers, the reason was that they were not providing proper accommodations. Speed up the bridge work, get the foundations in while the river was low, and hire more masons to carry up the piers. Move the materials faster—the 40 special stone cars the railroad had rigged up to run to the quarries sat around too long unloaded. They "should be kept constantly moving," Latrobe said.

The tactics apparently worked. Six months later, in the spring of 1839, the bridges were almost finished. They were covered with planks and supported on stone piers and abutments. The portals had pointed arches. The upstream bridge at Elysville had two 150-foot spans, and the lower bridge, nearer the mill, had three spans of 110 feet each. They were about 26 feet wide. The new timber bridges were not only quicker but also cheaper to erect than stone bridges; the total cost of the wooden superstructures at Elysville was just over $12,000.[11] Latrobe designed the timber trusses, using as a model the trusses that he and Lewis Wernwag had carried out for the bridge at Harpers Ferry. The trusses at Elysville were composite structures, principally of timber, but with cast-iron joint hardware and some wrought-iron tension members. They in turn served as models for the bridges built later between Harpers Ferry and Cumberland.

Parrs Spring Ridge required more extensive work. Steele's new alignment left the Old Main Line before plane no. 1 and headed northwest along a stream to the top of the ridge in a series of tangents and easy curves. On the other side it looped back down to meet the main line again between planes no. 3 and 4. Along the six-mile route there were several rock cuts, the worst of which was just before Henry Buzzard's new depot near the ridgetop.

William Slater was the contractor. Not much is known about him except that the summer of 1838 must have been his worst season in the construction business. Slater started work in mid-June with the best of intentions, sending more than 750 men swarming over the ridge with their horses, carts, plows, and special cars for carrying stone. They were supposed to be through in five months so that track could be laid before winter. By July, a third of the work had been completed. In August, Latrobe contacted Moncure Robinson and others to see if they were interested in buying the cog-and-sheave wheels from the B&O's inclined planes. "They are not likely now to be of any use to this company as the planes at Parrs Ridge are about to be superceded by a new location for locomotive power," Latrobe said.[12] But under the blistering sun, Slater's laborers began to sicken and die, even in elevated country away from the rivers. By mid-November 1838, when he was supposed to have the entire alignment finished, Slater was still working with the men he had left at the deep cut near the top of the ridge. They had dug a little over halfway down and stopped.

The excavation was a V-shaped trough about half a mile long and 55 feet deep at its greatest depth. The sides were to be sloped at 45 degrees. They were actually made steeper than that, perhaps 60 or 70 degrees, doubtless owing to the difficulty of construction. There were roughly 144,000 cubic yards of material to be removed. At 31 feet, Slater and his men hit two ledges of hard rock lying directly across their path about 100 yards apart. They were separated by a mass of earth and softer rock. When the workmen started to dig out the latter, they activated the springs beneath, producing a sticky gumbo dammed up by the two hard rock ridges. They began to blast.

Except for the invention of the safety fuse in 1831, the techniques of blasting had not changed much in the 50 years since James Rumsey's happy-go-lucky crews of brawling ex-convicts "used the powder Rather too Extravagent" at the Great Falls of the Potomac. Toward the end of the eighteenth century, Potomac Company superintendent Leonard Harbaugh had succeeded in hacking a canal around the Great Falls out of solid stone, with the help, the payroll says, of "Hercules," "Bob the Blaster," and "Monster Manley."[13] Blasting was, to say the least, an inexact science, and the experiments to see what black powder could do were often spectacular. On the Delaware and Hudson Canal in 1826, a contractor paid a visiting Irishman named Patten $5 to pack 70 pounds of gunpowder into a rock 40 feet high and almost as wide overhanging Rondout Creek and set it off. The explosion, "the greatest blast on record," laid the rock over onto the canal bank, right where the contractor wanted it—except for a "sliver" three feet square that rose like a mortar shell and buried itself in the earth a couple of feet from a spectator, "who was in a manner petrified from the shock." [14]

It was dangerous business for all concerned and especially for the laborers who set the charges. The procedure was to drill a hole in the rock, pour in black powder, and tamp down clay or soft rock around a thin, hollow iron rod that was used to introduce the fuse. But sometimes the iron tamping rod or the hollow needle for the fuse struck a spark and set off the explosion prematurely, with gruesome results. Even after copper rods and needles were introduced, workers often threw them away, preferring the iron ones. For the last step, a handmade paper tube, called a squib, filled with gunpowder or other combustible material, was stuck in the needle and ignited. If the blaster was lucky, he escaped before the charge went off. The safety fuse, invented in 1831, was machine-made paper or cord, wrapped around a core of gunpowder and covered with tar or pitch. It could be cut to any length, and it burned at a predictable rate. [15]

The dangers of blasting were exacerbated by the conditions of working in the "very long, deep and narrow gorge" at the top of Parrs Spring Ridge. The B&O committee that investigated Slater's claim for extra compensation pointed out the difficulties: "Whenever a blasting took place, and they were necessarily very frequent, the multitude of hands employed, in this confined spot, had to run for safety entirely out of the cut, and to return, as often, the whole distance, with a great loss of time, which had become the more valuable, from their number, the shortness of the days at that season, and the importance of bringing the work to an early completion." [16] McLane optimistically predicted in the B&O annual report in December 1838 that Slater would be through with the deep cut in January. In February, Slater was still hard at work with a reduced force, and he did not finish until June 1839. [17] Slater had taken the contract to do all the graduation and masonry work on the new alignment for a little over $130,000, pretty close to the engineers' estimates of the cost. But neither he nor Latrobe knew what was 30 feet underground. Slater claimed the job cost him $10,000 more than the contract price, mainly because of having to remove the unforeseen 6,000 cubic yards of hard rock from the deep cut. He requested reimbursement. The company ultimately turned him down. They said they, too, had been penalized by the construction delay and that, although they appreciated his efforts, no one had made him any promises. Slater requested reconsideration, but the railroad again denied his appeal.

The final test of the new alignment was having a locomotive pull a train over it. While Latrobe supervised the reconstruction of the Old Main Line, he was also conducting engine experiments to help determine the most appropriate type for the Baltimore and Ohio. One test was to see whether the locomotives would burn Cumberland coal. The engines of two manufacturers were then running on the railroad. They were Baltimore's Gillingham & Winans, and William Norris, of Philadelphia. The small Gillingham & Winans engines, the Crabs, had four wheels, upright boilers with horizontal cylinders, and burned anthracite coal. The Norris "one-armed Billy's" had six wheels in a 4-2-0 configuration, horizontal boilers, angled cylinders, and burned wood.[18]

The locomotives of Mathias W. Baldwin, Norris's Philadelphia rival, resembled Norris's in having the same horizontal boilers and wheel arrangement, but they differed in being "inside-connected"—that is, in having the cylinders, 11 or 12 inches in diameter, with a 16-inch stroke, linked to the inside of the drive wheels with long connecting rods and half-cranks. Baldwin made heavy freight locomotives that went 10 to 12 mph and faster passenger engines. The average weight for both types was about ten tons.[19] In the spring of 1838, Baldwin sent two locomotives down to Baltimore for trial, the Baltimore and the Carroll. Latrobe began the experiments with Cumberland coal in June and continued them for the next two months, during which the engineers ran the larger of Baldwin's engines, the Baltimore, and Gillingham & Winans's Isaac McKim, a Crab, out to the planes and back for the tests. They also tried Norris's Joseph W. Patterson, a "one-armed Billy," on the Washington Branch, its normal theater of operations.

Baldwin's Baltimore fared the worst in the tests. The coal seemed to melt rather than burn, dust and soot clogged several of the 150 copper boiler tubes, which were one and a quarter inches in diameter and seven feet long, and the engine failed to generate enough steam. Latrobe said, "The experiment was decidedly unsuccessful." Gillingham & Winans's Isaac McKim fared the best. The coal burned freely, and there was "No choaking of the tubes."[20] The engine had 450 vertical boiler tubes that measured one and one-half inches by four feet. Norris's Joseph W. Patterson, which normally burned pine, was an in-between performer. The combustion was better than in Baldwin's engine and the tubes remained clear, but the coal clogged the draft through the grate.

Latrobe's conclusion on the basis of these tests was that the vertical boilers and artificial draft of the B&O's anthracite-burning engines, the locally produced Crabs, made them the best locomotives for use with Cumberland bituminous coal. They were also the most economical in terms of fuel consumption. Thus advised, the board of directors, at the end of 1838, declined buying Baldwin's engines, and although they expressed a preference for Norris's wood-burners by buying two more, they also accepted another locomotive from Gillingham & Winans, the Mazeppa. The Baltimore engines had thus held their own in the competition with the more conventional locomotives. On Saturday, June 1, 1839, when the first train rode the new line over Parrs Spring Ridge, thereby avoiding the inclined planes, it was proudly led by Gillingham & Winans's Isaac McKim.

The following Monday, the passenger train from Baltimore went west over the ridge at 15 mph and the one eastbound from Harpers Ferry took it at 20 mph. Together, they cut an hour off the scheduled round trip running time between the two places. The Baltimore engines routinely pulled 60-ton freight trains over the hill in 30 minutes, saving fuel as well as time. "Such are the gratifying results of the improvement at the Ridge in connection with that at Elysville and the other minor ones upon the whole line," Latrobe told Knight.[21]

Altogether during 1838–39, nine miles of the B&O west of Baltimore, a mile at Elysville, and ten miles at Parrs Spring Ridge (six miles of new alignment and four miles of existing track at the western end) were rebuilt with the new H-rail from England. The remainder of the 80-mile Old Main Line to Harpers Ferry retained the original strap rail, some of it laid on stone. The reconstruction money came from a $450,000 fund produced by calling in the last $15 per share installment on the stock.

For the movement west, however, the summer of 1838 was a season of confusion as B&O officers and stockholders argued about whether to accept the Virginia law and to adopt the route through that state. In June, Latrobe sent Steele, who was familiar with the territory, out to the Ohio River with a crew to begin locating the railroad from Wheeling eastward. Latrobe later warned him to be discreet in voicing opinions about alternate alignments and depot sites as he and his men carried their bench marks and levels into Grave Yard Square near the market house on the northern bank of Wheeling Creek in the center of town.

The stockholders did not accept the Virginia law and the route until mid-November 1838, but within days, Latrobe had dispatched four more teams of surveyors to locate the line from Harpers Ferry to Cumberland. They set up their headquarters in a tent city at Martinsburg. Latrobe divided the 97-mile distance into divisions of 30 or so miles each, residencies of six to seven miles, and sections one mile long. Henry R. Hazlehurst received the first 32-mile division, through Martinsburg to Back Creek, which he had surveyed the previous year. John Small, Jr., took the next division, from there 25 miles to Sideling Hill Creek. The shortest section was given to Thomas C. Atkinson, just 17 miles to the South Branch of the Potomac, but it included a large tunnel. John Blount got the final part, 23 miles to the Maryland line above Cumberland, in the valley of Wills Creek. The surveyors were given detailed instructions. They were to try and avoid high construction costs and to end up with a line of moderate grades of 40 feet per mile, 0.7 percent, and curves of 800 feet radius, or about 7 degrees. After staking out the center line, they were to set boundary stakes for the cuts and fills and limit stakes to mark the legal 66-foot right-of-way. Latrobe said, "An accurate chain and compass survey of the lines from limit stake to limit stake will be made."[22] Latrobe requested more surveys of every property the railroad would cross, whether title had been conveyed or not. He also wanted maps for the lawyers and right-of-way agents showing the cultivated areas and how the tracks would divide the land. Damages should be kept to a minimum. The final maps and profiles were to indicate the positions of houses and other improvements, roads, and alternate routes with the amounts of excavation, embankment, masonry, and bridging for each one.

Latrobe issued equally precise instructions for the bridges. All the sites should be fixed at the time of location. Those with spans of less than 25 feet would be built of stone, with semicircular or elliptical arches, and the ones over 25 feet would have wooden superstructures. The surveyors were to inquire about the volume of the streams "in freshes," so that they could make the bridge openings large enough. In addition, they were to take soundings with an iron rod or augur to determine the nature of the bottom under the masonry piers and abutments. Duplicate drawings were to be made of each structure, one "a working drawing on rough strong paper for the contractors," and the other on fine paper for the office. Latrobe later decided to design the superstructures himself, patterned on the bridges at Elysville but adjusted to suit local conditions. "The preceding instructions have been made very minute in order to produce a systematic regularity and perfect uniformity in the proceedings of all of the parties operating in concert," Latrobe said, adding, "You are earnestly requested to use your best efforts to press on the location."[23]

Whenever he could, Latrobe joined the crews and introduced them to the right-of-way agents who were to be their coworkers along the line in Virginia. Most of the agents, like Thomas Jefferson McKaig and Andrew Hunter, were lawyers and politicians with good local connections and reputations. McKaig, a school principal turned lawyer, established a legal practice in Cumberland in 1839 with his brother, William Wallace McKaig, also a former teacher. One of their first clients was the Baltimore and Ohio Railroad. Thomas J. McKaig remained the B&O's Cumberland counsel for the next 39 years and aided the railroad in acquiring the right-of-way to Wheeling. In the mid-1850's, while Thomas served in the Maryland House of Delegates (he later became a state senator), William was mayor of Cumberland. Hunter was an attorney from Charlestown, Virginia, near Harpers Ferry. He first shows up in the B&O records in 1840 when the company paid him $1,750 for aid in acquiring land in that state. In 1844, Hunter was a director of the Winchester & Potomac Railroad, and had indeed represented them in one of their failed attempts to be taken over by the Baltimore and Ohio, but in 1847, as a member of the Virginia House of Delegates, Hunter again worked for the B&O in Richmond, assisting the railroad to get to Wheeling.

The trio from Martinsburg was quite a different lot. Judge Edmund Pendleton, John Pendleton Kennedy's uncle and law tutor, was old Virginia landed gentry. Charles James Faulkner was a Virginia state senator, later a lobbyist for the B&O, then a U.S. congressman. He helped McLane, Kennedy, and Nicholas obtain their 1838 legislative package in Richmond.[24] The third man, Charles C. Starbuck (known as "C.C."), was a conniver on the order of Caspar W. Wever. His previous job, as a C&O Canal superintendent, had been selling water power to mills located at locks. In the fall of 1837, more than a year before the railroad officially accepted and announced its new route through Virginia, and even before the trio of company representatives went to Richmond to seek enabling legislation, John H. B. Latrobe asked Starbuck his terms for obtaining right-of-way on the Virginia shore for the B&O. Under the agreement they soon signed, Starbuck was to get $10 a mile, plus $500 in expenses, for land he acquired gratuitously or on terms approved by the railroad along the routes surveyed in Maryland as well as Virginia. Where the property had to be taken under eminent domain, he was to procure testimony and assist the lawyers with the jury trials. Starbuck got the same $10 a mile whether the right-of-way was contributed or condemned.

As the survey crews spread out from Harpers Ferry to Cumberland, the right-of-way agents moved along with them. Faulkner, in the thorough manner of legal discovery, attempted to familiarize himself with the entire line. Starbuck, already an active field lieutenant, had more expedient measures in mind. He soon relayed them via Latrobe to McLane. Better means "must be adopted to prevent the extortions of landholders on the line of the road through Virginia," Starbuck said, and he proposed the ruse previously employed at the Thomas Viaduct. Believing the route locations were final, the proprietors tried to coerce the greatest possible amount in damages from the company; if there were alternative routes, "they would relinquish without compensation."[25]

Starbuck therefore recommended that a brigade of engineers survey dummy alignments on various sections where the owners needed further convincing to surrender their land at a decent price. Starbuck, McLane, and Latrobe were to be the only ones in on the secret. Latrobe thought it was reasonable and asked McLane for his opinion, but it is not known whether they actually put the scheme into practice. Starbuck's Martinsburg business failed not long after this, and he left the state owing several creditors, including the B&O, which later sued him and won a court judgment.

Meanwhile, Latrobe sought truer surveys with a new instrument, the transit, which was equipped with a telescope and was a vast improvement over the surveyor's compass, which only had sights. The transit combined the telescope's greater accuracy with the compass's utility, and it also incorporated aspects of the English theodolite, which, though highly accurate, was not popular among early American engineers because of its sluggishness in the field. Its telescope would not pivot, or "transit," on the horizontal axis. The ability of the telescope on the transit to pivot allowed a surveyor to sight behind the instrument as well as in front simply by rotating the telescope, without having to remove it from its mounts and reset it.[26]

The transit was invented in 1831 by William J. Young, of Philadelphia, and one of his first customers was the Baltimore and Ohio Railroad. At the time that Young, a London native, developed the transit, which he referred to as his "Improved Compass, with a Telescope attached," he had been making surveyor's compasses, levels, and other devices in Philadelphia for over 30 years. In fact, Young was well on his way to becoming the country's premier producer of mathematical instruments.[27] According to an 1833 testimonial given Young by the B&O's James P. Stabler, the railroad owned eight of Young's "improved compasses" and seven of his levels. Stabler, a Quaker relative of Philip E. Thomas's, was superintendent of construction from September 1831 to January 1833, when he resigned. He helped to put down the tracks into the city and out to Frederick. Stabler said that for laying rails, the instrument, "more recently improved with a reversing telescope, in place of the vane sights, leaves the engineer scarcely any thing to desire." He believed that when the transit became better known, it would be "as highly appreciated for common surveying."[28]

Latrobe wanted the instruments for that very purpose. He ordered a dozen transits and five levels from Young in the summer of 1839. "When may I expect the last order of six of which none have yet been received, and which are much wanted—please send them on in pairs at least—as fast as finished," Latrobe wrote urgently to Young in August.[29] He had them by fall. The seventeen instruments cost $2,433, or about $143 each. Latrobe also received eight levels from Edmund Draper at $140 each.

Some years earlier Latrobe had bought a theodolite from Young, which he admired. However, he pronounced one made by another manufacturer that measured distance, "a clumsy machine of whose practical value I have doubts."[30] He also experimented in the mid-1830's with a barometer to measure altitude. He found it accurate to within a foot at the Deep Cut near Baltimore, but when he took it to the top of the city's Washington Monument the next day, it was off by 26 feet. Therefore, the instruments used for the surveys between Harpers Ferry and Cumberland and over the mountains to Wheeling were the chain, for distance; the level, for elevations; and the new transit, for laying out the lines.

The five teams of surveyors stayed out through the winter of 1838–39. In February 1839, on McLane's orders, Latrobe shifted Steele from the remote Wheeling end of the line to a section where the location would be more difficult and where construction would probably start sooner. That was the Wills Creek–Casselman River area of Pennsylvania above Cumberland. Steele was to pitch his tents at Sand Patch, fix the position of the half-mile summit tunnel there, and carry his surveys down to Cumberland. "The part of the location thus entrusted to you is one of paramount interest, difficulty & importance, & I am sure yr energy & talents will be devoted to it with yr characteristic zeal & ability," Latrobe told him.[31]

By April, the location surveys for the Baltimore and Ohio Railroad between Harpers Ferry and Cumberland were finished with the exception of Harpers Ferry itself. The company was negotiating with federal government officials there to determine the route past the armory. "The corps of Engineers, under the direction of H. R. Hazlehurst, Esq., is now located in town, making up their reports and estimates," noted the Martinsburg press.[32] Latrobe advertised for contractors. "The line throughout is a fine one, & one of the handsomest and boldest portions of it will be the route across the North Mountain at Robbins Gap," he wrote Knight.[33] Latrobe also liked Steele's mountain railroad location, and he encouraged him to maintain the 66-feet-per-mile grade at the Sand Patch summit down to Wills Creek but not to worry about getting a precise balance between excavation and embankment: "There is a degree of approximation to perfection in these details with which we must be satisfied."[34] He dispatched two new survey parties to help Steele, and they pretty much followed what was then still the route of the C&O Canal. The B&O directors that summer adopted the canal's alignment from Cumberland to Connellsville as their own.

Construction bids started to come in. Thirty contractors got off the train at Harpers Ferry and flocked through Martinsburg to study the drawings and specifications and look over the job. By July 1839, the contracts had been awarded for the entire route to Cumberland except for the first section above Harpers Ferry, where the location was still unsettled. Some veterans of Parrs Spring Ridge took on the heavy construction around Martinsburg. Hundreds of laborers arrived to start working on the railroad. Their impact was noted before they lifted a shovel. Edmund P. Hunter, editor of the *Gazette*, the weekly Whig newspaper, wrote, "The constant application and competition for houses, the repairs of decayed buildings, the erection of new ones, the opening of new stores, taverns, etc. seem to indicate that Martinsburg may throw aside the torpor and lethargy of the past half century, and look to a better and brighter future."[35]

Latrobe shuttled between work in the office and visits to sites on the line, praising, criticizing, and arbitrating disputes among the surveyors and right-of-way agents, or between feuding brothers on a survey team, or in cases where one assistant had trumped another's location. He signed his letters, "In haste . . ." In March 1839, he was at Hancock; in July, Cumberland; and in late August, he was planning a ride up the Casselman River to visit the new survey parties. He requested accommodations and at the same time assured them, "I expect of course to fare in all aspects as you yourselves do."[36] Latrobe evidently was called back from Cumberland for a board of directors meeting before he could make the trip, but he had a good understanding of the topography nonetheless. He told Steele that he could visualize the surveyor's locale, even recall the features of the ground from his own surveys, "and with the aid of the map I have succeeded in understanding very well the position of the line as described by you. Still there is no map or description adequate to convey ideas so correct as those furnished by an actual view of the thing itself," he said.[37] Latrobe stopped in to see Atkinson at the Doe Gully Tunnel, which was going to cut off the first of the Potomac's big bends. There would be another, shorter tunnel at Paw Paw, the last of the bends. His instructions were: "I should like you to accompany me over your division that I may give my views as to the scites of the bridges and other matters . . . we will go down the line together."[38]

Construction started in August 1839 at scattered locations and immediately ran into delays, mainly because of farmers who refused to let the laborers on their land until they got in their crops or until they received damages for the right-of-way. Latrobe told the contractors they had the legal right to go to work. They should do as much as they could until the proprietors were paid, "keeping however out of cornfields if possible." The company hurried the survey work, but slowed construction because they were short of funds as the Panic of 1837 hardened into a deep depression. The railroad borrowed a total of $500,000 from every bank in Baltimore on a pledge of the city's 6 percent stock, issued in payment of Baltimore's $3 million subscription to the railroad. McLane left for London to dispose of the state bonds. Latrobe trailed from bank to bank in Baltimore, trying to keep his various accounts and checkbooks straight. He fended off suppliers like Edmund Draper, who had furnished surveying instruments, saying, "There is *just at this moment*, a scarcity of funds in the treasury."[39] He also had difficulty meeting the payrolls for the western survey crews. "Allow me to caution you against drawing until you have heard from me that the money . . . has been placed to your credit," he warned one of his assistant engineers.[40]

In October 1839, the Baltimore banks suspended specie payments again, creating more confusion. The directors voted to disband and recall the remaining survey parties in the west. Latrobe was at last on his way up the Youghiogheny River to see them when Knight caught up with him with the news. He was forced to turn back once again, this time for good, and he had to send letters to the four heads of the survey parties telling them they had a week to shut down their operations, discharge the workers, and store the equipment. His formal instructions implied that it might be some time before they passed that way again:

> While the field work is going on, the field books, notes, and drawings can be examined & corrected . . . and left in such a state as to be readily intelligible to those who may have occasion hereafter to use them. . . .
>
> In bringing the running of the line to a close for the present, care will be taken to leave such *plain & permanent* marks of its position upon the ground as will prevent any difficulty in the future resumption of the surveys: and of the character & position of these marks a full description will be recorded in the note Books, with references to known land marks or localities in the neighbourhood.[41]

"You will have perceived by the papers that Mr. McLane has returned and has been partially successful in the object of his mission," Latrobe ended his final letter to Steele, who had gone back to Wheeling. "It is hoped that the work between H. Ferry and Cumberland may now be prosecuted without interruption—West of Cumberland all is doubtful as yet—Let me hear from you occasionally."[42]

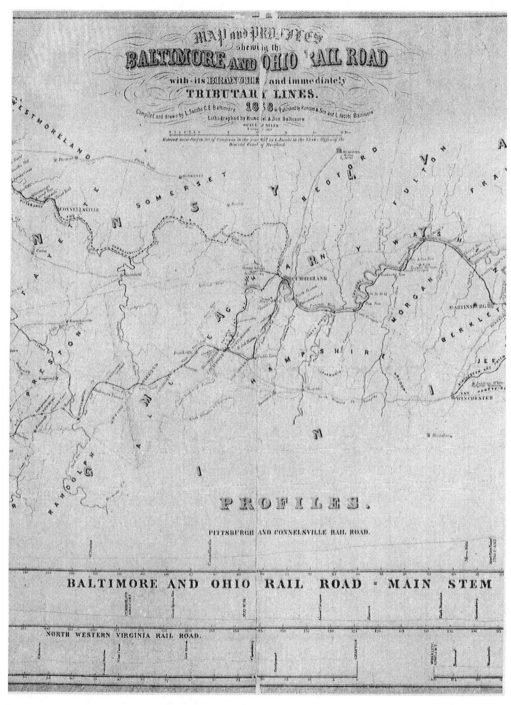

The bends of the Potomac River north of Paw Paw, the rich Georges Creek coalfield south of Cumberland (from Mount Savage to Westernport), and the virgin territory along the Youghiogheny and Cheat rivers were all opened to tourism and agricultural and industrial development by the B&O Railroad. *Special Collections, University of Maryland, College Park Libraries.*

Louis McLane was a politician, diplomat, and corporate statesman when the B&O chose him to run the company in 1836. An indifferent railroad man, and the weakest of the three B&O presidents during the early period, McLane extended the line from Harpers Ferry to Cumberland. *Lithograph, circa early 1850's, © The B&O Railroad Museum, Inc., Collection.*

Cultured, droll, a snappy dresser, politician-novelist John Pendleton Kennedy took up the pen on behalf of the B&O and stirred the company, weakened by its struggle with the canal and stalled at Harpers Ferry, into action. He later became a B&O director, but quit in a power struggle with McLane over the route of the railroad. *Archives of the Peabody Institute of the Johns Hopkins University.*

George Peabody, based in the City of London, handled the sale of Maryland State bonds issued on behalf of the C&O Canal while Louis McLane did the same for the B&O Railroad. Peabody helped to uphold Maryland's credit, made a fortune speculating in depreciated American securities following the Panic of 1837, and from humble beginnings became America's first great philanthropist. *Archives of the Peabody Institute of the Johns Hopkins University.*

Ross Winans was opinionated, cantankerous, and "a law unto himself" when it came to engineering matters. Winans designed several idiosyncratic locomotives for the B&O, including the Crab engine, which he developed in 1835. The Mazeppa, shown here *(bottom)*, was built by Gillingham and Winans in 1838. *Winans: © The B&O Railroad Museum, Inc., Collection; the Mazeppa: Herbert H. Harwood, Jr.*

Another new engine on the line was William Norris's Lafayette, weighing ten tons, with a four-wheel swiveling truck under its tall stack. The illustration is an 1837 advertisement for Norris's Philadelphia works. *Smithsonian Institution.*

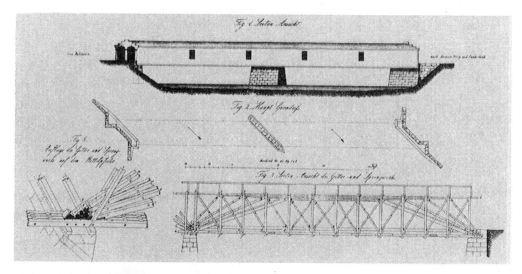

The B&O's main line at Elysville was realigned in 1839 with two new timber truss bridges over the Patapsco designed by Benjamin H. Latrobe, Jr., based on the bridge at Harpers Ferry. This is the upper span at Elysville, replaced by a Bollman truss bridge in 1852. Only the abutments and pier remain. *Herbert H. Harwood, Jr.*

The company town of Elysville (Daniels, Md.), with the railroad, the mill, and a highway bridge over the Patapsco leading to the houses of the workers, shown here in 1872, lasted until 1968. Very little remains, but the 111-year-old Daniels Community band still rehearses on Monday nights. © *The B&O Railroad Museum, Inc., Collection.*

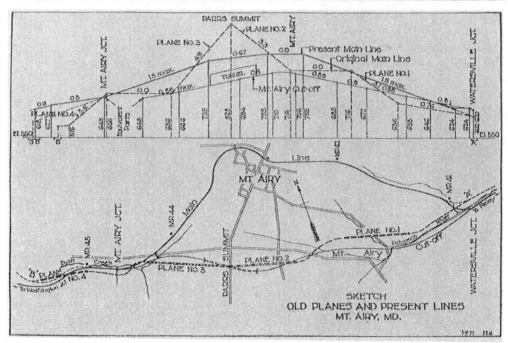

The main line was also shifted to avoid the inclined planes at Parrs Spring Ridge. The first train, pulled by a Gillingham and Winans Crab engine, went over it in June 1839. That line (through Mount Airy) has since been abandoned and the present main line tunnels under the ridge on an alignment that generally follows the location of the old inclined planes. *Map from the 1922 Corporate History of the B&O Railroad, © The B&O Railroad Museum, Inc., Collection.*

The B&O reached Martinsburg in 1842, and it quickly became a dining stop and railroad town with engine and machine shops. The shops shown here in 1872 are those that were rebuilt after the Civil War when Confederate forces destroyed the original ones. © *The B&O Railroad Museum, Inc., Collection.*

Cumberland was where the Baltimore and Ohio met the National Road, the C&O Canal, and coal. This stereoview, taken in the late 1870's, shows an engine roundhouse, with peaked roofs. *Wilgus Collection.*

The National Road *(above)*, the major highway between Baltimore and Wheeling, wound down off a hill east of Cumberland in this 1870's view, and then went west through the Narrows. *Wilgus Collection.*

The B&O built its first station *(opposite top)* in Cumberland in the 1840's next to a hotel where the National Road (Baltimore Street) crossed the tracks. When the trains stopped here in January 1853 on their way to Wheeling to open the line officially, the passengers dined at the Revere House. *The B&O Railroad Historical Society.*

A group of young miners is seen at the mouth of the Preston Mine *(opposite bottom)* near the state line in western Maryland in 1872. Economic development of the region's coal, iron, and lumber began with the railroad's arrival. © *The B&O Railroad Museum, Inc., Collection.*

The B&O's low coal rates were based on heavier and more powerful locomotives such as the Mud-digger, designed by Ross Winans. This engine may be the Cumberland, built by Winans in 1845. *Herbert H. Harwood, Jr.*

Ross Winans's earliest Camel engine appeared on the B&O in 1848. The celebrated Camels were the first coal-burning locomotives built in quantity for an American railroad. These were odd looking but ideal for hauling coal trains at slow speeds. Winans built hundreds of them for the B&O and affiliated lines. No. 80 was built in 1852 and photographed about 1866. © *The B&O Railroad Museum, Inc., Collection.*

Other B&O engines of this period were built by Matthias W. Baldwin of Philadelphia, such as his Dragon *(above)*, 1848, and by the New Castle Manufacturing Company of Delaware, whose 1848 Memnon *(overleaf)*, now in the B&O Railroad Museum, Baltimore, is the only original early American freight locomotive still in existence. *Herbert H. Harwood, Jr.*

The magnetic telegraph was first tested on the Washington branch on May 24, 1844, when Samuel F. B. Morse, from the Capitol, wired the famous "What hath God wrought?" message to his colleagues waiting in the B&O depot in Baltimore. *Circa 1864 photograph, National Portrait Gallery, Smithsonian Institution.*

19

Building on Promises

THE DECISION BY THE BALTIMORE AND OHIO RAILROAD
in November 1839 to issue its own scrip to finance the line from Harpers Ferry to
Cumberland meant that construction work, which had for some months been held
to a deliberately slow pace, could now move forward. There were 1,500 men and
a third as many horses spread out along the line. The approach was to undertake
the most difficult parts of the construction first. Despite holding back on the initial
work, there had been good progress on the embankments and tunnels, though not,
for some reason, on the bridges. Benjamin H. Latrobe, Jr., wanted the foundations
in before cold weather and the timber and iron assembled on the ground so that the
abutments and piers could be run up over the winter and the superstructures added
in the spring. At least, he wanted to see some activity on the part of the masonry
contractors. Most of them were from Pennsylvania.

There had been some effort at Opequon Creek, near Martinsburg, but Latrobe
informed Garvin & Johnson, the contractors there, "A more vigorous prosecution
of the work was & is expected from you." He went to Evitt's Creek, at Cumberland,
and wrote John Dougherty, "I found that no quarry had been opened or secured and
no step indeed of any kind taken for beginning the work upon the Bridge." To Henry
Wilton, of Wrightsville, the contractor for the viaduct over Patterson Creek, below
Cumberland, Latrobe wrote, "As neither you nor any person to represent you has
been on the ground since you were here and executed your contract early in August
last—I shall regard the work as relinquished unless I receive some assurance from
you to the contrary."[1]

Rather surprisingly, in view of the depressed economy, little labor violence was
reported on the railroad in 1839, the first year of construction. The worst riots took
place on the Maryland side of the Potomac at the C&O Canal's Paw Paw Tunnel,
where laborers had been burrowing into a slate ridge known as the Devil's Eyebrow
for three years and still were not through. The Paw Paw Tunnel was one of the main

reasons for the canal's impoverishment. It was 3,118 feet long, 24 feet in diameter, and 378 feet below the crest of the ridge. By cutting off two looping bends of the river, it saved five miles of heavy rock excavation. Crews were boring from both ends and using two vertical shafts to haul away the spoil. Work had started in June 1836 and was supposed to be done in two years at a cost of $33,500, but the rate of tunneling was much slower than expected and expenses had almost doubled over the contract prices.[2]

For three years, 1836–38, there had been annual riots on the canal; in 1838, when laborers threatened to destroy the work in a wage dispute at the tunnel, 130 troublemakers were blacklisted. More violence was brewing on the line in the summer of 1839 among the Irish laborers, Welsh miners, and German masons. A Baltimore correspondent who toured the canal and the railroad in August said the canal contractors at Fifteen Mile Creek were threatening to strike, claiming their estimates had been "doctored," and he quoted an unnamed engineer as saying that the C&O's new board of directors had not been able to breathe new life into "this superannuated piece of absurdity."[3] That month, the canal workers exploded. The Irish, their brains glowing with ancient hatreds, went on a rampage armed with several hundred rifles and pistols supplemented by a shipment of 50 large duck guns from Baltimore. They beat several Germans to death, killing one by throwing him into a fire. Charles B. Fisk, Latrobe's friend and counterpart on the Chesapeake and Ohio, called out the militia from Cumberland to bring the rioters under control.

In five days, during which the militiamen tramped through 81 miles of this lonely and isolated region, they knocked down 50 shanties, stove in as many barrels of whiskey, destroyed 200 firearms, and brought in 30 new rifles and muskets found at the bluff ten miles below Cumberland, along with 27 ringleaders, whom they lodged in the Cumberland jail. At the trial held at the end of September, there were almost 100 witnesses. Of the 20 tried, 14 were convicted and sentenced to jail terms, partly through the testimony of a labor spy named James Finney.[4]

A reporter for the Cumberland *Phoenix Civilian* wrote an account of the troubles:

> A fruitful source of all the outrages on the line of canal, is the existence of associations or banded confederations amongst the laborers called "Connoughtmen," "Longfords," "Fardowns," and "Corkmen." Each of these associations deserve no other name than a lawless Banditti.—They are banded together with pledges of brotherhood and have their secret signs and passwords. The "Connoughtmen" and "Longfords" are now and have been at war with each other, and with the most determined hostility. At a moment's warning, a leader will march, perhaps with 100 men, and in the most lawless manner, attack any of the other party, or any inoffending citizen against whom any prejudice exists, and assault them with guns, pickaxes or clubs sparing neither age nor sex, and burning and destroying stores, dwellings and shantees.

The troops confiscated the Connaughts' printed passwords and countersigns and the Cumberland press provided a sample:

Q. The winter is favorable.
A. So is friendship increasing.
Q. True Connoughtmen is valient.
A. Yes, and never will be defeated.
Quarreling Words
Q. That Connoughtmen may be steady.
A. And they will be respected.
Pass Words
Q. That all Connoughtmen may be nice.
A. Yes, without they may meet their enemies.[5]

After the riots died down, the Cumberland newspapers revived them as a political issue focusing on C&O Canal president Francis Thomas, Democratic candidate for Congress. When the Democratic *Alleganian* accused the Whig *Civilian* of running guest editorials, Whig editor Samuel Charles denied it. He had no such concerns about the *Alleganian*, he said—their editorials were so bad the editor must have written them.

As the 1839 construction season drew to a close, Benjamin H. Latrobe, Jr., toured the line with chief engineer Jonathan Knight, a resident engineer, and an important new addition to the staff, John Rudolph Niernsee. Niernsee, an amorous Austrian with a flamboyant mustache, was a Vienna-trained engineer who had emigrated to the United States the previous year. His first job on a southern railroad survey ended after six months; he then made his way to New York, where he anxiously searched for work. "No money . . . no income, no position and on top of it, in love again!" he scribbled in his diary. "I don't know what to do. I run around like a madman. But it does no good. I can't hunt down a single penny . . . I . . . am about to starve. I am thinking of powder and lead."[6] Fortunately, a job offer from Washington intervened. Bidding his "American beauty" good-bye in Manhattan, Niernsee boarded a train for the trip to the capital, and when he was laid off from that job in a month, Latrobe took him on, in August 1839, as official draftsman and office engineer for the Baltimore and Ohio Railroad.[7] Latrobe and the other three engineers went from Baltimore by rail in open cars with their horses. At Harpers Ferry they mounted up and spent the next four days in the saddle until they got to Cumberland. At the B&O's Doe Gully Tunnel, a couple of river bends downstream from the Paw Paw Tunnel, the railroad laborers were blasting their way through the red and green shale and sandstone.

Construction at Harpers Ferry, the last section of the new railroad to be put under contract, started early in 1840. The final arrangements brought to a close a year and a half of negotiations with the Winchester and Potomac Railroad and the federal government. The W&P Railroad's route left Harpers Ferry via the Shenandoah. The federal government owned the land at the arsenal, on the Potomac. Although the Baltimore and Ohio could have taken either alignment, in typical fashion it grasped simultaneously for both. The W&P Railroad offered to sell six miles of their line, leading out of town, for $150,000 and the B&O's board of directors, in September 1838, approved. There was some resistance on the part of the federal government, but Latrobe gained the confidence of the Inspector General and the superintendent of the arsenal by offering to construct an independent wall in the river to help support the tracks. This idea won out.[8]

Twice rebuffed, the Winchester and Potomac Railroad thereafter made things difficult for the B&O at Harpers Ferry. In October 1838, McLane personally obtained permission from War Secretary Joel Poinsett to cross the federal property. Six months later, the railroad was still vacillating between the two routes. It finally selected the one that was not only cheaper but also better suited for a depot, which would be built on filled land between the arsenal and the Potomac. The massive and handsome masonry wall began to rise in February 1840.[9]

As work on the railroad gathered momentum, the Chesapeake and Ohio Canal ground to a halt, its finances in disarray, its hopes near collapse. The $250,000 in scrip the company had issued to pay its bills had been unwelcome for some time. Francis Thomas, the embattled C&O president, looked in vain for new friends. As a Democratic congressman from Maryland who opposed paper currency, he had flooded his own district with "the very worst kind of shinplasters: if notes of . . . five dollars and not payable on presentation, can be called Shin plasters," the Frederick *Herald* reminded its readers.[10] Even the Washington *National Intelligencer*, the canal's most unwavering admirer, found the task overwhelming. The editors eagerly reported that the C&O had sold enough bonds in London to pay off its debts and have money left over to redeem its scrip, but there was still the fact of the company's credit. "Since that has failed, nothing that I could say would, I fear, have much effect," Francis Thomas said. He added that the C&O Canal did not plan to issue more scrip and would suspend construction.[11]

Cumberland, still skeptical of the efficiency of rail transport of coal, welcomed the project, "because the completion of the Canal will develop all our rich treasures."[12] Thomas acknowledged that the company would be unable to pay the interest on its loans unless it received more financial aid from the legislature; in fact, Thomas said, "The whole yearly income of the Canal Company does not exceed $50,000," and double that amount had been spent on salaries and repairs in 1839.[13] By comparison, the railroad had grossed close to $450,000 that year and its net revenues were $69,000. Thomas admitted that the canal had made interest payments from the proceeds of the sale of the Maryland bonds issued for construction, a repeat of its performance with the 1835 state loan of $2 million. A canal appropriation bill passed the Maryland House of Delegates that session but failed in the Senate. The Cumberland *Civilian* blamed Francis Thomas.

It was in this fiscal climate that the railroad began to issue its own stock orders, or scrip, in February 1840. The B&O hired four people to help McLane sign the first $100,000 worth. "I am gratified to say that despite the Gov's denunciations, our stock orders pass most freely," Benjamin H. Latrobe, Jr., told Knight. "The contractors take them gladly and the Banks are eager to get the dollar notes—The fives also pass well. . . . I now anticipate a ready & extensive circulation of this currency, whose security from the risk attending Bank paper, seems generally appreciated and to compensate for its irredeemability in coin."[14] The B&O readied a further issue of $100,000 in $2 and $3 notes. When the contractors complained about the inconvenience and lost time in coming to Baltimore to receive their monthly payrolls, McLane sent the scrip out to Martinsburg and Cumberland for distribution.

The heavy construction had continued despite the severe winter weather. There were now plenty of laborers, but Latrobe thought some of the Pennsylvania bridge contractors were still not moving ahead fast enough. For example, Charles Odell, a willing manager, was hampered by two sets of partners, one of whom worked while the other did not. After nine unsuccessful months of alternate threats and compliments to both groups, Latrobe annulled all their contracts and put their work on four bridges "into hands, in which it will be carried on with sufficient rapidity to make up for lost time." [15] Yet out of 150 construction contracts, the company had to re-let only seven because of neglect or misconduct.

Maryland and Pennsylvania interests—to some extent B&O competitors—completed two projects in the spring of 1840: the Baltimore and Susquehanna Railroad was extended from York, Pennsylvania, to Wrightsville, on the Susquehanna, and the Tidewater Canal was opened from there to Havre de Grace on the southwestern bank, completing the long-awaited connection with Pennsylvania's Main Line of Internal Improvements. These facilities opened new avenues for trade between the Susquehanna River and Baltimore.

In the city, the B&O had its first strike that summer, as a result of the company's attempt to withhold the back wages of workers who had been fired for negligence. The strike, which began July 23, was peaceful, but it did disrupt train service for several days. Accidents due to culpable negligence had been on the rise and firing the offending workers had not solved the problem. McLane recited a threnody of costly mistakes in the operation of the trains. In one, he said, a rope left dangling from a stone hoist at trackside broke a passenger's arm. In another, the coaches were thrown off by a loose rail when an employee failed to do his job. (Loose rails, or "snakeheads," were a particular hazard; they were known to curl up and spear through the bottoms of the wooden cars, creating havoc inside and halting the train, much the way snags and sawyers could impale and sink a river steamboat.) In a third accident, the agent at Relay ignored a crossed switch and derailed a train. After the last, "the individual guilty of such gross negligence was dismissed but became immediately employed in the vicinity of the road, and at equal wages, and in fact declared that his discharge put him to no inconvenience," said the frustrated B&O president. [16] Enginemen routinely set fences, barns, and the woods on fire through carelessness, McLane continued, and they crashed into one another with alarming frequency, usually as a result of excess speed. Most of these avoidable accidents produced claims for damages.

Since firing the workers whose mistakes could prove fatal seemed to have no effect, McLane thought that forfeiting their back wages might. He reasoned, correctly it seems, that poor men would be more concerned with collecting a few weeks' pay than in keeping their jobs. The lawyers prepared a contract authorizing the company to dismiss employees and retain their pay in cases of loss from neglect or inattention. Only those in positions of responsibility were expected to sign it. Many department heads, clerks and depot agents, and train conductors and brakemen did sign, but others refused, and on Monday, July 13, James Murray, who had been made machinery and repairs supervisor, and William S. Woodside, superintendent of transportation, informed McLane that they had been unable to collect all the signatures and that the contract was opposed. The workmen had various reasons for not signing: "It was stated that some objected to the forfeiture of wages under any circumstances,—some to forfeiture when the neglect was unintentional,—some required that the question of neglect should be submitted to arbitration, and be matter of proof pro and con—and many who were not required to sign the agreement objected to working under the immediate orders of anyone who did sign it."[17]

The workmen's representative, Zeigler, the machine shop foreman, was a good example of the situation the railroad executive was trying to correct. Testing a new engine on one occasion, Zeigler had violated orders and run into a burden (freight) train. He did not object when the company withheld the amount of repairs from his wages. Another time, after fixing an engine, he forgot to fill the boiler with water before firing it up and ruined the tubes. When Zeigler met with McLane to discuss the matter of signing the contract, he at first said that although he would like to sign, he had overcommitted himself with the men and could not retract his statements. McLane gave him and the workers until the end of the month to decide. Zeigler said they did not need any more time, and since he refused to sign the agreement, he quit. Zeigler then returned to the shops and convinced the workmen to walk off their jobs. They did so the next morning. After they prevented the evening mail train from leaving Mt. Clare for Washington, McLane called out the police.

The Baltimore *Sun* reported that it was a general strike: "But no act of violence was committed, and when the police arrived at the depot, they found nothing to do.—The men had simply ceased to work, and had betaken themselves to Hollins street market, to adopt peaceable measures of resistance against a demand deemed by them unjust."[18] The next day, McLane convinced some of the men to operate their trains and sent to Philadelphia for more enginemen. The strike was broken. Railroad operations soon returned to normal. Most of the strikers signed a simpler but equally comprehensive contract and went back to work unconditionally. McLane refused to negotiate with strikers who wanted their jobs back on their terms. The strike leaders were fired.

McLane had meanwhile begun preliminary discussions with the Barings in London to exchange some of the Maryland sterling bonds for the iron rails to be laid down to Cumberland. Although the price of iron was down to $39 a ton because of slack demand, the Barings counseled against disposing of the bonds "in the present flat state of our Market," preferring instead to advance the cash to buy the rails pending an eventual bond sale.[19] In that year's annual report, McLane was optimistic about the state of the railroad: construction was moving ahead at Harpers Ferry, the deep cuts at North Mountain were proceeding well, the Doe Gully Tunnel was over a third finished and "more than a moiety" was completed on its smaller companion at Paw Paw, and the bridge masonry along the entire line was at last "advancing as rapidly as can be desired."[20] McLane's fiscal analysis was equally optimistic. The construction from Harpers Ferry to Cumberland was being financed by bank loans ($500,000), scrip ($515,000), direct payment of city stock to contractors ($139,000), and sale of the Maryland 5 percent sterling bonds held by the Barings ($22,000). The last were sold in early 1840 at 85, leaving the rest of the bonds held by the Barings untouched, and there was no intention to use them, McLane said. The company paid its small dividend that year in stock orders and foreign bank notes.

The stock orders, or scrip, McLane said, would advance the railroad, protect Baltimore's credit, and keep the city from paying interest, as long as they remained unfunded. Of the $515,00 in stock orders issued, just $10,000 worth, or 2 percent, had been funded, that is, redeemed in city stock. He advised the municipality to seek state approval of the system. The scrip did not violate any law, because it was not real currency:

> The orders do not promise to pay money, nor, indeed, are they, in any respect, promissory in their character. They confer an absolute authority for the transfer of City Stock. . . . They, in fact, represent City certificates, though in smaller denominations; and in the requisite sums, may be funded, and converted into coin or bank paper, at the pleasure of the holder. They are, therefore, not liable to the risk, or any other objection to which irresponsible paper issues, professing to pay money, are exposed.[21]

The Baltimore banks, perhaps as confused as anyone, called on the company to pay off the city's loans, executed on a pledge of the city stock, which had been issued to pay Baltimore's subscription to the B&O Railroad. The B&O merely referred the banks back to the municipal finance commissioners. Governor Grason believed that the B&O and other corporations that issued scrip had no authority to do so. In his address to the legislature in January 1841 he said, as he had said before, that "shinplasters" were injurious to the public and prevented the circulation of specie, and Maryland was now running a deficit of more than $600,000. Grason said little about the B&O Railroad, other than that it probably would not add to the deficit, but he was frank about the Chesapeake and Ohio: "The canal is not only unfinished, but the company are without the means of continuing their operations. The debt, contracted for their use, is a dead weight on the state, and so it will remain till the whole line of canal is opened to Cumberland." He saw little hope of devising any practical scheme for continuing the work because the state was without the means of raising money for that purpose, and "it would appear to be a desperate expenditure to send a new set of bonds into the European market."[22]

The railroad requested and the General Assembly passed a state law allowing Maryland banks to receive and pay out the B&O stock orders. The company was not to issue more scrip than the amount of the stock turned over to them by the city, and for any violations under the law, the officers "shall be individually responsible to the full extent of their private fortunes."[23] The City of Baltimore passed similar legislation to receive railroad scrip in payment of local taxes and to pay its own bills with the same medium. Under prodding by the city council, the B&O decided to issue stock orders of smaller denominations than $1; they did so, down to a nickel.

The Maryland legislature's major accomplishment, at an extra session in 1841, was to enact a state property tax of 20 cents per $100 of assessed valuation, which was supposed to add half a million dollars a year to the state treasury. At the same session, the Chesapeake and Ohio Canal managed to convince the General Assembly one more time to appropriate $2 million to finish the work to Cumberland. And once again, it jettisoned the incompetents on the board of directors and brought in a new slate. In spite of the financial problems of the previous season, the C&O had managed to hole through the Paw Paw tunnel, and so, for a time, the canal lurched forward.

On the B&O, construction in April 1841 had progressed to the point where they could order the iron. The company wanted 8,014 tons of bridge rails, shaped like an inverted U. This was a total of 52,800 bars, each 20 feet long and weighing 340 pounds, or 51 pounds to the yard. Latrobe had thought earlier that the 15-foot, 300-pound H-rails used to rebuild the Old Main Line were about as much as the workmen could handle. Half the rails were to be delivered between July and November 1841, at a rate of 800 tons a month, and the rest were to be shipped starting in March 1842. McLane sent the Barings a full-sized drawing of the rail as well as a mahogany model. "I must ask your particular attention to have the iron well made, of a good quality, and sent to us in good condition," he wrote.[24] The Barings were to advance the sum of roughly $280,000 to pay for the rails. McLane hoped they would not have to sell the Maryland bonds at a loss to do so.

In May 1841, the Barings ordered 4,000 tons of rails from Thompson & Forman at $35 a ton—a low price—with an option to acquire the remainder in September at the same figure. But despite McLane's specific instructions, the iron that began to arrive that fall produced the usual complaints about size and quality. A civil engineer was appointed to inspect the rails before they left England. Not finding a better price, the Barings exercised the option to buy the remaining 4,014 tons from the same supplier. Joshua Bates, the Barings' American partner, passed through Baltimore at about this time on a grand tour of the Baring Brothers & Co.'s investments. He liked what he saw. "Dear Mildmay," he wrote his London partner, "While the railroad is only finished . . . about 70 miles, the route is so much the nearest to Ohio that every body takes it and the cars yesterday contained 300 or 400 people for Wheeling. . . . When the whole line is open, New York must suffer for the whole travelling to and from the West will be on this road."[25]

Out on the line, as the pace of construction quickened, the expenses rose to $100,000 a month, the same amount the canal had been spending a few years earlier. Latrobe still pursued a few malingering contractors, but there were no more intentional slowdowns because of tight money. Latrobe informed a Harford County lumber supplier, "On the score of payment there will be no difficulty—You cannot send it too fast."[26] Contracts were awarded for laying the rails between Harpers Ferry and Cumberland.

Just as the first 800 tons of British rails were being delivered on the pier in Baltimore in the fall of 1841, Congress began considering a duty on railroad iron. McLane dispatched a trio of lobbyists to Washington to seek an exemption for the B&O.

His more serious financial concern was that Maryland was about to suspend interest payments on the state bonds held by the Barings. The state's debt of over $15 million, almost all of it due to internal improvements, required an annual interest payment of $600,000. Maryland received almost no help from most of the internal improvement companies and hardly any at all from the C&O Canal, which had paid very little of the interest owed on its lion's share of the bonds. Since almost all the B&O's portion of the securities remained with the Barings unsold, its interest payments, although remitted, were of minor consequence. The Maryland property tax was supposed to make up the difference, but because the tax was proving uncollectible, there was a deficit.

McLane convened a special meeting of the board of directors to see whether there was any way the B&O could help the state. They discussed lending the railroad's net profits or advancing the dividend due Maryland for 1842. The B&O charter prevented the former, however, and the state treasurer rejected the latter course. Railroad scrip was the subject at an especially contentious board meeting in October 1841. John White, the city director, succeeded in imposing a $1.5 million limit on the issue of stock orders and requiring the City of Baltimore to pay the remainder of its B&O subscription in "bankable paper." The directors declared a dividend of 6 percent on the Washington Branch and 2 percent on the Main Stem.

McLane in his 1841 annual report assured the stockholders that the graduation, masonry, and bridging of the line from Harpers Ferry to Cumberland would be finished in a few months. Ten miles of timber had been laid down ready to receive the rails, and they were arching the tunnels, that is, lining them with brick, at Doe Gully and Paw Paw Ridge. As for the railroad scrip, McLane maintained that the stock orders had benefited the city and the public more than the railroad. Some $1,450,000 worth was then in circulation, and less than one percent had been redeemed in city stock. Although the orders were secure, the company was still worried about depreciation and had decided to stop issuing scrip, McLane said, but in the meantime, the B&O, like the city, would regard the notes as legal tender in the payment of debts. He promised that no matter how much the stock orders declined in value, the company would continue to redeem them at par: "Any loss which may, in this way, be sustained by the company, it is not doubted will be cheerfully borne in consideration of the vast advantages which, by the early completion of the work, will be conferred, not only upon the stockholders, but upon every citizen of the community."[27]

The public was not so confident. People became agitated over the scrip at public meetings in Baltimore and Virginia. McLane did his best to reassure everyone. Then on November 27, 1841, John S. Gittings, of the Maryland Loan Office in Baltimore, wrote to Baring Brothers & Co., London: "I regret that it is not in my power to remit by the Boston steamer the balance of exchange necessary to meet the interest due at your Banking House in the 1st of Jany upon the Bonds of the State."[28] And so Maryland suspended interest payments on its debt. It did not resume them until January 1848.

The City of Baltimore, too, was having trouble meeting its commitments. The railroad decided to demand the unpaid remainder of the city's $3 million stock subscription in monthly installments, borrowing money in the interim to pay the contractors. By December of 1841, the B&O's stock orders were being discounted in Baltimore at 12 to 14 percent. In their final act of the year, the B&O directors voted to turn over the whole matter of the stock orders to the city. Baltimore's response was to authorize a $500,000 loan to redeem an equal amount of railroad scrip. The city council passed another ordinance that would allow the municipality, after receiving its $60,000 dividend from the B&O, to give it back to the company as part of the installment on its stock subscription, thus providing funds for construction.

These convoluted finances were the subject of Governor Grason's January 1842 message to the legislature. This time, he was particularly critical of the B&O scrip: "This scheme has enabled the rail road company to dispose of city stock, to the amount of [$1.5 million] at its par value; and to transfer to the holders of their certificates the risk and loss, which they were not willing to encounter themselves of selling it in the market." Grason thought that the city and the railroad were the beneficiaries of the stock orders, but Marylanders wanted the return of specie payments, which the banks should be compelled to resume: "These [stock] orders are fast reaching the point of depression, at which they will cease to be a currency," he warned.[29] The governor laid the blame for Maryland's fiscal embarrassment squarely on the $7 million in state subscriptions and loans to the Chesapeake and Ohio Canal on which no interest would be paid until the canal reached Cumberland. The Baltimore and Susquehanna Railroad had started to pay interest on its $1 million state loan, but the Tidewater Canal, recipient of an equal amount, had not.

Maryland was one of the first to reject the B&O scrip when the state treasurer, a month after Governor Grason's speech, declined to receive the bonus from the Washington Branch in stock orders. In early March 1842 the shinplasters were being discounted in Baltimore at more than 25 percent. A lumber supplier said he could not continue deliveries "unless they are paid in such currency as their hands will receive and that Rail Road orders are not current with them etc."[30] When the B&O tried to pay its own employees in scrip, several workmen at Mt. Clare refused to accept it; they were fired, but then the board rescinded the rule. Finally, the railroad itself repudiated the stock orders, declaring that nothing "but funds current in Baltimore" would be acceptable for travel and transportation on the Baltimore and Ohio. This decision resulted from the resumption of specie payments by Maryland banks and a series of city and state laws aimed at removing the B&O scrip from circulation. But printing the shinplasters was easy compared with getting rid of them.

Many, like John M. Gordon, president of the Union Bank, considered the railroad scrip a "vile currency." Gordon was present at a meeting of Baltimore bankers when McLane asked them to redeem the depreciated stock orders in specie. Gordon recalled, "I told him that, as he had raised the devil, he might lay him, at which remark he became very much offended and never spoke to me afterwards." Gordon believed that the greatest burden of the depreciated scrip, which eventually fell to 50 percent of its face value, was borne by the laborers and shopkeepers who were stuck with the greatest amount of it.[31] Laws that authorized state banks to deal in railroad stock orders and the city to receive them in payment of taxes and debts were repealed, and the Maryland General Assembly further prohibited any state-chartered company from issuing notes intended to serve as currency.

The Baltimore city council, in a perverse move, decided to issue some itself. The city claimed in one of its ordinances that it had sustained the credit of the railroad scrip, implying that the state and the company had reaped the rewards. Baltimore now offered a 25 percent premium, payable in city scrip, to anyone who would pay cash for the B&O stock orders (up to $500,000 worth), trade them in for city stock, and show proof of the transaction. The city scrip could be used to pay taxes and debts. The first section of the law ended with the language, "The scrip to be issued on the presentation of the certificates of the amount funded, from the commissioners holding the stock for the redemption of the stock orders of the Baltimore and Ohio Rail Road Company."[32] People actually followed this incredibly complex roundelay of paper, involving currency, city and railroad scrip, and City of Baltimore stock, much of it of dubious value. Gradually, the B&O stock orders were removed from circulation.

McLane was absent from the board meetings with a kidney infection for all of March 1842, as his B&O scrip sank to a 35 percent discount in Baltimore. The chief engineer, Jonathan Knight, resigned to go back to the family farm in Pennsylvania and pursue a career as a consulting engineer and congressman. Knight received the usual encomium from the directors. Benjamin H. Latrobe, Jr., took over as chief engineer.[33]

Knight's last act was to issue a report, rife with figures, on freight and passenger traffic, both of which were down as a result of the depression and stiff competition from the National Road, the C&O Canal, and the new connections with the Pennsylvania improvements. The decline in passengers was due specifically to "the Franklin Rail Road connecting the Turnpike Road at Hagerstown, with Philadelphia, by way of the Pennsylvania Rail Roads," Knight said.[34] Knight recommended reduced rates to encourage business, according to the principles of *The Laws of Trade*, by Charles Ellet, Jr., an 1839 publication that had impressed him. Knight predicted, correctly, that all that was lost would be regained and then some once the railroad reached Hancock and Cumberland.

McLane returned after his illness to a company under great pressure from the city directors to cut salaries and positions. The officers at first felt this was a good idea, except when it came to themselves, and so the demand for retrenchment produced an abundance of information on employees and operations, culminating in spirited claims that the railroad was already being run as efficiently as possible. In the end, only one man, who had been in charge of the stock orders, was found expendable. The jobs, salaries, and duties of every employee were enumerated. Latrobe and Murray convincingly reported that the Baltimore and Ohio was operated at a lower cost than five other comparable railroads, and they implied that when it reached Cumberland, net revenues would double. McLane, stung by a recommendation from city director and traditional B&O antagonist James Carroll, Jr., that his president's salary should be reduced from $6,000 to $4,000 a year, issued a rejoinder defending his administration. Carroll later relented.

From the "wreck" that the B&O had been when he took it over in 1837, McLane asserted that in five years he had remade it into an efficient railroad: "Every branch of the service is in the best condition; the Road is in better state than it ever was before . . . and a larger amount of business is annually done, and at a reduced expense." Furthermore, these accomplishments took place "during a period of unparalleled stagnation and disorder, in which most other public works have been suspended, [while] the Baltimore and Ohio Rail Road has been prosecuted with the most gratifying success." McLane also pointed out that wages on the B&O were already lower than those on other railroads and that further reductions in personnel would endanger the public. "Why, under such circumstances it should be publicly attempted to retrench still further in all the departments without reference to the general economy of the service, it is difficult to conjecture," he concluded.[35]

The campaign to economize was forgotten in the excitement as the railroad reached Martinsburg, Virginia, on May 21, 1842.[36] The Martinsburg militia, whose members were engaged in a drill when the first train arrived, dropped their rifles and rushed off to witness the great event. The editor of the local *Gazette*, who had waited patiently for this moment, reported: "The engine and train came at dashing pace, smoking, whistling, and thundering through the hills up to the Pillar Bridge. A steam engine is a queer thing at best, but the appearance of one among the Opequon hills is a bit of an epoch."[37] The experimental trip to Martinsburg consisted of a short train with a single passenger car. Nine days later, an official train consisting of three coaches carrying the company officers, the mayor and city councilmen, and others, left Baltimore to open the line to Hancock. Not much happened when they got to Hancock—the railroad was across the river from the town and the real celebration was planned at Cumberland in the fall—but the whole town of Martinsburg turned out to greet them. They stopped and had dinner there on the way up and stayed overnight there on the return trip.

It is unclear why the railroad avoided a connection with the National Road at Hancock, where they might easily have recaptured the eastbound turnpike passengers they were losing at Hagerstown to the Franklin Railroad, and Philadelphia. The Baltimore and Ohio recommended a ferry or ford across the Potomac instead of a bridge. But the stagecoach lines that formerly ran from Frederick to Wheeling and Pittsburgh shifted their operations to Hancock anyway and cut ten hours from the trip to the west. The journey from Baltimore to Wheeling then took 41 hours— seven hours to go 123 miles to Hancock by train and 34 hours in a stagecoach for the remaining 173-mile trip. Later on in the summer of 1842, Lucius W. Stockton's stage company reduced the highway time by half, and it was possible, though not usual, to make the trip from Baltimore to Wheeling in just 24 hours.

This route soon became known as the Great Central Route. A traveler could go from the Chesapeake Bay to the Ohio River for $13, with meals at 37 and a half cents each. New York and Philadelphia investors planned to make it the centerpiece of a freight line that stretched from Boston to Wheeling and beyond, flanked by Eastern railroads and Ohio River steamboats. Travel to the west doubled, hotels and warehouses sprang up in Martinsburg and Cumberland, and the challenge was to finish the line before the money gave out. The railroad brought legal action to force the City of Baltimore to pay the rest of its stock subscription in cash. But eventually they compromised. The company agreed to accept the balance in city stock and use its own net revenues to get the rest of the way to Cumberland.

Because Maryland's suspension of interest payments made the sterling bonds almost worthless in the marketplace, the Barings refused to ship the second batch of iron rails unless the B&O found another way to pay for them. Through the Barings' American agent, Thomas Wren Ward of Boston, McLane arranged to pay back the advances at the rate of $50,000 a year for seven years, at 6 percent interest, from the railroad's net revenues. The Barings renewed the shipments, and 24 hours after landing on the wharf at the City Block in Baltimore, the iron was at the end of the line beyond Hancock, where the track crews laid it down at the rate of one mile a day.

The company, "in the present state of their finances," could not afford a public ceremony after they reached their destination. They would therefore offer politicians and stockholders one free ride apiece from Baltimore, McLane decreed in October 1842. His pride in the construction of 97 miles of railroad at a cost of $3,450,000, "during a period of unparalleled disaster in the monetary affairs of the country," illuminated his annual report that year. The report ended on an inspirational note: "Great enterprises are always attended with great difficulties, only to be overcome by persevering energy and unwavering fortitude."[38]

The first train to arrive in Cumberland left the Pratt Street depot in Baltimore at 7:00 A.M., November 3, 1842. The president, directors, and their guests were aboard, 30 to 40 passengers in all. For the first time, "the inhabitants of the wild regions of the Allegheny beheld a train of cars drawn by a smoking locomotive among their hills," a Baltimore correspondent wrote.[39] Crossing to the Virginia side of the river at Harpers Ferry, the train proceeded on trestles supported by stone piers and cast-iron columns and a massive stone wall, 1,700 feet long, that separated the armory from the rocky Potomac. A mile and a half above town, the train left the river by a 90-foot tunnel through a rock spur to follow Elk Run to the west. Two miles before Martinsburg, it passed 44 feet over Opequon Creek on a 165-foot-long wood and stone viaduct. The most striking bridge on the new line was the next one, the Pillar or Colonnade Bridge, crossing Tuscarora Creek into Martinsburg. It was 400 feet long, with a wooden covered superstructure like those at Elysville, supported on sixteen paired limestone columns in the Doric mode, each eighteen feet high and five feet in diameter. The bridge saved the expense of an embankment.[40]

At Robbins Gap, the train entered North Mountain via an excavation 1,500 feet long and 63 feet deep that had been blasted through a composite of shale, limestone, and fossil shells. After passing through a couple of short tunnels, it emerged from a smaller cut, 300 feet long and 75 feet deep, on the other side, into a wild, unsettled region with some of the most rugged scenery on the line to Cumberland. The line continued along a huge embankment, almost a third of a mile in length, over the floor of the valley to Back Creek, and crossed this on the only all-stone bridge on the new line, 230 feet long and 54 feet high, containing a single semicircular limestone arch of 80-foot span. On the far side, a bare, dark, forbidding set of cliffs fell away in a flat arc toward the Potomac.[41]

Proceeding over Sleepy Creek on a 240-foot viaduct, the train passed Hancock and entered a singular landscape of alternating high, steep, curving ridges, dotted with pine groves and waterfalls that pushed the tracks close to the river's shore and occasional broad bottomlands at some of the intervening creeks. There were no towns before Cumberland.

Round Top appeared, a distinctive landmark on the opposite side of the Potomac, and just beyond the 400-foot bridge over the green and slow-moving Great Cacapon was dam no. 6, the termination of the operating section of the Chesapeake and Ohio Canal. Past the gap at Sideling Hill, the cars went dark briefly in the tunnel at Doe Gully, 1,200 feet long, 21 feet in diameter, 110 feet below the summit. It was being lined with brick. The tunnel faces were finished with white sandstone from a nearby mountain. This tunnel marked the entrance to the largest of the Potomac bends. The line cut off the first, swept around the second and two more smaller bends, and emerged through another tunnel at Paw Paw. This one was 250 feet long, curved horizontally through a hill of soft slate with a radius of 750 feet, about 7.5 degrees. The tunnel was completely arched with brick and was fronted with white sandstone.

Beyond the flats of the Little Cacapon, crossed by a 143-foot viaduct, cloud shadows raced like rivers down Town Hill, and on the other side of the 400-foot bridge over the South Branch of the Potomac, patches of gauzy mist, heralding winter, blew over the finest and most extensive bottomlands on the route opposite Oldtown. Now the passengers could see the mountains at Cumberland. The Patterson's Creek viaduct was next, 150 feet, and less than two miles beyond it, the longest bridge on the line, 700 feet, over the Potomac proper and back into Maryland.

There was one final bridge to cross, of 100 feet, over Evitt's Creek. About 5:00 P.M., the train pulled through the crowd of spectators and musicians to the Cumberland depot at the National Road. All day, business had been suspended awaiting the train. McLane and several other directors left almost immediately in Thomas Shriver's bow-spring stagecoaches to visit the mines near Frostburg. Others went to Will's Gap, "The Narrows," a scenic and romantic spot above town.

Regular passenger travel to Cumberland began a week later. "Here at Last," Cumberland editor Samuel Charles headlined his newspaper article, and for once he did not mention the Chesapeake and Ohio Canal at all.[42]

20

Cumberland Coal and Iron

WITH THE APPEARANCE OF THE FIRST LOCOMOTIVE
in Cumberland in 1842, the three major ingredients of the industrial revolution, coal, iron, and the steam engine, came together at the most westerly point that had yet been reached by an American railroad. But Cumberland had had its hopes set on the canal, the Baltimore and Ohio was reluctant to invest heavily in an undeveloped industry, and the mining companies, the earliest of which had organized in 1828, had grown tired of waiting. Yet as coal started flowing and iron furnaces began producing, Cumberland, like Harpers Ferry before it, became an industrial center.

Ten years before the first train arrived, the residents of Cumberland numbered a little over 1,000. Less than ten years after, there were more than 6,000. In one eighteen-month period, the population doubled. New hotels, mills, and warehouses appeared along Baltimore and Mechanic streets, near the stage and railroad depots. On the other side of Wills Creek, away from the tracks, the stately homes of the merchants began their march over the top of the Washington Street hill. At mid-century, Horace Greeley said, "Cumberland is destined to become one of the largest inland towns in America, a rival of Pittsburgh and Lowell."[1]

Certainly the site was impressive. Cumberland was located in a pleasant valley circled by wooded hills where a loop of the Potomac River pushed the Maryland border almost as far north as it was at Hancock. Cumberland was spread out in an arc around the tip of the loop, where the Potomac was joined by Wills Creek descending from the north through the spectacular Narrows of Wills Mountain. Will, for whom the creek and mountain were named, was a friendly Shawnee who lingered to welcome the whites after the rest of his tribe deserted their village and fled westward. The Indians called the creek and the place Caiuctucuc. The Ohio Company built a trading post there in 1750 to which fortifications were added. A year later, Nemacolin, another agreeable native, helped Thomas Cresap survey one of the first roads over the mountains to the confluence of the Monongahela and Allegheny rivers. George Washington's small force improved the road during the first campaign of the French and Indian War in 1754, and in 1755 British General Edward Braddock and his troops turned it into a military road over which Braddock led the nation's first wagon train west to his fatal rendezvous at Fort Duquesne. Braddock named the installation at Wills Creek Fort Cumberland for the Duke of Cumberland. When his ill-fated expedition, which included Washington and Daniel Boone, left the fort, some of the troops followed Cresap and Nemacolin's path straight west over Wills Mountain. Others took the lower and easier route through the Narrows. Washington's military experience convinced him of the importance of the Potomac route to the West. The natural passageway into the mountains through the Narrows was subsequently chosen by the National Road and, much later, by the Baltimore and Ohio Railroad.

In 1774, when Lord Baltimore opened the lands west of Cumberland for settlement, the first to arrive were squatters, like John Friend, who established himself at the mouth of Bear Creek (Friendsville). After the Revolution, soldier lots, 50-acre tracts granted by Congress, were distributed to men who had fought in the war. In the early nineteenth century, the town of Cumberland began to serve the local farmers as a market center, just as the fort had sustained the nearby settlers when Indian marauders menaced the frontier in the aftermath of Braddock's disastrous encounter with the French. Cumberland was incorporated in 1815. In 1820, James Finley bridged turbulent Wills Creek with a wrought-iron chain bridge of more than 100-foot span. Finley's patented structures were America's first suspension bridges.

The federal government created the greatest potential impact on the local economy when it authorized a National Road from Cumberland to the vicinity of Wheeling in 1806. The controversial selection of Cumberland as the starting point, which favored Baltimore over Richmond and Philadelphia, was influenced by Maryland Senator Sam Smith. The congressional committee that reported the bill brilliantly paraphrased Washington's concept of consolidating a disparate population through domestic trade:

> Politicians have generally agreed that rivers unite the interests and promote the friendship of those who inhabit their banks; while mountains, on the contrary, tend to disunion and estrangement of those who are separated by their intervention. In the present case, to make the crooked ways straight, and the rough ways smooth will, in effect, remove the intervening mountains, and by facilitating the intercourse of our western brethren with those of the Atlantic, substantially unite them in interest, which, the committee believe, is the most effectual cement of union applicable to the human race.[2]

Political arguments over the terminus and a lack of funds delayed matters, but it was at last agreed that the route would start by following Braddock's Road and then veer off to Wheeling. Construction began at Cumberland in 1811 under superintendent James Shriver. It was finished seven years later. The 130 miles to Wheeling cost $1.7 million. Braddock's narrow, rutted, wagon track became a toll-free turnpike, a paved road with straight alignments, reduced grades, and substantial bridges over the streams. The National, or Cumberland Road, as it was known at first, had a 66-foot right-of-way. The roadbed was 30 feet wide and the pavement 20 feet. Grades were limited to five degrees, 462 feet per mile (almost 9 percent, four times the maximum permissible railroad grade). Benjamin H. Latrobe, who passed over the final section to Wheeling in February 1820 on his last trip to New Orleans, said that the stone-arched bridges added "very greatly to the beauty of this incomparably beautiful Country; & the road itself has all the grandeur & character of a national work."[3]

A string of separate turnpikes had been built over the years since 1806 between Baltimore and Cumberland via Frederick and Hagerstown. Gradually the missing pieces were filled in to create a continuous 135-mile, $1 million toll road. When it was finished in 1823, the road joined the National Road at Cumberland, and the first federally sponsored highway from the Atlantic seaboard over the mountains to the west was complete.[4]

When the B&O Railroad began, Jonathan Knight and Caspar W. Wever, as highway commissioner and superintendent, respectively, were busy extending the National Road through Ohio and Indiana. In his 1828 annual report on the highway, Wever described the McAdam system of construction, adopted earlier in that decade. The pavement was made up of three layers of stone, each layer three inches thick and each stone small enough to pass through a three-inch ring. The first layer was compacted by roller and the second by traffic before the third was added. But nine inches of so-called "metal" were hardly enough, considering the traffic. One traveler on the eastern stretch of road from Baltimore to Frederick in 1827 met or passed 235 large, heavily laden wagons in one day (seven per mile). Two commission merchants in Wheeling that year sent to Baltimore over 900 wagons loaded with 1,750 tons of produce.

Even before the road reached its destination, it had begun to deteriorate, and vandalism of one sort or another made it even worse. Logs were skidded over the surface, the faces of bridges and culverts were torn off for building stone, and fences and entire houses appeared on the right-of-way. Stage owners who reaped more benefit from the road than anybody also did more to ruin it, Wever reported. They defied the law by locking their wheels to slow their descent on hills and dug deep ruts in the pavement. East of the Ohio River, Wever said, the turnpike was headed for "complete and irretrievable ruin. . . . Is there not a saving power somewhere, and a disposition too?"[5] In the early 1830's, Congress authorized repairs, and the legislatures of Maryland and Pennsylvania passed laws to erect tollhouses. The federal portion of the road was transferred to the individual states. The citizens of Cumberland and Frostburg held a big procession to celebrate the 1834 relocation of the highway from its initial alignment following Cresap's and Nemacolin's trail over Wills Mountain to the route through the Narrows. The realignment made the approach to the coal mines easier.

Coal was too expensive to haul for any distance on the highway. Flour, whiskey, bacon, tobacco, and wool were all shipped east to be exchanged for dry goods and hardware going west, in loads that gradually increased from two to three to five tons. The freight moved in Conestoga wagons (named for an area near Lancaster, Pennsylvania, where they were developed), the beds of which were eighteen feet long, seven feet wide, and high enough inside for a man to stand up in. The wagon bodies were dished at the bottom to reduce the shifting of loads on the steep hills, and their head and tailboards were angled out to relieve the strain. This angle was carried upward to the peaks of the arched white canvas tops that extended fore and aft as weather protectors. Underbodies were invariably painted blue and upper woodwork, red. The rear wheels, ten feet in diameter, had four-inch wrought-iron tires. The wagons were pulled by six-horse teams, some of which had bells raised on iron hoops over their collars. They were the first vehicles of empire. Hezekiah Niles could not understand why German immigrants insisted on bringing their own wagons with them when such wonderful American ones were available, for roughly $250 apiece. Interspersed with the Conestoga wagons on the road were droves of horses and Kentucky mules, cattle from Illinois, merino sheep, Indiana hogs, Pennsylvania turkeys, and an occasional gang of slaves, roped together, all supervised by men on horseback.

The stagecoaches were equally distinctive as conveyances. The preferred Concord-style coach weighed about a ton and was pulled by four or six horses. Nine passengers rode inside on three lateral seats with their baggage either on top or in the boot. Thomas Shriver, of Cumberland, developed an elliptical spring that smoothed the ride, and brightly painted, plush-lined bow-spring coaches with names like Industry, Allegany, and Jackson maintained regular schedules from Cumberland over the turnpike to Wheeling. One of the most prominent "land admirals" was the legendary Lucius W. Stockton, originally from Flemington, New Jersey. In Baltimore in 1830, his firm, Stockton & Stokes, provided the B&O's first motive power: 36 horses and eight drivers at $50 a day "for doing the whole business," they said, "in the best possible style."[6] They owned the gray horse that raced Peter Cooper's engine and won. When the tracks reached a certain point, the company simply moved its stagecoaches farther west and subcontracted with the railroad to carry the mail up to the latest terminus. In that way, for the next twenty years, Stockton & Stokes skipped ahead of the railroad, first to Frederick, then to Hancock, and finally to Cumberland. When the Washington Branch opened in 1835, Stockton dropped his service on the Washington-Baltimore Turnpike and concentrated on the National Road. He ultimately shifted his headquarters to Uniontown, Pennsylvania, between Cumberland and Wheeling, and his National Road Stage Company became the biggest operator on the line. Stockton's major competitor was James Reeside, a native of Paisley, Scotland, who had also passed through Baltimore, where he served briefly as a contractor for the B&O Railroad, before migrating west. In the 1830's Reeside operated the June Bug and Good Intent lines of stagecoaches on the National Road.

Following his father's route of fifteen years earlier, John H. B. Latrobe took the turnpike to Wheeling in 1835, and his reaction was much as his father's had been: "The mountain scenery is magnificent: and the road is one which [deserves] its title of National, and of which any people might be proud."[7] A few months after that, on the other side of the Ohio River, a newspaper correspondent watched 140 families on the National Road pass by Lewisville, Indiana, in one day and sent a dispatch to his Baltimore editor: "The flood of Westward emigration, great as it has been in former years, is, this year, altogether unprecedented. . . . [The] great thoroughfare seemed constantly thronged with travelers on foot and horseback, going on to explore the 'Great West.' . . . The time is close at hand when the region west of the Alleghany mountains will sway the destinies of the nation."[8] The National Road cut the travel time for passengers between Baltimore and Wheeling from eight days to three and the wagon time for freight from five weeks to two. Rates were reduced proportionally. Before there was a turnpike, moving a ton of merchandise 265 miles from Baltimore to Wheeling cost about $120, which was more than ten times as much as it cost to ship the same cargo 3,000 miles across the Atlantic from Liverpool. After the National Road was finished, freight charges fell to $48 a ton in the 1820's and to $35 a ton a decade later. The National Road was of critical importance to the B&O from the very beginning in that it offered a raison d'être, a trajectory and destination, and a training ground for engineers, but when the railroad came, the highway was put out of business as a practical matter. The same fate overtook Virginia's Northwestern Turnpike, now U.S. Route 50. That road, tracing an Indian trail and wagon road, was completed from Winchester to Parkersburg in 1833. It was rendered obsolete only two decades later by the B&O's Parkersburg line, which paralleled it and appropriated its traffic.

But in Cumberland in 1842, where the tracks ended and the turnpike began, the high times were yet to come. The town also marked a geographic transition. On the far side of Dan's Mountain began the Allegheny Plateau whose shady woodlands, meadows, and icy streams provided scenic inspiration for the tourists who were beginning to frequent the Glades. Its special geological features, which put one viewer in mind of a "wonderful and sublime cosmogony," also held a thousand fortunes in undeveloped natural resources, for Cumberland sat at the eastern edge of extensive virgin forests and one of the nation's richest semibituminous coal fields, Georges Creek.

In 1842, the picturesque landscape still looked much the same as when Isaac Ridgeway Trimble reconnoitered it for the railroad, or, for that matter, as it did when Braddock's army marched off from Cumberland through "a realm of forests ancient as the world."[9] The Narrows, now traversed by the National Road, was still a "frightful chasm," and the Allegheny ridges to the west were still "covered with a dense growth of Pine, Spruce, Hemlock, Oak, etc. with scarcely a cultivated spot to indicate the abode of civilization," just as Trimble had found them in 1829. The spruce was so thick on Meadow Mountain west of Frostburg that it was impossible to see more than 100 feet into the woods. Beyond there, on Negro Mountain, the trees were big enough for hunters to use a hollow one as a shelter. Farther on stood a magnificent white oak, thirteen feet in diameter. As late as 1878, the high tableland west of Cumberland could still be described as "a grand park." Although commercial lumbering got a late start compared with coal mining, it was in full swing in the region by the 1890's, and from then on, indiscriminate cutting to produce mine props and tanbark as well as lumber greatly reduced the western forests. When the thirteen-foot white oak, the largest known tree in West Virginia, was felled early in the 1900's, its trunk was too large to travel by rail to the sawmill in Maryland, so it was first drilled and dynamited apart. The area where it stood was logged out in twelve years.

Coal, more than the inaccessible timber, was what first attracted the railroad and canal, according to their early reports.[10] Those documents described coal as inexhaustible, easy to get, and of superior quality. The Baltimore and Ohio's engineers on reconnaissance in 1828 said that Cumberland coal was particularly suited to making iron, and iron ore was also found in large quantities in the vicinity. C&O engineers thought that where the Potomac had exposed the veins on the mountainside near the Savage River only a chute would be needed to send the coal directly into the canal boats below. This intriguing concept was echoed and embellished in subsequent reports to the point where the chute was dispensed with and the fuel was shoveled from the coal bank right into the boat. Despite such eager anticipation, a century and more was to elapse between the first discoveries of western Maryland coal and the time when it reached the marketplace in any appreciable quantity.

The existence of coal was noted on maps as early as 1736 when two "colemines" were identified on the Upper Potomac. The first commercial application of Cumberland coal was in a Hagerstown nail factory in 1789. Mining activity increased during the early nineteenth century and transportation quickly became the ruling factor. Coal at Lonaconing revealed by a flood in 1810 found its way to Westernport and Washington, D.C. by water. When the construction of the National Road five years later uncovered more coal at Eckhart Mines, just outside Frostburg, it was wagoned to Cumberland and Baltimore. But the operation was mostly homegrown. Local farmers and itinerant entrepreneurs grubbed out the exposed coal with picks and sold it to a few residents and industries. A Cumberland glassworks tried some, but it turned the product green and they went back to using wood. Vestiges of this primitive mining system lasted at least until 1905. In that year, ten men were reported working a small mine with pickaxes near Frostburg, which had no rail connections. Mules hauled out the mine cars and the coal was loaded into wagons for local distribution as domestic fuel. By the 1820's, however, the coal trade was becoming significant. "Extensive beds of coal are now open and worked" in the vicinity of Savage Mountain, Trimble reported at the end of the decade. Alfred Cruger and Nathan S. Roberts of the C&O identified ten working mines on Braddock Run and four on Jennings Run, two streams that flowed into Wills Creek. Their broad valleys through Dan's Mountain west of Cumberland were to serve as natural arteries of transportation and commerce.

The coal was stockpiled on the riverbank at Cumberland and Westernport to await the spring floods. Along Wills Creek, an ancillary industry sprang up in the production of white pine flatboats, rectangular, with raked ends, to bring it down to Harpers Ferry and Georgetown. The craft were about 80 feet long and thirteen feet wide. Their shallow draft, of some two and a half feet, made it easy for them to be loaded and pushed off quickly when the Potomac approached the "boating stage." The flatboats carried roughly 50 tons of coal each and a crew of four—a "headsman" in the bow, two at the sweeps on either side, and a "steersman" who was also the captain. A fleet might consist of up to twenty such craft, and as many as 40 flatboats were known to leave in a single day, with crowds of sightseers cheering from the bank.

The crewmen would spend the next three to five days on the river, living on bread and bacon, washed down with whiskey. They played the fiddle a bit in the evenings while they moved in a leisurely fashion around the bends to Hancock, threaded the jagged shoals at Harpers Ferry, and finally, if they were lucky, passed through the locks at the Great Falls. A good bit of the coal and a few of the boatmen ended up on the Potomac's rocky bottom. Once they reached tidewater, both boat and cargo were sold and the coal-blackened crews of moonlighting farmers walked back to Cumberland. They frequently covered enormous distances in a day in order to make another $10–12 on a second trip back down while the big river was still running. Besides the Washington market, Cumberland coal began to supply Baltimore, which normally got its domestic fuel from Richmond and the eastern Pennsylvania anthracite fields. The boatmen also took keelboats downriver, sharp at both ends, carrying flour, grain, or whiskey, which they exchanged for cargoes of groceries or finished goods at Georgetown. Then they poled back up in eight to ten days, warping the craft past the rapids by passing lines through rings that the Potomac Company had attached to the rocks.

Corporate development of the Maryland coalfields began in the late 1820's when two companies were organized. They doubtless hoped to be in operation in time for the arrival of the railroad and the canal, which were just then setting out in a blaze of publicity. The first to go into actual production was the Youghiogheny (Yohogany) Iron Works. It began life in 1828 as the Allegany Iron Company and changed its name the following year. Despite their location in the middle of a coalfield, the operators first made iron with charcoal because hardwood was available and cheap, then switched to coal later on. The nearby hills also supplied the iron ore, which was hauled to the furnace by wagon. The site near Friendsville eventually included a forge, a foundry, a company store, and housing for 100 workers. Knight remarked that it was the sole sign of industry along his favorite Bear Creek route when he passed by on his 1835 reconnaissance.

The company successfully made iron posts, farm implements, and tools. They wagoned the pig iron they produced to Brownsville, Pennsylvania, where it could continue its journey by boat or highway. But transportation costs proved insurmountable. Deeply in debt, the struggling firm suspended operations temporarily in the 1830's and finally gave up in 1845. The Youghiogheny Iron Works set the pattern for the wildly fluctuating economy of western Maryland during the first half of the nineteenth century. Even more than on transportation, the iron industry depended on the tariff. When the tariff went down, so did production, and so, ultimately, did the communities.

The Maryland Mining Company also officially began in 1828, with a charter that allowed them to mine coal, build a railroad, and own a bank. For a decade nothing much happened besides an issue of $1 million worth of stock, but in 1836 the company said they intended to erect ironworks on their 2,000-acre property, which included the Eckhart Mines near Frostburg, and to build a rail line to move coal. However, their first real act was to open the Mineral Bank in Cumberland. The next entrepreneurs in the coalfields, when serious development began in the mid-1830's, were more successful. They made their intentions clear in the names of the companies: the Georges Creek Coal and Iron Company, and the Maryland and New York Coal and Iron Company. The 1836 prospectus of the Georges Creek company constituted one of the early scientific surveys of the western Maryland coalfields, and the town founded by this company the following year at Lonaconing was a model for those that followed. Incorporators John H. Alexander and Philip T. Tyson said in their prospectus that they owned a 10,000-acre tract called Commonwealth, on which was located an estimated 158 million tons of coal as well as ore containing up to 40 percent iron.[11] They planned to open mines, erect "mills and manufactories," and produce 7,000 tons of wrought iron a year. Part of their program was to build a railroad to Westernport, at the mouth of Georges Creek, where it would connect with the Chesapeake and Ohio Canal. The prospectus made no mention of the Baltimore and Ohio Railroad, which at that time was detained at Harpers Ferry, while the canal had surged far ahead and was expected yearly at Cumberland.

The operators estimated that the works, with several blast furnaces, a foundry, hammer and shears, puddling furnaces and rollers, a merchant mill, and steam engine, would cost $168,000 and return $610,000 in net profits. They concluded that "in no other place on earth has Providence allowed such returns for scientific research and honest enterprise, as are prodigally heaped up here." The "chorographic map" of their property turned out to be the first contour map printed in the United States. They illustrated a core, or section, of their stake at Dug Hill, Lonaconing, showing the alternate layers of sandstone, slate, coal, and iron shale with an early stratigraphic drawing. They also noted the presence of a fourteen-foot seam of bituminous coal, which would come to be known as the Fourteen-foot, or Big Vein. This was the famous Pittsburgh Seam.

The budding capitalists were well qualified for their new adventure, for they uniquely combined, as they so aptly expressed it, public research with private enterprise. Alexander was the state topographical engineer.[12] Tyson would become Maryland's agricultural chemist. One of their prime backers, Julius Timoleon (J. T.) Ducatel, was the state geologist. In 1833, Alexander and Ducatel had undertaken Maryland's first geological survey, for which Alexander drew the first official state map after borrowing the B&O's survey maps and profiles. During the course of the survey they visited every part of Maryland, paying particular attention to its natural resources. They were determined to prove their prediction: "The time will come when . . . the Western County of Maryland shall be looked upon as the Wales of North America."[13]

The property of these future industrialists, of some sixteen square miles, was located in the heart of Maryland's most valuable coalfield and atop the Pittsburgh Seam. Alexander compared the shape of the Georges Creek coal basin to that of a canoe. The basin is about twenty miles long and five miles wide, extending from the Pennsylvania state line to the Potomac River and defined by Dan's Mountain on the east and Savage Mountain on the west. Georges Creek itself flows in a south-westerly direction down the middle of the valley to the Potomac at Westernport. The creek starts at Frostburg, where Braddock and Jennings runs also begin their eastward journeys to join Wills Creek north of Cumberland. Frostburg, located on the National Road at the intersection of the valleys, became the unofficial capital of Georges Creek.[14] The Pittsburgh Seam occurs on either side of the creek, starting around Frostburg and running down to Lonaconing. At its southern end, the "breast" coal in this seam is 22 feet thick, and it was there, near a small stream called Koontz Run, that Alexander decided to build the ironworks and the town. He served as the company's first president.

The town was named for a local Indian chief, Lonacona, but it was feudal Europe rather than native America that provided the inspiration for Lonaconing. The Georges Creek Coal and Iron Company was incorporated in 1836.[15] British investors purchased much of its $300,000 worth of stock. The blast furnace was begun in 1837 and completed two years later. At that time, according to the historians of Allegany County, the valley of Georges Creek was "one continuous forest" between Frostburg and Westernport, except for perhaps half a dozen houses and a wagon track that forded the stream because there were no bridges. But forces had been set in motion that would transform it, in 50 years, into "one continuous street and town" from Mount Savage to Piedmont, lined with the houses of Welsh and Scottish miners and their families.[16] In 1839, some 700 people lived in Lonaconing, in 82 company-owned houses. Some of these were on Main Street in town and others were scattered up in the hollows, surrounded by well-cultivated farms, open pastures, and thick forests. They were double log cabins with each family occupying a single room and a garret. Among the 220 employees were 140 miners and 38 furnace hands. The two-story, brick Georges Creek company headquarters was close by, housing the company store and post office. There were also a church, a schoolhouse, a lumber mill, shops, and brick kilns. For a while Lonaconing was the second largest town in Allegany County, after Frostburg.

The focus of everything was the massive furnace at the foot of Dug Hill, a truncated pyramid 50 feet high. Each of its sides measured 50 feet at the base sloping in to 25 feet at the vertex. It was built primarily of sandstone. Some of the individual interior blocks weighed three and a half tons. It incorporated cast-iron beams and wrought-iron tie rods. Bricks produced on the site were used to face the sixteen-foot tuyere arches on either side and the main working arch in front, over which the masonry contractor proudly installed a stone tablet inscribed, "G.C.&I. Co./No. 1/ J.N. Harris/1837." In 1839, the furnace was making 75 tons of foundry iron a week and casting machine parts, agricultural implements, and stoves. They also made dowels for the lock walls of the C&O Canal and a set of gates for a Baltimore insurance company. The limestone flux and the ore, containing 34 percent metallic iron, were obtained from the adjacent Dug Hill and brought to the furnace by tramroad, laid with four-foot cast-iron plate rails. The fuel was coke, also produced nearby, and later on, raw coal. The furnace at Lonaconing was the first in the United States to use coke successfully to make iron.

The company ran the town as its private fiefdom, and for a little while it seemed that Georges Creek might indeed become "the Wales of North America." However, the company suffered severely from the constriction of British credit caused by the Panic of 1837 and was unable to transport iron except over the turnpikes at great expense. In August 1839, it blew out the furnace and at the end of the year suspended operations completely. "When our Legislators give us a Canal, our business will resume," a superintendent said. Yet when the company became active again in the 1840's, its products first moved on the railroad.

Meanwhile, the somnolent Maryland Mining Company had begun to stir. In 1838, they brought in Benjamin Silliman, professor of chemistry and mineralogy at Yale and editor of the *American Journal of Science and Arts* (popularly known as *Silliman's Journal*), to write a report.[17] His son, Benjamin, Jr., following in the footsteps that would lead him to his own Yale professorship and the editor's chair at the *Journal*, assisted him. Some of Silliman, Sr.'s, enthusiasm for the Cumberland coalfield was professional because his pamphlet, like Alexander and Tyson's, was designed to attract investors, but his commentary reflected his genuine interest in the countryside itself:

> The extremely varied surface of this beautiful region produces great richness of scenery, presenting bold and picturesque views that change with every movement of the observer. High mountain ridges form the outline, finished by dense slopes and crests of forest trees, and the vast swelling hills often cultivated in meadows and fields of corn and grain, delight the eye by the beauty of the surface, while they rarely give any distinct information of the mineral treasures that lie beneath the soil.

The geological structure of the coalfield was simple and intelligible, Silliman said. It resembled a stack of shallow canoes, sharply flared at the edges and without much rise at the ends, nested one inside the other, and representing successive layers of coal, shale, sandstone, iron ore, and limestone. The streams had cut down through these strata, exposing the various coal seams at different levels on the hillsides. The valleys drained the mines and provided routes for connecting railroads to the Potomac River where the canal would carry the coal to market. Thus the eye of the scientist saw past the geographic chaos to its usable, governing arrangement and even penetrated to the beautifully symmetrical concept below. "To an uninstructed observer, who should look only upon the surface of this region," the report went on, "there would be no indication of this regular structure beneath; he would see only the mountains, hills, and vallies, cheered by the fine skies of this grand and beautiful country."

The Pittsburgh Seam also lay under the property of the Maryland Mining Company. Silliman saw it at Eckhart's Mine. The farmers who excavated the original opening twenty or so years earlier had made it too broad, leaving a huge foyer, 40 feet wide and 200 feet deep, whose roof was supported by timber posts and beams. "Beyond that part, the mining has been carried on correctly by those trained to the business in Scotland," he said. "The coal is detached by the pickaxe and wedges; the pickaxe cuts it below by an operation called holing, and then laterally, on both sides, in a perpendicular direction; finally wedges cleave it from the top, when the masses fall and are ready for the car." The miners pushed the full cars out of the mine on a tram road. One man could bring out 150 bushels a day. He received a cent a bushel, so his daily reward for loading nearly five tons of coal was $1.50. The elite and interrelated Scottish miners could stand up straight in the Pittsburgh seam, but they actually preferred narrower ones, even those three feet high, in which they lay on their sides and swung their pickaxes horizontally.

While Silliman was making his inspection, in the summer of 1838, the Maryland Mining Company supplied the coal that was tested in the B&O locomotives. But again, lack of transportation made things difficult for the hapless firm. About this time, its president, Mathew St. Clair Clarke, a Washington lawyer, author, and former clerk of the House of Representatives, was ruined financially as a result of his heavy investment in its stock. In 1841, the canal failing to arrive as promised, C. M. Thruston, the new president of the Maryland Mining Company, asked the B&O to extend their rail line to Braddock Run to meet his. Nothing happened, however, and the company continued to send their coal to Cumberland on the National Road.

Silliman had found little iron ore on the property, but another company, the Maryland and New York Coal and Iron Company, incorporated in 1837, did find iron ore. This company had 3,000 acres of property that included large tracts at either end of Jennings Run. The first was an isolated hollow north of Frostburg where a confluence of streams had provided a level town site. The other was an open area six miles to the east where the broad valley met Wills Creek, offering a natural spot for a canal or railroad depot. The raw materials and the location were each potentially the best in the Georges Creek coalfield. The initial $500,000 investment came from England and the first owners and administrators were from New York. In its capitalization, rigidly organized company town, and technological innovation, the Maryland and New York Coal and Iron Company closely resembled its predecessor, the Georges Creek Coal and Iron Company.

There was already a town in the hollow above Frostburg, settled around 1825 by farmers who laid open the coal seams in the vicinity with their plows and mined them for their own use. In 1837, after Samuel Swartwout and his New York associates bought the 3,000 acres and resurveyed them, they aggregated the old soldier lots under a new name, Mount Savage, and began an aggressive marketing campaign. In the summer of 1838, Swartwout sent William Young down to look things over. Young was an experienced foundryman who had been making cast and wrought iron in America for over twenty years. He liked what he saw. He found the Mount Savage site "every way suitable for works on a large scale, there being sufficient ground for blast furnaces, refineries, rolling mill and forge, foundry, blacksmith and fitting-up shops, and workmen's dwelling-houses and gardens to each." [18]

The B&O had tested this company's coal as well and found it good. There was plenty of iron ore on the property, in nodules that could be mined with a crowbar. Young engineered a system by which the materials for each stage of production could be moved by gravity to the next level. The coal, ore, and limestone would flow by tram road from the mountaintop mines, ore banks, and quarries to the blast furnaces where they would be smelted into pig iron. This would descend to the puddling furnaces to be converted into wrought iron, which would then arrive at the rolling mills and be pressed into finished products. Young later got the chance to put his system into practice as president of the Maryland and New York Coal and Iron Company.

Swartwout next dispatched the Sillimans, who were even more excited than before by what they found. In the Mount Savage tract there were marble and hardwoods to build warehouses and towns, abundant farmlands and pastures for crops and cattle, maple trees to construct tramroads and to produce sugar for the "mining population," heat-resistant sandstone to erect iron furnaces and clay for firebricks to line them, limestone for flux, and most importantly, "inexhaustible supplies of coal and iron ores, both of the best quality." Mount Savage was also centrally located between "the ancient east, and the young and rising west," linked now by the "great national road," soon to have "the grand canal." After that would follow "an unlimited demand arising from the boundless wants of our great and rapidly-growing country, calling not only for fuel and iron, but for every product which can be manufactured by human skill and industry, managed by the dense population that will hereafter occupy this remarkable region." [19]

In August 1838, Swartwout packed up these two exuberant reports and sailed for England to seek investors. He had another reason for haste, for he was at the time under investigation in Congress for having used his position as the collector of the Port of New York to embezzle $1.25 million from the New York Custom House. He had spent the money speculating in land, canals, and railroads. The extent of his theft was still unknown, and no doubt he hoped to make up the shortfall in his accounts by disposing of his coal and iron lands in Europe. Swartwout was abroad until 1841. He found some investors and raised $500,000 in capital, though the stock issue was deceptive, according to a subsequent court suit. Finally, having surrendered his property to pay the claims, he returned to the United States after being promised he would not be prosecuted. In the meantime, the Maryland and New York Coal and Iron Company started to erect two blast furnaces in 1840, modeled on the one at Lonaconing, and had asked the Baltimore and Ohio about building a branch line to Mount Savage. Two years later, a little village had sprung up around the ironworks, consisting of 22 houses, a schoolhouse, and a company store.

Thus, of a dozen corporations chartered to do business in the western Maryland coalfields shortly before the railroad arrived in Cumberland, there were three major ones already engaged to some extent in mining coal, making iron, or both. All three—the Georges Creek Coal and Iron Company at Lonaconing, the Maryland Mining Company at Eckhart Mines, and the Maryland and New York Coal and Iron Company at Mount Savage—were much like the iron plantations of the previous century, such as Charles Ridgely's Hampton, expanded and institutionalized.

The market for local iron may have been uncertain at first, but Cumberland coal over the previous decade had floated down the Ohio River by flatboat to Cincinnati and poured from wagons into cellar windows in Wheeling and Pittsburgh. The federal armory at Harpers Ferry burned 3,600 tons of Cumberland coal a year and it was used also at the Antietam Iron Works ten miles up the river. There was speculation that the use of Cumberland coal would cut down boiler explosions on steamboats. Certainly it would have been more economical to burn than wood. A large Hudson River steamboat of the 1830's consumed up to 45 cords of wood (5,760 cubic feet), at a cost of $180, in making a single twelve-hour run from New York to Albany. The equivalent in coal would have been eleven tons, costing about $31, Cincinnati prices. A Maryland legislative committee in 1840 reported that Cumberland coal was twice as effective as pine for generating steam, "and consequently will be preferred in the navigation of our own waters by steamboats, or in the transportation over the railroads by locomotive engines."[20]

The Baltimore and Ohio used roughly 3,400 cords of wood in 1841. If factories are added to steam transportation, it is not difficult to imagine the fate of America's Eastern virgin forests. Half of the B&O's locomotives at the time burned coal, but not from Maryland. Although Latrobe had proved in 1838 that the Baltimore engines could run on Cumberland coal, the railroad's supply still came from eastern Pennsylvania through the C&D Canal. Therefore, the lack of transportation facilities for hauling coal now hindered the operations of the railroad itself. The railroad, however, still had much the same attitude expressed by Philip E. Thomas in 1836, shortly before he resigned: "It had not been the intention of our company to make any provision for the transportation of coal as that article can more appropriately be conveyed on the canal."[21] "The coal region is at present one of the unproductive regions of the State," a Baltimore newspaper observed in the summer of 1841, and, it added, the firms ready to do business in the western Maryland coalfields were still waiting for the canal, 50 miles away, or for the railroad.[22]

The railroad issued its new Cumberland timetable in the summer of 1843. Shortly thereafter a station of sorts, a two-story structure, the outboard half of which was the train shed, appeared alongside the Revere House near the intersection of the B&O's main line and Baltimore Street, the National Road. The passenger trains ran from Baltimore to Cumberland in a scheduled ten hours and Stockton's six-horse stages could get over the Alleghenies from there to Pittsburgh and Wheeling in about sixteen. By taking the railroad to Cumberland, a passenger going from Baltimore to Wheeling could cut the former all-turnpike travel time from 72 hours to about 24. The through ticket price had fallen from $18.75 (in the 1820's) to $11 (in 1844).

There was greater competition for passengers and the favor of the Baltimore and Ohio Railroad at Cumberland than at any of the railroad-turnpike junctions so far. Stockton & Falls, as the firm was then known, scrambled for business with Hutchinson & Weant's Good Intent and Pilot lines and several other operators. Thomas Shriver had acquired the Good Intent line from James Reeside in 1839, but he appears to have disposed of it the following year to Hutchinson & Weant, although he was listed in 1842 as the firm's agent. The inventor of the bow-spring coach was also a stagecoach manufacturer, and was interested in politics. In 1843, Shriver was the mayor of Cumberland.[23]

The railroad directors parried the stage companies' requests for exclusive contracts and tolerated their complaints about each other until the spring of 1843, when they adopted a standard $5 fare between Baltimore and Cumberland and dispensed with through rates. But then the stagecoaches raised their fares, and train travel fell off. The B&O committee handling the negotiations grew frustrated with "the vacillating and annoying course pursued by some of the stage companies now running from Cumberland to the Ohio River."[24] McLane himself was indecisive, first favoring one company, then changing his mind. But in the summer of 1843, Stockton's long association with the Baltimore and Ohio paid off when his firm and Hutchinson & Weant won contracts for the Wheeling traffic. Pittsburgh was left open to competition. Stockton was gone from the scene by November 1844, when the B&O signed a four-year contract with the National Road and Good Intent lines (both of which eventually came under the control of Moore N. Falls, Stockton's partner), and other stage companies. It dictated virtually every aspect of transportation from Cumberland to Wheeling and Pittsburgh and clearly revealed the railroad's control even over highway travel. The contract set the starting and running times for the stagecoaches (no more than 24 hours to Wheeling) and provided a $50 penalty for each infraction. It established the through fares and their division, reflecting the respective distances covered by train and stage. For instance, of the $11 through fare from Baltimore to Wheeling, the railroad got $5 and the stage company, $6. Passengers were limited to nine "inside and outside," and each could take 50 pounds of baggage free. The stage lines were to add extra coaches if travel increased.

When the Baltimore and Ohio Railroad reached Cumberland in November 1842, it had been carrying the mail to Washington, Frederick, and Harpers Ferry under agreements with the postmaster general, and between Frederick and Hancock as a subcontractor to Stockton & Falls. The last arrangement, made in June 1842, was worth $6,000 to the B&O, but McLane canceled it in November and the following month signed a contract with the federal government to carry the mail all the way to Cumberland. At the going rate of $300 per mile, the B&O's combined federal mail contracts were worth over $62,000 that year. They were renewed in 1844.

There was dramatic progress in the movement of freight. The first rail freight shipment sent from Baltimore to Wheeling was consigned to Shriver and Dixon, Cumberland commission merchants. The freight trains made the Baltimore-Cumberland run at that time in roughly 30 hours and the average rate was a little over $6 a ton. On its arrival, the three-ton shipment was wagoned to Forsythe and Son in Wheeling by Daniel Barcus in six days at $10 a ton. And so the former two-week wagon time for freight between Baltimore and Wheeling had been cut in half, and the rate of $35 a ton (in the 1830's), by more than that. When Barcus reached the Ohio River, the local merchants were so thrilled to get merchandise from Baltimore in just seven days that they met him at Steenrod's tavern near Wheeling Hill, escorted him into town, and held a grand public celebration.

Before the rails were laid to Cumberland, a group of businessmen from that city and Baltimore had urged the B&O to establish its own lines of wagons between the Potomac and Ohio Rivers. They would run day and night and reduce the travel time to just three days and the rates as well, they hoped. The board of directors turned them down, but later in the 1840's the railroad made agreements with private freight operations similar to those they had with the stagecoach lines. One was the "Great

Western four day line from Cumberland to Wheeling" that requested its own through rail freight car to Cumberland in 24 hours.

All this was good for the railroad. In 1843, a total of 150,000 people rode the trains and many of them arrived at the depot via stagecoach. The B&O transported 52,000 tons of freight eastward that year, much of it originating in Cumberland. Between 1841 and 1844, the railroad's net receipts from passengers and freight tripled. Immigrants were another valuable commodity. The first reference to them in the company records was in April 1840 when McLane received a letter saying that German immigrants were willing to ride in the burden cars at reduced rates. The B&O directors set a $2 fare for adults and half price for children. The next month they expanded the program to include "other" immigrants. When the trains were about to start running to Cumberland, the Baltimore newspapers recommended second class coaches to handle the heavy German immigration. In 1843, the railroad was transporting immigrant groups in parties of not less than twenty at $2.50 each.

One matter that might, in hindsight, be expected to have been a subject of greater discussion among the B&O directors in the early 1840's, considering its later significance in railroad operations and in general society, is the telegraph. Samuel F. B. Morse first approached Louis McLane with his scheme for an electromagnetic telegraph in the spring of 1843. McLane thought he was crazy. He referred Morse to John H. B. Latrobe, the B&O's lawyer, who knew him by reputation as a portrait painter. Reporting to McLane the next day, Latrobe told him that his future claim to fame might be that he had provided the venue for the first practical demonstration of the telegraph.[25] Chief engineer Benjamin H. Latrobe, Jr., also made a favorable report, and in April 1843 the board of directors authorized a trial of Morse's invention on the Washington Branch, provided that it did not interfere with railroad operations. They also wanted to have free use of the telegraph and the right to remove it if it proved troublesome.

Morse was the son of the famed New England Protestant minister Jedediah Morse, professor at Yale University, author of geographic texts and Indian studies, who became known as the Father of American Geography. Finley, as he was called, attended Yale and heard Professor Benjamin Silliman lecture on chemistry and galvanism. He also displayed a flair for art, and in 1811 he went to London with Washington Allston to study with him and Benjamin West, head of the Royal Academy. During his four years there, Morse won critical acclaim for his paintings and sculpture, and he returned to set up a studio devoted to historical art. In 1822, he unveiled *The Old House of Representatives*, a monumental work that showed Latrobe's domed chamber by candlelight with the members, 86 of whom sat for individual portraits, preparing for an evening session. Morse sent the painting on tour, hoping to profit from paid admissions, but there was little public response. He next founded the National Academy of Design in New York and became its first president. Meanwhile he attended occasional lectures on electricity. In 1829 he returned to Europe to pursue his art studies.

Encountering James Fenimore Cooper in Paris in 1832, Morse described to him the telegraph's basic principles, and during a scientific shipboard conversation on his way back to America that year, he announced, "If the presence of electricity can be made visible in any part of the circuit, I see no reason why intelligence might not be transmitted instantaneously by electricity."[26] Morse spent the remainder of the voyage in a fever of excitement, making drawings of an electromagnetic telegraph and devising a rudimentary code. In a one-room, fifth-floor apartment in lower Manhattan, subsidized by his brothers, which served as his workshop, studio, bedroom, and kitchen, the inventor began to assemble the components of his new device. He also continued to paint, and in 1833 completed another tour de force, *Gallery of the Louvre*, containing 38 identifiable masterpieces in miniature, but this, too, was little noticed. Morse had been made a professor of art at the institution that became New York University, but it was an unpaid position. Preferring poverty to debt, he took out his frustrations by writing several nativist tracts.

Meanwhile, he kept working on the telegraph. In 1835, he developed a relay to boost the signal. Two years later, he gave a successful demonstration. One of the witnesses, Alfred Vail, who worked in a New Jersey ironworks owned by his father, became Morse's partner, helped him to simplify the system, and provided needed capital. Morse filed a caveat with the patent office and left on a two-year trip to Europe to secure foreign patents. He brought back the daguerrotype, which he helped to introduce to the United States, but little else.

Even the Vails denied him funds as Morse struggled on. At the end of 1842, the House commerce committee, whose chairman was John Pendleton Kennedy, reported favorably on a bill to provide $30,000 for a practical test of the telegraph. Morse waited weeks for the measure to be called up in the same gallery he had painted twenty years before. "If the darkest time is just before day, daylight must be close at hand," he wrote an ally.[27] Finally, at the end of February 1843, Kennedy succeeded in bringing the bill to the floor. Many of the members mocked and ridiculed Morse's invention. One proposed a telegraph to the moon. Another corralled 22 votes for an amendment to use some of the money to study mesmerism and Millerism, a sect that believed in the second coming of Christ. But eventually the bill passed, with a majority of six. Ten days later, the Senate made it a law in the waning hours of the session. Morse publicly acknowledged Kennedy's role in the creation of the telegraph.

The New Jersey Railroad had already denied Morse the use of its right-of-way, fearing business would be done by wire rather than by rail. Morse's second choice was the turnpike or railroad between Baltimore and Washington. He chose the latter. Following British precedent and because he thought underground wires would be less subject to vandalism, Morse decided to enclose them in buried conduit. He advertised for 160 miles of copper wire, insulated with cotton twine, and 40 miles of half-inch inside diameter lead pipe. Former Congressman F. O. J. ("Fog") Smith, an early Morse supporter as well as an energetic opportunist, steered the contract for laying the pipe to his brother-in-law, and applied himself to setting up a system of supplier kickbacks. Smith also discovered Ezra Cornell, founder of Western Union and of the university. Cornell had developed a special plow.

The B&O allowed Morse and his crew to pay half-fares on the Washington Branch but balked at reducing the freight rates for construction materials. The trenching operation began in Baltimore in October 1843. Cornell's plow, pulled by a team of eight mules, cut a furrow two inches wide by twenty inches deep, laid the pipe enclosing the four wires, and pushed the dirt back, all in one operation. The rig moved so swiftly that the workmen joining the sections had trouble keeping up. By December, when they reached Relay, nine miles from Baltimore, they realized that heat generated by the process was destroying the insulation on the wires. With three-quarters of his appropriation spent, Morse, who knew the power of publicity, feared disclosure. So he stopped the work, pleading the lateness of the season. Recriminations began immediately among the three principals and there were long, late-night meetings at the Relay House, where they were staying.

Vail chose this moment to ask for a raise: "Even Mr. Vail, who has held fast to me from the beginning, felt like giving up just in the deepest blackness of all."[28] Congressman Smith, his illicit profits evaporating by the minute, turned into a treacherous enemy who pursued the inventor relentlessly. Said Morse, "Where I expected to find a *friend*, I find a FIEND."[29] Morse then abandoned the buried trench and adopted overhead wires. In March 1844, the unbarked chestnut poles, 24 feet tall and 200 feet apart, first appeared north of Washington, making an indelible imprint on the landscape and beginning a trackside march over the continent. "I hope for the best while I endeavor to prepare my mind for the worst," Morse said. When, the following month, the wires stretched to Beltsville, twelve miles from Washington, Morse told his brother, "A brighter day is dawning upon me."[30] The line was completed 22 miles to Annapolis Junction, just in time for the opening of the national Whig convention in Baltimore. Vail, operating at the junction, obtained the first report of Clay's nomination from the passing train and relayed it to Morse in the Capitol. When the passengers from Baltimore arrived an hour later, bringing what they thought was the latest convention information, they were stunned to find that it was no longer news.

The connection was made to Baltimore, and on Friday, May 24, 1844, Morse, seated in Latrobe's Supreme Court chamber in the Capitol, sent the famous message, "What hath God wrought?" to Alfred Vail at the B&O's Mt. Clare depot in Baltimore. (Later that day, the instruments were moved to the company's downtown depot at Pratt and Light streets, and transmissions continued from there.) The biblical text was supplied by the patent commissioner's daughter, Anne Ellsworth. Morse said she had been the first to inform him that his appropriation bill had passed the Senate. The formalities over, the mechanisms chattered back and forth.

Morse: "Stop a few minutes."

Vail: "Yes."

"Have you any news?" "No." . . . "What is your time?" "Nine o'clock, twenty-eight minutes." "What weather have you?" "Cloudy." "Separate your words more." "Oil your clock-work." "Buchanan stock said to be rising." "I have a great crowd at my window."[31]

The Baltimore *Sun* noted the event in two sentences, the longer of which read, "Several messages were sent to and fro with almost incredible dispatch, which, although unimportant in themselves, were most interesting from the novelty of the proceedings, forcing upon the mind the reality of the complete annihilation of space, in the fact that a distinct and well-defined conversation was actually going on with persons in a city forty miles distant." [32]

Three days after the first official message was wired to Baltimore, the Democratic national convention began in the city. "The conventions at Baltimore happened most opportunely for the display of the powers of the Telegraph, especially as it was the means of correspondence, in one instance, between the Democratic Convention and the first candidate elect for the Vice-Presidency," Morse wrote. This was Silas Wright, who declined in a telegraphed message from Washington. The Baltimore delegates adjourned in disbelief and sent a committee to meet with him to verify the information. For Morse, it was a triumph: "The enthusiasm of the crowd before the window of the Telegraph Room in the Capitol was excited to the highest pitch at the announcement of the nomination of the Presidential candidate [James K. Polk], and the whole of it afterwards seemed turned upon the Telegraph. They gave the Telegraph three cheers, and I was called to make my appearance at the window when three cheers were given to me by some hundreds present, composed mainly of members of Congress." Morse's triumph was complete when one of his former detractors in the House came up to him and confessed, "Sir, I give in. It is an astonishing invention." [33]

But the device that would revolutionize railroad operations was not used to control train movements until September 22, 1851, when Charles Minot telegraphed such an order to a conductor on the New York and Erie Railroad. In the interim, time governed the running of trains. Soon after the opening of the B&O Railroad to Cumberland, four daily trains were in operation between there and Baltimore, one passenger and one freight leaving each place every morning at staggered times. Three of them met at noon at Harpers Ferry, roughly the halfway point, although the eastbound freight from Cumberland had spent the night there. The new line was a single track, with quarter-mile sidings every seven or eight miles. There were other trains running to Frederick besides those on the Washington Branch, also a single-track line. What kept them all from colliding was simply the timetables and watches of their conductors, which were set according to the clock at the B&O's downtown Pratt Street depot.

The timetables fixed the speed (the top average was 18 mph) and established the meeting points of the trains. Where there was just one track, which was generally the case not only on most of the B&O line but on the majority of other railroads at the time, one of the trains of course had to be on a siding or a turnout for the other to go by. This made it imperative for the conductors to regulate and set their watches to the same time. The timetables also carried instructions about departures and schedules. No train was to leave the station before the time specified, and there were elaborate procedures for trains running behind schedule, "out of time," or "running wild," as it was called, owing to accidents or other reasons. A passing or opposing train not at the meeting place at the appointed time was genuine cause for alarm.[34]

An incident of this sort occurred the first week after the main line opened to Cumberland in November 1842. The turntable there collapsed under the weight of the engine, which fell into the pit and delayed the departure of the passenger train for several hours. The westbound passenger train left Harpers Ferry on schedule and, as the Martinsburg *Gazette* described it, "went slowly along, pawing, feeling and trembling to avoid collision in meeting until it found the downward train resting on a sideling beyond Doe Gully Tunnel. A train of burden cars leaving Baltimore on Sunday morning was less cautious, and meeting on a curve beyond Ellicotts Mills, the locomotives came in collision, grappled, and reared up like rampant dogs," causing considerable damage. It was unclear from the report whether the accident involved the same late passenger train from Cumberland.[35]

Morse had originally conceded to the B&O the right to use the telegraph when its proprietors were not, pending a decision by the federal government, but in 1845, when the postmaster general ratified the agreement, the railroad directors tabled it. Two years later, the Magnetic Telegraph Company, headed by Morse, and the Western Telegraph Company were incorporated in Maryland; the first was to operate between Washington and New York and the second between Baltimore and the western Maryland state line. The Townsends in 1845 had also proposed a telegraph along the B&O's right-of-way between Baltimore and Wheeling. In June 1848, the directors granted them the use of the rail line to Cumberland for a telegraph and arranged to transmit messages on it for a reduced price. The telegraph line opened a month later. (It actually followed the railroad only between Harpers Ferry and Hancock, proceeding the rest of the way along the National Road.) Newspapers, lottery agents, and brokers were quick to take advantage of the new system, but the railroads stayed with the clock and the timetable. Indeed, there was so little traffic the first few years on the Baltimore-Washington telegraph line that it was used to conduct chess games between the cities.[36]

∽21∾

This Noble Enterprise

LOUIS McLANE, SEEING GOOD PROFITS AHEAD,
was all optimism as the Baltimore and Ohio Railroad got to Cumberland. "The first
step should be to push the road without interruption into the heart of the coal and
iron deposits of Alleghany county," he said in October 1842.[1] The approved route
through the Narrows, north along Wills Creek and over the mountains to Connellsville, Pennsylvania, would take the railroad right past the valleys leading to Eckhart
Mines and Mount Savage. The estimated cost of building the necessary twelve and a
half miles of railroad was $250,000. McLane indicated that one of the mining firms
might furnish the necessary $70,000 worth of rails in exchange for transportation of
their other freight.

As soon as the first trains rolled into Cumberland in November 1842, the companies at the two locations renewed their requests for branch lines. The Maryland
Mining Company asked the price of transporting 100,000 tons of coal a year to
Baltimore and wanted to know whether or not, if they built their own railroad down
Braddock Run and across Wills Creek, the B&O would come up to meet them by
next summer. The ironworks at Mount Savage posed similar questions. But McLane,
apparently influenced by an "elaborate investigation" by James Murray, the railroad's
superintendent of machinery and repairs, had changed his mind. The directors declined either to make an agreement with the coal and iron companies or to extend
their railroad by "next summer or within any definite period."

Rather than make the necessary heavy investment in branch lines, engines, and
rolling stock to engage in the coal trade right away, McLane had decided to wait
and see how the market developed. Two more years would pass before even a trickle
of coal, but no iron, began to flow from western Maryland. The railroad, however,
made political capital out of the coal business from the very beginning.

The Chesapeake and Ohio Canal was still operating only to dam no. 6, some
134 miles from Washington and ten miles past Hancock, to which point it was opened

in the spring of 1839. Construction had moved ahead on the 50-mile stretch between there and Cumberland, especially at the tunnel, but in January 1843 work was suspended with eighteen miles and $1.5 million worth of construction still to go. The canal had an equivalent amount of liabilities. It was selling off property in Georgetown to stay alive and was back in Annapolis once again asking for the money to finish the job. But the state had no more means than the company to carry on the work. Hinting that William Gibbs McNeill would bring new energy and capital to the project, the canal hired the B&O's former engineer and antagonist as their president. The C&O's latest scheme called for the contractors to finance the construction. The canal, however, had become a political pariah. Its situation was remarkably similar to the railroad's when it was stranded at Harpers Ferry. Now that the B&O had won the race to Cumberland, it was in a position to offer itself as the final connecting link to the coalfields.

In December 1842, James Murray calculated that if the canal were completed to Cumberland, it could carry coal to Georgetown for $2.50 a ton. But if the Baltimore and Ohio brought the coal to dam no. 6 and transferred it to the canal at that point, the whole trip would cost just $2.56. The B&O was then charging two cents a ton per mile to carry coal. To finish the canal, the State of Maryland would have to issue $2 million worth of bonds, including back interest charges, Murray said. It was therefore cheaper to pay the six cents a ton extra, at least until the annual coal traffic reached 70,000 tons, which would not be for several years. Murray's statement, which appeared later in various forms, was turned into a powerful political argument against completing the canal.[2]

The C&O's affairs were "by no means encouraging," said incoming governor Francis Thomas—the former C&O Canal president—in reviewing its status and the state's debt in his first message to the legislature in January 1843. The state owed $10 million for internal improvements; it had suspended interest payments and was taxing its citizens to make up the deficit, and the taxes were not being paid. Thomas blamed the internal improvement companies for putting Maryland into debt and ruining thousands by issuing worthless scrip. There was talk of repudiation. Another scheme was to pay off the debt with the state's share of the federal government's Deposit Act, which Thomas called the Distribution Law. "It is as fruitless as ashes," he said. "Our public debt, if paid, must be paid out of our own resources. Whoever thinks otherwise, follows a phantom."[3]

The governor might have looked a little closer to home. As the past president of the canal, the designer of its free-wheeling finances, the man who had sold off the Maryland sterling bonds and issued his own worthless scrip, he was as much to blame as anyone for the state's fiscal dilemma. Thomas was an eloquent hypocrite. He was also one of the most remarkable chief executives in Maryland's long and amazing political history. He had served three terms in the Maryland House of Delegates in the 1820's, the last as speaker, and had spent the next ten years, from 1831 to 1841, in the House of Representatives. While a congressman, Thomas was a leader of Maryland's recusant electors, whom he called the "glorious nineteen." This was a group of Democrats who had challenged the Whigs in a bitter state party dispute in 1836 and lost, but whose actions resulted in legislative reapportionment and the direct election of the governor. It was during one of his terms in Congress, in 1839–40, that Thomas, a lawyer from Frederick, was president of the Chesapeake and Ohio Canal.[4]

McLane spent a good deal of time in Annapolis during the 1843 legislative session while the Whigs and Democrats argued over state taxes and methods of paying off Maryland's debt.[5] The Whigs wanted to settle it by selling the state's interest in the internal improvement companies. A law was passed to that effect, but it came to nothing because there were no buyers, particularly for the canal. That summer, a bipartisan Repudiation Party gathered strength in Maryland, especially in the southern counties of Worcester, Somerset, and Calvert, which had refused to pay state taxes, and in Harford and Cecil counties in the far northeast.

In June 1843, the new Chesapeake and Ohio Canal president, William Gibbs McNeill, and William Price, Governor Thomas's political opponent and a canal representative, asked the railroad to carry coal to dam no. 6. McNeill was advertising for contractors to complete the construction. They were to be paid in company bonds. The problem was that the contractors required a lien on the canal's revenues and the state already had one. Since leaving the B&O, McNeill had enjoyed a successful career as a railroad engineer on the Baltimore and Susquehanna and several New England lines, but he had lost none of his combativeness. He soon confronted the canal board, which preferred to await the action of the legislature before awarding contracts. In July 1843, while the directors were absent, McNeill broke into the company office in Frederick and signed up two contractors to complete the canal work to Cumberland. They had actually begun work by the time the board regrouped, annulled the contract, and fired McNeill. They replaced him with director James M. Coale. The canal was again at a standstill.

That September, McLane said the railroad would transport coal to the canal for two cents a ton per mile; they began to install $2,000 worth of switches and sidings at dam no. 6. William Young, now president of the Maryland and New York Coal and Iron Co., asked for rates on shipping 1,000 tons of coal a day, and also wondered whether the B&O would buy a rail line between Mount Savage and their proposed alignment through the Narrows, presuming that he built it. At cost and if they went that way, the company responded. But they were still not interested in investing substantial sums in branch lines, engines, and cars until there was more coal to haul.

The Allegany County coal trade began officially in December 1843. The first shipment from the Maryland Mining Company traveled via the National Road to Cumberland and by rail to dam no. 6. From there, it moved on the canal to Georgetown, where it was put aboard an ocean vessel for New York. That city, after a week of testing, pronounced it "the best species of bituminous coal in the world."[6] When people in Frederick started to use it for fuel about that time, Thomas C. Atkinson and Henry R. Hazlehurst, two of Latrobe's favorite assistant engineers, were prepared. As Atkinson and Hazlehurst, they had already been in business for a year, promising to deliver coal at any B&O depot at low prices, as well as grates and stoves from their Cumberland foundry in which to burn it.

Many such business connections arose between the railroad and the coal companies. McLane, for example, was a director of the Maryland Mining Company and owned stock in the Georges Creek Coal and Iron Company. For the latter firm, Ross Winans produced the running gear for the mine cars. Winans also manufactured engines, the Savage and the New York for the Maryland and New York Coal and Iron Company, and the Eckhart and the Mountaineer for the Maryland Mining Company.

Maryland had given up the idea of selling the canal, "a costly ruin," Governor Thomas told the members of the General Assembly at the end of 1843. Perhaps the legislators could find a way to finish it. The large state debt, most of it due to the C&O, was "a serious public calamity" that sat "like an incubus" on the population, Thomas said. He noted that there was still resistance to paying the taxes necessary to make up the deficit and claimed that the relationship between Maryland and its counties was analogous to the Continental Congress and the states under the old articles of confederation, when the congress passed revenue laws it was too feeble to enforce.[7]

In February 1844, the Baltimore and Ohio signed its first contract with one of the coal companies. William Young, of the Maryland and New York Coal and Iron Co., informed the B&O board that he had found the capital to build a branch line from Mount Savage to Cumberland. He wanted to ship coal, pig iron, castings, and fire brick to Baltimore. 175 tons a day, 300 days a year (52,500 tons annually), for five years. He asked again if suitable rates could be arranged. The railroad quoted him a price of one and a third cents/ton/mile to move the coal 188 miles from the mines to tidewater in Baltimore plus ten cents a ton for taking it through the streets of the city, or $2.61/ton total. They also said they would supply engines and cars. Young accepted and had the branch line built and running by the end of 1844.

While these negotiations were going on, the Maryland House of Delegates was querying McLane about the B&O's rates to dam no. 6 and the relative cost of transporting coal from Cumberland to Georgetown via the present combined system as opposed to the completed canal. At the quoted rate, McLane replied that it would cost half a cent *more* to move a ton of coal on the canal, if it were finished, than by the current train-boat arrangement.

These remarks introduced another round of bitter political infighting between the railroad and the canal. The C&O's legislative forces were pushing a bill calling for the waiver of the state lien and the completion of the waterway. They accused the Baltimore and Ohio of soliciting the House of Delegates inquiry in order to provide false answers. McLane maintained they were the same rates he had already given William Young at Mount Savage. Baltimore's mayor and city council and the city's delegation in Annapolis strenuously opposed the canal bill. The B&O's backers wanted the arrangement at dam no. 6 made permanent. Some of the issues were whether the railroad had the capacity to carry large amounts of bituminous coal and whether the slack demand for it on the Atlantic seaboard would generate enough revenue for the canal to pay off its debts, especially if the state lifted its lien to allow completion.

"The war between the interests of the two great projects, the canal and the railroad, to the west, is unhappily renewed," wrote Jeremiah Hughes, the editor of *Niles Register*.[8] The canal bill was defeated. Hughes blamed sectionalism. No internal improvement bill would pass the Maryland legislature unless the railroad and canal companies cooperated, he said. But why should they? John H. B. Latrobe asked Thomas Wren Ward that question during the summer lull. Ward was Baring Brothers & Co.'s American agent. Latrobe made him aware of the forces at work and why there would probably be no greater concurrence at the next session. The Barings hoped for a mutual understanding between the rival projects. However, Latrobe said, the railroad wanted nothing from the legislature and therefore had no motivation to collaborate with the canal. The Baltimore and Ohio could make a good profit hauling coal to dam no. 6 at one and a third cents/ton/mile, cheaper than the canal's rate, and they could probably do it for one cent. "Now this being the fact," Latrobe continued, "it at once strikes every one, that it will be far better to use the rail road, which is already in operation as a feeder to the Canal, at Dam No. 6, than to make any further outlay" for canal construction.[9] He was optimistic about the prospects for collecting taxes in Maryland and the state's resumption of interest payments to the Barings.

The lawyer was then approaching the crest of his career as a Baring Brothers & Co. lobbyist. He began it with Ward in 1842 after Maryland suspended interest payments on its debt. Latrobe's liaison was a brusque, flint-faced Boston Brahmin, who had supreme confidence in his opinions regardless of the subject and a stern sense of business propriety that must have been as anomalous in the nineteenth century as it would be in this one. Invited on one occasion to use his inside political knowledge to speculate in Maryland bonds on behalf of the Barings, Ward loftily replied, "Sir, the question is not what profit they may make, but what it becomes the House of Baring to do."[10] Ward came to Baltimore in early 1842 to check on his employer's investment. Latrobe took him on a tour of the B&O as far as Hancock, and he further ingratiated himself with the Barings by furnishing Ward with the full details of Maryland's financial situation. Ward forwarded them to London, and the Barings invited Latrobe to communicate regularly with their Boston agent. Overcome with gratitude for this princely notice, he unctuously agreed and became Ward's special agent; his assignment, to influence the State of Maryland to resume its interest payments.[11]

It was natural that the Baltimore and Ohio should work together with Baring Brothers & Co. for resumption, for unless the state paid its debt, the $3.2 million worth of Maryland sterling bonds held by the British bankers were useless to the railroad. The 1844 session was their first real campaign. Latrobe, now a Whig stalwart and an old hand in Annapolis, churned out articles for the press and bills for the legislative hopper. The resumption program failed that year. It got caught up in the renewed B&O–C&O hostilities, for one thing, but the primary reason was that Maryland's finances were still in too much disarray to allow the resumption of regular interest payments. Nevertheless, Latrobe and his cohorts laid the groundwork.

The railroad's low coal rates were based on a new engine built by Ross Winans that was 25 percent heavier and three times more powerful than any then working on the line. It represented a transitional stage, both for its designer and his sponsor, in their eccentric development of the locomotive. So many different machines were churning up and down the Baltimore and Ohio Railroad to Washington and Cumberland in 1844 that it must have seemed a little like the Rainhill trials or the B&O locomotive experiments all over again. A watchful spectator might have seen Phineas Davis's Grasshoppers, and George Gillingham and Ross Winans's Crabs, along with William Norris's "one-armed Billy's." The B&O had acquired several more of these since the Lafayette.

There were also some newer types, the company having grown weary of its existing complement and expanded the list of suppliers and styles. One of the first to respond was another Philadelphia manufacturer, Eastwick and Harrison. In September 1839, they provided the Atlas, a 4-4-0, that is, an engine with four drive wheels instead of two. Other than the extra pair of 50-inch drivers, the engine was similar to Norris's "one-armed Billy's," but with larger cylinders of 12.5 × 20 inches. Norris produced his first engine of this type, the Vesta, for the B&O two months later. In February 1840, Delaware's New Castle Manufacturing Company supplied another, the Arrow, an inside-connected 4-4-0, one of the first such engines they made. Between 1840 and 1842, Eastwick and Harrison built four more 4-4-0's for the Baltimore and Ohio. Norris furnished another in 1843 and Winans also built one that year, the Atalanta, in the same style.

The new firm of Andrew M. Eastwick and Joseph Harrison, Jr., was the first to promote the 4-4-0 engine. It became the standard nineteenth-century American locomotive. (Harrison, a mechanic, had begun his career with William Norris.) The prototype was the Gowan and Marx, an 1839 collaboration built for the Philadelphia and Reading Railroad. It was designed by the railroad's engineer, Moncure Robinson, and named for his English bankers. The Gowan and Marx incorporated Eastwick and Harrison's patented equalizing lever. This device improved the suspension of coupled locomotives by distributing road shocks between the driving axles and lessening the chance of damage or derailment. It later became a standard item in steam locomotive design. Planned for slow coal traffic, the eleven-ton Gowan and Marx, in early 1840, demonstrated its capacity by pulling a 101-car train weighing over 400 tons. This feat was one of the factors that ultimately resulted in the involvement of Moncure Robinson, Eastwick and Harrison, George W. Whistler, and Ross Winans and his sons, Thomas and William, in the lucrative and exotic task of building and equipping the first railroad between Moscow and Saint Petersburg, 420 miles long, for Czar Nicholas I of Russia.[12]

While the Russian project was still in the planning stages, Ross Winans was working on his own engine. By December 1840, he had the first version running. The B&O tested it in a gingerly fashion early the next year, sending the 19.3-ton locomotive over Latrobe's 150-foot timber truss spans at Elysville and measuring the deflection, which was five-eighths of an inch. The bridge resumed its normal position once the engine was across, but the railroad began strengthening the spans west of Harpers Ferry to support 20 tons. James Murray approved of Winans's new creation. It burned 30 percent more coal than the Crab engines, but it did three times as much work as the Norris "one-armed Billy's" and twice as much as Eastwick and Harrison's 4-4-0's. The B&O did not need additional motive power at the time and decided not to buy it, but they let Winans continue his trial runs on the railroad.

A seasoned observer who described this machine in March 1841 gave it high marks for power and efficiency. It had eight driving wheels, a vertical, coal-fired boiler, containing 650 tubes, and large cylinders, 14.5 × 24 inches. The locomotive was then working heavy trains between Baltimore and Harpers Ferry. However, the reporter said, "The appearance of the engine is remarkably plain, pleasing and imposing, while it is entirely without ornament, except the comeliness of its outline." [13] The new model had horizontal cylinders and spur gears, like Winans's Crab engines, of which it was a gigantic version. It had no name, but it did have a precedent, an eight-wheel connected engine built a few years before by the Camden and Amboy Railroad called the Monster. In September 1841, Winans sold one of these 0-8-0 engines to the Western Railroad of Massachusetts and over the next year or so he built three more of them for that line; he also talked Philadelphia's Mathias W. Baldwin, a conservative manufacturer enamored of the 4-2-0 design, into building them. "We do not look for beauty in a freight engine or a mudscow," the Western Railroad said rather defensively.[14] Still, it found the monsters unsatisfactory for reasons other than their appearance and soon retired them.

Winans's engine was, in truth, one of the ugliest mechanisms ever designed. Winans had always been indifferent to aesthetic refinement and good craftsmanship, and he almost seemed to like turning out awkward and even grotesque machines with rough finishes. But slow and ponderous though his engines were, they had the power to haul heavy coal trains. This might have seemed important to the B&O, but the company again declined, a year after their first test, to buy two of these engines, at $11,000 each. In July 1843, Winans patented his eight-wheeled locomotive, claiming it had greater traction and special suitability for curved railroads. He now found himself locked in competition with William Norris for the B&O's favor.

Early in 1844, Norris offered to sell four more 4-4-0 engines to the Baltimore and Ohio, but the directors wanted to investigate building locomotives in their own shops. In April 1844, they listened to a long report emphasizing that the railroad's low coal rates depended on using heavy freight engines with eight powered wheels and that the only person who knew how to assemble them was Ross Winans.[15] Winans's experience and the fact that the money would remain in Baltimore if he got the contract were strong reasons for giving it to him, the committee said. Their other bids were unacceptable. Philadelphia's Baldwin and Whitney wanted to build only six-wheeled engines and the New Castle Manufacturing Company's offer was too vague. Therefore, the battle was between Winans and Norris.

By that time, Winans had embraced conventional engineering practice at least to the extent of adopting the horizontal boiler. He was also using Eastwick and Harrison's patented equalizing lever. Norris and Brother, as that company was now known, and Winans engaged in a bidding war urged on them by the railroad. Winans was then asking $10,000 each for his locomotives; Norris had offered to build them for $8,500. Each maker consecutively dropped his price and there were complex negotiations concerning advances, patent payments, and so on. But the B&O wanted to give the contract to Winans, and at the end of April 1844, after Winans's price had dropped to $9,400, the railroad ordered from him six eight-wheeled, 20-ton engines.

For the first time in almost a decade, Ross Winans worked alone at the Mt. Clare shops. His partner, George Gillingham, had died that year. In June 1844, with the aid of James Murray and again after hard bargaining, Winans developed and sold to the B&O his idea for an improved coal car. By substituting cylindrical iron hoppers for wooden sides in their construction, Winans produced cars that were lighter, cheaper, and of greater capacity. They could carry almost three times their weight in coal. Winans's engines also began showing up on the line in the fall. They were promptly named "Mud-diggers," but at least they looked like locomotives and not rolling stills. They had a proper arrangement at last: a horizontal Bury-type (domed) boiler, a cab for the engineman in the rear, and a smokestack in front. The cylinders were very large, 17 × 24 inches, and the wheels quite small, 33 inches in diameter. Because of the spur gearing, the main and connecting rods still worked in opposite directions, producing the characteristic low-slung flurry of motion. (The name derived from the engine's tendency to churn up mud from the tracks.)

Over the next two years, Winans turned out a dozen of these innovative but highly idiosyncratic machines with names like Hercules, Gladiator, Elephant, and Elk. Nothing quite like them had ever been seen on an American railroad. For Winans, they served as technical studies for his final work, the celebrated Camel engines. They were certainly true reflections of their maker, an independent and opinionated personality if ever there was one. Winans was then approaching the midpoint of twenty years of litigation attempting to prove that he was the inventor of the eight-wheeled car. John H. B. Latrobe served as his attorney. He eventually lost in the courts, but as a critic observed, in engineering matters, "Ross Winans was a law unto himself." [16]

The Maryland and New York Coal and Iron Company was just starting to produce the rails for these new engines and coal cars to run on. When D. K. Minor, editor of the *American Railroad Journal,* toured the Mount Savage works in the summer of 1844, he found two blast furnaces, several puddling furnaces, and an "immense rolling mill" turning out 25 to 30 tons of rails a day. From raw materials to finished product, the operation flowed downhill, just as William Young had planned it. There was a further decrease in elevation between Mount Savage and Cumberland, "so that a locomotive will take down more loaded cars than it will bring back empty ones." Five hundred men worked in the mills, and 2,000 people lived in the town. The editor was delighted with it all, especially now that after Americans had sent millions of dollars to England to buy rails, the high tariff allowed them to make their own, "and, what is still better, as in this case, mainly with foreign capital." [17]

Mount Savage was then making the first heavy rails rolled in America. They were "bridge" rails, shaped like an inverted U, and weighing about 40 lbs/yard, similar to the British rails the B&O laid between Harpers Ferry and Cumberland.

The Maryland and New York Coal and Iron Company made roughly 500 tons of them in 1844. They used some to lay their branch line to Cumberland, which they completed about December. That month, Philadelphia's Franklin Institute examined an eighteen-foot bridge rail from Mount Savage and said, "This bar is well-proportioned, sound, and well finished; it is the first ever exhibited here of American make; we hail it with pleasure as the beginning of a new manufacture, and award to it A Silver Medal."[18]

McLane devoted a substantial portion of his October 1844 annual report to the coal trade. But now that he had the engines, cars, and even a rail line to the mines, caution had completely overtaken his initial enthusiasm. The B&O president emphasized the unsettled state of their route past Cumberland and the falling demand and low production of bituminous coal. So far, only 4,000 tons of coal and no iron at all had been offered for transportation. The railroad would have to ship 50,000 tons of coal a year to justify the expense of the specialized machinery and equipment necessary to make a serious commitment to the trade, he said. At the same time, however, McLane indicated a desire *not* to ship coal: the B&O had never particularly wanted to get involved in the coal trade, and because their main object was to get the line built to the Ohio River, they should leave coal to the canal. On the other hand, as long as they were stopped at Cumberland, there was no sense turning down business. McLane was an artful diplomat, and it was often difficult to tell where he stood on important issues.

At any rate, the B&O shortly began to haul coal for the Maryland and New York Coal and Iron Company from Mount Savage to Baltimore, but not at the low rates they quoted to the company and the inquiring legislative committee nine months earlier. Instead of 1.3 cents/ton/mile, or $2.61 total, the price was now 1.7 cents/ton/mile, or $3/ton overall. And they prepared for another round with the Chesapeake and Ohio in the Maryland legislature. McLane thought the state should take over the canal and when the fiscal situation improved, finish it to Cumberland and beyond, to the Savage River coal region. John H. B. Latrobe informed Thomas Wren Ward that although the election of Polk, a Democrat, had inspired increased talk of repudiation, the Whigs still controlled the state legislature. They would work with the Democrats to restore Maryland's honor, a noble aim that happened to coincide with the railroad's and the Barings' interests.[19]

Meanwhile, the state's financial condition continued to deteriorate. Governor Thomas in his final speech to the General Assembly at the end of 1844 reported that the treasurer had collected only 60 percent of the expected amount in state taxes the previous year and that there were now seven delinquent counties instead of three because the tax laws had not been enforced. Again Thomas singled out the C&O Canal as the chief malefactor. The company owed the state $2 million in back interest on its loans and had another $1 million in outstanding debts. Maryland was $1.5 million in arrears on its own interest payments. The canal had made little progress over the past five years, Thomas said. The law to sell Maryland's interest in the internal improvement companies remained a dead letter and he thought the state should foreclose on the canal's mortgage.[20]

The B&O and the Barings had great hopes for the new Whig governor, Thomas G. Pratt, who was inaugurated in January 1845. In 1836, as a Prince Georges County delegate, Pratt had led the fight against the Eight Million bill. For the 1845 legislative campaign, Latrobe hired a special assistant, Hugh W. Evans, a banker and former B&O director. Although measures were approved to facilitate the collection of state taxes, the resumption program again fell victim to the canal-railroad warfare. Over the B&O's objections, a law was passed providing for the completion of the canal to Cumberland. It removed the state's prior liens and allowed the C&O to issue $1.7 million in bonds. Wild rejoicing broke out in Georgetown, Alexandria, and western Maryland.[21] In England, the Barings, with some help from George Peabody, established a secret $4,000 slush fund to further their political cause in Annapolis. Latrobe and others administered it, actually spending about $3,000, mostly to aid the election campaigns of candidates friendly to resumption.[22]

The canal held public meetings to whip up enthusiasm and asked the Barings to help them market the new bond issue. The Barings declined, and the railroad countered by making arrangements with the City of Baltimore to run its engines in the streets and extend the tracks to tidewater to facilitate the coal trade. Washington, D.C., the canal's headquarters, retaliated by passing an ordinance that barred B&O locomotives from entering the city limits. The Washington city fathers also tried to get rid of the B&O's depot in the capital.

In the meantime, some interesting names started to show up in the coalfields. Brown Brothers & Co. of New York took over the Maryland Mining Company and brought in engineer Horatio Allen as president. They reportedly possessed $300,000 in capital, 2,000 acres of land (three-fourths of it containing coal), and a town of twenty houses, along with an office, store, and blacksmith shop at Eckhart Mines. Their nine-and-a-half-mile branch line was under construction to Cumberland and the company requested the same transportation rates as the B&O had given to Mount Savage. At that place, the Maryland and New York Coal and Iron Company had erected more than 200 stone houses in parallel rows on the hills, each with a small yard bordered by a stone wall. In one year, the population had grown 500 percent, to 3,000. The 500 workers burned 150 tons of coal a day, shipped an equal amount to Baltimore, and were turning out 200 tons of iron a week. Their wives could shop in Cumberland by taking the passenger trains that ran twice a day. The fare was 37 and a half cents.

At Mount Savage, the American industrial revolution, after lagging a century to a generation behind the British, came of age. In the summer of 1845, a "blowing engine" manufactured at the West Point Foundry (William Young's former employer) arrived in town, probably by rail, although that is not certain. The huge condensing engine, with a ten-and-a-half-foot-diameter cylinder and a ten-foot stroke, was installed to provide the blast for a third furnace and to fire the blacksmiths' forges. It was an American event that recalled the intricate and fascinating relationships among the Darbys, John Wilkinson, James Watt, and George and Robert Stephenson, the great ironmasters and coalfield steam engineers in England. Here, a steam engine delivered by a locomotive was used to power a blast furnace to make rails for other trains to ride on. The B&O signed a contract with the Maryland Mining Company to haul up to 52,500 tons of coal a year and drew up another with Georges Creek president John H. Alexander, to transport coal and iron. Cumberland coal was now being used in the steamship *Great Western*.

As the rebellious counties such as Worcester and Calvert began to pay their share of taxes, the state's finances slowly improved. John H. B. Latrobe, enjoying his role as a political analyst, sent cheery messages to Ward and Baring Brothers & Co. in the fall of 1845. The Barings' secret political fund had evidently been put to good use because the elections were over and the House of Delegates was Whig by a majority of four. The lawyer expected a resumption bill to pass during the coming legislative session. The only unknown factor was the canal, which proposed to let the work to contractors if they agreed to be paid in company bonds. Latrobe tried to convince the C&O's agent that unless the state resumed paying interest on its debt, "the bonds were blank paper." The contractors brought in heavy-duty lobbyist Daniel Webster. He tried peddling the securities to the Barings with assurances that his clients would strive to get the state to resume its obligations. However, the Barings had had enough of the C&O Canal and Webster sought greener fields.[23]

Although Latrobe had an idea that the canal company's eagerness to finish their project could be linked politically in Annapolis to the state's resumption of interest payments, he was skeptical of outright cooperation with the Chesapeake and Ohio. The Barings "have at times suggested a coalition between canal & Rail Road," he told Ward, but, as Latrobe well knew, "such things are not the most desirable in principle and have been largely odious in Maryland, whose present situation in pecuniary matters is owing to them."[24] Latrobe saw one possibility of compromise: a formal compact, enforced by the Barings, to divide the freight between the two rival works, coal on the canal and flour on the railroad. The Maryland Senate looked into some such arrangement but took no action.

The real fear of the B&O was the traditional one of competition. In a confidential report to Thomas Baring in October 1845, Latrobe admitted the canal could transport coal more cheaply than the railroad could, despite its earlier manipulation of the rates. The C&O could be finished to Cumberland at the contract price, he thought, and if the canal directors got the money, this time they would spend it on construction.[25] But coal was still in the railroad's future. The current fight with the canal was over flour. Flour was at that time the B&O's major commodity in terms of tonnage, as it had been from the beginning and as it continued to be until 1848, when coal overtook it. In fact, up to the mid-1840's, flour annually outweighed all other products coming east on the B&O combined. More than half a million tons of this staple of Baltimore commerce traveled on the railroad during the first two decades of its operation and much of it did so at cost, or less. The freight rates set by the 1827 Maryland charter, four cents/ton/mile eastward and six cents westward, although they may have seemed adequate at the time, did not cover the expense of moving flour, which was easily damaged in transit or spoiled by delay, and for that reason the state legislature in 1837 doubled the allowable freight rates, but exempted flour and other heavy products such as grain, coal, iron, and stone. By 1840, it cost the

B&O six cents/ton/mile to transport its major item of freight. But because the flour trade was so important to Baltimore and the state, as it had been since Revolutionary times, the railroad continued to carry it at a loss.

In 1841, the Maryland General Assembly relented and allowed the B&O to charge eight cents/ton/mile on flour and most other heavy items. (Some types of stone were left at the former rate.) But competition from other transportation facilities kept the railroad from making a profit on flour. The B&O had to contend not only with the C&O Canal and the National Road but also with the Cumberland Valley Railroad (the Franklin Railroad), which now extended all the way from Chambersburg, Pennsylvania, to Philadelphia. The B&O found itself unable to raise rates and keep the business. It tried six cents/ton/mile for a time, but soon regressed to the original four cents. At least it was no longer losing money. Having reduced expenses in the interim, the charge of four cents/ton/mile on flour—34 cents a barrel from Harpers Ferry to Baltimore—was cost in 1842.

Two years later, the railroad had advanced to 40 cents a barrel, but then it was forced back down to 25 cents in a rate war with the canal that, the B&O directors said, "threatens to divert the entire flour trade from Harpers Ferry, Frederick and the west . . . from Baltimore to Georgetown."[26] The Chesapeake and Ohio, of course, blamed the railroad for using similarly unfair tactics. A year after that, the Baltimore and Ohio still ran flour at reduced rates on the part of its line next to the canal. McLane tried to make some political profit, if no other, from the situation. At those prices, he said, the C&O could not make enough money to pay the interest it owed the state. Besides, they were taking trade away from Baltimore, a jurisdiction that Maryland hoped to tax to pay off the loan to complete the construction of the B&O's rival. The argument was clever, but it had no measurable effect on its target.

By late fall 1845, flour and grain were stacked up at Williamsport ready for shipment by water to the District cities. Contractors and workmen had assumed their positions along the canal line between dam no. 6 and Cumberland. "Day is dawning again after a long gloomy night," a reporter wrote.[27] The C&O had spent $9.8 million so far and had only eighteen more miles to build to reach Cumberland, 184 and a half canal miles from Georgetown. It had cost the B&O $7.6 million to construct its 178 miles of railroad between Baltimore and Cumberland.

In December 1845 the Maryland legislature listened to a report from Governor Pratt that was more optimistic than any the lawmakers had heard in years. For the first time since the state suspended interest payments in January 1842, the year's tax receipts exceeded the annual amount due on the public debt. Pratt was happy that terms for the completion of the C&O Canal, "which has for years rested as an incubus upon the legislation of the state," were finally settled.[28] Yet for the fulfillment of Maryland's great attempt to gain the trade of the West, the idea that had cost them so much, they must look to the B&O Railroad and its extension to the Ohio River, he said. The resumption bill failed again in the spring of 1846, despite strong efforts from lobbyists John H. B. Latrobe and Daniel Webster, and from Robert McLane, the B&O president's son and a promising Democratic member of the House of Delegates, who made a last-ditch effort to rescue it.

Nor was everything proceeding according to plan in the coalfields. The Mount Savage organization had run up a debt of $100,000 in rail transportation charges. At more or less the same time that the lawyer Latrobe was watching his bill go down to defeat in Annapolis, his brother the engineer was recommending the firm for a substantial B&O contract. Mount Savage was to provide half the rails to reconstruct the 80 miles of track between Baltimore and Harpers Ferry. Andrew Ellicott's Covington Manufacturing Company, in Baltimore, was the contractor for the other half. "Only let the tariff alone, and in a few years we would compete with England," the *Niles Register* said, "besides tracking our own wilderness with iron highways in all directions." [29]

Benjamin H. Latrobe, Jr., and his crews had rebuilt twenty miles of this distance in 1838–39, with 50-pound H-rail rolled in England, but the remainder of the line still consisted of the old strap iron, some of it laid on the original stone sills. In 1845, the board decided to replace the old roadbed with the same thing they used between Harpers Ferry and Cumberland: 51-pound bridge rails, shaped like an inverted U. But rather than ordering them from England, the B&O contracted with domestic manufacturers. More and heavier engines and trains, along with almost daily accidents that wrecked the rolling stock, disrupted operations, and cost the lives of railroad employees, had prompted a reconstruction study in the fall of 1845. Benjamin H. Latrobe, Jr., responded with a report within weeks. A ride on the old section of the line "imposes rather a penance upon, than affords a pleasure to the traveller," he noted carefully. Without being rebuilt, the track "will absolutely go down," he said. "It is already carrying three or four times the trade of any similarly constructed track in the country, and the iron, which has borne up well under 15 years hard use, is now beginning to break up." [30] Other reasons for replacement included the fact that tractive power was greater on edge rails than on plate rails, because of less resistance and more adhesion, and also lower maintenance costs. The railroad subsequently figured it could save as much as $73,000 a year in operations and repairs by rebuilding the old track.

As if to dramatize the need for action, the day Latrobe produced his report, an engine, tender, and house car full of merchandise went into the canal. Latrobe's old friend Charles B. Fisk, the C&O's chief engineer, kindly offered to drain the water from that section so they could drag the train out. By the end of 1845, the railroad directors had made up their minds to raise $1 million to reconstruct the line between Baltimore and Harpers Ferry.

It would take another decade for the B&O's accidental injuries to reach the level where official summaries of the mayhem out on the line read like battlefield casualty reports. But they were mounting seriously enough in the early 1840's to compel the company to do something about it. Employees were regularly being scalded, having their limbs broken, losing hands, arms, legs, and lives. Usually the B&O paid the medical bill and gave the worker a few months' wages, or bought the coffin and covered funeral expenses. In 1844, McLane set up an Invalid Fund to provide disability payments for injuries received in the company's service. He started it off with a first-time payment of $1,250, which the railroad had received from the Post Office

Department for carrying the President's message that year, but the fund was mostly financed by the workmen themselves, who contributed 1.5 percent of their wages. Workmen who did not subscribe did not receive benefits. The fund quickly ran out of money and the company advanced more. Later the directors tried to turn it over to the workmen, but changed their minds and the fund struggled on under corporate administration. The company experimented with other means. McLane interviewed a doctor who had removed the leg of a brakeman injured in an accident and said that "if a 'free ticket' were given him, he would attend to all amputations, wherever accidents might occur, without charge."[31] By a narrow margin, the board voted to try the system out for a year.

The reconstruction of the Old Main Line proceeded slowly. In early 1846, contracts were let to lay the first 30 miles of new track. However, the 6 percent, 20-year bonds the company issued to finance it could not be sold, except at a sacrifice, either in America or in Europe. The Barings turned them down, as they had the canal's, because the state had not yet resumed interest payments. The track work continued anyway, paid for by net revenues. It was virtually completed in 1849, by which time the eastbound track carrying the heavy traffic had been relaid with edge rail at a cost of $660,000.

In May 1846, the Maryland Mining Company began operating its branch line from Eckhart Mines to Cumberland and the B&O signed a new contract with them to haul 18,000 tons of coal annually. The mining company president, Horatio Allen, at first declined the railroad's offer of a 1.75 cents/ton/mile rate, but by July the coal was moving. At Mount Savage, 50 new buildings were going up and hundreds of frame houses now surrounded the mills, where the curious visitor could follow "every process of the manufacture of the ore from the mountain bed, through the blast and puddling furnaces, the annealer and trip hammer, until it comes out at the rolling mill in the form of the finished T rail."[32] The local mines still provided coal for the operation and for shipments east.

The B&O had at last established its capacity to transport coal "at cheap rates and at a good profit," McLane declared in the fall of 1846. Having finally made a commitment to the coal trade, he devised an elaborate plan to finance it. First, he wanted to obtain a tax exemption for the bonds and secure them with a $1 million mortgage on the B&O's property and revenues, similar to the one on the Washington Branch, thus making them more attractive to investors. Second, the president would pay these securities as dividends to stockholders, in effect reimbursing them for the $284,000 borrowed from net revenues in 1846 to reconstruct the Old Main Line and to buy the heavier engines and cars that were necessary to haul coal. If these things were done (and they were), the company's experiments in the coal trade would become part of their normal operations, McLane said (as indeed they did, in time). The B&O obtained an initial $105,000 in bank and private loans to help pay cash dividends to the small stockholders, reserving the bonds for the larger ones, such as the State of Maryland.

Thus the Baltimore and Ohio had begun to normalize its end of the trade, but in the coalfields, the situation remained unstable. The Maryland and New York Coal and Iron Company at Mount Savage dropped coal to concentrate on iron, whereupon the B&O canceled the coal-hauling agreement and tried to get the company to pay off its transportation debt in rails. There is no evidence that they did so. Mount Savage fell down on iron production too, and the B&O did not extend its contract for rails. McLane did make new arrangements with both Mount Savage and the Maryland Mining Company to operate their branch railroads with B&O equipment, but evidently it was Baltimore's Covington Manufacturing Company that provided the first domestically produced heavy rails for the Baltimore and Ohio. They were used in the reconstruction of the Old Main Line between the city and Harpers Ferry.

For the Mount Savage company, luck and timing could not have been worse. Summer floods destroyed about three miles of their railroad, including a bridge over Jennings Run, and the Tariff of 1846, which reduced average tariff rates in America to 27 percent, destroyed their iron business, as it did others in neighboring states. Of the three major companies then operating in the coalfields, Mount Savage was the hardest hit. John H. Alexander's Georges Creek Coal and Iron Company at Lonaconing was not connected by rail to the Baltimore and Ohio until 1850 and was a marginal producer of iron. The Maryland Mining Company's Eckhart Mines yielded only coal. Although the population at Mount Savage reached 4,000 in early 1847, the mills were a scene of "solitude and desertion" until that fall when the works were auctioned off. New owners, including Erastus Corning and John Murray Forbes, acquired the $1.6 million investment for $215,000. They renamed it the Mount Savage Iron Company. It slowly revived to the point where, in later years, Mount Savage did produce rails for the Baltimore and Ohio Railroad.

From Annapolis, the spring of 1847 brought better news. For the first time since the passage in 1836 of the Eight Million bill, which had marked the beginning of Maryland's fiscal problems, the railroad decided to cooperate with the C&O Canal on passing a law. The canal forces were told that if they did not go along, their project would receive no further state aid. John Pendleton Kennedy now occupied the speaker's chair in the House of Delegates, having arrived there with the help of John H. B. Latrobe. Both Whig leaders championed resumption. All the elements necessary for Maryland to resume interest payments on its debt were now in place. The new tax laws were being properly enforced, and, as Governor Pratt told the legislators at the new session, the state's revenues were more than adequate to meet current obligations. Without imposing new taxes, Maryland could begin to pay the accumulated interest, "and thereby cast off forever the reproach which for so many years has rested upon her and her people." [33]

The governor also made it clear that the C&O Canal now owed $2.5 million in back interest, whereas the B&O Railroad remained the state's sole hope for commercial prosperity. Still, Pratt was puzzled by the railroad's rationale for paying dividends to small stockholders in cash and to large ones such as the state in bonds. The treasurer of Maryland had refused to receive them, he noted. Although the City of Baltimore had accepted these bonds in payment of the dividend, the state argued that their $15,000 worth constituted an illegal conversion of the company's net revenues and discriminated against them. The *Niles Register* rejoiced that "the glorious day has dawned, when Marylanders can see their way clear to promise their creditors a faithful performance of their obligations upon the due day," which the lawmakers decided would be at the beginning of the new year.[34] Kennedy and Latrobe kept the troops in line and one delegate sober long enough to see the resumption bill passed on March 6, 1847. Maryland's fiscal dark ages were over.

John H. B. Latrobe's lobbying expenses for that year were $700, including travel, confidential payments, and fees to writers for favorable articles supplied to the Democratic newspaper, the Baltimore *Republican*. Altogether, over the five-year resumption campaign, he earned about $7,000 in lobbying fees, including expenses, from Baring Brothers & Co., roughly half the total amount the British financiers spent protecting their investment and encouraging the State of Maryland to honor its financial commitments.[35]

The Chesapeake and Ohio Canal announced shortly for the umpteenth time that it had raised the $1.1 million needed to finish construction. The Barings put up $300,000 of it, but once again pulled out because they were suspicious of the engineers' estimates and feared a recession in Europe. In the fall of 1847, the canal board reiterated that the contractors would accept the company bonds and finish the work in two years. Horatio Allen was one of the trustees named to oversee the operation.

Benjamin H. Latrobe, Jr., supported the president's strong performance in the B&O's 1847 annual report with an extensive document of his own incorporating numerous charts illustrating the railroad's growth since it began. Freight transportation rose 66 percent during the year, and passenger traffic, 20 percent, he said. Also, 22 million tons of freight came east and 6 million tons went west; the principal eastward tonnage consisted of 63,000 tons of flour and 50,000 tons of coal. The railroad had sufficient rolling stock to haul 90,000 tons of coal a year to Baltimore, at a profit of $50–60,000, but they could not do it until the tracks were extended to the south side of the inner harbor. Latrobe further reported that the Baltimore and Ohio had made $3 million in profits since it opened in 1830. One-third of this money had been distributed as dividends, and the remainder was invested in the railroad as new track, engines, cars, bridges, depots, "all of which remain as visible and tangible evidences that the portion of the income not directly given to stockholders, has not been squandered and sunk, but is existing, and in truth, if not in appearance, yielding them interest."[36]

The State of Maryland, inspired by the B&O's political opponents, sued the company over its application of net income to reinvestment in the railroad instead of dividends, but the general mood induced by the resumption of interest payments was euphoric. Few could have been happier than Jeremiah Hughes, the feisty Whig editorial heir to Hezekiah Niles. "No state," he said, "was surrounded with more embarrassments or had greater difficulties to encounter . . . than the state of Maryland. Not one." There was talk of repudiation, Hughes said, but "The people demanded the passage of whatever laws were necessary to retrieve the standing of the good old state of Maryland."[37] Governor Pratt hailed once again the imminent completion of the C&O Canal. As for the B&O Railroad, the governor repeated, "The prosperity of the state is deeply involved in the successful prosecution of this noble enterprise."[38]

22

The Trouble with Wheeling

THE BALTIMORE AND OHIO RAILROAD HAD SEVERAL
antagonists in the Virginia state house in January 1842. One was Richmond's James
River and Kanawha Canal Company. Another was Moncure Robinson, who was
associated with southern railroad lines seeking reduced fares on the B&O's Washington Branch to counter steamboat competition on the Chesapeake Bay. Then there
was the Winchester and Potomac Company, who, Benjamin H. Latrobe, Jr., said,
"will insist upon our buying their rotten road." But Wheeling was the worst of all.
"Wheeling is in the field against us and has declared war to the knife; as we expected," he told his brother.[1] Latrobe was sharing a room with Louis McLane at the
Exchange Hotel. McLane gave the speeches, aided by state senator Charles James
Faulkner, Latrobe prepared statements and law abstracts, and Samuel Cameron, a
B&O right-of-way agent, assisted them.

The Baltimore and Ohio wanted two things from the Virginia legislature, according to Latrobe: the $1,058,000 stock subscription they had been promised and
the restoration of their right to build the railroad to Parkersburg, where the Little
Kanawha River met the Ohio. That right was first granted in their 1827 Virginia charter, but the 1838 subscription act withdrew it and required the railroad effectively to
end its tracks at Wheeling. Now, Wheeling felt betrayed. One of its representatives, a
Colonel Thompson, was so hostile to the B&O in a speech to the House of Delegates
committee on roads that McLane was called upon to answer him, "which he did very
effectively as you may suppose," Latrobe reported. Other spokesman from Wheeling, Parkersburg, and northwestern Virginia took up the verbal sparring, and then
Thompson returned "with a long written argumentative tirade in which the company is convicted of a scandalous breach of faith towards Wheeling," and accused
of trying to steal Richmond's trade, Latrobe said.[2] If Wheeling could not have the
Baltimore and Ohio Railroad, nobody would, according to Thompson; they would
try to stop it at Cumberland. Their alarm was premature, for when the Baltimore

and Ohio reached that place at the end of 1842, no outside force was necessary to contain it. Even if the company had had the money and energy to push on, time was running out in the three states where the railroad was initially chartered. New laws were needed.

Maryland and Virginia shared the same situation. The time limits set at the beginning for completing construction, having been extended once, were due to expire again July 4, 1843. In Pennsylvania, too, the original deadline was up that year. That state had previously renewed the charter, but had included certain conditions that made the law unacceptable to the company. Maryland was the only state to extend the charter in 1843, and it did so contingent upon the sale of the state's interest in the internal improvement companies, which never took place. Despite McLane's and Faulkner's continued lobbying in Richmond in 1843 and again the following year, the Virginia legislature passed no B&O laws until 1845. The Virginia act of 1845 gave the company more time, but the B&O stockholders rejected it for other reasons. Pennsylvania in 1843, 1845, and 1846 produced B&O legislation, but again added restrictions, such as allowing intersections with the state's railroads, that made the laws either unacceptable to the company or otherwise inoperative. No effective charter extension was ever granted by Pennsylvania.

The railroad's major preoccupation in the mid-1840's was going farther west. The B&O considered three significant routes between Cumberland and the Ohio River during this period. The preferable one went to Parkersburg, located on an almost straight line between Baltimore and Saint Louis. The next was to Wheeling, already connected to Baltimore by the National Road. The last terminated at Pittsburgh, an industrial Goliath ideally situated for the Great Lakes trade. Tracing the remarkable changes of course that led the B&O ultimately to a destination whose attraction faded even as they approached, and analyzing the charges and counterclaims of its competitors, is like trying to understand the epicycles of the planets. In the railroad's case, three states and six municipalities orbited the corporation's eccentric path, leaving the most convoluted trail in the B&O's early history.

The company itself created a labyrinth of fact and deception. Partisan surveys and angry political confrontations seesawed between Virginia, then Pennsylvania, and back to Virginia again, with Maryland in the middle. Eastern cities plotted against each other—Baltimore against Richmond and Philadelphia—and hostilities were inflamed among those in the west. Wheeling fought Parkersburg as well as its traditional enemy, Pittsburgh. There was intrastate animosity between the eastern and western sections of Virginia and Pennsylvania (the Pittsburgh-Philadelphia contest was especially savage), while in Baltimore, an internecine struggle developed within the board of directors and the business community.

Elected officials acted as if the route of the B&O were a matter of commercial life or death for their home districts. Wheeling's politicians were particularly adamant. Newspapers pounced upon each suspect phrase uttered in an opposing camp. Campaigning hard for a Pittsburgh terminus, the Baltimore *American* sacrificed news propriety to the struggle. Things became so confused at one point that two sets of negotiations were going on simultaneously, official ones in Wheeling and unofficial ones with Pittsburgh. And in the center of it all was the enigmatic figure of Louis McLane, the consummate diplomat.

It took almost ten years for the B&O to make up its mind to go to Wheeling and another five for it actually to get there. McLane had left the railroad by then. The verdict, at least in Richmond, on his decade of dealing with state legislatures, city councils, and private companies was that the negotiations suffered from "an excess of ingenuity," as George Stephenson, the British railroad engineer, once said in another context.

The trouble really began in 1838. The Virginia legislature that year required the B&O in so many words to end its line at Wheeling but did not restrict its choice of route. The company accepted this law with some misgivings. The following year, the directors adopted a route through Pennsylvania to a point above Connellsville, where the main line was to continue to Wheeling with a branch going to Pittsburgh.

In June 1839, the Pennsylvania legislature, believing it had a captive railroad, passed an act extending the B&O's charter, but the act incorporated so many discriminatory provisions favoring Philadelphia that the B&O refused to accept it. McLane was particularly outraged by a requirement that Pennsylvania's Franklin Railroad be allowed to intersect the Baltimore and Ohio somewhere in Virginia between Martinsburg and Hancock. There were also several pages of rate restrictions. Since the only known route to Wheeling was through Pennsylvania, which had in effect withdrawn it, Wheeling became less desirable as a terminus for the Baltimore and Ohio. Virginia's subscription offers evaporated.

The B&O spent the years 1839–42 getting to Cumberland. In August 1843, they sent Latrobe, the chief engineer, to reconnoiter routes beyond there through Virginia, avoiding Pennsylvania, and terminating at points on the Ohio River between Wheeling and Parkersburg. He was also to look at western railroad connections. His itinerary followed the well-known path along the Potomac and Savage rivers, Crabtree Creek, and through the western Maryland Glades. In Virginia, the lines diverged. Latrobe's preferred routes went to New Martinsville by way of Fishing Creek and to Parkersburg via Clarksburg. When he returned two months later with a report, the directors were preoccupied with other matters and tabled it.

In May 1844, Jonathan Knight, then employed by Wheeling as their engineer, surveyed the opposite end of the line. Heading southeast, he followed Wheeling Creek, skirted the lower corner of Pennsylvania, and ended up at the Low Gap on Glover's farm, where a stream called Piles Fork began on the other side of the ridge separating the Monongahela and Ohio rivers. The following August, Latrobe and some Wheeling citizens joined Knight and continued the route down Piles Fork to its junction with Buffalo Creek at what is now Mannington, West Virginia. There, Latrobe's preferred line to New Martinsville branched off. He had found a new route, Knight told McLane. The B&O president replied that it was longer than Latrobe's, had very high grades, and would be costly.[3]

In the fall of 1844, delegates from eleven counties of northwestern Virginia met at Clarksburg to promote a Parkersburg alignment. The Baltimore and Ohio backed the convention and the engineer Latrobe monitored the proceedings for the company. At the end of the year, McLane outlined the company's status concerning its charter and possible routes to the Ohio River in a memorial to the Virginia legislature. He concluded by seeking more time and permission to strike the Ohio River at Parkersburg. Thus the stage was set for the semifinal event in Richmond.

The same antagonists were present in January 1845 that had harassed the president and his engineer three years before—Wheeling, the James River and Kanawha Canal Company, the Virginia railroads south of Washington, and the Winchester and Potomac Railroad—but as before, it was mostly a contest with Wheeling. Latrobe and Knight began a feud that continued for months over the intricacies of their respective routes and costs, leaving the rhetoric to McLane and his Wheeling opponent, James S. Wheate, who reminded the company of its "plighted faith" to his city, which the railroad denied. Latrobe hurriedly put together a survey report for McLane, pointing out that there were three routes to Wheeling through Virginia besides Knight's. They all followed creeks to the Ohio River south of the city and stayed along the edge of the river to Wheeling. Fishing Creek was 38 miles below town, then there was Fish Creek, 23 miles distant, and finally, Grave Creek, which ended at Elizabethtown, just eleven miles downriver from Wheeling. All three routes were longer than Knight's route via Wheeling Creek, but they were also more level and therefore less costly. Latrobe believed that his alignment along Fishing Creek to New Martinsville, besides offering better connections to Ohio's planned rail lines, would be $1.5 million cheaper to construct and operate than Knight's.

New Martinsville was about halfway between Wheeling and Parkersburg. If the last proved unattainable, the B&O would have settled for the first. But it soon became clear that no route was permissible that did not go directly overland to Wheeling without striking the Ohio River first. A political tug-of-war ensued. The railroad dug in its heels as far south on the river as it could get and the city of Wheeling dragged it inexorably northward. By the time they were through, the three insignificant creeks—Fishing, Fish, and Grave—would be as indelibly imprinted in the company records and the political annals of Virginia as the Point of Rocks and Harpers Ferry.

Pained and defiant by turns, McLane had the last word in Richmond in January 1845 in a speech to the House of Delegates' committee on roads. The B&O had been called a "foreign corporation," even a "Trojan horse," but its mileage was greater in Virginia than in Maryland, he pointed out. He had noticed the contest between Wheeling and Parkersburg over the route, and he wanted no part of it. McLane was especially stung by the assistance rendered in Richmond to Wheeling's James S. Wheate, in preparing his case against the railroad, by Jonathan Knight, "a former confidential officer of the company, until recently, exercising an important agency in its affairs, [who] has been by his side; to prompt to enquiry, to delve into the deepest recesses of the company's transactions, to develope all its mysteries and mistakes." As for Knight's alignment, McLane said, "This newly discovered route to Wheeling, shunning the river after getting within a few miles of its banks, climbing hills, creeping along precipices, and tunnelling mountains, in as many as seven places in a distance of some [35] miles . . . [is] impracticable." Moreover, the company would never adopt "a route productive only of embarrassment and loss." Concerning

Parkersburg and other possible destinations on the Ohio River south of Wheeling, McLane promised, "I am not given to pursue an object, however great, by sinister means, and I know those whom I represent to be equally scrupulous."[4]

McLane apparently convinced the committee to report a bill granting the company the right-of-way to Parkersburg. The Wheeling delegates, however, added enough amendments in the House to make it read more like a penalty clause than an enabling act. In February, the Virginia legislature passed the B&O law of 1845. It extended the charter, but the restrictions overcame the advantages. The railroad was forced to go to Wheeling directly, and branch lines to any point on the Ohio River below that city were forbidden. The State of Virginia would pay nothing (the former stock subscriptions were canceled), but it could tax the B&O's property and profits. Other railroads were permitted to intersect their line. The act imposed rate limits on local travel, on the Washington Branch, and on goods transferred between the B&O and the C&O Canal, along which certain freight depots were to be established. The company was also required to take over Virginia's Winchester & Potomac Railroad and pay off its debts.

There was no official reaction from the B&O until the stockholders met the following July. A month before that, President James K. Polk appointed McLane minister to England to deal with the Oregon question. Weary of the railroad and attracted by the $9,000 salary and an equal amount in expenses, McLane leaped at the chance. Money was always his prime mover. The B&O's board of directors refused to accept his resignation and appointed banker-politician Samuel Jones, Jr., president pro-tem at $3,000 a year, half McLane's former salary. McLane and his family took the Liverpool steamer from Boston on July 16, 1845. He was gone for sixteen months during a critical period when the railroad was literally trying to find its way.

More than the usual politicking went on for several weeks before the stockholders' meeting. Knight and some of Wheeling's leading residents spent two weeks in Baltimore, lobbying personally and in the press for the Virginia act's acceptance. McLane himself did not attend the meeting, but he recommended rejection in a letter to the stockholders. The Wheeling group asked for approval, or at least for the postponement of any adverse decision. A delegation from Pittsburgh argued that the next session of the Pennsylvania legislature was sure to pass an acceptable law guaranteeing the right-of-way to their city. The engineer Latrobe delivered a lucid exegesis of the Virginia legislation and made a striking comparison of the different alignments. Knight's route via Wheeling Creek, he said, the one prescribed by the law, was roughly 30 miles longer and would be $3 million more expensive to build and operate than the B&O's old alignment through Pennsylvania to Wheeling. It was also about 60 miles longer and $6 million more costly than the B&O line to Pittsburgh. In his opinion, the importance of Wheeling's location on the National Road had been exaggerated, and besides the problem of 48 river shoals between Wheeling and Parkersburg, a more southerly point on the Ohio would be better for trade.

The Baltimore and Ohio's old friend John Pendleton Kennedy also made a good case, cutting his way brilliantly through the thicket of laws, charters, and subscriptions of the three states and their effects on one another, but in his eagerness to promote an unrestricted right-of-way, he did say some things that were not quite true, such as that the company's intention when it began was to build a railroad to the Ohio River "without reference to any ascertained route, or definite point of termination." The 1827 "Proceedings of Sundry Citizens," the railroad's primary document, makes it clear that, from the outset, the idea was to parallel the National Road to Wheeling, which was specifically mentioned as a destination. At the same time, the company was thinking about Parkersburg, sanctioned by the Virginia charter that year, and it did not object to Pittsburgh, which was required by Pennsylvania's 1828 charter to be at least a branch line terminus. Clearly, the B&O's preferences had changed in the interim, as had also the liberal policies of the neighboring states, especially Virginia, where the lawmakers now wanted to deny the company a choice of routes, refuse financial aid, and require the railroad, which had been forced to relinquish its more direct access through Pennsylvania, "still to seek Wheeling over a circuitous and almost impracticable line, with great increase of cost," Kennedy asserted.[5]

Thus persuaded, the stockholders rejected the law by the resounding vote of 50,632 shares to two. (The two yes votes were reportedly cast by a Wheeling share-owner.) The result was to turn the eastern and western sections of Virginia and Pennsylvania against each other and to ignite the smoldering competition between Pittsburgh and Wheeling for the Baltimore and Ohio Railroad. Three-fourths of the western Virginia counties wanted the B&O's destination to be at Parkersburg. The James River and Kanawha Canal Company of Richmond opposed that destination on the theory that the farther south the railroad went on the Ohio River, the greater were the chances of Richmond's trade ending up in Baltimore. The same principle was at work in Philadelphia, which saw its Main Line Canal directly threatened by a railroad between Baltimore and Pittsburgh. Philadelphia was then talking about building its own rail line. In Pittsburgh, meanwhile, a mad passion flared for the Baltimore and Ohio. Wheeling bided its time.

The Ohio River, which was at the center of the noisy contest among the three states and six cities for one railroad, was by the 1840's one of the nation's great avenues of trade, as important to western Virginia as the Atlantic Ocean was to the eastern part of the state. Parkersburg, the youngest and smallest of the three Ohio River contenders for the B&O, was the terminus of the Northwestern Turnpike and the head of year-round steamboat navigation. Its marine and industrial development had barely begun, however, and with a population of just 1,400, the town was significant mainly in its potential. Parkersburg's real growth as a rail crossroads and oil refining center was ten or twenty years away. Wheeling, which Congress had made a port of entry in 1831, was a thriving distribution and production center fifteen years later. It had a population of about 11,000 and numerous manufacturers of steam engines, iron, glass, and paper. Wheeling was about to become the home of the world's first great wire suspension bridge. But both Virginia towns together could not equal Pittsburgh, population 70,000, the capital of the upper Ohio River Valley. In 1846, between 300 and 400 steam engines burned 2,500 tons of coal a day there to make cotton, glass, and iron. Fifty-one blast furnaces on the Allegheny River sent their pig iron to Pittsburgh. The city handled 60,000 tons of it that year, turning it into products for everything from bridges to steamboats. Ten of these a day called at Pittsburgh and there was daily packet service to Cincinnati as well as growing canal traffic to Erie and Cleveland.

In the months following the stockholders' meeting, Knight and Latrobe, former comrades, continued to snipe at each other with pamphlets. Knight accused Latrobe of magnifying the cost differences of their respective routes to induce the stockholders to reject the Virginia law, "a pretty serious charge against me, which I call upon him to substantiate," retorted Latrobe.[6] Each freely interpreted the company's survey history (which they had largely written) to prove his current thesis—that Wheeling was, or was not, an original destination of the Baltimore and Ohio Railroad.

The Virginia legislature early in 1846 postponed the extension of the James River and Kanawha Canal and chartered a railroad from Richmond to the Ohio River, and also refused to allow a private company, backed by the Clarksburg convention of northwestern Virginia counties, to build a rail line to Parkersburg. It was, as the lawmakers supposed, a B&O surrogate. Then, after carefully reviewing McLane's letter to the stockholders and other documents that figured in the rejection of the 1845 law, they passed another that they hoped would prove more acceptable. This act, passed in February 1846, did mitigate some of the offensive conditions of the 1845 law, such as state taxes, but it retained Wheeling as the terminus, which was the main reason the stockholders had rejected the previous version.

The more significant action for the company that year took place in the Pennsylvania legislature at Harrisburg, where representatives of the Baltimore and Pittsburgh city councils petitioned the members to pass a B&O right-of-way bill. The legislative session began with a Philadelphia-backed convention that opposed the Baltimore and Ohio and promoted a Central Railroad through Pennsylvania. Like Maryland, Pennsylvania had suspended payments on its debt, mainly because of its $10 million investment in the Main Line of Internal Improvements, the makeshift collection of railroads and canals stretching from Philadelphia to Pittsburgh. The system was now generally recognized as a technological and financial failure, and following the example of Baltimore, Philadelphia wanted to replace it with a railroad.

Yet despite the Main Line's shortcomings, a great deal of Pittsburgh's commerce moved on it. As the 1846 season opened, over 150 canal boats a month were leaving the city. Their cargo was hoisted painstakingly over the mountains on the Allegheny Portage Railroad, loaded once more onto canal boats on the other side and floated down to Harrisburg, where the freight was again transferred to rail cars for the rest of the trip. While the politicians were arguing in Harrisburg that year, more than 50,000 barrels of flour, 20,000 barrels of pork, 1,850 tons of bacon, and large amounts of lard, hemp, and tobacco were sent to market in this fashion. Two-thirds of Pittsburgh's trade going east came up the Ohio River from points south of Wheeling. If the Baltimore and Ohio reached that city, or Parkersburg, Pittsburgh's business would be ruined—or so the merchants felt in Pittsburgh, where they regarded Philadelphia's plans for the Pennsylvania Railroad as a ruse to prevent them from having a rail connection to Baltimore.

One gauge of the high feelings generated by the B&O's right-of-way bill, sponsored by Pittsburgh and western Pennsylvania politicians, was its zigzag course through the legislature. At the end of February 1846, after several days of heated debate, the Senate defeated the measure by one vote. "All the sophistry and blarney that Philadelphia may use from now till the close of the next century can never convince us against the teachings of experience and common sense," the Pittsburgh *Gazette* said editorially.[7] Three days later the Senate reconsidered its vote and passed the bill. In the House, the struggle continued for over a month, with the Pittsburgh *Gazette* erupting periodically to warn that if the legislature refused the right-of-way to the Baltimore company, western Pennsylvania ought to secede.

While the debate continued, nearly 400 delegates from twenty western counties met near Pittsburgh. Walter Forward, who addressed the convention, talked about the "selfish and stubborn folly" and "stupid blindness" of Pennsylvanians who wanted to keep the Baltimore and Ohio Railroad out of the state. It was an "unnatural and most unjust policy," he said: the western counties had the right to trade with anyone or build a railroad anywhere, and no one would make them "slaves to Philadelphia."[8]

A few days later, the Pennsylvania House of Representatives passed the B&O right-of-way bill, but it added a crippling amendment to the effect that if the newly authorized Central Railroad Company (the Pennsylvania Railroad) obtained $3 million in stock subscriptions and began construction at either end of the line by July 1, 1847, the grant to the B&O would be null and void. The measure was returned to the Senate, where Pittsburgh's George Darsie, a friend of Baltimore, tried to amend it so that the Pennsylvania Railroad could not comply, but his stratagem failed and the law was passed at the end of April 1846.

It was now clear that, inspired by the Baltimore and Ohio, the two states on either side of Maryland recognized the limitations of their outmoded canal systems and were ready to replace them with long-range railroads from their port cities to the west, within their own territory that stretched conveniently all the way to the Ohio River. Furthermore, both states were determined to make life difficult for their neighbor, Maryland, which needed an easement from one or both to reach the same goal.

In Pittsburgh, there was no gloom, only renewed determination. In less than two weeks, Darsie, Harman Denny, William Robinson, Jr., and others, with the B&O's connivance, had created a substitute. Their device was a dead-letter company known as the Pittsburgh and Connellsville Railroad. As subsequently revealed in a Wheeling analysis, the depth of their deception was breathtaking, even in those days of political legerdemain. A Pittsburgh group had chartered this railroad in 1837. Their immediate destination, 58 miles south on the Youghiogheny River, lay along the B&O's Pennsylvania route, near where the line would branch off to Wheeling. The law mandated that work start in five years, but nothing was done and the charter lapsed in 1842. The following year, the Pennsylvania legislature passed a bill entitled "an act for the relief of the overseers of the poor of the borough of Erie, and for other purposes." A rider was added reviving the Pittsburgh and Connellsville Railroad and providing for its extension beyond the original terminus.

In legislative parlance, a bill with such hidden provisions is known as a "snake," but this one was discovered before the governor signed it into law. The solons in Harrisburg then compounded their felony by adding an amendment to "a resolution legalizing the election of a justice of the peace in the borough of Dillsburg in the county of York, and for other purposes," that repealed the railroad charter provisions of "an act for the relief of the overseers of the poor of the borough of Erie," and so on. These statutes, known only to a few, lurked on the lawbooks of Pennsylvania until needed. In April 1846, with the Pennsylvania Railroad ascendant in Harrisburg, they were brought out. On private-bill day that month, the legislature approved "an act to authorize the court of quarter sessions of Alleghany county to vacate Delaware lane in said county, and for other purposes." The other purposes, by now familiar, were of course to resuscitate the Pittsburgh and Connellsville Railroad by repealing the previous act and reinstating the original one. This time the fraud went undetected, the governor signed the law, and its true nature was not revealed until after the session ended.[9]

During its erratic beginnings, the Pittsburgh and Connellsville had Latrobe draw up detailed plans for a rail line from Pittsburgh to Cumberland. Now that the current charter allowed the railroad to build to any point on the Youghiogheny River within Pennsylvania, the reconstituted company asked the Baltimore and Ohio for help. Samuel Jones, Jr., the B&O's president pro-tem, approved a $35,000 subscription to P&C Rr. stock. When a group from Pittsburgh arrived in Baltimore in the summer of 1846 for discussions with B&O officials, Jones further promised in writing that the company would meet them at the state line and provide "valuable pecuniary aid" to help construct the Pennsylvania portion of the route. The P&C Rr. named Latrobe their chief engineer. He sent Steele and Atkinson to begin surveys around McKeesport and they got ready to let contracts. Although the Baltimore and Ohio was vilified as a foreign monster that would destroy the state, there was no objection in Pennsylvania to the Pittsburgh and Connellsville Railroad.

In Virginia, alarmed by this activity, proponents of the Parkersburg route held a large right-of-way convention at Weston, south of Clarksburg, in September 1846. Their purpose, the same as before, was to inspire a surrogate firm to build the line. This gathering was also fomented by the B&O Railroad, which employed traveling agents and "outre and incongruous" handbills to stir up the local residents, according to their Wheeling opposition.[10] The delegates called Virginia's refusal to grant the B&O a route to Parkersburg "an act of injustice and oppression unparalleled in the history of legislation."[11] At that point Louis McLane returned from England.

His second tour as minister had been a qualified but not immediate success. The early negotiations on Oregon were conducted in Washington, leaving McLane with problems of his own in London. Many of his old friends were dead. He became ill but rallied, then used his diplomatic skills to help bring the stalemated negotiations to a successful end in June 1846. Before coming home, he asked the Barings for a $1 million B&O reconstruction loan, and was turned down because Maryland was still in default. The final insult was to have the Secretary of State job dangled before him, only to see it snatched away by circumstances. McLane returned reluctantly to the Baltimore and Ohio Railroad on October 1, 1846. The board reelected him president. McLane and Jones, rivals who disagreed on where the railroad should terminate, decided they would each write a statement for the annual report. McLane hedged on the line to Pittsburgh, saying that if it did not interfere with the B&O's construction "to its legitimate termination at a more southern point on the Ohio," the company and the people of Baltimore would support it. Meanwhile, he hoped they could obtain a better law from Virginia.[12] Jones, more optimistic, noted that the Pittsburgh and Connellsville Railroad was off to an energetic start and said it would be easy to build a short line from Cumberland to join it.

McLane's comments upset the P&C Rr. officials. They found his language "in striking contrast with the assurances of his predecessor," and ambiguous. The contretemps on their return to Baltimore for another meeting further disillusioned them. Darsie, Denny, Robinson, and Neville B. Craig arrived in the city in early November to see McLane. The president greeted them by saying he had tried to postpone the conference, but since his letter had not reached them in time, he would call a meeting that afternoon at four o'clock in the company offices. When the Pittsburgh committee got there, according to their version of events, Samuel Hoffman explained at length why the B&O could not now afford to help them financially. From his presentation, it seemed that McLane, Hoffman, and the other B&O directors were unfamiliar with the promises made by Samuel Jones, Jr.

Much more conversation "of a somewhat desultory character" took place, during which the P&C Rr. group urged the need to expedite their work and the B&O spokesmen said they definitely favored a Pittsburgh connection but were not prepared to make any further subscription. The meeting ended at a late hour. The disgruntled Pittsburgh delegation lingered for two extra days to lobby the B&O directors before the upcoming board meeting. They told McLane that if they went back empty-handed, their backers would be forced to seek an unwanted connection with Philadelphia. "The Pittsburgh and Connellsville Railroad Company cannot remain in its present state of doubt and uncertainty," they said.[13]

When the B&O directors met, they learned for the first time the P&C Rr.'s demands: a junction between Pennsylvania's Franklin Railroad and the B&O opposite Hancock, a $2 million subscription representing two-thirds of the construction cost from Pittsburgh to the Maryland state line, and the first $350,000 immediately. The B&O negotiators would not agree to those terms. They claimed that the Pennsylvanians were equally dissatisfied with the B&O's offer of financial aid when the money market improved and with their assurance that the P&C Rr. was second only in importance to a line farther south. The Baltimore and Ohio directors voted to submit the matter to the stockholders. The Pittsburgh and Connellsville delegates left town and never came back. Before the stockholders' meeting that was scheduled for February 1847, the B&O issued its own requirements for a reduced $600,000 subscription to P&C Rr. stock. There were to be no intersections with other lines without B&O consent, and additional caveats were provided respecting rates, start of construction, and so on. "Wholly inadmissable," rejoined William Robinson, P&C Rr. president.

The negotiations were now being conducted in the press. McLane's high-density reply ran for three and a half columns. It was full of feigned offense at Pittsburgh's peremptory tone, but it also revealed his primary reason for wanting to take the railroad elsewhere. Philadelphia had already raised nearly $1 million to build the Pennsylvania Railroad. Besides competing with the B&O at Pittsburgh, they might intercept its line before it got there. The Tidewater Canal was already siphoning off Baltimore's trade to Philadelphia, according to McLane, "and we would not be justified in aggravating the mischief by opening a more serious drain at another point. Indeed, not the least reason for declining to accept one or more of the Pennsylvania laws renewing our corporate franchise was the right of intersection reserved in favor of the roads of that state; and after rejecting these, and, by constructing our road on the Virginia side of the Potomac, escaping a connection with 'the Franklin Rail Road' at Hagerstown, we would scarcely be warranted in consenting to a connection by another work, at a far more dangerous point." [14]

McLane said the P&C Railroad's preferred "northern" route (very close to the existing alignment between Cumberland and Pittsburgh) could be intercepted more easily than the one the B&O liked at the time, which was a cheaper "southern" route leading to the place where the Youghiogheny River crossed the Maryland state line. (It was never built.) Under the P&C Rr. charter, the B&O had until April 1848 to decide whether to advance more money and construct the line. They should wait at least until the surveys were finished, McLane said. He added that there were prospects of obtaining better legislation in Virginia, and the B&O directors had not made any promises to Pittsburgh. The Pittsburgh newspapers immediately claimed they had been "humbugged." Robinson fired off an equally long reply to McLane, listing his grievances, which he summed up by saying, "You have, however, declined to meet us as we hoped to be met." [15]

The editorial opinion in both places was that the last chance for a rail connection had expired. In Baltimore, the *American* said the city, afraid of losing trade to Philadelphia, had dictated the B&O's tough stance toward Pittsburgh. The editors were skeptical of McLane's confidence that a better right-of-way awaited them in Virginia: "The grounds of that belief are not given, and so far as our knowledge goes, they are unknown to this community." [16]

But McLane knew. Within days of the P&C Rr. committee's departure in mid-November 1846, he held a quiet meeting with a man who professed to understand how the Virginia legislature really operated. This man, Alexander J. Marshall, of Warrenton, Virginia, claimed to have been invited to Baltimore by some of the railroad's major stockholders. A few days after his meeting with McLane, Marshall wrote a confidential letter to the B&O president in which he said he had had several years of experience as a "lobby-member" before the Virginia legislature on significant issues, although because of the necessary secrecy surrounding his current mission, he could not offer testimonials.

Marshall's notion was that, up to now, the Richmond-Wheeling axis and the Virginia canal and railroad companies had overcome the B&O's legislative program by logrolling and simply being present in large numbers and familiar surroundings to argue their case; without equal resources, the claims of the Baltimore company, although necessary and just, would be "mere sounding clamor in the hall. . . . The mass of the members in our legislature, are a thoughtless, careless, light-hearted body of men, who come there for the per diem, and to spend the per diem; for a brief space, they feel the importance and responsibility of their position; they soon, however, engage in idle pleasures, and on all questions disconnected with their immediate constituents, they become as wax, to be moulded by the most pressing influences."

According to Marshall, most of the members could vote with impunity on the B&O's right-of-way; the others would have to be influenced by "a corps of agents, stimulated to an active partisanship, by the strong lure of a high profit . . . give them nothing if they fail; endow them richly if they succeed." The company should know only a single agent and he would select the rest. In fact, Marshall and others were speculating in western Virginia land along the proposed B&O right-of-way, and that would be their ostensible reason for supporting it in Richmond. Marshall made it clear that a heavy outlay of cash would be necessary, requiring "a contingent fund of at least $50,000, secured to my order, on the passage of a law, and its acceptance by your company."[17]

McLane discussed Marshall's proposal in an unrecorded meeting at the railroad office on December 12, 1846, with a special committee of directors set up to obtain the right-of-way: James Harwood, William Cooke, Samuel Hoffman, and Columbus O'Donnell. Later that same day, McLane authorized Marshall to bribe the Virginia legislature with $50,000 for a route across the state to the Ohio River. McLane then invited the lobbyist back to Baltimore for further talks, the results of which were that Marshall was to get his money in 6 percent company bonds in five years if he obtained a law granting the right-of-way either to Parkersburg or to Fishing Creek (New Martinsville), for the B&O or for an independent company, and if the stockholders accepted it.

Before the 1847 legislative session in Richmond began, there was press speculation that talks were taking place between the B&O and Wheeling and that if the legislature stood firm, the railroad would go there by the prescribed route. McLane dismissed these stories as rumors; the railroad might stop at Cumberland or go to Pittsburgh, but "never" to Wheeling under the existing laws. Wheeling's James S. Wheate was skeptical. He asked his colleagues to reject yet another scheme for a substitute company to build a railroad to Parkersburg and to require the B&O to go to his city. (The Parkersburg proposal, backed by the Weston Convention, was an early casualty of the session.) Wheate blamed McLane's absence in England for the delay and agitation of the right-of-way question, and he dismissed the Pittsburgh and Connellsville Railroad as "an exploded scheme."[18]

When the B&O stockholders met in early February 1847 they took no real action because they were awaiting news from the Virginia legislature. They named a fact-finding committee on the Pittsburgh alignment and subscription issues, and passed a resolution saying they would never build a railroad to Wheeling according to Knight's route prescribed by the 1845 and 1846 laws. The Virginia legislature continued its session marked by backroom intrigue and sharp debate. Marshall and Duff Green, another B&O political operative, worked the cloakrooms and hallways. Out on the floor, Wheeling's D. M. Edgington and Andrew Hunter, the B&O's former right-of-way agent who was now a member, entertained their colleagues in the House of Delegates. The introduction of a new proposal that would take the railroad to Fish Creek, thirteen miles north of their agreed-on destination at Fishing Creek, coincided with a story in the Baltimore *American* quoting McLane as saying that a more northern terminus might be acceptable. Marshall wrote McLane: "I have taken the ground, that this paper has misrepresented you. . . . The argument of Wheeling, that you will go to that city . . . is greatly strengthened; they say that all you require is a change of the 'prescribed' route, and an assurance that you can do no better." Therefore, Marshall said, "It is necessary you should speak plain and speak at once; say you cannot extend your road, unless permitted to strike the Ohio, at least as low as Fishing creek." Furthermore, McLane should prepare himself to accept a compromise higher up: "This, of course, would cut me out; but that cannot be helped." [19] McLane did just that: he sent a public letter to the Baltimore *American* saying that no terminus above Fishing Creek was acceptable. Then he wrote privately to Marshall that if all else failed, the company might accept Fish Creek, in which case, McLane added magnanimously, "your compensation would apply to that." The Richmond *Enquirer* explained to its readers that "Fishing, not Fish, is the ultimatum of the company," and Hunter asked that his bill to construct the railroad to that place be taken up. Edgington referrred to McLane's recently published correspondence and asked for time to investigate an effort to influence the legislature.

The B&O stockholders met again at the end of February 1847 and listened to a lengthy analysis of the distances and costs of the various routes. The fact-finding committee said Pittsburgh was important, but not enough to be selected as a terminus "at this time." Its members were more intrigued with Parkersburg, even though it was also out of the running for the present. They liked Parkersburg because Baltimore, Parkersburg, Cincinnati, and Saint Louis were all within one degree of latitude of each other: "These cities are almost all in a direct line and the country from the Ohio River to St. Louis is fertile and level yielding produce in abundance and presenting a surface well adapted for a continuous rail road." [20]

After McLane presented his views, the stockholders again determined not to go to Wheeling without a subscription from that city and a terminus at Fishing Creek. They tried to keep interest alive in Pittsburgh by assigning Johns Hopkins (who became a B&O director later that year) and others to seek stock subscriptions for the P&C Rr. from the Baltimore City Council and the citizens. The lone dissenter was Wheeling advocate John H. Alexander, of the Cumberland Coal and Iron Company. Hearing this, the P&C Rr. ended negotiations, claiming the B&O was determined to run its line south of their city and was only using them to try to get a better law from Virginia.

In the House of Delegates in Richmond, the tug-of-war between Wheeling and the company over the railroad's destination was nearing a denouement. Hunter's bill was at last on the floor, the competing measure naming Fish Creek having been withdrawn. Reading aloud from the newspaper, Hunter enumerated the B&O stockholders' resolutions, which his bill incorporated: striking the Ohio River at Fishing Creek and calling on Wheeling for a $1 million subscription. He promised his listeners with a straight face that he had written it without any help from the B&O's officers. Edgington offered an amendment that not only reinstated Fish Creek as the route for the railroad but gave Wheeling the discretion to take it even higher, to Grave Creek (Moundsville). The approval of this amendment, 66–57, on February 24, 1847, was tantamount to passage of the act.

The Richmond press hailed the end of "one of the most 'vexed questions' that have ever come before our Legislature."[21] The Wheeling *Times* proudly saluted Edgington: "Our Delegate." Hunter declared that the railroad's interests were now in good hands, and there were congratulations all around. But there was no joy among the right-of-way agents. Thomas Swann, who would also become a B&O director later that year, showed up in Richmond toward the end of the session in a rescue operation. "I found the friends of the right-of-way disheartened, by the signal defeat which they had encountered," he said, "and almost indisposed to rally upon any new propositions."[22] Principle had triumphed over profit in the Virginia legislature. Despite his $50,000 bribery fund, Marshall had struck out.

The post-vote analysis showed that 16 out of 20 backers of Richmond's James River and Kanawha Canal Company, who had promised to support Hunter's bill, voted against it. "There have been many secret misrepresentations operating," said a close observer.[23] The B&O tried to salvage their program in the Senate, but the legislature was tired of being whipsawed. Even the company's friends were turning against it. The Richmond *Enquirer*, which had championed the railroad's free choice of a route, complained that McLane had been a little too diplomatic, "and we trust he will now desist." They called for an end "to this continued agitation, which has disturbed the peace of our own State, and so long delayed the great work."[24] When the Senate defeated an amendment that would have given the B&O Railroad a route to Parkersburg in exchange for 20 percent of the company's net revenues, the Richmond *Times* made it sound as if that had been an attempt to bribe the legislature, adding haughtily, "The state is not prepared to do what she conceives impolitic and unjust for a consideration."[25]

Virginia passed the right-of-way act on March 6, 1847. Marshall sent McLane a bill for $600; McLane paid it and they called it a day. Wheeling, victorious, professed an airy indifference. "We are frequently asked what is the news about the rail road?" said James E. Wharton, editor of the Wheeling *Times*. "We answer, once for all, we do not know or care." He said that after the B&O's four "violent efforts" to obtain a law (actually there had been at least half a dozen going back to 1842), the company would probably be unable to get a better one, "and they can either take it or stay where they are."[26]

The 1847 Virginia act authorized the B&O to build its line from the junction of Buffalo Creek and Piles Fork, where Knight and Latrobe had ended their joint survey in the summer of 1844 (now Mannington, West Virginia), to Wheeling. In a compromise worked out by Knight, they were allowed to strike the Ohio River at Fish Creek or Grave Creek. If the latter route proved more expensive to construct, Wheeling could pay the difference to have the railroad go that way. It was a slight improvement over Knight's far north Wheeling Creek alignment, but no more than that. Other jurisdictions had influenced the location. The line had to cross the Tygart Valley River within three miles of its confluence with Three Fork Creek in Taylor County. (This spot became Grafton, West Virginia, the most important division point on the early railroad after Cumberland.) The law canceled the state's former stock subscription but provided for a $1 million Wheeling subscription. It also extended the charter for fifteen years. Therefore, the company did get some of what it wanted, but it was denied the most important thing, a good route. McLane was in the position of the union leader who after a long and difficult bargaining process has to decide whether or not to accept the result, poor as it is, and if he does, how to sell it to the rank and file.

The Baltimore *American* dismissed the Virginia route as "entirely out of the question" and started beating the drums again for Pittsburgh. But Pittsburgh, so that city's press declared, had been insulted by the B&O's "disgraceful equivocation . . . now a Baltimore connection is by no means popular with our people." A spokesman for the Pittsburgh and Connellsville Railroad said that "no more diplomacy or demurring" would be tolerated from Baltimore because "procrastination has chilled every spark of enterprise" in Pittsburgh.[27]

There was a "little pique" in Pittsburgh, Kennedy admitted to the B&O stockholders at their first meeting, in March 1847, after the passage of the Virginia law. But he denied that the company was using the P&C Rr. only as a foil "to play off with Virginia for a route to Parkersburg or Fishing Creek." He had always been for Pittsburgh, Kennedy said, because he doubted that Virginia would ever provide a decent right-of-way. McLane's response was that rail lines to Parkersburg and Pittsburgh were compatible, but those to Wheeling and Pittsburgh were not. If one route was chosen, "Wheeling should be the terminus," he said.[28]

On Kennedy's recommendation, a committee including himself, Thomas Swann, Joseph W. Patterson, and Johns Hopkins was appointed to go to Pittsburgh and make amends, but they decided to write instead. The Pittsburgh spokesmen were not offended: they had had enough of committees and discussions that accomplished nothing. They left the door open just enough to say that if the B&O took the shortest and cheapest route between the two places, they could still do business. "On the other hand, if adverse counsels are to prevail in your city, those negotiations, which have [produced] only vexation and bad feelings will be forever terminated."[29]

Shortly after this, in April 1847, Kennedy and McLane clashed openly in front of the stockholders over the destination of the Baltimore and Ohio. Kennedy proposed that the Pittsburgh and Baltimore companies split the cost of the P&C Rr. line from Pittsburgh to Turkeyfoot (Confluence), Pennsylvania. The B&O would bring it on down to Cumberland along its own route, with financial help from Baltimore. Thomas Parkin Scott, an influential city director, derailed this idea with a substitute that toned down its provisions and left everything to the B&O directors. McLane, as usual, found fault with Pittsburgh's terms. He repeated his concerns about Philadelphia and the Pennsylvania Railroad and said that Baltimore's "true direction" was toward Cincinnati: in other words, reject Pittsburgh and confer with Wheeling.

But the Pittsburgh connection, whose primary function under McLane was to threaten Virginia, had acquired a life of its own. Baltimore businessmen, led by Robert Garrett among others, met to promote the Pennsylvania terminus. Garrett represented Robert Garrett & Sons, commission merchants who had extensive business dealings in Pittsburgh and throughout the Middle West. They were then becoming merchant bankers and developing a deep and abiding interest in the Baltimore and Ohio Railroad. The editors of the Baltimore *American* believed that building a line to Pittsburgh was the best way to extract a decent route from Virginia. Nobody was seriously considering going to Wheeling, at least through Virginia, they said.

Kennedy, fearing that the company would wind up with no route at all, appointed himself the B&O's minister without portfolio to the Pittsburgh and Connellsville Railroad. Their directors, by various means, let him know that his plan for constructing the line was acceptable. Kennedy so informed the B&O directors. "McLane was silent and surly," he said.[30] Although Kennedy had begun the month of April as a McLane supporter and had defended his lukewarm commitment to Pittsburgh and criticized the P&C Railroad's financial demands in a letter that was later published, by the end of the month he had turned against McLane and was making caustic journal notations about his political opportunism and erratic decision making. "A singular spirit has taken possession of McLane of late. He has become suddenly virtually opposed to me. This is because I have advocated the Pittsburg route to the stockholders," Kennedy wrote. "I am obliged to believe that his professions on this subject were insincere—that he never did wish to construct a branch to Pittsburg"; and later, "What has got into him!"; and finally, " *'He is not to be trusted'* as Mr. Clay once told me."[31]

Kennedy made it known through the Baltimore *American* "that the community of Pittsburgh, as well as the Pittsburgh and Connellsville Company, will negotiate with us," based on his plan for sharing the construction cost. Since Pittsburgh was now willing to furnish their part of the funds, "Under these circumstances, I presume, there will be no hesitation on the part of our city or Company to enter into the arrangement."[32]

But John Pendleton Kennedy was not the president of the Baltimore and Ohio Railroad. While Kennedy was negotiating on his own with the P&C Rr., McLane was in Wheeling, with T. Parkin Scott, Joseph W. Patterson, Samuel Hoffman, and Thomas Swann, winding up a week of official discussions with city officials and delegates from Ohio. William Robinson, Jr., president of the P&C Rr., responded that in light of the friendly attitude of Baltimore's merchants and citizens, they would make "one effort more" to effect an arrangement with the B&O and would welcome a conference committee in Pittsburgh, because they were ready to take action. It was what they always said when they wanted something to happen in Baltimore that never did.

McLane received Robinson's letter in Wheeling. Back in Baltimore, McLane convened a board meeting with a false sense of urgency, ostensibly to consider the Pennsylvania initiative but really to talk about Virginia. The delegation was on its way back anyway, the Wheeling conference having ended inconclusively because more surveys were needed. Latrobe was dispatched to conduct them. McLane said a Wheeling group would visit Baltimore to resume the negotiations.

At the board meeting on May 8, 1847, matters were further confused. Columbus O'Donnell and James Harwood tried to name yet another Pittsburgh visiting committee, but "there appearing to be no member of the Board willing to proceed to Pittsburgh," it was decided to open the negotiations by mail, only this time they could not even find anybody to write to Pittsburgh. Finally three volunteers, among the board's least-known members, were selected. Such was the official report of the meeting.[33] Kennedy's version, recorded in his journal, gives a different slant:

> The President (McLane) who has been with a committee to Wheeling to *beg* for favors, returned last night. . . . He now reports his progress in that matter—nothing. They won't allow us to go to Fish Creek, or any where on the river. McLane and his clique have, however, jumped Jim Crow, and are all for Wheeling: strange enough, this! After [haranguing] Virginia for ten years on this question, with so many protestations that nothing could induce him to recommend Wheeling to the company. We have new lights upon it now. He has worked up the board into an aversion to Pittsburgh. I refuse to go on the committee, and prophecy the failure of the negotiation. McLane and myself make speeches—at daggers. He black as thunder—I blacker.[34]

Kennedy continued to push for Pittsburgh in two more board meetings that month. At the first one, held in midweek, the directors voted down his resolutions, which he claimed embodied all the B&O's demands, 19–7. "Another angry discussion," he said. "We adjourn with declarations of war."[35] The two sides lobbied furiously over the weekend before the final confrontation on Monday. Kennedy had amended his proposal to meet every B&O objection and added new provisions to accommodate the P&C Rr.'s interests. On Sunday afternoon, at the home of director John Spear Nicholas, he encountered Samuel Hoffman, with the president's program. It was "the resolution with forty 'whereases' prepared by McLane, which Sam had in his hat, and was running around to read to every pliable director by way of preparation for tomorrow," Kennedy noted.[36] The argument over where to end the railroad had escalated into a full-blown proxy fight between the Pittsburgh and Wheeling factions on the board of directors for the control of the company. Each group was trying to unseat the other.

At Monday's special board meeting the former colleagues—two of the most eloquent, persuasive, and outstanding men of their age—confronted each other for the last time. McLane spoke first. He dismissed Pittsburgh's financial and route stipulations as novel and opposed to the B&O's best interests: if the company diverted its resources and energies now to construct a branch to Pittsburgh, it would "forever destroy their ability and their hope to extend the Main Stem of the road to a more Southern point on the Ohio River," he said.[37] Kennedy admitted in a lengthy reply that the latest proposals from Pittsburgh were not exactly what he expected, but he thought the negotiations could still be conducted in good faith, if they had not been designed in advance to fail. He did not want to see the company spend its money on a railroad to a terminus "too high for the South, and too low for the lakes." [38] But only five other directors agreed with him, while nineteen sided with McLane.

It was John Pendleton Kennedy's final appearance in an official capacity with the Baltimore and Ohio Railroad. The man who had been its most outspoken and selfless champion in trying times sold most of his 100 shares of B&O stock two days later. "I am afraid to hold it in the present state of the management," he said. [39] When Kennedy returned to Baltimore in the fall from a tour of Canada, he was defeated in his final race for Congress by Louis McLane's son Robert, the Democratic candidate. And he was eased out as a railroad director. "It was a useless piece of malice, as I had made up my mind, if I had been elected, to resign the seat," he commented. Kennedy added that he was "determined never to go to the board whilst McLane was president. My belief is that he will do the company infinite harm." [40]

But Kennedy's departure from the railroad failed to settle the controversy. The Pittsburgh connection refused to die. At the end of May 1847, Pennsylvania's venerable Andrew Stewart promised a large gathering of merchants in Baltimore that the P&C Rr. would contribute $750,000 and give the B&O control of their charter if they were met halfway. McLane was out of town, and since they could not get a committee from the railroad to go to Pittsburgh, the businessmen decided to send one themselves. Its seven members, including Robert Garrett and John Glenn, convinced a disillusioned audience of P&C Rr. stockholders in Pittsburgh not to abandon the charter or join forces with the Pennsylvania Railroad but to give them a little more time. If they were unable to talk the B&O into building the line from Cumberland to Pittsburgh, they would build it themselves, the business leaders declared grandly.

Back in Baltimore in early June, the merchants made a strong case for Pittsburgh at a public meeting at the Exchange. The Baltimore *American* gave their report five columns. Although mystification and obscurity had characterized the negotiations so far, it said, "The subject from the beginning seems to have possessed, in itself, entire simplicity." The businessmen echoed McLane's description of the Wheeling route of a few years back, "shunning the river . . . climbing hills, creeping along precipices and tunnelling mountains," and cited Latrobe's cost figures showing that it was 60 miles longer and $6 million more costly than the line to Pittsburgh. Moreover, the merchants said, "It has been twice rejected by the Baltimore and Ohio Railroad Company, whose Directors, having changed their views without having changed the nature of the route, now present it for consideration." They found the company's policy incomprehensible: "While the route to Pittsburgh is doomed to rejection . . . the official language of the company here has tantalized us, time and again, with hopes of a different consummation." They wanted railroad lines to Pittsburgh and Parkersburg. [41]

But McLane's mind was made up, and the next day, in his customary long, detailed, and ultimately persuasive fashion, he told the board that they should make location surveys, acquire the right-of-way, and put the railroad under contract from Cumberland to the Maryland state line 55 miles to the west. At that point, they would be near the Cheat River and the Northwestern Turnpike, and could go on to Wheeling, or perhaps, someday, to Pittsburgh. They should also extend the line from Mt. Clare to tidewater on Locust Point. Putting the best face on things, McLane said the Virginia law was "not unfavorable" except for the route and he hoped the Wheeling negotiations would improve that. The company's credit would cover the $1.6 million cost of the western extension. It would go through the coal and iron fields, and when the Locust Point line was finished the increase in trade in these products would more than pay the $96,000 annual interest on the loan.

By starting construction, McLane obviously hoped to stop the argument. The directors went along. Printing his speech in the newspapers, however, only fanned the flames. A correspondent said the president's argument was "weakest of all in the ingenuity by which it would conceal its weaknesses," and the *American* lashed out once again: "What is to be gained by this loss? Not much, certainly, by advancing [55] miles towards the Ohio, with no connections beyond, but with mountains and woods and a wilderness into which the road must debouche." They wrote off the Northwestern Turnpike as "a clay road to Parkersburgh," ridiculed the Cheat River by saying it was "utterly useless as a navigable stream," and maintained that even if the railroad managed to reach it through the mountains of Virginia, they would find there only "a forlorn hope of connecting the road in some imperfect way with the despised city of Pittsburgh."[42]

For a brief moment, the Baltimore City Council backed the Pennsylvania connection, and Henry S. Garrett and others went to work procuring stock subscriptions to the P&C Rr. At this point, toward the end of June, fortunately for McLane's forces, the Wheeling committee came to town. Among them was the B&O's recent legislative opponent, D. M. Edgington. Within a week they had signed an agreement with the railroad to build the line to their city, and in mid-July McLane and the other B&O negotiators presented the case for Wheeling to the board of directors. If their report could be summarized in a sentence, it might say that since they had to go there, Wheeling was just where they wanted to be.

Latrobe had returned to Baltimore a few days in advance of the delegation from the west. His five-week reconnaissance, conducted without instruments, showed that of the three routes to Wheeling legally left open to the railroad—via Fish, Grave, and Wheeling creeks—Fish Creek would be the cheapest. The City of Wheeling accepted this alignment, and also indicated that it would provide a $500,000 subscription to B&O stock, donate a free two-acre downtown depot site along with the right-of-way to it, and allow the use of locomotives within the city limits.

The B&O president and his colleagues did their best to make the agreement sound like the deal of the century. Wheeling, formerly scorned, was now seen to be a long-standing attraction. The evil restrictions of the previous Virginia laws that had caused their rejection (some of which remained in the present legislation) were spoken of as harmless conditions. In any case, the 1847 act was the most favorable the railroad was likely to get, they said. Fish Creek was only sixteen miles higher up on the Ohio River than Fishing Creek and was just as suitable for linking up with western railroads. Ergo, the conclusion: "It is obviously, therefore, the true policy of the company to arrest the trade and travel at *Wheeling*, instead of expending millions to force them to *Pittsburg*, to the fatal injury of the city and the ruin of the road."[43]

The board adopted the report and it was published in the newspapers. Alfred Kelley's less self-serving letters to McLane that appeared along with it were actually more convincing. Kelley had represented the Columbus city council at the Baltimore gathering. "No one railroad," he said, "can ever become the sole line of communication between the great basin of the Mississippi and the Atlantic seaboard."[44] There were northern and southern tiers, Kelley explained. Whereas the Great Lakes trade would always be linked with Canada and New York, Baltimore's proper sphere of influence extended to central Ohio and the middle sections of the states lying east and west of it. The western region's present trade over the National Road to Cumberland and then via the B&O to Baltimore would be vastly increased if rail service were extended into the interior of Ohio. Kelley believed that because the territory on the Ohio side of the river below Wheeling was rough and unpopulated, Wheeling was the best place to make the connection between the B&O and the new Central Ohio Railroad. Incorporated in July 1847, this line would run from Wheeling through Columbus to Cincinnati. Some sections of it were already in operation. (The Central Ohio Rr. eventually became part of the B&O system.)

As the Wheeling issues were being settled, news came that Pennsylvania's Central Railroad Company was meeting its financial requirements and starting construction at Harrisburg and Pittsburgh. Thus the Baltimore and Ohio Railroad's right-of-way through that state was formally voided. Latrobe left Baltimore with three parties of engineers to conduct location surveys to the western Maryland state line. The first group concentrated on the area between Cumberland and Westernport, 27 miles up the Potomac River. The second worked between there and the summit of Backbone Mountain, slowly running their lines on the rugged slopes bordering the Savage River and Crabtree Creek. The third surveyed "the easy and beautiful part of the route lying westward from the summit, through the glades."[45]

The company stockholders were the final obstacle to the complete acceptance of the Wheeling route. They were scheduled to consider it at the end of August 1847. Right up to the day of the meeting, the *American* continued to advocate Pittsburgh and question McLane's leadership; a correspondent pleaded that the meeting be held in a room large enough for everyone to be seated, rather than, as usual, in the board of directors' room.

The gathering, the culmination of the bitter proxy fight, had all the aspects of a carefully contrived event. It began at 10:00 A.M., Wednesday, August 25, 1847, in the cramped company offices. They were filled to capacity. Stockholders stood in the doorways and spilled out into the halls. The *American* reporter complained that the room was so packed that he could not take notes. McLane delivered the report of the Wheeling committee that he had presented the previous month to the board of directors, and for the rest of the morning there were arguments about whether or not to adjourn to await the arrival of one of the state directors and to find a larger room to meet in. They adjourned, and reconvened at 4:00 P.M. that afternoon, in the same room. McLane, meanwhile, had collapsed from the strain and had been carried away unconscious, and was under a doctor's care. The debate began with Tench Tilghman, the late arrival. He and the other state agent, Samuel Sprigg, voted $3.5 million in B&O stock held by the State of Maryland. Tilghman wanted the entire question of routes reexamined and reconsidered at a subsequent stockholders' meeting. It seemed that the state agents believed that the company had never seriously entertained a connection with Pittsburgh and they were worried about insufficient funds to build the line to Wheeling.

Their Baltimore counterpart was director T. Parkin Scott, who voted the 35,000 shares of B&O stock held by the city. Aided by Thomas Swann and others, Scott led the opposition. Since the state and city held equal amounts of stock, their votes would cancel one another and the decision would be up to the private stockholders. The arguments in the hot, confined boardroom continued until 9:00 P.M., when at last the Wheeling forces prevailed. The state agents' proposal was voted down 54,718 shares to 35,520, with most of the private stockholders such as Samuel Hoffman (who voted almost 9,000 shares, the majority of them proxies), siding with Scott. Then by an almost exact reversal of the count, the stockholders voted virtually unanimously to accept the 1847 Virginia act and build the Baltimore and Ohio Railroad to Wheeling.

McLane, taken aback by the fury of the opposition and worn out by his job as B&O president, had strength enough to justify his actions and to plead for harmony in his penultimate annual report. Although Kennedy dismissed it as "humbug," it was a strong defense of the president's stewardship over the past decade and a valiant effort at reconciliation. When he arrived at the Baltimore and Ohio in 1837, McLane said, the railroad's operating expenses were 95 percent of its gross receipts. That figure had now been reduced to 52 percent, which compared favorably with operating costs on a dozen newer New England railroads. A management reorganization with stricter accountability had also improved performance, he said. There could be no more thorough investigation and discussion of where to run the rail line west of Cumberland, McLane continued: "It is a great misfortune that ten years have already been spent in seeking the right to extend the road to the Ohio; but if, after obtaining it . . . ten years more are to be wasted in controversies respecting a route, or in excited struggles to reverse the decision already made . . . it would be . . . fatal." [46]

Following the stockholders' meeting and the appearance of the annual report, the route controversy quickly died. Even the *American* quieted down. The Baltimore citizenry fell to arguing instead over the best alignment for the railroad extension to the inner harbor, reminiscent of the old east side–west side dispute over where the B&O should enter the city. In November 1847, despite a last-ditch effort at revival by Andrew Stewart, Robert Garrett, and others, the P&C Rr. gave up when its supporters gathered once more in Pittsburgh, and, "amidst great confusion and the attempt of several gentlemen to address the meeting, it adjourned." [47] The Baltimore and Ohio concentrated on financing the line to Wheeling.

McLane appointed a select committee including Thomas Swann, Johns Hopkins, Samuel Hoffman, T. Parkin Scott, and George Brown, who had recently returned to the board as a state director, to find the necessary funds. He cautioned against disposing of the Maryland sterling bonds held by the Barings because, even though the state had resumed interest payments on its debt, investor confidence had not returned and the bonds would have to be sold at a loss. McLane thought they could do the job without sacrificing the bonds by applying the railroad's net revenues to construction. Rather than pay dividends to the stockholders, the company would furnish them with equivalent amounts of new stock. Contractors and suppliers might also be willing to accept stock certificates as payment, he said.

Swann, as chairman, delivered the group's report. First it went to the newspapers in a patent attempt to win back public favor. The document was an eloquent example of things to come. Swann credited McLane with taking over a company near bankruptcy and making it into an efficiently managed enterprise. He rearranged the facts in such a way that the $6 million line to Wheeling was now magically shorter and cheaper than the one to Pittsburgh. They at last had a route and it remained only to put down the tracks. Swann said that the railroad's prospects had never "been brighter or more flattering"; they would be more luminous still when they reached the Ohio River. In early January 1848, Swann presented the report to the board of directors, which voted to place the entire line to Wheeling under contract as soon as the location surveys were finished. They would use the annual net revenues for construction and deliver new shares to the stockholders proportionately until outside financing was arranged.

In a suitably bizarre conclusion to these strange events, Alexander J. Marshall sued the B&O Railroad for nonperformance under their contract to bribe the Virginia legislature. Marshall's contention was that since the company had accepted the law, he was entitled to his fee. His first audience was with John H. B. Latrobe, in April 1849, a year after he began pressing his claim. Latrobe's rather devious argument that the railroad's subsequent agreement with Wheeling made it a different law from the one that was passed failed to convince Marshall, who took his case to the public in July 1849 by initiating a pamphlet war.

If the B&O officials were embarrassed, they did not let on. In fact, their attitude was quite cavalier. (Marshall's attorneys were Wheeling advocate T. Parkin Scott, William L. Marshall, and Robert M. McLane, son of the B&O president.) The railroad had been trying for years to get a direct right-of-way across the state of Virginia, Thomas Swann said in reply, "and it is not remarkable that they should have been willing to pay a large contingent fee, to accomplish what they had deemed of such vital importance."[48] Three years later, concerned that the statute of limitations was about to expire on his claim, Marshall went to court. John H. B. Latrobe and Reverdy Johnson stated in the railroad's defense that a contract to bribe a legislature was illegal and therefore unenforceable, and they also argued that the law passed was not the one specified in the agreement. In November 1852, Judge Roger Brooke Taney of the U.S. Circuit Court in Maryland ruled in their favor. In pleading the moral turpitude of the agreement, the company was of course admitting to having made it. As for the law that was passed, a review of McLane's understanding with Marshall, the legislative history of the act itself, and the Wheeling agreement demonstrates that all parties eventually settled on Fish Creek as the Ohio River terminus of the railroad. McLane had even promised Marshall that he would be paid if that was where the line ended.

A few months later, Marshall claimed in a deposition that McLane misled him about the B&O's intention to go to Pittsburgh unless the company got the right-of-way it wanted from Virginia, and he called the Pittsburgh and Connellsville Railroad charter "a sham and a pageant." Marshall further stated that he had hired fifteen agents in Richmond in 1847 and arranged to pay them from $500 to $2,500 each. Marshall's own fee, paid by the railroad, was only $600, and in view of the fact that John H. B. Latrobe received just $700 the same year from the Barings for his successful lobbying on the resumption bill in the Maryland legislature in Annapolis, the lower figure is the more likely one. That would leave 85 percent of the $50,000 fund for other purposes. Neither Marshall nor the B&O Railroad admitted that they intended to bribe Virginia legislators, using instead the euphemism "contingent fees."[49]

Marshall lost his appeal of the case to the Supreme Court. The court in affirming the lower court's decision said that going into "a long and perplexed history" of the legislation and agreements "would require a map of the country, and tedious and prolix explanations." One of the dissenting justices said that the case, having no merit on either side, should not have been in court at all but rather should have been settled in an arena appropriate to the transaction. Congress, the majority pointed out, had outlawed champertous contracts that year (1853): "Bribes, in the shape of high contingent compensation, must necessarily lead to the use of improper means and the exercise of undue influence," which will "subject the state governments to the combined capital of wealthy corporations, and produce universal corruption, commencing with the representative and ending with the elector. Speculators in legislation, public and private, a compact corps of venal solicitors, vending their secret influences, will infest the capital of the Union and of every State, till corruption shall become the normal condition of the body politic, and it will be said of us as of Rome—*omne Romae venale*."[50]

Part III

Cumberland to Wheeling, 1848-1853

23

The Financier

THOMAS SWANN LEARNED POLITICS WITH
the Baltimore and Ohio Railroad. There were worse schools. When he began his term
as president in 1848, Swann was a 39-year-old lawyer, well connected but hardly
notable in the profession. After his term ended in 1853, he became the Know-Nothing
mayor of Baltimore, Unionist governor of Maryland, and after that, a Democratic
congressman for ten years. His record in private industry was the springboard for
his political career. Swann finished the B&O line to Wheeling.

His debut in company affairs occurred at the February 1847 stockholders'
gatherings when he was a member of the committee recommending that Pittsburgh
not be selected as a terminus "at this time," in favor of a more direct route to Parkersburg. He then went to Richmond to try to rescue the Virginia right-of-way legislation,
and from there to Wheeling to help negotiate the B&O's agreement with that city.
In mid-July 1847, he was elected to the board of directors.

At the shareholders' meeting the following month where McLane collapsed and
the private stockholders carried the day for Wheeling, Swann voted 1,640 shares, the
third largest number in private hands (after Samuel Hoffman and Edward Patterson). By the end of the year, he was issuing company policy statements to the press,
as chairman of a high-level committee charged with helping the president find the
money to get the railroad past Cumberland. Swann's January 1848 presentation to
the board of directors resulted in the decision to begin building again.

During the following year, as McLane withdrew more and more, Swann was
clearly being groomed as a successor. He differed politically with McLane, but supported him, he explained. On September 13, 1848, McLane's letter of resignation was
handed to the board of directors at a meeting he did not attend. The letter was ver-
bose and circumspect, but it nevertheless revealed his frustration at trying to build
the railroad to the west, rebuild the old track, and buy new engines and cars with only
the company's annual net revenues to spend. Without additional financial help, he

said, he could not "extend the work as expeditiously as would seem to be demanded." Therefore he was resigning.

The directors accepted McLane's resignation with a perfunctory statement and no real regrets. The stockholders thanked him for "rescuing them . . . from a very low state to their present prosperous one, with a fair prospect of an early completion of the road," and thus ended Louis McLane's eleven years with the Baltimore and Ohio Railroad.[1] Two days later, on October 11, 1848, the directors elected Thomas Swann president, at a salary of $3,000 a year, half McLane's salary. Swann said he did not consider the position permanent, nor did he seem to need or want the money. He took the job, he later recalled, "with the purpose ultimately to appropriate to myself no part of the salary which was assigned to it, I have had no object in view but the success of the company."[2]

Swann offered a welcome change from the bitter divisiveness of the previous administration. McLane had been an austere aristocrat even in the best of times; toward the end, he remained shut up in his office, declined to go out in the field, and would see no one, a critic said, "even on the business of the company, unless his name is first sent up by the porter."[3] Swann made a good impression on his required tour of the railroad. He had the confidence of the stockholders, the respect of the community, and he was accessible to everyone: "Moreover Mr. Swann is a Virginian," a Virginia editor said, "and will [understand] the importance of producing a closer identification than has heretofore existed of the interests of Virginia and Maryland."[4]

Swann differed from his predecessor in almost every respect. McLane, short, with high collars and an imperious gaze, always looked like a duke of some minor principality. His early political enemies referred to him as "the Dauphin." Swann was a big man. He had a thick shock of hair combed straight across his forehead, and when he was with the railroad he sported muttonchop whiskers. During his political days, he had a long, black, spade beard. As an elder statesman, he grew a full and imposing handlebar mustache. Although he was descended from some of Virginia's first families, one could say that he had the common touch. In fact, Swann was a skillful political opportunist, and not to his credit, after he retired from the B&O, he was taken up by the most bigoted and lawless members of the working class. His election as the nativist American Party's candidate for mayor in 1856, when mobs fought pitched battles in the streets with muskets and cannon and political clubs like the "Plug-Uglies," "Rip-Raps," and "Blood-Tubs" intimidated voters at the polls by stabbing them with shoemaker's awls, was the most violent in the history of Baltimore. In 1858, Swann was reelected by means of the same terrorist tactics and by a much larger plurality. Despite these infamous methods, or perhaps because of them, he proved to be a highly progressive leader, who inaugurated the city's street railway, fire department, and municipal park systems.

Swann's major stock-in-trade was his eloquence, and in the same way that his whole demeanor varied from his predecessor's, so also did his address. McLane had been a powerful advocate, who tended to give donnish lectures in which he examined every possible variation at great length until his auditors were overwhelmed by the extravagant profusion. Swann was a spellbinding orator who went for the punchline, like a politician. He was proud of his rhetorical ability, but his railroad papers are a hodgepodge of undated fragments of handwritten addresses, some ending in mid-paragraph, which amount to little more than a stockpile of usable phrases for various occasions.

Swann was born February 3, 1809, in Alexandria, Virginia. His father, Thomas Swann, was a prominent lawyer who served for a time as United States attorney for the District of Columbia. His mother, Jane Byrd Page, was a descendant of the Virginia Byrds. Swann attended the University of Virginia and studied law with his father, who had been the tutor of William Wirt. In 1833, Andrew Jackson appointed him to a minor diplomatic post in Italy. Back in a year, he married Elizabeth Sherlock, the niece of Robert Gilmor, Jr., a rich Baltimore businessman and art collector who had a heavy investment in the Baltimore and Ohio.

During the next few years, Swann was evidently practicing law and managing his expanding properties and portfolio. He moved to Baltimore from Washington in 1836 to occupy a new house he had built on Franklin Street near Cathedral. His municipal tax bill of 1842 indicates a net worth of almost $120,000. The house was assessed at $70,000 and there were other downtown properties as well as securities, including some B&O Railroad stock.[5]

Later on in the decade Swann acquired several other houses in his neighborhood, a pier and warehouse in Fells Point, and a lot on Preston Street where he planned to build a dozen houses. He also owned a 1,200-acre family estate, Morven Park, near Leesburg, Virginia, where he could while away the hot summer days plantation-style with a cool drink on the two-story Greek Revival porch that fronted the Georgian mansion. Swann freed his personal servant, Ramey Neale, in 1852, and the rest of his slaves before the Civil War. Swann subscribed to the right newspapers, the *American* and the *Patriot*, and he served on the Whig State Central Committee. He was a pewholder at St. Paul's Episcopal Church. He liked good whiskey, fine wine, and Havana cigars, but he could also drink beer with the workmen.

McLane smoothed the way in the boardroom for Swann's succession and also laid the groundwork in the field. By December 1847, the location surveys that Benjamin H. Latrobe, Jr., and his crews had started the previous fall from Cumberland across the Allegheny summit and through the Glades were finished to the Maryland state line. One survey team headed by assistant engineer Thomas Rowles pushed on, running experimental lines from the Glades down to the Cheat River in Virginia.[6] McLane sent the other two teams to the opposite end of the line. The B&O's veteran surveyor Thomas C. Atkinson moved eastward from Wheeling along Grave Creek. James L. Randolph surveyed Fish Creek, and Rowles carried the work farther east to Piles Fork of Buffalo Creek.

Latrobe, besides being chief engineer, was also acting general superintendent, and along with supervising the surveys, he provided management with detailed and optimistic economic forecasts that were increasingly important in justifying the construction program to stockholders and investors. In the spring of 1848, the company named Samuel Cameron their agent to acquire the Virginia right-of-way to the flats of Grave Creek. His Maryland counterpart was Thomas J. McKaig of Cumberland.

The board also hired engineers Jonathan Knight and John Childe of Boston to work with Latrobe in laying out the new line "to guard against any mistakes or errors . . . in a work of such magnitude and with so many difficulties to encounter."[7] One of the biggest hurdles, of course, was Wheeling. As long as the final route, via Fish or Grave Creek, was undecided, Wheeling could not be sure that it would be the B&O's terminus on the Ohio River. Therefore the choice of Knight was to some extent political, because he was consulting engineer to the City of Wheeling and also its land agent for acquiring the right-of-way.

The B&O had an understanding with Wheeling that it could choose whichever route was the cheaper. Anticipating a challenge and realizing he would have to justify his preference between Fish and Grave creeks, Latrobe cautioned his surveyors to be careful and impartial. He himself spent the spring and summer of 1848 on horseback with his survey crews and the consultants, Knight and Childe, traversing the shores of the Potomac, the Savage, and the Cheat.

Latrobe was 41 that year and had had eighteen years of experience with the Baltimore and Ohio. It was with a certain confidence, then, that he chose a route and built a line through 200 miles of mountain wilderness between Cumberland and Wheeling. Over the next five years, he directed a work force that at its peak consisted of nearly 5,000 men and 1,000 horses, overcame floods, landslides, a cholera epidemic, and two major riots, and supervised the construction of fourteen tunnels, including the three-quarter-mile Kingwood, the longest domestic tunnel up to that time, and 114 bridges, among them the largest iron truss bridge in America over the Monongahela River at Fairmont. This feat was one of the great achievements of nineteenth-century railroad engineering.

Good surveys were the first step, and soon Latrobe made the important discovery that the earlier surveyors of the Savage River route had erred in their estimation of the height and distance for the railroad's difficult ascent from the Potomac through Backbone Mountain to the Glades. The errors began with the estimate of the U.S. engineers in their 1825 surveys for the C&O Canal, which was quoted by Trimble in his 1828 memoir on the B&O reconnaissance, picked up by Knight in 1835, and then by Latrobe himself in 1844. Latrobe said, "In these documents, the distance from the Mouth of Savage River to the summit is stated as 16 1/2 miles and height 1685 feet, while by our late survey the distance turns out to be only 14 1/2 miles while the height is shown to be 1,709 feet."[8]

Two miles and 24 feet might not perhaps be considered critical, but the new figures indicated steeper grades of 116 feet per mile. Latrobe said that the B&O's operations on the Maryland Mining Company railroad, where ascents were 135 feet per mile, proved that locomotives could operate on such inclines, and thus the maximum permissible grade was established for the Baltimore and Ohio, which was later written into the charters of the transcontinental railroads. The original error, as Latrobe pointed out, lay not with the canal engineers, who located their project on the banks of the stream, but with the later assumption that the railroad would occupy the same ground. The new instrumental surveys, placing the railroad higher up on the slopes, corrected the matter.

In 1848, the rains came in July, and work in the rugged countryside turned soggy and uncomfortable. Yet on clear days, from the banks of the Potomac they could see the wind whip the great stands of oak and pine on the hillsides like mountain seaweed, and at dusk, high in the labyrinth of valleys beyond the Cheat, they watched the blue shadows settle over the land until the profiles of the jagged ridges merged into one and the potential pathways between them became all but indistinguishable. In January 1849, Latrobe told Swann, "The entire route to the Ohio river has now been surveyed." The engineers were preparing their drawings and calculations. The line began where the tracks ended on the Mount Savage Railroad, about half a mile west of the B&O's Baltimore Street ticket office in Cumberland. It traced the Maryland shore of the Potomac, climbed to "the summit dividing the eastern and western waters on Jonathan Wilson's farm," called the "Back Bone Summit" (Altamont, Maryland, elevation 2,629 feet), meandered through the Glades into Virginia, dropped down on another uniform 116-feet-per-mile grade to the Cheat River, went up the ragged slopes of Laurel Hill on the other side, and then passed through some very remote and broken country on the way to Wheeling.[9]

The engineers considered three possible alignments at Cumberland. The first was the Patterson Creek cutoff below town. (This alignment required an expensive tunnel through Knobly Mountain, and it was not built until 1903.) The second crossed the canal basin in Cumberland itself. The B&O therefore chose the third, which made a wide U-turn around the business district. The C&O at that time intended to push on past Cumberland to the Savage River coalfields, and it claimed the prior right to the Potomac's Maryland shore. The railroad had learned its lesson and declined to challenge the canal company, in town or on the river.

However, their selection of the alignment at the Ohio River end of the line reignited the controversy with the city of Wheeling. As provided for in the 1847 Virginia act and the B&O's agreement with Wheeling, Latrobe picked Fish Creek rather than Grave Creek. The chosen route called for moderate bridging and one tunnel. The Grave Creek route required four tunnels and 23 crossings of the stream in a single fourteen-mile section. Again there were three major alternatives, of which Fish Creek, Latrobe pointed out, was the longest in measured distance, the shortest in equated distance, the cheapest to build, occupied the middle range of expense for maintainance and working, and had the lowest overall cost.

In the spring of 1849, Swann sent the engineers' report to Charles W. Russell, the attorney for Wheeling. Russell shortly began questioning the comparative cost estimates, and before the board had a chance to adopt officially the preferred Fish Creek alignment, the B&O and Wheeling were at it again. But this did not deter Swann. When, in mid-March 1849, the directors approved the final report of the board of engineers (Latrobe, Knight, and Childe), containing their recommendation for the central portion of the route, Swann decided the time had come to address the board.

His analysis was to the point. The cost of building the railroad from Cumberland to Wheeling was about $7 million. The company's resources included Wheeling's $500,000 subscription, which would become available when they reached Fairmont on the Monongahela River. But Swann had no intention of stopping at Fairmont or anywhere else short of the Ohio "for a single day"; he wanted the whole line put under contract and finished in two years. "We may delay it for a season," he said, "but the result is inevitable and the longer we deliberate, the greater will be the loss to this community."

A successful conclusion to the ongoing negotiations with the Barings to sell the state securities would make it possible for the B&O to pay the contractors in cash, rather than in bonds or scrip, ensuring cheaper prices and faster work. A bond sale in the foreign market would avoid a tax on the local community. And if "we are thrown upon our unaided resources, is there a man in the city of Baltimore who understands the value and importance of this Road, who would not be disposed to contribute his aid?" Swann asked. "Can any one suppose that the completion of this great highway would not return every dollar . . . in the enhanced value of property throughout the city?" He set May 1, 1849, to begin work on the first twenty sections west of Cumberland.[10]

A final characteristic that set Swann apart from McLane was his penchant for aggressive fund-raising and particularly his attitude toward the Maryland bonds. They were "the company's great resource," something to be used, not held in reserve. Shortly after taking office, Swann gave the Barings his sales pitch. The railroad was in good condition and profitable. Trade and travel were increasing every year and would continue to do so, yielding 7 percent annual net revenues, he said. But the true impact of the railroad on the city would not be realized until it reached the Ohio River. "It is very important that our road should go forward without delay, and [therefore] we should make these bonds available," Swann said.[11]

The Barings activated their American agent, Thomas Wren Ward. Swann and John H. B. Latrobe met him in Boston and had a frank exchange of views. The substance of their interview was relayed to London, along with Swann's sunny assessment of the fiscal situation. Maryland's prompt payment of its liabilities and gradual liquidation of the state debt had given the local capitalists increased confidence. "Every day convinces us of the importance of an early completion of the Balto. & O. R. Road," Swann told the Barings.[12]

Swann sounded out George Peabody on handling the transaction and he entertained some domestic offers, but in April 1849 the Barings were the the first to sell 200,000 pounds of Maryland sterling bonds at 85 (about $856,000 worth). The sale had the expected effect on contractors, who reduced bid prices because they were confident of being paid, and on investors, who were encouraged by the linking of the cachet of the House of Baring with the credit of the State of Maryland. Henry Varnum Poor, the new editor of the *American Railroad Journal*, hailed the B&O's renewed activity: "The completion of the great trunk lines of railway from the Atlantic cities to the western navigable waters, will open a new era in the internal commerce of this country, as marked as that which followed the opening of the New York and Erie Canal."[13]

Swann had to defend his decision against the Pittsburgh faction, whose last-ditch denouncement of the expensive and impractical Virginia route with its high grades was forgotten when contractor James Quigg first broke ground in the valley of Crabtree Creek, 41 miles west of Cumberland (approximately Swanton, Maryland), on May 23, 1849, for the final extension of the B&O Railroad to Wheeling. Pittsburgh responded that the Pennsylvania Railroad would be finished in two years: "We want to hear the whistle of the locomotive from the heart of Ohio, and from Philadelphia, while Baltimore is still cooped up in the mountains." Here was a real race to the West.[14]

The B&O let construction contracts in three phases during the summer and fall of 1849. The first, in May, were for 20 one-mile sections in scattered locations, including bridges, tunnels, and rock excavation. In July, 24 more sections were let, covering the heaviest work on the entire line. In September, the board approved contracts for 58 additional sections, interspersed among the others and less difficult. The territory in question extended from Cumberland to the Northwestern Turnpike Bridge over the Tygart Valley River in Virginia (now Grafton, West Virginia), a little over halfway to Wheeling.

Latrobe had advertised for contractors as far away as Boston. Many who signed on were from Pennsylvania. Hundreds of Irish laborers began drifting in to the construction sites and putting up their shanties, accompanied by the usual whiskey vendors and sundry other camp hangers-on. As soon as the workmen got organized, they struck for higher wages and started fighting. Latrobe discounted the reports. The hands would settle down when they understood the system, he told Swann, and the rumored riots only came to an unruly celebration of the Fourth of July. Just a week after Latrobe filed his report, 50 men marched down a five-mile section of the line, threatening workers who came from traditionally hostile counties in Ireland and raiding the local chicken coops, gardens, and spring houses. Latrobe could not so easily dismiss the whiskey, "the chief cause of all the broils." But he admitted that the contract clause banning its use was unenforceable, because profits from the trade were high and safe harbors "for those who vend the poison are so readily found in that wild country" that the dealers were indifferent to the evils they visited upon their customers and, sometimes, "directly upon their own persons and property."[15]

Latrobe was now entering the high period of his career as a civil engineer. Separating him from the volatile youth who made himself sick with worry over his first bridge were 170 miles of railroad track, most of it well built and the rest improving. He went about this new task with a calm maturity and sense of purpose that inspired confidence in others. If his health still bothered him, he kept it to himself. William Parker, whom the company had hired as general superintendent from the Boston and Worcester Railroad, relieved Latrobe of his former responsibility for maintenance, depot facilities, reconstruction, engines and cars. The B&O considered the Boston and Worcester the best-managed line in New England and valued Parker's qualifications sufficiently to give him a $5,000-a-year salary, more than any other B&O employee, including the president.

About the time they brought in Parker, in February 1849, there was a huge landslide at the Doe Gully Tunnel, 60 miles past Harpers Ferry. It dumped a mass of broken slate 200 feet long and 20 feet deep at the western portal, bottling up the trains for ten days in the worst interruption to service since the company began operations. Wendel Bollman, master of road for the division, took charge of the cleanup. It was accomplished by 200 men working round the clock in freezing temperatures in the remote locale, supplied with provisions by rail from Cumberland. This marked Bollman's reemergence on the railroad. The B&O made him master of road for the entire line two years later and the ex-carpenter was poised for great things as an engineer.

Subordinates of this caliber gave Latrobe the freedom to plan the new work. He let the contracts for the heaviest sections first because he expected problems at the tunnels and bridges, and the sooner they appeared, the quicker he could deal with them. He avoided the inclination to choose the lowest bidders. Experience had taught him that these were often marginal operators who might give up too easily, and finding new contractors was time-consuming and expensive. Of the final batch of contract awards in 1849, less than 30 percent represented the low bid. For the Kingwood Tunnel, the single biggest construction project, Latrobe wisely passed over eight lower bidders to pick the ninth, Lemmon, Gorman, and Clark and McMahon. That tunnel proved to be one of the few large jobs that neither had to be let to new contractors nor taken over by the B&O.

In mid-1849, two very important route locations, the departure from Cumberland and the entrance to Wheeling, were still up in the air. The survey parties spent most of that first year of construction back in the field, pounding stakes into the ground in front of the contractors and trying to work out a joint location with the Chesapeake and Ohio. The canal had yet to make its way into Cumberland, but its proprietary interest in the territory on the other side expanded along with the railroad's plans to build west along the Maryland shore of the Potomac. There was a brief rapprochement, which disintegrated when the surveys revealed the extent of the problem. The first of several collisions occurred 21 miles above Cumberland, and Latrobe recommended crossing the Potomac into Virginia there, at Paddytown (now Keyser, West Virginia), and returning to Maryland nine miles farther up, at the Savage River. When the B&O adopted this route in the fall, it was the second (and last) time the canal forced its rival across the river and into Virginia.

Wheeling was a different matter. Many years earlier, Latrobe had noted that "the Wheeling people are wild for the extension of the railroad," and they still were. "There will be no delay, no management, no diplomacy, but work until the road is done," the local newspaper editorialists exulted as construction began in the summer of 1849.[16] But the city, isolated far up in the northwestern corner of Virginia between Ohio and Pennsylvania and more than 300 miles from the state capital at Richmond, had become very touchy over the long years of legislative warfare. Now that the prize lay almost within reach, the citizens feared more than ever that it might slip away.

As the first deep snow fell in the mountains in mid-November 1849, Latrobe reported that they were starting work at the Kingwood Tunnel. A little community sprang up there called Greigsville. The first real riots occurred there when about 300 Connaught men chased their rivals, the Corkonians and Fardowns, off the job and tore down and burned their shanties. The sheriff of Preston County summoned a posse of some 200 citizens who marched through the heavy snowstorm to find the ringleaders and take them to jail in Kingwood. The contractors, at Latrobe's suggestion, hired about 25 men at $1.25 a day to patrol the line armed with muskets and bayonets and, said the local press, "arrest persons engaged in riotous acts, dead or alive."

Over 2,000 men and 300 horses were strung out along the line. Although Latrobe seemed sure that they would complete the construction to Wheeling by June 1852, he was worried about some of the difficult parts of the work. Contractors had already walked off the job at several key bridge sites, including the Wills Creek viaduct in Cumberland, the Bloomington viaduct over the Potomac, and the Cheat River bridge. In fact, some of them had never even shown up after signing their contracts.

The Wills Creek viaduct was a massive stone structure. Five of its thirteen piers stood in the bed of the creek. The contractors had put in three of the easiest ones when the company took over the project, along with the stone quarry and the construction equipment, and therefore they were able to lay the foundations of the two remaining underwater piers before winter and avoid a serious delay. Latrobe planned to bring in new contractors for the Bloomington viaduct, another huge stone bridge located just above the place where the Savage River entered the Potomac. This bridge was expanded from two to three arches to accommodate the canal that never reached it. Latrobe re-let the other river crossings to the contractors who were working on adjacent sections of the railroad.

As Swann's first full year in office drew to a close, he and his chief engineer could point to several accomplishments. The Baltimore branch line to Locust Point, a year in the making, was finished and the first coal shipments had left the company's wharf in March. The eight-acre facility had 2,000 feet of waterfront and could accommodate fifteen to twenty ships at a time. Coal cars ran out on trestles to load the ships. Panama was a frequent destination. Cumberland bituminous coal was now regarded as superior to all other types for steamships. The railroad hauled more than 100,000 tons of it in 1849.

The Locust Point branch was designed to handle bulk export commodities, avoiding the slow and costly trip through the streets to the City Block. Although locomotives could operate within the city limits, they were restricted to nighttime hours. Because of operational problems, the railroad still employed horsepower, but engines could run freely on the Locust Point branch. In January 1850, the company closed its City Block operation and moved across the harbor. The Ellicotts' iron furnaces were near the B&O property on the north side of the Locust Point peninsula, and the Baltimore and Cuba Copper Smelting Company was located on the south side. The latter firm had erected several brick houses for its workers and a church "to keep everything in order." Steam ferry service was planned to Fells Point on the opposite side of the harbor. Thus began the industrial and residential community of Locust Point, a place that before the coming of the railroad had existed in name only.

The track to Locust Point was the B&O's first to be laid with rails placed directly on the ties, dispensing with wooden stringers and undersills. The local Avalon Company rolled the rails. The new track was the result of two years of study by Latrobe and Parker that was given early impetus by a spate of collisions, derailments, and engine failures in late 1847. In the worst one an entire train went off the track at North Mountain above Martinsburg. A congressman had his arm broken and some railroad employees were injured in the wreck, which was traced to a decayed oak stringer under the rail.

There was also the human factor. John Keller, a farmer at Cherry Run, near the wreck site, was so incensed when another train ran over his cow that he dragged the carcass back on the track, added some heavy timber, and threatened the lives of the B&O workmen in the neighborhood when they tried to remove them. Two trains, including an eastbound passenger run, passed over the obstacles but held the tracks before Latrobe was able to have the farmer arrested and the mess cleared away.

There were at the time five different kinds of track on the B&O, including the ancient types in the Patapsco River Valley. Most of the track was light 40-pound bridge or T-rail laid on wooden stringers and ties, sometimes with an undersill; the wooden stringers provided needed support under the joints of the iron rails, which were subject to tremendous concussion from the passing wheels. Eliminating them would require stronger and heavier rails and improved fixtures for fastening the joints. After monitoring experiments on other lines, Latrobe decided to try this in early 1849, for both new and reconstructed track. He tested a three-part, compound rail of his own invention, but it was not a commercial success. Swann meanwhile negotiated with the Barings to buy the rails in England. Latrobe's specifications called for 22,000 tons of 60-pound T-rails, enough iron to lay 211 miles of single track, with sidings, from Cumberland to Wheeling. They decided to pay for it with 6 percent company bonds, backed by a mortgage. Thompson and Forman of London were again the suppliers. The cost to the B&O, including freight and commission, was about $40 a ton.

With construction under way in the mountains, the rail order well advanced, and Latrobe's favorable cost-revenue breakdown in hand, Swann radiated confidence and inspiration on November 14, 1849, when he delivered to the board of directors the greatest speech of his railroad career. He began in the usual way by noting the activities of their rivals, that is, the Erie Railroad, which was then under construction from New York, and the Pennsylvania Railroad, which was making good progress from Philadelphia. "The avenues of trade, when once established, often become fixed and permanent," Swann warned. They had to keep going before Baltimore lost the Western trade to the competition, because "there is a point," he said, "where the revenue of the road cannot be interfered with, where its destiny will be forever established, and where the only question [will be] the ability of the company to accommodate the trade and travel. That point, gentlemen, is the Ohio river."

Because the construction bids had come in lower than Latrobe's estimates, Swann now believed they could build the line to Wheeling for $6.3 million. Their financial resources were the proceeds from the sale of the state sterling bonds ($3 million), the B&O's net revenues during the course of construction ($1 million), the Wheeling subscription ($500,000), and the company's rail bonds ($650,000). That left $1.1 million to raise. Swann proposed to do this by issuing a preferred stock or long-term company bonds. The rewards would be great if they finished the railroad in three years, for it "would be the first avenue opened to the trade of the West." On the other hand, "Delay would be as fatal at this critical juncture as the total abandonment of the enterprise." The annual net revenues once they reached the Ohio River—$1,350,000, according to Latrobe—would be more than adequate to meet the annual interest payments on the debt and the $500,000 cost of equipping the new line with engines and cars, Swann said.

Swann's peroration—"The completion of a stupendous work, binding together two grand extremes of our Union, and promising so largely to the future advancement of the city of Baltimore, in every department of her industrial pursuits, and indirectly to the whole State of Maryland, might well excite the ambition of all classes and interests, having an eye to our common welfare and prosperity"—so electrified George Brown that he jumped to his feet and offered a resolution calling for the whole line to the Ohio River to be put under contract. The approval was unanimous.[17]

At almost the same time as this meeting in the B&O boardroom, the city of Wheeling, 380 railroad miles away, was celebrating the opening of Charles Ellet's Wheeling Suspension Bridge. The B&O directors were invited, but they did not attend. The Wheeling officials would understand why, "when you are apprised that the board that day passed a resolution instructing the president to put the whole line of their road to your city under contract without a moment's delay," Swann wrote.[18]

The ceremony that took place on the next day, November 15, 1849 (the day after Swann spoke to the board), had been well planned by the Wheeling citizens to reflect the significance of the event. This was the first clear span over the Ohio River, and at 1,010 feet, the world's longest suspension bridge. Cannon reports punctuated the "soul-inspiring" sounds provided by a band from Zanesville, Ohio, that drew crowds all day. "A continuous train of human beings moved along the work from 3 o'clock until dark," the Wheeling *Times* reported: "At 6 o'clock, the thousand lamps, hung upon the wires, were lighted almost simultaneously and presented an elegant and graceful curve of fire, high above the river, that was never excelled in beauty. It forcibly reminded one of Mr. Clay's remarks, a few days since, when looking at the work from a distance, while his face glowed with pride and exultation—'Take that down! you might as well try to take down the rainbow.'"[19]

Even as it opened, however, the bridge was being objected to by Wheeling's long-standing rival, Pittsburgh, which claimed that the span obstructed navigation; the matter was headed for the Supreme Court. The bridge was also involved in the renewed argument between Wheeling and the B&O over the railroad's route. Although the span was built to carry the National Road traffic across the Ohio River, Ellet had designed it for railroad use as well, and both he and the city of Wheeling intended it to form the strategic link in the great central route between Baltimore, Cincinnati, and Saint Louis. In other words, the real argument with Pittsburgh was less about steamboats and navigation than about railroads and, ultimately, the control of transportation in the upper Ohio River valley.

Ellet had proposed in October 1847 that the bridge floor, 24 feet wide, would hang from twelve four-inch-diameter cables of iron wire resting on two stone arched towers that rose 60 and 70 feet, respectively, from the abutments at the east and west ends. For an additional $30,000, four more wire cables could be added and a wider and heavier floor installed, strengthening the bridge enough to support a single locomotive or a horse-drawn train. The Central Ohio Railroad, coming east from Columbus and connecting to Cincinnati and Saint Louis, would "strike the river at Wheeling, where the Baltimore and Ohio will carry it on to tide water," Ellet explained: "The vast trade which will be brought by this great line and its tributaries, will cross over the Suspension Bridge, and probably, at no distant day, require that bridge to be modified so as to pass the cars forward without any transhipment of persons or property."[20]

Ellet, the builder, was as controversial as his bridge. He was a mercurial genius, who was his own best advertisement and worst enemy. Besides introducing the wire suspension bridge to the United States, Ellet was the first to advocate a comprehensive system of navigation improvements, flood control, and power generation for the rivers of America by the use of upland reservoirs, or dams, to impound excess water. The Tennessee Valley Authority is an heir of this farsighted concept. Ellet got the idea, as a way to maintain sufficient depth for steamboats, while he was measuring the flow of the river for his work on the Wheeling bridge. Ellet was a prolific writer and a skilled polemicist; he published 46 separate titles before dying in 1862 of wounds suffered during the Battle of Memphis when he commanded a fleet of Union steam rams, his final obsession.

Ellet, the son of an eccentric, litigious, dour Quaker farmer from Penns Grove, near Philadelphia, was himself a maverick, irascible engineer, a tall man—six feet, two inches—blade-thin, intelligent but humorless. Distant visions fired his eyes; he vibrated with tense energy. He spent his twenty-first year attending the Ecole des Ponts et Chaussées in Paris and observing suspension spans under construction. On his return, he quickly presented plans for wire suspension bridges that were bold and unprecedented, one to Congress in 1832 for a 600-foot Potomac River span at Washington, D.C., and another four years later to the Saint Louis city council for a bridge twice as long over the Mississippi. Congress declined to act and Saint Louis rejected his views as "extravagantly wild and unsafe."

By the time he got to Wheeling, his headquarters from 1848 to 1853, Ellet had spent twenty years as surveyor or engineer for the C&O Canal, the Erie Railroad, and the James River and Kanawha Canal among others. (The last did not renew his contract as chief engineer because he was said to have been occasionally "dictatorial if not sarcastic" to the board.)[21] He published several pamphlets, including one on suspension bridges, and a book called *Essay on the Laws of Trade* (1839), which attempted to encourage transportation companies to adopt scientific principles in setting rates and thereby maximize revenues. (Jonathan Knight admired the book, which introduced Ellet as a railroad economist.) Ellet got his first real chance to show what he could do in Philadelphia in 1842 when he replaced Lewis Wernwag's Colossus bridge, which had burned four years earlier, with a 357-foot wire suspension bridge over the Schuylkill River at Fairmount, the first of its kind in America. On this project he encountered his great rival, John A. Roebling. They argued about the proper way to make up wire cables.

Ellet undertook the project for the Wheeling and Belmont Bridge Company in July 1847. His fee for the design and supervision was a modest $5,000, but as he said, his object was "to associate my name honorably with the edifice." The final cost for the planned $145,000 structure was $210,000. In November of that year, he signed another contract to build a railroad suspension bridge between America and Canada over the Niagara River gorge below the falls. Ellet competed aggressively with Roebling for both of these important commissions and he worked on them simultaneously. In March 1848, at the falls, having slung a wire cable over the gorge, he climbed into a small iron basket equipped with pulleys and hauled himself over and back in fifteen minutes. "The wind was high and the weather cold, but yet the trip was a very interesting one to me—perched as I was [240] feet above the Rapids, and viewing from the centre of the river one of the sublimest prospects which nature has prepared on this globe of ours," he said.[22]

Four months later, as women fainted and men stood aghast in the crowds on either side, Ellet crossed the chasm again, this time by driving a spirited horse and carriage, standing up, chariot-style, over a swaying, wooden-planked service bridge that was only seven and a half feet wide and lacked most of its railings. Nothing he did thereafter at the falls equaled that dramatic demonstration of personal courage and faith in the wire suspension bridge. Ellet's completed temporary span proved such a popular and lucrative tourist attraction that a disagreement arose between the engineer and the bridge company over the tolls. At one point, Ellet backed his claim by mounting cannon at the bridge. But he gave up the contract at the end of the year and the company hired Roebling, who finished the Niagara suspension span in 1855, using Ellet's structure as a scaffold, which he then removed. Roebling's bridge carried heavy railroad traffic on its upper deck and highway traffic on its lower one for over 40 years. It was the only important railroad suspension bridge ever built.

Work started on the Wheeling span in the summer of 1848. Baltimore masons, carpenters, and riggers made up part of the construction crew. Before it opened, the State of Pennsylvania sued the Wheeling bridge company on behalf of Pittsburgh steamboat interests. The contention was that the bridge, 92 feet above low water and 44.5 feet above high water, would block the passage of steamboats that had high stacks. The Supreme Court in 1852 ruled in favor of the steamboats (Chief Justice Roger B. Taney provided a key dissenting opinion), but Congress later that year declared the bridge part of a post road and therefore beyond the court's jurisdiction.

The Wheeling Suspension Bridge was not perfect, but it was the greatest triumph of Ellet's engineering career and he never built another. The deck, inadequately trussed and stayed, blew down in a tornado in May 1854. Tall steamboats normally cleared the bridge by lowering their hinged stacks and when a Pittsburgh boat did so derisively on passing the wreckage, the Wheeling citizens stoned it. However, the deck was replaced by Ellet and William K. McComas in two months and the bridge was reopened. Still standing and in use, it is the country's oldest highway suspension span.[23]

At the time it was built, the bridge symbolized Wheeling's struggle for railroads against its traditional rival, Pittsburgh. Ellet himself said emphatically: "The action against the bridge was commenced, avowedly for the purpose of preventing the Baltimore and Ohio Rail Road from forming its connexion with the rail roads of the West, at any point south of Pittsburg. The parties who first agitated the subject were the principal officers of the Ohio and Pennsylvania Rail Road Company—a Company having no possible interest in the river navigation, but owning a rail road line running from Pittsburg, westwardly." [24]

When he designed the Wheeling span in 1847, Ellet was so impressed with the B&O's stated intention to build their line to the city that he favorably quoted their annual report in his bridge proposal. The Wheeling committee read the document another way. In a protest pamphlet, they argued that the railroad's real aim was to terminate the line at Fish Creek, establish a depot there, and attract the Ohio railroads to a point 23 miles below town, leaving Wheeling at the end of a branch line. When Swann sent Latrobe's route report favoring Fish Creek to Wheeling in the spring of 1849, their suspicions were confirmed. By the time his bridge opened in the fall, Ellet had joined the fight to get the railroad to adopt the Grave Creek route, which met the Ohio River only eleven miles below Wheeling.

During most of the next year, Ellet was busy in the pamphlet war. He criticized Latrobe's principles of location and cleverly played on Wheeling's paranoia in a report to their city council. Ellet found it hard to believe that the B&O would be allowed to adopt a line eleven miles longer, $1.25 million more expensive, "and which, instead of securing to your city 'the practical benefits of the western terminus of the road,' will inevitably build up another city, rival to your prosperity, [23] miles below you." [25] Preparing for the final legislative battle, Charles W. Russell, the Wheeling city lawyer, stopped off in Baltimore on his way to Richmond and had a long talk with Swann. Russell emerged convinced that the reason the railroad wanted to reach the Ohio via Fish Creek was not to save money but to avoid Wheeling. They had begged the company for two years to honor its obligations, he complained to Wheeling stalwart James S. Wheate, the city clerk, but it was a waste of time to solicit "mere justice from a corporation of trade" or to rely on "the conscience of this company; that being a metaphysical entity which we have not yet been able to discover." [26] Swann, though assuring Russell that he was "the friend of Wheeling," nonetheless argued that Wheeling's object was to get the company to relinquish any route that they thought was unsuitable, and since freedom of choice was the major concession gained in their compromise, the B&O would not give it up.

The two sides met again in Richmond in February 1850, before the Committee on Roads of the House of Delegates. Benjamin H. Latrobe, Jr., led off by defending his principles for selecting the Fish Creek route, particularly the use of equated distances. Russell, speaking for Wheeling, dragged in Alexander J. Marshall and the B&O's $50,000 bribery fund, which was then becoming public knowledge, and he praised the city's new hero, Charles Ellet, whose triumphal arch, he said, was more beautiful than the Ohio River itself. Wheeling even called out Daniel Webster, who obligingly charged the B&O, his former client, with fraud in a written opinion. John H. B. Latrobe offered a succinct legal review of the case and Swann put it all in perspective.

The 1847 act said that the railroad should be built to Wheeling on the most feasible and practical route as determined by instrumental surveys, he told the committee. Those routes were via Fish and Grave creeks. The law provided that if Fish Creek proved the cheaper, Wheeling could still compel the adoption of the Grave Creek route by paying the difference in construction cost. But in their subsequent agreement, Wheeling had waived that right, allowing the company to adopt the cheaper route without qualification. If Wheeling had not compromised, the railroad would have been built to Pittsburgh, he maintained. Swann countered Webster's charge of fraud, and answered Ellet's criticism "that in estimating the comparative cost of the Grave and Fish creek routes, the Chief Engineer of this Company had committed a fatal blunder in his calculations" by praising Latrobe's professional ability. He denied that the B&O ever intended to establish the depot and terminus of the line at any point other than Wheeling. If the city succeeded in the legislature and appealed to the courts, "Where would be the end of litigation?" he asked.[27]

Jonathan Knight had drafted the confusing section of the 1847 act regarding the two routes, believing, as he still did, that the Grave Creek alignment favoring Wheeling was the cheaper and would ultimately be built. It was also clear that both sides had read the law and the agreement according to their own interests from the beginning, the company assuming all along that they would construct the Fish Creek route. To avoid "an angry and expensive controversy," the Virginia legislators passed a law establishing a three-man board of engineers to act as arbitrator. The members could not be residents of Maryland, Virginia, or Pennsylvania. They were to investigate the evidence, undertake additional surveys if needed, and make a decision. If the railroad company lost and tried to build its preferred route regardless, then Wheeling could sue.

Swann gave the law a highly critical review in an address to the B&O stockholders, but he acknowledged that the company had no real objection to it and they unanimously approved the act on May 1, 1850. Ten days later, Ellet delivered his second report to the Wheeling city council, a stinging denunciation of the engineering principles that Latrobe had developed over the past fifteen years. Friction, resistance, grades, power, velocity, gravity, the angle of repose—Latrobe had got them all wrong. Ellet reserved his greatest scorn for "the elastic nature of the 'equation of distances'" that Latrobe had invented to cover any contingency. It resulted in "aboriginal deductions," he said.

When Ellet had finished correcting what he considered his colleague's sloppy work, the Grave Creek route had amazingly become twelve miles shorter than Fish Creek (in equated distance) and $1.9 million cheaper to build and operate. The Wheeling city council must be aware, their engineer concluded, "that there has never been any stability in the estimates offered to you by this Railroad Company, which, from the outset to the end, are as shifting as the sands of the Missouri."[28] Latrobe, probably wisely, declined to answer this philippic, nor did he react when John H. Alexander, the western Maryland coal and iron entrepreneur and Wheeling advocate, reworked many of Ellet's charges in another screed for the Wheeling city councilmen.

In early July 1850, the three-man board of engineers—Dennis Hart Mahan of

West Point, New York; John McRae of Charleston, South Carolina; and Meriwether Lewis Clark, of Saint Louis, Missouri—assembled in Wheeling. Latrobe spent several weeks with them. His opponents must have had equal time, because the lobbying was severe. Ellet and Knight submitted a list of captious complaints disavowing the use of equated distances (of which Knight had been an early proponent) in favor of adopting the finished part of the railroad as a guide for making comparative cost estimates. "The question at issue has assumed many shapes," Russell told the board of engineers, "but it has always been, in substance, whether the western terminus of the road should be at Wheeling." Therefore, the best route was the one that assured the city of being the terminus: Grave Creek. The lawyer appealed to the arbitrators to make their decision according to the intention of the law, which was that Wheeling be the final destination of the Baltimore and Ohio Railroad.[29]

John H. B. Latrobe answered that the company had agreed to construct its line to Wheeling if the city yielded its legal right to control the route. Wheeling knew "that the Company desired to have the right to take the Fish Creek route, should it prove to be the cheapest," he said. His argument was that Wheeling believed that by bridging the Ohio it would attract the Western rail lines no matter where the B&O arrived at the river, because there was no other crossing, and when the Western railroads failed to appear on their doorstep, Wheeling started worrying about the B&O's route. Swann also addressed the board of engineers.[30]

Did the B&O really intend to bypass Wheeling and meet the Ohio railroads at a point 23 miles below the city? Probably they did, although the company records are inconclusive, for they discuss termini and potential rail connections at both places. The arbitrators ended the matter in September 1850. Their one-paragraph decision said the "true and proper route" for the railroad according to the 1847 Virginia act would strike the Ohio River at Grave Creek. Latrobe said it was no reflection on his engineering ability, since the arbitrators did not rule on the relative cost of the routes. The board of engineers seemed more concerned with the political and legal ramifications of the dispute. They did not explain their decision.

The railroad shortly advertised for contractors. The new 33-mile alignment called for seven tunnels, including one nearly half a mile and another almost a quarter-mile in length, several deep cuts and embankments, and numerous bridges. Wheeling's intransigence ultimately cost the Baltimore and Ohio more than $400,000 in extra construction costs, six months of time, and the race to the Ohio River with the Pennsylvania Railroad.

The B&O's other prime antagonist at last reached Cumberland that fall. Swann forgot to tell the B&O directors that they had been invited to the official opening of the Chesapeake and Ohio Canal on October 10, 1850. By the time he remembered, it was too late. That was unfortunate because the railroad officials missed one of the most remarkable celebratory speeches ever uttered.

"Many of us were young when this great work was commenced, and we have lived to see its completion only because Providence has prolonged our lives until our heads are gray," William Price, the Cumberland lawyer, said to the assembled crowd from the deck of a canal boat. "Thousands have been ruined by their connection with this work, and but few in this region have any cause to bless it." Price's tone brightened as he hailed the end of state subsidy and the beginning of profitable operations.[31] Five canal boats loaded with coal set off in a race to Washington. Two got stuck above dam no. 6 on account of low water, but they all arrived a week later to the accompaniment of more band music, artillery reports, fireworks, and speeches. The anticipated financial windfall was never forthcoming.

The presence of Charles Fenton Mercer, the Chesapeake and Ohio's creator, was not noted at the opening. James M. Coale, the C&O president, gave the keynote address. He made the obligatory comments about someday extending the project to the Ohio River, as the original plan called for, but the waterway's spokesmen seemed greatly relieved just to have got to Cumberland.[32]

One necessary element was still missing from the railroad's program to reach its objective. In the summer of 1850, Swann reopened negotiations with the Barings to sell the rest of the Maryland sterling bonds while economic conditions were favorable. The mutual confidence and understanding that they had built up over the years should be continued until the railroad was completed, he said. One of the Barings' responses to Swann was at once so typically guarded, urbane, and magisterial, and such a model of its type, that it is worth quoting at length:

> Sir,
>
> We have the pleasure to acknowledge the receipt of your valued letter of the 8th Inst. the contents of which have our careful attention. We beg you will accept our best thanks for the friendly expression your letter contains and we beg to assure you that it has always been our desire to facilitate by all the means in our power the completion of your great enterprise believing it to be very important to the welfare of the shareholders as well as to that of your City and State. With these views we had addressed to Mr. Ward our instructions to treat with you for the purchase of the state bonds, but owing to the very threatening state of German politics, we desired him to delay making positive engagement until we should be able to advise him whether we were to have peace or war. In the latter case, we are of opinion that the value of money would increase and there would be no probability of disposing of American stocks at present high prices. For ourselves, we cannot believe we are to have a continental war and we hope in the course of ten days to be able to advise Mr. Ward that he may go on with the negociation . . .
>
> We remain
> Sir Your Obedient
> Baring Brothers[33]

Swann met Ward in Boston and again in New York after the Barings gave their approval and events accelerated to a sudden conclusion. But for most of November and December, 1850, the burgeoning correspondence made its tedious rounds on the steamers between London and Baltimore and Boston. The railroad president wrote the British bankers that he had had offers for a large amount of the bonds in New York and for some in Baltimore, but would prefer to make a satisfactory arrangement with them.

On Christmas Day 1850, Ward summoned Swann to New York with the news that the Barings would take roughly half of the $2 million in state sterling bonds remaining unsold at a mutually agreeable rate and the rest in six months. But the Barings' agent was, if possible, even more prudent than his employers: "You will, I think, be prepared for a price corresponding to [changed] circumstances in making a sale to Messrs. Baring Brothers and Company," he warned.

What happened over the next ten days stunned the Barings and brought the Baltimore and Ohio Railroad once again into the financial orbit of their competitors. Early in January 1851, Swann wrote a brief letter to London that began: "Gentlemen: The Board of Directors of this Company have sold the whole amount of sterling bonds of the State of Maryland . . . to Messrs. Brown Brothers and Company," and he asked the Barings to suspend further sales. Swann later explained that he had gone to New York, talked to Ward, and then received an offer from the Browns to take roughly half the bonds at 91. Ward came back with 90. Swann said he could do better, hoping Ward would offer to take all the bonds at a fixed rate, because that was the arrangement he wanted to make. Ward's instructions from the Barings did not permit that, but even so, Swann returned to Baltimore prepared to advocate the Barings' proposition to the board of directors. However, before they met, Brown Brothers offered to take the whole amount of state sterling bonds at 91, "the money to be paid as required by the company, and without conditions of any sort." Although Swann felt the Barings might be encouraged to make the same offer, he left the choice up to the directors, and on January 4, 1851, they quickly accepted the Browns' proposal.

The Barings, taken by surprise, were not amused. Why had they safeguarded the bonds for a dozen years, not only protecting Maryland's credit but lobbying to have the state resume its obligations? Why had they arranged to purchase the iron to lay the track from Harpers Ferry to Wheeling? Why had they been a constant financial friend to the railroad when there was no competition for its securities, if not to benefit from their final sale? There was the principle of the thing and then there was the money. Swann had offered the Barings a 5 percent commission for handling the bond sale, worth roughly $100,000 (about $850,000 in present-day funds).

Swann tended to blame their overcautious intermediary, Thomas Wren Ward, for the Barings' missed opportunity, but Ward was severely handicapped by the distance. His superiors were in London, a two-to-three-week steamship run away, whereas the Brown Brothers & Co. representatives were on the scene in New York. "In justice to the Board, I must say, that they could not have acted otherwise than they did," Swann told the Barings in an apologetic letter. "Their obligations amounted to $200,000 per month, and without a sale of the whole amount of Sterling bonds, they might have been subjected to a risk, which would have involved the safety of their work. The condition insisted on by Mr. Ward satisfied the Board, that even your great House, entertained doubt of the future, and were not prepared to run so great a risk; and with such a warning, they would have had no excuse to make to their stockholders, if with an absolute offer before them, they had postponed action."[34]

The relationship between the House of Baring and the Baltimore and Ohio

Railroad cooled somewhat after that. There was communication, but apparently no further aid during Swann's tenure.[35] Four days after the sale of the last $2 million worth of Maryland sterling bonds, the B&O directors approved contracts to build the final 33 miles of railroad to the Ohio River, the sections that had been delayed by the dispute with Wheeling.

24

Tracking the Wilderness

AS THE MAJOR POLICY QUESTIONS OF ROUTE
and financing were being settled, Benjamin H. Latrobe, Jr., grappled with his own
problems. He could deal with failing contractors and a fractious labor force, but
a countryside that was inhospitable for railroads, weather that only made things
worse, and cholera that visited the line each autumn—these were difficulties beyond
his control.

The construction program that tentatively began in May 1849 and continued
without interruption through the winter, mainly at the tunnels and bridges, expanded
dramatically the following year. In the spring of 1850, Latrobe took steps to improve
the performance of the contractors. Most of them were men of good reputation but
slender resources. To carry on their work, they needed profits as they went along
equal to the 20 percent of the price retained until their contracts were completed, or
if not that, access to outside financing. Many had neither and were constantly on the
verge of failure. Proposing that the company serve as their bank, Latrobe arranged
with Swann to reimburse, at Latrobe's discretion, a portion of the retained funds.
Even so, by the time the work was finished, 88 of the 200 one-mile sections and 28 of
the 114 bridges had had to be re-let to new contractors at increased prices, some
of them two and three times. In the end, the company took over and completed nine
of the most difficult sections of railroad along with five of the biggest bridges.

A strike for higher wages during the first two weeks in March 1850 resulted in
a pay raise for laborers to 87 and a half cents a day and the reestablishment of the
private police. The force regrouped at the Kingwood Tunnel after strikers threatened
and shot at the men who remained at work deep in the tunnel shafts. They managed
to preserve the peace and keep the job going throughout the strike. The guards hired
in the fall of 1849, when the Irish first rioted at the tunnel, had disbanded because the
contractors stopped paying them after the disorders subsided. When the riots started
up again, Latrobe reasoned that a permanent police force might be able to keep the

laborers from killing each other at least in places where the greatest numbers of them were concentrated, specifically on the twelve miles along the Cheat River, site of the most difficult work on the new line. The company would share with the contractors the cost of hiring twelve men, one for each mile. Latrobe thought that if they could pacify that area, they could dispense with police elsewhere. Each guard was to receive the same $1.25 a day as before, and Latrobe estimated the B&O's total expense at roughly $5,000. Management went along, but as events proved, armed guards became necessary at both ends of the line, at a cost of more than $20,000. The Pennsylvania Railroad adopted a similar system.

In the summer of 1850, workmen at the Kingwood Tunnel pushed on faster than expected. However, the company had to take over the troublesome Section 77 leading up to it, where the line crossed deep ravines in the Cheat River Valley. The B&O hired contractors that summer for 65 more sections west of the Northwestern Turnpike bridge over the Tygart Valley River (Grafton, West Virginia). Yet only a few months passed before they had to reclaim a major project in the new territory, the greatest bridge on the line over the Monongahela River at Fairmont. "This bridge was let to a highly recommended firm of Pennsylvania contractors," who for unexplained reasons, Latrobe said, "waived the work, after causing much loss of time by feints towards its commencement." The contractors may have discovered what the company did not yet know, that a mass of tangled timber lay buried in mud several feet below the surface of the water near the location of the eastern pier.[1]

Latrobe's second idea for maintaining harmony among the laborers had at first quite the opposite effect and resulted in the establishment of another armed police force near Cumberland. One faction of Irishmen was then in control of the entire line and was preventing the hiring of members of other factions, so it was difficult to increase the work force. By contacting immigration agents and societies and offering lower immigrant fares on the railroad, Latrobe planned to import enough workmen from different counties of Ireland to even the sides. Over the winter of 1850–51, more than 2,500 Irish recruits arrived at Cumberland from New York. The B&O laborers already on the job, all construction-hardened veterans, immediately began attacking the new men moving out over the line in a series of bloody assaults, clubbing and cursing them back to town. Latrobe reported that "many of the newcomers were severely beaten altho' it is not yet certain that any were killed." He brought in more private police, and with their help the company was able to shift the old hands to other sections. The new arrivals made it as far west as the Cheat River, but over half disappeared without reimbursing the railroad for the cost of their transportation.

They were hardly to be blamed. These were young men who had been lured by the prospect of a decent job in America to depart a starving country—1850 was the year after the potato famine ended but the height of Irish emigration—and had endured weeks of wretched food aboard a lurching steamship followed by sleepless days and nights in an immigrant car, only to arrive at their destination cold, hungry, and exhausted to find the welcome worse than the trip. The recruiters had not mentioned bleeding under a railroad bridge or serving as a target in a dim tunnel on some godforsaken Virginia hilltop. Some of those who stayed were totally inexperienced with construction work and had to be trained. Nevertheless, they turned out to be good workers. Latrobe considered the experiment a success. He had expanded the labor force and broken the power of one Irish faction to dictate who was hired. In the summer of 1851, when there was more violence in the Kingwood Tunnel area, he imported additional laborers from New York. Disturbances erupted simultaneously near Wheeling, where the hands were constantly "turbulent," and Latrobe called in additional armed guards there. John C. Watson, the captain of a special force of 25–30 men at the western end of the line, settled a fight at Grave Creek as late as December 1852 as the railroad was reaching the Ohio River.

Latrobe's reports to Swann on these matters were factual and uniformly positive. He always said that there had been some problems but they were past and order again prevailed on the line. Because no one ever disciplined the Irish for very long, labor unrest never ceased during the entire three and a half years of construction, yet the worst was over with the Kingwood Tunnel riots in the winter and spring of 1849–50 and the violence at Cumberland a year later. Labor was plentiful as construction drew to a close on the C&O Canal in 1850 and began in earnest on the railroad. Later on, competing public works in Ohio and other states, as well as the unceasing factional strife among the Irish, made it more difficult to keep up the numbers. Latrobe noted that the men "always take advantage of a desire on the part of the company to press on the work, to demand higher wages, and lose much of their time in strikes and suspensions." The work force reached its peak—4,870 men and 995 horses—in November 1851, and thereafter Latrobe did not again resort to bringing in immigrants.[2]

The company's monthly expenses for construction reached their highest point, $200,000, in July 1851. By then, five of the seven major bridges between Cumberland and Wheeling were finished. They included a pair of large but conventional masonry viaducts at Cumberland and Bloomington. In between was a bizarre manifestation of the railroad's experiments over the past few years with iron, a new primary structural material for bridges. Beyond the Glades were two more iron structures, over the Youghiogheny and the Cheat. The unfinished spans were those farthest west, the Monongahela River Bridge at Fairmont and the one over Wheeling Creek at the destination.

The investigation of iron as a major component of bridge trusses was supervised by Benjamin H. Latrobe, Jr. He contributed the strange-looking example, but the experiment was most successfully carried out by his two assistants. Their combined deliberations made a significant contribution to American civil engineering. Latrobe had incorporated cast-iron joints and wrought-iron tension members in his wooden truss bridges as early as 1835. Ten years later, the directors asked him to look into the cost of an iron bridge to repair a fallen span at Harpers Ferry. In 1847, they again requested him to examine two new iron highway spans over the Jones Falls in Baltimore to help them determine the best means of replacing a pair of stone bridges on the Washington Branch that had been washed away by a flood in October of that year.

Latrobe discovered that the failures of these bridges, one over the Little Patuxent River at Savage and the other over the northwest branch of the Potomac (the Anacostia River) at Bladensburg, were due to insufficient waterway, insecure foundations, and inferior masonry, "unskilfully or carelessly put together." He took this as further evidence of Caspar Wever's shoddy work. Temporary trestles were erected to carry the trains, but not much else was done until the fall of 1849, when Swann noted in the annual report that the bridges on the Washington Branch were being rebuilt in stone and iron. Latrobe also chose masonry and iron for the new bridges west of Cumberland, but he said the larger ones would have timber trusses, a clear indication that the railroad did not yet trust metal for long spans.

Very soon, however, two men emerged in the company's affairs who forever changed such notions: Wendel Bollman and Albert Fink. Bollman, a Baltimore-born, first-generation American of German parentage, was 35. He was an engineering autodidact. Fink, only 22, was an immigrant from Germany who had been graduated in 1848 with a degree in architecture and engineering from the polytechnic school at Darmstadt. Bollman had been around the B&O at the start and had been dropping in at ten-year intervals after that. He helped to lay the first tracks in Baltimore in 1829 and to rebuild the wooden bridge at Harpers Ferry a decade later. He was back in 1849 as master-of-road. In between times, he worked as a carpenter. Fink left Germany for America in 1849, "after the failure of the agrarian revolution," according to a biographical sketch among his papers, and found his way to Baltimore and into the B&O's engineering department. Three years later, Latrobe described him as his "principal office assistant."

Between 1849 and 1852, Latrobe and his colleagues successfully redesigned the American railroad truss bridge in iron. Wendel Bollman became the pioneer builder of such bridges. Albert Fink created the first widely adopted truss system and also the earliest iron railroad viaducts. And the Baltimore and Ohio, the sponsor, adopted this new bridging material as a matter of policy before any other railroad company in the United States. There was no single inspiration for the early designs. One point of origin lay in the wooden truss bridges at Harpers Ferry and Elysville, for which Latrobe and Lewis Wernwag had replaced the supplemental timber arch with straight members in the form of diagonal struts. In designing their "suspension trusses," Bollman and Fink, in a manner of speaking, turned these structures upside down and reproduced them in metal. Charles Ellet's Wheeling suspension bridge, which all three engineers would certainly have seen, was equally important.

The replacement bridge that appeared in 1850 at Savage on the Washington Branch was the earliest example of the Bollman truss. William Parker, the B&O general superintendent who helped to create the new bridge designs, described the bridge as novel, "embodying valuable mechanical features, and holding out the fullest degree of encouragement as to its success and reliability."[3] The bridge was quite an original arrangement in the best B&O tradition. There was no bottom chord and the load was transmitted by wrought-iron diagonals to the tops of the cast-iron columns at the ends. These were kept from inclining toward each other by a cast-iron member that Bollman called a "stretcher." One latter-day analyst said of it, "Bollman's intention in this highly redundant and bewildering array of separate pieces was undoubtedly to combine the truss with a mode of support comparable to that of the suspension bridge."[4]

The significance of the Savage span was greater than its modest 76-foot length would indicate. In his report, Parker alluded to the failure of an iron bridge on another railroad, which had panicked that company's directors into denouncing all iron bridges. To Parker's mind, that catastrophe should have made people more skeptical of contractors' plans for cheap structures, but on the other hand ought not "destroy our confidence in a material so nearly essential to the success of mechanical practice in almost every department of art and science."[5] The bridge in question was one on the Erie Railroad that collapsed under a cattle train in July 1850. It was an all-iron variation of a Howe truss, built by a contractor who apparently had little understanding of iron or trusses. He was charged with gross negligence. After this disaster, the Erie Railroad set out in precisely the opposite direction as the B&O, removing its other metal bridges, replacing them with wood, and giving up all faith in iron for the next fifteen years.

Bollman completed his replacement bridge at Bladensburg in 1851. He also erected a 124-foot version at Harpers Ferry to replace the timber Winchester span. This bridge was a composite structure with granite columns, iron trusswork, and wooden floor. Bollman explained: "By this combination of cast and wrought iron, the former is in a state of compression, the latter in that of tension, the proper condition of those two metals. It unites the principals of the Suspension and of the Truss Bridge." He patented his design in 1852. It did have a major drawback in that the diagonals, being of different lengths, expanded and contracted unequally with temperature changes, and therefore the bridges were difficult to keep in alignment.[6]

While Bollman, under Parker's tutelage, built truss bridges east of Harpers Ferry, Fink, at Latrobe's request, worked on an improved design for the bridges west of Cumberland. The result was essentially a variation of the Bollman truss. It, too, was a suspension truss without a lower chord, having wrought-iron diagonals and posts and chords of cast iron. Because the Fink truss was symmetrical, however, it was not subject to distortion caused by temperature changes, and it was also more economical in its use of metal. The first documented major bridge on the Fink plan, over the Youghiogheny River, appeared on the new line just past the recently founded town of Oakland, Maryland. To avoid the need for two bridges there, the Little Youghiogheny was diverted into an old channel and made to enter the larger stream just above the new span. The January 1851 issue of the *American Railroad Journal* described what it said was the plan of this bridge—on which the masonry was being finished—but their description is definitely not that of a Fink truss. Perhaps the bridge was not constructed as planned. In any case, the Youghiogheny River bridge was finished in July 1851. In November 1853, Latrobe said it was a single, 180-foot span on white sandstone abutments 25 feet over the water with a superstructure of timber and iron, "upon Fink's plan of suspension truss."[7]

A bridge quite similar to the one reported in the *American Railroad Journal* actually was built over the Potomac below Paddytown (Keyser, West Virginia). Latrobe was its designer. The Youghiogheny River bridge at Oakland, according to the magazine, was to have had four eighteen-foot stone towers. These were four feet square at the base and battered, each masonry course composed of a single stone. Spanning the distance between the towers across the stream were two "solid built beams"—the wooden stretchers. From each one hung an iron suspension chain in a catenary curve. These chains passed through iron castings attached to timber trusses between the stretchers and the bridge deck, which consisted of timber floor beams that carried the track. Horizontal struts running from post to post gave the appearance of a lower chord, but this was nonfunctional, as in the Bollman and Fink trusses. Although the *Railroad Journal* described this structure as "a beautiful application of the suspension principle to railroad bridges," what it really amounted to was a bad compromise between suspension and truss forms. It lacked the rationale for the former—the need to span great distances without intermediate piers—and the stiffness of the latter. It was a pastiche of influences, principles, and materials, and structurally illogical.

The version of this bridge that Labrobe designed to cross the Potomac River at Paddytown must have been very odd looking. He planned the bridge in October 1850 as a timber structure but said it was to be built on a "new principle." It was completed in July 1851, at the same time as the one over the Youghiogheny at Oakland, and Latrobe said it had been "well tested and shows abundant strength and stiffness." A year later, the *American Railroad Journal* referred to it as a "wooden suspension bridge ingeniously designed" by Latrobe.[8] In 1853, Latrobe himself listed it as a timber and iron bridge of two 156-foot spans resting on limestone piers and abutments. "The trusses are supported by a wrought iron, parabolic, suspension chain, stiffened by diagonal rods," he said. The structure had a sheet iron roof and weather-boarding on the sides; at the west end was the foundation legend: "Potomac Bridge, 1851; Designed by B.H. Latrobe, Chief Engineer; Executed by A. Fink, Assistant Engineer; J.C. Davis, Carpenter."[9]

Latrobe must have had faith that at least some of these experiments would be successful because in the spring of 1850 he arranged for a new $10,000 shop at Mt. Clare to produce the 350–400 tons of iron superstructures for the spans on the line past Cumberland. This was before any of the iron suspension truss bridges had been erected, except possibly Bollman's at Savage, Maryland, and certainly before they had been tested under operating conditions. Latrobe was determined to buy ballast and cross ties for the track from those working on or living near the railroad and not, as he had done before, by advertising for bids. He had discovered that under the old system, the contractors colluded and fixed prices.

The first 60-pound T-rails arrived from England and by the spring of 1851, when they began laying them west of Cumberland, Latrobe had devised a new system for that, too. Instead of being by contract, the work would be done by a company force directed by Roseby Carr. Carr had worked as a contractor on rebuilding the Old Main Line at Elysville and Parrs Spring Ridge, and he was now an energetic B&O division superintendent. He drilled the new men until they could put down half a mile of rails in a day. Toward the end, they were laying track at the rate of a mile a day, no mean feat in the mountains.

Joshua Hartshorne, a Baltimore iron founder, furnished 350 tons of wrought iron to make "clamp chairs" for the ends of the rails, and the new Mt. Clare ironworks produced them. Smith and Tyson, also of Baltimore, provided a million pounds of railroad spikes. They were low bidders with the best product, handmade and sharpened by convicts in the state penitentiary. Locomotives hauled the construction materials and boarding cars for the men out to the end of the track; Latrobe said, "The whole line to Wheeling is to be pushed forward in this way by transporting the iron over the new road as fast as it is finished."[10]

The worst construction problem between Cumberland and Piedmont, their first objective, was Section 21, a deep rock cut just before Latrobe's combination truss and suspension bridge over the Potomac. Latrobe put on a night crew, but heavy landslides that began in October 1851 and continued because of the wet weather for the next several months hampered construction and therefore the work was not completed until the following summer. Meanwhile, they laid tracks around the cut, with an inclined plane, and went on.

Besides simply moving forward, the company had another reason for wanting to reach Piedmont: coal. The site lay at the foot of the highest ridge in the Allegheny Mountains and in the center of the Georges Creek coal basin. Duff Green, a major speculator in the region, had bought cheap land there some years before but lost control of it temporarily about the time the railroad arrived. Piedmont in the spring of 1851 was not much more than a flat several hundred yards wide in a bend of the river opposite Westernport and the mouth of Georges Creek, but it had great potential as a rail depot and a town. The coal trade, and extra power needed for trains to ascend the high grade, would require a concentration of engines there. Buildings would be necessary to house and repair them. While Latrobe got work started on the engine house, an original landowner began laying out the town.

Latrobe also located the rail line from the Georges Creek Coal and Iron Co. at Lonaconing, in the heart of the coalfield, to Westernport and arranged for the B&O to provide the rails. It was under construction in 1852. By then the Piedmont engine house was finished. This represented another collaboration between Latrobe and Albert Fink. The brick building, 150 feet in diameter, had sixteen sides and could accommodate as many engines. Iron columns on stone pedestals angled steeply upward to the lantern, like the poles of a tepee. These supported a high, conical iron roof and a low, flat sheet-iron roof laid on wooden rafters that flared out to the exterior walls. When other such buildings were added, they gave Piedmont the aspect of an industrial Indian village.

The locomotives destined to assemble here were already being built by Ross Winans. They represented the culmination of his engineering career. Winans had spent decades with the B&O perfecting his ideas through trial and error. The result in his case was the Camel engine, the first coal-burning locomotive produced in quantity for an American railroad. Its acceptance was gradual and controversial, however, the B&O having become increasingly skeptical of Winans's eight-wheeled Mud-diggers, first introduced in the mid-1840's. Latrobe complained that the Mud-diggers were built larger than originally contemplated, "and by a gradual accumulation of weight had become too unwieldy and too liable to get out of repair, to be efficient,"[11] and in late 1847 he advertised for bids for four twenty-ton, eight-wheeled, coal-burning engines. The contracts were spread among several builders, including Matthias W. Baldwin of Philadelphia, the New Castle Manufacturing Company of Delaware, the B&O's own shop, and Winans.[12]

Early in 1848, the railroad decided to buy five more of these engines and gave Baldwin the contract, but they rejected his first machine that fall for not meeting specifications. Baldwin eventually supplied three engines and the company authorized Winans to build two substitutes. In the meantime, Winans had begun manufacturing locomotives for the western Maryland coal companies. In 1848–49, he built the Mount Savage, the Eckhart, and the Mountaineer, the last for the Maryland Mining Company. He had also introduced on the Baltimore and Ohio in June 1848 the first Camel engine.

The Camel was a stylistic regression for Winans, but he cared nothing for appearance anyway, or even for efficient, well-built locomotives. Ruggedness, reliability, and power were his criteria. Despite its looks, the Camel was the machine for the B&O, which wanted coal-burning engines to haul heavy coal trains at slow speeds over steep grades. The first one had a horizontal boiler with a large steam dome behind the stack that resembled the hump of a camel. The engineer rode in a cab on top of the boiler, which contained 103 iron tubes, two and a half inches in diameter and a little over fourteen feet long. Cantilevered from its rear was a huge firebox, nearly seventeen square feet. The cylinders, 17 × 22 inches, were mounted horizontally under the smokebox, and for the first time in a Winans locomotive were directly connected, without intermediate gearing, to the eight 43-inch-diameter wheels. The whole ensemble weighed a little over 25 tons, stretched as many feet in length, and perched on a wheelbase that was only eleven feet three inches long. The locomotive was "the most peculiar engine in use in the United States," one contemporary authority said. "In every detail of construction" it was "alike peculiar and in the strongest possible contrast with the proportions, arrangement, and workmanship of the standard American engine."[13]

The Baltimore and Ohio Railroad, evidently impressed by the design, agreed to buy several more Camels from Winans in the fall of 1850. A few weeks later, the initial controversy concerning them erupted. It revolved around a newspaper article that compared Winans's latest engine with one built in the company shops by Thatcher Perkins. Perkins, formerly the shop foreman, had replaced James Murray as the B&O's master of machinery in 1847. His company-built, eight-wheeled locomotive was comparable in size and power to the Camel, but its elements were conventionally deployed. The directors called for a test of the engines to determine the relative cost of operation, repairs, and so on. At the same time, Perkins threatened to resign unless his salary was increased to $2,500 a year. In early 1851, the B&O accepted Winans's offer to build 24 more locomotives. They also adjusted Perkins's salary, but he quit anyway to make engines in Alexandria, Virginia.[14]

Locomotive performance was compared, but what was really tested on the railroad's first excursion over the new line to Piedmont on July 22, 1851, was the engines themselves. The public demonstration of their capacity to climb the high grades of the Alleghenies was reminiscent of the successful steam-powered ascent of the inclined planes at Parrs Spring Ridge staged for the Baltimore city council fifteen years earlier. Latrobe had promised that the railroad would be open to Piedmont by July 4 (the tracks had actually reached there June 28), but Swann had decided against a large celebration in favor of an informal outing for the governor, the mayor, and the city council. They and the other guests left Baltimore the day before on an express train to Cumberland. On Tuesday, July 22, in five coaches pulled by Engine no. 71, a Winans Camel, they rode out over the new line. The first bridge they crossed was the Cumberland Viaduct, passing the streets of the town on a curve and then moving straight across Wills Creek. The abutments and piers were built of limestone and sandstone. The fourteen elliptical arches, spanning 50 feet each, were of brick. The bridge was 850 long, eighteen and a half feet wide, and 28 feet above the stream.

They had a panoramic view of the Potomac in the vicinity of Latrobe's strange combination timber truss and iron suspension span. At Piedmont, 28 miles past Cumberland, they waited while one of the passenger coaches was detached and five gondola cars filled with iron were added. The tracks had been laid to the Everett Tunnel, four miles ahead. The train proceeded, followed by another consisting of eighteen gondola cars loaded with iron rails, drawn by no. 72, the Perkins company-built, eight-wheeled engine. The excursionists crossed the Potomac again on the Bloomington Viaduct, a white sandstone structure approximately 200 feet long and 50 feet over the water. Its piers rested on bedrock or timber pilings and each of the three semicircular arches spanned 56 feet. The company had built this as well as the other two bridges. Just beyond it, the tracks began their climb up Backbone Mountain.

Latrobe rode on the locomotive where he could hide in the smoke if they did not make it, and Swann stood "at an open door of the car, with a view to a more ready access to the woods," the railroad president remembered later.[15] But the Winans Camel engine took the 117-ton train up the last few miles of the steepest part of the grade, 116 feet per mile, in eight minutes, at almost 18 mph. Perkins's locomotive followed, pulling its load of 234 tons gross weight at about 8 mph. Both engines, with comparable loads, had gone up at the slower speed the day before. There was no longer any doubt that these locomotives could pull passenger trains over the steep grades, said a knowledgable observer.

Back in Piedmont, during an after-dinner speech in one of the new depot buildings, Swann reminded the guests that the New York and Erie Railroad had just been completed at a cost of $27 million. This six-foot, broad-gauge line, running 467 miles from Piermont, on the Hudson River 25 miles above New York City, to Dunkirk, on Lake Erie, had opened officially a few months before, on May 17, 1851; it was the first of the four great Eastern trunk lines to be finished. But the cost of completion of the B&O to the Ohio River would be only $16 million, Swann said, and their road would be second to none.

The preceding February, the legislators in Richmond had at last granted a charter to the Northwestern Virginia Railroad Company to build a line from Three Fork Creek in Taylor County (Grafton, West Virginia) to Parkersburg on the Ohio River;

Swann called it "the greatest railroad charter that has ever emanated from a Legislative body." [16] He predicted that the company would be organized, the line surveyed, and the railroad opened within a year after the B&O reached Wheeling. [17] Yet the Parkersburg line was no sooner announced than it awakened all the old jealousies and animosities. Philadelphia sought an alliance with Wheeling via the Hempfield Railroad. This line was proposed from a point on the Pennsylvania Railroad southeast of Pittsburgh to Wheeling. From there, a connection was planned to follow the western shore of the Ohio River down to Marietta and link up with a railroad coming east from Cincinnati. Although Swann was skeptical about all this, less than a month after his speech the Cincinnati line had been diverted from its original destination, Belpre, opposite Parkersburg, to Marietta, ten miles north, and it probably surprised no one when Swann noted that the Pittsburgh and Connellsville Railroad had again raised its head. [18] Swann thought that if the Baltimore and Ohio had not accepted Wheeling as its terminus in 1847, the state of Virginia would never have chartered an independent company to build the Parkersburg line. Wheeling was the ultimate political expedient. He never believed it was the best place to be on the Ohio River, but rather "the best that could be accomplished." [19]

By the time Swann issued the B&O's annual report that fall, the Winans Camel engines were working heavy trains daily over the mountains and through the Glades to Oakland, but the coal traffic from Georges Creek and Piedmont was sluggish. The railroad therefore primed the pump by transferring the operation at Locust Point in Baltimore from the already "totally inadequate" company facilities, including the B&O's deteriorating coal wharf, to private wharves. They offered a drawback (rebate) of six cents a ton on coal shipped to them from Cumberland. Swann also negotiated the sale of the final batch of securities whose proceeds were needed to complete the railroad to Wheeling. In the fall of 1849, Swann had identified a $1.1 million gap in their construction financing, which he planned to fill by issuing stocks or bonds. A year later, in an effort to raise some of these funds, the B&O offered for sale $500,000 worth of company 6 percent coupon bonds. Over the next several months, they sold $360,000 worth, most of them to board members, at rates of 95 or better.

In October 1851, the company advertised the sale of the remainder of the bonds, $760,000 worth. They accepted the bid of Josiah Lee and Company, Baltimore bankers, to take the whole amount at 80. It was the lowest rate offered, but it was the only proposal to buy the entire lot. (There were three other bids for smaller amounts, totaling $32,500, at rates concentrated at 81–83 percent.) The transaction aroused a storm of criticism and Swann threatened to resign. He decided instead to make a public statement defending his fiscal policy to the board of directors at the end of the year. It was another grand production.

When he took over, the president said, B&O stock was selling at 28 percent of its list price and the company's bonds had no fixed marketable value. The railroad had then embarked on a $6 million, 200-mile construction program. So far, they had spent $4.3 million, all of it provided since November 1848 on advantageous terms. But they still needed more money. Swann explained that the company employed nearly 5,000 laborers and 1,000 horses. "To work up to the very period of their wants, with such a family to provide for [i.e., to delay raising money until the bills were due], in the hope that the money market would become easier," would, he said, have "risked the safety of the company on a mere contingency." He went on to review the lackluster sales of the first $500,000 worth of coupon bonds and said that when they initially offered the second batch of $760,000, the total response was for $12,000 at rates no higher than 90. It was not company policy to contract large floating debt, he said, and a discount on the face value of the bonds was preferable to hypothecation, or borrowing large sums at high interest for short periods.

Swann further acknowledged that in their emergency, he had considered appealing to the citizens of Baltimore "by going from door to door, and soliciting their aid and cooperation" but had rejected that idea in favor of one last effort to attract capitalists. The members of the finance committee pledged their credit and the railroad directors continued to invest in the bonds. These measures so strengthened public confidence that when the securities were advertised for a third time, Josiah Lee made a bid for all of them and the directors accepted it. "Had the board declined this offer of 80 per cent, in the hope of accomplishing some 5 per cent more and had they subsequently failed to negotiate on any term, what would have been the situation of the company?" Swann asked rhetorically. "Would $35,000 have compensated for the suspension of the work, and the ruin that must have resulted from the depression of their labor, and a delay and expense of getting it back again, when a more auspicious period would have arrived?" The president added grandly, "I have not regarded fractions where I have had vast results to deal with," and summarized his fiscal approach to building railroads: "Money must be had, whenever it may be needed, at whatever may be its market value."[20]

Out in the mountains, Latrobe and his assistants and their "family" of 5,000 contentious Irish laborers persevered. Their next goal was Fairmont, on the Monongahela River. When they reached it, the B&O would be eligible to collect Wheeling's $500,000 subscription. In April 1851, Latrobe had promised the Baltimore city council that the tracks would be at Piedmont on July 4, Fairmont in a year, and Wheeling by January 1, 1853. They had achieved the first objective, but in the fall of 1851 the engineer's usually sanguine monthly reports turned somber. A particularly malignant form of cholera struck in the west. That winter, the landslides continued at Section 21 upriver from Cumberland and other places. With the spring of 1852 came heavy rain and flooding on the Monongahela.

The weather, labor disturbances, and machinery problems regularly interrupted work at the Kingwood Tunnel. Even so, the largest undertaking on the new line continued to make the most consistent progress. Latrobe had able assistants and good contractors who brought in miners to do the work. Tunnels were their business. Thomas Rowles, the surveyor of this section and later the division engineer, helped convince Latrobe when they began construction in the fall of 1849 that they should lay out a temporary rail line over the top of the hill in case the tunnel was not ready when the tracks got there. They did so and resorted to it on numerous occasions. The contractors grasped the importance of the project and started right in. The miners found that the materials they had to excavate, mostly slate and sandstone, made the job somewhat easier, but the slate was also a curse in that, although it stood up well when first exposed to the air, it crumbled with time. Because of the slate, the tunnel had to be arched later on, which proved very costly in terms of men and money.

Their common task was to build a 4,100-foot-long tunnel, 24 feet wide and 22 feet high, straight through the hill and 223 feet below its crest. It dropped 53 feet from east to west and required deep cuts, 72 and 65 feet, respectively, at either end. Again moving from east to west, the three shafts had to be dug 180, 175, and 167 feet down. Latrobe figured it would take them until the summer of 1852.

Engineers with the customary transit, level, and chain first aligned the tunnel by surveying a straight line over the top of the hill and making an accurate profile of it. They staked the line out on the ground and positioned the shafts by selecting three sites, roughly equidistant, at the lowest possible points on the ridge. The middle shaft, for example, was near a deep trough cut by a streambed.

The tunnel men who took over next were a clannish breed in the nineteenth century, as they are today; few jobs are more specialized or dangerous. Of these laborers, one contemporary admirer wrote: "Of all branches of construction, it is one of the most difficult. A barbarous people may, perhaps, develop a high degree of perfection in the mere art of open-air building, where stone can be piled on stone, and rafter fitted to rafter, in the light of day; but it takes the energy, knowledge, experience, and skill of an educated and trained class of men to cope with the unknown dangers of the dark depths to be invaded by the tunnel-man."[21] They started with the 15-by-20-foot excavations for the shafts, using hammer, drill, and black powder. As they worked their way down through solid rock, they lined the pits with heavy timbers to prevent cave-ins. Other crews simultaneously began cutting the western approach. They soon ran into limestone, more difficult to remove but more stable as a tunnel roof.

The shifts worked around the clock and the digging went quickly that first winter of 1849–50, even with riots and wet weather that impeded the operation of the horse gins used for lifting out the spoil. These were huge winches, mounted horizontally on a heavy timber framework. They were connected by ropes to a pair of pulleys suspended over the mouth of the shaft and by wooden cranks to two horses that walked slowly in circles, drawing up a full container of dirt and rock while simultaneously lowering an empty one. A total of 90,000 cubic yards of material were removed from the tunnel through the shafts and 110,000 from the openings at either end. It didn't go far. The place where they dumped the spoil for Shaft no. 1 was right beside it. The shafts and the western portal were finished in eight months and work started on the headings. These were smaller excavations, about eight feet high, twenty feet wide, arched, and driven horizontally to connect the bottoms of the three shafts and the cut for the western portal. Tunneling therefore proceeded from seven points at once. These openings, or breasts, represented the top of the tunnel. Later on, the bottom would be removed.

One of the difficulties was keeping the tunnel aligned. As the shafts were sunk, they were held from deviating vertically with a plumb line and rule; the chain determined the proper depth. In the tunnel headings, nails were driven into the ceiling and a string stretched between them, each succeeding nail being centered exactly with the transit. Since it was generally not possible to see more than 100 feet in a tunnel, a man stood behind the farthest nail with a light. (Later on, special plummet lamps were developed for this purpose.) The level established the proper slope in each section. The tunnelmen worked in eight-hour shifts in the dim lamplight, drilling and blasting, four hammers to a breast. Their natural enemies, water and gas, were absent here, but there were other dangers. The first fall of rock from the unsupported roof of the tunnel occurred near the middle shaft. The miners' wage was $1 for eight hours. Common laborers made 87 and a half cents for eight hours below or eleven hours top labor.

In October 1850, at the end of the first full year of construction, Latrobe reported they had driven 1,500 feet of heading, more than a third the total distance, at a rate of 300 feet per month, which would complete the work ahead of schedule. Excavation now began at the eastern tunnel entrance, where hard rock was also found. The crews moved ahead so fast they could not get the rock out quickly enough, so at the second and third shafts, Latrobe substituted steam engines for the horse gins and also used them to power fans to ventilate the tunnel.

By January 1851, the 300 hands at work under the watchful eyes of a dozen heavily armed security guards had driven half the length of the tunnel. Greigsville had become a town of 80 houses, seven stores, two churches, two schools, and a post office. But the weather again interfered. That winter, as the first headings came together, the hoisting machinery broke down and Latrobe could not attract good machinists to the remote site. The next summer, a drought shut off the supply of water to the steam engines. The succeeding winter of 1851–52 was bitter cold. In Morgantown, Virginia, the temperature dropped to 18 degrees below zero. At Greigsville, the tunnel shafts filled with ice. The lack of water and an accident stopped one of the steam engines. Then, on January 16, 1852, they holed through the last heading. It was the worst recorded disaster at the Kingwood Tunnel. Two crews on opposite sides of the final section of rock to be removed had a wager on which would be the first to get through. The customary blasting signal either was not given or was ignored and the explosion blew out the other side, killing an Irish laborer and wounding several others. Sheer recklessness was to blame, Latrobe said.

They laid the track over the hill atop the tunnel that winter. By spring, when the rains came, locomotives were climbing the steep grades to haul rails, bridge components, and construction materials to the other side. On one trip, a heavy car broke loose from an engine, came hurtling back down the incline, and was prevented from crashing into the boarding cars where the workmen were eating lunch only by a dragging chain that snagged a tie. Latrobe reported that the tunnel was completed and the track laid through it on May 8, 1852, in accordance with his prediction. The cost was $460,000. It was two years and eight months after they had started construction, but they were not through yet. As the trains began running regularly through the tunnel that summer, they put timber supports under the worst sections of the roof.

Twice Latrobe assured Swann that it was secure and twice it fell in, halting traffic and forcing trains to be rerouted to the steep grades and switchbacks over the top.[22]

An even more exciting adventure for passengers was Section 77, which began five miles east of Kingwood Tunnel and led up to it. Here, the railroad made its way across several deep gorges while climbing the steep side of the Cheat River Valley. When the company took over this section from dilatory contractors and began building it in June 1850, Latrobe was thinking of a simple and economical way to pass the ravines. For the two deepest ones, he and Albert Fink devised the nation's first iron railroad viaducts. Section 77 offered some of the most spectacular mountain scenery on the line. For years, excursion trains stopped there and passengers got down to admire the view. Bands played and speakers tried in vain to do justice to the awesome surroundings. Writers, artists, and photographers dramatically portrayed the streams rushing down from the heights underneath the slender iron viaducts that clung precariously to the hillside. Others entertained themselves by flinging stones at the coffee-colored Cheat River hundreds of feet below until it was time for the coaches to lurch off again.

The scores of Irish workmen on Section 77 saw it for two long years from below looking up. They first built large culverts over the watercourses, and then, on top of them, constructed massive stone walls to support the iron viaducts that would hold up the tracks. Despite a shortage of masons in the spring of 1851 and heavy rains and landslides a year later that affected the retaining walls, the rails were laid over Section 77 in March 1852.

Once past the Cheat River bridge, the track climbed 450 feet in five miles to the Kingwood Tunnel, crossing the first ravine, Kyer's Run, 76 feet deep, on an earth embankment. Buck-eye Hollow, which came next, was 108 feet down and 400 feet across. The way over was first built as a timber trestle supported on a stone wall, but by 1853, the wooden trestle had been replaced by an iron viaduct 340 feet long and 46 feet high. The greatest of the ravines was Tray Run, where the track level was 150 feet above the streambed and extended 600 feet from side to side. It, too, was first crossed by a masonry-supported timber trestle. The iron viaduct that took its place in 1853 was 445 feet long and 58 feet high. Finally, there was Buckhorn Run, 90 feet deep, and crossed again by an earth embankment.

The feelings of the passengers who rode over those first high, spindly wooden structures may be imagined, as the trees, hillside, and the ground on either side suddenly dropped away and the train proceeded out over the valley floor far below seemingly with no support at all. One early traveler wrote: "Perceiving the slow movement of the cars I rushed to the window, and it seemed as though we were flying through the air. Looking down I could hardly see the ground. I asked the conductor where we were. He replied that we were 'going over the great section called 77' . . . it appeared that the track was hung upon the clouds."[23]

By the fall of 1852, the workmen were erecting the iron viaducts at Buck-eye Hollow and Tray Run, using components produced by the Mt. Clare foundry. The viaducts were finished a year later. "These structures are of cast iron connected by wrought iron bolts and rods," Latrobe said. "They consist of columns, inclined so as to give greater width of base and more stability, connected by arches of open work, the whole system firmly united by proper ties. The columns rest on pedestals supported on the stone walls built across the deep beds of the two ravines mentioned, and which walls it was originally designed to continue up to the road level." The iron viaduct at Buck-eye Hollow cost $24,000 and that at Tray Run, $36,000. Instead of the narrow, single-track timber trestles, the double track was now laid on a floor of heavy planks 28 feet wide between four-foot-high parapet railings on either side. For the design of the Cheat River cast-iron viaducts, Latrobe credited Albert Fink, "whose talents and taste have been nowhere displayed to greater advantage than here." [24]

In addition to the advantage of saving time and labor by erecting the iron viaducts rather than carrying the masonry up to track level, Latrobe also noted another benefit: "The experience we have had in the use of these structures for several months past is very satisfactory as regards their stability and now that the broad platforms by which they are covered interpose between the eye of the passenger and the chasm beneath, there will be no more nervous apprehensions experienced, as the viaducts are in truth as strong and safe as any part of the road." [25]

Forty miles on the other side of the Kingwood Tunnel, the company was not having much better luck with their principal bridge, over the Monongahela River at Fairmont, than the builders who surrendered it in the fall of 1850 had had. The original plans called for four 156-foot timber trusses here. The first winter was spent quarrying stone. A year later, with the abutments started, Latrobe reported delays and problems in laying the foundation for the eastern pier. They had found the timber buried in the river bottom. Work on the abutments continued, but frigid temperatures in the winter of 1851–52 and ice in the river kept them from doing much more. Early in the spring, a foot of snow fell in the mountains. Latrobe wrote, "We have pressed on, however, without faltering, through all the obstacles thus thrown in our way."

Heavy rains melted the snow and the Monongahela flooded on April 5, 1852. Latrobe reported on the situation from Fairmont. Most of the destruction was on the west fork, which rose ten feet higher than the crest of the worst previous flood. The Northwestern Turnpike bridge at Clarksburg was swept away and the entire river town of Worthington below it slipped its moorings and sailed past Fairmont in pretty much the same arrangement in which it stood on solid ground, he said. There was only slight damage to the railroad itself. Part of the grade and a bridge scaffold disappeared on Three Fork Creek. But the floods caused landslides and held up construction at several points along the line. Latrobe had promised to have the rails in Fairmont that month. Now they would need more time, he told Swann, and he added that their prospects "are much clouded at this moment as it has been raining hard and incessantly for 30 hours," and the river was rising again. "This is extremely discouraging," Latrobe said. Then he sent Roseby Carr and his entire track-laying force to repair the gaps. At the end of the month the rails passed the washout on Three Fork Creek (Grafton, West Virginia). [26]

On June 5, 1852, they reached the east bank of the Monongahela River. Latrobe formally notified Swann of the fact and of their intention to push on to Wheeling so that the B&O, having fulfilled its obligations, could qualify for the $500,000 subscription from that city. (Wheeling subscribed for 5,000 shares of B&O stock on June 16, 1852.) Their immediate goal was Fairmont, a mile down the river. That was the destination for the excursion Swann had scheduled for June 21. Latrobe's current plan was for an iron bridge there with three spans of 200 feet each, but because only the abutments were finished, they would first put up a temporary timber trestle. While that was being built, they ferried the rails over the Monongahela in boats, and kept going.

The great bridge at Fairmont took another year to complete. The company crew finished the western pier in November 1852 and immediately erected that part of the iron superstructure. It had been fabricated at Mt. Clare and sent west on the railroad. They installed the cofferdam for the eastern pier, but raising the stonework took another six months of work through the winter ice and springtime floods that constantly threatened the temporary timber trestle. The site was in deep water. Before they reached bedrock 22 feet below the surface, they had extracted more than 100 logs and tree trunks and tons of sand.

Latrobe's note to Swann on June 7, 1853, expressed the relief that he and the exhausted laborers felt when they were done: "I am happy to be able, at length, to report the completion of the iron viaduct over the Monongahela river at Fairmont, the strength, durability and beauty of which will I trust be regarded as a compensation for the unavoidable delays which have attended its progress and the increased expense they have occasioned." [27] It was the largest iron bridge in America, a monumental structure of heavy ashlar masonry and handsome Fink trusses, 600 feet long, 38 feet above the water, and skewed at 36 degrees. "The whole structure is painted a light green color, and when viewed from a neighboring eminence, nothing can surpass it for beauty and harmonious proportions," a contemporary critic said. [28] At $138,200, it was by far the most expensive bridge on the new line, greater than the all-masonry Cumberland and Bloomington viaducts combined, an indication of its torturous construction. Again Latrobe credited Albert Fink for his aid "in the design and execution of most of the bridge structures and buildings upon the line, and which are alike creditable to his skill as an engineer, and his taste as an architect." [29]

The president's excursion was the engineer's nightmare. The elements and the Irish could not depress Latrobe for long, but safe passage for several hundred politicians and other important passengers over 124 miles of newly laid rails and raw structures between Cumberland and Piedmont gave him pause. With the Cheat River trestles and the Kingwood Tunnel barely completed and just five days before the first train was due to pull into Fairmont, the engineer wrote Swann, "I arrived here last night and found our road promising to be completed in time to let us cross the river and bring our company to the town without the passage of which I have been somewhat in fear." In other words, the trestle bridge over the Monongahela was not yet finished, but it would be by the time the train got there. The Fairmont courthouse could not accommodate 300 guests, Latrobe continued, so the journey would end at the company's lot half a mile below town, "on the river bank, a beautiful spot," where they would erect a shed, fill it with tables, and hope for good weather.[30]

Unlike Piedmont, Oakland, Rowlesburg, and Grafton, which did not exist before the coming of the railroad, Fairmont was an established settlement when the B&O arrived. The town, spread out on steep hills on both sides of the river just below where the West Fork and Tygart Valley rivers join to form the Monongahela, originated around 1819 as a halfway stop on the new Virginia highway between Clarksburg and Morgantown. It began as two towns, Middletown on the west bank where hotels and mills were located, and Palatine on the east bank, the site of a copper and machine works. In 1843, when the two towns incorporated as Fairmont, Middletown had 70 houses, five stores, and several hotels and taverns, while Palatine had most of the industry. A wire suspension bridge connected the two. Fairmont, even then, was a gritty coal town.

The train left Baltimore early in the morning on June 21, 1852, and arrived late in the afternoon at Cumberland for the customary overnight stay. Latrobe was aboard when they set out the next day for Fairmont. The cars passed the 2,629-foot summit on Wilson's farm, the highest main line railroad crossing of the Allegheny Mountains, crept out over the timber trestles beyond the Cheat River—"singular," said a newspaper reporter—and approached the Kingwood Tunnel.

When they were almost there, Latrobe was informed that another rock fall had taken place "and that the only way left open to the excursion train was over the top of the hill instead of through it. The news somewhat disconcerted me at first, but I soon saw in it an opportunity," he said. Coolly directing the track to be reconnected to the steep, switchback line to the top, the engineer turned what could have been a genuine disaster into yet another triumphant demonstration of locomotive power. The line over the summit left the main track before the eastern tunnel portal and ascended on a grade that increased to 10 percent near the top, five times steeper than the B&O's toughest main line grade at Backbone Mountain. It curved sharply around the spoil bank at Shaft no. 1 into a switchback, then descended on a lesser grade with easier curves along a creek to the other side and returned to the main track. The engine employed was a slightly bigger version of the first Winans Camel. The new model, a "medium-furnace Camel," weighed 28 tons, had a larger, sloping firebox, and 19-by-22-inch cylinders.[31]

The standard procedure was to place a single car in front of the locomotive so that the engineman could keep an eye on it, get a good running start on the level, charge up the first part of the incline, slow down around the tunnel portal to build up steam, and then make an all-out rush for the top through the final 1,200 feet of 10 percent grade and the tight, 300-foot-radius curve. If John C. Jacobs, the nervy master engineman who conducted most of the runs at the tunnel hill, was at the controls and the track was dry, over they went, and backed the train down the other side. In this way, passengers and construction materials traveled west of the tunnel in the spring of 1852. If the tracks were wet, the engineman leaned heavily on brakes, sand, and prayer.

Sometimes not only did they fail to make it, but the entire consist, with wheels locked, would slide back through the sharp curve (which helped to slow it down), all the way to the bottom of the 10 percent grade. "One or two serious accidents occurred to persons upon the train who jumped off on such occasions, while those who kept their places were unhurt, as the engine always brought up where the grade slackened at the tunnel portal, and left the track in but one or two instances," Latrobe said matter-of-factly.[32] But they had clearly reached the upper limit of steam power and passenger composure.

The engineer took no chances with the excursion guests. They disembarked and walked to the top of the hill, while the engine took the seven cars over one by one. "Everything was favorable to the success of the exhibition, the weather being fine, the rails dry and the engine in good condition," and the guests witnessed a novel display of steam power before going on to enjoy the rest of the festival, according to Latrobe.[33] The reporter for the Baltimore *American* was equivocal. "The sur-mounting of this extremely steep grade is said to be the greatest steam locomotive achievement ever accomplished," but he found the delays "mortifying." Following an evening glimpse of the falls on the Tygart Valley River and a nighttime crossing of the Monongahela on the wooden trestle bridge, they arrived at 9:00 P.M., "greatly to the disappointment of the visitors and the inhabitants of the town of Fairmont, who had turned out in full force," he said.[34]

Expecting a great increase in business when they reached the Ohio River in six months' time, the directors ordered 24 new engines and 1,000 freight cars from outside sources in addition to two engines and 200 cars from the company shops. The contracts totaled $840,000. As usual, most of the work went to local firms. Ross Winans received an order for fifteen first-class tonnage engines at $9,750 each. A. (Adam) and W. Denmead & Sons, whose downtown Monumental Foundry with several hundred employees was the largest in the city, got to build five second-class engines, 100 house cars, and 200 gondola cars. Their total contract was worth almost $200,000. Other local foundries receiving substantial car-building orders from the B&O were Murray and Hazlehurst, Poole and Hunt, and Benjamin S. Benson. If the new equipment were strung together, it would make a train seven miles long, said a Wheeling editor. The B&O paid for it by selling $700,000 worth of company bonds in March 1852 at an average rate of 87.

The directors simultaneously planned new station buildings for the ends of the road. The B&O's first real station in Washington, D.C. was completed in fall of 1852. Their original depot there, a former three-story boardinghouse at Pennsylvania Avenue and Second Street that the company first occupied in 1835, and to which it added a belfry and car shed, had grown outmoded and filthy and the city wanted to demolish it in order to improve the streets in the vicinity. In 1850, municipal officials and the railroad agreed on a new depot site at New Jersey Avenue and C Street, the inner limit for locomotive use. The new building was designed by John Rudolph Niernsee and James Crawford Neilson, the former B&O engineers who in 1848 had formed an architectural firm, Niernsee and Neilson. It was a brick, brownstone and stucco structure in the Italianate style with a 70-foot tower, backed by Wendel Bollman's 340-foot, iron-roofed train shed. The station's gas-lit interior featured wood paneling and armchairs and benches with crimson plush seats.

Also in June 1852, the B&O board members defined the need for a new Baltimore station. The downtown depot at Pratt and Light streets was too constricted, and Mt. Clare being too far away for convenient freight operations, the company still had to rely on horsepower to bring goods into the city during the daytime. The previous year, the B&O had received 500,000 barrels of flour in Baltimore and they expected 800,000 in 1853. A million barrels would require more than 400 drays per day, working 300 days a year, to move it. Besides clogging the streets, the horse and wagon system was expensive. "If such embarrassments be produced by this one article, what shall be done when the thousands of hhd's of Tobacco, of bbl's of provisions, of bushels of grain, of tons of iron, and numerous other articles are to be distributed?" the directors wanted to know.[35]

They decided to consolidate the passenger and freight operations at a central depot fronting on Camden Street between Howard and Eutaw streets, which would be convenient both to the inner harbor and to the center of the city. The directors approved the purchase of five blocks of property, from Camden to Lee streets, for almost $600,000. "No act of this board," Swann said, "has been received with more favor by the entire community, than the location of this noble station," and he added that the city had allowed locomotives to be used on the approaches. The B&O sold the old depot property at Pratt and Charles streets for $80,000, cleared the land at Camden Street, and by early 1853 new tracks connected the Locust Point Branch to the station site.[36] The company then called for plans for a station building. Renderings published at the time showed a Norman-style structure reminiscent of James Renwick's 1849 Smithsonian Castle in Washington, D.C. The main building had a vaguely five-part plan, a central tower flanked by two smaller ones, and three train sheds with semicircular iron roofs in back. A perimeter wall surrounded the property. But nothing was built that year except some wooden, iron-roofed freight and passenger sheds and a modest engine house designed by Niernsee and Neilson.[37]

Wheeling agreed early in 1852, after a year of negotiations, to provide a site for a depot at the mouth of Wheeling Creek. The station was to be constructed on Water Street, on the Ohio River levee at the north side of the creek. The train shed would back out over the creek itself, supported by the last of the seven major bridges to be built on the new line. Clearing the land for the station took place that summer, while contractor William McGowan was beginning the excavation for the bridge abutments. McGowan had supervised some of the difficult contracts on Section 77 and he wanted to finish the Wheeling bridge in time for the B&O's official opening in January 1853.

He ran into trouble almost immediately. The bridge design called for two spans of 75 feet each, 39 feet above the water. It required massive abutments—the northern one formed the retaining wall for the station—and large piers in the middle of the creek. Laborers worked around the clock seven days a week during the fall of 1852 to get in the foundations during low water, but accidents and the weather frustrated their efforts. Mark Connelly, a workman, was badly hurt when a pair of shears fell.

Heavy rains inundated the excavations. A floating crane collapsed, but the laborers escaped injury by leaping into the creek. The high water returned. Yet by the end of the year, the foundations for the abutments were laid and a chain pump was emptying the cofferdam for the central pier. Because there was no hope of completing the bridge in time for the railroad to cross it, a temporary timber trestle was erected similar to the one at Fairmont.

Latrobe had also secured about ten acres two miles below Wheeling Creek for the engine houses and workshops of the outer depot. Additional facilities were planned on the south side of the creek. Work on the bridge and the various depot buildings continued through 1853. At the end of the year, the engineer reported that the inner station was essentially finished and that temporary engine houses and shops had been erected at the outer depot pending the completion of permanent ones. The foundations of the gray sandstone bridge piers and abutments rested on timber piles protected by sheet piling and heavy stone riprap. Above them, Albert Fink's iron deck trusses carried two passenger and three freight tracks over Wheeling Creek. The two-story brick passenger station with its 60-foot tower, designed by Niernsee and Neilson in the Italianate style, had a waiting room paved with flagstones, offices on the second floor, and a 290-foot-long shed covering the passenger tracks on the bridge. Next door was the freight house, fronting on Quincy Street. Stone pillars supported its timber and iron roof and the tracks passed through it to the warehouses of the Forsythes and other Wheeling forwarding merchants. Altogether, the Wheeling bridge and station buildings cost more than $100,000.[38]

The railroad relied on the river to move passengers and freight between Wheeling and Cincinnati and Saint Louis. To counter the daily packets operating between Pittsburgh and Cincinnati, it supported the Union Line of Steamboats, a Wheeling venture. In the summer of 1852, as the directors ordered rolling stock and station facilities, they at the same time approved a through ticket from Baltimore to Cincinnati and Louisville, via the Union Line. The backers of this line included James S. Wheate, the city clerk, who had parlayed his opposition to the railroad's other routes through Virginia into a job as the B&O's lawyer in Wheeling; John McLure, hotel operator and partner in the firm that built the steamboats; and Thomas Sweeney, president of the Union Line. Swann reasoned that a traveler from the west would choose Wheeling over Pittsburgh, because in the day's time that it would take him to go by steamboat between those cities, he could reach Baltimore by rail. He predicted that the Union Line boats would be superior to any on the western waters, and because they would be timed to sail with the arriving and departing cars, the B&O would carry more through traffic than any other railroad.

The steamboats took shape in the summer and fall of 1852 amid the ring of hammers and the chatter of saws at the McLure, Dunlavy & Co. shipyard. The H. W. Phillips foundry provided the machinery. The *Baltimore* was launched on Saturday, December 18, 1852. "She glided off beautifully," a Wheeling reporter wrote, "like a majestic Queen of the Waters." He further noted, "The cabin, Texas and baggage room are built quite sharp in front, offering little or no resistance to a head wind, and her bow and stern are sheer as a knife."[39] The boat was 302 feet long with a 35-

foot beam. Its four boilers and 30.5-inch-diameter cylinders with a nine-foot stroke powered a paddle wheel 36 feet in diameter. The *Thomas Swann* followed a week later. Then came the fitting out: Queensware from England stamped "Wheeling and Louisville, Union Line," silver from Philadelphia, cutlery from New York, and glassware provided by T. Sweeney, Wheeling. With the *City of Wheeling*, these were the three fastest of the seven-boat fleet.[40]

Separating the railroad's temporary end of the line at Fairmont from its final goal on the Ohio River were 77 miles of wilderness, including some of the most remote and picturesque countryside the B&O had yet encountered, wilder even than the valley of the Cheat. This region, extending for 33 miles between Littleton, on Fish Creek, and Moundsville, on the Ohio, was the area of the Grave Creek route dictated by Wheeling, which ended up costing the company so much. Latrobe had split the final 77 miles into two roughly equal parts at Littleton. By the end of 1850, he had let all the remaining contracts for the railroad between Fairmont and Wheeling. As usual, he concentrated initially on the toughest parts of the line. There were to be three major tunnels: at Glover's Gap, through the ridge separating the Monongahela and Ohio river systems; the Pettibone Tunnel, later called Board Tree, just beyond Littleton between the two branches of Fish Creek; and the Welling Tunnel, dividing Fish and Grave creeks.

Work continued through the labor disturbances during the summer of 1851. The hands were particularly fractious at the western end of the line, but the private police were able to keep them under control. By fall of that year, the tunnels were well along. The workmen had sunk two 160-foot shafts at the Pettibone Tunnel and were proceeding horizontally from four points. They had started taking out the heading at the west end of the Welling Tunnel. Then the cholera hit, "in quite a malignant form," said Latrobe. "Not much short of 100 deaths must have resulted from the experience at various points at which it broke out, and the panic which it occasioned cost much time to the work," he reported prosaically. They lost two months at Pettibone Tunnel, where the epidemic was most severe. Although Latrobe said it would not jeopardize the opening of the line to Wheeling by January 1, 1853, disease was a major factor in delaying the completion of the tunnel itself.[41]

The heavy rains and flooding in the spring of 1852 caused landslides at Glover's Gap, a recurrent problem there, and disrupted operations at other locations along the line west of Fairmont, but not at Pettibone and Welling tunnels. These, however, had developed internal problems. Clay slate in horizontal strata was the material to be excavated, the same as at Kingwood, but it was more treacherous here. At the Pettibone Tunnel, the situation was even worse. The tunnel men drilled and blasted in constant danger of falls, and they also had to cope with "bad air" deep inside the mountain. But they persisted, putting up timbers as they went, and by the time of the excursion to Fairmont in late June 1852, they had let the daylight through.

As he had at Kingwood, Latrobe decided to build a line over the top of the hill at Pettibone Tunnel so that the rails and construction materials could go forward in case the bore was not finished by the time the tracks got there. He had to replace Pettibone, the tunnel contractor, who had fallen so deeply into debt that his creditors were seizing his horses and he could no longer keep the work going. Cholera threatened on a few sections and as quickly disappeared. It was a good thing, Latrobe said, for there was no more margin for error. The work force was down to 2,000 men and 550 horses.

By October 1852, the new rails had reached Littleton through the completed 383-foot tunnel at Glover's Gap. Hitchcock, Humbird and Company, its successful contractors, took over the work at Pettibone Tunnel, which thereafter was known as Board Tree, named after a local stream. Latrobe realized that it could not be finished in time for the opening of the railroad. Therefore, with Charles P. Manning, division engineer, Benjamin D. Frost, the resident engineer at the tunnel, and Mendes Cohen, a 21-year-old assistant, he laid out the track over the hilltop.[42]

Other than the downward slope of the tunnel from east to west, there was little resemblance between Kingwood and Board Tree. The latter ridge rose to a sharp peak 300 feet over the tunnel and the shape of the surrounding ground was quite different, and therefore instead of a single switchback, as at Kingwood, the engineers laid out seven, two on the east side and five on the west. This effectively reduced the grades from 10 to 6 percent and doubled the efficiency of the locomotives, which would no longer be in danger of sliding back down the hill in wet weather with their wheels locked. The rails were not laid through the single-track, 2,360-foot Board Tree Tunnel until March 28, 1853. The construction had taken over two years and had cost $265,000.[43]

In the meantime, contractors were at work grading the line south of Wheeling. Latrobe sent 500–600 tons of rails and the 1835 Grasshopper engine, the George Washington, over the Pennsylvania Main Line of Internal Improvements to Pittsburgh for shipment down the Ohio. He also dispatched Roseby Carr and part of the company's track-laying force to Wheeling to start laying rails eastward. The locomotive shortly arrived and was put to work hauling ballast and ties. The Wheeling *Intelligencer* editors climbed aboard and reported, "We have actually taken a ride on the Baltimore and Ohio Railroad within the precincts of the city of Wheeling." Soon, they said, the trains would be running "between the great Bridge city of the West and the Monumental city of the East."[44]

The rails crossed the summit of Board Tree Tunnel hill in November 1852, and that same month the 1,250-foot Welling Tunnel was completed. Less than three feet of water in the Ohio River channel, however, slowed the delivery of ties to the workmen below Wheeling. "There are still about 37 miles of track to lay, but with all obstructions out of the way and with two parties of layers, this can be accomplished in the six weeks of the year still remaining, and it must and shall be done," Latrobe promised Swann. The work force had shrunk to 1,000 men and 420 horses, mainly concentrated at the Board Tree Tunnel, with the company's track gangs stretched out beyond there.[45]

For most of the 77 miles between Fairmont and Wheeling, especially in the central portion along Fish and Grave creeks, there were no towns of any size. Most of the few settlements there were, such as the 100 or so shanties at Board Tree Tunnel hill that housed 700 workers and their families, existed because of the railroad or because of a new highway being constructed at the same time. This highway, the Ohio River and Maryland Turnpike Road (now West Virginia Route 250), paralleled the B&O line from Fairmont to Littleton, then abandoned the stream valleys for the ridge tops until it reached Moundsville, and from there followed the B&O tracks to Wheeling.

The territory in between where the rails were still to be laid, from Board Tree to the Ohio River, was virgin countryside. The tunnel district, less than half a mile from the Pennsylvania state line, marked the stark and desolate beginning of it. Black hills and patches of dirty snow were what the tunnel men saw every day as they trudged between the job site and the warm fires and boisterous family life in the shanties. But they were also alert to the primitive beauty of the place. Waterfalls playing off the rocks left gleaming icicles in the dark grottoes, ridge tops bristled with the bare spikes of trees while the wind sighed in the hemlock, and an occasional hawk or turkey vulture floated overhead above streams that glowed like quicksilver in the pale sun as they threaded their way down to the Ohio. In the creek valleys and the marshy glades below, beaver dams dotted the creeks, deer wandered the right-of-way, and cardinals flickered among the sentinel pines and white beeches and sycamores.

Soon this neighborhood echoed with the shouts of the advancing track crews. Not long after they went through, a new contingent arrived with saws and axes. Raw communities began to emerge from the woods and spread up the slopes through fields of stumps, anchored by a center strip of two-story clapboard buildings with fresh coats of paint and wooden sidewalks that faced each other across a right-of-way exactly 66 feet wide bearing the grand designation, "Railroad Street."

In early December 1852, the temporary trestle bridge was going up over Wheeling Creek, the Grasshopper engine was eight miles below town, and the rails were moving smartly out in front of it. Engines were climbing the grades over Board Tree Tunnel. The tracks had reached Loudenslager's (now Loudenville, West Virginia), about halfway between the tunnel and the Ohio River. "The two parties working towards each other should complete this in about 16 working days, which would bring the track to a close a day or two before Christmas, leaving the week between that and New Year as a margin for contingencies," Latrobe reported.[46]

Latrobe estimated correctly. On Christmas Eve, the track gang working east under superintendent R. Cass, Jr., and the one moving west led by Roseby Carr met at an isolated spot in the valley of Grave Creek eighteen miles below Wheeling. Beside a natural block of stone the size of a small house, they closed the track at 6:05 P.M. Carr commemorated the historic moment with a humble speech: "We have laid the last rail of the long line of Railroad which connects the Chesapeake Bay and the water of the Ohio; and I call upon all to give three hearty cheers for our President Thomas Swann, and three more for our Chief Engineer Benjamin H. Latrobe." The hills resounded with the yells of the united track crews, who added three more for Roseby Carr. "This done, the men, tired with a hard day's service, retired to their camp."[47]

The first through train left Baltimore about five o'clock on the afternoon of Friday, December 31, 1852, and arrived in Wheeling at roughly eight o'clock the next evening, New Year's Day, 1853. It was four hours late, having been delayed by a landslide at the Glover's Gap tunnel. The next train did better, pulling in at 5:45 P.M., Sunday evening. The Wheeling *Intelligencer* said, "The company have thus redeemed their pledge," but at the request of the Wheeling city council, the celebration of the official opening of the railroad was postponed until January 11.[48]

Thomas Swann, in his final annual report in October 1852, anticipated the conclusion in alluding to the twenty-six years that had passed since the Baltimore and Ohio Railroad Company made its first annual report to the enterprising stockholders. "Of those who stood prominent in its early organization," he said, "few have survived the delay which has attended the progress of this road, or will be present to rejoice with us in the work of final completion. In the animating prospects of the future, it becomes us, however, not to forget what is due to those who have borne a part in the conception of the grand idea which it embodies. History will do justice to the past as well as the present."

His extended comments, though fashionably rhetorical, were nonetheless accurate:

> After years of delay, surrounded by embarrassments, and staggering under the vastness of the undertaking, with a credit almost exhausted, its few remaining friends scattered and disheartened, a community over-taxed, and an opposition rendered formidable by the honesty of the convictions under which they acted, this great work entered upon its extension from Cumberland to the City of Wheeling, a distance of more than 200 miles. Through every vicissitude of climate, obstructed by interminable rocks, or opposed by a succession of mountain barriers, altogether without a parallel in the progress of similar enterprises, by day and by night, it has pressed forward in such a march as human labor is seldom called to encounter, sustained only by that determined spirit which so strongly marks the character of the age in which we live, until it is now within reach of the goal for which it has been so long striving.
> To this noble City what a prospect it discloses![49]

25

The Work Is Done at Last

OF THOSE WHO BEGAN THE BALTIMORE AND OHIO
Railroad a quarter-century before, just a handful were left in 1853 when the railroad
reached Wheeling, its original destination on the Ohio River. George Brown, then
65, was the only one to attend the celebration. He carried with him a flag used during
the July 4, 1828, cornerstone-laying ceremonies. His partner in the formation of the
B&O, Philip E. Thomas, its first president, whose health had prevented him from
participating in the ceremony in the field near the Gwynns Falls, pleaded the same
excuse at the end. So did his brother Evan. Louis McLane, Thomas's successor, sent
his regrets. Thomas Ellicott, incorporator, member of the original board of directors,
and disgraced head of the Union Bank, did also.

"I have the Silver Trowel in the office which was used by Charles Carroll of
Carrollton on the same occasion," company treasurer Joshua I. Atkinson informed
B&O president Thomas Swann a few days before the Wheeling excursion: "I can
send it to you, so that you can put it in your trunk."[1]

Three hundred eighty railroad miles away, Wheeling prepared to welcome those
who for years had resisted their strident invitations. Mr. Carroll, proprietor of a new
hotel on Market Street patterned on New York's Astor House, barely managed to
open it in time for the affair. After buying several thousand dollars' worth of cutlery and household goods in Baltimore, all stamped "McLure House," he confessed
that he still was not ready. He would accommodate the guests who came and then
close again until further notice. Wheeling journalists wondered if they would hear a
cannon fired at Grave Creek, ten miles down the river, when the train got there.

The morning of the great event, a crowd that eventually grew to an estimated
10,000 people "of all ages, colors, and conditions" began to mill around the unfinished depot structures. A chartered steamboat brought celebrants from Marietta,
Ohio. Another tied up at the levee with a military company of Steubenville Grays. The
Bridgeport Artillery was on hand, as were around twenty editors and numerous pick-

pockets. "By noon a dense crowd was assembled along the line of the track in Centre Wheeling, as far as the eye could see, awaiting the arrival of the cars."[2] But there was no train at noon, when it was first expected. A dispatch received in the morning said it had reached Cumberland the previous night and was now due at Wheeling by late afternoon. The military and fire companies accordingly lined up on the south side of Wheeling Creek about 2:00 P.M. There followed another long wait, as unrewarding as the first. In the early darkness, "the Suspension Bridge was brilliantly illuminated along its entire length with 1010 lights, and its long curve of radiance stretching in mid air," said a reporter, "looked really like a triumphal Rainbow."[3]

When the mail train pulled in at 8:30 P.M. with about 50 passengers, mostly from Baltimore, the crowd cheered, thinking they were the official party. Disappointed, the military companies retired and the country people went home. It began to rain. But things were still lively around midnight at the McLure House. There were visitors from Cincinnati, Louisville, and the other river towns, all in a high state of excitement. The pickpockets busily worked the crowd. Three were arrested, "caught in the act."

The two excursion trains with roughly 500 celebrants had left Baltimore's new Camden Station at 9:15 A.M., Monday, January 10, 1853, fifteen minutes past their scheduled departure time. Each train consisted of six passenger coaches along with refreshment and baggage cars, pulled by a pair of the company's wood-burning engines. Several thousand people stood along the tracks between the depot and Locust Point Junction. As the flags on the new cars fluttered in the breeze, Captain Holland's Independent Blues Band, in the front car of the lead train, struck up the "Railroad Quickstep."

The Maryland and Virginia governors and their entourages, 110 members of the legislatures of the two states, judges, and the press were assigned to the first train. The second carried the B&O directors and present and former members of the Baltimore city council with their invited guests. Everyone was aboard except Maryland's governor Enoch Louis Lowe who, apparently not aware of the Camden Street depot, had gone first to Pratt Street, then to Mt. Clare, and had missed the train. Swann sent a telegram telling him to take a later one and they would meet him at Fairmont. As it turned out, the governor had plenty of time to catch up.

A thousand workmen from the B&O's Mt. Clare shops wished the travelers a safe journey. At the small towns in the lower Patapsco River Valley and at Ellicotts Mills, people stood outside in the mild weather to cheer and wave flags while the coaches rolled by. Inside the train, the refreshment cars were busy as waiters dispensed snacks to the passengers en route from tables running down the center aisles. William Guy, proprietor of the United States Hotel in Baltimore, handled the catering. He brought with him 100 servants, besides the cooks, to serve the celebration banquet in Wheeling.

The guests stopped for dinner at Frederick Junction, where more politicians climbed aboard. Past the Point of Rocks, the once-thriving mill town of Weverton looked deserted. The old mill there had been destroyed in 1850, allegedly by sparks from the engines, according to Caspar W. Wever, who filed a claim with the company for remuneration. Government armory workers turned out in large numbers at Harpers Ferry, but the trains paused only long enough for the Baltimore *Sun* correspondent to file his first dispatch. Telegraphed to the new Sun Iron Building at Baltimore and South streets, the story appeared in the next morning's paper. It became the definitive account of the journey.

At 3:00 P.M., the entire population welcomed them to Martinsburg, where they took on wood and water. It was a place, too, where passengers could get out and stretch their legs, walking on the platform, looking at the engine and the train. Under way once again, the cars accelerated as they rolled past North Mountain down through sparsely populated country to the tree-lined shores of the Potomac, and the passengers experienced the unique compression of the landscape when viewed from a speeding train:

> You catch a distant glimpse perhaps of a haystack on the brow of an eminence miles away before you. As you proceed, a farm-house, with its outbuildings and granaries to follow, marches right out of the haystack, and takes up its position at the side. Then the angles all change as the line of vision is altered. The farm-house expands, shuts up again, turns itself completely round, a window winks at you for an instant under one of the gables, and then disappears; presently the farm-house itself vanishes, and a rough, half-shaved cornfield, with sturdy sheaves of wheat staggering about its back, comes running up out of a coppice to overtake the farm. . . . A pit yawns into a pond; the pond squeezes itself longways into a thin ditch, which turns off sharply at a corner, and leaves a dreamy-looking cow occupying its place. Then a gate flies out of a thicket; a man leaning over with folded arms grows out of the gate, which spins round into a lodge, and then strides off altogether; while the trees slink away after it, and a momentary glimpse is caught of a fine mansion perched upon rising ground at the back, and which has become suddenly disentangled from the woods surrounding it. . . . Then comes the open country again—a purple outline of distant hills, with a cloud or two resting lazily upon them; a long-drawn shriek from the valve-whistle, a few moments of slackened speed, and a gradual panoramic movement of sheds, hoardings, cattle-trucks, and piled-up packages, and we emerge upon a station, with a bustling company of anxious passengers ranged along the platform eager for our arrival.[4]

At 6:30 P.M. an immense crowd greeted the excursion trains at the Cumberland depot. The guests had supper at the trackside Revere and Virginia houses, strolled around town for a few hours visiting their friends, and at 10:00 P.M., when the whistle blew, climbed back aboard. The *Sun* correspondent posted his second dispatch. Soon, he said, they would "enter the gorges of the Allegany, speeding our way to the top of the mountain range as merry and joyous a party as ever followed in the wake of a locomotive." They expected to eat breakfast at Fairmont, courtesy of Mr. Guy, and get to Wheeling by noon, "in time for the dinner." Fires tended by laborers burned for nearly 100 miles in the Alleghenies that night, like Japanese lanterns strung at half-mile intervals between the Potomac and the Monongahela, casting light over the heavy mountain grades and tunnels "and producing the most magnificent effect I ever beheld," said the *Sun* reporter. The sleepy passengers were in Fairmont at 8:00 A.M.

Tuesday, had breakfast, and left an hour later. They expected to be in Wheeling by mid-afternoon.

North of the town, the trains turned left, away from the Monongahela, along Buffalo Creek, a dark, quiet stream about the size of the Patapsco. The railroad crossed it seven times on Fink deck trusses. This was sheep-grazing territory. Then all of a sudden, around 10:00 A.M., just before Mannington, while rounding a sharp, half-mile curve, the first tender in the lead train broke an axle, throwing the tender and the second locomotive off the track. The engineers stopped the train and managed to keep the engine from going down the bank and into Buffalo Creek. Passengers Benjamin H. Latrobe, Jr., Wendel Bollman, and Isaac Ridgeway Trimble organized 100 of the local laborers into a work party and had the wrecked tender and disabled engine cleared from the tracks in four hours. During the interim, Governor Lowe arrived in the mail train and there was an impromptu dinner and reunion in the cars. The mail train continued on to Wheeling, with the *Sun* correspondent, who decided he would rather spend the next several hours at the McLure House than in the train crossing the Board Tree Tunnel hill at night.[5]

The expedition reached the Board Tree Tunnel shortly after sundown of the warm and springlike second day. A gentle rain was falling, just enough to make the rails slippery. Eyes bleary from lack of sleep, the long-suffering excursionists could make out, through the evening mist, ten "huge, black, unearthly looking" machines waiting for them, with steam up. These were the Winans Camels, under the supervision of John C. Jacobs, the engineman who had conquered the steep grades at the Kingwood Tunnel hill. The trains were separated into sections and each engine took two cars through the seven switchbacks. Recent rains had caused the newly laid roadbed to shift, deranging the track on the curves, which is what had caused the accident at Mannington. Some of the locomotives did not traverse well as they ground their way in contrary directions up and down the inclines, tacking ponderously over the hill. Occasionally, they left the track on the curves, resulting in further delays.

"But the scene was grand," one eyewitness wrote:

> We were composed of nine or ten caravans. I was in the third, and night was settling on the broad landscape as we began the ascent. Before us were two parties slowly climbing their zig-zag way far above us, upon different elevations, and their panting iron horses . . . spit out volumes of black smoke and sparks against the blackened sky. . . . The summit gained, we halted for a short time, which gave us an opportunity of surveying the picture. What a magnificent scene! Around and beneath us were stupendous hills, far as the lurid shadows of evening could be pierced, while far down the mountain side, from terrace upon terrace, the upheaving locomotives glowed, and then away in the deep valley, a hundred torches gleamed from the hands of workmen leaving their alloted task in the depths of the tunnel below.

The more cautious groped their way on foot across the mountain in the dark and as the cars and hikers passed the laborers' cabins, "each with a phantom looking torch, stood out in the valleys and along the mountain sides, giving to the scene the appearance of magic."[6]

Traversing the Board Tree Tunnel hill took most of the night. It was not until two o'clock in the morning of the third day after their departure from Baltimore that the lead train arrived in Wheeling. The brass bands and the thousands of welcomers had long since left, and the exhausted tourists stumbled from the coaches into a cold, driving rain. The members of Captain Holland's Independent Blues Band put their instruments to their lips and did their best to cheer them up as they plodded up the hill to the McLure House. When the second train pulled in about two hours later, the new arrivals were given breakfast there before they retired.

At noon that day, Wheeling entrepreneur James S. Wheate met the visitors outside the hotel and led a procession to the courthouse for the formal reception. It was packed to the galleries, which were filled with women. Mayor Morgan Nelson officially welcomed the group to Wheeling. Swann responded but seemed to be conserving strength for his big speech later on. There were other speeches, interspersed with selections by the indefatigable Blues Band. Maryland's Governor Lowe, just 32 years old at the time of the Wheeling opening, professed a youthful dislike of speech making, but his graceful address expressed all the appropriate sentiments. He congratulated the Baltimore and Ohio Railroad for always paying the interest on its Maryland loan and not becoming a burden on the state, and he predicted that Baltimore, having established a railroad connection with Wheeling, would soon reach the Great Lakes through Pittsburgh, and San Francisco via Cincinnati and Saint Louis. "Who can measure her destiny?" Lowe asked. "The hopes of this nation, and of unborn millions of men of every clime, are bound by mysterious links to these highways of commerce. . . . The blows of fanatacism shall fall harmlessly upon a Union thus held together by the iron ties of interest, as well as by the more sacred bonds of affection and a common nationality."[7]

The banquet began that evening at 6:00 P.M. on the upper two floors of Washington Hall, a new three-story building at Market and Monroe streets. Altogether, there were nearly 1,000 guests, evenly divided between the two halls. The B&O president, the mayor of Wheeling, Virginia's Governor Johnson, Benjamin H. Latrobe, Jr., and George Brown sat at the head table in the lower hall, on a raised platform near which hung the flag of the new Union Line steamboat, the *Thomas Swann*. On the upper floor, Governor Lowe of Maryland and John H. B. Latrobe mingled in the crowd. The members of the Maryland and Virginia legislatures and the Baltimore and Wheeling city councils were distributed equally between the rooms, along with local merchants such as John McLure, J. H. Forsythe, and Thomas Sweeney.

Captain Holland's Baltimore band on the lower level vied with the German band of Wheeling on the upper. Dinner was served at 7:00 P.M. It "consisted of every delicacy that the palate could desire."

Stewed Oysters: Vol au Vent of Oysters.

Entrees—Hot
Lamb Chops with Green Peas; Form of Rice, à la Financier; Cutlets of Veal,
Truffle Sauce; Buffalo Tongues, Gardineer's Sauce.

Cold and Ornamental Dishes

Beef, à la mode; Boned Turkey, with Truffles . . . Ham decorated with Jelly;
Chicken Salad, French style; Game Patta, modern style; Lobster Salad, New York
style; Fillets of Chicken, En Belveue; Beef Tongue, decorated with Jelly; Pressed
Corned Beef, Maryland style; Rounds of spiced beef, decorated with Pickles;
Turkey Olio.

Roast Dishes

Turkey, Chicken, Beef, Saddle of Mutton, Capons with Mushrooms.

Ornamental Dishes

The Horn of Plenty, Emblem of Commerce, The Alleghany Mountains over
Pettybone's Tunnel.

At eight o'clock, "The brisk popping of champagne corks was our signal for
retirement," said S. Siegfried, the moralizing editor of the Morgantown, Virginia,
temperance weekly. "It is much to be regretted that these public occasions are not
allowed to pass off in a manner congenial to the refined taste of the community. Our
public men are decidedly behind the great mass of society in their habits of dissi-
pation and excess." He and about 100 other teetotalers rose dramatically and left
the room.[8]

The speeches began. There were 36 toasts. Swann, holding the silver trowel that
Charles Carroll of Carrollton had wielded at the ground breaking, told of his shock
on experiencing for the first time in 1849, on horseback, the beginning 60 miles of the
new line let for contract past Cumberland. If the people of Baltimore could have seen
the country they were trying to build the railroad through, it would have been abandoned, he said. The president had high praise for Benjamin H. Latrobe, Jr., whose
support had sustained him and whose modesty and skill distinguished him as a man
and as an engineer.

The gathering listened attentively as George Brown delivered an intelligent and
concise address recounting the company's early history. His talk was the testimony
of a man who conceived the Baltimore and Ohio and was familiar with its growing
pains, and it has come to be appreciated by railroad historians as well. At its conclusion, Brown held up the Union flag that he said had been originally displayed on Evan
Thomas's sail car Aeolus, which appeared on the tracks during the experimental days.

The thirteenth toast brought up Benjamin H. Latrobe, Jr. He said he had been
too busy finishing the railroad to prepare a speech. "I have been commended for the
success of the grades, and for the tunnels and the bridges of this road; but there is a
source of pride more grateful to me just now, in that I have been enabled to complete
the line at the precise time I had promised," he said. "I have not, however, a right
to call it finished. No Rail Road, indeed, is finished while the trade for which it was
constructed continues to grow; and progress is the genius of our people. But this road
is unfinished in a stricter sense."

John H. B. Latrobe, in his turn, spoke of how the Baltimore company was the
first to begin a railroad between the Atlantic and the Ohio and the first to com-

plete one on which a train could operate "without the aid of stationary engines," an important qualification. This was strictly true. Yet with regard to its two most important rivals, New York and Philadelphia, Baltimore, though the first to start, was the last to finish. The Erie Railroad had been opened officially on May 17, 1851. The first through train over the Pennsylvania Railroad from Philadelphia had reached Pittsburgh November 29, 1852. Had Wheeling not compelled them to take the Grave Creek route, the B&O would have beaten the Pennsylvania to the Ohio River by six months, according to the engineer Latrobe.

The Pennsylvania system still employed the inclined planes and stationary engines of the old Allegheny Portage Railroad between Hollidaysburg and Johnstown, but they were due to be replaced by a new line with 90-feet-per-mile maximum grades within a year. In truth, as Benjamin H. Latrobe, Jr., intimated, the Baltimore and Ohio was every bit as incomplete as the Pennsylvania. The Board Tree Tunnel, the bridges at Fairmont and Wheeling, and several of its depots were unfinished. The line was incapable of handling freight. But it was time for someone to say, "The work is done at last." John H. B. Latrobe did, and so it was.

J. H. Sullivan, president of the Central Ohio Railroad, promised that in a week, his company would finish a 58-mile line between Zanesville and Columbus. It would connect those cities with "the whole Railway system of the West," including Cleveland, Chicago, and Cincinnati. And within eighteen months, he went on, they would extend their line east from Zanesville to the Ohio River about three miles below Wheeling. Yet the Central Ohio still intended to make Wheeling their terminus. Meanwhile, Sullivan said, before sitting down to wild applause, "afar from its starting place at the tide water sweeps the mystic train into this fair Valley of the West."[9]

A bachelor toasted "The Ladies of Wheeling and Baltimore." Then someone else, unnamed, raised his glass: "Mr. Roseby Carr—The man who laid the rails and his army of sappers and miners." Carr, in acknowledgment, said, "Mr. President, I am no speaker. Let the long line of road I have laid in so short a time, and under so many difficulties, speak for me. But let me say, three cheers for Benjamin H. Latrobe, Esq." The hall rang with shouts. There were several more speeches upstairs and down, and around ten o'clock, the banquet was over. "The company dispersed at a late hour," read the official account, "long to remember the celebration of the opening of the Baltimore and Ohio Railroad at Wheeling."

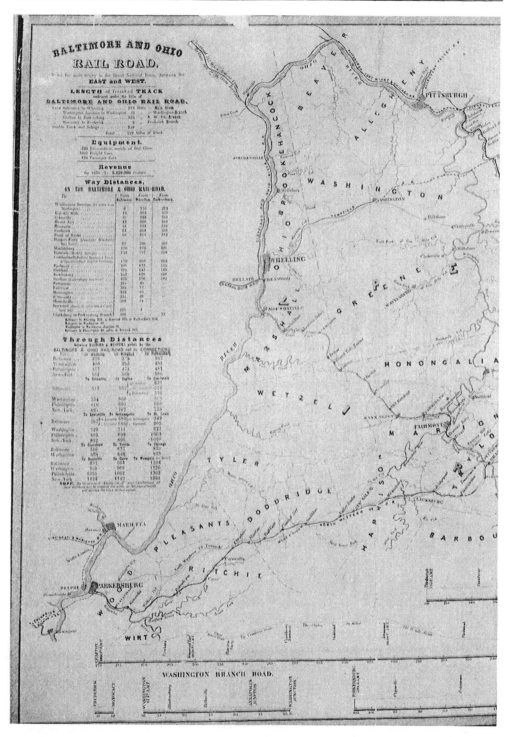

The final stretch of the B&O Railroad passed through 200 miles of mountain wilderness between Cumberland and Wheeling; both politically and physically, it was the most difficult section to build. *Special Collections, University of Maryland, College Park Libraries.*

Thomas Swann, wealthy stockholder and budding politician, was the new B&O president in 1848 who got the job done. © *The B&O Railroad Museum, Inc., Collection.*

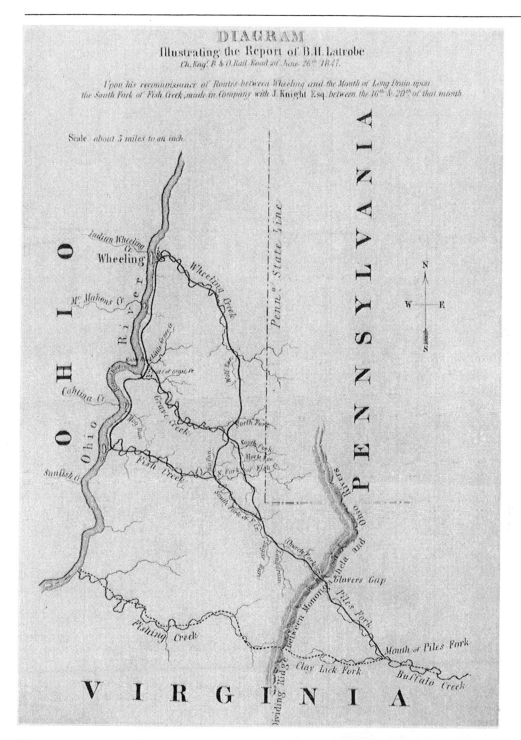

The map drawn by Benjamin H. Latrobe, Jr., for the 1847 B&O annual report shows the series of creeks flowing into the Ohio that the B&O and the City of Wheeling argued over for years as the proper route for the railroad. The city preferred Wheeling Creek, the railroad Fishing Creek; they compromised on Grave Creek. © *The B&O Railroad Museum, Inc., Collection.*

The masonry Cumberland Viaduct, whose fourteen arches raised the railroad over the streets of the town and Wills Creek, was the first major structure on the line leading west to Wheeling. *Smithsonian Institution.*

Engine houses such as this one gave Piedmont, which the B&O reached in 1851, the aspect of an industrial Indian village. Here the B&O line connected with the Georges Creek coal lines. *Wilgus Collection.*

(Opposite, top) The Bloomington Viaduct across the Potomac River marked the beginning of the Baltimore and Ohio's ascent of Big Savage Mountain, the Allegheny backbone. © *The B&O Railroad Museum, Inc., Collection.*

(Opposite, bottom) The B&O's bridge at Rowlesburg across the Cheat River was based on a truss designed by Albert Fink. This is probably the original masonry, iron, and timber structure dating from the early 1850's; it was photographed in 1872. © *The B&O Railroad Museum, Inc., Collection.*

(Above) Past the Cheat, the railroad paralleled the river, climbed the steep side of the valley, and crossed several deep ravines, the most dramatic of which was Tray Run, shown here looking west. It became a favorite stop for sightseers to view the spectacular mountain scenery. *Maryland Historical Society, Baltimore.*

To cross Tray Run and another ravine, Benjamin H. Latrobe, Jr., and Albert Fink designed America's first iron railroad viaducts. They were produced by the B&O's Mt. Clare foundry in Baltimore and shipped west on the railroad. *Peale Museum, Baltimore City Life Museums.*

The Tray Run Viaduct from the top with the iron railings added to allay the fears of railroad passengers. The bridge tender's cottage is at the left and a Civil War blockhouse is on the far side in this 1872 view. © *The B&O Railroad Museum, Inc., Collection.*

(Above) This 1860's view looking east shows the primitive nature of the first railroad in the Cheat River Valley, with its winding track and telegraph poles that look like crosses. This may be the earth embankment at Kyer's Run, scene of the worst accident in the early history of the B&O. *Maryland Historical Society, Baltimore.*

(Opposite) In March 1853, a few months after the railroad opened, the last two cars of the eastbound passenger train were thrown off the track at Kyer's Run and rolled down the incline, killing eight people and injuring twice as many. An account of the accident was published in the *Illustrated News*, and for years afterward the B&O had to counter the publicists of competing rail lines who warned against "the terrors of the Cheat." *Peale Museum, Baltimore City Life Museums.*

An impressive amount of rock cutting was necessary to get the railroad over the mountains, as shown in this 1860's view, again looking east, higher up in the Cheat River Valley. *Maryland Historical Society, Baltimore.*

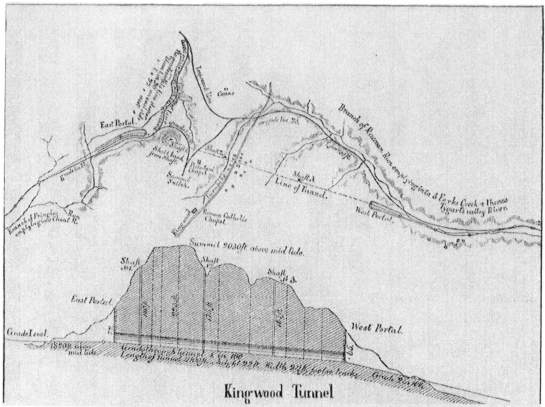

Kingwood Tunnel

Moving west, the railroad route next passed through the 4,100-foot Kingwood Tunnel, the longest in the nation when it was completed in 1852. Benjamin H. Latrobe, Jr.'s map shows the profile of the hill and the switchback route over the top that moved construction materials and passengers while the tunnel was being built. *Railroad Gazette, Dec. 15, 1874, p. 473.*

The western portal of the Kingwood Tunnel as it appeared in the *Illustrated London News* in 1861. © *The B&O Railroad Museum, Inc., Collection.*

With smoke rising from the chimneys and picket fences climbing the hills, the new town of West Grafton, Virginia, struggles from the wilderness in 1858, six years after the B&O tracks reached the then-unnamed location. The Parkersburg Branch, the through route to Saint Louis, left the Old Main Line here. *Maryland Historical Society, Baltimore.*

Albert Fink's great bridge over the Monongahela River at Fairmont, finished in 1853, was the largest iron bridge in the country at the time. It took the workmen three years, battling winter ice and springtime floods, to raise the stone piers. *Maryland Historical Society, Baltimore.*

The Board Tree Tunnel, with a train entering the bore through the mountain and others zigzagging over the top of the hill, was shown in the May 15, 1861, issue of the *Illustrated London News.* © *The B&O Railroad Museum, Inc., Collection.*

The narrow and confined nature of the early railroad tunnels in the Alleghenies is obvious from this photograph *(right)*, taken probably in the late 1860's, of the approach to Board Tree. The telegraph poles mark the line of the temporary track that traversed the hilltop with seven switchbacks; the need for so many is illustrated by Latrobe's profile and map *(below)* drawn for the December 1874 *Railroad Gazette. Photo: Peale Museum, Baltimore City Life Museums.*

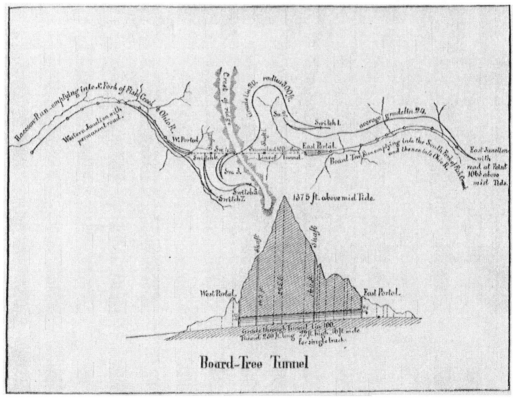

Board-Tree Tunnel

John Monahan *(left)*, an Irish immigrant who settled in Wheeling, was twenty years old when his crew closed the tracks between Baltimore and Wheeling on Christmas Eve 1852 at a remote spot in the valley of Grave Creek. The recorders of the event on a huge rock nearby *(below)* misspelled the name of Roseby Carr, head of the track gang. *Monahan: Private collection of Margaret Brennan; Roseby's Rock: © The B&O Railroad Museum, Inc., Collection.*

While the line was being finished, the company planned three new major depots, designed in the popular Italianate style by Niernsee and Neilson, house architects for the B&O. The one in Washington *(opposite, top)* was completed in the fall of 1852, and Wheeling's *(opposite, bottom)* late the following year. A rare view of the latter *(above)*, from the west, shows the train shed backing out over the wide bridge that spanned Wheeling Creek. Baltimore's Camden Station *(left)* was built between 1857 and 1867; it is the only one still standing and has been restored, awaiting a use. *Washington: © The B&O Railroad Museum, Inc., Collection; Wheeling: Smithsonian Institution and Peale Museum, Baltimore City Life Museums; Baltimore: © The B&O Railroad Museum, Inc., Collection.*

The B&O Railroad stretched 380 miles across the Alleghenies from the company piers at tide-water on Locust Point in Baltimore *(above)* to their depot on the Ohio River levee in Wheeling *(overleaf)*, with Charles Ellet's suspension bridge in the background. *1872 photographs,* © *The B&O Railroad Museum, Inc., Collection.*

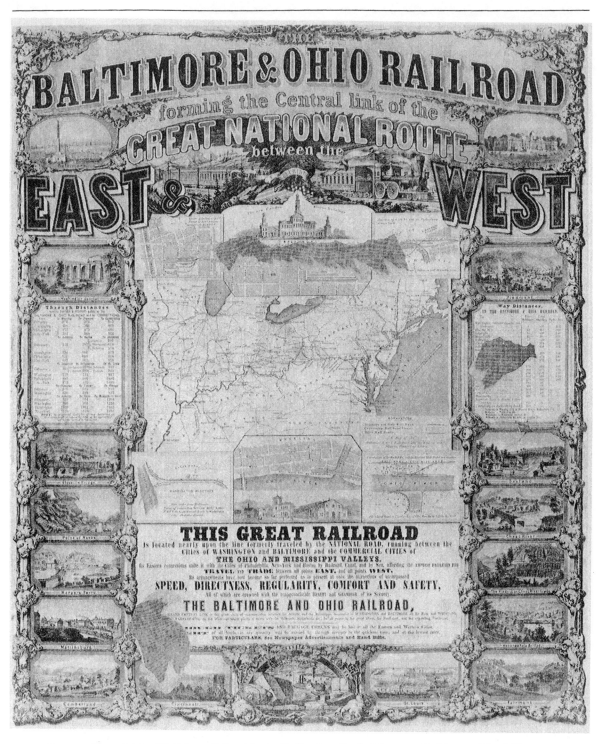

Poster, circa 1860's. *T. Edward Hambleton Collection, Peale Museum, Baltimore City Life Museums.*

Epilogue

AFTER THE GREAT CELEBRATORY BANQUET,
the Baltimoreans expected to return home immediately, but because heavy rain and melting snow had caused a landslide in the mountains, they waited a day and spent their time visiting Charles Ellet's suspension bridge, the Union Line steamboats, and various Wheeling industries. They toured meat packing plants and learned what "whole hog" meant, watched in fascination as German glassblowers at T. Sweeney and Sons puffed out decanters at the ends of their long tubes like molten whole notes, and observed English puddlers passing red-hot iron back and forth through the rollers to be fashioned into nails. That night they attended a grand ball at Washington Hall, and the following morning, Friday, through a great crowd of spectators stretched between the inner and outer depots, they left on the excursion trains. They arrived back in Baltimore on Sunday morning.

Wheeling when the railroad came was in transition from a frontier town of rivermen, teamsters, and Western outfitters to an industrial and commercial center, the most important on the Ohio River between Pittsburgh and Cincinnati. The town had been settled in 1769 by the Zane Brothers, incorporated in 1806, and chartered as a city 30 years later. The name was an anglicization of an Indian word of uncertain origin. In 1816, Henry M. Shreve built the prototypical Western steamboat, the *Washington*, at Wheeling. The iron industry, which would become Wheeling's largest, started in 1832 when Pittsburgh ironmasters Peter Agnew and David Schoenberger opened the Wheeling Iron Works and began turning 1,000 tons of Pittsburgh pig iron a year into nails and boiler plate. The works were located on the river at the north end of town, beyond the sweeping curve of the National Road that brought stagecoach travelers and wagon freight around the high sandstone cliff and onto the narrow riverbank that comprised Wheeling proper; it was known as the "Top Mill" to distinguish it from other ironworks built lower down. This and the other early iron and glass plants used bituminous coal mined from the nearby hills.

Wheeling combined the latest puddling and rolling techniques with mechanical nail cutters. Over the next few decades, foundries making cast-iron machine parts, and steam engine manufacturers also became established: the Virginia Mill was built at Wheeling Creek in 1847, the Belmont Iron Works came on line in 1849, and the La Belle Iron Works started in 1851. All three produced nails. The Eagle Wire Mill started up in 1852, and the following year the Crescent Manufacturing Company, another ironworks, was organized. Breweries and distilleries, makers of cigars and fire brick, sawmills and lumberyards, leather firms, carriage makers, silk, cotton, and woolen mills, were some of the other major employers in Wheeling. The population in 1853 of about 18,000 included a substantial number of foreign-born, mostly German, with some Irish and Welsh.

Commercial exploitation of the Wheeling coalfields did not take place until after the Civil War, but Swann was well aware of the immediate needs of the Georges Creek companies. Two weeks before the first train reached the Ohio River, in his next-to-last major address to the board of directors, Swann made it clear that he would not temporize regarding the coal business as McLane had. "It is useless," he told the members, "to make partial arrangements to accommodate a few of the many operators who are now beating at your door. You must decide the question at once, whether you will promptly respond to the demands of this large and increasing trade and make provision accordingly."[1]

Maryland and Baltimore were both deeply interested in developing the coal business, and Swann thought the railroad might transport a million tons a year. The mining companies were asking for hundreds of daily hopper and gondola cars. The Cumberland Coal and Iron Company, which had recently acquired the old Maryland Mining Company, was investing $100,000 in barges and propellers to run coal from Baltimore to New York, Swann said, and the Parker Vein Company, another new firm, was building ten steamships to do the same thing.

Indeed, Swann said, "There is no mineral region in this country that can come into competition with the vast and inexhaustible coal fields of our own state." The B&O Railroad offered "its only reliable avenue to market." The directors approved the president's request to issue $2.5 million in bonds to finish the railroad, lay a second track, and acquire more power and rolling stock primarily to accommodate the coal trade. They selected Adam Denmead to build four new first-class engines, and decided to order an additional 500 iron hopper cars, 200 gondola cars, and 30 locomotives. To start off, the B&O would add 100 more miles of second track between Baltimore and Piedmont.

Swann also delivered his usual optimistic review of the railroad's finances. With the new bond issue, the company's total debt would be $9.7 million, the annual interest, $600,000, and their anticipated annual gross revenues, $4 million. He recommended that the Washington Branch loan, due in 1854, be extended for twenty years and that a sinking fund be established to reduce their other obligations, but after April 1, 1853, when the new line was to be in full operation, the dividends that had been paid in stock since 1847 in order to finance construction should again be paid in cash. "The first thing to be cared for is the road. If this be protected by a judicious system of repairs, the stockholders may calculate on dividends," Swann promised.[2]

But the burdens of running a new railroad took precedence over everything else. General superintendent William Parker admitted that the transportation offered at first was embarrassing: "Not only was a vast thoroughfare to be opened through a comparative wilderness," with an unfinished roadway and bridges, with no buildings to house or repair engines and cars, without adequate sidings for trains, "or any of the comforts of life for our officers and hands," he said, "but our organization was to be suddenly and vastly increased," at a time when the demand for skilled and experienced personnel by all railroads greatly exceeded the supply.[3]

One of the first things the directors did in 1853 was to alter the system of assigning train crews. This resulted in a raise in salary for conductors and baggage masters, who, "being better paid and being relieved from the petty annoyances of the way may be expected to be in better temper to deal with the travelling public." The board turned aside a request for a pay increase from the workmen at the Mt. Clare shops, but after they struck three days later, the members reconsidered and by a one-vote majority approved a 15 percent raise for carpenters, woodworkers, and machinists. The wage dispute took almost a month to settle, during which time work was delayed on the 30 engines and 700 cars needed for the coal trade and for regular freight operations on the new line west of Cumberland. Orders for most of this equipment had to be given to outside contractors, and the work force at Mt. Clare was reduced and restricted to repairs. The Lawrence Manufacturing Company of Massachusetts supplied five of the engines, and the Bay State Rolling Mills signed a contract for 5,000 tons of rails at $75 a ton to lay 50 miles of second track. The board also authorized construction of a $25,000 magnetic telegraph line from Hancock to Wheeling, which the railroad planned to use for train control. Another new venture was an agreement with Adams & Co. for an experimental Western express. Adams was a Boston firm with important Baltimore connections that were gradually expanded throughout the South and West. In 1854, it incorporated as the Adams Express Company, which still exists.

The directors also reformed the old system of giving the agents at way stations a percentage of the charges on goods they received and delivered for the railroad. The B&O had been almost the only company to use this method, which was subject to abuse and caused customer dissatisfaction. According to Parker, the agents used railroad cars for warehouses, and because they had no incentive to protect the company's interests, they could not be relied on to detect irregularities by train hands or even to make proper business reports. The board decided to pay the agents at way stations and to encourage the construction of warehouses by allowing them to charge for storage. Even at the major depots, however, the agents had grievances. J. B. Ford, who took over the Cumberland depot in 1848, protested having to do business in a single small room crowded with the clerks who weighed the coal and the drovers who were were responsible for the thousands of hogs that had been driven over the mountains for shipment to Baltimore. In response to Ford's complaints, the railroad finally agreed to put a second story on the building.

The Baltimore and Ohio transferred Ford to Wheeling in the fall of 1852 to prepare for the opening of the line, but several months later he was still improvising under the burden of freight "poured in upon us to the extent of filling up any available space on the landing & adjoining vacant lots & all that was consigned to the company was at the risk of the agent." In fact, for years, until the railroad was double-tracked throughout its length and the Ohio was bridged at Parkersburg and at Benwood, below Wheeling, operations were sometimes interrupted, if not brought to a standstill, by rock falls in the tunnels, landslides along the line, and the more normal obstructions of low water in the summer and ice in the winter, which made movement across the Ohio uncertain.

Ford reported that his tiny office at Benwood became so crowded with passengers waiting to cross the Ohio that he had to stop work. A collapse in the Board Tree Tunnel in 1856 forced crews to drive stock over the mountain in the hot July weather. Often the Central Ohio Railroad could not pay its freight charges, so that he was obliged to go to Zanesville, Columbus, or Cincinnati to collect. Ford regularly complained of the "extraordinary services" he had to perform for the company, his need for "reliable clerical help which was never furnished," and "the insatiate greed of the managers of the road in thus imposing overwhelming duties upon their agents."[4]

Ford's greatest challenge, and his greatest service to the company, came early in his career at Wheeling when, at around three in the afternoon of Sunday, March 27, 1853, the eastbound passenger train was thrown off the track on the Cheat River grade, killing eight and injuring about twice as many, some seriously. It was the worst accident in nearly a quarter-century of B&O operations, and it could not have come at a worse time, when the railroad was just opening for normal business. (Only two days later, the passenger train from Baltimore, instead of zigzagging over the top of the hill, went through the Board Tree Tunnel, making the trip to Wheeling in 24 hours. Two days after that, the Baltimore and Ohio was officially declared finished.)

Accidents were no rarity on the B&O. For years, employees had been killed and injured in the line of duty. Enginemen and firemen had been scalded to death beneath overturned locomotives, brakemen had been maimed while turning brake wheels or dealing with the treacherous link and pin car couplers, and once in a while bystanders or trespassers had been run down and killed; but this was the first B&O accident in which passengers had died.

The accident occurred at Kyer's Run, one mile west of the railroad bridge over the Cheat River (now Rowlesburg, West Virginia), in the first of the Cheat River ravines.[5] The line crossed a 76-foot-deep earth embankment there, and the curve was sharp and the grade particularly steep. The train consisted of two locomotives, one large and one small, a baggage car, and three passenger cars. The large engine forced the spikes from the ties, causing the track to separate, and the last two cars, containing 50–75 passengers, left the rails. The cars turned over four times as they rolled down the 100-foot incline before coming to rest. Meanwhile, the stoves tore loose from their moorings and scattered burning coals about the interiors.

Rachel Ogle of Philadelphia was lying on a sofa in the saloon of the ladies' car when she felt the jolt. She remembered it all distinctly—the gradual sloping of the car and the slow revolutions as it rolled over and over down the hill, while she caromed alternately off the sides, top, and bottom, protected by the cushions she had grabbed from the sofa. Then she found herself outside, not knowing how she got there, bruised and burned but not badly hurt. She heard the terrifying screams and groans of the rest and went to help them.

Daniel Holt, an oyster dealer from Baltimore who had been in Wheeling on business, was standing on the platform talking with Captain Rawlings, the conductor, when the accident occurred. Rawlings leaped off on the uphill side and saved himself, but Holt went down with the coach, was thrown among the rocks, and "terribly torn and mashed." He died three hours later, lucid, composed, resigned. Among the other fatalities were a Miss Isaacs, of Indiana, Lewis Deline, a French emigrant returning from California, and a daughter of Ernest Giese and his wife, of Louisville, who were traveling with their four children, the only small children in the cars. The one was killed instantly, another was injured, and the parents were both badly hurt. But Mrs. Giese, acting "most nobly and coolly," though her face streamed with blood, picked up her surviving children "and went to the creek nearby and washed them so that they soon revived."

Conductor Rawlings, hindered by a badly cut hand, worked for the next three hours to get the survivors out of the wreckage, up the hill, and back on the train, which continued on to Cumberland. The dead and those too badly hurt to travel were left in shanties and dwellings in the neighborhood. The next morning the railroad sent a doctor, Thomas A. Healey, in a special car out to the Cheat River from Cumberland. He returned that evening with the bodies of the dead and the rest of the injured except two whose wounds were particularly severe, Gardner, a brakeman, from Baltimore, and a Dr. Cadwallader, of Indiana. The Hebrew Society of Baltimore, supposing from the name that Miss Isaacs was Jewish, confirmed the fact by telegram and took the necessary steps to have her remains sent to her friends.

The railroad also dispatched J. B. Ford to the scene from the other end of the line. He had a particularly delicate mission. By the time he got to Cumberland, a Dr. Dunbar from Baltimore was there helping the local physicians and nurses care for the survivors. All were accounted for except Dr. Cadwallader, who, burned from head to foot, his leg broken in three places, and suffering from chest injuries, had been considered too far gone to recover and had been left in an Irish laborer's log cabin to die. Besides being "the most dreadfully injured," said Ford, "Doct. Cadwallader was much embittered against the company by reason of the killing of Miss Isaacs, an elegant young lady, a ward of his."

Ford, acting for the company, interviewed the persons who had been taken to Cumberland. One man, S. F. Clise, was "injured in the genitals, the scrotum was cut, and the testicles protruded, being only held by their cords, this was a case of the most intense suffering, and required the utmost care, and skill of the surgeons to get him in condition to return to his home in Wisconsin." A Col. Sanders, from Kentucky, "had the crown of his head burned, severely cut in the face, a number of his teeth displaced, an arm and ribs broken, suffered intensely, was en route to Washington to contest for a seat in Congress," Ford reported. A. Brady, of Mississippi, with "the sinews under his arms burned," was also in extreme pain. When Ford told the surgeons why he was there, they said he was wasting his time because the injured passengers blamed the railroad and threatened to sue. And yet, through constant care and attention, "they recuperated rapidly and we gained their fullest confidence," said Ford. "They were unanimous in acknowledging . . . that they could not have had such attention in hospitals or at their homes, and in further evidence of their sincerity they unhesitatingly signed releases exempting the company from suit for damages."

All, that is, but two: a company employee (probably Gardner, the brakeman), and Dr. Cadwallader, who had not died after all and had been taken to Cumberland. Nearly a month had passed since the accident, which so far had cost the B&O $2,623.87 for private medical care. Ford returned to his duties in Wheeling. Col. Sanders sent an attorney to Cumberland, who "upon investigation found no cause for action, the company's agent had not exercised undue influence to get his release."

But there had been little real investigation of the cause of the accident. The Baltimore *Sun*, in the lead paragraph of its first article about it, exonerated the company. "So far as it is possible at this time to make an inference from the facts which have reached us, the occurrence is purely accidental, and attributable to causes unforeseen and which might have produced the same result upon any hill side tracks." When the first group of survivors got to Baltimore the next day, "they uniformly expressed themselves as satisfied of an entire absence of any real culpability on the part of those connected with the road," the newspaper said.

J. B. Ford knew better. He was sure that the accident was the result of negligence on the part of the workman who was in charge of keeping the track in a safe condition for the passage of trains on Section 76. Ford's report was detailed and very clear: "He [the workman] was informed by the man on the train passing over the road a short time prior to the one to which the accident occurred that the track over the Kyers run fill had sunken so much that if not put in place, would throw off the train going east. To this he replied that it was Sunday and he would attend to it on Monday morning. He was admonished that it should be done without delay, he failed to do it, and the consequence was the loss of eight lives with a large number of terribly wounded."[6] Ford also described his business with the injured doctor: "When Doct. Cadwallader was in condition to resume his journey east I was detailed to accompany him to Baltimore with reference to a settlement with him." The two doubtless knew each other by that time. In any case, Ford must have rehearsed his overture carefully. When he approached the injured man, he found him "fully posted as to the cause of the accident, and the inability of the company to defend themselves against the most exemplary damages, he demanded ten thousand dollars."

After they got to Baltimore, Dr. Cadwallader immediately began negotiations with the board of directors, then meeting at 23 Hanover Street, via agent Ford and general superintendent William Parker. Dr. Cadwallader wanted $12,000 (that is, $10,000 plus previous expenses), and he gave them 24 hours to decide. The first official mention of the Cheat River accident in the company records is on this occasion, June 8, 1853 (more than ten weeks after it occurred), when the new president,

William G. Harrison, who had replaced Thomas Swann, considered Dr. Cadwallader's ultimatum and decided to postpone action.

So informed, Dr. Cadwallader said he would withdraw his request for settlement and sue the railroad for $100,000. He had consulted some of his Baltimore merchant friends in the interim who thought he would have no trouble collecting, owing to "the severity of his injuries and the defenseless position of the company." Ford remonstrated, "reminding him of the unflagging interest and care the company had exercised for him and of their having restored his losses," and the doctor agreed to settle for $10,000 if it was paid promptly. Parker convinced the railroad president of the need for immediate action.

Dr. Cadwallader shortly received $11,275.75, which, with his previous expenses, brought the total to $12,000 (about $100,000 in today's money). It was the largest single payment of a claim against the Baltimore and Ohio Railroad to date for any purpose, including right-of-way, property damage, personal injury, contractor's cost overrun, or patent infringement. With two other smaller claims that were settled for a total of $4,900, and their earlier costs in Cumberland, it brought the company's medical expenses for the Cheat River accident to roughly $19,500. The company thanked Ford for his discreet management in saving them more than $100,000. Probably it was much more, for had the case gone to trial, the true cause of the accident would have emerged and opened the door to other suits.[7]

But the Cheat River accident proved very costly in terms of adverse publicity. Three weeks after it happened, the *Illustrated News*, one of the new American pictorial newspapers that made use of dramatic woodcut illustrations of events, showed the cars rolling down a steep hill in a fanciful (but not too fanciful) sketch captioned, "Frightful accident on the Baltimore and Ohio Railroad."[8] Even though the wreck did not occur on the soaring iron viaducts that spanned the deepest of the chasms, the various dangers of the Cheat River became one in the public mind. The railroad studiously ignored the accident in its official documents, except that Benjamin H. Latrobe, Jr., made a veiled reference to it in his annual report that year:

> The bed of the Road from Cumberland to Wheeling is in good condition, the heavy embankments having become so far consolidated as to be quite safe *when properly attended to*. [Emphasis added.] The great bugbear of the traveller, turned from his intention to pass over the B&O Rr. by the "runner" of some rival route, who has described the terrors of the Cheat River trestle work, in terms such as one of his craft could alone compose, has at length disappeared. . . . Under these circumstances the fears of the public which have been excited by the unscrupulous assertions of the agents of other lines, must soon subside, and this magnificent route over the mountains become as popular a highway for travel as any of its competitors.[9]

To ensure that it did, William Prescott Smith, a new B&O employee, took to the road to try to win customers through public relations. Although Smith was as clever with a pen as Ford was at diplomacy, Smith found his task strenuous. Many of those who knew anything at all about the B&O line had real concerns. Smith was the anonymous author of *A History and Description of the Baltimore and Ohio Railroad*, the country's first railroad history, which was published in the spring of 1853. That was about the time the company hired him as assistant master-of-road and sent him west. His datelined dispatches from Cincinnati and Saint Louis and later reports from Baltimore to general superintendent William Parker offer a candid and often amusing portrayal of a major American railroad on the ragged threshold of imposing its economic, social, and political dominion over the hinterland. Smith began his tour in Wheeling in May 1853. The river freight there was landed on the levee and manhandled up and down the steep incline between the steamboats and the depot. Smith thought there was a need for covered wharves and platforms, and cranes or cars running on inclined planes.

He met with Thomas Sweeney, John McLure, and James S. Wheate, the backers of the Union Line. Their boats were then running to Louisville, and they—especially Sweeney—were desperate to extend their line to Saint Louis. They told Smith that they were providing Western freight and passengers to the B&O, but the railroad was not reciprocating. The provisions for through service were inadequate and the B&O did not appreciate the strength of their competitors. "Suffice it to say, that every Boat and Car interest in the West, is in opposition to the Union Line, and also to our Road," Smith reported after listening to their complaints, "and that beyond Louisville, for the remaining [400] miles on the Ohio, and for the [1,200] miles on the Mississippi from New Orleans to St. Louis, there is no Boat upon which a through ticket can be had, except by going through Pittsburg." [10]

Smith told of one woman who on her way east to Harpers Ferry was warned to avoid the B&O line at Wheeling, so she bought a ticket over the Pennsylvania Railroad to Philadelphia, then had to go south to Baltimore, and then travel 80 more miles west to Harpers Ferry at an additional expense. "With such influences at work against them, it will be next to impossible for the Company to obtain its share of the travel from the West," Smith said. He argued for a new steamboat line between Louisville and Saint Louis.

Yet to the Baltimore and Ohio, steamboats were an expedient, like stagecoaches. They had to be dealt with (usually dictated to) until the railroad could extend its own lines through to the destination. Then the riverboats, like the stages before them, retreated farther west. That was the fate of the Union Line. For the remainder of 1853, Sweeney and the other officials importuned the B&O for a subscription to extend their line to Saint Louis. They also requested a guarantee on passengers and freight to protect them against loss and asked that a B&O delegation at least visit them and ride the riverboats. All the requests were denied, while, in the meantime, the railroad made overtures to the Pittsburgh steamboat companies. Sweeney finally got an agreement by going to Baltimore and demanding one.

By November 1854, the Baltimore and Ohio had through rail connections, via the Central Ohio Railroad, to Columbus and points west. In July 1857, with the opening of the Northwestern Virginia Railroad, it gained access directly to Cincinnati and Saint Louis. By that time, "not a packet of the Union Line remained on the Ohio, all having answered the call of the West." Although steamboats continued to serve Pittsburgh, Wheeling, Parkersburg, Cincinnati, and Louisville throughout the remainder of the nineteenth century and into the twentieth, their period of real prosperity was brief.[11]

When Smith took the Union Line steamboat down the Ohio River from Wheeling in May 1853, he met 35 passengers from the East and not one from Baltimore. "This is another complaint of the Boat folks, that the Baltimoreans . . . go West by the Pennsylvania and other Northern routes. This is a melancholy truth." One of the steamboat passengers "complained badly of the surliness of our baggage-master, who would not give him information asked for about time of starting, etc. etc. There needs to be a radical reformation in the manners of many of those who go upon our Passenger trains."

Falling in with a Kentucky railroad president who was also a newspaper editor and was hostile to the B&O because of its alleged cavalier treatment of his state at the Wheeling celebration and elsewhere, Smith attempted to mollify him by giving him a free railroad pass. The Kentuckian promised to use it on his next trip east, although he had planned to go by other routes, "partially through fear of danger on our line, and partly from the prejudice he acknowledged he had formed against it, and against our city." Smith also diplomatically placed an ad for the B&O in the man's newspaper, the Maysville *Eagle*, as he did in other papers from Wheeling to Memphis. In Cincinnati, he met the press proper. "I also presented each full member of the corps editorial with a general pass, and a copy of the history of the Road, and took care to give as good account of things as possible," he said. "I was much surprised to find so great a degree of downright ignorance about the Road existing all over the West, the editors themselves not excepted." Smith found the Cincinnati merchants of whiskey, flour, pork, livestock, tobacco, cotton, hemp, and dry goods were well disposed toward the Baltimore and Ohio Railroad, but sorry that it was not better prepared to do business. One large shipper had lost $5,000 because of a seven-week delay in moving his pork from Wheeling. Others were withholding freight because they thought the railroad was unable to accommodate it.

After four exhausting days in Cincinnati, with J. H. Forsythe, the Wheeling merchant, as his guide, Smith felt overwhelmed: "I had thought, upon starting from home, that this undertaking of going through the West would prove something of a pleasure jaunt as well as an affair of business, but by the time that I get home at night from my tramps in the ardent pursuit of knowledge under difficulties, I am too tired to read or to write."

The steamboat vibrated so badly between Louisville and Saint Louis that Smith could not write anything at all. On disembarking, he found plenty of new material. Anonymously, he asked their "pretended Agent" in Saint Louis about through tickets over Eastern railroads. "He answered me, by enumerating all, *excepting* the Baltimore and Ohio Rail Road. I asked him whether I could not go to Baltimore by the Ohio and through Wheeling? He said yes, there was a line of steamers he believed, but the Rail Road was not in a fit state to be used with safety, and he never recommended . . . any one to go by that route, they had better go to Cleveland or to Crestline and through Pittsburg," Smith noted. "He said that the Road was not desirable or safe, because it was a new and very heavy work, and having been built in winter had not yet 'settled,' and it was the opinion of all Rail Road men that it would not be in a good condition for travel for two years at least. . . . I recommend that this ticket agent be 'settled' at once."

William Prescott Smith ended his trip at Saint Louis, having "sailed through the great oceans of Pork and Whiskey," only a generation later and a few miles from where Stephen H. Long and his companions had set out to navigate a sea of grass on their exploration of the American West.

Benjamin H. Latrobe, Jr., put the final cost of building the 201 miles of main track and 22 miles of sidings through the mountains between Cumberland and Wheeling, along with the tunnels, bridges, and depots, at $8,065,385. It was a little more than 6 percent over his original estimate and, as he put it, "a moderate increase upon a work of such magnitude, complication and difficulty."[12]

Altogether, by 1853, the Baltimore and Ohio Railroad had invested about $22.2 million in building and equipping its plant. The figure included $18.3 million in construction costs: $8.8 million for building the line from Baltimore to Cumberland, $8 million for the section from there to Wheeling, and $1.5 million for the Washington Branch. In addition, they had spent $513,000 on adding second tracks, $798,000 for stations, and $2.6 million for engines and rolling stock. Even in its imperfect state, the railroad was a money-maker, just as it had been at the beginning, when it operated with horsepower. The receipts for just six months of 1853, when the Ohio River averaged less than 30 inches of water, were $1.3 million, more than for the entire previous year before the B&O reached Wheeling.

Thomas Swann resigned the presidency of the Baltimore and Ohio in April 1853. He took a trip to Europe, returned in the fall, and became a B&O director. Swann defended his fiscal policy, which was again under attack, one last time before a board riven with factionalism between Whigs and Democrats. He indicated then that he had been forced out and had no friends among the directors. But as he said when he retired, he had promised to stay only long enough to get the railroad open to the Ohio River. His predecessors, Philip E. Thomas and Louis McLane, had left their jobs exhausted men near the end of their professional careers. Not Thomas Swann. He was just beginning. Ahead was a successful political career at the local, state, and national levels.

Swann's resignation speech to the board of directors was long and not one of his best. The railroad had opened "under embarrassments," but "there is a limit to human power in these matters," he said. "No road in this country has been more securely or substantially built." He called George Brown to the chair, handed his letter of resignation to the secretary, and left the room.

The board accepted the resignation "with deep regret," and the customary committee was appointed to make the appropriate comments. This one included old and new B&O directors. Among its members were former Congressman Benjamin C. Howard, an original incorporator of the railroad who had recently returned as a director representing the state, and Henry S. Garrett, a new board member whose brother John Work Garrett would become the Baltimore and Ohio's greatest president and its dominant force during the Civil War and the postwar period of expansion.

Their comments supplied all the eloquence that Swann's had lacked. "At length the great object is accomplished," the committee said. "Man has triumphed over the mountains whose lofty summits and deep chasms appeared to forbid every species of transit. The little streams which meandered through the deep gorges of the Alleghany, seemed to be the only moving things allowed by nature to interrupt her profound silence, until human skill and boldness, under your decisive management, pierced the hills and spanned the ravines.

"Of all the monuments which the ancient Romans erected, those only remain which led, by durable roads, from the Capital to the circumference; showing that the wisdom of making such lasting structures was fully appreciated at an early day, and has received the commendations of twenty successive centuries.

"How long is the road to last, which you have had such an active participation in building? Will twenty centuries continue to praise the sagacity which planned and the firmness of purpose which executed it? Whatever may be the answer to these questions, it is quite certain that this road rises into an object of national importance, knitting together States and districts of country by imperishable ties." [13]

REFERENCE MATTER

NOTES

For full names of authors, complete titles, and publication information of sources cited in abbreviated form in the Notes, see Works Cited, pp. 449–52.

CHAPTER 1

1. Baltimore *American*, June 21, 1828. Also July 7, 1828, reprinted as *Detailed and Correct Account of the Grand Civil Procession in the City of Baltimore on the Fourth of July, 1828 . . .* (Baltimore: Thomas Murphy, 1828). The olive green half-pint whiskey bottles depicted a horse on a track pulling a cart loaded with barrels, surrounded by the legend, "Success to the Rail Road."

2. The 1809 parade had been modeled on the one held in Baltimore on May 1, 1788, to celebrate Maryland's ratification of the U.S. Constitution. On that occasion, 3,000 of the town's 13,000 residents participated in a "grand procession" from Fells Point to Federal Hill. The parade included a full-rigged miniature ship, the *Federalist*, and featured 40 mechanics' groups displaying their tools and occupations. Similar pageants took place in other cities at the time.

3. Brown, *History of First Locomotives*, p. 93.

4. B. Tuckerman, ed., *Diary of Philip Hone*, p. 132 (1835 entry).

5. The site, at the foot of Catherine Street off Wilkens Avenue, is now a junkyard. The first stone itself is in the B&O Railroad Museum.

6. [W. P. Smith], *History and Description, B&O Railroad*, p. 127.

7. John H. B. Latrobe, *The Baltimore and Ohio Railroad. Personal Recollections*, p. 9.

8. There are several versions of Carroll's famous quote concerning the significance of laying the railroad cornerstone. This is George Brown's from [W. P. Smith], *History and Description, B&O Rr.*, p. 164.

9. Philip E. Thomas to Thomas Kennedy, Thomas Letterbooks, July 3, 1828.

CHAPTER 2

1. Jared Sparks, "Baltimore," *North American Review* 20 (Jan. 1825): 99–138. Sparks's literary and scholarly pursuits culminated in multivolume works on Washington and Franklin. As Harvard's first professor of modern history, he guided Francis Parkman's independent study. He later became president of the university.

2. Augustine Herrman, "Virginia and Maryland . . ." Map, 1670, Library of Congress, Washington, D.C.

3. Albert Gallatin, "Report of the Secretary of the Treasury on the Subject of Public Roads and Canals made in pursuance of a resolution of the Senate, March 2, 1807," Apr. 4, 1808, p. 20.

4. House Report, 19th Congress, 1st Sess., Report no. 228, "Chesapeake and Ohio Canal," May 22, 1826, p. 2.

5. Washington's Diary of September 1784, in Hulbert, *Washington and the West*, p. 28.

6. Ibid., p. 43.

7. Ibid., p. 68.

8. House Report no. 228, 1826, pp. 2–3.

9. Hulbert, *Washington and the West*, p. 100.

10. House Report no. 228, 1826, p. 30.

11. Coria Bacon Foster, "Early Chapters in the Development of the Potomac Route to the West," *Records of the Columbia Historical Society* 15 (1912): 157.

12. Ibid., p. 164.

13. Hulbert, *Historic Highways*, vol. 13, *The Great American Canals*, p. 64.

14. Hulbert, *Washington and the West*, p. 192.

15. Gallatin, "Report on Roads and Canals," 1808, pp. 93–94, 96.

16. Dunbar, *History of Travel in America*, p. 772.

17. Gallatin, "Report on Roads and Canals," 1808, p. 7.

18. Ibid., pp. 22–23, 40, 44.

19. Ibid., pp. 82, 106.

20. Ibid., pp. 118–19.

21. John H. B. Latrobe, *The First Steamboat Voyage on the Western Waters*, Fund Publication no. 6 (Baltimore: Maryland Historical Society, Oct. 1871). The three earthquakes centering on New Madrid that took place between December 1811 and February 1812 are considered the most powerful that ever occurred in North America; evidence suggests their magnitude was greater than eight on the Richter scale. The shocks rang church bells in Boston and terrified Indians as far west as the upper Missouri River.

22. Hulbert, *Historic Highways*, vol. 14, *The Great American Canals*, pp. 78, 102.

23. Dunbar, *History of Travel in America*, p. 780.

24. John Eager Howard, Jr., "Remarks on the Intercourse of Baltimore with the Western Country . . ." 1818, B&O Rr. Pamphlets.

25. *Report by the Maryland Commissioners on a Proposed Canal from Baltimore to Conewago* (Baltimore: Fielding Lucas, Jr., 1823), p. 31.

26. The canal was eventually built, in part anyway, along the southwest shore of the Susquehanna River from Wrightsville, Pennsylvania, opposite Columbia, to Havre de Grace, Maryland. Backed by Baltimore capital, the Susquehanna and Tidewater Canal opened in 1840 and did a substantial business. The portion between Havre de Grace and Baltimore was never constructed. The route later became a railroad line.

27. *Report of the Commissioners appointed to examine into the practicability of a canal from Baltimore to the Potomac together with the Engineers Report.* 1823.

28. Baltimore *American*, letters from "Clinton," Feb. 17, 23, Mar. 2, 10, 25, May 7, 1825. "Clinton" may have been Minus Ward, an early Baltimore railroad promoter, pamphleteer, and locomotive designer.

29. Ibid., May 2, 9, 1825.

30. For comments on the Erie Canal opening, see ibid., Oct. 27, 29, Nov. 4, 1825.

31. "The State Convention on Internal Improvements . . ." Baltimore, Dec. 14, 1825, p. 15, B&O Rr. Pamphlets.

CHAPTER 3

1. Goodrich, *Government Promotion*, p. 55; Taylor, *Transportation Revolution*, p. 33. Hulbert, however, refers to the Erie Canal as "merely the lengthy application of a principle already perfectly understood"; see *Historic Highways*, vol. 13, *The Great American Canals*, p. 195.

2. McMaster, *History of People of the U.S.*, 5: 142.

3. Strickland, *Reports on Canals, Railways*, p. 30.

4. Quoted in Rubin, *Canal or Railroad?*, p. 28.

5. Baltimore *American*, Sept. 17, 1825.

6. Ibid., Feb. 2, 1828; Baltimore *Gazette*, Jan. 22, 1831.

7. Livingood, *Philadelphia-Baltimore Trade Rivalry*, p. 37.

8. John Eager Howard, Jr., "Remarks on the Intercourse of Baltimore with the Western Country . . ." 1818, pp. 10, 19, 20, 25, B&O Rr. Pamphlets.

9. Carter, Van Horne, Formwalt, eds., *Journals of Benjamin Henry Latrobe*, 3: 219.

10. "The State Convention on Internal Improvements . . ." Baltimore, Dec. 14, 1825, p. 41, B&O Rr. Pamphlets.

11. Abner Lacock and C. F. Mercer, "Great National Object. Proposed connection of the Eastern and Western Waters, by a communication through the Potomac Country," Nov. 1, 1822, B&O Rr. Pamphlets.

12. James Shriver, *An Account of Surveys and Examinations, with Remarks and Documents, relative to the projected Chesapeake and Ohio and Lake Erie Canals*, 1824.

13. Deep Creek was dammed in 1925 to create Deep Creek Lake, now a prime recreational facility in western Maryland.

14. *Maryland Gazette and State Register*, June 16, July 14, 1825.

15. From a letter signed "Torquatus Silansus," Baltimore *American*, Dec. 16, 1825. A copy of the newspaper article, with "C&O Canal Essay" written on it in ink, is among Benjamin C. Howard's business papers: Benjamin Chew Howard Papers, MS 469, Maryland Historical Society.

16. Baltimore *American*, Mar. 10, 1826.

17. House Report, 19th Congress, 2nd Sess., Report no. 10, "Message from the President of the United States, transmitting a report from the Secretary of War with that of the Board of Engineers for Internal Improvement, concerning the proposed Chesapeake and Ohio Canal," Dec. 7, 1826.

18. *Washington National Journal* quoted in Baltimore *American*, Aug. 9 and Sept. 2, 1826.

19. House Report, 19th Congress, 1st Sess., Report no. 228, pp. 10, 20.

20. "Report of the Committee appointed on the 6th of December, 1826, by the Chesapeake and Ohio Canal Convention . . ." p. 71, B&O Rr. Pamphlets.

21. Baltimore *American*, Jan. 8, 1827.

22. Ibid.

23. "Report of the Directors of the Baltimore and Ohio Railroad Company to the Legislature of Maryland," Jan. 3, 1831, pp. 4–5. It has been postulated that Baltimore chose the railroad because it doubted the legality and route of a connecting waterway to link the city with the C&O Canal. See the reply of "Maryland" to an article in the Washington *National Intelligencer* in the Baltimore *Gazette*, June 2, 1831; and William M. Franklin, "The Tidewater End of the Chesapeake and Ohio Canal," *Maryland Historical Magazine* 81 (Winter 1986): 295–96.

There were such doubts, and the C&O Canal convention on December 8, 1826, did defeat Benjamin C. Howard's effort to eliminate them by having Congress enact a law providing for a connector canal from Georgetown to Baltimore. On the other hand, Thomas and the others did not wait for William Howard to finish his survey of the route before deciding on the railroad. The high cost and impracticality of the Chesapeake and Ohio Canal, the difficult terrain surrounding the city for a waterway to the Susquehanna or to the Potomac, and the current publicity about railroads, all led to the decision in Baltimore: B&O Rr. Annual Report, 1830, pp. 6–7.

CHAPTER 4

1. There is some question about when, exactly, this dinner occurred. John H. B. Latrobe describes the dinner at Belvidere in *Baltimore and Ohio Railroad. Personal Recollections* but does not give the year. George Brown remembered the railroad discussions as beginning in earnest in July 1826, while Evan Thomas was still in England: see [W. P. Smith], *History and Description, B&O Rr.*, p. 163.

2. Quoted in Perkins, *Financing Anglo-American Trade*, intro. by Alfred D. Chandler, Jr., p. 23.

3. *Proceedings of Sundry Citizens of Baltimore . . .* (Baltimore: William Wooddy, 1827). I quote from this 38-page document at length in the paragraphs that follow.

4. Smiles, *Lives of George and Robert Stephenson*, p. 131.

5. The total cost of building the 184-mile C&O Canal from Washington, D.C. to Cumberland in 1850 was approximately $11.1 million, or some $60,000 per mile. The total construction cost of the 379-mile railroad from Baltimore to Wheeling in 1853 was roughly $18.3 million, or about $48,000 a mile.

6. The other members of the 25-man committee were Thomas Tenant, John McKim, Jr., Talbot Jones, James Wilson, George Hoffman, William Steuart, George Warner, Solomon Etting, W. W. Taylor, Alexander Fridge, James L. Hawkins, John B. Morris, Luke Tiernan, Alexander McDonald, and Solomon Birckhead.

7. Baltimore *Gazette*, Feb. 23, 1827.

8. Mason, *Life of McMahon*, pp. 26, 27.

9. McMahon's final year in public office was 1828. He subsequently declined party nominations for Congress and the Senate and for the office of attorney general in the Harrison and Tyler administrations, as well as offers of important judicial posts in Maryland. His stated reason was the fear of discharging the duties of high office under public scrutiny and ultimately of failure. He also intimated a fastidious distaste for politics. "The odor of honesty . . . hung around him," said his biographer. Finally the offers stopped coming, and "the great McMahon" spent his later career and forensic eloquence in the relative obscurity of the state courts where he remained an electrifying speaker. Handsome and histrionic, he was known to swoon dramatically into the arms of an associate on reaching the emotional peak of an address; the effect on women in the courtroom was pronounced. At the opening of the tumultuous 1840 Whig convention in Baltimore for Harrison and Tyler, it was McMahon who announced, "The mountains have sent forth their rills, the hillsides their streams, the valleys their rivers, and lo! the avalanche of the people is here!"

10. "An Act to incorporate the Baltimore and Ohio Rail Road Company," *Laws and Ordinances, B&O Rr.*, p. 24 and passim.

11. The tax exemption was a major reason for the Baltimore and Ohio Railroad's longevity as a separate corporation after it became affiliated in 1962 with the Chesapeake and Ohio Railway to create the Chessie System, and after Chessie's merger with the Seaboard Coast Line to form the CSX Corporation in 1980.

12. Quoted in [W. P. Smith], *History and Description, B&O Rr.*, p. 16.

13. Baltimore *Gazette*, Feb. 28, Mar. 2 and 6, 1827.

14. Baltimore *American*, Mar. 2, 1827.

15. Mason, *Life of McMahon*, p. 55; John H. B. Latrobe, *Baltimore and Ohio Railroad. Personal Recollections*, p. 6.

16. John H. B. Latrobe, *Baltimore and Ohio Railroad. Personal Recollections*, p. 6.

17. Two 1827 stock ledgers at Baltimore's B&O Railroad Museum contain the actual signatures of the buyers or their attorneys.

18. *Niles Register* 32 (Mar. 17, 1827): 33.

19. Baltimore *American*, Mar. 14, 26, Apr. 30, May 25, June 25, 1827.

20. Ibid., May 8, 11, 1827.

21. The steamboat incident is related in Riley, *History of the General Assembly of Maryland*, p. 334.

CHAPTER 5

1. B&O Rr. Minute Books, Apr. 24, 26, May 4, June 22, 1827.

2. Hill, *Roads, Rails, and Waterways*, pp. 4, 47.

3. Baltimore *American*, Jan. 27, July 21, 1825.

4. Bernhard, *Travels Through North America*, 2: 187–91.

5. *Report of the Committee appointed by the [B&O Rr. Co.] to Examine the Mauch Chunk and Quincy Rail Roads* (Baltimore, 1827).

6. *Niles Register* 32 (June 9, 1827): 248. Three years after the B&O committee visited Mauch Chunk, the Lehigh Coal and Navigation Company finished the canal to Easton. It was eventually replaced by the Lehigh Valley Railroad.

7. For reports of these surveys, see Wm. Gibbs McNeill, "Descriptive Memoir of the Country comprising the proposed summit level of the Ohio and Chesapeake Canal," Dec. 29, 1824; McNeill, "Descriptive Memoir in relation to the eastern section of the summit level of the C&O Canal," Dec. 28, 1825, in "Letters Received by the Topographical Bureau of the War Department," Records Group 77, M 506, National Archives; House Report, 19th Congress, 2d Sess., Report no. 10, "Message from the President of the United States . . ." Dec. 7, 1826; "Letter from the Secretary of War transmitting a report upon . . . an extension of the National Road from Cumberland to the District of Columbia," 1826; "Letter from the Secretary of War transmitting a report on the James River and Kanawha Canal Route," Mar. 24, 1828, B&O Rr. Pamphlets. The copy of the last pamphlet is inscribed, "Philip E. Thomas, Esq. from his friend Wm. G. McNeill."

8. Edwin James, *Account of an Expedition from Pittsburgh to the Rocky Mountains . . .* 2 vols. (Philadelphia: Carey and Lea, 1823; Readex Microprint, 1966). Long defined the region he explored as "The Great Desert" on a map that accompanied the publication. The designation continued to appear on maps as late as the 1850's. Long was later blamed for creating the myth of the "Great American Desert," but he was merely reinforcing ideas already spread by Pike, and it was an honest judgment of what appeared to him to be the case at the time.

9. House Report, 19th Congress, 2d Sess., Report no. 105, Stephen H. Long, "A Report upon . . . a National Road from Washington to Buffalo," 1827.

10. Ibid. It was several years before Long's theories were widely recognized: "It appears to be generally unknown that a road which goes round a hill may be actually . . . shorter than the one which goes over it," Baltimore *Gazette*, Nov. 15, 1834.

11. Ibid.

12. *Niles Register* 32 (July 14, 1827): 333. The letter is dated Apr. 16, 1827. Long amplified his theories in another letter to Thomas dated Nov. 12, 1827: Baltimore *American*, Nov. 21, 1827.

13. B&O Rr. Minute Books, July 2, 1827; Thomas to Long, McNeill, and Howard, July 2, 1827, Thomas Letterbooks.

14. Vose, *Manual for Railroad Engineers*, p. 13.

15. Thomas to Knight, July 2, 1827, Thomas Letterbooks.

16. House Report, 19th Congress, 2d Sess., Report no. 74, "Letter from the Secretary of War transmitting reports and drawings relative to the National Road from Wheeling to . . . Missouri," Feb. 1827.

17. Andrew B. Barker to Alexander Brown, May 10, 1827, Baltimore and Ohio Railroad Company Papers, MS 1135, Maryland Historical Society.

18. Undated newspaper clipping, ca. June 1827, B&O Rr. Pamphlets.

19. Thomas to James E. McFarland, Aug. 14, 1827, Thomas Letterbooks.

20. Thomas to McFarland, Jan. 15, 1828, ibid.

21. Ibid.   22. B&O Rr. Minute Books, Aug. 14, 1827.

23. Ibid., Nov. 5, 1827.   24. Ibid.

25. The 188-page report was printed in 1828 by William Wooddy, Baltimore. The quotes in the several paragraphs that follow are drawn from this printed version.

CHAPTER 6

1. Philip E. Thomas to Board of Directors, June 2, 1828, Baltimore and Ohio Railroad Company Papers, MS 1135, Maryland Historical Society.

2. Both Long and McNeill were also receiving government pay as Army engineers, a practice Congress later abolished.

3. Wever to Thomas, Apr. 17, 1828, B&O Papers, MS 1192, Maryland Historical Society.

4. Alex. Brown and Sons to Wm. and James Brown and Co., May 29, 1828, *The Early Correspondence of Alex. Brown and Sons with regard to the building of the Baltimore and Ohio Railroad* (Baltimore, 1927), p. 7.

5. In 1817, the West Point curriculum was revised and Claudius Crozet, a graduate of France's famed École des Ponts et Chaussées, was brought in as professor of engineering. The reforms were based on the Ecole Polytechnique and the intellectual atmosphere at the Military Academy became grounded in French rationalism. Most of the textbooks and many of the teachers were from France. The only foreign language taught was French, the language of early nineteenth-century science. Other West Point instructors at the time were Jared Mansfield, surveyor of the Northwest Territory, and Andrew Ellicott, who laid out the city of Washington, D.C.

6. At least seven of the ten engineering assistants from West Point who worked on the B&O reconnaissance and surveys became railroad engineers.

7. Alex. Brown and Sons to Wm. and Jas. Brown and Co., May 29, 1828, *Early Correspondence of Alex. Brown and Sons*, p. 7.

8. Baltimore *American*, Mar. 17, 1828.

9. Long's *Manual*, designed as a pocket guide, was the first American work on railroads. Long recommended or used other angle-measuring devices such as the theodolite, more accurate but more cumbersome than the surveyor's compass, the pocket sextant, and the pocket compass. The mathematics and instruments have become more sophisticated, but there is a direct correspondence between Long's basic system for laying out curves on the ground and the one used today.

10. A one-degree curve is, roughly speaking, a 100-foot segment of a circle with a radius of over a mile, in other words, a very slight curve. More precisely, it is the arc of a circle with a radius of 5,730 feet, defined by a 100-foot chord that subtends an angle of one degree. As the radius of the circle becomes smaller, the degree of curvature increases; thus, a 14.5 degree curve has a radius of less than 400 feet. Railroads at the time, both in England and America, had curves as sharp as 250-foot radius. Modern standards call for no more than 12-degree curves for freight lines, and three, two, or one-degree curves for high-speed passenger lines. Long's system for laying out curves, based on the work of Walter B. Guion and Jonathan Knight, made use of "versed sines" (offsets). These were lines of varying length measured off on the ground, either from the chord or from the tangent to the arc, to produce a series of points defining the sweep of the curve: Vose, *Manual for Railroad Engineers*, pp. 27–33; Trautwine, *Civil Engineer's Pocket-Book*, pp. 874–81; Rubey, *Route Surveys*, pp. 58–65.

11. B&O Rr. Minute Books, Sept. 30, 1830.

12. The peninsula gradually disappeared as the Middle Branch was filled in around it; the site of the shipyard was on Russell Street between Bayard and Worcester streets.

13. [James Carroll], "The Claim of the Western Navigation of the City of Baltimore to a Railroad Deposit" (by "A Friend to the Railroad") (Baltimore, 1829), p. 19, B&O Rr. Pamphlets.

14. Etting to Thomas, May 26, 1828, printed in the Baltimore *Gazette*, June 21, 1828.

15. Ibid.

16. Thomas later confirmed that the City of Baltimore threatened to withdraw its support for the railroad unless it came in along the proper alignment. Besides Etting, those who owned property along the route eventually taken by the railroad included Luke Tiernan, incorporator; J. B. Morris, director; William Howard, civil engineer, and two of his brothers, James and Charles: B&O Rr. Annual Report, 1831, map by T. Poppleton.

17. B&O Rr. Minute Books, June 24, 1828.   18. Baltimore *Gazette*, June 13, 1828.

19. B&O Rr. Minute Books, May 12, 1828.   20. Ibid., May 23, 1828.

21. John H. B. Latrobe, *Baltimore and Ohio Railroad. Personal Recollections*, p. 22.

22. Thomas to John V. L. McMahon, May 23, 1828, Thomas Letterbooks.

23. The Deep Cut is where the railroad crosses the present City Line at Patapsco Avenue. Gadsby's Run, now called Herbert's Run, is just before Relay, as is the second crossing of the Washington Turnpike (Route 1); the first is between Parksley and Whistler avenues in Baltimore.

24. S. H. Long, Wm. Gibbs McNeill, *Narrative of the Proceedings of the Board of Engineers of the Baltimore and Ohio Railroad Company . . .* (Baltimore, 1830), p. 43.

25. Thomas to Knight and McNeill, Liverpool, Dec. 28, 1828, Thomas Letterbooks.

26. Alex. Brown and Sons to Wm. and Jas. Brown and Co., Jan. 29, 1829, Brown Letterbooks, Library of Congress, Washington, D.C.

27. Alex. Brown and Sons to Wm. and Jas. Brown & Co., Dec. 31, 1828, ibid.

28. The prototype of the Winans friction wheel car was illustrated in the *Franklin Institute Journal* 3 (1829): 231–39, and the later model in the B&O Rr. Annual Report, 1831.

29. B&O Rr. Minute Books, Dec. 1, 1828.

30. Long, McNeill, *Narrative*, p. 114.

31. Alex. Brown and Sons to Wm. and Jas. Brown, June 12, 1829, Brown Letterbooks.

32. Long, McNeill, *Narrative*, p. 116.

33. William Howard's letter printed in *Niles Register* 35 (Feb. 21, 1829): 432; author's interview with John H. White, Jr.

34. Thomas to John L. Sullivan, New York, May 26, 1832, Thomas Letterbooks.

35. Rolt, *Railway Revolution*, p. 140.

36. *Niles Register* 40 (Apr. 23, 1831): 132.

37. Alex. Brown and Sons to Wm. and Jas. Brown and Co., Dec. 18, 1829, Brown Letterbooks.

38. Wever officially listed the cost of the Gwynns Falls Bridge (the Carrollton Viaduct) at $58,000 and that of the Patapsco River bridge (the Patterson Viaduct) at $36,000. Whistler claimed the actual prices were $70,000 and $45,000, respectively. Ten years after the fact, Latrobe indicated that the Carrollton Viaduct might have cost well over $100,000. Probably no one will ever know what the real figures were.

39. *Niles Register* 36 (Apr. 4, 1829): 92.

40. Baltimore County wills, DMP 14, Folio 128, Aug. 8, 1829, Maryland Hall of Records.

41. Second Annual Report of the Board of Engineers, 1829, p. 24. The Carrollton Viaduct, the first railroad bridge built in America, is still standing.

42. Baltimore *Gazette*, Dec. 4, 1829. The Patterson Viaduct was located a little more than half-way between Relay and Ellicott City. A flood in 1866 destroyed three of its four arches, leaving one of the roadway arches, which remains. The viaduct was replaced the following year by a single-span Bollman truss. This was in turn replaced during a major realignment of the Old Main Line in 1903 by the present steel truss, slightly upriver.

43. The major sources for the discussion that follows are the B&O Rr. Minute Books, Jan. 4, 1830, Long and McNeill's *Narrative*, and the B&O Rr. Annual Report, 1830, pp. 109–23.

44. *Niles Register* 36 (Aug. 8, 1829): 386.

45. Ibid., 37 (Sept. 12, 1829): 43.

46. Alex. Brown and Sons to Wm. and Jas. Brown and Co., Sept. 28, 1829, Brown Letterbooks.

47. George W. Whistler to Joseph G. Swift, New York, Oct. 24, 1829, Joseph G. Swift Papers, New York Public Library.

48. B&O Rr. Minute Books, Oct. 5, 1829.

49. This account of the committee hearings is based on Long, McNeill, *Narrative*, pp. 262–64.

50. B&O Rr. Minute Books, Jan. 4, 1830.

51. Ibid.

52. *Niles Register* 37 (Oct. 17, 1829): 124.

53. Long, *Bridges*, p. 44. Long's bridge, which was located on what is now Washington Boulevard between Parksley and Whistler avenues, survived until after the Civil War. The structure has been replaced several times since then, but the area still bears the name Jackson Bridge.

54. Baltimore *Gazette*, Dec. 29, 1829.

CHAPTER 7

1. These monstrous Cornish engines can still be seen "in steam" at the Kew Bridge Steam Museum, London.

2. *Niles Register*, addenda to vol. 3, 1813.

3. Ibid. Jesse Hollingsworth was the Baltimore legislator.

4. Ibid. Latrobe's primary objection to the steamboat at the time was the weight of the engine, he explained in his report, which the American Philosophical Society published in 1809, minus the denunciation of Evans: "Improvements in Steam Engines," *Transactions of the American Philosophical Society* 6 (1809): 89–98. "What a pity they did not also reject his demonstrations respecting steam boats! for notwithstanding them, they have run, are now running, and will run; so has my engine and all its principles completely succeeded—and so will land carriages," Evans retorted ten years after the event: *Niles Register*, addenda to vol. 3, 1813.

5. "Artists' Excursion over the Baltimore and Ohio Railroad," *Harper's Magazine* 19 (June 1859): 3. Hezekiah Niles remembered that when he was a small boy (around 1787) Evans was a frequent visitor in his father's house and that he thought him "cracked" for saying that the Ohio and Mississippi rivers would some day be covered with steamboats and that a rail traveler would go from Philadelphia to Boston in a day by steam power. Besides printing Evans's recollections, Niles often reminded readers of the inventor's various prophecies as they became reality.

6. The main sources for the discussion of Trevithick and his engine are Rolt, *Railway Revolution*, p. 38; Smiles, *Lives of George and Robert Stephenson*, p. 72; Robert H. Thurston, *A History of the Growth of the Steam Engine* (New York: Appleton, 1897), pp. 159–60, 174–77; and H. W. Dickinson, *A Short History of the Steam Engine* (Cambridge University Press, 1939), pp. 93–97.

7. Smiles, *Life of Trevithick*, quoted in Thurston, *History of the Steam Engine*, p. 177.

8. The standard biography is Smiles, *Lives of George and Robert Stephenson*, first published in 1874.

9. Booth, *Liverpool and Manchester Railway*, p. 15.

10. Charles Sylvester, "Report on Rail Roads and Locomotive Engines, to the chairman of the committee of the Liverpool and Manchester Railroad," 1825, B&O Rr. Pamphlets.

11. Alex. Brown and Sons to Wm. and Jas. Brown and Co., Oct. 20, 1828, Brown Letterbooks.

12. George W. Whistler, Liverpool, to Joseph G. Swift, New York, Feb. 10, 1829, Swift Papers, New York Public Library.

13. Knight, McNeill, and Whistler to Philip E. Thomas, from Manchester, Dec. 9, 1828, Baltimore and Ohio Railroad Company Papers, MS 1192, Maryland Historical Society.

14. Knight, McNeill, and Whistler to Philip E. Thomas, from Liverpool, Feb. 4, 1829, printed in *Niles Register* 36 (Apr. 4, 1829): 92.

15. Knight, McNeill, and Whistler to PET, from Darlington, Jan. 26, 1829, in ibid.

16. Knight, McNeill, and Whistler to PET, from Manchester, Dec. 9, 1828, B&O Rr. Co. Papers, MS 1192, Maryland Historical Society.

17. Ibid.

18. Robert Stephenson and Joseph Locke, "Observations on the Comparative Merits of Locomotive and Fixed Engines as Applied to Railways . . ." (Liverpool, n.d.), p. 32, B&O Rr. Pamphlets. Thompson's stationary engine idea may have been an extension of mining practice; in any case, a system remarkably like the one he described was in use in Maryland's Georges Creek coal mines 75 years later: W. B. Clark, et al., *Coals of Maryland*, p. 542.

19. Stephenson, Locke, "Observations," p. 33.

20. James Walker, "Report to the Directors of the Liverpool and Manchester Railway, on the

comparative merits of Locomotive and Fixed Engines as a Moving Power," 1829, p. 30, B&O Rr. Pamphlets.

21. Rolt, *Railway Revolution*, p. 158.

22. Stephenson, Locke, "Observations." See also Robert Eugene Carlson, *The Liverpool and Manchester Railway Project 1821–1831* (Devon, England: David & Charles, 1969), pp. 212–14.

23. Booth, *Liverpool and Manchester Railway*, pp. 73–74.

24. Liverpool *Mercury*, Oct. 9, 1829, reprinted in *Niles Register* 37 (Nov. 28, 1829): 222.

25. *London Mechanics' Magazine*, Oct. 10, 1829, reprinted in *Journal of the Franklin Institute* 5 (March 1830): 186–210.

26. *Liverpool Mercury*, Oct. 9, 1829, reprinted in *Niles Register* 37 (Nov. 28, 1829): 222.

27. *Liverpool Mercury*, Oct. 17, 1829, reprinted in *Niles Register* 37 (Nov. 28, 1829): 222. Reports of the Rainhill trials were widely circulated in the United States via newspapers and pamphlets. The Baltimore and Ohio published its own version: "Experiments on Railroads in England . . ." 1829, B&O Rr. Pamphlets.

28. Although some railroad historians believe this engine was lost at sea, B&O correspondence indicates that it survived whatever misfortune it was involved in: see PET to Wm. and Jas. Brown and Co., Jan. 2, 1830, Thomas Letterbooks; Evan Thomas to PET, Apr. 30, 1830, B&O Papers, MS 1192, Maryland Historical Society.

29. Alex. Brown and Sons to Wm. and Jas. Brown and Co., Dec. 30, 1829, Brown Letterbooks.

30. [James Carroll], "The Claim of the Western Navigation of the City of Baltimore . . ." 1829, B&O Rr. Pamphlets.

31. The name Canton was popularized by John O'Donnell, an Irish ship captain and merchant, who brought the first goods imported from China to Baltimore in 1785, settled in the city, and acquired property in the area. Peter Cooper traded his interest in the land for Canton Company stock in 1832. He leased his Canton Iron Works in 1833, and later sold it to Horace Abbott of Boston; the Abbott Iron Works made the armor for the *Monitor*.

The Canton Company earned an early reputation as a haven for speculators. There was some suspicion that the bidding on the lots in 1833 and at later sales was "collusive and fictitious" in order to inflate the stock price. In the 1850's, Daniel Drew and other New York speculators manipulated the shares of the Canton Company. Some investors did not know its purpose; others thought it had something to do with China. There was not much more knowledge of its operations in Baltimore. Nevertheless, the Canton Company achieved its original goals and existed as a corporate entity until the early 1980's. One can still see the vestiges of its pier, warehouse, and railroad operations, and Canton is today one of Baltimore's largest and best-known communities.

32. Address to the Master Mechanics Association, New York, May 12, 1875, *Railway Gazette* 15 (Apr. 13, 1883): 225.

33. Cooper to John H. B. Latrobe, Oct. 7, 1880, MS 34, Special Collections, Eisenhower Library, the Johns Hopkins University.

34. Baltimore *Gazette*, Aug. 25, 1830.

35. Address to the Master Mechanics Association, New York, May 12, 1875, *Railway Gazette* 15 (Apr. 13, 1883): 225.

36. Letter from Benjamin H. Latrobe, Jr. to Wm. H. Brown, Aug. 4, 1869, in Brown, *History of the First Locomotives in America*, p. 111.

37. John H. B. Latrobe, *Baltimore and Ohio Railroad. Personal Recollections*, pp. 17–18.

38. Baltimore *Gazette*, Sept. 22, 1830.

39. Baltimore *Sunday Herald*, July 9, 1882.

40. The only known contemporary illustration of Cooper's locomotive appeared in a Mayger and Washington advertisement in Matchett's Baltimore City Directory, 1831.

41. B&O Rr. Annual Report, 1830, pp. 35, 12.

42. At no place on the B&O route from Baltimore to the inclined planes at Parrs Spring Ridge was the grade greater than one percent, and it averaged about half that; the situation was the same on the other side of the planes. On modern, first-class railroads, grades of 0.3–0.6 percent are

considered acceptable, and on mountain and industrial railroads, 2–3 percent. About a third of the 68-mile route between Baltimore and the Potomac River consisted of curves with radii ranging from 955 feet down to 400, or 6 to 14 degrees, and there were two in the 320-foot, 18-degree range. Chevalier, in *Channels of Communication of the U.S.* (1841), wrote "Concerning curves, this railroad is quite daring."

43. B&O Rr. Minute Books, June 4, 1832.

44. For the basic theory regarding Cooper's involvement with the Baltimore and Ohio, I am indebted to John Hankey, chief curator, B&O Railroad Museum. The story of Cooper's adventures in Baltimore was a collective effort written by the protagonist and his admirers many years after the event. It is impossible now to determine who suggested what to whom, or even to analyze the situation without quarreling with the witness. Although he never departed from the outline, Cooper elaborated on the details until they almost achieved burlesque, and owing to subsequent repetition by his many biographers, the whole affair has become shrouded in myth. Contemporary accounts, which an early biographer implied were more reliable than Cooper's selective memory, are partial and inconclusive.

In 1855, in reply to a letter from John H. B. Latrobe seeking information, Cooper said he could not remember much about the engine itself, but stated his reasons for coming to Baltimore and building it, the same ones he repeated later, with variations. Latrobe then picked up the narrative in his 1868 speech to the Maryland Institute. In 1871, Latrobe ran into Cooper in Newport, and asked if he would like a printed copy of the speech. "He sent me the address and it gave me information which I was not aware existed," Cooper said. That same year, William H. Brown published his *History of the First Locomotives in America*, incorporating John H. B. Latrobe's account of the race, accompanied by a dramatic, foldout illustration, and letters from Benjamin H. Latrobe, Jr., and Ross Winans discussing the engine. The two Latrobes and Winans collaborated on some drawings for the book that remain the most accurate depictions of the locomotive.

Cooper's talk to the Master Mechanics Association in 1875 was a relatively straightforward rendition. He related the story of his life, in which the Maryland episode always figured prominently, on numerous occasions after that, each seemingly more fanciful than the last, but there were two major ones. The first is the "Autobiography" that Cooper gave to John G. Zachos, the librarian at Cooper Union, in conversations in 1876, which was published the following year. Then there were the *Reminiscences*, 200 pages of which Cooper dictated to a stenographer in 1882, when he was 91 years old. These were relied upon by his next biographer, Thomas Hughes, whose 1886 book was suppressed by Cooper's daughter, supposedly because of its cavalier treatment of her father. Only 50 copies were printed, of which some were circulated. Original transcriptions of this material have been altered or have disappeared. Four of Cooper's more recent biographers—Rossiter W. Raymond (1901), Allan Nevins (1935), Edward C. Mack (1949), and Miriam Gurko (1959)—quoted parts of the *Reminiscences* relating to his engine, either from the original or from published versions. Since both the "Autobiography" and the *Reminiscences* contain statements by Cooper that are clear exaggerations of what he said earlier, this account is based mainly on his 1875 speech.

45. Baltimore *Gazette*, Nov. 13, 1829.

46. It has often been stated that the South Carolina Railroad was the first planned for steam power, the first to operate a "practical" locomotive, and therefore by implication, the first "real" American railroad (see, e.g., Haney, *Congressional History of Railways*, p. 192). This canard may have started with Horatio Allen in his published letter to William H. Brown, *History of First Locomotives* (1871), pp. 168–70. It was repeated the next year in Greeley et al., *Great Industries of the U.S.*, p. 917, and has since become received wisdom.

However, it is one thing to plan a railroad for steam power after the Rainhill trials had demonstrated the locomotive's effectiveness, and another to begin construction before the motive power question was settled. John H. B. Latrobe's claim in his 1868 pamphlet, "In the beginning, no one dreamed of steam power upon the road," is contradicted by contemporary statements such as George Gillingham, superintendent of machinery, in the B&O Rr. Annual Report, 1832 (p. 108):

"From the very commencement of the Baltimore and Ohio Railroad, it was fondly anticipated . . . that steam power should be used in transportation." Indeed, the B&O's primary document, the February 1827 *Proceedings of Sundry Citizens*, as well as the April 1828 "Report of the Engineers on the Reconnoissance and Surveys," contemplated the use of locomotives, but no one knew then whether they were practical.

By any standard measure: incorporation, ground breaking, official opening, and operating the first locomotive, the Baltimore and Ohio preceded the South Carolina Railroad. Besides the latter's peculiarities of construction—it was built on wooden pilings that caught fire and caused serious accidents—the line never crossed the mountains.

47. B&O Rr. Minute Books, Jan. 18, 1831.

48. Baltimore *Gazette*, June 29, 1831.

49. B&O Rr. Annual Report, 1831, p. 23.

50. Philip E. Thomas to Phineas Davis, Dec. 14, 1831, Thomas Letterbooks.

51. *Niles Register* 32 (Mar. 17, 1827): 33.

CHAPTER 8

1. Washington *National Intelligencer*, July 7, 1828, quoted in Hulbert, *Historic Highways*, vol. 13, *The Great American Canals*, p. 103.

2. Baltimore *American*, July 8, 1828.

3. Ibid.

4. [W. P. Smith], *History of the B&O Rr.*, p. 19.

5. During the Civil War, Trimble was one of Stonewall Jackson's favorite generals. He led the left wing of Pickett's Charge at Gettysburg, was wounded, captured, had his leg amputated, and at age 61 organized an escape attempt from a Union prison camp.

6. Second Annual Report of the Board of Engineers to the Baltimore and Ohio Railroad, 1829, p. 42.

7. Ibid., p. 41.

8. Chesapeake and Ohio Canal Annual Report, 1829, appendix.

9. House Report, 22d Congress, Report no. 18, C&O Canal Co. Memorial, Dec. 19, 1831, pp. 114–15, 133.

10. Unidentified, undated news clipping, B&O Rr. Pamphlets.

11. John H. B. Latrobe, "A History of My Connection with the Baltimore and Ohio Railroad Company," Latrobe Collection, MS 523, Maryland Historical Society.

12. "Report of the Directors of the Baltimore and Ohio Railroad Company to the Legislature of Maryland," Jan. 31, 1831, p. 14.

13. C&O Canal Annual Report, 1830, p. 9.

14. H. H. Walker Lewis, "The Great Case of the Canal vs. the Railroad, 4 Gill & Johnson 1 (1832)," *Maryland Law Review* 19 (Winter 1959): 1.

15. Anna Boyd to John McHenry, Aug. 6, 1819, in Browne, *Baltimore in the Nation*, p. 259.

16. Philip E. Thomas to Charles F. Mercer, Mar. 9, 1829, Thomas Letterbooks.

17. B&O Rr. Annual Report, 1829, p. 10.

18. PET to Mercer, Feb. 19, 1830, B&O Rr. Pamphlets.

19. B&O Rr. report to the Maryland Legislature, Jan. 3, 1831, p. 23.

20. C&O Canal Memorial to the General Assembly, Jan. 1, 1829, C&O Canal Annual Report, 1829, appendix.

21. PET to John V. L. McMahon, Jan. 12, 1829, Thomas Letterbooks.

22. William Wirt to Elizabeth Wirt, July 24, 1829, William Wirt Papers, MS 1011, Maryland Historical Society.

23. This and the quotations that follow are taken from "The Chesapeake and Ohio Canal Company vs. the Baltimore and Ohio Rail Road Company," 4 Gill & Johnson 1, 1832, pp. 32–37.

24. J. Semmes, *John H. B. Latrobe*, p. 202.

25. William Wirt to Elizabeth Wirt, July 27, 1829, William Wirt Papers, MS 1011, Maryland Historical Society.

26. "Argument Delivered at Annapolis by William Wirt, Esquire . . ." Aug. 18, 19, 1829.

27. Quoted in J. Semmes, *John H. B. Latrobe*, p. 202.

28. "The Chesapeake and Ohio Canal Company vs. the Baltimore and Ohio Rail Road Company," 4 Gill & Johnson 1, 1832, p. 55.

29. "The Correspondence between the Chesapeake and Ohio Canal and the Baltimore and Ohio Rail Road Companies, and the proceedings of the former in relation to a compromise of the conflicting claims of these companies to the left bank of the river Potomac, between the Point of Rocks and Harpers Ferry or Williamsport" (Washington, 1831), p. 73. The railroad had published its version the previous year: "Correspondence Between the Chesapeake and Ohio Canal Company, and the Baltimore and Ohio Rail Road Company in relation to the dispute between those companies concerning the Right of Way for their respective works along the Potomac River" (Baltimore, 1830).

30. B&O Rr. Minute Books, Jan. 19, 1830.

31. PET to W. A. Bradley, June 5, 1829, Thomas Letterbooks.

32. Nathan S. Roberts to Mercer, Apr. 11, 1830, "Correspondence" (C&O Canal version), p. 103; "Correspondence" (B&O Rr. version), pp. 29–30.

33. S. H. Long and Wm. Gibbs McNeill, *Narrative of the Proceedings of the Board of Engineers of the Baltimore and Ohio Rail Road Company . . .* (Baltimore, 1830), p. 347. McNeill resigned from the B&O Apr. 9, 1830.

34. Roberts to Mercer, Apr. 11, 1830, "Correspondence" (C&O Canal version), p. 105.

35. Roberts to Mercer, May 17, 1830, ibid.

36. Report on the joint surveys by Roberts and Knight, B&O Rr. Annual Report, 1830, pp. 135–44.

37. Mercer to Thomas, Nov. 6, 1830, "Correspondence" (B&O Rr. version), p. 65.

38. C&O Canal Annual Report, 1831, pp. 4–9.

39. Baltimore *Gazette*, Aug. 1, 1831.

40. Quoted in ibid., Oct. 1, 1831. Gales was mayor of Washington, 1827–30, and chairman of the stockholders' committee of the C&O Canal. Seaton, Gales's brother-in-law, was mayor of Washington, 1840–50. Besides being printers for the federal government, Gales and Seaton also published numerous C&O Canal documents.

41. The High Court of Chancery and the Chancellor's powers were based on British models. Bland was, for example, the keeper of the Great Seal of the State. The Maryland court dated from colonial times; Leonard Calvert was the first Chancellor. Bland was the fourth appointed by the Governor after the court was reestablished under the State Constitution of 1776: William L. Marbury, "The High Court of Chancery and the Chancellor of Maryland," *Proceedings of the Maryland Bar Association* 10 (1905): 137–48.

42. There was ill feeling between the two courts. The Court of Appeals judges resented the fact that although they were the higher court and could overrule the Chancellor, he enjoyed a substantially larger salary. John Buchanan, the chief judge of the Court of Appeals, had been passed over for the Chancellor's post before Bland was appointed. (He was the younger brother of Thomas Buchanan, who had issued the canal's first injunction in the Washington County court.)

43. Quoted in J. Semmes, *John H. B. Latrobe*, p. 373.

44. Many years later, Webster wrote Latrobe (Jan. 2, 1845): "A few plants, and only a few, survive from those roots, which you sent me, so long ago; and those flourish very well. They stand by the side of a frequented summer path, I never see them, without remembering . . . our acquaintance at Annapolis, always a most agreeable recollection with me." In another letter (July 10, 1851), he said: "We attended to our professional duties, I hope, with diligence, but I remember that we had a good deal of general conversation. . . . We talked of Shakespeare and the Players edition of his plays. . . . I remember also that you Kindly arranged to send me some Scotch Broom, then

growing near Annapolis and which is now flourishing at Marshfield." Latrobe Collection, MS 523, Maryland Historical Society.

45. Baltimore *Gazette*, Jan. 2, 1832.

46. Ibid., Jan. 4, 1832.

47. "The C&O Canal Co. vs. the B&O Rr. Co." 4 Gill & Johnson 1, 1832, p. 86.

48. Benjamin C. Howard to John H. B. Latrobe, Jan. 15, 1832, Benjamin Chew Howard Papers, MS 469, Maryland Historical Society.

49. The Maryland law relieving the company from this obligation was passed Mar. 10, 1832: *Laws and Ordinances, B&O Rr.*, pp. 41–42.

50. Benjamin C. Howard to Robert Gilmor, Jan. 11, 1832, Benjamin Chew Howard Papers.

51. Alfred Cruger, "Report of the Committee appointed on the 28th April 1832, by the Stockholders of the Chesapeake and Ohio Canal Company," B&O Rr. Pamphlets.

52. PET to Caspar W. Wever, Feb. 25, 1832, Thomas Letterbooks.

53. PET to Benjamin C. Howard, Jan. 24, 1833, ibid.

54. *Niles Register* 43 (Jan. 12, 1833): 319.

55. Mercer to Bernard Nose, Feb. 22, 1833, Charles James Faulkner Papers, West Virginia and Regional History Collection, West Virginia University, Morgantown.

56. *Laws and Ordinances, B&O Rr.*, p. 60.

57. Ibid., p. 257.

58. Baltimore *American*, May 11, 1832.

59. C&O Canal Annual Report, 1833, p. 15.

60. B&O Rr. Annual Report, 1834, pp. 14–15.

CHAPTER 9

1. B&O Rr. Minute Books, June 30, 1836.

2. Baltimore *Gazette*, Nov. 8, 1827.

3. John Barney to Philip E. Thomas, Apr. 6, 1828, B&O Railroad Company Papers, MS 1192, Maryland Historical Society.

4. PET to Sam Smith, Apr. 16, 1828, Thomas Letterbooks.

5. Joseph W. Patterson to Sam Smith, Apr. 16, 1828, B&O Rr. Pamphlets.

6. Baltimore *Gazette*, Apr. 29, 1828, reprinted in *Niles Register* 34 (May 5, 1828): 154.

7. Thomas Ellicott to president and directors, B&O Rr. Co., May 3, 1828, B&O Rr. Pamphlets.

8. B. H. Latrobe, Jr., Journals, Sept. 4, 1833, Mrs. Gamble Latrobe Collection, MS 1638, Maryland Historical Society.

9. Although the ten-hour days of gleaning and condensing information and packaging it into sixteen pages of small-type newsprint every week often left him exhausted, Niles liked nothing better than to sit in his living room after dinner in what he called "freedom's chair" (which had belonged to a participant in the Boston Tea Party), light up a Cuban cigar, and, further stimulated by coffee and Madeira, conduct a "fireside conversation" with his subscribers. They included, at one time or another, John Adams, Jefferson, Madison, and Jackson. Mathew Carey, the editor's Philadelphia colleague and fellow protectionist, considered the *Register* "the best periodical work ever published in America." Niles carried it on pretty much as a one-man operation for 25 years, although his son, William Ogden Niles, shared the editorial duties from 1827 to 1830. Subsequently the son and others continued it until 1849, ten years after Niles's death. The bound volumes, with indexes, constitute a thorough and impartial compendium of American affairs during the period and for years were considered standard equipment for libraries and American diplomats: Luxon, *Niles Weekly Register*, pp. 1–65, 107–18, 124.

Roland K. Hoke, a Baltimorean, copied verbatim from the *Register*, with citations, hundreds of articles dated between March 1825 and February 1834 pertaining to the Baltimore and Ohio, railroads in general, and related subjects. The typescript is at the B&O Railroad Museum and I have made extensive use of it.

10. "General Convention of Agriculturists and Manufacturers and others friendly to the encouragement and support of the domestic industry of the United States," July 1827, B&O Rr. Pamphlets.

11. Baltimore *Gazette*, Apr. 29, 1828.

12. *Niles Register* 34 (May 5, 1828): 154.

13. PET to John Barney, May 8, 1828, Thomas Letterbooks.

14. "Memorial of the Inhabitants of Philadelphia to the House of Representatives," May 8, 1828, B&O Rr. Pamphlets. The Philadelphia *Aurora* blamed "a Baltimore ironmaster," who could only have been Ridgely, for indirectly sponsoring the memorial. The Baltimore *Gazette* denied it and the newspapers continued the argument for days after Congress had settled the issue: *Gazette*, May 30, June 1, 3, 6, 19, 1828. With the substitution of foreign steel for English rails and the addition of American union rhetoric, 1980's protectionist arguments were remarkably similar to those of the 1820's.

15. Henry B. Chew and James Tucker to James Buchanan, May 12, 1828, B&O Rr. Pamphlets.

16. John Barney to PET, May 15, 1828, ibid.

17. The site of Northampton furnace, three miles north of Towson, is now submerged under Loch Raven Reservoir. The land and ironworks were the basis of the Ridgely fortune. Three men, all known as Charles Ridgely of Hampton, created it. The first, the colonel, bought land at Northampton and started the furnace in 1762. The second, his son, a sea captain, traded pig iron and other colonial products for British finished goods, later profited by selling iron kettles, shot, and cannon to the American forces during the Revolution, and used the money from these and other ventures to build Hampton. Slaves and indentured servants worked on the mansion for seven years. Captain Ridgely expanded the estate by buying up confiscated British property, including competing ironworks. He spent several terms in the Maryland legislature and became the political boss of Baltimore County. The captain died in 1790, the year the house was finished, leaving the property to his nephew, Charles Ridgely Carnan, on condition that he change his last name to Ridgely. This man, the third Charles Ridgely of Hampton, served a term as governor of Maryland, 1815–17, and then retired to the homestead. After Charles Carnan Ridgely died in 1829, the estate was broken up. In his will, he freed most of his slaves.

18. PET to Barney, May 17, 1828, B&O Rr. Pamphlets.

19. Alex. Brown and Sons to Wm. and Jas. Brown and Co., Feb. 24, 1827, Brown Letterbooks, Library of Congress.

20. The 1828 Tariff Act, which was manipulated by the Jacksonians in an attempt to embarrass Adams, placed high duties on raw materials and finished goods. It displeased both New Englanders and Southerners; the latter named it the Tariff of Abominations.

21. PET to Wm. and Jas. Brown and Co., Nov. 26, 1828, Thomas Letterbooks.

22. PET to John Bolton, June 3, 1829, ibid.

23. PET to Alex. Brown and Sons, Sept. 25, 1829, ibid.

24. PET to Wm. and Jas. Brown and Co., Jan. 21, 1830, ibid.

25. Robert L. Stevens, son of the builder of America's first trial locomotive and some of its earliest steamboats, invented the modern T-rail. It had parallel top and bottom edges, in profile, and a broad base that was fastened directly to the ties with hook-headed spikes. Stevens had the first such rails rolled in England in 1830 and installed the following year on New Jersey's Camden and Amboy Railroad; the system was later adopted throughout the United States and Europe and with minor modifications it is still the railroad track used today.

The idea of the stone rails seems to have originated with Chevalier Joseph de Baader, who claimed to have built such a track in Germany in 1825 and published a paper on it a year later. Minus Ward, a Baltimore railway advocate and engineer manqué, said he thought of it first and described it in the Baltimore *American* in 1825, before the Quincy Railroad was built. De Baader's claim appears to have priority, however.

26. George W. Whistler to Joseph G. Swift, Oct. 24, 1829, Swift Papers, New York Public Library.

27. B&O Rr. Annual Report, 1830, p. 21. James Stimpson claimed that he developed the coned wheel and by extension the inside flange and furthermore that in December 1829 he convinced Thomas and Knight to adopt them on the B&O: James Stimpson, "A Dissertation upon the running gears of rail-road carriages . . ." 1836, B&O Rr. Pamphlets. However, James Wright, another Baltimorean, really deserves the credit for developing the coned wheel.

28. Alex. Brown and Sons to Wm. and Jas. Brown and Co., Jan. 29, 1830, Brown Letterbooks.

29. B&O Rr. Minute Books, July 15, 1830.

30. Knight to Steel, July 20, 1830, Archives, B&O Rr. Museum.

31. B&O Rr. Annual Report, 1830, p. 70.

32. Ibid., pp. 77–85.

33. *Niles Register* 39 (Aug. 28, 1830): 12.

34. [Boardman], *America and the Americans*, p. 262.

35. Wittke, *Irish in America*, p. viii.

36. A. Roger Ekirch, "Exiles in the Promised Land: Convict Labor in the Eighteenth-Century Chesapeake," *Maryland Historical Magazine* 82 (Summer 1987): 95.

37. "Report of the Board of Managers of the Lehigh Coal and Navigation Company presented to the Stockholders, January 12, 1829," B&O Rr. Pamphlets.

38. Ward, *Early Development, C&O Canal*, p. 90.

39. C&O Canal Annual Report, 1830, pp. 5, 29.

40. PET to Walter Smith, Oct. 22, 1829, Thomas Letterbooks.

41. Undated, unidentified news clipping, B&O Rr. Pamphlets.

42. Baltimore *Gazette*, May 28, 1829.

43. *Niles Register* 36 (Aug. 22, 1829): 409, and 37 (Aug. 29, 1829): 1; Baltimore *American*, Aug. 25, 1829.

44. Baltimore *Gazette*, Dec. 2, 1829.

45. PET to Upton S. Heath, Feb. 24, 1830, Thomas Letterbooks.

46. Charles Warfield, "Protest against the Baltimore and Ohio Railroad taking possession of part of his lands for their line of road" (Baltimore, 1828), B&O Rr. Pamphlets, Evergreen House, the Johns Hopkins University.

47. John H. B. Latrobe, *The Baltimore and Ohio Railroad. Personal Recollections*, p. 11.

48. Nor were the granite sills a joy to ride on. Traveling on them in springless cars was accompanied by the sound of rolling thunder and an "excessively disagreeable" sensation, something like being pushed in an iron wheelbarrow down a row of curbstones.

49. B&O Rr. Annual Report, 1830, pp. 26–27.

50. "Report of the Directors of the Baltimore and Ohio Railroad Company to the Legislature of Maryland," Jan. 31, 1831, p. 42.

51. Ibid., p. 65.

52. B&O Rr. Minute Books, June 28, 1831.

53. B&O Rr. Annual Report, 1831, p. 45.

54. Baltimore *American*, July 21, 1831.

55. B&O Rr. Minute Books, Sept. 5, 1831.

56. Portions of the stone track in the Patapsco River Valley were exposed in June 1972 by Hurricane Agnes. They were mostly covered up again by new ballast in the rebuilding of the modern track that was damaged by the flood, but some of the original granite rails, minus the iron, can still be seen on the old railroad alignment at Daniels, Maryland, and at other spots along the line: John H. White, Jr., and Robert Vogel, "Stone Rails Along the Patapsco," *Journal of the Society for Industrial Archeology* 4 (1978): 1–14.

CHAPTER 10

1. The barrister, so called to distinguish him from several other Charles Carrolls, was active in pre-Revolutionary politics in Maryland and served in the state's General Assembly as did his distant cousin, Charles Carroll of Carrollton, with whom he has been often and understandably confused, even by historians.

2. James Carroll's offer of land and the company's response are summarized in the B&O Rr. Minute Books, Sept. 28, 1830. Carroll first proposed the land deal in March 1828; the first official mention of his donation of ten acres for a depot occurs in the Minute Books, Oct. 5, 1829. Thomas excised the section concerning the land deal from the Board of Engineers Report dated June 1, 1829: S. H. Long and Wm. Gibbs McNeill, *Narrative of the Proceedings of the Board of Engineers* (Baltimore, 1830), pp. 160–61. Carroll deeded the land to the railroad Dec. 1, 1830: W.G. 208, Folio 448, Baltimore County Deed Book, Maryland Hall of Records. The company accepted the nine plus acres for a depot "near to Pratt street," Dec. 6, 1830: B&O Rr. Minute Books.

Carroll's land constituted the heart of the B&O's Mt. Clare property, its first depot in the city. Anna Boyd granted them an additional block of land nearby in May 1829, and in June 1835 the railroad bought 11 more acres in the vicinity from Ramsay McHenry for $25,000. By then, locomotive and car building were well under way at Mt. Clare. The site was gradually expanded to roughly 30 acres. In the 1920's, the work force numbered 3,000, and as late as the 1960's, the B&O's extensive repair facilities still covered the area. The shops closed in 1974 and most of the acreage has since been cleared. The B&O Railroad Museum and a shopping mall now occupy Mt. Clare.

3. Report of the Bd of Eng'rs, B&O Rr. Minute Books, June 24, 1828, published in the Baltimore *American*, June 26, 1828.

4. B&O Rr. Minute Books, Feb. 2, 1829; Baltimore *Gazette*, same date. "Civis," "Consistency," "Z" criticize the route: *Gazette*, Feb. 16, 23, 24, 28, 1829.

5. B&O Rr. Minute Books, Aug. 26, 1830.

6. "Address to the Citizens of Baltimore relative to the contemplated extension of the Rail Road down Pratt street to the City Block . . ." Sept. 30, 1830, B&O Rr. Pamphlets.

7. B&O Rr. Annual Report, 1831; B&O Rr. Minute Books, Feb. 14, 1831; PET to Mayor and City Council, Feb. 7, 1831, Thomas Letterbooks.

8. Newspaper clippings of James Carroll's letters to the editor, signed "Civis, "C," "Graviora Manent," and "GM," appear in the company records, which identify him as the author: B&O Rr. Pamphlets. See also "Civis" in Baltimore *Gazette*, Feb. 15, 16, 1831. James Stimpson devised street corner turntables for the railroad that were actually used for a time.

9. Undated, unidentified news clipping, B&O Rr. Pamphlets.

10. B&O Rr. Minute Books, Feb. 21, 1829.   11. Baltimore *Gazette*, Mar. 14, 1831.

12. B&O Rr. Minute Books, Mar. 26, 1832.   13. Ibid., Aug. 23, 1832.

14. In 1836, James Stimpson, the developer of the horse treadmill that ran into the cow, patented a grooved iron rail for street running as well as improvements to his turntable: James Stimpson, "A Dissertation upon the Running Gears of Rail-Road Carriages," 1836, B&O Rr. Pamphlets.

15. Baltimore *Gazette*, Mar. 7, 19, 1835.

16. Few of the city tracks still remain, but the two-mile extension of the main line from Mt. Clare down Pratt Street to the City Block was in service until 1972 and sections of it are still visible. For all practical purposes, the City Block was the end of the line for the B&O in Baltimore in 1832, but the Baltimore and Port Deposit Railroad, laid out by Benjamin H. Latrobe, Jr., continued from that point down along the deepwater harbor and made the rail connection with the Canton Company that James Carroll was so opposed to. It began operations in 1835. Later, as the Philadelphia, Wilmington and Baltimore Railroad, it became part of the continuous rail line between New York and Washington. A third historic railroad, the Baltimore and Susquehanna, subsequently known as the Northern Central (Baltimore to York and Harrisburg, Pennsylvania), was extended along Central Avenue to the City Block area in the mid-nineteenth century. The sole remaining evidences of the meeting place of these three primary rail routes entering the city from the west, north, and east are the old yards between Lancaster and Aliceanna streets and the head house of the PW&B's President Street Station, built in 1850. Rail service continued at the yards until the 1980's. The station's abandoned appearance belies its significance as the oldest metropolitan rail terminal in the United States. (A vigorous station preservation effort is now under way, however.)

The vicinity of Carroll's Point is now known, ironically, as the Carroll Industrial Park. Although it acquired rail service in the 1850's, the area remained a backwater. A forest of concrete piers supporting an elevated expressway now rises out of the Middle Branch, blocking what James Carroll hoped would be Baltimore's premier port facility.

17. PET to Knight, Jan. 18, 1831, Thomas Letterbooks.

18. The B&O built a two-story stone depot, similar to the one at Ellicotts Mills, at All Saints and South Carroll streets in Frederick in 1832. Five years later, it opened a ticket office at All Saints and Market streets, and in 1854 it built a new Italianate depot at that location. The later depot still stands, but the first one was torn down in the early 1900's.

19. PET to Caspar W. Wever, Oct. 12, 1831, Thomas Letterbooks.

20. B&O Rr. Annual Report, 1831, p. 109.

21. Parrs Spring, source of the west branch of the Patapsco River, is located south of Ridgeville off Route 27, at the intersection of Carroll, Howard, Montgomery, and Frederick counties.

22. Robinson's system is illustrated in Chevalier, *Channels of Communication of the U.S.*, map 3.

23. Long and McNeill, *Narrative*, appendix, p. 42.

24. The inspection tour was reported in the Baltimore *American*, Nov. 15, 1831, and the Frederick *Herald*, Nov. 19, 1831.

25. These grades were relatively modest. Those on the Allegheny Portage Railroad ranged from 7 to 10 percent.

26. Baltimore *American*, Dec. 2, 1831.

27. *Niles Register* 44 (July 20, 1833): 338. Niles also reported on this date an incident in which a horse fell while a car was descending Parrs Spring Ridge, but the car was stopped and the animal was put back in the traces. Although Niles believed accidents might result from human carelessness and that the inclined planes themselves were not dangerous, the planes in fact were dangerous, mostly because of runaway trains resulting from parted lines or brake failures. There were serious accidents on most of the systems of inclined planes in America, and their use in England resulted in the death or injury of hundreds of men and horses: C. F. Dendy Marshall, *A History of British Railways Down to the Year 1830* (London: Oxford University Press, 1938), p. 163.

28. Quoted in Williams and McKinsey, *History of Frederick County*, p. 230. The account of the official opening of the Frederick Branch is drawn from the Baltimore *American*, Nov. 15, Dec. 2, 5, 1831; Frederick *Herald*, Nov. 19, Dec. 2 (?), 1831, B&O Rr. Pamphlets; B&O Rr. Annual Report, 1831, pp. 106–7; [Latrobe], *Picture of Baltimore*, pp. 208–10; Varle, *Complete View of Baltimore*, pp. 117, 119; and Williams and McKinsey, *History of Frederick County*, pp. 229–31.

29. White, *American Railroad Passenger Car*, pp. 9–11.

30. The depot at Ellicotts Mills, now Ellicott City, is the nation's oldest railroad station. In 1828, the Ellicotts offered the B&O a little over an acre of land, some right-of-way, and quarrying rights in exchange for a depot. In 1830, when they conveyed the land, the railroad approved a bridge over the Patapsco and a siding to the Ellicotts' mills, and provided engineers and materials.

31. PET to A. G. Chapman, Feb. 21, 1832, Thomas Letterbooks.

32. PET to Peter H. Schenck & Co., N.Y., Mar. 20, 1832, ibid.

33. "Diary of John Rudolph Niernsee, Architect, 1838–1841," p. 32, translated by M. Albrecht, typescript, Vertical File, Maryland Historical Society.

34. B&O Rr. Minute Books, Nov. 7, 1838. The old main line of the B&O at Parrs Spring Ridge was relocated in 1902 to pass under it in a tunnel, but the vestiges of the inclined planes can still be seen. For an excellent description of their location, see Harwood, *Impossible Challenge*, pp. 409–10; 437–40.

35. B&O Rr. Annual Report, 1832, p. 4; *Niles Register* 42 (Apr. 28, 1832): 153; Williams and McKinsey, *History of Frederick County*, p. 231.

CHAPTER 11

1. Baltimore *Gazette*, Feb. 11, Apr. 8, 1828; Haney, *Congressional History of Railways*, p. 258.

2. "History of Julia Latrobe," Latrobe Papers, American Philosophical Society, Philadelphia.

3. *Niles Register* 34 (May 3, 1828): 155.

4. R. Semmes, *Baltimore Visitors*, p. 112, 113.

5. A century later, the reputation of Route 1 between Baltimore and Washington was even worse. In the 1930's, this highway, lined with billboards, juke joints, and cheap motels, was one of the most heavily traveled and dangerous stretches in the nation, and motorists could spend up to four hours driving the 29 miles between the cities; in 1951, 44 people died in auto accidents on this section of road. In recent years, most of the intercity traffic has shifted to the Baltimore-Washington Parkway and Interstate 95, and Route 1 is enjoying a resurgence: Michael Kelly, Baltimore *Sun*, Nov. 9, 1986.

6. Baltimore *Gazette*, Sept. 29, 1829.

7. Ibid., Nov. 17, 1830.

8. George Brown said the B&O built the Washington Branch as a substitute for not being able to extend the line to the west because of the court contest with the C&O Canal; the management wanted to maintain public support by demonstrating the worth of a successful and profitable rail line: [W. P. Smith], *History and Description, B&O Rr.*, p. 165.

9. Philip E. Thomas to Benjamin C. Howard, Jan. 13, 1831, Thomas Letterbooks.

10. B&O Rr. Minute Books, Jan. 5, 1831.

11. Patrick Macaulay to Benjamin C. Howard, Jan. 5, 1831, Howard Papers, MS 469, Maryland Historical Society.

12. William Howard to Benjamin C. Howard, Jan. 9, 1831, ibid.

13. B&O Rr. Minute Books, Jan. 22, 1831.

14. Unidentified news clipping, ca. Jan. 29, 1831, B&O Rr. Pamphlets.

15. Charles Howard to Benjamin C. Howard, Jan. 22, 1831, Howard Papers, MS 469, Maryland Historical Society.

16. B&O Rr. Annual Report, 1831, p. 91.

17. Baltimore *Gazette*, Jan. 28, 1831.

18. Wm. Howard to B. C. Howard, Jan. 29, 1831, Howard Papers, MS 469, Maryland Historical Society. The idea of building a "cross-cut," as it was later called, to connect Baltimore with the C&O Canal at Georgetown or somewhere north of there was revived in the late 1830's, in the 1850's, and for the last time in the 1870's. The proposal was always linked to the chronic political battles and to competition for trade between the B&O Railroad and the C&O Canal: Sanderlin, *Great National Project*, pp. 172–75.

19. Philip E. Thomas, "Washington Rail Road," B&O Rr. Pamphlets.

20. The $2.50 one-way fare on the Washington Branch in the 1830's, established by Maryland law, provided ample profit for both the railroad and the state. The same one-way ride today costs $5, and on a monthly commuter ticket, just $2.50. The latter figure is evidence not of the lack of increase in railroad fares over the past 150 years, but of the exorbitant nature of the original fare.

21. B&O Rr. Annual Report, 1833, p. 8.

22. Knight's report dated July 27, 1833, in ibid., pp. 41–167. Reviewing committee report dated Sept. 23, 1833, in ibid., pp. 24–27.

CHAPTER 12

1. Philip E. Thomas handwritten memo, Oct. 15, 1833, B&O Rr. Pamphlets.

2. John H. B. Latrobe, "Benjamin H. Latrobe," *American Architect and Building News*, Jan. 29, 1876. Yale University Press has recently published Benjamin H. Latrobe's journals, sketchbooks, and letters, many of which are housed at the Maryland Historical Society, as are the journals of his two sons.

3. J. Semmes, *John H. B. Latrobe*, p. 285.

4. Hamlin, *Benjamin Henry Latrobe*, p. 181.

5. William Gibbs McNeill's stone viaduct for the Boston and Providence Railroad at Canton, Mass., which opened July 28, 1835, just a few weeks after the Thomas Viaduct was finished, was

also a multispan railroad bridge built on a slightly curving alignment. It was 615 feet long, 22 feet wide, and 70 feet above the Neponset River. Most of its arches were filled with stone, however, and it has little of the grace and power of Latrobe's structure: E. D. Galvin, "The Canton Viaduct," *Railroad History* 129 (Autumn 1973): 71–85.

6. Condit, *American Building Art*, p. 73.

7. The Sankey Viaduct was shown in I. Shaw's *Views of the Most Interesting Scenery on the line of the Liverpool and Manchester Railway*, and T. T. Bury's *Coloured Views on the Liverpool and Manchester Railway*, both published in 1831.

8. Benjamin H. Latrobe, Jr., Journal, Aug. 22, 29, 1833, Mrs. Gamble Latrobe Collection, MS 1638, Maryland Historical Society. Perronet was the first engineer to apply the concept of inter-dependent arches, whereby the outward thrust of each arch is transferred from pier to pier until it is met and contained at the abutments. The idea translated into flatter arches, thinner piers, and lower profile bridges.

9. Ibid., Sept. 4, 7, 9, 1833.

10. B&O Rr. Annual Report, 1835, p. 114.

11. BHL, Jr., Journal, Sept. 6, 1833.

12. Ibid., Sept. 3, 6, 1833.

13. Ibid., Sept. 6, 1833; BHL, Jr., "Professional Memoranda," Mrs. Gamble Latrobe Collection, MS 1638, Maryland Historical Society, Oct. 4, 1834.

14. BHL, Jr., Journal, May 17, 1834; Nov. 26–28, 1833.

15. Ibid., Dec. 19, 1833.

16. Ibid., Sept. 6, 12, 1833.

17. BHL, Jr., "Professional Memoranda," Sept. 6, 1833.

18. Ibid., Feb. 5, 1834.

19. BHL, Jr., Journal, May 17, 24, 1834; June 8, 1835.

20. Ibid., July 15, 1834.

21. Ibid., July 17, 1834.

22. Ibid., July 8, 1834.

23. BHL, Jr., "Professional Memoranda," Oct. 4, 1834.

24. BHL, Jr., Journal, Sept. 3, 1834.

25. Ibid., Sept. 26, 30, Mar. 13, 1834.

26. Ibid., Oct. 14, 1834.

27. Baltimore *Gazette*, Nov. 10, 1834.

28. BHL, Jr., Journal, Feb. 20, 1835.

29. Ibid., June 13, 1835.

30. Benjamin H. Latrobe, Jr. may have suffered from a psychosomatic condition, or in current medical parlance, "an anxiety disorder with prominent somatic symptoms." His syndrome was remarkably similar to that described by Civil War soldiers and reported by J. M. DaCosta, "On Irritable Heart; a Clinical Study of a Form of Functional Cardiac Disorder and its Consequences," *American Journal of the Medical Sciences*, Jan. 1871, pp. 17–52. Dr. DaCosta considered over 300 cases of soldiers who complained of cardiac pain, palpitations, rapid pulse, respiratory problems, vertigo, headaches, and digestive disorders. He noted that the problems mostly affected those aged 20–25, were caused primarily by hard field service, and cured mainly through rest. For the tentative diagnosis and the 1871 article, I am grateful to L. Randol Barker, M.D., Associate Professor of Medicine, the Johns Hopkins University, Baltimore, and to Michael J. Weaver, M.D., Fitzsimmons Army Medical Center, Denver.

31. Latrobe had been named chief engineer of the Baltimore and Port Deposit Railroad in December 1833, at $1,500 a year. The B&O paid him the same amount and for the next fifteen months or so, during the time he was working on the Thomas Viaduct, he made $8 a day, "as much as a Congressman," he said. In May 1835, the other company raised his salary to $3,000 a year. For a short time after he returned to the B&O, he again drew a double salary and a very high one for the time.

The Baltimore and Port Deposit Railroad reached Wilmington in 1837 and Philadelphia the following year. It then became known as the Philadelphia, Wilmington, and Baltimore Railroad, and for a dozen years, off and on, in an uneasy arrangement, it shared the B&O's downtown depot, bounded by Pratt, Light, Camden, and Charles streets. The PW&B had agreed to pay the B&O

$2,500 to use the B&O's tracks between the City Block and downtown and to occupy the depot's west side, but after the B&O complained of interruptions, delays, and track damage from the PW&B's four daily trains, the two companies reached a compromise whereby the PW&B moved its freight depot east of the Jones Falls and ran only two passenger trains a day into the joint depot. There were a few more squabbles, but until the PW&B opened its new President Street Station in 1850, passengers could transfer from one line to the other by walking across the platform. In the 1880's, the PW&B fell under the control of the Pennsylvania Railroad, later Penn-Central. The right-of-way is now owned by Amtrak as part of their main line between Washington and New York. Latrobe's original location through Canton was superseded by other routes in the city, but roughly from the city line in east Baltimore to the Susquehanna River, Northeast Corridor Amtrak passengers today ride on virtually the same alignment he first laid out in the 1830's.

John McCartney showed up again briefly in 1840 to work for Latrobe on the B&O line west of Harpers Ferry, where he and some others forfeited their contracts for violating the railroad's prohibition against whiskey.

32. In 1876, the B&O planned to straighten the Washington Branch between Halethorpe and Elkridge by rerouting the line and bypassing the Thomas Viaduct. The realignment would have followed pretty closely the lower route rejected in the 1830's. In the 1890's, the company acquired the right-of-way and began construction, but the project was postponed for economic reasons. It has been periodically revived since then, even as late as the 1960's, but the costs have always been prohibitive. In 1972, the railroad sold this right-of-way to the neighboring Seagram Distillery and shelved the project for good: Harwood, *Impossible Challenge*, pp. 243–45, 399.

CHAPTER 13

1. Van Deusen, *Jacksonian Era*, p. 66.
2. Swisher, *Taney*, p. 292.
3. B&O Rr. Minute Books, Mar. 11, 1834.
4. In 1842, the directors authorized Louis McLane, then the B&O president, to execute a deed covering the $1 million loan for the Washington Branch: ibid., Sept. 7, 1842.
5. John H. B. Latrobe Diaries, Mar. 24, 1834, MS 1677; Benjamin H. Latrobe, Jr., Journal, Mar. 24, 1834, Mrs. Gamble Latrobe Collection, MS 1638, Maryland Historical Society.
6. JHBL Diaries, Dec. 20, 1833.
7. Ibid., Jan. 9, 16, and Feb. 5–8, 12–15, 17–19, 1834. In 1836, the United States Bank offered the Pennsylvania legislature $2 million in cash in exchange for a charter, which was granted: Reginald Charles McGrane, *The Panic of 1837* (Chicago: University of Chicago Press, 1924), pp. 72–78.
8. JHBL Diaries, Mar. 24, 28, 1834.
9. BHL, Jr., Journal, May 27, 1834.
10. *Niles Register* 48: 418, quoted in Scharf, *History of Maryland*, 3: 179.
11. Browne, *Baltimore in the Nation*, p. 123.
12. George Brown to PET, B&O Rr. Minute Books, Feb. 3, 1834. My chief sources for the bank war and the B&O Rr.'s role in it are: Schlesinger, *Age of Jackson*, pp. 74–125; Swisher, *Taney*, pp. 207–85; Hammond, *Banks and Politics*, pp. 286–450; Scharf, *History of Maryland*, 3: 176–82; Browne, *Baltimore in the Nation*, pp. 119–25; and J. Semmes, *John H. B. Latrobe*, pp. 399–411. For the similarity between the stock manipulation and fraud at the Bank of Maryland and the recent savings and loan scandals, see Eric N. Berg, " 'Running Wild' at First Maryland Savings and Loan," *New York Times*, Apr. 18, 1988.

Historical opinion has traditionally been divided concerning the bank war. Hammond (*Banks and Politics*, p. 325) feels that the Jacksonians destroyed the monetary order provided by Biddle's Bank of the United States out of stupidity and self-interest and that succeeding administrations had to recreate its centralized banking functions through other institutions. Swisher (*Taney*) argues that a more balanced judgment "must take into account not merely so-called laws of money, but also the actions, the motives, the emotions, and perhaps the illusions of such men as Andrew Jackson and Nicholas Biddle . . . Roger B. Taney and Louis McLane, and a host of others who were involved in the conflict" (see esp. pp. 164–65).

John H. B. Latrobe, a minor participant, twice changed his mind on the issue. He started out in favor of the Bank of the United States, turned against it for political reasons when he became convinced that Taney's state banking system would work as well, and after it did not, again favored a U.S. Bank. "One may pay too dear for abstract principles in government," he said: JHBL Diaries, May 3, 1838.

13. Philip E. Thomas to John B. Morris, Feb. 4, 1834, Thomas Letterbooks.

14. PET to George Mackubin, Apr. 5, 1834, ibid.

15. B&O Rr. Minute Books, Apr. 7, 1834.

16. PET to Isaac McKim, Jan. 9, 1834; to John B. Morris, Feb. 4, 1834, Thomas Letterbooks.

17. PET to Charles S. Ridgely, Mar. 10, 1834, ibid.

18. PET to Clement Dorsey, Apr. 7, 1834, ibid.

19. BHL, Jr., Journal, Jan. 27, 1834. See also *Niles Register* 45 (Feb. 1, 1834): 382.

20. Belt, "a genteel young man of a speculating turn," according to Benjamin Latrobe (BHL, Jr., Journal, Oct. 18, 1833), began his association with the B&O by providing a right-of-way through his land and, in a pattern that was often repeated, became successively a company manager, a contractor, and the proprietor of a water station established near his store at the junction of the railroad and the turnpike. It is the site of present-day Beltsville.

21. Jessop was also a company manager, contractor, and water station proprietor. Prisoners at the Maryland House of Correction, located at what is now Jessup, Md., still refer to it as The Cut.

22. The area where the murders occurred is known to B&O trainmen today as Watson's Cut. It is a silent, eerie place. There are no houses nearby. The details of events at the shanty came mainly from the Frederick *Herald*, reprinted in *Niles Register* 47 (Dec. 20, 1834): 272; the Baltimore *Gazette*, Nov. 21, 1834; and the Baltimore *American*, Nov. 21, 22, 1834, and Jan. 31, 1835.

23. PET to John Contee, Sept. 30, 1834; PET to Amos A. Williams, Nov. 23, 1834, Thomas Letterbooks.

24. Baltimore *American*, Nov. 28, 1834.

25. PET to Amos A. Williams, Nov. 26, 1834, Thomas Letterbooks.

26. Baltimore *Republican*, ca. Dec. 2, 1834, B&O Rr. Pamphlets.

27. Carter, Van Horne, Formwalt, eds., *Journals of Benjamin Henry Latrobe*, 3: 71.

28. *Niles Register*, Sept. 5, 1835, quoted in Schlesinger, *Age of Jackson*, p. 210; see also Scharf, *History of Maryland*, 3:178.

29. Handbill, Aug. 9, 1835, Benjamin C. Howard Papers, MS 469, Maryland Historical Society.

30. BHL, Jr., Journal, Aug. 9, 1835.

31. "A Virginian and his Baltimore Diary," Dec. 22, 1835, John M. Gordon Papers, MS 1584, Maryland Historical Society.

32. *National Gazette* quoted in *Maryland Gazette*, Aug. 27, 1835.

33. White, *American Railroad Passenger Car*, pp. 10–14, 56–60.

34. *Niles Register* 49 (Sept. 19, 1835): 35.   35. Ibid., 48 (Aug. 29, 1835): 449.

36. Baltimore *Gazette*, Aug. 26, 1835.   37. BHL, Jr., Journal, Aug. 25, 1835.

CHAPTER 14

1. Davis, in *The Shenandoah*, p. 19, was unable to find an exact translation of the Indian term, but noted that "Daughter of the Stars" was commonly accepted by the people who lived in the valley.

2. Hahn, *Towpath Guide to the C&O Canal*, section 3, p. 4. By 1850, 3,000 people lived in the town, many of them workers at the federal arsenal. Harpers Ferry was a much different place after John Brown's abortive raid to free the slaves in 1859. The first man killed in the raid was the B&O Rr. station porter, Heyward Shepherd or Shepherd Heyward, a free black. During the Civil War, Stonewall Jackson's forces and northern armies fought for control of the strategic site, burned the

arsenal, and destroyed the railroad bridge several times over. Washington Roebling, of Brooklyn Bridge renown, was at Harpers Ferry as a Union soldier in 1861, helping to construct suspension bridges. "This is a mean little town," he said: McCullough, *The Great Bridge*, p. 158.

Things improved somewhat after the war, but Harpers Ferry never really recovered. The armory did not reopen. Major floods in 1870, 1878, 1889, 1924, 1936, and on up to the present, devastated the town. By the mid-twentieth century, when the National Park Service began a restoration program, the population had dwindled to several hundred. Harpers Ferry remains an important railway junction and river crossing, seeing perhaps a dozen trains a day. The B&O Rr. bridge there has fallen down, been blown up, or destroyed by fire or flood at least a dozen times since it first opened in 1836. The present one dates from 1931. Very little remains of the Virginius Island factories on the banks of the Shenandoah. The armory site on the Potomac has been obliterated by successive railroad improvements. The major industry today is tourists, who visit the Harpers Ferry National Monument.

3. The B&O's depot policy was still evolving at this time, but basically the railroad had two types, public and private. At major towns, such as Ellicotts Mills and Frederick, the company accepted free land for public depots, erected substantial buildings, and hired agents. Private depots were located in between the public ones. These were mills or small villages, horse relay stations, or locomotive water stops, with ambitious proprietors. After receiving a donation of land, the company usually agreed only to drop off and pick up goods. The private agent, appointed by the local community, was encouraged to construct his own building and operate the depot himself, in exchange for a percentage on the handling charges. This was two thirds on material forwarded, and one third on that received. The company's charge for receiving goods at Buckeystown, in the Monocacy Valley, was just 30 cents a ton, but in quantity and over time the fees added up, judging from the controversies that arose.

The Point of Rocks was a private depot. Jessup and Beltsville on the Washington Branch, and Sykesville, Ijamsville, Brunswick (formerly Berlin), and Weverton on the Old Main Line are other examples of Maryland localities whose growth, if not creation, was largely due to the railroad. Brunswick was literally a company town. Although they were often subject to abuses by the agent (as indeed were the public ones), the private depots were maintained until 1853 when the B&O reformed the system.

4. Benjamin H. Latrobe, Jr. to John H. B. Latrobe, Nov. 21, 1830, Mrs. Gamble Latrobe Collection, MS 1638, Maryland Historical Society.

5. B. H. Latrobe, Jr., Journal, Jan. 10, 1834, Mrs. Gamble Latrobe Collection.

6. *Niles Register* 44 (June 15, 1833): 263.

7. Maryland Heights (Harpers Ferry Narrows) is as confined now as it was in the 1830's. Near Sandy Hook, the railroad is still located between the remains of the C&O Canal and the county road, so close to the latter that ballast spills onto the pavement and a pedestrian runs his own gauntlet between the automobiles and the trains.

8. Philip E. Thomas to John Bruce, Aug. 21, 1833, Thomas Letterbooks.

9. PET to William Gunton (a C&O Canal director), Oct. 17, Dec. 21, 1833, ibid.

10. PET to William Gunton, Jan. 11, 1834, ibid.

11. BHL, Jr., Journal, July 6, 1834.

12. Ibid., Apr. 12, 1834.

13. PET to F. A. Schley, May 17, 1834, Thomas Letterbooks.

14. B&O Rr. Annual Report, 1833, p. 5. Virginia's James River and Kanawha improvements were first planned as a combined canal-railroad system, like Pennsylvania's. A few sections of the canal were built above Richmond before 1800. In the early nineteenth century, Benjamin H. Latrobe proposed a railroad to bring the coal from the nearby mines to the James River below the city. William Gibbs McNeill surveyed a route for a canal, or railroad, or both between the James and the Kanawha in 1827 when he was working on the B&O surveys. The James River and Kanawha Company was incorporated in 1832 and organized in 1835. It planned a hybrid trans-

portation system that would extend from Richmond to Covington by canal, from Covington to the Kanawha River by rail, and from there to the Ohio at Point Pleasant by an improved river navigation. Five years later, the canal was finished to Lynchburg. It was extended to Buchanan in 1851 and did a substantial business up until 1860. The State of Virginia and the company itself were divided over whether to continue the line by canal or rail, but by the 1870's, the Chesapeake and Ohio Railroad was under construction over the entire route. It is now a major component of the CSX Corporation.

15. Ithiel Town (1724–1844), an architect, patented his popular lattice truss bridge in 1820. Its top and bottom chords were separated by a diagonal web of timber.

16. BHL, Jr., Journal, Jan. 30, 1834, Nov. 14, 1835. As the engineer of the Philadelphia and Reading Railroad, Robinson in 1839 designed a powerful locomotive for that line, the Gowan and Marx. The following year, he turned down the job of civil engineer for the Russian railroads. In the late 1840's, he was president of the Richmond and Potomac Railroad and served as a consultant on the Bay Line of steamboats between Baltimore and Norfolk.

17. See PET to John Bruce, June 16, 1834, Thomas Letterbooks.

18. PET to John Bruce, July 9, 1834, ibid.

19. *Niles Register* 46 (May 3, 1834): 148.

20. George P. Grimsley, *The Baltimore and Ohio Railroad*, 1933 (XVI International Geological Congress), p. 15.

21. *Maryland Gazette*, Apr. 5, May 8, 10, June 7, 21, July 26, Aug. 16, 30, and Sept. 10, 27, 1832.

22. C&O Canal Annual Report, 1833, p. 1.

23. *Encyclopaedia Britannica*, 1910 edition.

24. Sanderlin, *Great National Project*, p. 95.

25. Ibid.

26. Asiatic cholera is caused by a curved bacillus, *Vibrio cholerae*, which infects fecal material and is most commonly spread by a contaminated water supply. It has a short incubation period, which accounts for the explosive nature of a cholera epidemic.

27. Baltimore *American*, Nov. 26, 1834.

28. J. P. Donleavy, *The Ginger Man* (New York: Dell, 1977), p. 14.

29. BHL, Jr., Journal, Feb. 1, 1834.

30. B&O Rr. Minute Books, Dec. 11, 1834.

31. Ibid., Aug. 4, 1834.

32. PET to Wever, Nov. 20, 23, 1834, Thomas Letterbooks.

33. Baltimore *Gazette*, Dec. 3, 1834. William Gwynn Jones acquired the *Gazette* in July 1834, from William Gwynn, who had published it for the past 21 years. Jones turned it into an inferior sheet, replacing much of its hard news with society matter and other filler material. His editorial career ended abruptly in May 1835, when he was caught stealing letters from the post office, where his special privileges had enabled him to make off with hundreds of items over the previous several months, including notes and drafts that netted him about $2,000. After Jones's arrest, William Gwynn again assumed control of the *Gazette*, and published it until December 1837. The following year, the *Gazette* was merged with the *Patriot*. Jones was also suspected of setting the February 1835 fires that destroyed the Atheneum, where John H. B. Latrobe had his office, and the Courthouse: Scharf, *Chronicles of Baltimore*, pp. 87–88, 481–82; Scharf, *History of Baltimore City and County*, 2: 609.

34. BHL, Jr., Journal, Dec. 22, 1834. The B&O's minimum 400-foot-radius curves (14 degrees) and maximum 30-feet-per mile grades (0.6 percent) throughout the twelve-mile distance from the Point of Rocks to Harpers Ferry were established by Maryland law in 1833 and approved as built by the engineers and officials of the canal and the railroad. Many physical changes have taken place in the area since then, especially in this century, as the canal expired and the railroad predominated, but enough of the original structures still exists to suggest how closely run was the early race between these chariots of empire.

Originally, at the narrow passes, the single track of the railroad followed the canal around the cliffs. The railroad was to be a minimum of 20 feet wide, the canal at least 40. In 1868, at the lower and upper Point of Rocks, tunnels big enough for a double-tracked rail line were built—the Point of Rocks and Catoctin tunnels. They were rebuilt in 1902, when the brick tunnel faces were added. In 1978, the tunnels were single-tracked to accommodate larger trains and a second line was added around the outside, again occupying the original railroad alignment and the partly filled in canal bed.

35. B&O Rr. Minute Books, Dec. 3, 1834.

36. B&O Rr. Annual Report, 1832, pp. 47, 52–53, 120–21; B&O Rr. Minute Books, Jan. 7, 1833.

37. B&O Rr. Annual Report, 1833, p. 33.

38. Evan Thomas echoed these sentiments about the same time in a letter to Edward Pease, of England's Stockton and Darlington Railway: *Railroad History* 90 (May 1954): 157–61.

39. B&O Rr. Annual Report, 1833, p. 33. The spur gear was placed on a separate shaft instead of on the driving axle as it was on the Atlantic, an arrangement that caused the gear cogs to break. The new design, which gave solid bearing to the cranks and countered the motion of the springs on the main axles, was adopted in subsequent Grasshopper engines. Ross Winans was involved in the conversion.

40. Unsigned, undated document, Winans Papers, MS 916, Maryland Historical Society. The probable author is John Elgar.

41. B&O Rr. Annual Report, 1834, pp. 25–26.

42. If the outer circumference of the wheel mold is made of iron rather than sand, the molten metal that touches it is cooled faster than the rest and crystallized, producing a hard, long-wearing surface. Phineas Davis accomplished the same thing by casting the rim of the wheel around a ring of cold wrought iron: B&O Rr. Annual Report, 1834, p. 38; White, *History of the American Locomotive*, p. 81. Edward Gillingham and Joseph W. and Edward Patterson, the sons of William Patterson, made the wheels, axles, and journal boxes for the B&O at this time.

43. Benjamin H. Latrobe, Jr., "Phineas Davis and the 'Grasshopper Engine,'" *Railroad Gazette*, Mar. 8, 1873, pp. 93–94. Of a dozen Grasshopper engines that were manufactured, a third were still running 40 years later. The *Railroad Gazette* editor observed: "We doubt whether there are any locomotives in existence which have done an equal amount of service."

44. BHL, Jr., Journal, Oct. 17, 1834.   45. Ibid., Sept. 11, 1834.

46. B&O Rr. Minute Books, Dec. 3, 1834.   47. Ibid., Sept. 1, 1835.

48. PET to John Bruce, Mar. 23, 1836, Thomas Letterbooks. His locomotive-building career cut short, Charles Reeder returned to fabricating marine steam engines. His son, Charles Reeder, Jr., had entered the firm in 1832 and five years later it became Charles Reeder and Sons. For the next 50 years, they provided the machinery for several ocean-going steamships and built hundreds of engines for river and bay steamers. The elder Reeder retired in 1842 to serve on a government commission aimed at the prevention of steam-boiler explosions. For information on Charles Reeder's early career, I am grateful to Baltimore historian Randolph W. Chalfant.

49. PET to Joshua Jones, Jan. 7, 1835, Thomas Letterbooks.

CHAPTER 15

1. Baltimore *American*, Feb. 13, 21, 1834.

2. Philip E. Thomas to J. P. Ingle, July 7, 1834, Thomas Letterbooks.

3. Baltimore *American*, Oct. 28, 1834, and Baltimore *Gazette*, Nov. 22, 1834.

4. PET to George C. Washington, Nov. 6, 1834, Thomas Letterbooks.

5. Unidentified, undated news clipping, ca. Nov. 1834, B&O Rr. Pamphlets.

6. The Pennsylvania Main Line of Internal Improvements, consisting of the Philadelphia and Columbia Rr., the Pennsylvania Canal, and the Allegheny Portage Railroad, opened officially in October 1834.

7. "Journal of the Internal Improvement Convention which assembled in the City of Baltimore on the 8th day of December, 1834," p. 36, B&O Rr. Pamphlets.

8. "Report to the Executive," B&O Rr. Minute Books, Jan. 6, 1835.

9. A Citizen of Maryland, *A Short History of the Public Debt of Maryland and of the Causes which Produced It*, 1845, p. 45.

10. C&O Canal General Committee of the Stockholders Report, June 15, 1835, B&O Rr. Pamphlets.

11. Williamport *Banner*, quoted in *Niles Register* 48 (Apr. 25, 1835): 129.

12. In 1867, the route Latrobe surveyed was used to build the B&O's Hagerstown Branch. This branch was abandoned in 1978.

13. *Niles Register* 48 (June 13, 1835): 25.

14. PET to John Bruce, Mar. 11, 1835, Thomas Letterbooks.

15. PET to G. B. Wager, Mar. 12, 1835, ibid.

16. PET to N. H. Swayne, Sept. 1, 1835, ibid.

17. Benjamin H. Latrobe, Journals, Sept. 18, 19, 1835, Mrs. Gamble Latrobe Collection, MS 1638, Maryland Historical Society.

18. Wernwag's Belvedere Bridge in Baltimore (1818) over the Jones Falls had combined timber arches and trusses. The bridge was rebuilt in 1819 and stood until it was demolished in 1880.

19. For discussions of the design and influence of the Schaffhausen bridge, built in 1758 at a cost of $40,000, see Tyrrell, *Bridge Engineering*, p. 124; and H. Smith, *World's Great Bridges*, p. 61.

20. BHL, Jr., Journal, June 15, 1835.

21. The engine may have been the George Washington, which was being tested on the Washington Branch the day before Davis was killed: B&O Rr. Annual Report, 1835, p. 11.

22. Ibid., p. 22.

23. *Niles Register* 49 (Sept. 12, 1835): 17.

24. Baltimore *American*, Nov. 12, 1835.

25. PET to George Sweeney, Nov. 13, 1835, Thomas Letterbooks.

26. John H. B. Latrobe Diaries, Nov. 7, 1835.

27. See the Baltimore *American*, issues of Dec. 11, 12, 14, 15, 17, 19, 1835, and Mar. 11 and 22, 1836, letters from "A Man of the Times." Kennedy was never identified as their author and there was no editorial comment until the issue of Dec. 29, 1835, when the newspaper endorsed his opinions. Five of the December letters appeared the following year in a pamphlet, "Letters of a Man of the Times to the Citizens of Baltimore," attributed to John Pendleton Kennedy.

28. B&O Rr. Minute Books, Dec. 17, 1835.

29. These estimates are from George C. Washington, C&O Canal Memorial to the General Assembly of Maryland, Jan. 27, 1836, B&O Rr. Pamphlets.

30. PET to J. W. McCulloh, Mar. 6, 1836, Thomas Letterbooks.

31. John H. B. Latrobe, "A History of My Connection with the Baltimore and Ohio Railroad Company," Latrobe Collection, MS 523, Maryland Historical Society.

32. Baltimore *American*, Mar. 11, 1836.

33. The four counties bypassed were Charles, St. Mary's, and Calvert on the western shore and Talbot on the eastern shore.

34. Baltimore *American*, Mar. 11, 1836.

35. Ibid.

36. Ibid., Mar. 10, 1836; *Niles Register* 50 (Mar. 12, 1836): 17.

37. Baltimore *American*, Mar. 11, 1836.

38. Baltimore *Chronicle*, Mar. 16, 1836. The Baltimore ordinance provided that when the railroad and city officials certified that no legal obstacles existed to prevent the company from completing the work "in an unbroken line from the city of Baltimore to the western waters," the city could subscribe to $3 million in B&O stock, borrow the money by creating a 6 percent city stock, and levy a property tax that, with the dividends, would pay the interest: *Laws and Ordinances, B&O Rr.*, p. 144–46.

39. BHL, Jr., Journal, Apr. 3, 1836.

40. Baltimore City Council report, "Baltimore and Ohio Rail Road Locomotive Engines," Mar. 23, 1836, quoted in B&O Rr. Annual Report, 1836, pp. 24–27.

41. Reverdy Johnson and John V. L. McMahon argued the case for the indemnity for several days before the General Assembly passed the bill.

42. Baltimore *American*, Mar. 30, 1836.   43. Baltimore *Gazette*, Apr. 1, 1836.

44. BHL, Jr., Journal, Apr. 2, 1836.   45. Baltimore *Gazette*, May 25, 1836.

46. Maryland House of Delegates, "Report of the minority of the Joint Committee appointed to inquire into the manner in which the loan of 1834, for completing the Chesapeake and Ohio Canal to Cumberland had been appropriated, etc.," May 29, 1836, B&O Rr. Pamphlets.

47. C&O Canal Co. Memorial to the Maryland legislature, May 27, 1836, C&O Annual Report, 1836, pp. 12–15.

48. Citizen of Maryland, "Short History of the Public Debt of Maryland," 1845, p. 34.

49. Baltimore *Gazette*, June 2, 1836.

50. Wheeling *Gazette*, June 10, 1836, quoted in Baltimore *American*, June 14, 1836. A curious sidelight on the Eight Million Bill was the role of another Merrick, Joseph I.—possibly related to the bill's protagonist, the chairman of the House ways and means committee. Joseph I. Merrick was a lawyer in Hagerstown and a delegate in 1825 to the Maryland General Assembly and in 1827 the first secretary of the state board of public works. During the 1833 legislative session, the B&O paid him $1,000, a healthy fee at the time, for his help in working out the compromise with the canal company. Two years later, the C&O gave him $3,000 for helping them get the $2 million loan from the state. And in 1836 each company agreed to pay Merrick $10,000 to arrange the passage of the Eight Million bill. The sum of $20,000 was a very large amount (it would be eight to ten times as much in today's money), and it could have had only one purpose: bribery. In January 1836, Thomas, a member of a special committee of B&O directors established "to employ such assistance as they may deem necessary towards obtaining the requisite funds," offered James W. McCulloh $5,000 to help pass a money bill in Annapolis. McCulloh said it was difficult, that he would need help, and demanded $10,000. Thomas and the committee agreed to retain McCulloh for $500, and to pay him $9,500 later on if the railroad obtained a $3 million state stock subscription. McCulloh offered the assignment and the contingency fee to Joseph I. Merrick, who accepted in March 1836. When the bill passed, the C&O paid its $10,000 but the B&O did not, saying that it was an ad hoc arrangement unsanctioned by the board. Very little of this information appeared in the company records until May 12, 1840, when a select committee investigating Merrick's claim for reimbursement made its report. Merrick filed suit in 1841; some arrangement was apparently made out of court, but Merrick continued to try to collect the whole sum at least up until 1853 (he died in 1854). See B&O Rr. Minute Books, May 12, 1840, and William Price, "To the President and Directors of the Baltimore and Ohio Railroad Co.," Oct. 26, 1853, B&O Rr. Pamphlets.

51. PET to Richard Potts, May 23, 1836, Thomas Letterbooks.

52. B&O Rr. Minute Books, June 30, 1836.   53. Ibid., July 5, 1836.

54. BHL, Jr., Journals, May 27, 1836.   55. Ibid., Aug. 10, 1836.

56. Ibid., Mar. 6, 1837. The Potomac Viaduct was listed as unfinished in the B&O Rr. Annual Report in October 1836. The earliest notice of its completion was Benjamin H. Latrobe's visit in January 1837. The company never gave an official cost for the structure.

57. B&O Rr. Minute Books, May 3, 1837. The investigating committee's major report appears in the Minute Books, May 30, 1837. Skewbacks are the inclined "steps" or bearings at the tops of the piers that receive the bridge trusses and absorb the horizontal thrust from the arches or, in this case, inclined struts.

58. B&O Rr. Minute Books, Oct. 4, 1837. In September 1844 and again in March 1845, the failure of some of the wooden arches of the Harpers Ferry bridge owing to defective workmanship and rotten timber caused accidents that injured crewmen and precipitated engines and cars into the river. In 1851, the railroad began to rebuild the bridge in iron, and replaced the 124-foot Winchester span with an iron Bollman truss. By 1870, the entire wooden superstructure of the Potomac Viaduct

had been rebuilt with similar trusses, erected on the same piers. This bridge was carried away by a flood in 1936. Besides the piers, its huge abutment and wing walls are still visible on the Harpers Ferry side of the river. In 1894, the B&O Rr. tunneled Maryland Heights and built a new bridge on a new alignment with easier curves, which today carries the Valley Branch trains. Then in 1931, the mouth of the tunnel was widened and the B&O's present main line bridge was constructed, easing the curvature still further. The B&O Railroad crossing is on the National Register. As each new railroad bridge was added, the older one was converted to partial highway use. The traditional road crossing at Harpers Ferry, which dated back to the Wagers in the 1830's, finally ended with the construction of new highway bridges on new alignments over the Potomac and Shenandoah rivers in the 1940's. The old Shenandoah highway bridge to Harpers Ferry, which dated to about 1885, was swept away in one of the subsequent floods; its piers remain. On the Maryland side, the county road, after passing through Sandy Hook, now follows the old railroad alignment around the cliff.

CHAPTER 16

1. J. Semmes, *John H. B. Latrobe*, pp. 359–63.

2. Philip E. Thomas to Richard Potts, Jan. 9, 1837, Thomas Letterbooks; *Niles Register* 51 (Dec. 31, 1836): 274.

3. J. W. Patterson to McLane, May 6, 1837, Thomas Letterbooks.

4. Munroe, *McLane*, p. 448; Swisher, *Taney*, p. 179.

5. Augustine Herrman received title to the land in 1660 from Lord Baltimore in exchange for drawing a map of his patron's domain in the new world. The original Bohemia Manor comprised some 20,000 acres: Scharf, *History of Maryland*, 1: 429.

6. Munroe, *McLane*, p. 267.

7. Catherine M. McLane, "Louis McLane of Delaware, 1786–1856," typescript, McLane-Fisher Papers, MS 2403, Maryland Historical Society.

8. Quoted in Swisher, *Taney*, pp. 162–63.

9. The State of New Jersey took over the Morris Canal in 1922 and later sold off most of the property: *New York Times*, Apr. 9, 1989.

10. Louis McLane, "Report of the Executive Officers of the [B&O Rr. Co.] on the subject of retrenchment," May 4, 1842, B&O Rr. Pamphlets.

11. In his review of the 1833 canal-railroad compromise, Sanderlin, in *Great National Project*, pp. 102–13, does not mention the B&O's stipulation regarding the Potomac route. He dismisses, as its usual deceptive tactics, the railroad's consideration of an alternative route to the Ohio River and perhaps to New Orleans via the Winchester & Potomac Rr. and Virginia's James River and Kanawha improvements. "The railroad even revived talk of abandoning its road to the West in favor of a line down the Shenandoah Valley," Sanderlin says (p. 103), and he adds in a note: "It seemed to be a routine proposal used by the railroad to lull the canal into a sense of security and to demonstrate to the [Maryland General] Assembly the railroad's selfless efforts to accommodate its adversary. There is no evidence that the railroad seriously considered the project at this time."

The record shows that the B&O between 1833 and 1836 did indeed give serious consideration to this alternate route; however, Philip E. Thomas was so fixed on the Potomac alignment as the only possible one that he could not accept the middle ground beyond Harpers Ferry that lay between the unattainable preferred route and the remote secondary one. The intermediate route, a line across Virginia to Cumberland, was the one the company adopted shortly after Thomas resigned. It had been available to the railroad all the time. See Reizenstein, *Economic History B&O Rr.*, p. 36. On the Hagerstown route, see Martinsburg, Virginia, *Gazette*, May 9, 1839, and Williams, *History of Washington County, Maryland*, 1: 228.

12. *Laws and Ordinances, B&O Rr.*, p. 58.

13. B&O Rr. Annual Report, 1835, p. 7.

14. *Laws and Ordinances, B&O Rr.*, p. 79.

15. "Report of the Joint Committee of the City Council on Internal Improvement," ca. Mar. 15, 1836, B&O Rr. Pamphlets.

16. "Report of the General Committee of the Stockholders of the [C&O Canal Co.], Richard S. Coxe, Chairman," July 18, 1836, B&O Rr. Pamphlets.

17. [A Citizen of Maryland], "A Short History of the Public Debt of Maryland, and of the Causes which Produced It," 1845, p. 45.

18. Scharf, *History of Maryland*, 3: 208. See also Sanderlin, *Great National Project*, pp. 173–75.

19. The private agreement gave the C&O engineers the right to determine the slope of the river walls of the canal wherever it paralleled the railroad and required the B&O's permanent bridges to be at least seventeen feet above the waterline.

20. *Laws and Ordinances, B&O Rr.*, p. 82.

21. George Peabody to Gwynn Harris, Jan. 12, 1837, quoted in Franklin Parker, "An Abstract of George Peabody, Founder of Modern Philanthropy," Ph.D. diss., Peabody College for Teachers, 1956, p. 166.

22. B&O Rr. Annual Report, 1835, p. 41.

23. Benjamin H. Latrobe, Jr., Journal, Aug. 1, 1836. This spot may have been the notorious "Shades of Death," a dark pine grove on the National Road between Frostburg and Grantsville, Md., that was a favorite haunt for highwaymen. The mail stage had been robbed there two years earlier.

24. B&O Rr. Annual Report, 1836, p. 60.

25. Jonathan Knight to Philip E. Thomas, Jan. 18, 1837, Thomas Letterbooks.

26. B&O Rr. Annual Report, 1837, p. 27.

27. McLane to Knight, Nov. 9, 1837, Thomas Letterbooks.

28. B&O Rr. Annual Report, 1837, p. 3.

29. Parker, *Peabody*, p. 27.

30. McMaster, *History of People of the U.S.*, 6: 407.

31. Quoted in McGrane, *Panic of 1837*, p. 44.

32. Message of Governor Francis Thomas to the Maryland legislature: *Niles Register* 63 (Jan. 14, 1843): 314–15.

33. J. W. Patterson, B&O Rr. Annual Report, 1836, p. 15.

34. William Brown to George Peabody, June 26, 1837, quoted in M. Hidy, *Peabody*, p. 87. The major factor in rescuing the Browns was a $10 million loan from the Bank of England.

35. McGrane, *Panic of 1837*, p. 130. The C&O Canal riots occurred in January and April 1836, May and June 1837, and January, May, July, and August 1838.

36. McMaster, *History of People of the U.S.*, 6: 404.

37. Swisher, *Taney*, p. 344.

38. See the description by Knight in B&O Rr. Annual Report, 1836, pp. 22–23.

39. "Locomotive steam engines adapted to undulating and curved roads," July 29, 1837, Winans Papers, MS 916, Maryland Historical Society.

40. B&O Rr. Minute Books, Sept. 11, 1837.

41. William Norris started as a dry goods merchant in Baltimore and went on to locomotives, but he was a promoter rather than a businessman, and after suffering severe financial losses during the Panic of 1837 he was forced to close his factory for a time. In the spring of 1844, William was eased out of the business by his brother Richard, formerly a Baltimore wholesale druggist, who, with a third brother, Septimus, rescued the firm. Richard was a manager and Septimus, an engineer. Under Richard's guidance, the Norris Locomotive Works in the 1850's was the largest producer of engines in the world: White, *History of the American Locomotive*, p. 456; John H. White, Jr., "Once the Greatest of Builders: The Norris Locomotive Works," *Railroad History* 150 (Spring 1984): 17–57.

42. See the Baltimore *American*, Jan. 23, 1838, for Buchanan and Emory's report to the Governor of Maryland, and ibid., Feb. 12, 1838, for McLane's testimony to the Ways and Means

Committee of the Maryland House of Delegates. See also *Laws and Ordinances, B&O Rr.*, p. 100.

43. "Report upon the Surveys for the Extension of the [B&O Rr.] from its present termination near Harpers Ferry, on the Potomac, to Wheeling and Pittsburg, on the Ohio River," 1838, B&O Rr. Pamphlets.

44. Ibid., pp. 6–7.

45. Ibid., p. 88.

46. Ibid., p. 121.

CHAPTER 17

1. On summer vacation, the youthful Kennedy traveled by horseback from Baltimore to Virginia, "first to Martinsburg or The Bower, where my uncle Dandridge lived, and thence into the mountains . . . the perfection of enjoyment," he said. "I have always had such a vivid relish for country scenery, such a keen perception of the beauty of the landscape, that my delight in these journeys was of the highest artistic character, and for years afterward I could sketch pretty well, from memory alone, the scenes I had witnessed." H. Tuckerman, *Kennedy*, in *The Collected Works*, 10:45.

2. Ibid., pp. 71–80.

3. Quoted in J. Semmes, *John H. B. Latrobe*, p. 431.

4. "Report to the House of Delegates of Maryland by the Committee on Internal Improvement," etc., Feb. 11, 1822, B&O Rr. Pamphlets.

5. In 1838, Kennedy was elected to his first term in Congress and in 40 days wrote *Rob of the Bowl*, his best novel and most successful attempt to blend fiction and history. By that time he and Washington Irving were friends; they subsequently took to calling each other "Geoffrey Crayon" and "Horse-Shoe." Kennedy's literary career continued with the publication in 1840 of *Quodlibet*, a political roman à clef based on the "bank war." Ten years later, he published the two-volume *Life of William Wirt*, a well-documented but rather dull biography of the U.S. attorney general. This work sold well and went through six editions.

Looking back in 1854, Kennedy thought he should have worked harder at his writing. By that time he had finished his third term in Congress, returned to the Maryland House of Delegates for a single term (as speaker), and served as secretary of the navy. Even his most enthusiastic admirers considered him a dilettante in his legal, literary, and political careers, yet few of his contemporaries made as great a contribution to America's emerging national literature or were such reliable political witnesses to the times. Kennedy's papers, which he left to the Peabody Institute in Baltimore along with his 5,000-volume library, fill 130 manuscript volumes and 27 microfilm rolls.

6. "Trip to Richmond with Louis McLane and Spear Nicholas on the affairs of the Rail Road," March 1838, John Pendleton Kennedy Journals, George Peabody Library of the Johns Hopkins University, Baltimore.

7. McLane admitted routing the B&O through Virginia to avoid a connection with the Franklin Railroad at Hagerstown in "Address of Mr. McLane, President, to the Stockholders of the [B&O Rr. Co.] at their meeting on the 5th of April, 1847, respecting a proposed subscription to the capital of the [B&O Rr. Co.]," p. 11, B&O Rr. Pamphlets.

8. McLane's proposed compromise was that the B&O would spend $600,000 to build the Hagerstown branch and a railroad connection across the Potomac River at Hancock, if Washington County paid the balance: B&O Rr. Minute Books, Feb. 6, 1839. The Hagerstown *Torch Light* reflected the town's frustration in an article reprinted in the Martinsburg, Virginia, *Gazette*, May 23, 1839. Under the 1841 Maryland law, the state reserved the right to require the B&O, after it reached the Ohio River, to construct the Hagerstown branch.

9. B&O Rr. Minute Books, June 19, 1839. The city and state stock subscriptions entitled each jurisdiction to appoint an additional six railroad directors; as factions developed, politics began to play a major role in boardroom decisions.

10. Ibid., July 3, 1839.

11. Louis McLane to Joshua Bates, Apr. 23, 1839, "Letters Received, General, 1833–1839," Baring Brothers & Co. Papers, National Archives of Canada (NAC).

12. McLane's commission of one-half of one percent was double the state agents' commission. Buchanan and Emory would have split $20,000 if they had sold the entire $8 million bond package. The railroad had offered them a total advance of $6,000.

13. B&O Rr. Minute Books, July 10, 1839.

14. R. M. Blatchford to Joshua Bates, Aug. 24, 1839, "Letters Received, General, 1839–1841," Baring Brothers & Co. Papers, NAC. Two years before, McLane had introduced Blatchford to Bates as the confidential agent of the Morris Canal and Banking Co.

15. Munroe, *McLane*, p. 480.

16. The British lionized Peabody, granted him the rare privilege of the freedom of the City of London, and when he died in 1869, wanted to bury him in Westminster Abbey, the highest honor that can be bestowed on a British subject and one never before accorded to an American. Peabody's will, however, said that his body was to be returned to the United States. This was done, after a period of lying-in-state at Westminster Abbey.

17. Parker, *Peabody*, p. 2.

18. Peabody in London was an imposing figure—tall and well dressed, formal and reserved—and his business was his life. "The prince of merchant princes" lived unostentatiously at a private club in Regent Street, carried his sandwich to the office in a metal lunchbox, and "lacked rest, ate the bread of watchfulness, and worked till nine o'clock at night," according to a friend (quoted in Parker, *Peabody*, p. 66). In the evenings he often dined at Morley's Hotel in Trafalgar Square with his friend Henry Stevens, a rare book dealer from Vermont. "How are books today?" he would say to Stevens, as a commodities broker might ask the price of wheat (quoted in Kenin, *Return to Albion*, p. 93).

19. Sanderlin, *Great National Project*, p. 133.

20. "Letters Received, General, 1839–1841," Baring Brothers & Co. Papers, NAC.

21. M. Hidy, *Peabody*, pp. 160, 170.

22. Ibid., p. 163.

23. Louis McLane to Louis McLane, Jr., Sept. 28, 1839, McLane-Fisher Papers, MS 2403, Maryland Historical Society.

24. R. Hidy, *House of Baring*, p. 83.

25. M. Hidy, *Peabody*, p. 157. Baring Brothers & Co., Ltd., is still located at 8 Bishopsgate, but in a modern, 20-story building.

26. Ziegler, *Sixth Great Power*, p. 85.

27. R. Hidy, *House of Baring*, p. 4.

28. B&O Rr. Minute Books, Feb. 14, 1843.

29. R. Hidy, *House of Baring*, p. 281; M. Hidy, *Peabody*, p. 167.

30. *Niles Register* 73 (Jan. 1, 1848): 284. Peabody was not the only one stuck with Mississippi bonds. Many were held by middle-class British investors. The Peabody Trust Fund in 1914 retaliated by returning, as its contribution to education in Mississippi, some of the state's worthless securities. The London bondholders continued to try to collect, as they had since 1868, on $7 million worth of Mississippi bonds issued in 1841. Finally, in 1989, they gave up. With interest, the debt had ballooned to more than $10 billion. The Mississippi state treasurer announced his intention to sell the bonds in his possession as collector's items. The proceeds were to be used to fund scholarships: Baltimore *Sun*, Mar. 12, 1989.

31. B&O Rr. Minute Books, Nov. 27, 1839.

32. B&O Rr. Annual Report, 1839, p. 12.

33. From 1839 to 1840, Maryland's interest payments on its internal improvement loans more than doubled while its receipts from the various canal and railroad companies declined by almost two-thirds: Hanna, *Financial History of Maryland*, p. 100.

34. *Niles Register* 57 (Jan. 4, 1840): 290–93.

35. "Report of the Select Committee . . ." B&O Rr. Minute Books, Jan. 13, 1840.

36. Baltimore *Sun*, Jan. 21, 1840; John Pendleton Kennedy Journal, Jan. 26, 1840, George Peabody Library of the Johns Hopkins University.

37. See, for example, Buchholz, *Governors of Maryland*, p. 130.

CHAPTER 18

1. J. Knight and Benj. H. Latrobe, "Report upon the plan of construction of several of the Principal Railroads in the northern and middle states . . ." 1838, pp. 46–47, B&O Rr. Pamphlets.

2. Benjamin H. Latrobe, Jr., to H. R. Hazlehurst, Mar. 1, 1838, Letters to Assistant Engineers, B&O Rr. Museum.

3. All railroads were concerned about the preservation of wood, and Latrobe frequently discussed the matter with engineers of other lines. One process, called Kyanizing, after its inventor, involved saturating the timber with a corrosive sublimate, but Latrobe was as concerned with the health of the workers engaged in the process as he was in its effect on the wood. Other methods involved soaking the timber in coal tar (creosote), sulphate of iron, or limewater.

4. The negotiations to acquire the right-of-way through Carroll's Doughoregan Manor began amicably but ended in claims and arbitration. "The business is not a pleasant one, and I do not want to have any occasion for another discussion of it," Philip E. Thomas told Caspar W. Wever, Jan. 28, 1832, Thomas Letterbooks. Wever's section of the B&O Rr. Annual Report, 1832, p. 72, notes the railroad's payment to Carroll.

5. B&O Rr. Minute Books, Oct. 5, 1833.

6. BHL, Jr., to Charles W. Hood, General Letterbook no. 1, B&O Rr. Museum.

7. BHL, Jr., to Knight, July 12, 1838, ibid. Elysville, twenty railroad miles from Baltimore, was beautifully situated in a bend of the river framed by a bowl of hills curving away to the west. The town, founded in 1819, took its name from the owners. Later on in the 1860's, it was known as Alberton and in this century as Daniels. One hundred years ago, the mill property consisted of 1,800 acres, a four-story granite main building with a bell tower (the mill housed 228 looms and 9,000 spindles), a company store, school, churches, and 70 brick dwellings for the millworkers. The manager's mansion was fronted with ornamental shade trees, rare flowers, and fountains. The town lasted until 1968. In that year, the owners of Daniels, in a final act of paternalism, destroyed the 118 substandard workers' dwellings rather than improve them. In 1972, Hurricane Agnes effectively ended the life of the mill. Today, only the bucolic setting and a few structures remain of this nineteenth-century Brigadoon. The 111-year-old Daniels Community Band, however, still rehearses on Monday nights: Scharf, *History of Baltimore City and County*, 1: 408–9; Fisher, *Country Walks Near Baltimore*, pp. 37–44; "Upbeat with the Down Beat," Robert A. Erlandson, Baltimore *Sun*, Dec. 9, 1990.

8. BHL, Jr., to Charles W. Hood, Apr. 27, 1838, General Letterbook no. 1.

9. BHL, Jr., to Caleb Moore, Aug. 2, 1838, Letters to Assistant Engineers.

10. BHL, Jr., to James Murray, Mar. 25, 1839, ibid.

11. Tyrell, *Bridge Engineering*, pp. 140–41; Harwood, *Impossible Challenge*, p. 38. The wooden superstructures have disappeared, but the bridge abutments and piers, exhibiting beautiful stonework, are still plainly visible at Daniels. The present railroad alignment dates from the turn of the century; the original one can still be traced on the Patapsco River's south side.

12. BHL, Jr., to John Alter, Philadelphia, Aug. 2, 1838, General Letterbook no. 1.

13. "George Washington's Patowmack Canal," *National Geographic*, June 1987, p. 751.

14. Baltimore *American*, Apr. 25, 1826.

15. Drinker, *Tunneling*, pp. 102–4.

16. B&O Rr. Minute Books, Dec. 11, 1839.

17. In 1902, as part of another campaign to straighten out the Old Main Line, the B&O once again rebuilt the sections at Elysville (Daniels) and at Parrs Spring Ridge (Mount Airy). At the

latter place, the present tunnel under the ridge follows essentially the alignment of the old inclined planes. The 1838 route avoiding the planes remained in service for much of the twentieth century serving the town of Mount Airy, which grew up around Henry Buzzard's depot complex. This line is now abandoned, but most of it, including the deep cut at the summit excavated by William Slater and his men, can still be traced. The stone-arched, brick-lined bridge at the eastern end dates from the 1902 realignment.

18. In the system of locomotive classification by wheel arrangement devised by Frederic M. Whyte in 1900, "the first numeral represents the number of leading wheels; the second figure the number of driving wheels; and the final figure the number of trailing wheels": White, *History of the American Locomotive*, p. 33.

19. Ibid., pp. 34, 449–50; Clark and Colburn, *Recent Practice in the Locomotive Engine*, pp. 49–50; J. Knight and Benj. H. Latrobe, "Report Upon the Locomotive Engines . . ." 1838, pp. 32–33, B&O Rr. Pamphlets.

20. BHL, Jr., to C. M. Thurston, July 2, 1838, General Letterbook no. 1.

21. BHL, Jr., to Jonathan Knight, June 17, 1839, ibid. The B&O was remarkably successful in being able to operate locomotives over a 755-foot elevation with grades of 80 feet per mile, or 1.5 percent, but they were not the first to have done so, despite the claims of some local newspapers. That honor belonged to Isaac Ridgeway Trimble, the B&O's former topographical engineer. Trimble located various sections of the Baltimore and Susquehanna Railroad in the broken country on either side of the Maryland-Pennsylvania line using grades of 84 feet per mile, 1.6 percent, to overcome an elevation of 800 feet. He began running trains over them in the fall of 1838 when he was chief engineer of that railroad. Trimble described his triumph in a personal memoir owned by his great-grandson, William C. Trimble, of Brooklandville, Md., and in a printed address to the annual meeting of the Association of Graduates at West Point around 1884. The claim of some Baltimore newspapers in June 1839 that the grades at Parrs Spring Ridge were the steepest yet crossed by locomotives was disputed on Trimble's behalf by the York *Gazette* in *Niles Register* 56 (June 22, 1839): 263.

22. BHL, Jr., to H. R. Hazelhurst [sic], Nov. 15, 1838, Letters to Assistant Engineers.

23. Ibid.

24. Boydville, Faulkner's plantation-style mansion in Martinsburg, which Lincoln spared from being burned by Union troops during the Civil War, is now an inn.

25. BHL, Jr., to Charles J. Faulkner, Feb. 5, 1839, General Letterbook no. 1.

26. Benjamin Henry Latrobe, the architect, supposedly brought the first theodolite from England to the United States. The theodolite and the transit were both goniometers, or angle-measuring devices. Later on in the nineteenth century, their various features were combined in one instrument, the "transit-theodolite," or engineer's transit. "The Engineer's Transit is the most useful and universal of all surveying instruments. Besides measuring horizontal and vertical angles it will read distances by means of the magnetic needle . . . and do levelling by means of a bubble attached to the telescope. It is therefore competent to perform all kinds of service . . . and is sometimes called the 'universal instrument.'" Johnson, *Theory and Practice of Surveying*, p. 83.

27. Deborah Jean Warner, "William J. Young: From Craft to Industry in a Skilled Trade," *Pennsylvania History* 52 (April 1985): 53–68.

28. *American Railroad Journal* 3 (Sept. 13, 1834): 576.

29. BHL, Jr., to J. Young, Aug. 14, 1839, General Letterbook no. 1.

30. BHL, Jr., Journal, Jan. 25, 1836, Mrs. Gamble Latrobe Collection, MS 1638, Maryland Historical Society.

31. BHL, Jr., to Steele, Feb. 18, 1839, Letters to Assistant Engineers.

32. Martinsburg *Gazette*, July 18, 1839.

33. BHL, Jr., to Knight, Apr. 20, 1839, General Letterbook no. 1. Hazlehurst originally ran the alignment to the Potomac near Little Georgetown, then around the mountain by the river. In the final location, however, he shifted it through the gap with a couple of short tunnels (which later became deep excavations) and brought the line back down to the Potomac near Fort Frederick. In

1903, the railroad constructed a line that basically followed Hazlehurst's original alignment; it is now known as the "low grade."

34. BHL, Jr., to Steele, Apr. 23, 1839, Letters to Assistant Engineers.

35. Martinsburg *Gazette*, July 18, 1839.

36. BHL, Jr., to William Matthews, May 30, 1839, Letters to Assistant Engineers.

37. BHL, Jr., to Steele, June 13, 1839, ibid.

38. BHL, Jr., to Atkinson, Aug. 14, 1839, ibid.

39. BHL, Jr., to Edmund Draper, Aug. 19, 1839, General Letterbook no. 1.

40. BHL, Jr., to Albert M. Lea, Sept. 19, 1839, Letters to Assistant Engineers.

41. BHL, Jr., to Lea, Oct. 23, 1839, ibid.

42. BHL, Jr., to Steele, Nov. 9, 1839, ibid.

CHAPTER 19

1. Benjamin H. Latrobe, Jr., to Garvin & Johnson and John Dougherty, Oct. 4, 1839; to Henry Wilton, Oct. 5, 1839, General Letterbook no. 1, B&O Rr. Museum.

2. Work was suspended owing to a lack of funds for five years, between 1842 and 1847, and the Paw Paw Tunnel was not finally completed until 1850, at a total cost of over $600,000.

3. Martinsburg *Gazette*, Aug. 15, 1839.

4. The riots were described in *Niles Register* 57 (Sept. 14, 1839): 37.

5. Cumberland *Phoenix Civilian*, Sept. 7, 21, 1839.

6. John Rudolph Niernsee, trans. E. Albrecht, "Continuation of my Diary from May 1st, 1838 till," typescript, vertical file, Maryland Historical Society. For additional information on Niernsee, I am grateful to Baltimore historian Randolph W. Chalfant.

7. The prefabricated iron roofs that Niernsee designed a few years later for B&O depot buildings in Washington and Frederick are the earliest known examples of composite iron roofs in the United States. In 1848, Niernsee and James Crawford Neilson, another B&O engineer who began as a $3-a-day draftsman and had prepared the maps and profiles for Latrobe's massive survey report of 1838, left the railroad to form an architectural firm that for a time was the largest and most successful in Baltimore. Niernsee and Neilson designed the B&O's Camden Station and several other important buildings in the city.

8. BHL, Jr., "Description of the proposed Route thro Government grounds at Harpers Ferry Va. Submitted to Cols. Lucas & Talcott, Sept. 19th, 1838," loose correspondence, B&O Rr. Museum.

9. The B&O Railroad's river wall has been featured in numerous illustrations of Harpers Ferry over the past two centuries. Nature has reclaimed most of the site, but the lower end of the wall near the old bridge abutments is still plainly visible.

10. Frederick *Herald* quoted in the Hagerstown *Herald of Freedom*, Nov. 20, 1839.

11. Washington *National Intelligencer* quoted in *Niles Register* 57 (Jan. 11, 1840): 311; Cumberland *Phoenix Civilian*, Jan. 10, 1840.

12. Cumberland *Civilian*, Jan. 18, 1840. (The newspaper dropped the word *Phoenix* from its title with this issue.)

13. Hagerstown *Mail*, Feb. 14, 1840.

14. BHL, Jr., to Knight, Feb. 8, 1840, General Letterbook no. 1.

15. BHL, Jr., to Charles Odell, Oct. 2, 1840, ibid.

16. B&O Rr. Minute Books, July 24, 1840.

17. Ibid.

18. Baltimore *Sun*, July 24, 1840.

19. Baring Brothers to President, B&O Rr., June 30, 1840, Letters Received, British North America, Baring Brothers & Co. Papers, National Archives of Canada (NAC).

20. B&O Rr. Annual Report, 1840, p. 9.

21. Ibid., p. 12.

22. *Niles Register* 59 (Jan. 9, 1841): 293.

23. *Laws and Ordinances, B&O Rr.*, p. 112.

24. B&O Rr. to Baring Bros., Mar. 8, 1841, Letters Received, General, Baring Brothers & Co. Papers, NAC.

25. Joshua Bates to Humphrey St. John Mildmay, May 13, 1841, ibid.

26. BHL, Jr., to Herman Stump & Co., July 5, 1841, General Letterbook no. 1.

27. B&O Rr. Annual Report, 1841, p. 17.

28. John S. Gittings to Baring Bros. & Co., Nov. 27, 1841, Letters Received, General, Baring Brothers & Co. Papers, NAC. Gittings was a banker, Baltimore homebuilder, and future B&O Rr. director.

29. *Niles Register* 61 (Jan. 15, 1842): 305–7.

30. B&O Rr. Minute Books, Mar. 2, 1842.

31. John M. Gordon, "An Account of the First Carnival in the City of Washington . . ." 1871, pp. 8, 24, B&O Rr. Pamphlets, Evergreen House, the Johns Hopkins University.

32. *Laws and Ordinances, B&O Rr.*, p. 158.

33. Latrobe placed Knight among the first rank of American civil engineers and recalled his longtime associate's knowledge of basic mathematics, his enlightened views on trade, agriculture, and politics, and his sarcastic humor in Stuart, *Lives and Works*, pp. 239–42.

34. "Report of the Chief Engineer of the Balt. & Ohio Rail Road Co. on the transportation of passengers and tonnage on that road," Mar. 31, 1842, p. 24, B&O Rr. Pamphlets.

35. Louis McLane, "Report of the Executive Officers of the [B&O Rr. Co.] on the subject of retrenchment," May 4, 1842, pp. 7–9, ibid.

36. Martinsburg, founded in 1778, was the Berkeley County seat and a thriving Shenandoah Valley market town when the B&O Railroad surveyors first arrived in 1836. By 1852, Martinsburg had become a flour and woolen manufacturing center, dining stop, and railroad town complete with an engine house and machine shops. The original shops were destroyed during the Civil War; the remaining shop buildings were built shortly after the war.

37. Martinsburg *Gazette*, May 26, 1842.

38. B&O Rr. Annual Report, 1842, pp. 12, 22.

39. Baltimore *American*, Nov. 5, 1842.

40. Stonewall Jackson's forces burned the Colonnade Bridge during the Civil War. It was eventually replaced by solid masonry.

41. The Confederates destroyed the stone-arch bridge at Back Creek in 1861. The next year, the Union Army built a blockhouse on the dark cliffs overlooking the bridge and the tracks. Its outline is still visible. Some of the original masonry can also still be seen in the bridge abutments along this portion of the Old Main Line. Iron superstructures were substituted for the wooden ones in the nineteenth century, and these in turn were replaced by stone arches or steel plate girders in the twentieth.

42. Cumberland *Civilian*, Nov. 10, 1842.

CHAPTER 20

1. Thomas and Williams, *History of Allegany County*, 1: 153.

2. Ibid., p. 182.

3. Benjamin H. Latrobe to John H. B. Latrobe, Feb. 18, 1820, Mrs. Gamble Latrobe Collection, MS 1638, Maryland Historical Society.

4. The original route of the National Road from Baltimore to Wheeling can still be traced for most of its 265-mile length by following Maryland Route 144 or U.S. Route 40.

5. United States Road in Ohio under the superintendency of C. W. Wever, Annual Report, Nov. 18, 1828, B&O Rr. Pamphlets.

6. B&O Rr. Minute Books, May 20, 1830.

7. John H. B. Latrobe Diaries, June 7, 1835, Latrobe Collection, MS 523, Maryland Historical Society.

8. Baltimore *American*, Nov. 11, 1835.

9. Parkman, *France and England in North America*, 2: 986.

10. My main sources for the early lumbering and coal industries in western Maryland were: Kline, Jr., *Tall Pines and Winding Rivers*; Gutheim, *The Potomac*, pp. 217–20; W. Clark et al., *Coals of Maryland*, pp. 221–24, 513–18; and Stegmaier et al., *Allegany County*, p. 121.

11. John H. Alexander and Philip T. Tyson, "George's Creek Coal and Iron Company," 1836, George Peabody Library of the Johns Hopkins University, Baltimore.

12. Alexander, the most interesting member of the group, was just 24 years old when he started out as a civil engineer with the Baltimore and Susquehanna Railroad. He was a graduate of Saint John's College, Annapolis, and very versatile—a trained mathematician, a fluent linguist, and a budding author who would produce works on such diverse subjects as the Maryland iron industry (1840) and the Delaware Indian language. He once spent a month in a brickyard learning to make bricks and he took this same experiential approach in western Maryland. When Alexander died in 1867, he was buried according to his instructions at midnight by torchlight at St. Paul's Cemetery, Baltimore.

13. J. T. Ducatel and J. H. Alexander, "Report on the Projected Survey of the State of Maryland . . ." 1834, p. 34.

14. Of the five Maryland coal basins, Georges Creek is the only one that contains, to any extent, the Pittsburgh Seam, so designated in 1856. There are other valuable coal seams in this basin, but because of its extent and accessibility, the Pittsburgh Seam was exploited first and provided most of the coal shipped from Georges Creek during the nineteenth century, an estimated 132 million tons. Early estimates of the original reserves are confusing because the Big Vein and the Georges Creek basin were inconsistently defined, their extent but sketchily understood, and variable units of measurement were employed. In 1829, C&O Canal engineer Nathan S. Roberts guessed there were about 143 million tons of coal in some 20 square miles of the Big Vein, or roughly seven million tons per square mile. Cruger of the C&O thought that it would take 400 years to exhaust one such square mile at the then-current rate of mining. Alexander and Tyson, in 1836, believed there were 158 million tons in their 16-square-mile section, or around ten million tons/sq. mi. The Pittsburgh Seam was later determined to occupy about 50 square miles of the Georges Creek basin, so these early figures, if projected, would represent estimates ranging from 350–500 million tons of coal.

Whatever amount was there originally, the Pittsburgh Seam was clearly not inexhaustible. In 1905, when the seam was being heavily mined, it was thought the coal would soon be gone. Now it just about is: there are an estimated three million tons left. The mid-nineteenth-century estimates for the entire 100-square-mile Georges Creek coalfield ranged from 22 to 32 million tons/sq. mi., or a whopping 2.2 to 3.2 billion tons for the whole area. A current educated guess, by James R. Brooks, economic geologist for the Maryland Geological Survey, is that, of an original 1.4 billion tons, 354 million tons remain.

The four largest coal producers in Georges Creek strip-mined 371,000 tons of coal in 1988; of this, 129,000 tons, or 35 percent, came from the Pittsburgh Seam. Some went by truck to other destinations, but most was shipped by rail to Baltimore. CSX Corporation, of which the former B&O Railroad is now a part, is the nation's largest coal-hauler, deriving 38 percent of its revenue from this source.

15. The following discussion of the Georges Creek Coal and Iron Company was derived mainly from: Gutheim, *The Potomac*, pp. 223–24; Stegmaier et al., *Allegany County*, p. 132–35; and Harvey, *Best-Dressed Miners*, pp. 130–38. See also Katherine A. Harvey, "Building a Frontier Ironworks: Problems of Transport and Supply, 1837–1840," *Maryland Historical Magazine*, summer 1975, pp. 149–66, and the same author's Maryland Historical Trust survey form and National Register nomination records on the Lonaconing Furnace in Ware, Edwards, Henry, and Ridout, *Green Glades and Sooty Gob Piles*, pp. 225–27. The furnace has recently been restored, and some of the company's original buildings still stand at Lonaconing. Although strip mining still goes on in the vicinity, it is not obvious to the casual observer from the appearance of the hills, which are dotted with farms as they were in the 1840's.

16. Thomas and Williams, *History of Allegany County*, 1: 536; Scharf, *History of Western Maryland*, 2: 1439.

17. The quotes in the following section are from this report: Benjamin Silliman and Benjamin Silliman, Jr., "Extracts from a Report made to the Maryland Mining Company," 1838, George Peabody Library of the Johns Hopkins University, Baltimore.

18. William Young to Samuel Swartwout, Aug. 14, 1838, in Benjamin Silliman and Benjamin Silliman, Jr., "Extracts from a report made to the Maryland and New York Coal & Iron Company," etc., 1839, p. 44, George Peabody Library of the Johns Hopkins University, Baltimore.

19. Ibid., p. 39.

20. Radoff, ed., *Old Line State*, p. 283.

21. Philip E. Thomas to Col. U. S. Heath, Mar. 25, 1836, Thomas Letterbooks.

22. Baltimore *Sun*, Aug. 7, 1841, quoted in Scharf, *History of Western Maryland*, 2: 1434.

23. In 1840, Thomas Shriver, as the leader of the Allegany County Whigs, helped to construct a huge wooden ball, twelve feet in diameter, that became a main prop in that year's circus-style Harrison-Tyler campaign. Covered with red, white, and blue cloth and political slogans, and equipped with devices for rolling it along the highway, the ball traveled to the huge Baltimore Whig convention, then on to Philadelphia, New York, and Boston. "Keep the ball rolling" entered the nation's lexicon.

24. B&O Rr. Minute Books, Apr. 21, 1843.

25. J. Semmes, *John H. B. Latrobe*, pp. 321, 548–56.

26. *Appleton's Cyclopaedia of American Biography* (New York: D. Appleton & Co., 1888), s.v. "Morse."

27. Mabee, *The American Leonardo*, p. 254.

28. Ibid., p. 271.

29. Morse, ed., *Morse, Letters and Journals*, 2: 212.

30. Ibid., p. 218.

31. Prime, *Life of Morse*, pp. 496–97.

32. Baltimore *Sun*, May 27, 1844.

33. Morse, ed., *Morse, Letters and Journals*, p. 224.

34. For an appreciation of the crucial importance of time to pretelegraph railroad operations, I am grateful to Ian R. Bartky, whose articles over the past decade in *Railroad History*, *Scientific American*, and *Technology and Culture* have explored virtually every aspect of the subject.

35. Martinsburg *Gazette*, Nov. 10, 1842.

36. Morse's successful experiment with the telegraph on the B&O's Washington Branch signaled the start of a close relationship between railroads and instant communications that culminated some 150 years later with the placing of fiber optics cables along the same right-of-way.

CHAPTER 21

1. B&O Rr. Annual Report, 1842, p. 17.

2. James Murray to Louis McLane, Dec. 28, 1842, Letters Received, General, 1841–43, Baring Brothers & Co. Papers, National Archives of Canada (NAC).

3. *Niles Register* 63 (Jan. 14, 1843): 314–15.

4. In 1841, Thomas, 42, married Sally McDowell, a woman less than half his age who was the daughter of the governor of Virginia. While Thomas was governor of Maryland, 1842–45, their marriage broke up and the bitter estrangement became a political cause célèbre. Thomas wrote an extraordinary pamphlet about it, was sued for libel and divorce, and lost both cases. Unnerved by the experience, the governor, who was once considered presidential material, became a semi-recluse for the next twenty years. Thomas made a political comeback in the 1860's as a Radical Republican and served three more terms in Congress. In 1876, he was run down and killed on his Frederick County estate by a B&O Rr. locomotive. See Buchholz, *Governors of Maryland*, pp. 136–43, and Gutheim, *The Potomac*, pp. 237–43.

5. My sources for the events of 1843 are: McLane to Joshua Bates, Mar. 25, 1843, Letters Received, General, 1841–43, Baring Brothers & Co. Papers, NAC; B&O Rr. Minute Books, June 7, Sept. 6, 1843; and *Niles Register* 64 (July 29, 1843): 342–43, and 65 (Dec. 2, 1843): 216.

6. New York *Herald*, quoted in *Niles Register* 65 (Dec. 16, 1843): 242.

7. *Niles Register* 65 (Dec. 30, 1843): 274–77.

8. Ibid., 66 (Mar. 16, 1844): 33. Jeremiah Hughes, former editor of the Annapolis *Republican*, acquired the *Register* in 1839, the year Hezekiah Niles died. Three years before that, Hezekiah Niles's son, William Ogden Niles, had taken over the newspaper, moved it to Washington, and renamed it *Niles National Register*. He concentrated on national news and congressional reporting but was an ineffective editor, and when his father died, the paper was sold. Hughes had been a friend of Hezekiah Niles. Like his mentor, he was a staunch Whig and a vigorous editorialist.

9. John H. B. Latrobe to T. W. Ward, July 27, 1844, Letters Received, General, 1843–45, Baring Brothers & Co. Papers, NAC.

10. Quoted in J. Semmes, *John H. B. Latrobe*, p. 460.

11. Baring Brothers & Co. to JHBL, Sept. 3, 1842, in ibid., p. 458; JHBL to Baring Brothers & Co., Sept. 27, 1842, Letters Received, General, 1841–43, Baring Brothers & Co. Papers, NAC.

12. Robinson in 1840 had turned down the job of civil engineer for the Russian railroad. Whistler accepted it in 1842 and offered the mechanical work to his former B&O colleague, Ross Winans. Winans declined but sent his sons, Thomas, a talented mechanic, and William, to Russia in 1843 with a demonstrator locomotive. Thomas Winans formed a company with Eastwick and Harrison that won a five-year, $7 million contract to produce the engines and rolling stock for the Russian line. They established a plant at Alexandrovsky, near Saint Petersburg, where they built hundreds of engines and cars, completing the work a year early. Thomas Winans and Joseph Harrison, Jr., returned to the United States as wealthy men. Whistler, demoralized by dealing with corrupt Russian bureaucrats and the thousands of starving serfs used as construction workers, succumbed to cholera the year before the railroad line opened in 1850. In 1857–58, the Winans firm was recalled to Russia for more mechanical work. John H. B. Latrobe went along as their legal adviser. Alexandroffsky, Thomas De Kay Winans's fantastic Baltimore estate, now demolished, and the Crimea, his summer house, still standing in Leakin Park, were the local monuments of this Russian adventure.

13. *American Railroad Journal*, Mar. 15, 1841, p. 189.

14. White, *History of the American Locomotive*, p. 221.

15. B&O Rr. Minute Books, Apr. 18, 1844.

16. Sinclair, *Development of the Locomotive Engine*, p. 447.

17. *Niles Register* 67 (Sept. 14, 1844): 20.

18. Ware, Edwards, Henry, and Ridout, *Green Glades and Sooty Gob Piles*, p. 227.

19. JHBL to Baring Brothers & Co., Nov. 28, 1844, Letters Received, General, 1843–45, Baring Brothers & Co. Papers, NAC.

20. *Niles Register* 67 (Jan. 4, 1845): 276.

21. Ibid., 68 (Mar. 15, 1845): 23, 24.

22. R. Hidy, *House of Baring*, pp. 326–27; M. Hidy, *Peabody*, pp. 282–84; JHBL to T. W. Ward, Boston, Mar. 16, 1847, Letters Received, General, 1845–48, Baring Brothers & Co. Papers, NAC.

23. JHBL to Baring Brothers & Co., Sept. 13, 1845; Daniel Webster to Baring Brothers & Co., Oct. 14, 1845; JHBL to T. W. Ward, Boston, Dec. 19, 1845, Letters Received, General, Baring Brothers & Co. Papers, NAC; R. Hidy, *House of Baring*, p. 327.

24. JHBL to T. W. Ward, Oct. 7, 1845, Letters Received, General, 1845–48, Baring Brothers & Co. Papers, NAC.

25. JHBL to Thomas Baring, Letters Received, General, 1845–48, Baring Brothers & Co. Papers, NAC.

26. B&O Rr. Minute Books, Oct. 9, 1844.

27. *Niles Register* 69 (Nov. 8, 1845): 147.

28. Ibid., 69 (Jan. 10, 1846): 291.

29. Ibid., 70 (Mar. 28, 1846): 64.

30. "Report of the Chief Engineer upon the expediency of resuming the reconstruction of the [B&O Rr.] between Baltimore and Harpers Ferry . . ." Nov. 12, 1845, B&O Rr. Pamphlets.

31. B&O Rr. Minute Books, May 15, 1846.   32. Baltimore *American*, May 2, 1846.

33. *Niles Register* 71 (Jan. 2, 1847): 278–79.   34. Ibid., 71 (Feb. 6, 1847): 353.

35. JHBL to T. W. Ward, Boston, Letters Received, General 1845–48, Baring Brothers & Co. Papers, NAC; R. Hidy, *House of Baring*, p. 329.

36. B&O Rr. Annual Report, 1847, p. 59.

37. *Niles Register* 73 (Jan. 1, 1848): 273.

38. Ibid., p. 284.

CHAPTER 22

1. Benjamin H. Latrobe, Jr., to John H. B. Latrobe, Jan. 17, 1842, Mrs. Gamble Latrobe Collection, MS 1638, Maryland Historical Society.

2. Ibid.

3. Benjamin H. Latrobe, Jr., "Abstract of the Report of the Chief Engineer to the President of the Baltimore & Ohio Railroad Company, Upon the Route to the City of Wheeling, through Virginia, and avoiding Pennsylvania . . ." Jan. 6, 1845, B&O Rr. Pamphlets.

4. "Concluding Reply of the President of the [B&O Rr. Co.] to the rejoinder on the part of the City of Wheeling . . ." Jan. 18, 1845, pp. 1, 3, 21, ibid.

5. Baltimore *American*, July 14, 1845.

6. "Reply to the review of Jonathan Knight, Esq. made at the request of the City of Wheeling on the report presented to the stockholders of the [B&O Rr. Co.] at their meeting of July 12th, 1845, by Benj. H. Latrobe, C.E." Jan. 5, 1846, p. 16, B&O Rr. Pamphlets.

7. Quoted in Joseph S. Clark, Jr., "The Railroad Struggle for Pittsburgh," *Pennsylvania Magazine of History and Biography* 48 (1924): 8.

8. Baltimore *American*, Apr. 14, 1846.

9. "Memorial of the City of Wheeling . . ." Dec. 7, 1846, p. 10, Association of American Railroads Library, Washington, D.C.

10. Ibid.

11. *Niles Register* 71 (Oct. 17, 1846): 99.

12. B&O Rr. Annual Report, 1846, p. 13.

13. P&C Rr. Annual Report, 1846, unidentified news clipping, ca. Dec. 14, 1846, John Pendleton Kennedy Papers, item 63, George Peabody Library of the Johns Hopkins Library.

14. Baltimore *American*, Jan. 1, 1847.

15. Ibid., Jan. 20, 1847.

16. Ibid., Jan. 21, 1847.

17. Marshall v. Baltimore & O. R. Co., 16 Fed Cas. 828 (Case no. 9,124) (1852).

18. Wheeling *Times*, Jan. 8, 16, 1847.

19. Ibid.

20. B&O Rr. Minute Books, Feb. 22, 1847.

21. Richmond *Republican* quoted in Baltimore *American*, Feb. 26, 1847.

22. "Letter of Thomas Swann, Esq. President of the [B&O Rr. Co.] on the claim of A. J. Marshall, Esq. of Va. with accompanying documents." 1849, p. 28, B&O Rr. Pamphlets.

23. Pittsburgh *Gazette* quoted in Wheeling *Times*, Mar. 5, 1847.

24. Richmond *Enquirer* quoted in ibid., Mar. 6, 1847.

25. Richmond *Times* quoted in Baltimore *American*, Mar. 9, 1847.

26. Wheeling *Times*, Mar. 17, 1847.

27. Pittsburgh *Commercial Journal* quoted in ibid., Mar. 19, 1847; Neville B. Craig to Edward Gray, Mar. 17, 1847, and to John Pendleton Kennedy, Mar. 27, 1847, Mendes Cohen Scrapbook, B&O Rr. Museum.

28. Baltimore *American*, Mar. 23, 1847.

29. Ibid., April 1, 1847.

30. Journal entry, Apr. 14, 1847, J. P. Kennedy Papers, item 7.

31. Ibid., Apr. 19, 1847.
32. Baltimore *American*, May 4, 1847.
33. B&O Rr. Minute Books, May 8, 1847.
34. Journal entry, May 8, 1847, J. P. Kennedy Papers, item 7.
35. Ibid., May 12, 1847.
36. Ibid., May 16, 1847.
37. B&O Rr. Minute Books, May 17, 1847.
38. Baltimore *American*, May 19, 1847.
39. Journal entry, May 19, 1847, J. P. Kennedy Papers, item 7.
40. Ibid., Oct. 12, 1847.
41. "Baltimore and Pittsburgh. Report of the Committee of citizens of Baltimore who were appointed to visit Pittsburgh, with a view to confer with the Pittsburgh and Connellsville Railroad Company." Pamphlet, June 8, 1847, pp. 5, 6, 20, 21, George Peabody Library of the Johns Hopkins University.
42. Baltimore *American*, June 16, 17, 1847.
43. Report to the board of directors, July 16, 1847, by T. Parkin Scott, J. W. Patterson, Sam'l Hoffman, Thomas Swann, Louis McLane, in B&O Rr. Annual Report, 1847, p. 81.
44. Ibid., p. 87; Kelley to McLane, July 2, 1847.
45. Latrobe in B&O Rr. Annual Report, 1847, p. 60.
46. McLane, ibid., p. 20.
47. Baltimore *American*, Nov. 18, 1847. Despite its fraudulent beginnings, the Pittsburgh and Connellsville Railroad was too good an idea to die completely. It came to life again in the 1850's, was brought under B&O control in the following decade, and after many vicissitudes, the first train from Baltimore arrived in Pittsburgh in 1871. B&O President John W. Garrett and Benjamin H. Latrobe, Jr., who served for many years as president of the P&C Rr., led the celebration. Amtrak's Capitol Limited between Washington and Chicago follows this old route today. The line to Parkersburg, built by a B&O surrogate, the Northwestern Virginia Railroad, was opened in 1857. Until the 1980's, it served as main-line trackage to Saint Louis. Latrobe's favorite line to New Martinsville was added in 1901. Of the B&O's four major destinations on the Ohio River discussed in the 1840's, only Wheeling no longer sees the company's trains.
48. "Letter of Thomas Swann, Esq. President of the [B&O Rr. Co.] on the claim of A. J. Marshall, Esq. of Va. with accompanying documents." 1849, pp. 6, 7, B&O Rr. Pamphlets.
49. Deposition of A. J. Marshall, "Testimony received by the special committee on the subject of the Baltimore and Ohio Railroad," Feb. 26, 1853, Thomas Swann Papers, MS 1826, Maryland Historical Society.
50. Marshall v. Baltimore and Ohio Railroad Co., 16H, U.S. Supreme Court, December Term, 1853.

CHAPTER 23

1. B&O Rr. Minute Books, Oct. 9, 1848.
2. Draft of a letter, ca. Nov. 18, 1851, Thomas Swann Papers, MS 1826, Maryland Historical Society.
3. Undated pamphlet, signed "Philo," ca. May 1847, "No. 2. To the Stockholders of the [B&O Rr. Co.] and the Citizens of Baltimore generally," B&O Rr. Pamphlets.
4. Winchester, Virginia, *Republican*, Nov. 3, 1848, Thos. Swann Papers, MS 1826, Maryland Historical Society.
5. "City Taxes," Oct. 24, 1842, ibid. Swann's tax papers reveal that in 1842, of the total tax rate of 83 cents per $100 of assessed valuation, 63 cents was for internal improvements. Most of this tax was levied to pay for Baltimore's $3 million contribution to the $3.6 million cost of constructing the railroad from Harpers Ferry to Cumberland. The late Howard E. Simpson, a twentieth-century B&O president, expressed surprise when he learned that the people of Baltimore and the State of

Maryland had been taxed heavily to build the original line to Wheeling, most of which is still in service.

6. The place where the B&O Rr. crossed the Cheat River is now Rowlesburg, West Virginia.

7. B&O Rr. Minute Books, May 10, 1848.

8. Benjamin H. Latrobe, Jr., "Reports, B&O Rr. Co." Apr. 8, 1848, B&O Rr. Museum.

9. Ibid., and Jan. 9, 1849; B&O Rr. Annual Report, pp. 37–40.

10. B&O Rr. Minute Books, Mar. 14, 1849.

11. Swann to Baring Brothers and Company, Dec. 5, 1848, "Letters Received, General, 1845–1848," Baring Brothers & Co. Papers, National Archives of Canada (NAC).

12. Ibid., Feb. 8, 1849.

13. *American Railroad Journal* 22 (Mar. 24, 1849): 185.

14. Pittsburgh *Gazette*, quoted in Wheeling *Times*, May 16, 1849.

15. B&O Rr. Annual Report, 1849, p. 39.

16. Wheeling *Times*, Oct. 5, 1949.

17. *Address of Thomas Swann, Esq. (President), to the directors of the [B&O Rr. Co.] on the importance of an early completion of their road to the Ohio River . . .* (Baltimore: James Lucas, 1849); B&O Rr. Minute Books, Nov. 14, 1849.

18. Wheeling *Times*, Nov. 21, 1849.

19. Ibid., Nov. 17, 1949.

20. Charles Ellet, Jr., *Report on the Wheeling and Belmont Suspension Bridge, to the City Council of Wheeling* (Philadelphia: John C. Clark, 1847), pp. 27, 38.

21. Lewis, *Charles Ellet, Jr.*, pp. 44–45.

22. Stuart, *Lives and Works*, p. 275.

23. John A. Roebling, the designer of the Brooklyn Bridge, completed other projects that Ellet had first proposed, including the suspension bridge at Cincinnati, but he was not called in to rebuild the Wheeling span, as has sometimes been said. McComas reconstructed the cables in 1860 and Washington Roebling made further improvements in 1871. There was a $2.4 million renovation in 1983. Electric lights were later added, recreating the nighttime effect of the grand opening of the bridge in 1849, which was repeated to celebrate the B&O Railroad's arrival four years later.

John Roebling did, however, realize at the time that high winds could produce a series of undulations in the floor of a suspension span lacking the inherent stiffness provided by stays and trusswork, which could magnify until the bridge literally shook itself to pieces. Ellet did not anticipate such a possibility—nor, indeed, was the lesson learned until the twentieth century. In 1940, a similar fate befell the Tacoma Narrows Bridge, the famous "Galloping Gertie," over Puget Sound in Washington state.

24. Lewis, *Charles Ellet, Jr.*, p. 124.

25. Charles Ellet, Jr., "Report on the Location of the Western Portion of the [B&O Rr.] to a committee of the City Council of Wheeling," Dec. 10, 1849 (Philadelphia, 1850), B&O Rr. Pamphlets.

26. "Contract between the City of Wheeling and the [B&O Rr. Co.] with a recent correspondence between the president of the company and a committee of the city, etc." (Richmond, 1850), p. 23, ibid.

27. "Statement of Thomas Swann, Esq. . . . with accompanying documents, laid before the committee on roads and internal navigation of the Virginia Legislature, in relation to the Grave and Fish Creek routes to the City of Wheeling" (Richmond, 1850), p. 10, ibid.

28. Charles Ellet, Jr., "Second Report on the Location of the western portion of the [B&O Rr.] to a Committee of the City Council of Wheeling," May 10, 1850 (Philadelphia, 1850), pp. 11, 34, 90, 100, ibid.

29. Charles W. Russell, "Considerations respecting the true and proper route for the [B&O Rr.] submitted by the Counsel of Wheeling," July 1850 (Wheeling, 1850), p. 6, ibid.

30. "Answer of the Counsel of the [B&O Rr. Co.] to the Argument of Charles W. Russell . . ." (Baltimore: John Murphy and Co., 1850), p. 26, ibid.

31. Thomas and Williams, *History of Allegany County, Maryland*, 1: 215.

32. For nearly three-quarters of a century after it opened, the C&O Canal competed with the railroad for trade in flour and especially coal, but it gradually fell under the B&O's complete domination. It was not until 1869 that the C&O's annual revenues exceeded expenses, by $160,000. Maryland, which held 60 percent of the canal's $8.4 million in stock, and Virginia, another stockholder, immediately began a court contest to see which was entitled to the proceeds.

The 1870's and 1880's were the most prosperous decades for the C&O, during which its administrators waged effective political warfare against the B&O Railroad and enjoyed profitable operations. (The extension to Pittsburgh was considered in 1876 and again in the 20th century.) But devastating floods in 1877 and 1889 almost wrecked the C&O Canal. After the second one, the B&O Railroad, having acquired control by buying C&O bonds, repaired and operated the canal until 1924 when that year's flood put the waterway out of business for good. In 1938, the railroad turned the property over to the federal government for a public park. The late Supreme Court Justice William O. Douglas spearheaded efforts to ensure that it remained a park instead of becoming a parkway in the late 1950's. Congress, largely because of his efforts, declared the ditch and towpath the C&O Canal National Park in 1971. Although recent floods have damaged the canal, segments of it have been rewatered and tourists can ride on real canal boats near Georgetown.

33. Baring Brothers & Co. to Swann, Nov. 29, 1850, Thomas Swann Papers, MS 1826, Maryland Historical Society.

34. Swann to Barings, Feb. 25, 1851, Baring Brothers and Company Papers, "Letters Received, General, 1849–1853," NAC.

35. It was all in a day's work for the Barings. In October 1852, Thomas Baring, one of the partners, passed through Baltimore. "I had a long interview with Mr. Swan [sic] who evidently feels hurt about the last sale of Bonds but I told him that bygones were bygones," he reported to the London office. In 1870, the Barings handled the sale of 800,000 pounds in sterling bonds on behalf of the B&O Railroad. Thomas Baring to Baring Brothers and Company, Oct. 1, 1852, Baring Brothers & Co. Ltd., Archives.

CHAPTER 24

1. B&O Rr. Annual Report, 1850, p. 50.

2. Benjamin H. Latrobe, Jr., "Reports, B&O Rr. Co." Aug. 12, 1851, B&O Rr. Museum.

3. B&O Rr. Annual Report, 1850, William Parker's report, p. 30.

4. Condit, *American Building Art*, pp. 120–21.

5. B&O Rr. Annual Report, 1850, William Parker's report, p. 30.

6. *Iron Suspension and Trussed Bridge as constructed for the [B&O Rr. Co.] at Harpers Ferry, and on the Washington Branch of this road. Designed and patented by Wendel Bollman* (Baltimore: John Murphy and Co., 1852), p. 6. Bollman left the B&O in 1858 to form one of America's first bridge-building firms, W. Bollman and Co., and later, the Patapsco Bridge and Iron Works. He continued to build bridges for the railroad, using his truss design. They included 160-foot spans at Harpers Ferry and all but the channel span of the fourteen-span, one-and-a-half-mile crossing of the Ohio River at Bellaire, below Wheeling. He also designed bridges for other clients in the East, Middle West, and South America. As part of his bridge work, Bollman developed the concept for the "Phoenix column," a wrought-iron column made up of smaller rolled sections riveted together, an important contribution to nineteenth-century building technology. The use of the Bollman truss was mainly confined to the railroad that sponsored it, and its subsidiaries. The design lasted for about 25 years before being supplanted by others that required less metal. The only existing Bollman truss bridge is at Savage, Md., near where the first one was located. It is not the original; the present double-tracked bridge was built elsewhere in 1869 and moved to its present location in 1888.

7. *American Railroad Journal* 24 (Jan. 4, 1851): 12–14; B&O Rr. Annual Report, 1853, chief engineer's report, p. 22.

8. *American Railroad Journal* 25 (July 3, 1852): 428.

9. BHL, Jr., "Reports, B&O Rr. Co." July 8, 1851, B&O Rr. Museum; B&O Rr. Annual Report, 1853, chief engineer's report, p. 22; [W. Prescott Smith], *History and Description, B&O Railroad*, p. 108.

10. BHL, Jr., "Reports, B&O Rr. Co.," Apr. 7, 1851.

11. B&O Rr. Minute Books, Nov. 11, 1846.

12. The New Castle Manufacturing Co. built two locomotives for the B&O in 1848. One of them, the Memnon, was a conventional 0-8-0 engine, weighing 23.5 tons with 43-inch drivers and 17-by-22-inch cylinders. The original machine, housed in the B&O Railroad Museum in Baltimore, is the sole surviving product of the New Castle works and the only early American freight engine still in existence.

13. D. Clark and Colburn, *Recent Practice*, p. 50. Zerah Colburn, a gifted technical writer, was mechanical editor of the *American Railroad Journal* in the early 1850's. His books on locomotives are considered classics.

14. After building locomotives in Alexandria for eight years, Perkins returned to the B&O as master of machinery, 1859–65.

15. [W. Prescott Smith], *History and Description, B&O Rr.*, 1853, p. 160.

16. Baltimore *American*, July 26, 1851, in Thomas Swann Papers, MS 1826, Maryland Historical Society.

17. The Northwestern Virginia Railroad Company was organized in July 1851. Latrobe completed his surveys in early 1852 and construction began in December of that year. Swann was company president, ca. 1853–56, but the line was not finished until July 1, 1857. It was 104 miles long from Grafton to Parkersburg, with 23 tunnels, and had cost $5.4 million. The B&O had lent the company $1 million in bonds. The City of Baltimore provided $1.5 million worth. By the time it opened, the management of the Northwestern Virginia Railroad Company had been taken over by the B&O. The line was henceforth known as the Parkersburg Branch.

18. Benjamin H. Latrobe, Jr., thought that the Pennsylvania legislature's passage of the Hempfield Rr. charter in 1850 was as surreptitious as its earlier chartering of the Pittsburgh and Connellsville. Charles Ellet, Jr., served as the Hempfield's chief engineer from 1850 to 1855 and collaborated with Jonathan Knight on its notable Wheeling viaduct and tunnel. The B&O acquired the line in 1861, eventually extending it from Washington, Pa., to Pittsburgh; it was recently abandoned. Despite the intervention of Swann and Latrobe in Ohio railroad affairs as advocates of the competing Cincinnati, Hillsborough, and Parkersburg Rr., the Belpre and Cincinnati Rr. was transformed into the Marietta and Cincinnati Rr. with the assistance of Chillicothe, and with the financial aid of Marietta, Wheeling, and the Pennsylvania Railroad. The line was in receivership by 1857, however, after completing 157 miles of track from Loveland, near Cincinnati, to Marietta. The one-hour ferry trip on the Ohio River that separated it from Parkersburg, along with the B&O's sanctions against the company in favor of the Central Ohio Railroad near Wheeling, made its situation worse. The B&O in 1868 took over the Marietta and Cincinnati, which was known thereafter as the B&O Southwestern. A bridge over the Ohio at Parkersburg, and direct rail connections between there and Belpre, and points west, were completed in the 1870's. Distance and topography combined to make the planned link between Marietta and Philadelphia via Wheeling inadvisable. Swann, in the B&O Annual Report, 1852, p. 30, said the section from Marietta to Wheeling "must rise like an exhalation, from the beautiful river," and noted that "it needs no penetration to see that the project of a road to connect the southern portion of the State of Ohio with the City of Philadelphia via the Hempfield Road, would be utterly fruitless." And so it was, except for Philadelphia and the Pennsylvania Railroad, which had achieved their goal of frustrating the rival Baltimore and Ohio.

19. *American Railroad Journal* 24 (Aug. 2, 1851): 485–87. The July 1851 excursion to Piedmont was covered in this issue.

20. B&O Rr. Minute Books, Dec. 10, 1851. William Prescott Smith, the B&O's first historian, considered this bond sale a turning point in the progress and success of the railroad: W. Prescott

Smith, *Great Railway Celebrations*, p. 49. Swann restated his financial theory in a letter to an official of the Cincinnati, Hillsborough, and Parkersburg Rr. "My own policy in regard to the negotiation of bonds intended to accomplish a great enterprise like the one over which you preside, is to ensure certainty. If you can negotiate a sufficient amount of your bonds at a limit of 5 per cent to make your road and place it in a position to make a return, I do not think that I would be deterred by the loss of half a million of dollars. . . . The great and necessary object is to build your road and this I would do upon the most advantageous terms but build this road I would upon some terms.": Swann to Trimble, Apr. 15, 1853, Swann Papers, MS 1763, Maryland Historical Society.

21. Drinker, *Tunneling*, p. 32.

22. The story of the construction of the Kingwood Tunnel was taken mainly from Drinker's work, which includes an account of the building of the Pennsylvania Rr.'s Allegheny Tunnel, 1851–55, and from Latrobe's engineering reports. The timbering of the roof of the Kingwood Tunnel was completed in November 1852. A year later, Latrobe recommended that the tunnel be arched as soon as possible. Drinker says (p. 956): "The arching of this tunnel was not commenced until 1855, and in three years which had elapsed since its excavation, the roof and sides had become much decomposed and bore heavily upon the supporting timbers. The work of arching was therefore both difficult and dangerous. To expedite it, a cast-iron arched rib was used in the worst sections, the side walls having first been erected of stone."

The iron arches, cast an inch thick and three feet wide, in two sections that formed a semicircle, were carried into the tunnel on frames mounted on special cars from which they were raised up and spread until their bases rested on the side walls and their crowns were bolted together. A rough masonry arch was turned atop the iron one. From this the roof was propped up, and the cavity, in some places 30 feet high, was closely packed with stone. Other sections of the tunnel were arched in brick. Meanwhile, trains were routed over the top of the hill on Latrobe's improved track location. This track work was completed in 1859 under the direction of Wendel Bollman and his assistant, John T. Wilson. It brought the total cost of the tunnel to $724,000.

From 1866 to 1869, Latrobe served as a consultant to the Hoosac Tunnel, a 4.75-mile railroad tunnel in Massachusetts, built 1852–73 at a cost of nearly 200 lives. In 1869, he was named one of the experts to assess John A. Roebling's design for the Brooklyn Bridge.

A new, slightly longer and larger Kingwood Tunnel, also double-tracked, was built in 1910–12 at a cost of $1.5 million. The original tunnel was eventually closed up, but the names of those who finished it can still be seen above the western portal.

23. Clarksburg *Register*, quoted in Morgantown *Monongalia Mirror*, Oct. 23, 1852.

24. B&O Rr. Annual Report, 1853, chief engineer's report, pp. 23–24.

25. BHL, Jr., "Reports, B&O Rr. Co." Oct. 11, 1853, B&O Rr. Museum. In the Cheat River Valley today, one can still see some of the original masonry and rechanneled streams left from the first heavy construction. The Buck-eye Hollow viaduct was removed in 1885 and replaced with a massive masonry substructure. In 1887, a steel trestle was built at Tray Run. This was supplanted in 1907 by the present stone viaduct; some of its materials probably came from the first one.

26. Ibid., Apr. 10, 18, 25, 1852.

27. Ibid., June 7, 1853.

28. Ele Bowen, *Rambles in the Path of the Steam Horse* (Philadelphia, 1855), p. 323.

29. B&O Rr. Annual Report, 1852, chief engineer's report, p. 77; see also ibid., 1853, p. 24, for a description of the bridge. Albert Fink supervised the construction of bridges and buildings on the Northwestern Virginia Railroad (the B&O's Parkersburg Branch) in 1853–55. He left the company in 1857 to become construction engineer of the Louisville and Nashville Rr., but after building several more important bridges, he became a railroad administrator. His 1874 report on the cost of transportation is considered to be the foundation of railway economics. In 1877, as commissioner of the Trunk Line Association, he helped to mitigate the disastrous rate wars among the Eastern railroads. Fink was perhaps proudest of his accomplishments with the B&O Railroad under Latrobe, particularly the viaduct at Tray Run and the bridge over the Monongahela River at Fairmont. A biographical sketch (of which he was probably the author) among his papers at the

Library of Congress contains an immodest though not exaggerated account of them. Confederate forces destroyed the B&O bridge at Fairmont during the Civil War.

30. BHL, Jr., "Reports, B&O Rr. Co." June 17, 1852, B&O Rr. Museum.

31. The larger Winans engines provided the prototype and eponym for between 200 and 300 similar machines that followed. The Reading and Northern Central railroads bought them in number, but like the Bollman truss, the use of the Camel engine was largely restricted to the B&O and its subsidiaries.

In late 1852, Winans quarreled with Samuel J. Hayes, the B&O master of machinery who had replaced Thatcher Perkins, over the economy and efficiency of the Camel's performance compared with that of the company's engines, the so-called Hayes Ten-Wheelers, which were Camels with a four-wheel leading truck and other improvements. Road tests showed that the company's engines were more efficient, but Winans claimed his had more power and took the grades faster even though they consumed more fuel and water. Winans's most bitter and prolonged engine controversy was also his last. It concerned his refusal in 1856–57 to build the conventional 4-6-0 locomotive desired by Hayes's replacement as master of machinery, Henry J. Tyson. Winans was determined to go on building Camels, but the B&O refused to buy any more of them and he was forced to close his works in 1860.

32. *Railroad Gazette*, Dec. 5, 1874, p. 471.

33. Ibid., p. 472.

34. Baltimore *American* quoted in *American Railroad Journal* 25 (July 3, 1852). The rock falls in the Kingwood Tunnel began a day or two before the arrival of the excursion train and continued for some time afterward.

35. B&O Rr. Minute Books, June 29, 1852.

36. B&O Rr. Annual Report, 1852, pp. 8, 9.

37. The renderings of Camden Station appeared in Ele Bowen's 1853 Prospectus and also in his *Rambles in the Path of the Steam Horse* (1855). Niernsee and Neilson submitted plans for a station building in 1855, but again nothing was built. Camden Station was finally constructed in 1857–67 in the Italianate style with a five-part plan and three towers, under the supervision of Joseph F. Kemp, who was also partly responsible for its design. The building still stands, recently restored to its early appearance, but vacant.

38. Niernsee and Neilson's 1853 passenger station was taken down about 1908 when a new B&O station was built in Wheeling. The original bridges and freight house were also removed, and, more recently, the tracks and the railroad's entire presence. The huge masonry retaining walls and a newer bridge pier can still be seen. The 1908 station building, once the third largest on the B&O system, is now West Virginia Northern Community College.

39. Wheeling *Intelligencer*, Dec. 20, 1852.

40. Ibid., Jan. 6, 1853.

41. BHL, Jr., "Reports, B&O Rr. Co.," Nov. 11, 1851, B&O Rr. Museum.

42. Manning lent his name to Mannington, West Virginia. Mendes Cohen, scion of a prominent Baltimore family, began his distinguished engineering career in Ross Winans's locomotive works. Later, after his stint with Latrobe, he became president of the Pittsburgh and Connellsville Railroad. Cohen was president of the Maryland Historical Society and the American Society of Civil Engineers and wrote an excellent engineering account of the B&O's early days: ASCE *Transactions* 26 (June 1892): 535–58.

43. After its completion, the well-timbered Board Tree Tunnel continued in operation for two or three years and the switchback line over the hilltop was abandoned. In the meantime, the slate roof deteriorated to the point where the rock settled so heavily on the wooden supports that they began to fail and endanger passing trains. In 1856–57, the tunnel was arched with stone and brick, a very dangerous piece of construction that required blasting the slabs of rock resting on the timbers in order to remove them. Often the entire ceiling collapsed. Five men were crushed to death by the fall of one such slab, and the arching was done "at the perpetual risk of life and limb" to the miners and laborers. The total cost of the tunnel rose to $520,000. While the work was going on, trains

were again run over the top of the ridge: Benjamin H. Latrobe, Jr., note in Drinker, *Tunneling*, pp. 958–60.

44. Wheeling *Intelligencer*, Oct. 30, Nov. 11, 1852.

45. BHL, Jr., "Reports, B&O Rr. Co.," Nov. 9, 1852, B&O Rr. Museum.

46. Ibid., Dec. 6, 1852.

47. Wheeling *Intelligencer*, Dec. 28, 1852. The rock was later inscribed: "Rosbby's Rock, Track Closed, Christmas Eve, 1852, Hobbs & Faris." The inscribers may have been still celebrating at the time, or perhaps they were merely indifferent spellers; in any case, they misspelled Carr's first name. The events here gave rise to a small community called Roseby's Rock, which still exists and whose members are proud of their role in the B&O's history.

48. Ibid., Jan. 4, 1853.

49. B&O Rr. Annual Report, 1852, p. 35.

CHAPTER 25

1. Atkinson to Swann, Jan. 8, 1853, Thomas Swann Papers, MS 1826, Maryland Historical Society.

2. Wheeling *Intelligencer*, Jan. 12, 1853.

3. Ibid.

4. This description is from an anonymous article in *Harper's Magazine* 2 (Dec. 1850): 195.

5. Baltimore *Sun*, Jan. 11, 12, 1853.

6. [W. P. Smith], *History and Description, B&O Rr.*, p. 148.

7. Governor Lowe, a Southern sympathizer, spent most of the Civil War in Virginia and Georgia aiding the Confederate cause. His speech at the Wheeling courthouse and the account of the banquet are from the Wheeling *Intelligencer*, Jan. 14, 15, 17, 1853, and [Smith], *History and Description, B&O Rr.*, pp. 149–90.

8. *Monongalia Mirror*, Jan. 22, 1853.

9. The Central Ohio Railroad was opened between Columbus and Bellaire, on the Ohio River, November 1, 1854. A ferry service linked it to the B&O at Benwood, Virginia. Wheeling filed a court suit against this connection, which was four and a half miles below the city, but lost. In 1871, the B&O bridged the Ohio River at Parkersburg and at Benwood Bellaire. Wheeling therefore never became the transfer point between the Eastern and Western railroads that it had hoped to be when Charles Ellet built the suspension bridge.

EPILOGUE

1. B&O Rr. Minute Books, Dec. 18, 1852.

2. Ibid.

3. B&O Rr. Annual Report, 1853, William Parker's report, p. 32.

4. J. B. Ford Legal Papers, ca. 1877, MS 292, West Virginia and Regional History Collection, West Virginia University, Morgantown.

5. The following account of the accident is based on the J. B. Ford Legal Papers and reports in the Baltimore *Sun*, Mar. 29, 30, 1853.

6. J. B. Ford Legal Papers.

7. B&O Rr. Minute Books, June 8, July 13, 1853.

8. *Illustrated News*, Apr. 16, 1853.

9. B&O Rr. Annual Report, 1853, chief engineer's report, p. 11.

10. Smith's accounts are from "Reports made to the General Superintendent of the [B&O Rr.] by the assistant master of transportation," May, June, 1853, B&O Rr. Pamphlets.

11. Ambler, *History of Transportation, Ohio Valley*, p. 197.

12. B&O Rr. Annual Report, 1853, chief engineer's report, pp. 9, 19.

13. B&O Rr. Minute Books, Apr. 13, 1853.

WORKS CITED

The Baltimore and Ohio Railroad Museum contains a vast amount of archival material on the history of the company. The following sources, frequently cited in the Notes, were particularly valuable to this study:

Baltimore and Ohio Railroad Annual Reports, 1830–53
Baltimore and Ohio Minute Books, 1827–53
Baltimore and Ohio Pamphlets
Philip E. Thomas Letterbooks

BOOKS AND ARTICLES

Ambler, Charles Henry. *A History of Transportation in the Ohio Valley*. Glendale, Calif.: Arthur H. Clark, 1932.

Bernhard. *Travels Through North America During the Years 1825 and 1826 by his highness, Bernhard, Duke of Saxe-Weimar Eisenach*. 2 vols. Philadelphia: Carey, Lea, and Carey, 1828.

[Boardman, James]. "A Citizen of the World." In *America and the Americans*. London, 1833.

Booth, Henry. *An Account of the Liverpool and Manchester Railway* . . . Liverpool, 1831.

Brown, William H. *The History of the First Locomotives in America*. New York: D. Appleton, 1871.

Browne, Gary L. *Baltimore in the Nation, 1789–1861*. Chapel Hill: University of North Carolina Press, 1980.

Buchholz, Heinrich Ewald. *Governors of Maryland from the Revolution to the Year 1908*. Baltimore: Williams & Wilkens, 1908.

Carter, Edward C., II, John C. Van Horne, and Lee W. Formwalt, eds. *The Journals of Benjamin Henry Latrobe, 1799–1820, from Philadelphia to New Orleans*. 3 vols. New Haven, Conn.: Yale University Press, 1980.

Chevalier, Michel. *History and Description of the Channels of Communication of the United States*. . . . Paris, 1841.

Clark, Daniel Kinnear, and Zerah Colburn. *Recent Practice in the Locomotive Engine*. . . . London, 1861.

Clark, William Bullock, George C. Martin, J. J. Rutledge, B. S. Randolph, N. Allen Stockton, W. B. D. Penniman, and Arthur Browne. *Report on the Coals of Maryland*. Maryland Geological Survey. Baltimore: The Johns Hopkins Press, 1905.

Condit, Carl W. *American Building Art: The Nineteenth Century*. New York: Oxford University Press, 1960.

Davis, Julia. *The Shenandoah*. New York: Farrar & Rinehart, 1945.

Drinker, Henry S. *Tunneling, Explosive Compounds, and Rock Drills.* . . . New York: John Wiley, 1878.

Dunbar, Seymour. *A History of Travel in America*. New York: Greenwood Press, 1968 [1915].

Fisher, Alan. *Country Walks Near Baltimore*. 1981.

Goodrich, Carter. *Government Promotion of American Canals and Railroads, 1800–1890*. New York: Columbia University Press, 1960.

Gray, Thomas. *Observations on a General Iron Railway* . . . London, 1825.

Greeley, Horace. *The Great Industries of the United States*. Hartford, Conn., 1872.

Gutheim, Frederick. *The Potomac*. New York: Rinehart, 1949.

Hahn, Thomas. *Towpath Guide to the C&O Canal*. York, Pa.: American Canal and Transportation Center, 1973.

Hamlin, Talbot. *Benjamin Henry Latrobe*. New York: Oxford University Press, 1955.

Hammond, Bray. *Banks and Politics in America from the Revolution to the Civil War*. Princeton, N.J.: Princeton University Press, 1957.

Haney, Lewis H. *A Congressional History of Railways in the United States*. New York: Augustus M. Kelley, 1968 [1908, 1910].

Hanna, Hugh Sisson. *A Financial History of Maryland, 1789–1848*. Baltimore: Johns Hopkins University Press, 1907.

Harvey, Katherine A. *The Best-Dressed Miners: Life and Labor in the Maryland Coal Region, 1835–1910*. Ithaca, N.Y.: Cornell University Press, 1969.

Harwood, Herbert H., Jr. *Impossible Challenge: The Baltimore and Ohio Railroad in Maryland*. Baltimore: Barnard, Roberts, 1979.

Hidy, Muriel Emmie. *George Peabody, Merchant and Financier, 1829–1854*. New York: Arno Press, 1978.

Hidy, Ralph W. *The House of Baring in American Trade and Finance*. Cambridge, Mass.: Harvard University Press, 1949.

Hill, Forest G. *Roads, Rails, and Waterways: The Army Engineers and Early Transportation*. Norman: University of Oklahoma Press, 1957.

Hulbert, Archer Butler. *Historic Highways of America*. 16 vols. Cleveland: Arthur H. Clark, 1903.

———. *Washington and the West*. New York: Century, 1905.

Johnson, J. B. *The Theory and Practice of Surveying* . . . New York: John Wiley, 1895.

Kenin, Richard. *Return to Albion: Americans in England, 1760–1948*. New York: Holt, Rinehart & Winston, 1979.

Kline, Benjamin F. G., Jr. *Tall Pines and Winding Rivers*. 1976.

Latrobe, John H. B. *The Baltimore and Ohio Railroad. Personal Recollections. A Lecture Delivered before the Maryland Institute . . . March 23d, 1868*. Baltimore: Sun Book and Job Printing, 1868.

[———]. *Picture of Baltimore,* . . . Baltimore: F. Lucas, Jr., 1832.

Laws and Ordinances relating to the Baltimore and Ohio Railroad Company. Baltimore: John Murphy, 1850.

Lewis, Gene D. *Charles Ellet, Jr.; The Engineer as Individualist*. Urbana: University of Illinois Press, 1968.

Livingood, James Weston. *The Philadelphia-Baltimore Trade Rivalry, 1780–1860*. Harrisburg, Pa.: Historical and Museum Commission, 1947.

Long, Stephen H. *Description of Col. Long's Bridges* . . . Concord, N.H., 1836.

———. *Rail Road Manual* . . . Baltimore: W. Wooddy, 1829.

Luxon, Norval Neil. *Niles Weekly Register: News Magazine of the Nineteenth Century*. Westport, Conn.: Greenwood Press, 1970.

Mabee, Carleton. *The American Leonardo: A Life of Samuel F. B. Morse.* New York: Knopf, 1943.

McCullough, David. *The Great Bridge.* New York: Simon & Schuster, 1972.

McGrane, Reginald Charles. *The Panic of 1837 . . .* Chicago: University of Chicago Press, 1924.

McMaster, John B. *A History of the People of the United States from the Revolution to the Civil War.* 8 vols. New York: D. Appleton, 1907.

Mason, John Thomas. *Life of John Van Lear McMahon.* Baltimore: John B. Piet, 1880.

Morse, Edward Lind, ed. *Samuel F. B. Morse, His Letters and Journals.* 2 vols. Boston: Houghton, Mifflin, 1914.

Munroe, John A. *Louis McLane: Federalist and Jacksonian.* New Brunswick, N.J.: Rutgers University Press, 1973.

Parker, Franklin. *George Peabody: A Biography.* Nashville, Tenn.: Vanderbilt University Press, 1971.

Parkman, Francis. *France and England in North America.* 2 vols. New York: Library of America, 1983.

Perkins, Edwin J. *Financing Anglo-American Trade: The House of Brown, 1800–1880.* Cambridge, Mass.: Harvard University Press, 1975.

Prime, S. I. *The Life of Samuel F. B. Morse, LLD.* 1875.

Radoff, Morris. L., ed. *The Old Line State: A History of Maryland.* Annapolis: Maryland Hall of Records Commission, 1971.

Reizenstein, Milton. *The Economic History of the Baltimore and Ohio Railroad, 1827–1853.* Baltimore: The Johns Hopkins Press, 1897.

Riley, Elihu S. *A History of the General Assembly of Maryland.* Baltimore, 1905.

Rolt, L. T. C. *The Railway Revolution: George and Robert Stephenson.* New York: St. Martin's, 1962.

Rubey, Harry. *Route Surveys.* New York: Macmillan, 1951.

Rubin, Julius. *Canal or Railroad? Imitation and Innovation in the Response to the Erie Canal in Philadelphia, Baltimore, and Boston.* Philadelphia: American Philosophical Society, 1961.

Sanderlin, Walter S. *The Great National Project: A History of the Chesapeake and Ohio Canal.* Baltimore: Johns Hopkins University Press, 1946.

Scharf, J. Thomas. *The Chronicles of Baltimore.* Port Washington, N.Y.: Kennikat Press, 1972 [1874].

———. *History of Baltimore City and County.* 2 vols. Baltimore: Regional Publishing, 1971 [1881].

———. *History of Maryland.* 3 vols. Hatboro, Pa.: Tradition Press, 1967 [1879].

———. *History of Western Maryland . . .* 2 vols. Philadelphia, 1882.

Schlesinger, Arthur M. *The Age of Jackson.* Boston: Little, Brown, 1945.

Semmes, John E. *John H. B. Latrobe and His Times, 1803–1891.* Baltimore: Norman, Remington, 1917.

Semmes, Raphael. *Baltimore as Seen by Visitors, 1783–1860.* Baltimore, 1953.

Sinclair, Angus. *Development of the Locomotive Engine.* Cambridge, Mass.: MIT Press, 1970 [1907].

Smiles, Samuel. *The Lives of George and Robert Stephenson.* London: Folio Society, 1975 [1874].

Smith, H. Shirley. *The World's Great Bridges.* New York: Harper & Row, 1953.

[Smith, William Prescott]. "A Citizen of Baltimore." *A History and Description of the Baltimore and Ohio Railroad . . .* Baltimore: John Murphy, 1853.

———. *The Book of the Great Railway Celebrations of 1857.* New York: D. Appleton, 1858.

Stegmaier, Harry, Jr., David Dean, Gordon Kershaw, and John Wiseman. *Allegany County: A History.* Parsons, W. Va.: McClain, 1976.

Strickland, William. *Reports on Canals, Railways, Roads and Other Subjects, made to the Pennsylvania Society for the Promotion of Internal Improvements.* Philadelphia: Carey & Lea, 1826.

Stuart, Charles B. *Lives and Works of Civil and Military Engineers of America.* New York: Van Nostrand, 1871.

Swisher, Carl Brent. *Roger B. Taney.* New York: Macmillan, 1935.

Taylor, George Rogers. *The Transportation Revolution, 1815–1860.* New York: Rinehart, 1951.

Thomas, James W., and T. J. C. Williams. *History of Allegany County, Maryland.* 2 vols. 1923.

Trautwine, John C. *The Civil Engineer's Pocket-Book.* Wallingford, Pa.: Trautwine, 1922.

Tuckerman, Bayard, ed. *The Diary of Philip Hone, 1828–1851.* New York: Dodd, Mead, 1899.

Tuckerman, Henry T. *The Life of John Pendleton Kennedy,* in *The Collected Works.* 10 vols. New York: Georg Olms Verlag, 1969 [1871].

Tyrell, Henry Grattan. *Bridge Engineering.* n.p. 1911.

Van Deusen, Glyndon G. *The Jacksonian Era: 1828–1848.* New York: Harper & Row, 1959.

Van Horne, John C., and Lee W. Formwalt, eds. *The Correspondence and Miscellaneous Papers of Benjamin Henry Latrobe.* 2 vols. New Haven, Conn.: Yale University Press, 1984.

Varle, Charles. *A Complete View of Baltimore.* Baltimore: Samuel Young, 1833.

Vose, George L. *Manual for Railroad Engineers.* Boston: Lee and Shepard, 1881.

Ward, George Washington. *The Early Development of the Chesapeake and Ohio Canal Project.* Baltimore: Johns Hopkins University Press, 1899.

Ware, Donna M., Mark R. Edwards, Geoffrey B. Henry, and Orlando Ridout V. *Green Glades and Sooty Gob Piles.* Crownsville, Md.: Maryland Historical & Cultural Publications, 1991.

White, John H., Jr. *A History of the American Locomotive.* . . . New York: Dover, 1979.

———. *The American Railroad Passenger Car.* Baltimore: Johns Hopkins University Press, 1978.

Williams, Thomas J. C. *A History of Washington County, Maryland* . . . 2 vols. Baltimore: Regional Publishing, 1968 [1906].

Williams, T. J. C., and Folger McKinsey. *History of Frederick County, Maryland.* Baltimore: Regional Publishing, 1967 [1910].

Wittke, Carl. *The Irish in America.* New York: Russell & Russell, 1970.

Ziegler, Philip. *The Sixth Great Power: Barings, 1762–1929.* London: Collins, 1988.

INDEX

In this index an "f" after a number indicates a separate reference on the next page, and an "ff" indicates separate references on the next two pages. A continuous discussion over two or more pages is indicated by a span of page numbers, e.g., "57–59." *Passim* is used for a cluster of references in close but not consecutive sequence.